THE NATIONAL
GEOGRAPHIC TRAVELER

FRANCE

Rosemary Bailey

Contents

How to use this guide

See back flap for keys to text and map symbols

The National Geographic Traveler brings you the best of France in text, pictures, and maps. Divided into three main sections, the guide begins with an overview of history and culture. Following are eight regional chapters with featured sites selected by the author for their particular interest. Each chapter opens with its own contents list.

The regions and sites within the regions are arranged geographically. Some regions are further divided into smaller areas. A map introduces each region, highlighting the featured sites. Walks and drives, plotted on their own maps, suggest routes for dis-

covering an area. Features and sidebars give intriguing detail on history, culture, or contemporary life. A More Places to Visit page generally rounds off the regional chapters.

The final section, Travelwise, lists essential information for the traveler—pre-trip planning, getting around, communications, money matters, and emergencies— plus a selection of hotels, restaurants, shops, and activities.

To the best of our knowledge, all information is accurate as of the press date. However, it's always advisable to call ahead when possible.

Floors We have used the French convention when referring to the floors of a building. Hence, in this book ground floor refers to the first floor, the first floor refers to the second, and so on.

Metric measurements In this book metric equivalents are given in parentheses after imperial measurements.

140

Color coding

Each region is color coded for easy reference. Find the region you want on the map on the front flap, and look for the color flash at the top of the pages of the relevant chapter. Information in **Travelwise** is also color coded to each region.

The Louvre

🅰 53 D3
✉ Palais du Louvre
☎ 01 40 20 51 51
🕐 Closed Tues.
💲 $$ ($ from 3 p.m.; free for those under 18)
🚇 Métro: Palais-Royal–Musée du Louvre

Visitor information

Practical information for most sites is given in the side column (see key to symbols on back flap). The map reference gives the page number of the map and grid reference. Other details are address, telephone number, days closed, entrance charge in a range from $ (under $4) to $$$$$ (over $25), and nearest metro stop for sites in Paris. Other sites have information in italics and parentheses in the text.

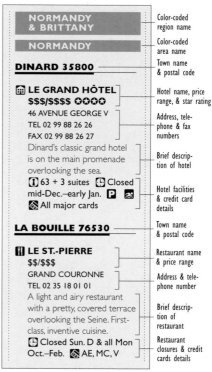

TRAVELWISE

NORMANDY & BRITTANY	Color-coded region name
NORMANDY	Color-coded area name
DINARD 35800	Town name & postal code
🏨 **LE GRAND HÔTEL** $$$/$$$$ ✪✪✪✪	Hotel name, price range, & star rating
46 AVENUE GEORGE V TEL 02 99 88 26 26 FAX 02 99 88 26 27	Address, telephone & fax numbers
Dinard's classic grand hotel is on the main promenade overlooking the sea.	Brief description of hotel
🛏 63 + 3 suites 🕐 Closed mid-Dec.–early Jan. 🅿 🌊 🃏 All major cards	Hotel facilities & credit card details
LA BOUILLE 76530	Town name & postal code
🍴 **LE ST.-PIERRE** $$/$$$	Restaurant name & price range
GRAND COURONNE TEL 02 35 18 01 01	Address & telephone number
A light and airy restaurant with a pretty, covered terrace overlooking the Seine. First-class, inventive cuisine.	Brief description of restaurant
🕐 Closed Sun. D & all Mon Oct.–Feb. 🃏 AE, MC, V	Restaurant closures & credit cards details

Hotel and restaurant prices

An explanation of the price ranges used in entries is given in the Hotels & Restaurants section beginning on p. 346.

REGIONAL MAPS

- A locator map accompanies each regional map and shows the location of that region in the country.
- Adjacent regions are shown, each with a page reference.

WALKING TOURS

- An information box gives the starting and ending points, time and length of walk, and places not to be missed along the route.
- Where two walks are marked on the map, the second route is shown in orange.

DRIVING TOURS

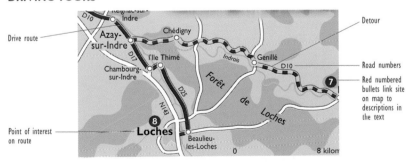

- An information box provides details including starting and finishing points, time and length of drive, places not to be missed along the route, and tips on the terrain.

THE NATIONAL GEOGRAPHIC TRAVELER
FRANCE

About the author

Rosemary Bailey fell in love with France 20 years ago when she stayed on a rose farm in Provence. Since then she has traveled all over France and has written and edited a number of guides to the country and its regions, including the Côte d'Azur, Burgundy, and the Loire Valley, as well as contributing many articles to publications including *The Sunday Times* and *Elle*. Her other books include guides to Italy and New York and a family memoir, *Scarlet Ribbons*.

Rosemary Bailey divides her time between London and Southwest France, where she and her husband, author Barry Miles, are restoring a Romanesque monastery, and her son attends the village school.

With contributions by:
Professor Colin Jones, professor of History at Warwick University: pages 17–30
Dr. Julian Petley, lecturer in Sociology, Brunel University: pages 10–16 & 31–45
Elizabeth Carter, restaurant critic and author: pages 46–50
Jo Sturgis, editor of a number of travel guides, author of a *Guide to France for Children*, and editor/producer of the AA CD-Rom *Paris*: pages 51–102
Helen Varley, travel writer and journalist, founder of *Time Out* city guides, and author of *Weekends across the Channel*: pages 103–132

History & culture

Edward I of England pays homage to Philippe IV of France (a book illustration by Jean Fouquet).

France today

THE BOUNDARIES OF FRANCE ARE LARGELY NATURAL: THE ENGLISH Channel and the Ardennes hills in the north; the Atlantic Ocean in the west; the Pyrenees in the southwest; the Mediterranean Sea in the south; the Alps in the southeast; and the Jura and Vosges Mountains and the Rhine River in the east. To these striking natural features we must also add the Massif Central, where huge extinct volcanoes dominate the landscape; the wide, graceful rivers of the Loire, Seine, Rhône, Saône, and Garonne; and the dramatic gorges cut by the Ardèche, the Tarn, and other rivers through the strange, lunar, limestone plateaus south of the Massif Central.

THE LAND

France is the largest country in Western Europe at 211,150 square miles (547,020 sq km) and the 37th largest in the world; at the same time it is actually slightly smaller than the state of Texas. Although twice the size of the United Kingdom, it has roughly the same population—57 million. It is a largely rural country: 56 percent of the land is farmed and 25 percent forested. Agriculture, the country's largest industry, has been described as France's *pétrole vert* (green oil). France has by far the largest cultivatable area, and the biggest agricultural output, of any state in the European Union. Big cities are few and far between; Paris is the largest, with a population of 2.1 million, followed by Lyon (1.2 million) and Marseille (1.1 million)—all of them small cities by European standards.

Regional diversity

The first feature that strikes any visitor traveling through France, aside from its rurality, is its remarkable regional diversity. France is the only European country that covers both the north and south of the continent. Significant regional differences in climate, geology, geography, and culture have given rise to the extremely varied and rich agriculture that contributes so strikingly to the diversity of the French landscape—and, of course, produces France's fabled cuisines and wines. Again, these are above all regional: The cuisine of Périgord is as unlike that of Normandy as the wines of Champagne differ from those of Bordeaux.

Village life

For all the splendors of Paris, and of provincial cities such as Bordeaux, Lille, Nice, and Toulouse, France is above all a country of villages. There are 33,000 *communes* (the smallest administrative unit in France), each embracing a number of villages. Again, these vary from region to region: From the gray, granite fishermen's cottages of Brittany shielding themselves against the rolling Atlantic breakers, to the thatched and half-timbered Normandy hamlets nestling among apple orchards dotted with cows, to the flat, Roman-tiled, red roofs of sleepy Provençal hill villages clinging in terraces to the steep slopes.

At first sight, many of these villages and their rural surroundings may appear to have changed little over the centuries. But changes there most certainly have been. In 1789 the population of France was 27 million, 22 million of whom lived in the countryside. Since the middle of the 19th century, there has been a steady flight from the land and, since 1945, 6 million people have left for the towns and cities, driven away by dramatic changes in farming practice. In 1939, 35 percent of France's active population worked on the land; now the proportion is down to about 5 percent and expected to fall further. Hardest hit of all has been the smallest farmer, the *paysan* or peasant—unknown in America, already extinct in many European countries, and in almost certain terminal decline in France. In the brave new world of agribusiness, GATT (General Agreement on Trade and Tariffs), and European Union farm subsidies, the peasant farmer and his tiny, much-divided smallholding is simply being modernized out of existence. Subsidy farming and the remote,

The village of Pernand-Vergelesses in the Côte-d'Or, Burgundy, thrives among its vineyards, a source of considerable wealth.

absentee landlord-business person have become unattractive but increasingly common features of the French countryside. The evidence can be seen in the vast, eerie prairies that now clothe parts of the north and center, unbroken by the outline of a single house, let alone a village. This is less an empty countryside than an emptied one. Traveling through

Some rural activities have not changed for centuries: Truffles in Périgord are still found by the keen noses of trained pigs.

France, and especially through poorer parts such as the Auvergne or the Ariège, it is hard not to be struck by the number of ruined houses left as the visible sign of this exodus.

But, while it is important to understand the forces that have made the French countryside what it is, one should also beware of romanticizing the peasant past—a considerable body of French literature exists to suggest that most of us would actually have loathed to have lived in it! And in recent times French villages have undergone something of a revival, as French people and foreigners have bought rural vacation houses or even set up small businesses, thus bringing new forms of work and encouraging fresh varieties of rural economic activity.

THE PEOPLE
As with the French landscape, the keynotes here are again diversity and regionality.

Although the French are famously patriotic (Chauvin was a Frenchman, after all), a French person referring to *mon pays* may very well mean the area in which he or she lives rather than France as a whole. It can be quite disconcerting to discover just how little acquainted some French people are with parts of the country other than their own. In its most pronounced form, this identification with region over country has led to separatist demands—largely peaceful (albeit illegal) in Brittany, less so in Corsica and the Basque region of the Pyrenees. Language is also a symbol of regional independence—Breton in Brittany (see p. 154), and Occitan in Provence and Languedoc (as in "tongue of oc," see p. 317), are both experiencing a revival.

Nothing illustrates so clearly the enormous diversity of France as the differences between its peoples. The Celtic Bretons are dramatically distinct not only from the Mediterranean people of Provence and Languedoc, but also from their Norman neighbors—and so on all around France. A gulf still exists between Parisians and the rest of France. Parisians may think of themselves as urban sophisticates, but there are those outside the capital who regard them as haughty and arrogant. Parisians may enjoy having their *maisons secondaires* (second houses) deep in rural France, but for some the word "provincial" is still virtually a term of abuse. Even celebrated writers such as François Mauriac (Bordeaux) and Gustave Flaubert (Normandy) frequently seem to have harbored distinctly ambivalent feelings about their own provincial backgrounds. There can be few more poisonous portrayals of small town bourgeois life than Flaubert's *Madame Bovary* (which makes it all the more surprising that various Normandy villages vie with each other in claiming to be the model for Flaubert's suffocating town of Yonville).

Not surprisingly, given its colonial past (in Algeria, Morocco, Indochina, French West Africa, and so on), France also has many communities of different ethnic origins. From the mid-1950s to the mid-1970s, furthermore, labor shortages led to massive recruitment campaigns not only in North Africa but also in poorer European countries such as Greece

Spain, and southern Italy. Many of these foreign workers chose to settle permanently. In spite of that famous French saying, "*Vive la différence!*" France is not free of racism. It has been exploited by the Front National, with considerable success in some areas. Almost unbelievably, the beautiful Provençal city of Orange is now controlled by this overtly racist political party. Tourists are unlikely to encounter this side of France, however, unless they visit the run-down housing projects on the fringes of cities.

France remains a deeply civilized country, nevertheless, and the liberal majority are disgusted by this particular blot on their nationhood. Indeed, no one can visit France and fail to notice the role that courtesy, decorum, and good manners play in everyday life (except, unfortunately, behind the wheel of a car). Shaking hands and kissing on the cheeks—two, three, or even four times, depending on the region and how well those kissing know each other—are indispensable and graceful social rituals. Anyone entering a store, café, restaurant, or waiting room will greet the assembled company with a "*Bonjour Messieurs-Dames,*" and "*Monsieur*" and "*Madame*" are routinely added to any conversational remark, even if it is only "*merci*" or "*pardon.*" Understandably, foreign tourists often do not realize how important these niceties are to the French.

It is also impossible to visit France without immediately becoming aware of the importance of style. Looking good really matters, and not only in super-fashionable Paris. Chairs outside French bars and cafés often face outward, not toward each other: You are there to watch the passersby. People don't spend all that money on their image simply to be ignored! Immensely stylish, too, is the presentation of food. One of the joys of walking down any French street is not simply the sheer variety of small shops, but also the virtuoso window displays, particularly of food—mouth-watering works of art in their own right. And even in simple restaurants, dishes are frequently presented with a style and flair that completely belie the modest prices charged.

The French are extremely proud of their rich cultural heritage. Intellectuals and artists are listened to and even revered: It is not insignificant that the 200 franc note carries the image of the philosopher Montesquieu, the 100-franc one the painter Delacroix, and the 50-franc the writer Saint-Exupéry. A significant number of politicians are writers, too—and not simply of the usual turgid, self-serving memoirs.

Les Bains **club in Paris, once public baths, requires you to be famous, dress with chic, or just look amusing if you want to join the packed dancers on the floor.**

In this increasingly global era, the French do tend to feel that their very Frenchness is under threat, be it from GATT, American films and hamburgers, or the conditions for European monetary union, and they are quite prepared to take to the streets to defend it. In France, with its revolutionary tradition, direct action is seen not as inimical to democracy, but rather as an integral part of it. There is particular concern that French culture—be it food, fashion, film, or even the very language itself—is under threat from an Anglo-Saxon invasion. On the other hand, no European country has done more than France to celebrate the best of American culture: its jazz in the twenties and thirties, "hard-boiled" crime writing in the forties, Hollywood in the fifties, and so on. And it is France—not, as might be expected, Anglo-Saxon Great Britain—which plays host to the European Disneyland.

FESTIVALS

France has a large number of public holidays, (for details see p. 343) when everything is closed. Seven of these are religious ones. As France has been a secular state since 1905, the existence of so many religious holidays may seem curious. Only about 14 percent of the French go regularly to Mass, and although this may rise to 80 percent in traditionalist rural areas, it drops to 10 percent in Paris and 4 to 5 percent in certain industrial centers. The flight from the land has contributed significantly to the decline of religious observance. On the other hand, a majority of French people are still nominally Christian, and about half of all children are baptized. Furthermore, the organized church is still a formidable force. A Socialist government discovered this to its cost when in 1984 it tried to integrate Catholic schools into the state system, thus sparking off one of the biggest demonstrations ever seen in postwar Paris.

Aside from the national holidays, there is a myriad of local religious festivities. Perhaps

The Tour de France bicycle race, France's major sporting event, lasts three weeks. Each year, towns and villages compete to have the tour route go through them.

the most striking is the Gypsy Pilgrimage held every year on May 24–25 at Stes.-Maries-de-la-Mer in the Camargue (see p. 311).

Given the importance that the French accord to culture, it is hardly surprising that the country abounds in cultural festivals. Best known is the Cannes film festival, but enlightened local, regional, and national attitudes to what the French call the *septième art* insure funding for a whole host of smaller (and many would say better) film festivals.

Every form of art is catered to in France's festivals: classical music at Aix-en-Provence, Montpellier, and Prades; jazz at Juan-les-Pins; rock at Bordeaux and Rennes; graphic art at Angoulême and St.-Malo; theater at Avignon. And these are but a fraction of the hundreds of festivals that take place each year, especially in summer. ■

Food & drink

GASTRONOMY, OR THE ART AND SCIENCE OF GOOD EATING AND DRINKING,
is more than a national pastime: In a country where the population spends more of its
income on the pleasures of the table than on anything else, food is a way of life.

France's gastronomic and regional diversity is probably greater than that of any other country. An exasperated Charles de Gaulle once famously remarked "How can anyone be expected to govern a country that produces 265 different cheeses?" (The official tally is nearer 400.) And a gastronomic pilgrim traveling the southwest coast from La Rochelle to the Spanish border (a distance of some 300 miles, or 480 km) could encounter more than 500 different seafood dishes.

The French pleasure in food is most apparent at the street markets. For the visitor, a tour of a French market is an education in the nature of Gallic society. Established food shops are also busiest on market days; French butchers and fishmongers are masters of their craft, and dispense verbal recipes with each purchase, while sellers of cheese or fruit will ask if your purchase is for that evening or the next day, and select the produce accordingly.

Although daily marketing at local shops and markets is still the general rule in France, giant supermarkets filled with prepackaged bread, vegetables, diet cuisine, and frozen foods are hugely popular, and there is concern that individual shops will eventually find it hard to compete. *Boulangeries* (bakeries) are a case in point. The traditional French baguette is made with no fat and goes stale in a matter of hours. As bakers become increasingly reluctant to bake twice a day (early morning and again in the afternoon), so the French have changed their habits, buying their bread once a day instead of, as was customary, twice. And so the baguette seems to get flabbier as preservatives are added. The faster-paced lifestyle of modern France is fueled by microwaveable meals and chains of fast-food restaurants (McDonalds is known as Macdo).

Curnonsky, the famous French gastronome and author of the 32-volume *La France gastronomique,* described four distinct types of French cookery: "la Haute Cuisine, la Cuisine Bourgeoise, la Cuisine Régionale, et la Cuisine Improvisée." Half a century later, these categories still stand.

Haute cuisine is professional cooking by chefs of the highest achievement. In current terms, it describes accurately the cooking of multi-Michelin-starred chefs such as Guy Savoy and Alain Ducasse. Nouvelle cuisine is (or was) a modern interpretation of haute cuisine. Top chefs reconstructed classic French dishes in response to the 1980s' demand for lighter dishes containing less butter and cream, and fewer heavily reduced sauces. In its original form the style was short-lived, but nouvelle cuisine has left its mark on French haute cuisine; classic dishes are prepared in a much lighter vein than 20 years ago. By contrast, cuisine improvisée is peasant in origin. This cuisine comprises farmhouse dishes of hams, sausages, stews, and omelettes.

But it is the two remaining categories that have most shaped the culinary map of France. Cuisine bourgeoise is the simple and unbeatable ordinary middle-class French cookery. Cuisine régionale consists of the great regional specialties of France in classic dishes such as bouillabaisse from Provence, coq au vin from Burgundy, and *cassoulet* from Toulouse.

Restaurants vary greatly. At their simplest, they are small, family-run affairs offering home-style cooking, with local cheeses and desserts probably brought in from the local patisserie. Wine is offered by the carafe, with a small selection available by the bottle.

Then come brasseries, lively restaurants serving a limited menu at any time of day and often fairly late at night. Beer remains a feature (brasserie means brewery), with some brasseries offering an extensive selection. Typical dishes include *steak pommes frites* (frequently described as the national dish of France); *estouffade de boeuf;* and *blanquette de veau,* as well as cold meats and cheeses.

**Waiter and patron are as likely to discuss
issues of the day as the menu.**

The first taste of this year's wine is a moment to be enjoyed by all.

Most distinguished are top-flight restaurants offering classic haute cuisine in a refined setting. Prices are higher, but often there will be a fixed-price menu representing surprisingly good value, especially at lunchtime. Some specialize in creative, modern cooking, others in seafood or regional classics, and all will offer an extensive wine list, possibly with a sommelier to give advice on what to order.

And then there are cafés, those picture windows for observing everyday life, as French as the baguette. No village is complete without one. To adopt the café lifestyle, just learn how to nurse a beer or coffee for hours.

Regional differences are marked, and defended vigorously and with pride. In the cool north, where dairy produce is paramount, butter, cream, and cheese form the basis of a rich cuisine. Traveling south, the emphasis shifts, with chestnuts, walnuts, and truffles dominating dishes that rely on duck

and goose fat. The market gardens of the Mediterranean provide the olive oil, garlic, tomatoes, and peppers for dishes reflecting the influence of Spain to the southwest, and of Italy to the east.

WINE

Climatic differences also distinguish French wine. Thousands of properties all over the country make wines of all complexions, though, in general, northern vineyards produce the stunning white wines, and those farther south make the great reds. In the United States the names of a handful of grape varieties such as Chardonnay and Merlot are used as the ready reference for wine. But in France, more complex traditions prevail: Wine is known by its origin, not by the grape.

CIDER & BEER

Not all French people drink wine with their meals. In Normandy and Brittany farmers brew a range of ciders. Beer, too, is popular in northern France and neighboring Belgium. ■

History of France

THE DISTINCTIVENESS AND STYLE ASSOCIATED WITH FRANCE AND Frenchness are rooted in an extraordinarily rich and diverse history—a history, moreover, that is full of contrasts. Contemporary France stands as an object lesson in state centralization, its carefully honed administrative procedures an example to the world. Yet it has always also been a bastion of stubborn resistance to bureaucracy, of regional diversity, of decentralization, and of localism, individualism, and idiosyncrasy.

France's past has often seemed inextricably linked with the peasant, rural orientation of its society. Yet at the same time, this apparent rootedness belies the extent to which the country has been built up through a rich accretion of other peoples. As much as other richly diverse states, such as the United States, France is a melting pot on whose history a dazzling succession of peoples have left their mark: Celts and Romans in earliest times, Germans and Scandinavians in the Middle Ages, Africans and Asians in the 20th century, and spasmodically the English, the Spanish and Portuguese, the Jews, and many other groupings have all affected the composition and temperament of French society.

France is sometimes seen as a supremely land-based state, its destiny linked intrinsically with that of continental Europe; yet it is in reality an amphibious power, as much at home at sea as on land. Its naval and commercial strengths have made it a crucial player in the fates of parts of North America, Africa, India, Southeast Asia, and the Pacific.

PREHISTORY

At every stage of its history, from the very earliest times, France's role in the development of Western civilization and culture has been crucial. The prehistoric cave art found in the Dordogne area and in the Pyrenees, dating back 20,000 years or so, is among the richest in Europe.

THE ROMANS

The Romans infused a sense of collective identity into the diverse and belligerent Celtic tribes who had developed a powerful Iron Age culture. The Roman Empire had brought the Mediterranean fringe of France under control in 125–121 B.C., but it was Julius Caesar who conquered the warlike Celts. Though the last resisting chieftain, Vercingétorix, defeated by Julius Caesar at Alésia in Burgundy in 52 B.C., was to become something of a national hero, the establishment of the *pax romana* brought new wealth and prosperity to the region.

THE FRANKS

With the collapse of the Roman Empire in the fourth and fifth centuries, Roman Gaul gave way to Francia—the kingdom of the Franks. The Franks were originally just one among a tribal swarm of Germanic societies outside the Roman Empire whom the Romans dubbed "barbarians." They were well placed to benefit from the slow crumbling of imperial power. In the late fourth and fifth centuries, one Frankish grouping, the Merovingians, took over northern France and extended their power south. Their ruler, Clovis, chose Paris as his capital, and in A.D. 496 became a Christian, thus assisting the spread of Frankish power over the Christian south.

CHARLEMAGNE

In the eighth century, the Frankish prince Charlemagne founded the Carolingian dynasty, building up a European power bloc centered on what would later be France and Germany. In 800, he was crowned emperor (the first since Roman times) by the pope. The centrifugal tendencies within feudalism, together with new incursions by Saracens from north Italy, by Magyars from central Europe, and by Norsemen (or Vikings) from Scandinavia, cut short the life of the Carolingian Empire. In the Treaty of Verdun of 843, the empire was subdivided into three units: the Germanic kingdom of the East Franks; the

The prehistoric artists in the caves at Lascaux used the rock contours to increase the lifelike effect of their animal paintings.

kingdom of the West Franks, which was to become the historic core of France; and an intermediary bloc, Lotharingia.

In 987, West Francia, or Francia as it was increasingly called, passed into the hands of Hugues Capet, founder of the Capetian dynasty. Branches of this family provided the French ruling house down to the 19th century.

Louis XII (R.1489–1515) leaving the city of Alexandria on the way to Genoa (an illustration from *Le Voyage de Gênes* by Jean Marot).

His authority was initially meager—he ruled directly over a tiny region in the Île-de-France around Paris, a power base dwarfed by the territory and war bands possessed by feudal lords throughout France. One of his vassals, William, Duke of Normandy, became king of England, following a successful invasion in 1066. The English kings built up an empire stretching from Berwick-upon-Tweed on the Scottish border to the Pyrenees. The Capetians gradually—through a combination of military force, diplomacy, skillful marriage alliances, and outright chicanery—rolled back the power of the English and their other over-mighty subjects.

CRUSADES

From the 11th century to the 13th, French kings were in the forefront of the West's Crusades to rescue the Holy Land from the infidel. One monarch, Saint Louis (Louis IX), even died on a Crusade. The extension of Capetian power into southwest France into the 13th century came through an internal Crusade authorized by the pope against the so-called Albigensian heresy. Now the authority of kings of France was imposed, almost for the first time, in the Mediterranean as well as in the northern zones.

The increasing political power of the Capetian monarchy was accompanied by economic prosperity. Much newfound wealth was channeled into cathedral building, and the Gothic style that Capetian rulers sponsored was widely copied throughout Europe. The towns also saw the emergence of the first universities. The university in Paris, where Pierre Abélard and Thomas Aquinas taught, soon achieved wide renown.

HUNDRED YEARS' WAR

But in the early 14th century, there were already signs that the economy was failing, and the Black Death of 1348 came as a final hammer blow. The disease killed perhaps one-third of France's population, which in many regions took centuries to rise again to pre-plague levels. The epidemic caused unparalleled damage to the economy, though the ensuing labor shortage did lead to the erosion of feudalism, as lords were obliged to lessen the feudal burden on their serfs. At this critical moment, English claims to French lands triggered the Hundred Years' War (1337–1453), with the English forming an alliance with the dukes of Burgundy, who were angling for autonomy from France.

The wars frequently went badly for the French. English feats of arms—most famously at the Battle of Agincourt in 1415—humiliated the French kings. By the early 15th century, the power of the the the latter was negligible, and the country seemed on the verge of partition. With the charismatic Jeanne d'Arc at the helm—notably in 1429–1430—the French king fought back. Despite sacrificing Jeanne to the Anglo-Burgundians, Charles VII drove the English back to the English Channel, and he and his successors brought Burgundy to heel. Its integration into the French kingdom in 1477 was complemented by that of Provence in 1481 and Brittany in 1491.

THE RENAISSANCE

In 1494, Charles VIII invaded the Italian peninsula, thus inaugurating the Italian wars that would last to 1559. Though they were fought on Italian soil, the main targets of French aggression were the Habsburg rulers who held the title of Holy Roman Emperor in Germany and who also ruled Spain. The struggle, eventually a stalemate, marked a period of cultural and economic vitality as well as political recovery in France. Italian Renaissance masters such as Leonardo da Vinci and Benvenuto Cellini worked for the French King, François I, and the spectacular court culture that François developed gave rise to important building projects. The most outstanding of those were in the Loire Valley, resulting in a dazzling spread of both new châteaux such as Chambord, Chenonceau, and Azay-le-Rideau, and up-to-date additions to older ones, like Blois.

WARS OF RELIGION

The Renaissance was accompanied by religious reformation. France was split between two antagonistic camps, as Protestants and Catholics fought no fewer than eight Wars of Religion between 1562 and 1598. The struggle was marked by terrible bloodshed—most notoriously in the infamous St. Bartholomew's Eve Massacre of 1572. In Paris alone 2,700 Protestants were slaughtered (more than the Revolutionary Tribunal was to manage in two years of the Terror between 1792 and 1794), with as many as 20,000 more deaths in other French cities. Only the conversion from Protestantism to Catholicism of Henri IV, first of the Bourbons, accompanied by the military defeat of his ultra-Catholic foes and erstwhile Protestant allies, was to bring the religious struggles to an end. The Edict of Nantes in

1598 established an uneasy truce between the two sides.

By rallying his subjects around the notion of religious tolerance and social welfare after the horrors of civil war—his ideal of every peasant having a "chicken in the pot" was an enduring propaganda image—Henri IV sealed his reputation as Good King Henry. But from

Even the king joined in the *bals masqués* and theatricals at Versailles. This costume was designed for Louis XIV, the Sun King, to portray Apollo, the Sun God.

the 1620s on, the Cardinal Ministers, Richelieu and Mazarin, who successively wielded great power, sought to defeat the Austrian Habsburg monarchy in Europe and to establish a centralized absolutist state. This placed severe strains on French society—the tax burden rose threefold between 1630 and 1648. The discontent of the poor, amplified by the grievances of nobles and religious dissidents, exploded in riots and rebellions.

SUN KING

Despite these alarms, the groundwork for a strong centralized monarchy had been laid by 1661, when Louis XIV achieved his majority and began his personal rule.

The reign of the "Sun King" was to be one of the longest in French history, mingling glory and ingloriousness in equal measure. The elaborate court society that Louis installed and led in his huge new palace at Versailles became the envy of Europe. It was also the base from which Louis pursued

The pattern of court life at Versailles was as rigidly formal as the geometric design of the gardens and the classical facade of the palace itself.

European power and a colonial empire, notably in Canada.

This was the period in which some of the greatest creative talents in French cultural history—Descartes, Corneille, Racine, Molière —flourished, and lent luster to France's *Grand Siècle* (Great Age), when France was Europe's

greatest power. From the 1680s on, however, Louis lurched into an increasingly desperate struggle against an alliance of his principal European foes, the English and the Dutch. He added to his problems by revoking the Edict of Nantes in 1685 and launching a repressive campaign against France's Protestants.

THE ENLIGHTENMENT

If the cultural achievements of 17th-century France centered on Versailles, those of the 18th-century Enlightenment largely flowed through the network of organs and institutions that characterized the bourgeois society now emerging as trade and manufacturing increased. Salons, coffeehouses, academies, novels, periodicals and newspapers, masonic lodges, and political clubs all now proliferated. Thus developed an urbane and humane culture that did not shrink from criticism of hidebound court-based hierarchy. There was an international, pacifist flavor to the French Enlightenment, too—English and Scottish philosophers were honorary members, as were

Americans Benjamin Franklin and Thomas Jefferson. In contrast, the dynastic wars of kings seemed both primitive and cruel.

The Enlightenment fostered a widespread taste for freedom and social improvement, which the monarchy did little to satisfy. The crown became increasingly indebted, even though for most of the century the economy

A contemporary view of the taking of the Bastille by Dubois, in the Musée Carnavalet, Paris

boomed. Foreign policy was directed for the most part against France's commercial rival England, and this antagonism was to remain the fulcrum of European international relations from the last wars of Louis XIV in 1688 to the overthrow of Napoleon in 1815. For most of the century, France was losing the struggle. The only significant success it managed—when French armed forces helped England's American colonies achieve their independence (1775–1783)—was so expensive that it bankrupted the state. Financial crisis, combined with a social crisis caused by a succession of poor harvests in the late 1780s, drove the state toward something more drastic than reform: revolution.

THE FRENCH REVOLUTION

The French Revolution was to provide the seeds of European liberal democratic traditions. The values of liberty, equality, and fraternity, enshrined in the Declaration of the Rights of Man of 1789, established an ideal both for political action and for the political culture within which most European states have evolved. The decade from 1789 to 1799 saw a kind of fast-forward scramble through five types of government: absolutist monarchy of the Ancien Régime type, constitutional monarchy, authoritarian republicanism (and "The Terror"), liberal republicanism, and finally—with the advent of Napoleon Bonaparte—military dictatorship.

It was probably asking too much of the well-meaning but ineffectual Louis XVI to mutate from an absolute monarch to a liberal ruler working within strict constitutional limits. His queen, the implacably anti-Revolutionary Austrian Marie-Antoinette, did not help, encouraging him to view his principal duty as lying more toward the old nobility than toward the new political nation.

The king's tireless efforts to sit on the political fence were doomed following the declaration of war against Austria. His failure to give his full support to the national war effort led to his overthrow in August 1792 (he was executed the following January), and to the establishment of a republic that became increasingly authoritarian as the war became more desperate.

By early 1793, France was fighting virtually the whole of Europe. The Enlightenment had put religious tolerance on the agenda, so it was perhaps surprising that religion became a major bone of contention too, with the church supporting the Ancien Régime and the Revolutionaries tempted into ever more anti-clerical policies.

THE TERROR

The Committee of Public Safety, with Maximilien de Robespierre as its mouthpiece, set out to assure the defense of the Republic against internal and external enemies through policies of internal terror (combined with radical social legislation aimed at eliciting support from peasants and urban workers) and national mobilization. The so-called *levée en masse* of August 1793 was the closest that any state came to mass warfare prior to the 20th century.

However, Robespierre and his faction seemed to want to intensify the Terror even as the war threat receded. In July 1794, his fellow deputies in the National Assembly deposed him in order to move toward a more liberal republic, enshrined in the Constitution of 1795. The period known as the Directory failed to impose internal harmony on warring factions or to bring the external war to a successful conclusion. In November 1799, the régime fell to a coup d'état by the Revolutionary Corsican general, Napoleon Bonaparte. A new constitution was organized, but within a couple of years Napoleon's de facto dictatorship had become a de jure imperial regime.

THE NAPOLEONIC EMPIRE

To a considerable degree, Napoleon only continued what the Revolutionaries had already started. Through brilliant generalship and astute diplomacy, he built an empire encompassing a good deal of western and central Europe. He also famously redrew the map of Europe in order to provide sufficient new states for the members of his extensive family to rule.

The spread of French power under Napoleon was far from a victory for the Rights of Man. Though he accepted and consolidated some of the gains of the Revolution—notably equality before the law, religious tolerance, economic freedom, and the abolition of feudalism—in many respects he represented an absolutism even more absolute than that of his Bourbon predecessor. The Napoleonic Civil Code was a signal achievement, though it demonstrated that the emperor was concerned even less with the rights of women than with the Rights of Man.

As long as he could insure that the costs of warfare fell on his enemies rather than on the people of France, Napoleon remained popular. After his disastrous Moscow campaign of

1811–12, however, he was always on the run. The main European states combined forces against him, and encouraged dissent within territories under French rule. By 1814, he had been deposed, and though he made a brief return from exile, he was defeated definitively by the Duke of Wellington at the Battle of Waterloo (in Belgium) in 1815.

François Gérard (1770–1837) painted Napoleon in the robes in which he crowned himself emperor in 1805.

AFTER NAPOLEON

The factionalism and acrimony of French politics in the Revolutionary and Napoleonic periods did not go away after 1815. The restoration of the Bourbon dynasty in 1815 failed to satisfy all but dyed-in-the-wool enthusiasts for "Throne and Altar" since they had learned nothing from the preceding 25 years. The revolution of 1830 brought a more liberal regime under a cadet Bourbon branch, the Orléanists. But this, too, failed to find general favor.

A further revolution in 1848 brought a flirtation with more radical policies, but the president of the new Second Republic—Louis Bonaparte—stayed true to his uncle's political sympathies. He seized power in a coup d'état in 1851, and in 1852 installed the Second Empire. This, too, failed to put down strong enough roots to survive defeat by the

Gen. Charles de Gaulle (1890–1970), here in French Equatorial Africa in 1941, led the Free French forces during World War II. Later, as president, he established the Fifth Republic and achieved political stability.

Prussians in 1870–71, and the loss of Alsace and Lorraine, which were incorporated into the new Germany.

SOCIAL & POLITICAL CHANGE

A republican regime seemed to be the type of government that divided the country least, though in the early days of the Third Republic many believed that it would preface the

restoration of the monarchy. Fearing this, the people of Paris seized power and set up the Commune to rule the city. Its brief rule ended in massive loss of life as the communards fought the government forces street by street for the city. The monarchy was not restored, but French political life remained venomously divided. The emergence of organized working-class parties, some of which proudly laid claim to a revolutionary tradition, brought fresh lines of division.

While politics oscillated frantically, French society was changing under the impact of industrialization. The process was slower than in neighboring England, but less painful too. The growth of towns and the development of industry neither spelled the end of peasant farming nor utterly transformed the countryside. By the last years of the century, moreover, industrialization was bearing fruit for a large proportion of the population. Middle- and even working-class life was transformed by the processes of modernization. Writing on the eve of World War I, the writer Charles Péguy claimed—with a certain amount of accuracy—that the world had been transformed more radically since his own school days in the 1880s than it had between then and the time of the Romans.

PARIS RENEWED

Paris was the beacon of the new, its Tour Eiffel, constructed in 1889 for the international exhibition to commemorate the centenary of the Revolution, towering over the city. That city enjoyed wide new boulevards and was famed for fashion houses, department stores, art nouveau styles, and glamorous sites of all imaginable pleasures. The elegant belle epoque had its dark and pessimistic side, however. As realist novelists such as Émile Zola showed, working-class conditions were appalling, and yet the Third Republic took little interest in social questions.

CONFLICT WITH GERMANY

France had lost its colonial empire to England during the Revolutionary and Napoleonic wars. In 1830 it conquered Algeria and began to amass a new one. The bulk of imperial acquisitions were made after the 1870s, and amplified tensions with other European

After the long years of the Occupation in World War II, the Allied troops were welcomed across France. This woman at Belfort joyfully greets an American soldier.

powers, notably Great Britain. Nevertheless, the prime target for French aggression was now Germany, which in economic and military terms seemed to be outstripping France down to the outbreak of World War I in 1914.

France benefited from being on the winning side of that war. Alsace and Lorraine were restored to the Third Republic at the Treaty of Versailles in 1919, but the victory was won at a massive price. France lost more men in the war—1.3 million—than any other nation. Much of the northern part of the country was devastated by the passage of the Allied and German armies as first one side and then the

other gained a few miles of country in the fruitless struggle of trench warfare. Modernization meant not only more consumer goods and more elegant lifestyles, but also murderous new forms of mechanized and mass warfare.

French men and women still found it difficult to sleep soundly at night, moreover. The German call for revenge became ever more threatening in the interwar years, as Hitler and the Nazis came to power in Germany in 1933. France had its own Fascist movement too, against which was pitted a revolutionary Communist movement linked to the Soviet regime established in Russia in 1917.

The Third Republic still had its charms: Foreigners such as writers Gertrude Stein, Ernest Hemingway, F. Scott Fitzgerald, and Ezra Pound; black jazz musicians; and a variegated range of painters and sculptors found Paris in particular a welcoming center of cultural dynamism. But the Third Republic's political accommodation and compromise would not be sufficient to deal with the new challenge of war in 1939.

OCCUPATION & DECOLONIZATION

In the middle decades of the 20th century, France had to cope with two profound traumas: firstly World War II and secondly the process of decolonization.

The French defeat at the hands of Nazi Germany in 1940 brought German occupation, at first in the northern half of the country and then, from 1942 on, throughout the whole country. It also involved collaboration with the Nazis. Under Maréchal Pétain, a World War I hero, Jews and Communists became the prime targets of the Vichy regime's collaborationist zeal.

Resistance was at first marshaled from London by the self-exiled Gen. Charles de Gaulle, and from the early 1940s was spearheaded by a wide range of political activists, with Communists to the fore. The Allied landings on the Normandy beaches in 1944 found Resistance movements coming out into the open to mop up the retreating German forces. After the war, France united around the new Fourth Republic (which granted women the vote for the first time). Yet painful memories of collaboration remained, rising spasmodically to haunt the national conscience.

The process of decolonization had a similar effect. From the early 1950s, the liberation movements in North Africa and Indochina elicited a military response from the French. Their defeat at the battle of Dien Bien Phu in Indochina (which Vietnam was then part of) in 1954 by the Communist Viet Minh led to the complete withdrawal of the French from the Far East. Civil war flared up in Algeria and threatened political stability within France itself.

Political crisis triggered by the events in Algeria brought General de Gaulle to power as president of the new Fifth Republic, which accorded him extensive powers. His solution to the crisis—complete independence of Algeria, plus the repatriation of the colonists (or *pieds-noirs*)—left lasting rancor on both sides of the Mediterranean.

THE "MAY EVENTS"

These political scars should not blind us to the way in which France has come to terms with some of its thorniest problems in the second half of the century. Most notably, it has achieved an almost undreamed of political stability. During de Gaulle's lifetime, many political thinkers suspected that the structure of the Fifth Republic was such that only a right-wing figure could operate effectively within it. In the event, however, the regime has proved able to accommodate the death of its founder; the election of a Socialist president, François Mitterrand, in 1981; and since then a general acceptance of the principle of alternation (*alternance*) between left- and right-wing governments and presidents.

The only time the regime has appeared to be in danger was during the extraordinary and quite unclassifiable "May Events" of 1968, when student protests, escalated by working-class and liberal professional militancy, almost brought down de Gaulle's government. With its 40th birthday now behind it, however, the Fifth Republic has become the second longest-enduring regime in French history since the 18th century, after the much-underestimated Third Republic.

EUROPEAN COOPERATION

The second specter to be exorcised from French political life since World War II is that

The venerable Pont des Invalides across the Seine in Paris witnessed an impromptu party when rock and roll first hit Paris in the fifties. Like jazz to an earlier generation, rock and roll was all the rage for young French people.

of an aggressive Germany. From the 1860s to the 1940s, French foreign policy was constructed around hostility to Germany. But Germany's defeat in war led farsighted individuals in both countries to work toward Franco-German cooperation. Starting with the Coal and Steel Union of 1951, France and Germany have been at the forefront of every stage of European cooperation, up to the establishment of the European Union, the acceptance of a common currency, and beyond.

This is a situation in which France has generally prospered. The end of World War II in 1945 initiated the so-called Thirty Glorious Years, which saw the French economy modernizing and expanding at a faster rate than ever before, in a period which some commentators have dubbed the real French Revolution. Impressive rates of economic growth and an unparalleled baby boom were combined with a thorough shake-up in infrastructure and services, the widespread diffusion of consumer durables and other commodities, the growth

Despite the pressures of modern high-speed living, Paris retains its traditions of pleasure and leisured joie de vivre.

of mass leisure, and a new affluence that put a question mark against hallowed customs and conventions.

Though opinion polls sporadically reveal anxiety about social development and economic performance in France, it remains true that most people find the country an attractive one to live in or visit. Paris, beneficiary of a

policy of cultural grandeur (as exemplified by the Centre Pompidou, the Opéra National de Paris-Bastille, the Musée d'Orsay, and other projects), is still outstanding among cities.

Equally striking has been the dynamism of a number of provincial cities such as Lyon, Montpellier, Lille, and Nîmes. A growing concern for regionalism, multiculturalism, and for gender issues suggests a broadening of political and cultural options at the beginning of the 21st century, in the context of a general respect for the country's heritage. ■

The arts

HARDLY SURPRISINGLY, GIVEN ALL THE RICHES, THE FRENCH ARE EXTREMELY proud of their cultural heritage. Education is highly valued, and discussion of artistic and intellectual matters is taken for granted as part of everyday life.

ROMAN ERA (56 B.C.–A.D. 476)

It was with the Romans that the first signs of "modern" civilization appeared in France. Their architecture symbolized the power of their empire, and can still be seen to striking effect in the amphitheaters at Arles and Nîmes, the temples at Nîmes and Vienne, and the aqueduct of the Pont du Gard.

ROMANESQUE PERIOD (11TH–12TH CENTURIES)

After the fall of the Roman Empire, France plunged into the Dark Ages until the coming of the Carolingian dynasty in the eighth century. This period has left few visible remains: For these one looks to the flowering of Romanesque ecclesiastical architecture in the 11th century. Here timber roofs give way to stone vaulting, buttresses take the increased weight, and the use of decoration grows.

The Romanesque style spread throughout France and developed regional features—especially in Burgundy, where you can appreciate an excellent example of the Romanesque at Vézelay (see p. 202).

Fortresses were the other major buildings to survive from the Romanesque era, but most have been either reduced to ruins or have been modified or rebuilt. Angers (see p. 184–85) retains its massive curtain wall, and Langeais still has a medieval exterior (see p. 188)

The main themes of this period's literature, which was mostly in verse, are faith and chivalry. Particularly important are the *chansons de geste* or heroic songs. A favorite theme was Charlemagne's wars against the infidel, as in the *Chanson de Roland* (circa 1098), which recounts the death of the Carolingian hero while defending the pass at Roncesvalles against the Saracens.

The first courtly romances appeared in the 12th century—narrative poems concerned with idealized and chivalrous conceptions of love. The classical influence was strong, and the most famous romance writer, Chrétien de Troyes (died circa 1183), saw himself and his contemporaries as inheritors of the literary traditions of the Greeks and Romans. In the 13th century, courtly romances were preoccupied with the Arthurian legend; the genre also produced the most influential work of the Middle Ages, the *Roman de la Rose*, a dream-allegory of courtly love.The same theme dominated the lyric poetry of the Provençal troubadours, who made a significant contribution to the development of French music.

GOTHIC PERIOD (12TH–15TH CENTURIES)

Gothic architecture had strong upward aspirations (see pp. 114–15); Gothic churches and cathedrals have high, pointed arches, flying buttresses, and large traceried windows filled with stained glass, which reach their apogee in the rose window, as at Chartres cathedral (see pp. 98–99). Interiors became more highly decorated and elaborate, with rood and choir screens, altarpieces, and statuary.

Book decoration and illustration, known as illumination and best represented by the books of hours, containing prayers to be said at the canonical hours, reached its zenith in the 14th century. At the same time, easel painting arrived. In its attention to detail and concern with representing space convincingly, French art of this period shows the influence of the more developed Italian and Flemish schools. The major figure is Jean Fouquet (circa 1420–circa 1481), painter to Louis XI.

Medieval France's main contribution to music was through the monasteries, which preserved the tradition of the plainchant and elaborated it into polyphony. The Burgundian court also had a key musical role, employing a huge number of musicians, and composers such as Guillaume Dufay (circa 1400–1474) flourished under its patronage.

The arch at La Défense, one of the "Grand Projects" that have transformed Paris

The 15th century saw France's most outstanding medieval lyric poet, François Villon, who used conventional verse forms but invested them with the spirit of the *fabliaux* (bawdy popular tales) to draw a vivid picture of low-life in 15th-century Paris.

The most interesting prose writers of the time are the chroniclers, of whom the best

The Roman arena at Arles is still used for performances, as it was 2,000 years ago.

known is Jean Froissart, the chief historian of the Hundred Years' War; in particular he compiled a remarkable eyewitness account of the Battle of Crécy (1346).

THE RENAISSANCE (16TH–17TH CENTURIES)

French campaigns in northern Italy at the end of the 15th century brought the aesthetics of the Italian Renaissance to the attention of French artists and architects and their patrons. This can be seen most clearly in the building of châteaus by the royal family and nobility that marked the final stages of the castle's progression from fortification to elaborate residence. Living quarters were extended, windows became larger, and moats, keeps, and turrets became purely decorative as opposed to defensive features. The castle descended

from hilltop to riverside, where its watery reflection further enhanced its splendor. The château was supposed to harmonize with its natural surroundings but, increasingly, formal grounds were integrated into the grand design. The Renaissance influence made for increasingly regular and symmetrical designs although châteaus exhibit a number of different styles. Thus Cheverny, built in 1634, is classical in its purity of line, while Blois (see p. 167), built between the 13th and 17th centuries, reflects the development of secular French architecture from feudalism to classicism. Chambord (see pp.168–69), the largest of the Loire châteaus, is a superb example of Italian Renaissance style.

The spirit of the Renaissance began to permeate literature in the 16th century, as scholars rediscovered the classical Greek and Latin writers. Under their renewed influence a broader outlook began to challenge the rigid theological thinking of the late medieval period. The first printing press was established in Paris in 1470, and by 1515 some 100 operated in France. This had a huge impact on the development of vernacular literature. The work of François Rabelais is the supreme expression of this newfound freedom, vitality, and enthusiasm. His *Gargantua* and *Pantagruel* were parodies of chivalric romances, but also addressed serious philosophical issues.

Equally a Renaissance man, but far more methodical and rationalist, was Michel de Montaigne, whose three books of *Essais* (literally "tryings out") gave the form its name. Montaigne's remark that "each man bears the complete stamp of the human condition" perfectly sums up the humanist spirit of Renaissance thought.

The key poet of the 16th century, and the leader of a group of writers known as the Pléiade, was Pierre de Ronsard (1524–1584). The Pléiade broke with medieval poetic forms and looked to Greece and Rome for models. The 12-syllable line, the Alexandrine, began its long dominance of French poetry.

CLASSICISM (17TH CENTURY)

Classicism started during the reign of Louis XIII and reached its apogee with his successor, Louis XIV. The absolutism of the age is expressed in its architecture by grandiosity, stress on order and symmetry, and evocation of the glory of Greece and Rome. The zenith of the early Louis XIV style is undoubtedly the Château of Vaux-le-Vicomte, built in 1656–1661 for Nicolas Fouquet, finance minister in Mazarin's time. Louis XIV was so envious that he hired the same design team (led by Louis le Vau) to build a château a hundred times bigger—Versailles.

In 1648, the Royal Academy of Painting and Sculpture was founded, a key instrument for imposing "official" standards and principles of taste. It enshrined the classical idea that the practice and appreciation of art are rational activities that can be reduced to rules and precepts, and thus be taught and learned.

Italian influence

In painting, Italy was the influential center of Europe. Especially important was Caravaggio for his rich colors, deep shadows, and dramatic compositions, and his introduction of a disturbing realism into conventional religious subjects as in his "Death of the Virgin" (in the Louvre). His influence is clearly visible in the work of leading French 17th-century painters like Moïse Valentin, Georges de La Tour, and Simon Vouet. But the two French painters who best express the classical spirit are Claude Lorraine and Nicolas Poussin. Lorraine's landscapes are Arcadian, evoking the pastoral serenity of a golden age bathed in a glorious light. Poussin dealt with noble themes from classical mythology treated in a pastoral mood, but developed a more austere classicism in works that exude a monumental simplicity, lucidity, and calm.

Elaborate ballets were the main form of musical entertainment at court, and a young Florentine, Lully, became one of the principal dancers and composers. Italian opera was not popular, and *tragédies lyriques* (a form of sung play with balletic elements) proved more to French tastes. Lully composed a large number of these; he also greatly influenced church music and wrote solemn motets for the royal chapel, with soloists, chorus, and orchestra. This form was also developed by Gustave Charpentier, François Couperin, and Michel-Richard Delalande with strict counterpoint enriched by sonorous harmonies.

Literature

French classical literature was built on the foundations laid by Montaigne. He saw literature as a part of the enlightened study of human nature, a search for its universal features, inseparable from what we would now think of as philosophy. Furthermore, Descartes's conception of man as essentially

The vividly illustrated *Chronicles* of Jean Froissart (circa 1333–circa 1404) cover the history of the Hundred Years' War.

rational, endowed by the Creator with reason to be used in the pursuit of truth, had a massive impact on all forms of intellectual life. Their literary followers were preoccupied with the purity of language and style, and the dramatic unities of time and place. They divided literature into discrete genres such as comedy and tragedy, and founded the Académie Française in 1634 to safeguard French language and literature. The century also saw the growth of salons, hosted by noblewomen such as the Marquise de Rambouillet, in which literary matters were discussed.

Some of the most interesting writers of the age dealt in nonfiction. For example, La Rochefoucauld's *Maximes*—such as "hypocrisy is the homage which vice pays to virtue" and "we are all strong enough

to bear other people's misfortunes"—give off a certain sense of cynicism and moral pessimism. Madame de Sévigné's *Lettres* paint a lively picture of daily happenings and also communicate a vivid sense of the writer herself. Finally, the *Lettres provinciales* and the *Pensées* of Blaise Pascal provide a welcome antidote to the narrow, overly neat, and self-confident rationalism of much 17th-century thought. His famous saying, "the heart has its reasons of which Reason knows nothing," marks him as a precursor of Romanticism.

Drama

The chief poetry of the 17th century is in its drama (although one should not forget the sly and sometimes cynical *Fables* of Jean de La Fontaine, which borrow heavily from Greek fabulist Aesop's originals). The plays of Pierre Corneille and Jean Racine insured that tragedy was the supreme genre. Corneille's tragedies such as *Le Cid* and *Polyeucte* are highly formal, concentrated dramas about passion versus moral duty, peopled by superhuman figures who are less three-dimensional, psychological

The classical exterior at Versailles contrasts with the extravagant interior exemplified by the Galérie des Glaces.

characters than symbols of nobility and heroism. Racine took the theme of duty versus desire to even greater heights in *Andromaque*, *Phèdre*, and other classically inspired plays, but he was the greater poet; his characters are not just ciphers but passion-filled human beings, the language has an incantatory power, and the dramatic action has a remorseless intensity.

Comedy

Comedy flourished at the same time, thanks to Jean-Baptiste Molière. The first French playwright to use the genre for social commentary, he is, along with William Shakespeare and Ben Jonson, a key figure in the development of European comedy.

Molière's plays mingle farce, ballet, and the comedy of manners, and they have a satirical edge that sometimes caused trouble with the authorities. His attack on intellectual pretension, *Les Précieuses ridicules*, offended the habitués of the salons and earned him enemies there. *Tartuffe* attacked religious hypocrisy, but was taken as an attack on religion and banned for five years. But his masterpiece, *Le Misanthrope*, shows that Molière was not simply a deft satirist but also a master of the comedy of character who knew that the line between comedy and tragedy was indeed a fine one.

Molière as Caesar in "La Mort de Pompée," painted by Pierre Mignard (1612–1695)

FRENCH ROCOCO (18TH CENTURY)

Inevitably there was a reaction against the austere grandeur of the Louis XIV style. In architectural terms, interiors became smaller, more intimate, and highly decorated, with elaborate furniture to match. There was an abundance of curved lines, exotic woods, lacquered paneling, floral marquetry, and gilt.

The paintings of Antoine Watteau, François Boucher, and Jean Honoré Fragonard best express the rococo spirit. Watteau may have been influenced by Rubens, but he is quintessentially 18th-century French. Painting in colors that are rich, yet also soft and light, he depicts an exquisitely delicate and artificial world of *fêtes galantes* in dreamy, pastoral settings. After this, Boucher, Madame de Pompadour's favorite artist—several of his most famous paintings are of Louis XV's mistress—and the epitome of the elegant superficiality of the mid-18th-century French court, seems rather frivolous. His pupil, Fragonard, painted lightly erotic works such as "The Progress of Love"—full of verve, sparkle, color, and wit—for Madame du Barry, a later mistress of Louis XIV; they are the very embodiment of the rococo.

NEOCLASSICISM & THE ENLIGHTENMENT (18TH CENTURY)

After the frivolity of the rococo, there was a return to the classical. In painting, the Académie Française insisted on a new seriousness, reviving heroic and edifying themes from antiquity. The most notable exponent of the new manner was Jacques-Louis David, whose subjects displayed self-sacrifice and moral duty in a suitably severe, even austere, style. He had strong Revolutionary sympathies, later becoming Napoleon's official painter and, indeed, the principal artist of the Revolution. One of his best-known works, "The Death of Marat" (1793), depicts the Revolutionary hero assassinated in his bath.

In philosophy and literature, the spirit of free, rational inquiry was predominant, and there was a widespread belief in progress through enlightenment. This was the century of the *philosophe*, the progressive-minded individual involved in cultural and artistic activity as well as social and scientific thinking. In literary terms the treatise and the essay were equally important as the novel, play, or poem—marking the beginnings of a literature of thought.

Philosophical thought

Montesquieu epitomized the Enlightenment spirit. In his *Considérations sur les causes de la grandeur des Romains et de leur décadence* he laid down a rational, theoretical approach to the study of history, arguing that "it is not chance that dominates the world, but general causes, either moral or physical." Similarly *L'Esprit des lois* is an early example of political theory that attempts to explain why the laws of different countries vary; characteristically it enthrones reason as "the most noble, the most perfect, the most exquisite of our senses."

Voltaire

Equally important was Voltaire (1694–1778). His *Lettres philosophiques*, based on two years' exile in England, show an admiration (shared by Montesquieu) for tolerance and liberalism, as epitomized for them by English political and religious institutions. His *Essai sur les moeurs* was a survey of world history showing peoples' slow progress from superstition to rationality. But today Voltaire is best known for his satirical philosophical tales. The most famous, *Candide*, hilariously satirizes the then-influential philosopher Leibniz and his idea that God had created the best of all possible worlds. As a philosopher Voltaire made social thinking popular, and even fashionable.

The key product of the Enlightenment is the 17-volume *Encyclopédie*, edited by Denis Diderot and his assistant Jean d'Alembert, which laid out the latest positions in science and philosophy and aimed to "change the general manner of thinking."

In the theater, the *drame bourgeois*, written in prose and with contemporary characters, began to replace the outmoded classical forms. This was first attempted by Beaumarchais, whose fame rests on the plays *Le Barbier de Séville* and *Le Mariage de Figaro*, the latter being the box office hit of the century. These topical comedies, tinged with risqué democratic sentiment, restored a vitality to the genre that had been missing since Molière.

Rousseau

However, the 18th century also saw a reaction against rationalism and a foreshadowing of Romanticism. Nobody illustrates this better than the philosopher Jean-Jacques Rousseau, who proclaims the natural over the civilized, emotion over reason, the individual over society. Largely self-taught, Rousseau exerted an enormous influence on every field he entered. His *Discours sur les sciences et les arts* elaborated the theory of natural goodness, the *Discours sur l'inégalité* the virtue of primitive society. The novel *La Nouvelle Héloïse* is the key work of the "sentimental revolution," which dethroned reason and reestablished the claims of the heart. It was the century's publishing sensation, going through 70 editions in its first 40 years. *Émile*, part novel, part treatise, and wholly a defense of nature as the

greatest educator, was a key text of progressive education, as *Le Contrat Social* was of democracy. Finally, Rousseau's devastatingly intimate *Confessions* virtually defined the modern autobiography.

The sentimental revolution also expressed itself in novels concerned with libertinage. Typical is *Manon Lescaut* by the Abbé Prévost. The novel's ostensible purpose is to show "the disastrous effects of the passions," but it is so ambiguous and bizarre that it is almost a celebration of *l'amour fou*. Similarly, Pierre Choderlos de Laclos's much-adapted *Les Liaisons dangereuses* presents as a moral lesson its story of two libertines who seduce two innocents, but what emerges is also a study of the seductive fascination of evil. In the novels of the Marquis de Sade, the idea of presenting libertinage so as to deliver a moral message is taken to such hyperbolic and pornographic extremes that it has the opposite result.

ROMANTICISM (19TH CENTURY)

French Romanticism was at its height from 1820 to 1850, but cultural movements are never neat and there are important precursors (already noted) and late blooms. It was a reaction against the rationalism of the Enlightenment and its attendant classicism, and proposed the primacy of unfettered, individual imagination. Romantics rejected external reality to seek solace and inspiration within themselves, or in exotic or imaginary locales. Particularly via the writer Madame de Staël, who spent much time in Germany, interest grew in German writers such as Goethe, Schiller, and Novalis. Meanwhile, English influence ceased to be philosophical and rationalist and became lyrical and picturesque thanks to such writers and artists as Byron, Scott, Constable, Turner, and the hitherto neglected Shakespeare.

Painting

Théodore Géricault was the archetypal Romantic, even dying young (at 33). His "Raft of the Medusa" is typical in its macabre subject (dying castaways on a raft), Romantic brio, swirling movement, and energetic handling of paint. Even more important, however, was Eugène Delacroix. Influenced by Rubens and the English painters Bonington,

Gainsborough, and Constable, he specialized in emotionally charged and often exotic subjects; his technical virtuosity, freedom of brushwork, and richness of color were extraordinarily influential, way beyond the confines of Romanticism.

Music & opera

The rigid institutionalization of music in France made it difficult for outsiders to break in, and the Romantics were outsiders by temperament. But German composer Christoff Gluck had helped to pave the way for Romanticism when he worked on his operas in Paris in the 1770s, and in the next century the French, no longer musically insular, welcomed the arch-Romantics Franz Liszt and Frédéric Chopin.

France produced a key Romantic composer, indeed Romanticism personified, in the shape of Hector Berlioz. A composer with the grandest of ideas and a formidable sense of drama, his *Symphonie Fantastique*, with its

Jean-Auguste-Dominique Ingres (1780–1867), one of the great French classical artists, painted his voluptuous "La Grande Odalisque" in 1814.

evocations of a violent storm, a march to the scaffold, and a climactic witches' sabbath, broke all the bounds of what a symphony was "supposed" to be. Berlioz's *Mass* and *Te Deum* are works on a truly gargantuan scale, and had he completed *Les Troyens*, it would have been the equivalent of Wagner's *Ring* cycle. His *Memoirs* are one of the great heroic expressions of the Romantic era, but it would be a mistake to regard their author simply as the archetypal Romantic rebel and outsider, disdaining all formal procedures. Berlioz also wrote one of the definitive treatises on orchestration, and introduced the finest Romantic music to France. He was not only a key Romantic but also a pioneer of modern music.

Romanticism had a longer life in music than elsewhere. Gounod's *Faust* (1859) was for

Even in 1806, the French led the world in fashion: Empire dresses illustrated in the *Journal des Dames et des Modes* **would have inspired many dressmakers.**

many years the best loved French opera; Massenet, the most popular opera composer of the second half of the century, specialized in grand but rather prettified and sentimental Romantic spectacles such as *Manon*. In orchestral music, the influence of Liszt was clearly felt in the symphonic poems of Camille Saint-Saëns and César Franck. For example, Saint-Saëns in *Danse macabre* portrays Death playing his violin in a churchyard at midnight whilst skeletons dance around, while Franck's *Le Chasseur maudit* paints a noisy picture of a huntsman doomed to be chased forever by the hounds of Hell as a punishment for hunting on the Sabbath. After 1880 the German Romantic influence was further intensified by the seemingly irresistible lure of Wagner, which tends sometimes to make itself felt in a rather un-French grandiosity. However, French classical restraint, albeit tinged with Romantic feeling, reasserted itself in the work of Gabriel Fauré and Henri Duparc who, among other things, transformed the drawing room *mélodie* into an art song that can stand comparison with the great German lieder.

Literature of Romanticism

Some of the finest expressions of French Romanticism can be found in the poetry of Lamartine, de Vigny, Hugo, and de Musset. Here, poetry is the expression of primarily personal feelings and emotions. Intensely lyrical and introspective, it allows the imagination full play, and uses the outside world, especially nature, as a reflection of inner feelings. This kind of Romantic poetry helped to establish the image of the poet as the tortured artist.

In the theater, Romanticism is best exemplified by the historical verse dramas of Victor Hugo and, in prose, those of Alexandre

"Algerian girls in their apartment" by Eugène Delacroix (1798–1863), in the Louvre

Dumas père. Hugo rejected the classical unities of time and place, attacked the artificial separation of the tragic and the comic, and demanded more natural language and local color. His picturesque historical dramas *Hernani* and *Ruy Blas* feature noble characters battling against all odds.

The confessional tales of Chateaubriand, *Atala*, and *René* (1802) clearly prefigure the doomed Romantic hero, and Benjamin Constant's *Adolphe* (1806) is a bleakly Romantic story of *le mal du siècle*. But it is in the historical novel that the Romantic impulse is clearest: Alfred de Vigny's *Cinq Mars*, Hugo's *Notre-Dame de Paris*, and the colorfully exotic works of Prosper Mérimée, whose *Carmen* was the source of Bizet's opera, and whose *Colomba* is the story of a Corsican vendetta. However, it was Dumas père who developed the Romantic past into something really popular in his Musketeers trilogy and *The Count of Monte Cristo*.

Nineteenth-century French culture can be seen as a dialogue between Romanticism and Realism, and the novels of Stendhal (Marie-Henri Beyle) and Honoré de Balzac straddle

both. Stendhal was a Romantic in his fascination with Italy, his championship of Shakespeare, his interest in the theme of love, and his novels' proud, young, egotistical heroes. The ambitious Julien Sorel in *Le Rouge et le Noir* enters the priesthood in order to climb the social ladder in contemporary France, and Fabrice in *La Chartreuse de Parme* becomes embroiled in the intrigues of the court at Parma. But society is portrayed with a profundity, irony, and sharpness that is more realist than Romantic. Meanwhile, Balzac's vast *Comédie humaine*, which includes 80-odd novels and stories and covers French life from the Revolution until 1840, has an extraordinary, even obsessive, realism of detail. At the same time the novels often seem to be infused by a shadowy, Romantic aura.

REALISM (19TH CENTURY)

In art, an interest in unadorned nature and in ordinary people began to appear in the middle of the century. There is still something of the Arcadian in Camille Corot's misty, soft-edged paintings, but he did attempt to represent

Manet painted fellow-Impressionist Monet at work in a boat at Honfleur in 1874.

nature without idealization or romanticization. Théodore Rousseau, Charles Daubigny, Jean-François Millet, and others painted direct from nature and formed the Barbizon school, named after the village in the Fontainebleau forest in which they painted. Millet's scenes from rural life emphasize its tough side, and he invested ordinary people with weight and dignity. His "Angélus" was the most frequently reproduced painting of the century, but because of the religious nature of its subject matter, it also earned him an unjust reputation for pious sentimentality.

The chief realist painter is undoubtedly Gustave Courbet. A Socialist who was imprisoned for his part in the 1871 Commune, he concentrated on the tangible reality of things and people. Conventional opinion regarded his pictures as crude and ugly, but his influence was tremendous, not least on the cubists.

The Impressionists also belong under the realist banner. They were not a unified school, but a loose association of artists with a certain community of outlook. They came together between 1860 and 1886 for the purposes of exhibiting in a largely hostile environment.

They included Monet, Renoir, Sisley, Pissarro, Dégas, and Manet who, though often interested in different subject matter, shared the rejection of the Romantic ideal. In particular, they wanted to capture immediate, fleeting impressions of color and light rather than the permanent aspects of a subject. Thus, for example, Monet's series of paintings of poplars, haystacks, and the west front of the cathedral at Rouen, in which he tried to capture the impression of the same subject under different climatic conditions and times of day.

Realist literature

Gustave Flaubert's *Madame Bovary,* published in 1857, marks the arrival of the realist novel, although formally it also prefigures modernism. However, his notion that the author should be like God, omnipresent but invisible, is certainly realist. Flaubert's hostility to Romanticism is underlined in the novel by Madame Bovary immersing herself in escapist Romantic fantasies as compensation for the ghastliness of provincial Normandy life. The Normandy countryside is also the setting for many of the best stories of Guy de Maupassant, the acknowledged master of the realist short story.

In Émile Zola, realism developed into naturalism. He believed that the novel should be an illustration of the laws of scientific

Nijinsky and the Ballet Russe danced to the *Prélude à l'après-midi d'un faune* in 1915, shocking and scandalizing the French establishment.

determinism that govern human nature through heredity and the environment. He put this theory into practice in his huge *Rougon-Macquart* series of 20 novels—a vivid and imaginative panorama of the whole Second Empire.

In musical terms, Georges Bizet's *Carmen*, based on a novel by Mérimée and, almost unbelievably, a flop at its first performance in 1875, is an interesting mix of realism and Romanticism. The Spanish setting may have exotic connotations, but its treatment of passionate (as opposed to simply romantic)

feelings is realistic, as is the inclusion of speech between the music.

MODERN TIMES

In the first half of the 20th century, France became a hotbed of artistic modernism, and its culture was further enriched by the novelists, poets, artists, and composers who flocked there from across the world. These included Aaron Copland, Ernest Hemingway, Henry Miller, Ezra Pound, and Gertrude Stein. However, modernism's roots lie firmly in 19th-century France.

Architecture

During the Second Empire, Baron Haussmann laid the basis of modern Paris. He replaced the narrow streets of festering slums with the wide boulevards of today. This wasn't entirely philanthropic; Paris had seen three uprisings in 50 years, and, in any future trouble, the boulevards would facilitate rapid troop movements and provide clear fields for artillery fire. The year 1889 saw the opening of the Eiffel Tower, which demonstrated spectacularly the architectural potential of steel, and helped to usher in the modern era.

Today we tend to blame modern architects for creating inhuman, alienating environments. But one of the founding figures of architectural modernism, the Swiss Le Corbusier, was almost utopian in his vision of the social benefits of a functional, rationally planned urban environment, with its skyscrapers, gridlike street systems, wide-open spaces, and rings of satellite towns. That vision is exemplified by the Cité Radieuse in Marseille (see p. 301). Also worth visiting are La Roche Villa (now the Le Corbusier Foundation, *10 square du Docteur-Blanche*) in Paris and the extraordinary Chapelle de Notre-Dame-du-Haut in Ronchamp in the Jura (see p. 210), one of the few great modernist religious buildings.

Even in these supposedly postmodernist times, France has never shied from promoting unapologetically modern architecture; nor has it been afraid to use considerable public funds in doing so. Indeed, both presidents and local mayors regard bold architectural commissions as an excellent means of leaving a visible mark. The acclaimed results encourage an increase in tourism and other forms of business, and are thus popular. Consequently, no visitor to France can ignore its modern architecture, be it the Grande Arche de la Défense, the Tour Montparnasse, the Beaubourg Center, the Parc de la Villette, the Institut du Monde Arabe, the Louvre Pyramid, or the Bastille-Opéra building in Paris; the new national library in Marseille; Futuroscope outside Poitiers (see p. 237); the Eurolille complex; or Roissy, near the Charles-de-Gaulle airport.

Modern art

In the early 20th century, Paris was accepted as the world center of contemporary art. The Impressionists and other painters of the time had begun to liberate art from the merely representational and photography had made the straightforward copying of reality redundant. The founding figure of modern art is undoubtedly Paul Cézanne, who was concerned above all with analyzing the underlying structural forms of nature. His influence is incalculable, but can be seen at its clearest in the cubism of Picasso, Braque, Léger, Delaunay, and others. A key precursor of later abstract art, cubism abandoned the traditional notions of perspective and tried to represent objects not as they appear at a particular moment and from a particular angle, but analytically and from all sides at once, as it were, as if the eye could take in simultaneously every facet and plane.

Everywhere, non- and indeed antinaturalism was the order of the day. Paul Gauguin and Vincent van Gogh had been extraordinarily influential, in their different ways, in nonnaturalistic use of color. Furthermore, van Gogh had taken to its ultimate extreme the use of the external world to express the inner; his strong, vivid colors and bold lines not only communicate the artist's tortured state, but the thickly laid-on paint pushes ever closer toward purely abstract patterns and shapes. The influence of the way these artists used color is visible in the *fauves* (literally, wild beasts), who included Henri Matisse, André Derain, Georges Braque, and Georges Rouault and who used vivid, nonnaturalistic colors for emotional or decorative effect.

Music

Musical modernism also owes a great deal to France. In Paris in 1913 the émigré Igor Stravinsky's ballet *The Rite of Spring* caused

Behind the scenes at the showing of Dior's collection in 1955. His 1947 New Look revived the fashion industry after the war.

one of modernism's great scandals. But just as important is Claude Debussy, and especially his *Prélude à l'après-midi d'un faune* (1894). Though deceptively easy on the ear it actually marks the beginnings of modern music. The piece is by no means atonal, but already conventional harmonic relationships are giving way, and at times the key is in doubt. Debussy does not take a clear-cut theme and develop it in consecutive, goal-directed fashion; rather the overall impression is improvisatory. There are fluctuating tempi and irregular rhythms, and orchestral color is no longer an ornament but increasingly an end in itself. Debussy was to develop these ideas much further but, without this seemingly innocuous piece, it would be hard to envisage the more obviously

modern compositions of the great 20th-century French composers, Olivier Messiaen and his pupil Pierre Boulez.

Surrealism

One modernist movement that spread across all the arts, and still has an influence on much contemporary culture, was surrealism. Again, this has its roots in the 19th century—in the extraordinary symbolist paintings of Odilon Redon and Gustave Moreau (whose Parisian house is now a gallery devoted to his art). It

can also be seen in the hallucinatory, transgressive writings of Joris Karl Huysmans, Gérard de Nerval, and Lautréamont (the pseudonym of Isidore Ducasse) and especially in the intensely subjective, language-stretching poetry of Charles Baudelaire, Arthur Rimbaud, and Paul Verlaine.

Surrealists were fascinated by the unconscious, the bizarre, and the irrational. Clearly influenced by Freud, they wanted to challenge the dominance of reason and the conscious mind. They were inspired by Lautréamont's

Models at a 1980s Emanuel Ungaro fashion show. The world still looks to Paris for new directions in haute couture.

definition of beauty: "the chance encounter of a sewing machine and an umbrella on an operating table." Two of the key French poets of the 20th century—Louis Aragon and Paul Éluard—emerged from surrealism, and it also left a distinct mark on the scriptwriter Jacques Prévert and the films of Jean Cocteau, particularly *Le Sang d'un poète*.

Cinema

Cocteau brings us to cinema, the quintessentially modern medium, which the French christened *le septième art*, the seventh art. French pioneers Étienne Marey and Felix-Louis Regnault played a key role in the prehistory of the cinema, while the Lumière brothers laid the basis for the documentary and Georges Méliès for fantasy genres.

Film might have been regarded early as an art in France, but its commercial possibilities, too, were rapidly realized by Gaumont and

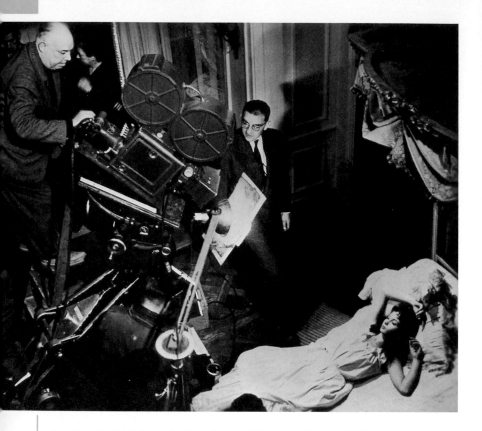

Jean Renoir directs Françoise Arnoul in *French CanCan*, released in 1955.

Pathé, although after World War I France, like other European countries, felt the effects of Hollywood imports. Nevertheless, French cinema managed to thrive, as evidenced by the immensely varied work of directors such as Marcel L'Herbier, Jean Epstein, René Clair, Jacques Feyder, Jean Renoir (the painter's son), and Marcel Carné, among many others.

After World War II, and in spite of the country's economic difficulties, interesting new figures such as Henri-Georges Clouzot, Jean-Pierre Melville, Jacques Tati, and Georges Franju appeared. By the early fifties a number of critics grouped around the journal *Cahiers du Cinéma* argued for a more personal and contemporary form of cinema. They reexamined Hollywood cinema, and argued that the works of Alfred Hitchcock, John Ford, and Harold Hawks, among others, were *authored* movies, with a strong personal content.

Soon *Cahiers* critics such as Jean-Luc Godard, Claude Chabrol, François Truffaut, and others were putting their ideas into practice by making their own highly personal movies. This *Nouvelle Vague* (New Wave), as it was called, rapidly became the new French art cinema, envied and imitated around the world. Indeed, by inspiring directors like Scorsese, Coppola, and De Palma, it later helped to revitalize the American cinema, which had helped to give birth to it in the first place.

By the end of the sixties the filmmakers of the *Nouvelle Vague* had largely dispersed, although they carried on making distinctive films, Godard in particular. Today it would be difficult to isolate any one trend or school. However, thanks to its enlightened system of state support, France remains one of the key filmmaking countries. ■

At the core of France is the Île-de-France, at whose heart lies Paris. Since Clovis established his capital here in the fifth century A.D., Paris and the Île-de-France have been the pivot around which the fortunes of this great country have turned.

Paris & the Île-de-France

Sign of the Moulin Rouge nightclub

Paris

Paris has an unrivaled reputation for being one of the most beautiful, exciting, and romantic cities in the world. Often called the City of Dreams, Paris has been a mecca for aspiring artists, writers, thinkers, and adventurers since the earliest times. Stroll down almost any street in central Paris and you pass evidence of its past in the narrow, twisting medieval streets and awe-inspiring churches; in the ornate 17th-century Renaissance palaces that flaunt incredible wealth; in Napoleon's classically inspired monuments; and in the sweeping, tree-lined boulevards of Baron Haussmann's 19th-century revamp of Paris. Packed into the center are some of the greatest museums in the world, the most beautiful buildings in France, and all possible luxuries.

Looking east over the Île St.-Louis from atop Notre-Dame

A game of *boules* in the Bois de Vincennes, east of Paris

Paris is still a vibrant, living city, the economic and cultural center of France. The creativity of today is evident in the exciting new buildings and modern painting and sculpture that sit alongside the treasures of the past. With dozens of museums and galleries, beautiful parks, stunning stores displaying world-famous fashions, and irresistible cafés and restaurants, the visitor can happily occupy every moment.

Over the centuries, the city has played host to a procession of performing artists. Kings and nobles acted as patrons to playwrights, musicians, and actors. Today the capital still offers a vast choice of entertainment: theaters, rock venues, nightclubs, and bars—although just wandering the streets of so lively a city can be entertainment enough. ■

C D E F

Musée de Montmartre
Basilique du Sacré-Cœur
CIMETIÈRE DE MONTMARTRE
PLACE DU TERTRE
Bal du Moulin Rouge
SQUARE DES BATIGNOLLES
BLVD. DE CLICHY
BLVD. DE ROCHECHOUART
BOULEVARD DE LA CHAPELLE
Gare du Nord
Parc de la Villette
18
BOULEVARD DES BATIGNOLLES
0 1 kilometer
0 ½ mile

St.-Augustin
Gare St.-Lazare
RUE DE CHATEAUDUN
RUE LA FAYETTE
Gare de l'Est
BOULEVARD HAUSSMANN
Folies Bergère
Hôpital St.-Louis
4
Opéra Garnier
Musée Grévin
10
PLACE DE LA MADELEINE
La Madeleine
BLVD. MONTMARTRE
Palais de la Bourse
2
Conservatoire de la National des Arts et Métiers
PLACE DE LA RÉPUBLIQUE
20
Bibliothèque Nationale de France Richelieu
PL. DES VICTOIRES
Hôtel des Postes St.-Eustache
3
Jeu de Paume St.-Roch
AVENUE DE LA RÉPUBLIQUE
PLACE DE LA CONCORDE
Orangerie
Comédie Française
Palais Royal
Les Halles
Beaubourg/Centre Georges Pompidou - Centre National d'Art et de Culture
Archives Nationales
Cimetière du Père Lachaise
Assemblée Nationale-Palais Bourbon
Musée du Louvre
Bourse de Commerce
Forum
Musée Picasso
JARDIN DES TUILERIES
Théâtre Musical de Paris
Tour St.-Jacques
Théâtre de la Ville
Musée Carnavalet
3
Musée d'Orsay
École Nat. Supérieure des Beaux-Arts
Institut de France
Conciergerie
Hôtel de Ville
PLACE DES VOSGES
St.-Germain des Prés
Préf de Police
Île de la Cité
Hôtel Dieu
PLACE DE LA BASTILLE
Hôtel Matignon
St.-Sulpice
Cathédrale Notre-Dame
Île St.-Louis
Opéra de Paris Bastille
12
Musée de Cluny
2
Palais du Luxembourg
Sorbonne
Institut du Monde Arabe
JARDIN TINO-ROSSI
Bois de Vincennes
JARDIN DU LUXEMBOURG
Panthéon
JARDIN DES PLANTES
Gare de Lyon
Tour Montparnasse
Hôpital Val de Grâce
Mosquée
5
Palais Omnisports de Bercy
Gare Montparnasse
CIMETIÈRE DU MONTPARNASSE
Muséum National d'Histoire Naturelle
Gare d'Austerlitz
BLVD. DE BERCY
14
Observatoire
Manufacture des Gobelins
13
Bibliothèque Nationale de France François Mitterrand
PLACE DENFERT ROCHEREAU
PLACE D'ITALIE
1

The Gothic Cathédrale Notre-Dame stands at the heart of Paris above the Seine River.

Île de la Cité

The oldest and most celebrated part of Paris is the Île de la Cité, an island in the Seine, little more than half a mile (1 km) long. Here, on a sandbank at a crossing point on the river, the Parisii, or boat people, had built a fortified town by the third century B.C.

Under Roman rule the settlement, called Lutetia Parisiorum, prospered, becoming the hub of a network of roads that crossed the northern part of the Roman Empire. In the third century A.D. it was destroyed by barbarians, so when the Parisii restored it, they built a thick stone wall to create an island fortress. By A.D. 508, Paris was the seat of the kings of the Franks. When Hugues Capet was declared King of France in 987 (see p. 22), Paris, as the capital city, became ever more important.

The Île de la Cité was the residence of the French kings from the 10th to the 14th cen-turies. In a display of wealth and power by the Church, the medieval streets were overshadowed by the new cathedral of Notre-Dame. Royal power was equally evident in the huge palace, so vast that it now forms the Conciergerie, the Palais de Justice, and Ste.-Chapelle. When the court left in the 14th century, the Île lost its significant place in French affairs.

The island, connected to the mainland by bridges, was later linked to the nearby Île St.-Louis. In the 16th and 17th centuries, the Île St.-Louis became fashionable and noblemen built their beautiful mansions here. ■

Notre-Dame

ON A SITE THAT HAS BEEN OCCUPIED SINCE ROMAN TIMES, the Cathédrale Notre-Dame is the essence of the city. Between 1163 and 1375, armies of craftsmen labored to create a masterpiece of Gothic architecture. The cathedral became a meeting place for the craftsmen's guilds and a place of education renowned throughout Europe. On these foundations, Paris's world-famous university, the Sorbonne, was based.

**Cathédrale
Notre-Dame**

📍 53 D2

✉ place du Parvis
Notre-Dame, Île de
la Cité

☎ 01 42 34 56 10
Towers

💲 $$

🚇 Métro: Cité

Changing fashions, neglect, and political vandalism took their toll on the cathedral, particularly in the 18th century. The Revolution saw carvings removed and statues beheaded. By the time Napoleon crowned himself emperor here in 1804, the cathedral had fallen into a very sorry state.

Victor Hugo's 1831 novel *Notre-Dame de Paris* was instrumental in prompting restoration plans, and work by historian-architect Eugène Viollet-le-Duc began in 1844, bringing back the cathedral's past splendor. Today, Notre-Dame remains a masterpiece of French Gothic style, still seen much as it was originally designed. It displays several steps in the development of Gothic cathedrals (see pp. 114–15)

PLACE DU PARVIS NOTRE-DAME

Medieval houses and narrow streets were swept away in a 19th-century scheme to enlarge this square overlooked by Notre-Dame's magnificent west front. Parvis, derived from the Latin *paradisus,* was a name given to an open space in front of a cathedral or church. People could stand here to study the biblical carvings on the facade—a valuable introduction to Bible stories in an age when congregations were largely illiterate.

WEST FACADE

Crowned by two early Gothic towers, the west facade has three imposing portals. In the Middle Ages the statues and sculptures here would have been brightly painted. The central portal depicts the Last Judgment, with Christ and the celestial court. The cathedral's oldest sculptures (1165–1175) are on the right-hand portal. They illustrate the life of St. Anne, and include one of the Virgin Mary showing Jesus to a kneeling King Louis VII (who consecrated the cathedral in the 12th century) and to the founder, Bishop Sully. The Virgin's portal, on the left, depicts her coronation, resurrection, and assumption, surrounded by saints, angels, and signs of the zodiac.

Above the portals is the Galerie des Rois (Gallery of Kings). The present 21 statues of Old Testament kings are reconstructions. The originals, damaged by revolutionaries who mistook them for French monarchs, were rediscovered in a 1977 excavation. Fragments are in the Musée de Cluny (see p. 61). Higher still, above the magnificent rose window, is the Galerie des Chimères, a balustrade embellished with grotesque stone figures of demons, birds, and weird beasts. The gargoyles, together with Quasimodo, the hunchback of Notre-Dame, feature memorably in Victor Hugo's *Notre-Dame de Paris.* Redesigned by Viollet-le-Duc, the gargoyles were intended to drain water from the roof (and, perhaps, to deter evil spirits). Climb the towers to see them close up.

TOWERS

Originally designed to be sur-
mounted by spires, the towers are
226 feet (69 m) high. Climbing the
238 steps to the north tower is hard
work; a further 140 steps lead to the
top of the south tower, but the
spectacular views over the city
make the climb well worthwhile.

In the south tower hangs the
13-ton bell "Emmanuel." The only
one of the cathedral's bells to
escape destruction in the Revolution, it is famous for its pure tone.
It was recast in bronze in 1686 and
eight people are needed to ring it.

FLYING BUTTRESSES

The famous flying buttresses, so
typical of a high Gothic cathedral,
were originally built between 1220
and 1230. Each incorporates a
channel to allow rainwater to run
off. Those at the east end have a
span of 49 feet (15 m). The chapels
between the buttresses date from
1250–1325.

INTERIOR

The traditional Gothic layout of
Notre-Dame's interior consists of a
nave of ten bays flanked by double
aisles continuing around the choir.
The walls are lined with 37 chapels,
added during the 13th and 14th
centuries. Stand at the crossing of
the transepts for the best view of
the rose windows.

Windows

The cathedral has three magnificent
rose windows. The north window,
which certainly should not be
missed, measures an amazing 69
feet (21 m) across. Almost all its
medieval glass remains. It depicts
the Virgin encircled by figures
from the Old Testament. The west
window, above the main door,
was completed in the 1490s, but
restored in the 19th century. It also
portrays the Virgin. The south rose
window, which has kept
some original 13th-century
glass, shows Christ
surrounded by angels,
saints, and the 12 Apostles.

The original stained
glass of the nave windows
survived until 1771, when
Louis XV, declaring stained
glass outmoded, had it
replaced with clear panes.
These were changed in
1965 to modern abstract
stained glass by Jacques Le
Chevallier.

South tower

Portals

Left: This 14th-century Virgin and Child stands against a pillar at one side of the chancel entrance.

Great Organ

With 110 stops and 6,000 pipes, this is the largest organ in France. Some pipes survive from the late Middle Ages, but most are 18th century. In 1868 the master organ-builder Aristide Cavaillé-Coll improved the mechanism and pipework in an attempt to make it as expressive and versatile as a symphony orchestra. Free organ concerts are given on Sunday afternoons.

Chancel & choir

At one time a tall, beautifully carved, 14th-century stone screen shut off the nave from the chancel. Much of it was moved in the 17th century; only parts survive in front of the first three north and south bays. Inside the chancel are the choir stalls, with scenes from the life of the Virgin carved on their backs. Bishops lie in their tombs around the ambulatory and below the choir. The sacristy, on the south side of the choir, houses the Treasury of medieval manuscripts, gold and silver sacred dishes, and caskets for the relics of saints. ■

Clerestory

Rose window

Flying buttress

Nave

Triforium

The high Gothic features of Notre-Dame are displayed in this drawing, which has been cut away to reveal the three-story nave. Flying buttresses help to support the roof vault weight, enabling the nave pillars to be elegantly slender.

Strolling the islands

The Île de la Cité and the Île St.-Louis are the oldest parts of Paris. This walk takes you around both islands, past their most historic features, and offers wonderful views up and down the river.

Start from Place Louis-Lépine, whose colorful flower market (one of Paris's last remaining) makes way for the Marché aux Oiseaux (bird market) on Sundays.

Walk along Rue de Lutèce to the ornate gates of the vast **Palais de Justice ❶** (*Tel 01 44 32 79 15*). Since the 16th century the palace has been the seat of the *parlement* (law court). After repeated fires and damage during the Revolution, most of the palace was rebuilt in the 19th century.

Before turning left along Boulevard du Palais, look up for a glimpse of the soaring spire of **Ste.-Chapelle** (*Tel 01 53 73 78 51*). One of the jewels in Paris's crown, this lovely Gothic chapel, built for Louis IX (St.-Louis, R. 1226–1270) in 1248, is tucked away in a courtyard within the precincts of the Palais de Justice. The entrance is on Boulevard du Palais. Take binoculars for close-up views of the amazing stained-glass windows, which depict more than 1,000 biblical scenes in an area of almost 7,000 square feet (620 sq m).

At Pont St.-Michel turn right along Quai des Orfèvres. Turn right again to cross quaint Place Dauphine, whose huge trees shade a *boules* pitch. A narrow medieval street, Rue Henri Robert, leads to Pont Neuf.

Beyond the bridge is a fine equestrian **statue of Henri IV.** Steps lead down to **Square du Vert-Galant ❷**, on the island's tip. This little tree-shaded park, a peninsula in the middle of the Seine, offers marvelous views, especially at sunset. Picasso's 1943 painting of this view is in the Musée Picasso (see pp. 86–87).

Walk east along Quai de l'Horloge, in the shadow of the turreted **Conciergerie ❸** (*Tel 01 53 73 78 50*). The oldest part of the former royal palace, it was rebuilt in about 1300. The Salle des Gens d'Armes, the largest hall in medieval Europe, could accommodate the entire palace staff—some 2,000 people. In 1358 the palace was stormed and the king was forced to move the royal residence away from the island. An important noble was appointed

concierge (caretaker). From 1391 until 1914 the building was a prison. Prisoners here during the Revolution included the queen, Marie-Antoinette. Her cell is one of several that have been reconstructed and can be visited.

At the far end of Quai de l'Horloge, notice the Conciergerie's famous clock tower; the clock dates from 1370 and still works today. Continue along Quai de la Corse and Quai aux Fleurs, where typical Parisian stalls, *bouquinistes*, sell books and artworks. Across the river is the **Hôtel de Ville**, a neo-Renaissance building of 1882.

Cross **Pont St.-Louis ❹** on to the Île St.-Louis. Follow Quai d'Orléans past magnificent 17th-century town houses—look out for superb courtyards, wrought iron, and carved heads. The Île St.-Louis has long been a sought-after residential area of Paris. Turn left onto Rue des Deux Ponts, then right onto Rue St.-Louis-en-l'Île. Pass the island's richly

Boats on the Seine

Many of the most memorable views of Paris are from the river, so be sure to see the city this way. Sightseeing trips in glass-roofed boats take in the stretch of the Seine between the Eiffel Tower and the Île St.-Louis, passing the Grand Palais, the Louvre, the Musée d'Orsay, Notre-Dame, and other legendary landmarks.

Most trips last about an hour, departing half-hourly in summer (hourly in winter) from 10 a.m. Some of the larger boats offer longer lunch or dinner trips—a wonderful (though expensive) way to see the city.

The large **Bateaux-Mouches** (*Tel 01 42 25 96 10*) depart from Pont de l'Alma (Right Bank), while **Bateaux Parisiens Tour Eiffel** (*Tel 01 44 11 33 44*) leave from the quay near the Eiffel Tower. **Vedettes du Pont-Neuf** (*Tel 01 46 33 98 38*) are smaller boats, departing from the western tip of the Île de la Cité by Pont Neuf. ∎

The lower chapel of Ste.-Chapelle, where servants and commoners once worshiped

decorated church, **St.-Louis-en-l'Île 5,** and turn left on Quai d'Anjou. Continue along Quai de Bourbon then, at Pont Louis-Philippe, turn left and recross Pont St.-Louis to approach **Notre-Dame 6** (see pp. 55–57) through a small park. Walk to **Place du Parvis Notre-Dame 7,** at the west end of the cathedral. Here a bronze star marks the official center of Paris, from where all distances on French roads are measured. Below the parvis, in the **Crypte Archéologique** (*Tel 01 43 29 83 51*), lie the remains of 16th- and 18th-century houses, the church of St.-Étienne, and fragments from Lutetia, the

Gallo-Roman city. From the parvis, take Rue de la Cité back to Place Louis-Lépine. ∎

- See area map p. 53
- Place Louis-Lépine (Métro: Cité)
- 2.5 miles (4 km)
- 2 hours
- Place Louis-Lépine

NOT TO BE MISSED
- Ste.-Chapelle
- Conciergerie
- Notre-Dame

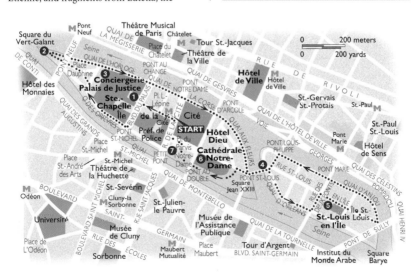

Flower displays in the Jardin des Plantes beside the Natural History Museum

Left Bank

The Left Bank—the famous Rive Gauche—is a lively area south of the Seine. Stretching from the Jardin des Plantes to the Champ de Mars, it encompasses the narrow streets of St.-Germain in the Quartier Latin (Latin Quarter—until the Revolution teaching at the Sorbonne was in Latin), the quieter, grander areas around the Panthéon and the Palais du Luxembourg, the Musée d'Orsay, and the Assemblée Nationale.

For both tourists and Parisians there is an endless attraction to the cozy, medieval streets of St.-Germain, their little shops and cafés frequented by writers, artists, and students from the Sorbonne and the École des Beaux-Arts. The Latin Quarter, alongside the Île de la Cité, is where Paris first spilled onto the mainland. Scattered Roman remains show how extensive the city then became. The Musée de Cluny houses a stunning collection of Roman and medieval artifacts while the Roman-style Panthéon nearby is a mausoleum for many of France's most revered historical figures. Napoleon Bonaparte, perhaps the greatest, is also laid to rest in this area of Paris—farther west, in the magnificent Église du Dôme in Les Invalides. Finally, soaring over central Paris is La Tour Eiffel—the Eiffel Tower, a monument to the Parisian flair for innovation in design and technology. ■

Musée de Cluny

BUILT FOR VISITING BENEDICTINE MONKS FROM CLUNY, in Burgundy, in the late 15th century, the former Hôtel de Cluny stands beside the remains of Paris's oldest Roman baths. The mansion, one of France's finest examples of Gothic domestic architecture, was owned after the Revolution by art collector Alexandre de Sommerard. His acquisitions form the basis of the Musée National du Moyen Age et des Thermes de Cluny. Don't miss this unique combination of Gallo-Roman ruins, medieval mansion, and one of the world's finest collections of medieval art and crafts.

Musée de Cluny
- 53 D2
- 6 place Paul-Painlevé
- Closed Tues.
- $$
- Métro: St.-Michel, Odéon

On display are medieval furniture, clothes, and accessories; textiles, including examples of Byzantine and Coptic work as well as European; and some magnificent tapestries. One series, "La Vie Seigneuriale," illustrates the life of a noble household in the Middle Ages. Also in the museum are the 21 mutilated stone heads of the Kings of Judah, carved around 1220 for the west front of Notre-Dame but defaced and then lost during the Revolution.

ROMAN BATHS

On the ground floor are the remains of second-century baths: three stone chambers for steam, tepid, and cold baths, and a gymnasium. The vaulted ceiling of the cold bath (*frigidarium*) rises over 45 feet (14 m). The capitals of the pillars supporting the vaulting are ships' prows, which suggests that the baths were built for the Nautae, the wealthy corporation of Paris boatmen.

HÔTEL DE CLUNY

On the first floor is the abbot's chapel, with fan-vaulting radiating from a central pillar. One room has been restored as a medieval living room with wooden shutters, candelabra, armor, and tapestries.

Also on this floor is a superb collection of goldwork and jewelry including belts, bracelets, rare votive Visigoth crowns, and two 13th-century double gold crosses.

The most famous of the treasures are the six allegorical tapestries "La Dame à la Licorne" (the lady with the unicorn), displayed in a circular room. Exquisitely woven, they are in 15th-century millefleurs style, noted for its graceful depiction of plants, animals, and people. Five of the tapestries show the lady acting out the five senses, while the enigmatic sixth presents her in front of the motto "À mon seul désir" (to my only desire). ∎

Surrounded by flowers, birds, and little animals, her pet dog on her lap, the lady spins while listening to a reading in one of "La Vie Seigneuriale" series of tapestries.

Latin Quarter walk

Enjoy the special buzz of the Latin Quarter on this walk through its student-thronged streets and quiet backwaters.

Starting from the Pont au Double beside Notre-Dame, cross the Quai de Montebello. Walk through the small garden facing you; a false acacia here is reputedly the oldest tree in Paris. Pass beside the little 13th-century church of **St.-Julien-le-Pauvre** ❶.

Turn right down Rue St.-Jacques and cross to Rue de la Huchette. Once the heart of the Latin Quarter, the street is now dominated by Greek restaurants but still retains the famous Caveau de la Huchette jazz club at No. 5. At the end of the street turn left onto Rue de la Harpe, with its cafés and clubs. This area is at its most vibrant when crowded with students on a warm evening.

Cross Boulevard St.-Germain and walk up the hill on Boulevard St.-Michel, past the remains of some Roman baths. Turn left into Place Paul-Painlevé for the **Musée de Cluny** ❷ (see p. 61).

From the museum, cross the small square and walk up to Rue des Écoles. Turn left past

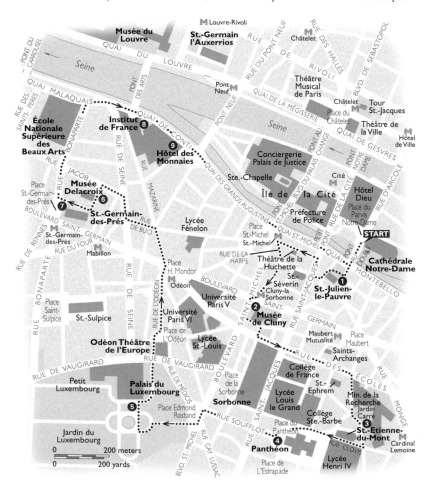

the buildings of the **Sorbonne,** Paris's world-famous university, founded in 1253.

At the junction of Rue des Écoles and Rue de la Montagne de Ste.-Geneviève, turn right and walk up the steep hill. Named after the patron saint of Paris, the street was part of the Roman road linking Lutetia (Paris) with Italy.

At the fork, take Rue Descartes. Turn right into Rue Clovis, named after the king of the Franks who defeated the Romans and founded France. On your right is the charming church of **St.-Étienne-du-Mont ③,** well worth a brief visit to see the intricately carved 16th-century rood screen, flanked by spiral staircases. Rue Clovis opens onto the Place du Panthéon. Walk around the square to

---

🅐 See area map p. 53
▶ Pont au Double (Métro: Maubert-Mutualité)
🔁 3 miles (4.5 km)
🕐 2 hours
▶ Pont au Double

NOT TO BE MISSED
- Musée de Cluny
- Panthéon and St.-Étienne-du-Mont
- Jardin du Luxembourg
- Hôtel des Monnaies

go inside the **Panthéon ④** (*Tel 01 44 32 18 00*), burial place of Voltaire, Rousseau, Hugo, and other French luminaries. Walk down Rue Soufflot to the **Jardin du Luxembourg ⑤.** The 17th-century promenades offer some relaxing strolls.

Leave the gardens to the right of the **Palais du Luxembourg** (seat of the French Senate) to reach the 18th-century Odéon-Théâtre de l'Europe. Continue downhill to Boulevard St.-Germain and cross to Rue de l'Ancienne Comédie. On the right is Le Procope (*13 rue de l'Ancienne Comédie, tel 01 40 46 79 00*), Paris's first café (see p. 70), now a restaurant.

Turn left on Rue de Buci and right on Rue de Seine. This whole area is full of small stores, many selling antiques and works of art. Turn left on Rue Jacob and left again on Rue Furstemberg. In a corner of elegant Place Furstemberg is the **Musée National Eugène Delacroix ⑥** (*Tel 01 44 41 86 50, closed Tues.*), based in the last home of the major Romantic artist, who died in 1836.

Turn right from Rue Furstemberg and continue to Place St.-Germain-des-Prés. Beside the old abbey church of **St.-Germain-des-Prés ⑦,** a little garden contains Picasso's sculpture, "L'Hommage à Apollinaire."

Place St.-Germain-des-Prés offers the chance of a reviving drink at one of Paris's best-known cafés, such as **Les Deux Magots** or **Café de Flore** (see p. 70). From the square, go down Rue Bonaparte, lined with interesting little stores and galleries. On the left is the École Nationale Supérieure des Beaux-Arts (School of Fine Art).

Having reached the Seine, and the splendid view of the Louvre, turn right on Quai Malaquais and walk past the **Institut de France ⑧.** This is where the historic French academies, including the exclusive Académie Française, carry out their research. Farther along, in the former mint, the **Hôtel des Monnaies ⑨,** is the Musée de la Monnaie (*Tel 01 40 46 55 35, closed Mon.*), which traces the history of coinage from 300 B.C.

Go down steps from Quai des Grands-Augustins to the lower embankment of the Seine, away from the busy road (but usually closed at night). Return to Pont au Double. ∎

One of the Latin Quarter's many cafés

Musée d'Orsay

Musée d'Orsay

53 C3

rue de la Legion d'Honneur

01 40 49 48 14

Closed Mon.

$$

Métro: Solférino

The gilded belle epoque station clock times art lovers now, not passengers.

OPENED IN 1986, THE MUSÉE D'ORSAY SOON BECAME ONE of Europe's top art museums. The unconventional building—a converted Left Bank hotel and railroad station—lent itself to imaginative displays, winning wide acclaim. The collections cover the period from 1848 to 1914, an exciting and dynamic time for the art world, with Paris very much at the helm. All the great names are here.

THE STATION

The original hotel and station were built for the 1900 Universal Exhibition on the site of the Palais d'Orsay, burned down in the Commune uprising of 1871. Functional iron-and-glass railway architecture would have looked wrong in this elegant part of Paris, so a monumental stone facade was built, effectively concealing the building's purpose. The ornate belle epoque reception areas, restaurant, and ballroom are still intact.

Within 40 years the station was obsolete, its platforms too short for modern trains. Temporary uses for the building included a mailing center, film set, and hostel for prisoners of war. By the 1960s demolition plans were well advanced when the present innovative conversion was proposed. This allowed various important art collections, covering the period from 1848 to 1914, to be regrouped, including the famous Impressionist works from the overcrowded Jeu de Paume across the Seine. The Musée d'Orsay thus filled a natural gap between the Louvre and the contemporary collections of the Centre Georges Pompidou (Beaubourg).

GROUND FLOOR

Visitors in a hurry may be tempted to head for the Impressionist works upstairs. Resist, if you have time: The ground floor, mostly covering the period 1848–1870, traces some of the developments that paved the way for 20th-century painting and sculpture. In the central gallery, devoted to sculpture, look especially at the work of the influential Jean-Baptiste Carpeaux (1827–1875), whose bronze group "Count Ugolino" gave Rodin ideas he used in "The Thinker."

Mid-19th-century paintings occupy the side galleries on this floor. To the right (as you enter) are later works by the conservative Ingres, devotee of classical ideas and technical precision, and the Romantic Delacroix, for whom imagination and the use of color became more important.

Highlights of the galleries on the opposite (north) side include pictures by realists Millet and Courbet. Note especially Millet's deliberately mundane portrayal of three peasant women, "The Gleaners," and Courbet's "Burial at Ornans," considered vulgar to the point of offensiveness when it was first shown. Many such works illustrate the important move away from heroic, stylized subject matter toward depictions of ordinary people and everyday themes. Equally revolutionary approaches to color and light characterize the pre-1870 pictures by painters such as Monet, Pissarro, Manet, and Renoir that can be found toward the northeastern end of this floor.

UPPER LEVEL

The core of the museum's world-famous Impressionist collection is on the Upper Level. Many familiar images include Manet's "Déjeuner sur l'Herbe," Monet's "Poppies," and Whistler's portrait of his mother. All the great artists of the period are well represented; there are works by Renoir, Cézanne, Pissarro, and Degas. Some fine van Gogh paintings are here, including "Bedroom at Arles," "Church at Auvers," and several self-portraits. Van Gogh was in Paris from 1886 to 1888, meeting and exchanging ideas with all the major artists.

Some of the rooms at the western end of this floor show pictures by the Pont-Aven school, a breakaway group led by Paul Gauguin. They emphasized two-dimensional patterns from memory rather than nature. A nearby room is devoted to the nabis, another genre of late 19th-century painters including Bonnard and Vuillard, named for the Hebrew word *nabi* (prophet). Their flat, linear forms, and arbitrary use of color paved the way for early 20th-century abstract art.

MIDDLE LEVEL

Make time, if you can, to visit the varied collections here. Some—such as the early photographs, the art nouveau glass and ceramics, or the sumptuous ballroom of the former hotel—offer a complete contrast with exhibits on other levels. Other galleries return to themes already explored: There are larger works by the nabis (such as Bonnard's "The Croquet Party"), some sculptures by Rodin, and rooms of naturalist and symbolist paintings. ■

Carpeaux's bronze group "Count Ugolino" influenced later sculptors, notably Rodin.

Hôtel des Invalides

Hôtel des Invalides

🅰 52 B2

✉ esplanade des Invalides

☎ 01 44 42 54 52. Guided tours: 01 44 42 37 72

💲 $$

Ⓜ Métro: Varenne, Latour Maubourg

Son et Lumière

🕐 March–mid-Oct. (phone for further information)

MONUMENTAL EVEN BY THE STANDARDS OF THE SUN King, the Hôtel des Invalides was founded by Louis XIV to care for his veteran soldiers, many of them sick or disabled and desperately poor. The impressive classical building, with its huge severe facade, was completed in 1676. The Église du Dôme, whose gilded and painted cupola now stands over Napoleon's tomb, was added in 1706.

The huge **Cour d'Honneur** is lined with two-story arcades. "The Little Corporal," a statue of Napoleon I originally on the column in the Place Vendôme, stands above the south side. Trophies, flags, guns, and heraldic symbols

armies at the end of World War I. Directly under the stately dome is the centerpiece, the **tomb of Napoleon I.** In 1840 his ashes were brought back to Les Invalides. In order to place the tomb directly under the dome without disturbing the architectural symmetry, an open crypt was dug. At its center a red porphyry sarcophagus stands on a green granite base. Inside are Napoleon's ashes. Twelve colossal marble Victory statues and a star-shaped floor mosaic recall the emperor's principal victories.

MUSÉE DE L'ARMÉE

The Musée de l'Armée, housed on both sides of the Cour d'Honneur, is one of the world's largest military collections. Weapons,

The arcaded Cour d'Honneur in the Hôtel des Invalides contains the Musée de l'Armée.

adorn four pavilions, and in the four corners, at roof level, carved horses trample emblems of war. At the end is the entrance to the soldiers' church, **St.-Louis-des-Invalides,** its interior hung with captured regimental standards.

The **Église du Dôme** alongside is a mausoleum to the military heroes of France, among them Maréchal Foch (1851–1929), commander-in-chief of the Allied

artillery, emblems, offensive and defensive armor, flags, uniforms, historical souvenirs, and paintings trace the evolution of warfare from prehistoric days to World War II. A fascinating separate collection, the **Musée des Plans-Reliefs** displays scale models of fortified towns and fortresses in France and along the borders. Some of the models date back as far as 1668. ■

Tour Eiffel

Tour Eiffel

52 A3

Champ de Mars

01 44 11 23 23 or
01 44 11 23 45

$$

Métro: Bir-Hakeim

Statistics

- Height (including antenna): 1,051 feet (319 m)
- Height increase on hot days from metal expansion: up to 6 inches (15 cm)
- First platform at 187 feet (57 m)
- Second platform at 377 feet (115 m)
- Top platform at 905 feet (276 m)
- 1,585 steps
- 5 million visitors per year

The intricate metalwork of the Tour Eiffel seen close up is as impressive as a view of it in its entirety.

RISING FROM THE GREEN EXPANSE OF THE CHAMP DE Mars, a former military parade ground established 140 years before its construction, the Tour Eiffel (Eiffel Tower) is Paris's most enduring symbol. Built for the centenary of the Revolution in 1889, it was feted by almost half a million people at its own centenary celebrations in 1989.

When plans for the Eiffel Tower won first prize in a competition organized for the 1889 Universal Exhibition, Gustave Eiffel pronounced that France would be the only nation with a 300-meter flagpole. The precision of his plans, with exact measurements for more than 15,000 metallic parts, enabled it to be completed by 300 workers in just over two years (January 1887 to March 1889). A staggering 2.5 million rivets were used. For some time after its completion, the tower remained the tallest building in the world. An immediate success, it was visited by almost two million people during the exhibition. Within a year it had recouped most of its building cost.

The tower was due to be pulled down in 1909, but by then it had become indispensable in the world of telecommunications, particularly for the first transatlantic radio telephone service.

You can reach the first platform by 360 steps or by one of four elevators that travel diagonally up the legs (one serves only the restaurant). A small museum on the first floor runs a short film about the tower's history, with footage of famous visitors. A video gives visitors details about the building including how much it sways on a windy day (just 5 inches, 12 cm).

The panorama from the top platform is breathtaking. On a very clear day the horizon can extend to 45 miles (72 km). Directly below is the Seine and, on the opposite bank, the Palais de Chaillot. At night the tower is lit from within, making a glittering spectacle so evocative of Paris's romantic image. ■

Musée Rodin

Musée Rodin

🅰 52 B3

✉ 77 rue de Varenne

☎ 01 44 18 61 10

🕐 Closed Mon.

💲 $

Ⓜ Métro: Varenne

FOR THE LAST NINE YEARS OF HIS LIFE, THE SCULPTOR Auguste Rodin (1840–1917) had his studio in the Hôtel Biron, an elegant rococo mansion near Les Invalides. Built in 1730, the house and its lovely garden were owned by a dedicated horticulturist, Maréchal de Biron, who died on the guillotine. Subsequently a dance hall, convent, and school, the Hôtel Biron became artists' studios in 1908. Rodin stayed here from then until his death, paying the rent with his works. After he died, the house became a museum for the collection he left to the nation.

Rodin gained fame only in his forties, but his output was prolific, and the museum possesses several thousand sculptures and fragments as well as many drawings. Works from Rodin's youth include a bust of his father, and the charming terra-cotta "Young Woman in a Flowered Hat" (circa 1865). The sculptor's first major commission, in 1880, was "The Gates of Hell." Intended as a bronze door for the planned Musée des Arts Décoratifs, the work was not cast until 1929, after Rodin's death, but many of the figures that he made for this project developed into independent sculptures. Versions of these—which include some of Rodin's most famous pieces, such as "The Thinker" and "The Kiss"—can be seen in several of the rooms and in the garden.

Alongside Rodin's own works in the museum are works by his contemporaries, notably his talented but tragic mistress, Camille Claudel. She never recovered from Rodin's rejection in 1898, spending her last years in a mental institution.

Wild and beautiful in Rodin's day, the gardens have become a perfect setting for large casts of some of his important pieces. "The Thinker," formerly outside the Panthéon, was moved here in 1922. Not far away are "The Gates of Hell," finally assembled in 1937. Several works in marble, such as the monument to Victor Hugo, are now protected by glass. With their roses, well-placed seats, and summer café, the gardens make an agreeable end to a visit to the museum. ∎

Rodin's "The Kiss," one of the highlights of the Rodin Museum

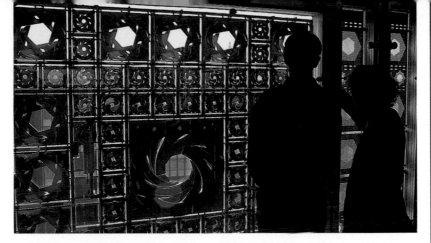

Metal screens, inspired by Arab designs, control the light in the Institut du Monde Arabe.

More places to visit on the Left Bank

ASSEMBLÉE NATIONALE
The lower house of the French parliament sits in the Palais Bourbon. The library ceiling, by Delacroix, depicts the history of civilization. 🅰 53 C3 ✉ Palais de Bourbon, quai d'Orsay ☎ 01 40 63 60 00 🕐 Tours Sat. 10 a.m., 2 p.m., & 3 p.m. (when parliament is not in session) Ⓜ Métro: Assemblée Nationale

LES CATACOMBES
The world's largest depository of human bones has over six million skeletons in many miles of former Montparnasse quarry tunnels. 🅰 53 C1 ✉ 1 place Denfert-Rochereau 🕐 Closed a.m. Tues.–Fri. & all day Mon. 💲 $ Ⓜ Métro: Denfert-Rochereau

CIMETIÈRE DU MONTPARNASSE
Montparnasse in its heyday drew literary and artistic figures. Baudelaire, Saint-Saëns, Sartre, Ionesco, and many others are buried here. 🅰 53 C1 ✉ 3 boulevard E. Quinet ☎ 01 44 10 86 50 Ⓜ Métro: Edgar Quinet

LES ÉGOUTS (PARIS SEWERS)
Haussmann's vast 1850 network of sewers has become a popular tourist attraction. 🅰 53 B3 ✉ opposite 93 quai d'Orsay 🕐 Closed Thurs., Fri., & Jan. 💲 $ Ⓜ Métro: Alma Marceau

INSTITUT DU MONDE ARABE
An innovative 1987 building, with light-sensitive windows and transparent elevators. A museum displays Islamic metalwork, ceramics, and carpets. 🅰 53 E2 ✉ 1 rue des Fossés St.-Bernard ☎ 01 40 51 38 38 🕐 Closed Mon. 💲 $ Ⓜ Métro: Jussieu, Cardinal Lemoine

JARDIN DES PLANTES
The huge variety of plants here includes two trees planted in 1636—the year after the adjacent natural history museum was founded. 🅰 53 E1/2 ✉ 57 rue Cuvier 🕐 Museum closed Tues. ☎ 01 40 79 30 00 💲 $ Ⓜ Métro: Monge, Gare d'Austerlitz

JARDIN TINO-ROSSI
Relax among trees, lawns, and sculpture in this peaceful area beside the Seine, with views across to the Île St.-Louis. Avoid after dark. 🅰 53 E2 ✉ quai St.-Bernard Ⓜ Métro: Gare d'Austerlitz

LA MOSQUÉE
The courtyards of this mosque, inspired by the Alhambra, hide a *hammam*, or Turkish bath. 🅰 53 D1 ✉ rue Daubenton 🕐 Closed Fri. Ⓜ Métro: Monge

TOUR MONTPARNASSE
The 688-foot (210-m) tower offers panoramic views from its 58th floor. 🅰 53 C1 ✉ place Rault-Dautry 💲 $$ Ⓜ Métro: Montparnasse-Bienvenue ■

Cafés & café life

For Parisians the café has a special place in their lives: It is here that they meet friends, discuss the affairs of the day, and watch the world go by. For some the café is virtually a second home. Many Parisian cafés have famous histories as melting pots for artists and intellectuals to exchange and develop ideas. Traditional café culture is as strong today as it ever was, though the number of cafés in Paris has dropped significantly in recent years.

Historical cafés

The first café to open its doors in Paris, in 1686, was Le Procope, on the Left Bank. (It still exists, but as a restaurant.) It soon became the meeting place of actors from the Comédie-Française and later of philosophers Voltaire and Rousseau, revolutionaries Danton, Robespierre, and Marat, and 19th-century writers, including Balzac and Hugo.

The broad, sweeping Grands Boulevards of the 19th century moved café life onto the sidewalks. The Café de la Paix, one of the first of these, still retains much of its Second Empire glory. Parisians delight in sitting outside where they can watch the passing street life. In the summer, the streets buzz with people crowded at outdoor café tables. Even in winter people can be seen muffled up at tables on the sidewalk.

By the 1920s café society had moved to Montparnasse where the likes of revolutionary photographer Man Ray and controversial novelist Henry Miller frequented La Rotonde, Le Dôme, and Le Select. In 1939, Picasso was a patron of Café de Flore in St.-Germain, followed in 1940 by Jean-Paul Sartre and Simone de Beauvoir. Sartre developed the philosophy of existentialism during the many hours he and Simone de Beauvoir spent there—from 9 a.m. until well into the night. Nearby is Les Deux Magots, named for its two statues of Chinese mandarins, *magots,* which sit inside

Popular cafés change little through the years. Aux Deux Magots in the 1950s (above) looks almost the same as Les Deux Magots today (top); only the name has changed. The wicker chairs, round tables, dress of the waiters, even, apparently, the clientele remain the same.

on a pillar—a reminder of the café's original function, selling silks. Les Deux Magots attracted the key figures of a whole postwar generation of philosophers and writers, including Ernest Hemingway, André Breton, and André Gide.

Cafés today

Modern cafés are keeping tradition alive. Many still attract an artistic clientele while acting as a showcase for superb design. The

If you want to read a magazine, have a snack, discuss the meaning of life, or just sit and watch, a café is the place to go.

Café Beaubourg, on the square outside the Centre Pompidou, was designed by Christian de Pontzamparc and is a fashionable rendezvous for artists, critics, and gallery owners. On the Left Bank, La Palette is popular with students from the École des Beaux-Arts, and retired Parisians and the fashionable elite go there to be seen. It offers a wonderful tree-shaded terrace in summer.

One very popular café for people-watching is the Café Marly, in the Louvre courtyard overlooking the pyramid. Expensive but delightful, it must boast the most stylish toilets ever seen in a café. At the other end of the spectrum are the local cafés, where working people eat a quick snack at lunchtime and local residents meet in the evening. You can find plenty of these around Montmartre and Pigalle.

Most visitors to Paris also enjoy sitting on a café terrace. Cafés open early in the morning, in time to serve the traditional *grand crème* (large cup of white coffee) with croissants to people on their way to work. Throughout the day they also serve wine, beer, and pastis—a strong aniseed spirit diluted with water—and, of course, espresso coffees. Drinks are cheaper *au bar* (standing at the bar) than *en salle* (sitting at a table). They are more expensive again if you sit at a table outside, but this increase in price never seems to worry anyone intent on soaking up the atmosphere. ■

The Louvre is both one of the world's great museums and an extremely elegant building.

Right Bank

The wealthy have favored this area north of the Seine ever since Charles V moved the royal residence here in the late 14th century. Palaces, elegant squares and gardens, sweeping boulevards, and grand town houses are their legacy. Recent decades have brought imaginative rejuvenation schemes to areas such as Les Halles, Beaubourg, and the Marais. Cultural life on the Right Bank (Rive Droite) ranges from the Opéra Garnier to a series of museums including the Louvre, the largest museum in the world.

As Paris grew in importance, so did its grand buildings—including the Tuileries, built for Catherine de Médicis but destroyed by fire in 1871, and the Palais-Royal, which began life as the residence of Cardinal Richelieu. Napoleon encouraged neoclassic schemes such as La Madeleine and the Arc de Triomphe to glorify his growing empire. The *grands projets* of the 19th century swept away earlier housing to create sweeping vistas along Les Grands Boulevards in Baron Haussmann's major exercise in town planning.

For elegance of the modern kind, look no further than the designer shops, jewelers, and galleries of Rue St.-Honoré and Place Vendôme. This is the hallowed center of the world of high fashion. The Right Bank can be seriously chic. ■

Champs-Élysées

Champs-Élysées

 52 B4

Métro: Champs
Élysées Clemenceau,
Franklin Roosevelt,
George V

**The lights of the
never ending flow
of traffic mark
out the Champs-
Élysées as it rises
to the Arc de
Triomphe.**

From an unpaved track across swampy ground, the Champs-Élysées has evolved into one of the most famous avenues in the world. The process was begun by Marie de Médicis in 1616. Her avenue was already a fashionable carriage drive by the time landscape designer André Le Nôtre planted trees to frame the long westward vista from the Louvre. By 1836, when the view was crowned by the Arc de Triomphe, the Champs-Élysées had become an elegant promenade with cafés, fountains, and lighting.

Brash modern commerce may have taken its toll on the dignity of the Champs-Élysées, but the scene remains memorable. The avenue excels as a powerful setting for state occasions, from General de Gaulle's triumphal return to Paris, in 1944, to the spectacular procession celebrating the 1989 Bicentennial. ■

Arc de Triomphe

Arc de Triomphe

 52 A4

✉ place Charles de
Gaulle

☎ 01 55 37 73 77

💲 $$

Métro: Charles de
Gaulle-Étoile

This great Paris landmark dominates the axis leading east down the Champs-Élysées and west down the Avenue de la Grande Armée toward La Défense. In Baron Haussmann's 19th-century transformation of the city, the Arc de Triomphe became the central point of 12 radiating avenues. Now known as the Place Charles-de-Gaulle, it is a perpetual maelstrom of swirling traffic.

Napoleon I commissioned the triumphal arch in 1806 as a tribute to his Grande Armée. It was finally completed in 1836, and Napoleon's remains passed under the arch on their way to Les Invalides in 1840.

The arch is 164 feet (50 m) high and has four massive sculptures carved on its main facades. They portray victories won during the 1789 Revolution and the First Empire. Round the top are shields inscribed with the names of the Grande Armée's battles. Inside, an elevator and stairs lead up to the viewing platform with panoramas in all directions over the city. A small museum in the crosspiece has video displays about the arch.

The Unknown Soldier was buried beneath the arch in 1920. A flame is relit daily at 6:30 p.m. in a remembrance ceremony. ■

A walk from the Opéra Garnier

To see Paris at its most supremely elegant, follow this walk from the Opéra to the Champs-Élysées, then through the Jardin des Tuileries to return past the Palais-Royal.

Equally lavish inside and out, Paris's legendary **Opéra Garnier** (newly restored) ❶, opened in 1875, is now devoted to ballet. From the Place de l'Opéra, take Rue de la Paix past glittering jewelry stores to the equally classy Place Vendôme, dominated by the Ritz Hotel.

Cross the square to Rue de Castiglione and turn right on Rue St.-Honoré, celebrated for its designer shops. Fork right on Rue Duphot to Place de la Madeleine. **La Madeleine** ❷, with its 52 Corinthian pillars, commands a stunning vista down Rue Royale to Place de la Concorde.

From Rue Royale, turn right on Rue du Faubourg St.-Honoré, past the **Palais de l'Élysée** ❸, the French president's official residence since 1873 (not open to the public).

Turn left on Avenue de Marigny and walk across the Champs-Élysées to Avenue Winston Churchill, between the **Grand Palais** ❹ and the **Petit Palais,** both built for the 1900 Universal Exhibition. The Petit Palais houses the varied art collections of the City of Paris (*Tel 01 42 65 12 73, closed Mon.*). In the west wing of the Grand Palais is the **Palais de la Découverte,** a well-displayed and informative science museum and planetarium (*Tel 01 56 43 20 21, closed Mon.*).

Cross Cours la Reine to view the Seine from the elaborate Pont Alexandre III. Turn left along the embankment to **Place de la Concorde** ❺. This splendid square, designed in 1757, witnessed thousands of executions during the Reign of Terror in 1793–94. The 3,000-year-old Egyptian obelisk in the center overlooks eight symbolic statues representing the major French cities.

Go through elaborate iron gates into the **Jardin des Tuileries,** originally landscaped for Catherine de Médicis's palace here in 1564. The Tuileries palace was destroyed by the Communards in 1871, but its gardens have changed little since then.

The octagonal pond is flanked by two art galleries. The **Galerie National du Jeu de Paume** ❻ (*Tel 01 47 03 12 50, closed Mon.*),

built in 1878 as a tennis court, was until 1986 the home of the fine Impressionist collection now in the Musée d'Orsay. Temporary art exhibitions are held here. The **Musée de l'Orangerie** ❼ (*Tel 01 42 97 48 16, closed Tues.*), built in 1852, will be closed for major renovations until 2002.

Continue through the gardens, which display over 100 statues, toward the Arc de Triomphe du Carrousel, built to commemorate Napoleon's victories of 1805. Here, look back for the vista to the more famous Arc de Triomphe at the top of the Champs-Élysées.

Cross the gardens and go through the arch beneath the Louvre's north gallery to Rue de Rivoli. Turn right to Place du Palais-Royal, then left into Place des Pyramides, home of the **Comédie-Française,** still the venue for classic French theater. Walk beneath the theater's arcades to reach the precincts of the **Palais-Royal 8.** Cardinal Richelieu's palace (now government offices) is not open, but the gardens are a pleasant meeting place, just as they were in the 18th century. The striped columns and water features in the Cour d'Honneur are a 1980s innovation by installation artist Daniel Buren, worth seeing at dusk.

Walk past the arcade of shops to the left of the gardens, then turn right and left on Rue Vivienne, passing the rear of the former **Bibliothèque Nationale de France**

Richelieu, whose 12 million books are now at Bercy. At Rue du Quatre Septembre, opposite **La Bourse 9** (Stock Exchange), turn left to return to the Opéra. ∎

- See area map p. 53
- ▶ Place de l'Opéra (Métro: Opéra)
- ↔ 3.25 miles (5 km)
- ⏲ 2½ hours
- ▶ Place de l'Opéra

NOT TO BE MISSED
- La Madeleine
- Grand Palais and Petit Palais
- Place de la Concorde
- Jardin des Tuileries
- Jardin du Palais-Royal

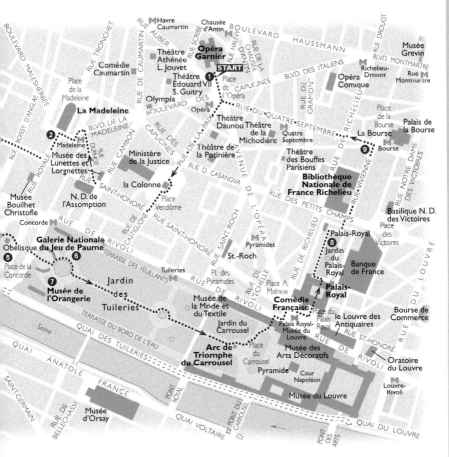

A shoppers' paradise

From tiny boutiques in medieval streets to elegant, world-famed department stores, Paris is a shopper's paradise. Whatever you wish for is here in this Aladdin's cave of a city—at a price! If your purse does not stretch to haute couture or diamond necklaces, it is still fun to browse through the arcades and hunt for bargains in markets or among the stalls alongside the Seine.

Specialty shopping
Some streets and areas have particular specialties. On the Île St.-Louis you will find unusual boutiques and restaurants (and the capital's best ice cream, at Berthillon). The *bouquinistes*, booksellers, with their ramshackle stalls along Quai de Montebello, are a particular Parisian delight. Flowers, birds, and animals are for sale in Place Louis-Lépine and on Quai de la Mégisserie.

The area around the chic Boulevard St.-Germain brims with galleries and antiques, especially on Rue Bonaparte and Rue des Sts.-Pères, while collectors of first editions head for Rue Jacob.

In the Marais, the Rue du Temple and the parallel Rue des Archives are known for leather goods and jewelry, while the arcaded shops of the Place des Vosges sell antiques, art, fashions, and books.

Fashion capital
For centuries the world has been influenced by fashion trends from Paris. It is still home to the most prestigious couturiers and a mecca for the design-conscious. Serious haute-couture seekers head for Avenue Montaigne, where nearly all the top names have their premises. Chanel, Givenchy, Dior, and Cartier are all here. Fabergé maintains a long tradition of displaying jewelry at astronomical prices.

Rue du Faubourg St.-Honoré is ultra-fashionable and wealthy. Expensive antiques galleries, furriers, perfumeries, crystal and caviar shops, and designers Gucci, Hermès, Lagerfeld, and Lacroix all encourage the well-heeled to part with their francs. Exclusive jewelers, such as Van Cleef et Arpels, line Rue de la Paix and Place Vendôme, their proximity to

the Ritz Hotel's diamond-studded clientele surely not coincidental. Less expensive are the dress shops on the arcaded Rue de Rivoli, which is unfortunately also crammed with tacky souvenir shops.

Galleries and arcades
In the 19th century fashionable Parisians shopped in the 140 covered galleries of the Right Bank. Fewer than 30 now remain. Hardly changed since they were built, the Galerie Véro-Dodat, Galerie Colbert, and Galerie Vivienne make harmonious settings for restaurants, galleries, and antiques and contemporary design shops.

The area between Rue de Rivoli and Boulevard de Sébastopol is crisscrossed with glass-roofed walkways, such as the passages Molière, des Princes, des Panoramas, and du Claire. Also relics of a veritable warren of 19th-century arcades, they now shelter a host of specialty shops and unusual eating places.

Department stores & shopping centers
Paris's celebrated department stores lay emphasis on elegance and fashion in clothes, accessories, and household goods. Au Printemps and the glass-domed Galeries Lafayette are near the Opéra district, known as the *quartier des grands magasins*. Bazar de l'Hôtel de Ville (BHV), excellent for household and do-it-yourself items, is on Rue de Rivoli. By the river, La Samaritaine is famous for its art nouveau interior and for the views from its rooftop terrace. Au Bon Marché, on the Left Bank, has a fine food section.

Covered shopping continues to be popular, and there are modern underground complexes at Forum des Halles (site of the former central market) and the Carrousel du Louvre, off Avenue du Général Lemonnier. The Galeries des Champs-Élysées are worth exploring for their elegant boutiques, while Les Quatre-Temps at La Défense is one of the largest shopping centers in Europe. ∎

The giant glass dome of Galeries Lafayette lights three floors of enticing merchandise.

The Louvre

ONCE THE LARGEST PALACE IN THE WORLD, THE LOUVRE was first a showcase for art during the reign of François I, who was eager to display his Italian paintings. Subsequent rulers acquired new works of art and the Louvre in the end became one of the world's largest museums, with exhibits spanning more than seven millennia.

The Louvre

- ⚠ 53 D3
- ✉ Palais du Louvre
- ☎ 01 40 20 50 50. Recorded information: 01 40 20 51 51
- 🕐 Closed Tues.
- 💲 $$ ($ from 3 p.m.; free for those under 18)
- 🚇 Métro: Palais-Royal–Musée du Louvre

Left: The Louvre Pyramid is I. M. Pei's famous solution to the problem of access to this most popular of museums. Beneath it, steps lead down to the main reception hall.

Right: The winged Victory of Samothrace from the second century B.C. stands beside the stairs to the first floor of the Denon Wing.

The palace began as a fortress in the medieval city walls. Philippe-Auguste enlarged this tower in about 1200, creating a keep surrounded by a moat. Already called the Louvre, his fortified building served as a prison and arsenal. Excavations beneath the Cour Carrée in 1984–85 revealed some of its foundations, which have been opened to visitors as a fascinating exhibit in the Sully Wing.

The Louvre's transformation into a palace began in 1385, when Charles V began to turn it into an elegant royal residence with large windows, a grand entrance, and luxurious apartments. The result was a Gothic palace fit for the king and his possessions, including his magnificent library.

Succeeding monarchs preferred more fashionable residences in the Marais or on the Loire River. Not until the reign of François I (R.1515–1547) did the Louvre regain royal favor. The cultured François had begun to collect paintings and sculptures on his travels in Italy, and he encouraged Italian Renaissance artists such as Leonardo da Vinci and Benvenuto Cellini to come to France. Toward the end of his life, he began to plan a complete rebuilding of the Louvre, in Renaissance style, as a fitting home for his collection. It already included the museum's most famous exhibit—Leonardo's "Mona Lisa."

François's project was continued by Henri II. After his death in 1559, his widow, Catherine de Médicis,

moved the official royal residence from the Hôtel des Tournelles to the Louvre. Between 1595 and 1607 Henri IV realized Catherine's plans for a long gallery beside the Seine, joining the Louvre to the neighboring Tuileries.

Building work in the 17th century included much of the Cour Carrée and the Colonnade at the eastern end. Progress slowed after Louis XIV moved his court to Versailles in 1682, but a great benefit of the Sun King's reign was a tenfold increase in the size of the royal art collections. Many of the Louvre's key works by major artists including Raphael, Titian, Rubens, and Holbein were acquired during this period.

The 18th century saw the Louvre

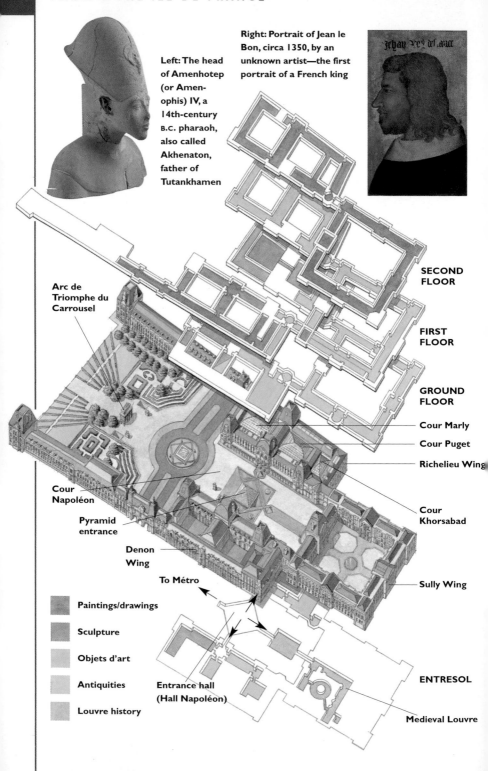

Left: The head of Amenhotep (or Amenophis) IV, a 14th-century B.C. pharaoh, also called Akhenaton, father of Tutankhamen

Right: Portrait of Jean le Bon, circa 1350, by an unknown artist—the first portrait of a French king

SECOND FLOOR

FIRST FLOOR

GROUND FLOOR

Arc de Triomphe du Carrousel

Cour Marly

Cour Puget

Richelieu Wing

Cour Napoléon

Cour Khorsabad

Pyramid entrance

Denon Wing

To Métro

Sully Wing

Paintings/drawings

Sculpture

Objets d'art

Antiquities

Louvre history

Entrance hall (Hall Napoléon)

ENTRESOL

Medieval Louvre

neglected and lacking a focus. Its apartments were put to various uses, from sheltering homeless artists to housing the French academies. Eventually, in 1793, the Musée Central des Arts was inaugurated at the Louvre, which soon became the home of many treasures acquired by Napoleon I from his victories in Europe. (A large proportion of them were returned after his defeat.) Napoleon III finally completed the museum's symmetrical "grand design" and created state apartments. The Louvre continues its tradition of change, most recently in the radical 15-year reorganization and expansion program of the 1980s and 1990s, known as the "Grand Louvre" project.

FINDING YOUR WAY

The Louvre's main entrance, in the Cour Napoléon, is through I. M. Pei's ingenious 793-panel glass pyramid. Visitors go down into the gleaming marble underworld of the spacious reception area, known as the Hall Napoléon.

Here are the entrances to the museum's three wings: Sully (enclosing the Cour Carrée), Denon (alongside the Seine), and Richelieu (beside the Rue de Rivoli). Each wing has four levels: entresol, ground floor, first floor, and second floor. (A fourth entrance brings visitors into the Louvre from the Carrousel du Louvre, a huge underground shopping complex, and the Métro.)

With up to 30,000 artworks to choose from, the first thing you need when visiting the Louvre is some idea of what you would like to see. The second thing you need is a floor plan, available from the information desk in the Hall Napoléon. Audio guides and frequent guided tours are also offered.

The museum consists of seven departments: Oriental Antiquities;

Egyptian Antiquities; Greek, Etruscan, and Roman Antiquities; Objets d'Art; Sculptures; Paintings; and Prints and Drawings. Within each department there are several collections.

The Sully Wing is a good place to start your tour. Here, at the entresol (lower ground) level are the impressive remains of Philippe-Auguste's medieval fortress, unearthed in the corner of the Cour Carrée in the "Grand Louvre" project. The dungeons, the base of the twin towers, and the support for the drawbridge over the moat can be seen, together with displays of pottery and royal artifacts found during excavations.

ANCIENT WORLD

The recently expanded galleries of the Egyptian Antiquities department, on the lower floors of the Sully Wing, are easily reached from the Medieval Louvre exhibition through the Crypt of the Sphinx. The collection has two parts: the ground floor, arranged by theme (The Nile; Writing and Scribes; Music and Games), and the first floor, arranged by date. This starts with a 5,000-year-old ceremonial dagger with an intricately carved ivory handle. Room upon room of mummies, friezes, exquisite fabrics, papyrus texts, jewels, and statues (including the fine "Seated Scribe") make up the largest Egyptian collection outside Cairo.

The main collections representing ancient Greece and Rome are also in the Sully Wing, where you (and very many other visitors!) will find the instantly recognizable "Venus de Milo," elegant as ever, on the ground floor. Don't miss the huge collection of Greek terra-cotta vases in the Galerie Campana (first floor) and the lovely Greek and

Leonardo da Vinci's haunting portrayal of John the Baptist

"The Cheat with the Ace of Diamonds" (circa 1635) by Georges de La Tour (1593–1652)

Roman glassware nearby in the newly laid out Salle des Verres. Not far away, in Napoleon III's former stables (Denon Wing, entresol), is an exciting new gallery devoted to Pre-Hellenic Greece. Look especially at the Cycladic sculptures, amazingly modern-looking figures whose smooth, simple shapes belie their early date (2,000–3,000 B.C.). Two floors up from here, presiding over the sweeping Daru staircase, is the Louvre's second world-famous Greek statue, the graceful marble "Winged Victory of Samothrace" (circa 190 B.C.).

PAINTINGS

The Louvre's enormous collection of paintings spreads into all three wings. The second floor of the Richelieu Wing may be the best place to start. It can be reached by I. M. Pei's imaginatively designed escalator—a 1990s answer to the grand staircase of bygone days.

The northern European paintings, occupying the western part of the wing, include works by important Dutch and Flemish masters such as van Eyck, Rembrandt, the Brueghels, and Vermeer. The large Médici Gallery is a fine setting for the most ambitious work here, Rubens's epic 24-panel sequence depicting scenes from the life of Marie de Médicis. Designed to adorn the Palais du Luxembourg, the enormous paintings were completed in a mere three years between 1622 and 1625. Nearby galleries include a small but significant collection of meticulously observed 15th- and 16th-century German pictures by Dürer, Cranach, Holbein, and others.

A broadly chronological sequence of French pictures, from the 14th to the 19th centuries, starts at the eastern end of this area and continues clockwise round the entire second floor of the Sully Wing. Among the paintings in the Richelieu Wing's galleries, notice two early royal portraits: the anonymous "Portrait of Jean le Bon" (circa 1350) and Jean Fouquet's life-size portrait of Charles VII

(1445–1450). Works worth seeking out later in this long sequence are Watteau's enigmatic "Pierrot" (1718–19), Fragonard's "The Bathers" (1764), and paintings by Ingres, including the technically brilliant portrait of publisher Louis-François Bertin (1832) and the well-known "Turkish Bath" (1862). A number of pictures by Corot, including "The Church at Marissel" (1866), show revolutionary developments in subject matter and light. Such new thinking was soon to be the basis of the Impressionist movement.

The Italian collection is based in and around the Grande Galerie on the first floor of the Denon Wing, beside the Seine. It starts with Cimabue and Giotto panels and continues through all the great Renaissance names. Be sure to see Botticelli's delicate 15th-century frescoes from the Villa Lemmi near Florence, and Raphael's sensitive portrait of his friend Baldassare Castiglione (1515).

Titian and Tintoretto are represented in these galleries not only through their own paintings, but also by Veronese, who is said to have depicted his fellow artists among the musicians in his huge picture "The Wedding Feast at Cana" (1563). Close by is the world's most famous enigmatic smile—that of the "Mona Lisa" (1503–06), known in France as "La Joconde." Don't neglect Leonardo's other masterpieces here, "The Virgin of the Rocks" (1483–86) and "The Virgin and Child with St. Anne" (1510).

SCULPTURE

French sculptures are housed on the lower floors of the Richelieu Wing, where three new glass-roofed courts were laid out during the recent conversion of the wing from government offices. The Cour

Marly is named after the grand château and park that Louis XIV created just outside Paris. The Sun King commissioned many fine marble statues for his retreat, including "Fame Riding Pegasus" (1699–1702) by Antoine Coysevox. The Louvre's collection of more than 20 statues from Marly also includes the later "Horses of Marly," carved by Guillaume Coustou around 1745. Exhibits in the nearby Cour Puget include sculptures by Pierre Puget (1620–1694). His most famous work, the dynamic "Milon of Croton" (1671–1682), was commissioned by Louis XIV for Versailles. Foreign sculpture is covered on the lower two floors of the Denon Wing, where Michelangelo's two powerful (even though unfinished) "Slaves" (1513–15) are the most sought-after exhibits.

DECORATIVE ARTS

The Galerie d'Apollon, on the first floor of the Denon Wing, is the place to view the most glittering display in the whole collection—the crown jewels of France. They include the golden scepter made for Charles V about 1380, and the coronation crowns of Louis XV and Napoleon. On view also is one of the purest diamonds in the world, known as the Regent, worn by Louis XV at his coronation in 1722.

For a further view of French regal life and an insight into style of the Second Empire at its peak, visit the sumptuously decorated and lavishly furnished state apartments of Napoleon III, at the west end of the Richelieu Wing's first floor. Two new museums have recently opened, the Musée de la Mode et du Textile, and the Musée de la Publicité, devoted to advertising. ∎

One of Michelangelo's "Slaves," which were intended for the tomb of Pope Julius II

A walk around the Marais

Architectural gems of the 17th and 18th centuries—several of them now museums—
highlight this walk through a recently rejuvenated area of the city.

The Marais (marsh), a swampy area on the Right Bank, was enclosed by King Philippe-Auguste's great wall of Paris. In the 1200s, the marsh was drained and building began. Today the area is a delightful medley of narrow medieval streets, grand 17th-century *hôtels,* and chic little shops, galleries, and bars.

Start from the **Place de la Bastille ❶,** famous as the site where the Bastille fort was stormed on July 14, 1789, marking the start of the French Revolution. A more recent event, in the 1980s, was the building of the **Opéra National de Paris-Bastille** on the southeast corner. Its appearance, and its cost, provoked much criticism. The 164-foot (50-m) column towering above the square commemorates the July 1830 Revolution.

Walk west along the busy Rue St.-Antoine and turn right on Rue de Birague for the spectacular square Louis XIII, better known as **Place des Vosges ❷.** Commissioned by Henri IV, with two royal pavilions, the square

▲ See area map p. 53
► Place de la Bastille (Métro: Bastille)
↔ 2.25 miles (3.5 km)
⏱ 2 hours
► Quai des Célestins (Métro: Pont Marie)

NOT TO BE MISSED
- Place des Vosges
- Musée Carnavalet
- Musée Cognacq-Jay
- Musée Picasso
- Hôtel de Sens

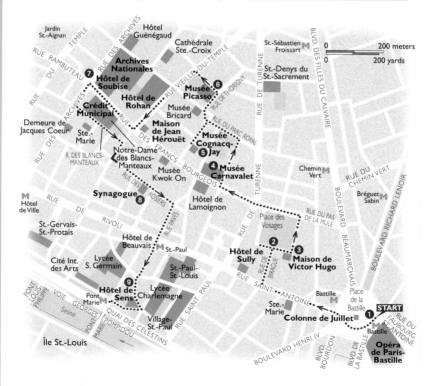

was completed in 1612. It quickly attracted new residents such as Cardinal Richelieu and the playwright Molière. **Maison de Victor Hugo** ❸ at No. 6 is a museum in memory of the writer who lived here 1832–1848 (*Tel 01 42 72 10 16, closed Mon.*). On the southwest corner is an entrance to the **Hôtel de Sully,** perhaps the most magnificent private palace in the Marais, dating from about 1630 (*Tel 01 44 61 20 00, weekend guided tours only*). Stroll around the square to admire its perfect symmetry, perhaps stopping to browse in galleries or shops, or to have lunch or a drink under the arcades of Ma Bourgogne (No. 19).

Leave the square on Rue des Francs-Bourgeois. Turn right on Rue de Sévigné for the **Musée Carnavalet** ❹ (*Tel 01 42 72 21 13, closed Mon.*). Part of the museum occupies the Hôtel Carnavalet, a 16th-century mansion that was the home of aristocratic writer Madame de Sévigné (1626–1696). Her vivid accounts of life in the era of Louis XIV are still absorbing today. The museum brings to life the turbulent history of Paris, from Roman times through the Renaissance and the Revolution to the early 20th century. The extravagant decor typical of the 17th and 18th centuries can be seen in the beautifully renovated interiors here. Some were rescued from buildings demolished by Baron Haussmann in his 19th-century remodeling of Paris.

Continue north up Rue de Sévigné, past typical 17th-century Marais gardens. Turn left on Rue du Parc Royal and take the second left, on Rue Elzévir, to visit the remarkable **Musée Cognacq-Jay** ❺ (*Tel 01 40 27 07 21, closed Mon.*). Here, in the exquisite Hôtel Denon, is a superb collection of 18th-century paintings, furniture, and decorative items such as snuffboxes. Retrace your steps to Rue de Thorigny and the Hôtel Salé, now the impressive **Musée Picasso** ❻ (see pp. 86–87).

Turn left onto Rue des Coutures-St.-Gervais and left again down Rue Vieille-du-Temple. Pass the carved gates of the Hôtel de Rohan and, on the corner of Rue des Francs-Bourgeois, the picturesque turret of the Maison de Jean Hérouët (private).

Turn right on Rue des Francs-Bourgeois, known for its eclectic shops, elegant mansions, and the Crédit Municipal (municipal pawnshop) at No. 55. Across the street is the impressive courtyard of the **Hôtel de Soubise** ❼. Housing part of the National Archives, the imposing *hôtel* is of interest for its sumptuous architecture. Rebuilt in 1709 from a 14th-century manor for the Princesse de Soubise, the interiors were decorated by the most talented artists of the day.

Turn left down Rue des Archives, then left on Rue des Blancs-Manteaux to the covered market. On the far side of the market take Rue des Rosiers. This is the central Jewish quarter, full of specialist shops as far as Rue Pavée. Walk past the **Synagogue** ❽ designed in 1913 by Hector-Germain Guimard, known for his art nouveau Métro stations, then turn right at Rue Pavée. Cross Rue St.-Antoine and follow Rue du Figuier to the 15th-century **Hôtel de Sens** ❾ near the Pont Marie. This medieval building was home in 1605 to Henri IV's first wife, Queen Margot, who had one of her suitors beheaded on its steps. It now houses the Bibliothèque Forney, a decorative arts library (*Tel 01 42 78 14 60, open Tues.–Fri. 3:30–8:30, Sat. 10 a.m.–8:30*). ∎

Beaubourg

This formerly run-down area between Les Halles and the Marais gained an exhilarating new lease of life from the construction of the Centre Georges-6 Pompidou (*rue St Martin, tel 01 44 78 12 33, closed Tues.*) during the 1970s. With its external glass-walled escalators, colored pipes, and massive steel struts, this innovative cultural center stands out as a landmark of high-tech style in the middle of historic Paris. Beside it is the Place Igor Stravinsky, famous for its colorful moving water sculptures.

The museum re-opened in 2000 after a two year revamp. More space has been given to the excellent (and growing) collections of the Musée Nationale d'Art Moderne, covering major contemporary art movements, from cubism to conceptualism and from dada to minimalism.

Other parts of the building are devoted to temporary exhibitions, industrial design, the performing arts, and film. The reference library remains, and visitor facilities include innovative new restaurants. ∎

Musée Picasso

AN OUTSTANDING 17TH-CENTURY TOWN HOUSE IN THE Marais is now the showcase for the world's largest Picasso collection. The paintings, collages, sculptures, drawings, and ceramics are complemented by letters, photographs, and other archival material. Picasso's collection of works by his contemporaries, including Cézanne and Matisse, is also on show here.

Musée Picasso
- 🅰 53 E3
- ✉ Hotel Salé, 5 rue de Thorigny
- ☎ 01 42 71 25 21
- 🕐 Closed Tues.
- 💲 $$
- Ⓜ Métro: Chemin Vert

The ornate elegance of the Hôtel Salé, built for a salt tax collector in 1656, makes a perfect backdrop to the works of this great 20th-century master. Though Picasso (1881–1973) was born in Spain, his adult life was spent almost entirely in France. During his long and productive career he had kept many of his own works, resulting in a huge inheritance tax liability when he died. The French state claimed this in the form of works of art amounting to a quarter of the artist's collection, and then undertook a lavish refurbishment of the Hôtel Salé as a museum for them.

With more than 250 paintings, 3,000 drawings, and 100,000 archival items, the collection is much too big to be displayed all at once. A carefully chosen selection representing Picasso's hugely varied output over some 70 years is always on show. The sequence is broadly chronological, so visitors can trace the artist's development through different phases—though there was much overlapping of styles.

The collection begins with works produced after Picasso's first visit to Paris from Spain in 1900, among them the bleak "Self Portrait" (1901), a masterpiece of his famous Blue Period, and "Celestine" (1904). Many of the works of this period (1901–1904) were inspired by tragic figures he saw on the streets of Paris: prostitutes, beggars, and drunks. Picasso used varying shades of blue to express feelings of intense melancholy and his preoccupation with life and death following the suicide of his friend, the poet Casagemas, who had accompanied him to Paris.

Poignant sadness continued to pervade Picasso's work through his so-called Rose Period (1904–1906), though his harlequins and circus performers are portrayed in lighter, warmer colors than those of the Blue Period. The impression is of a greater tranquility, seen, for example, in "The Two Brothers" (1906).

The rapid developments in Picasso's work during his twenties and thirties were influenced by key events in his life. In Paris, artists of the day such as Matisse, Cézanne, Braque, and Rousseau made a powerful impression on him. He often visited the Louvre, where he got to

Picasso's sculptures are as strong as his paintings: "Bust of a woman" (1931).

know classical art. His travels, notably to Rome, Spain, and the Mediterranean, brought new themes. Primitive art from French colonies in Africa and the South Seas was becoming the object of serious interest. It is possible to trace these different influences in a host of works from Picasso's middle years including "The Bathers" (1918), "Three Women at the Fountain" (1921), and the early studies for the key painting "Les Demoiselles d'Avignon" (now in New York).

In his mid-twenties, Picasso, together with Georges Braque and Juan Gris, began to develop cubism, a style that aimed to depict the complete structure of an object from different angles by breaking it down into geometrical units. Picasso's paintings from this phase of his life include "Man with a Mandolin" (1911).

Among the great variety of later works in the museum look for "The Crucifixion" (1930), the menacing "Cat Catching a Bird" (1939), and "Portrait of Dora Maar" (1937).

Dora Maar was one of many women in Picasso's life; others included Françoise Gillot and Jacqueline Roque. They figure strongly throughout the collections, giving the museum a personal feel (these are, after all, the works he chose to keep for himself).

COLLAGES & CERAMICS

By 1912, Picasso had begun to produce collages, using materials such as wood, chair caning, and wallpaper. Collages in the museum include "Still Life with Chair-caning" (1912) and "Man with a Pipe" (1914).

In 1948, Picasso began working with ceramics at Vallauris in Provence. His relish for this medium is evident in the relaxed and joyful pots, jugs, plates, and figures he created during this period. In one year, he produced over 2,000 ceramic pieces, at first using traditional techniques, then indulging in ever bolder artistic experiments—a familiar trend in the work of this great genius of 20th-century art. ■

"Femmes à leur toilette" (Women dressing), 1938

Montmartre & Sacré-Coeur

Basilique du Sacré-Coeur

🅰 53 D5

✉ place du Parvis du Sacré-Coeur

💲 Crypt & dome $

🚇 Métro: Abbesses, Anvers, Lamarck-Caulaincourt

THIRTY WINDMILLS ONCE DOTTED THE MONTMARTRE skyline. The steep hill that Parisians call "La Butte" now has an even more distinctive landmark: the great white Basilique du Sacré-Coeur. Although tourists flock to Montmartre today, it is still possible to stroll in quiet backwaters where streets and squares have retained a village atmosphere.

The white dome of Sacré-Coeur rises above the bustle of the Place du Tertre in Montmartre.

Its commanding position overlooking Paris ensured Montmartre's importance from early times. The Roman temple here probably gave the district its name (from Mons Martis, "hill of Mars"). The 12th-century Benedictine abbey church is one of Paris's oldest; **St.-Pierre-de-Montmartre** still overlooks the Place du Tertre.

Quarries and vineyards supported Montmartre, and it remained a separate village until the quarries (and their associated windmills) had to close because of collapsing tunnels. By 1860 Montmartre had become the 18th arrondissement of the city of Paris.

The late 19th century saw Montmartre as it is most often

pictured now—a focus of exciting, if lurid, bohemian life, inhabited by poets and painters. Many great names from this period can be seen on the gravestones in the **Cimetière de Montmartre** on Avenue Rachel. They include composers Hector Berlioz and Jacques Offenbach (who wrote the famous cancan), writers Stendhal and Émile Zola, and painter Edgar Degas. The film director François Truffaut and the Russian dancer Vaslav Nijinsky are also buried here.

Today the creative ferment of the belle epoque has been replaced by the street artists of the **Place du Tertre,** a prime stop on the sightseeing circuit.

Visible from almost anywhere in Paris, the **Basilique du Sacré-Coeur** was started in 1876 to honor the 58,000 killed in the Franco-Prussian War and to atone for the "crimes" of the Commune. Pillars had to be driven deep into unstable rock to support the enormous church, which was finally consecrated in 1919. Inside, the chancel vaulting is decorated with a colossal square mosaic (1912–1922) by Luc-Olivier Merson. It depicts the French nation worshiping the Sacred Heart of Christ.

Steep spiral stairs lead to the dome, where an exterior gallery commands a spectacular panorama of Paris. The views at ground level are almost as stunning. ■

Artists in Montmartre

Paris has long been an inspirational magnet for artists, both French and foreign, who have come here and made it their home. With its picturesque streets, bohemian ways, and cheap lodging houses, Montmartre began to attract impoverished artists in the 19th century. Legendary cafés and clubs—Le Chat Noir, Au Lapin Agile, La Nouvelle Athènes—became known as literary and artistic meeting places.

The Moulin Rouge, on Boulevard de Clichy, opened its doors in 1889. Henri de Toulouse-Lautrec was a regular visitor, often sketching and painting as he sat in the dance hall. Dancers and cabaret *artistes* of the louche Montmartre world, such as Aristide Bruant, Jane Avril, and Yvette Guilbert, were immortalized in his posters. Another Montmartre dance hall, the Moulin de la Galette, was the subject of paintings by Renoir, Bonnard, and others.

Montmartre's streets are peppered with memories of famous artists. Boulevard de Clichy, painted by van Gogh and Renoir, was a focal point. Seurat, Signac, and, later, Picasso all had studios here. Degas died at No. 6 in 1917. The squalid Bateau-Lavoir building, where Picasso lived from 1904 to 1909, was shared by 30 other residents, many of them artists. The building (at No. 13 Place Émile-Goudeau) is gone now—but the clowns and harlequins of the Montmartre circus world live on in Picasso's paintings. ■

Toulouse-Lautrec caught the atmosphere in the cabaret halls of Montmartre with just a few deft strokes.

La Défense

Grande Arche

- 🅰 52 A4
- ✉ esplanade de la Défense
- ☎ 01 49 07 27 57
- 💲 $$
- Ⓜ Métro: Grande Arche de la Défense

Dôme IMAX

- ☎ 01 46 92 45 50

Musée de l'Automobile

- ☎ 01 46 92 45 50
- 💲 $$

The Grande Arche is reflected in the colored parvis below.

PARIS HAS FREQUENTLY HIT THE HEADLINES FOR ITS daring new architectural exploits, such as the Opéra-Bastille and the Centre Georges Pompidou (see p. 85). But of all of these *grands travaux*, none has been more ambitious than the controversial space-age development at La Défense, dominated by the truly monumental Grande Arche.

The entirely modern district of La Défense, located to the west of Paris across the Pont de Neuilly, takes its name from a statue in the central square, symbolizing the defense of Paris during the 1870 Franco-Prussian War.

A broad pedestrian avenue, the Esplanade du Général de Gaulle, rises in steps from the Pont de Neuilly to give access to office towers, apartment blocks, the vast shopping complex of Les Quatre-Temps, and the CNIT. The oldest building on the site (1958), the triangular CNIT building is now an international business and conference center. Roads and railroads run beneath the buildings, leaving the main areas traffic free. More than 70 works of contemporary sculpture punctuate the concrete landscape.

The focal point of La Défense is the colossal **Grande Arche.** Designed by Danish architect Johann Otto von Spreckilsen, it was completed for the Bicentennial of the Revolution in 1989. Shaped like a huge hollow cube and faced with glass and white marble, this "window on the world" is so vast that Notre-Dame would easily fit beneath it. The walls of the arch contain government and company offices. External glass elevators take visitors up to the roof to admire the views over Paris from a height of more than 300 feet (100 m). Be sure to look to the southeast, where a dramatic corridor cuts a swath straight across the city. Stretching to the Arc de Triomphe and beyond, it continues along the same axis to the Place de la Concorde and the Bastille. The Grande Arche was deliberately aligned on this historic "Triumphal Way."

At the base of the arch, fountains and cafés enliven the square of La Défense. Beside the Grande Arche, the spherical **Dôme IMAX** encloses one of the world's largest cinema screens. Next door is the **Musée de l'Automobile,** which traces a century of motoring. ∎

Parc de la Villette
🅰 53 E5
☎ 01 40 03 75 03
🚇 Métro: Porte de la
  Villette

Cité des Sciences
et de l'Industrie
✉ 30 avenue Corentin
  Cariou
☎ 01 40 05 72 23
🕐 Closed Mon.
💲 $$$
🚇 Métro: Porte de la
  Villette

The Géode in
front of the Cité
des Sciences has a
hemispherical
screen showing
special wide-
angle films.

Parc de la Villette & Cité des Sciences

AN ASTONISHING TRANSFORMATION HAS TAKEN PLACE here in northeast Paris. The former livestock market and slaughter-houses of La Villette are now a futuristic cultural park and interactive science museum. Allow a full day to make the most of a visit—there is lots to see and do.

Adults and children alike will be enthralled by the Parc de la Villette's star attraction, the **Cité des Sciences et de l'Industrie.** This vast science museum occupies the former cattle auction hall, innovatively converted by Adrien Fainsilber. Notice how his designs play with the light reflected off water, steel, and glass.

Explora, the main exhibition, invites visitors to find out about the universe, from space to volcanoes and the oceans, through its range of interactive presentations. Green-houses and the aquarium focus on the living world. To see the stars, go to the **Planétarium** on the second floor. Its 10,000-lens astronomical projector throws images of some 5,000 stars onto the 68-foot (21-m) hemispherical dome.

Children will love the robots and rockets, the sound bubble, and the room of optical illusions. In addition, the **Cité des Enfants** (ages 3–12) and the **Technocité** (age 11 and up) encourage children to experiment with scientific theories and techniques. In the **Inventorium** they can build a house or program computers.

Reflecting sky and water in front of the building is the shiny steel of the **Géode,** which contains an enormous curved IMAX cinema screen. Beside the Géode lies the submarine *Argonaute*, built in 1957. The interior is fascinating, but not for the claustrophobic.

Bridges across the Canal de l'Ourcq lead into the landscaped southern area, with playgrounds and cafés. Part of the original cattle market, the Grande Halle, is now an exhibition and concert hall, while the Zénith is a venue for rock concerts. The **Cité de la Musique** (*Tel 01 44 84 44 84*) is a resource center for music and dance. ■

RAOUL DUFY
La Fée Electricité 1937

Art on a grand scale at the Musée d'Art Moderne de la Ville de Paris

More places to visit in Paris

BOIS DE BOULOGNE

This huge expanse of parkland, forest, and lakes offers boating, fishing, cycling, horseback riding, horse racing, and a popular children's playground, the Jardin d'Acclimatation.

🅰 52 A4 🗺 Métro: Porte d'Auteuil (south), Les Sablons or Porte Maillot (north)

CHÂTEAU & BOIS DE VINCENNES

Set in a large landscaped park east of Paris, the château has a moated 14th-century keep, a Gothic chapel, and royal apartments. More recent additions include a Buddhist center, a theater complex, and a zoo. The **Musée des Arts d'Afrique et d'Océanie** (*293 avenue Daumesnil, tel 01 44 74 84 80, closed Tues.*) displays art from former French colonies.

🅰 52 F2 $ $$ 🗺 Métro: Château de Vincennes

CIMETIÈRE DU PÈRE-LACHAISE

Out of the city center, but worth the trip, this vast cemetery is full of fantastic tomb designs and memorials to the famous (Héloïse and Abélard, Chopin, Molière, Victor Hugo, Édith Piaf, Oscar Wilde, and Jim Morrison).

🅰 52 F3 🖂 boulevard de Ménilmontant
$ $ 🗺 Métro: Père Lachaise

MUSÉE D'ART MODERNE DE LA VILLE DE PARIS

A showcase for living artists, this collection also covers earlier 20th-century art movements such as the École de Paris, cubism, and 1960s pop art. Artists represented include Picasso, Matisse, Dufy, and Utrillo.

🅰 52 A3 🖂 11 avenue du Président Wilson
☎ 01 53 67 40 00 🕒 Closed Mon. $ $
🗺 Métro: Iéna, Alma Marceau

MUSÉE MARMOTTAN

Not to be missed, this museum housed in an elegant 19th-century mansion has a substantial Monet collection, including some of the "Water Lilies" paintings. Renoir, Sisley, and Gauguin are also represented. And there are sculptures, furniture, and medieval manuscripts.

🅰 52 A3 🖂 2 rue Louis-Boilly ☎ 01 42 24 07 02 🕒 Closed Mon. $ $$ 🗺 Métro: La Muette

PALAIS DE CHAILLOT

The curved wings and vast terrace of this 1937 edifice form the backdrop of many classic pictures of the Eiffel Tower. Inside, the **Musée de l'Homme** (*Tel 01 53 65 69 69*) traces the story of humanity; the **Musée de la Marine** (*Tel 01 53 54 69 69*) is a maritime museum; due to open soon is the **Centre Musée National de l'Architecture.**

🅰 52 A3 🖂 place du Trocadéro
🕒 Closed Tues. $ $$
🗺 Métro: Trocadéro ■

The Île-de-France

Not literally an island, though largely bounded by rivers, the Île-de-France comprises the region ruled over by Hugues Capet when he was declared king of France in 987. Although his kingdom nominally extended over all of western and southern Gaul, he actually controlled an area of only 60 by 120 miles (100 by 200 km) around his capital, Paris. Well populated even during Roman times, it is an area rich in art and architecture. St.-Denis was the site of the first French cathedral and a royal burial place. Sèvres is famous for its 18th-century porcelain factory, and Meudon has a museum dedicated to the works of Rodin. The elegance of Meaux and the charm of medieval Provins demonstrate the area's cultural richness.

This is the royal heartland of France, littered with sumptuous châteaus. The most grandiose of all, of course, is the palace of Versailles, closely followed by its precursor, the magnificent château of Vaux-le-Vicomte. A great number of smaller châteaus testify to the popularity of the area as a country retreat. The intimate Malmaison was home to the Empress Josephine in her last years, while Champs-sur-Marne belonged to Madame de Pompadour, mistress of Louis XV. The forest and château of Fontainebleau have inspired generations of painters. ■

Angels mourn on a royal tomb in St.-Denis.

Château de Versailles

IN 1661, LOUIS XIV DECIDED TO BUILD THE ULTIMATE royal residence at Versailles, 12 miles (17 km) from Paris. For nearly 50 years the greatest artists of the time worked on the château: Louis Le Vau and then Jules Hardouin-Mansart were the architects; André Le Brun supervised the interior decoration; and André Le Nôtre designed the gardens.

Château de Versailles

- 🅰 93 B2
- ✉ 12 miles (17 km) southwest of Paris
- ☎ 01 30 84 78 00
- 🕐 Closed Mon.
- 💲 $$
- 🚇 RER line C: Château de Versailles

The king and his court—some 5,000 people, rising later to 20,000—moved in during 1682. Versailles became the political heart of France until October 1789, when the revolutionary mob invaded the palace and triumphantly carried Louis XVI and Queen Marie-Antoinette off to captivity in Paris. During the Revolution, the palace furniture was sold, its paintings sent to the Louvre, and its buildings abandoned. In 1837, Louis-Philippe converted it into a museum of French history; in 1919, the Treaty of Versailles, bringing to an end World War I, was signed in the Hall of Mirrors. Only after that did any serious restoration begin.

The château was built around Louis XIII's small hunting lodge, whose low brick front is still visible in the middle of the Marble Courtyard. Le Vau built the first enlargement in the 1660s, a series of wings which expanded into an enlarged court-yard. Columns were added to the west facade and a great terrace was created on the first floor. In 1678, Hardouin-Mansart added the huge north and south wings, and created the Hall of Mirrors from Le Vau's terrace.

The private apartments of the King and Queen are arranged around the Marble Courtyard. In the north wing the Great Staircase leads visitors up to the "Grands Appartements," extravaganzas of colored marble, gilt bronze, silk and velvet drapes, trompe l'oeil murals, and rich paintings and sculptures. Each state room is dedicated to an Olympian deity. The Salon de Diane, with its marble decor based on the themes of Diana and hunting, once

A Passemant astronomic clock in the Clock Room gives date, time, moon phases, and planet movements.

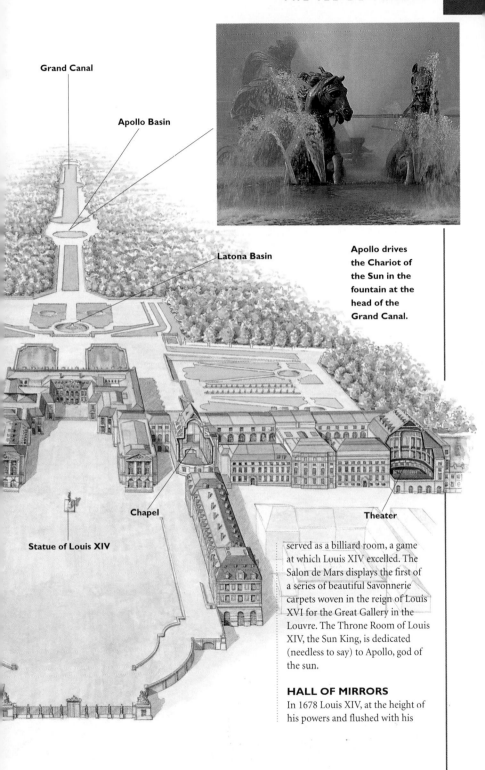

Grand Canal

Apollo Basin

Latona Basin

Apollo drives the Chariot of the Sun in the fountain at the head of the Grand Canal.

Chapel

Theater

Statue of Louis XIV

served as a billiard room, a game at which Louis XIV excelled. The Salon de Mars displays the first of a series of beautiful Savonnerie carpets woven in the reign of Louis XVI for the Great Gallery in the Louvre. The Throne Room of Louis XIV, the Sun King, is dedicated (needless to say) to Apollo, god of the sun.

HALL OF MIRRORS

In 1678 Louis XIV, at the height of his powers and flushed with his

The King's Bedchamber is sumptuously decorated as it was for Louis XIV.

military victories, built the Galerie des Glaces to enhance the magnificence of the palace and glorify his own absolute power.

Flanked on either side by the ornate salons of "War" and "Peace," this vast room, 230 feet (70 m) long, has 17 huge mirrors—an ostentatious display of fabulous wealth in the days when mirrors were staggeringly expensive. Further embellishments included great crystal chandeliers, silver furniture, gilded candelabra, damask curtains, even potted orange trees, and a silver throne.

In Louis XIV's time, this dazzling space was rarely used for great ceremonies, despite all the expense and magnificence.

King's Bedchamber

From 1701, Louis XIV was in the habit of granting private audiences and dining informally in the royal bedchamber. The ceremonies of the king's *levée* (rising) and *couchée* (retiring), with their arcane rituals, were also held here, and it was here that Louis XIV died in September 1715 after reigning for 72 years. The bed alcove is lined with crimson velvet and gold, silver, and crimson brocade; the paintings, with one exception, are still those chosen by Louis XIV.

The Queen's State Bedchamber, with its balustrade, canopied bed, and silk hangings, has been restored to look as it did when Marie-Antoinette left in 1789, never to

return. In this room, in full view of members of the court, various queens of France gave birth to 19 royal children.

The two-story baroque chapel, dedicated to St. Louis and finished in 1710, was Louis XIV's final addition to Versailles. Here, Masses were said for military victories and the baptisms and weddings of princes were celebrated, the royal family and the members of highest nobility sitting on the upper floor with the courtiers below. The interior of the chapel is richly decorated in white marble, gilding, and baroque murals.

The Opéra was inaugurated in 1770 for the wedding of Marie-Antoinette to Louis XVI. The theater formerly seated 1,000; today there is room for an audience of 700 spectators. As was usual with court theaters, it also doubled as a ballroom.

Louis-Philippe's museum, consisting of some 8,000 paintings and sculptures devoted to the history of France in the 17th and 18th centuries, is housed in the north wing. The huge Battle Gallery is lined with paintings celebrating French feats of arms from 496 to 1809.

Fountains

🕐 The fountains play Sun., May–Sept. 11:15–11:45 a.m. & 3:30–5 p.m.

THE GARDENS

Landscaping work on some 2,000 acres (815 ha) of grounds created an extensive series of formal gardens with statues and fountains, an orangery, kitchen gardens, a vast artificial lake, and even a zoo.

Laid out by Le Nôtre, the 247 acres (100 ha) of gardens radiate from the west facade of the château. The apotheosis of 17th-century French formal style, their rigid symmetry and relentlessly tamed version of nature reflect the classical ideals of the period. The Grand Canal serves as the focal point, with ponds, fountains, sculptures, flower beds, lawns, wooded groves, and

shady retreats placed around it. Gilded gondolas once plied its waters, and today rowboats can be still rented.

The most impressive of Versailles's 300 statues grace the Water Garden, the Pyramid Fountain in the North Garden, and the Apollo Fountain in the Apollo Basin at the end of the Royal Avenue and start of the Grand Canal. The allegorical references to the Sun God Apollo that pervade the palace's decorative scheme inside and out are magnificent in the elaborate statues of the fountains—above all in the superb figure of Apollo rising triumphantly in the Chariot of the Sun.

Beyond the North Garden, the Water Avenue leads to the Basin of Neptune, the central figure bordered by 22 fountains, each with a marble basin supported by charming bronze statues of children.

Concealed within the garden's highly formal design are a variety of follies, including a grove decorated with shells, rock gardens, and ornamental lamps where the court danced in summer. Also here, a circular marble colonnade provided an elegant setting for the palace's famous festivities.

Grand & Petit Trianon

The Italianate Grand Trianon was built for Louis XIV in 1687 as a retreat from court life. The Petit Trianon was built for Louis XV's mistress, Madame du Barry. Louis XVI presented this jewel of neoclassic architecture to Marie-Antoinette. She transformed its grounds into a romantic English-style park and built her famous hamlet, complete with a farm, in which she and her court playacted an idealized form of rural life.

Due to storm damage in 1999 some of the gardens will be closed for some time to come. ■

Chartres

Chartres

⚑ 93 B2

Visitor information

✉ place de la
Cathédrale

☎ 02 37 21 75 02

**Musée des
Beaux-Arts**

✉ Cloître Notre Dame

☎ 02 37 36 41 39

🕐 Closed Sun. a.m.
& all Tues.

💲 $

THE MODEST TOWN OF CHARTRES, LOCATED ABOUT 45 miles (75 km) southwest of Paris just outside the Île-de-France, boasts a magnificent cathedral considered one of the greatest surviving examples of 13th-century Gothic architecture. Its asymmetrical spires rise majestically above the town and the surrounding countryside, a perfect monument to the medieval fervor for building to the glory of God.

Dedicated to the Virgin Mary, the first cathedral was built (reputedly on the site of a Druid temple) to house a precious relic of her veil donated by Charles the Bald in the late ninth century. It is still

The rose window in the south transept shows Christ in Majesty.

displayed in the Treasury. Chartres immediately became an important center of pilgrimage, which it remains to this day. Fire destroyed that first shrine and four successive churches, the last in 1194, but contributions to the rebuilding poured in from every side. Completed in a

record 30 years, the new cathedral preserves the Romanesque west front and the south tower of the earlier building. The rest of the cathedral, with its characteristic flying buttresses, is pure Gothic.

The triple portal of the west front and its recessed statues, devoted to the glory of Christ, are superb examples of Romanesque carving. The sculptures on the north portal (circa 1230) are devoted to the Old Testament and those on the south (1225–1250) to the New Testament.

The Clocher Vieux, at 345 feet (105 m), is the tallest Romanesque steeple in existence; the Clocher Neuf has a slightly taller Gothic spire, added after lightning damage in the 16th century. A strenuous 378-step climb up the tower leads to tremendous views from the top.

THE INTERIOR

The breathtaking interior is illuminated by 176 incomparable stained-glass windows, covering a total area of 27,000 square feet (2,500 sq m). Most date from the 13th century, though the west facade contains three that survived the fire of 1194. The rose windows depict the events of the Apocalypse, the life of the Virgin, and the Last Judgment.

The floor of the nave features a circular labyrinth (usually obscured by chairs) representing good and evil, with paradise at its center. Medieval pilgrims would crawl the 920-foot-long (280-m) path.

The unusually broad choir is surrounded by a stone wall sculpted with a filigree pattern and with scenes from the life of Christ and the Virgin arranged in 41 groups of about 200 figures. Behind the choir, in the Chapelle St.-Piat, is the Treasury. The 11th-century crypt, entered via the Maisons des Clercs, is the largest in France, and encloses another crypt dating from the ninth century.

The Eure River creates a picturesque backdrop to the quiet town, with old washhouses and drying lofts along its banks. The medieval town has some fine architectural features, particularly on Rue du Cheval Blanc and also at 35 Rue des Ecuyers and 12 Rue des Grenets. The former bishop's palace, which still has some state rooms, now houses the **Musée des Beaux-Arts**, with collections including enamels, tapestries, 18th-century French paintings, notably by Chardin and Fragonard, and contemporary works, including a room of Vlamincks. Amateurs of the bizarre will enjoy **Maison Picassiette**, where Raymond Isidore devoted his life to decorating every surface and object with fragments of china and glass. ∎

Maison Picassiette
- ✉ 22 rue du Repos
- ☎ 02 37 34 10 78
- 🕐 Closed Tues. & Sun. a.m.

The asymmetric spires of the cathedral rise above the town of Chartres.

The splendor of the Galerie François I with decorations from the school of Fontainebleau (1532–1570)

Château de Fontainebleau

THIS LOVELY CHÂTEAU, SITUATED 37 MILES (60 KM) SOUTH of Paris, started life in the tenth century as a hunting lodge in the huge forest of Fontainebleau, and quickly became a favorite retreat of the kings of France. Beginning in 1527, François I rebuilt it as a château, importing Italian artists to design the interior. Within a few years, their mannerist style became known as the school of Fontainebleau, subsequently exerting a major influence on French painting.

Many French monarchs were born at Fontainebleau and several died here. The château also witnessed the fateful revocation of the Edict of Nantes in 1685 (see p. 25) and Napoleon's abdication as Emperor of the French in 1814.

The interior is magnificently decorated with paneling, stucco, and frescoes, most famously in the Galerie François I. Other highlights include the 98-foot-long (30-m) Salle de Bal, the Galerie Henri II, and the salon of Marie de Médicis. The apartments of Napoleon I are in pure Empire style.

The beautiful forest of deciduous woodland offers opportunities for walking, cycling, horseback riding, and rock climbing. ■

Fontainebleau
🅰 93 C2

Château de Fontainebleau
☎ 01 60 71 50 70
🕐 Closed Tues.
💲 $$

Barbizon
🅰 93 C2
Visitor information
✉ 55 Grande Rue
☎ 01 60 66 41 87

Maison Jean-François Millet
✉ 27 Grande Rue, Barbizon
☎ 01 60 66 21 55
🕐 Closed Tues.

Barbizon school

The mid-19th century saw a move toward greater realism in landscape painting, pioneered by Jean-Baptiste Corot and Gustave Courbet in France, and the British artist John Constable, among others. Strongly influenced by their ideas, a group of painters, led by Théodore Rousseau, settled in the village of Barbizon in Fontainebleau forest. Working outdoors and taking scenes from peasant life as their subject, they produced such shimmering landscapes and touching tableaus as Jean-François Millet's famous "Gleaners" (1857). The village remains a fashionable retreat for Parisians, and a popular tourist destination where you can visit the house in which Millet lived. ■

Short excursions from Paris

CATHÉDRALE ST.-DENIS

According to legend St. Denis was beheaded on Montmartre in A.D. 262. He then picked up his head and walked 6,000 paces north before expiring. There the abbey church of St.-Denis was built, his tomb becoming a shrine. Clovis, king of the Franks, was buried here in 511 to be joined the following year by Ste. Geneviève, patron saint of Paris, and subsequently by other French kings. By 1143, a great Gothic cathedral stood here, the first example of the new style in Europe. Massively damaged during the Revolution, the cathedral was partially restored in the 19th century. Today only the choir and west front authentically reflect the original. Apart from its importance to French architecture, the cathedral is the mausoleum of the French monarchy, with some 60 funeral monuments carved by the greatest sculptors from the 13th century onward. St. Louis commissioned monuments for his predecessors, the most remarkable being King Dagobert's tomb. The later graves are very elaborate, particularly the Renaissance monument of Catherine de Médicis and Henri II. The crypt contains the collective grave of the Bourbon dynasty.

🅐 93 C3 ✉ rue de la Légion d'Honneur
☎ 01 48 09 83 54 💲 $$

CHANTILLY

The Chantilly châteaus (see p. 116) make a pleasant day's outing from Paris.

CHÂTEAU DE MALMAISON

Empress Joséphine, first wife of Napoleon, bought the elegant 17th-century château of Malmaison in 1799, and died there in 1814. Now a museum, it houses an extensive collection of Empire paintings and decorative arts. The Château Bois-Préau, next door, is devoted to souvenirs of Napoleon.

🅐 93 B2 ✉ avenue du Château, Rueil-Malmaison ☎ 01 41 29 05 55 🕐 Closed Tues. 💲 $$

CHÂTEAU DE RAMBOUILLET

Since 1897, the château of Rambouillet has been the presidential summer residence, but it is open to the public when the president is not there. Only the round tower of the original 1375 fortress remains. The rest was rebuilt in 1706 for Louis XIV's illegitimate son, the Count of Toulouse. Here Louis XVI bred the noted Rambouillet sheep, known for their resistance to heat and drought, and built a dairy and grotto in the park for the amusement of his wife, Marie-Antoinette.

🅐 93 B2 ☎ 01 34 83 00 25 🕐 Closed Tues. 💲 $$

CHÂTEAU DE VAUX-LE-VICOMTE

The inspiration for Versailles, this outstanding baroque château built by Nicholas Fouquet, one of Louis XIV's ministers, was the first project on which the formidable team of architect Louis Le Vau, painter Charles Le Brun, and landscape gardener André Le Nôtre worked together. On the château's completion in 1661 Fouquet held a lavish party and banquet, to which he invited Louis XIV. Supper was served on 432 gold plates and 6,000 silver plates; 1,200 fountains framed the entertainment, written and performed by Molière and his troupe; and the evening culminated with spectacular fireworks. Unfortunately, just before the feast, Louis was told that Fouquet had embezzled state funds. Fouquet was promptly arrested and Vaux-le-Vicomte confiscated. Try to attend one of the breathtaking candlelight tours (*Sat. May–Sept., 8–11 p.m.*), lit by over 1,000 flickering candle flames.

🅐 93 C2 ✉ Maincy 🕐 Fountain displays 2nd & last Sat. April–Oct. 3–6 p.m. 💲 $$–$$$

DISNEYLAND PARIS

The vast theme park and resort of Disneyland Paris covers nearly 5,000 acres (2,000 ha), one-fifth the area of Paris, at Marne-la-Vallée. RER line A4 whisks visitors from the Gare de Lyon in central Paris directly into the park. The Magic Kingdom offers over 50 rides in Fantasyland, Adventureland, Discoveryland, and Frontierland. Pirates, a haunted house, a giant treehouse, characters from the Disney movies and the famous Main Street U.S.A. parades add to the fun. Within the resort are seven themed hotels, wooded campsites, restaurants, cafés, stores, a golf course, tennis courts, and plenty of nighttime entertainment.

 93 C2  Marne-la-Vallée, about 12 miles (19 km) east of Paris  01 60 30 60 30  $$$$$. Entrance fee includes all rides

GIVERNY & MONET

The village of Giverny, in the Seine Valley between Paris and Rouen, contains the house where Claude Monet lived from 1883 until his death in 1926. Gardens (including the famous water garden), studios, and house, lovingly restored as Monet himself designed them, are open to the public. All are a delight: the house with its fresh yellow walls and tiled floors, Monet's own furniture and collection of Japanese prints, the shutters and garden furniture still painted in the exact green chosen by the master.

Visitors today can wander the paths of the garden and admire the same palette of bright colors that Monet painted. The gallery sells reproductions of the works painted here, and the shop sells seeds and plants.

Also in Giverny is the **Musée d'Art Américain** (99 rue Claude Monet, tel 02 32 51 94 65, closed Nov.–March), devoted to American impressionist artists, many of whom came to France seeking inspiration, including Winslow Homer, Lila Cabot Perry, John Singer Sargent, and Mary Cassatt, the only American to exhibit with the Impressionists.

Fondation Claude Monet (Monet's house & gardens)  105 C3  Rue Claude Monet, Giverny  02 32 51 28 21  Closed Nov.–March except Easter & Whitsun  $$

ST.-GERMAIN-EN-LAYE

Just west of Paris lies the pleasant residential town of St.-Germain-en-Laye. Here you'll find the fortress of St.-Germain-en-Laye, home of French kings from François I to Louis XIV. Napoleon III restored the Renaissance castle, establishing the **Musée des Antiquités Nationales** (tel 01 39 10 13 00, closed Tues.). Exhibits in the museum range from the Paleolithic period to the Dark Ages, including a reconstruction of the Salle des Taureaux (Hall of Bulls) at Lascaux (see pp. 254–55). The tremendous **Grande Terrasse** provides a sweeping overview of the Seine Valley. Also of interest is **Ste.-Chapelle,** a Gothic masterpiece similar to the chapel of the same name in Paris (see p. 58). Nearby, the **Musée du Prieuré** (rue Maurice Denis, tel 01 39 73 77 87, closed Mon.–Tues.) contains Postimpressionist art, including paintings of the nabis movement.  93 B2 ■

The bridge over the pond in Monet's garden at Giverny features in several of his paintings.

Great cathedrals across northern France show how Gothic architecture evolved. In the northeast lie two wine regions, Champagne and Alsace. And from Flanders to the Marne, mementos of war scatter the landscape.

Northern France

Fleur-de-lis detail from the "Fontaine de Neptune" in Place Stanislas, Nancy

Northern France

SOME OF FRANCE'S GREATEST WINES, EARLIEST AND MOST MAGNIFICENT
Gothic cathedrals, and most valued art collections are to be found in the five northern
regions: Nord-Pas-de-Calais, Picardie, Champagne-Ardenne, Alsace, and Lorraine. These
are France's borderlands with Germany, Switzerland, Luxembourg, and Belgium, and—
mediated by the narrow Manche or English Channel—with Britain.

A mix of languages, cultures, and traditions
testifies to the historic impermanence of
France's frontiers. Calais, for example, was
once English; Alsace and most of Lorraine
have intermittently been part of Germany; and
Flandre (Flanders), now in the Nord-Pas-de-
Calais region, was part of a medieval state that
included much of Belgium. It scarcely seems
credible that these frontiers were being fought
over only half a century ago, in wars that drew
the world's greatest nations to battle in
northern France.

WINE COUNTRY

Stained-glass windows in Reims's cathedral
depict vine cultivation and wine production,
for Reims is capital of the Champagne
region, where wine has been made since
Roman times. It was here that the renowned
sparkling wine is thought to have been
developed about 300 years ago. Champagne is
France's most northerly wine-growing district,
and the cool climate is a factor in the success
of its great wine.

The main area of production centers on
the vineyards around Reims and Épernay,
where the major *maisons de champagne* are
located. Most invite you to tour their *caves*—
the labyrinthine cellars where the wine is
fermented, blended, and stored—and taste
the champagne before buying (see p. 119).
Another delightful part of a visit to the
Champagne region is to tour the charming
villages, abbeys, churches, and castles of the
area along the signposted Route Touristique
du Champagne (see p. 120).

Wine has also been made since Roman
times in Alsace. You can follow the signposted
Route du Vin for about 130 miles (200 km)
along a scenic route that winds through the
foothills of the Vosges Mountains, through
vineyards dotted with charming old towns
and villages, churches and castles.

CRADLE OF THE GOTHIC STYLE

Gothic architecture grew up here: Picardie
alone has six major cathedrals. The former
bishop's palace and medieval abbeys and
churches still cluster round Strasbourg's
cathedral and the early Gothic Cathédrale de
Notre-Dame in the old town of Laon. The
Treasuries of these ancient cathedrals preserve
centuries-old relics, gold and silverware,
paintings, sculptures, and church ornaments.
The magnificent cathedral of Reims was the
coronation cathedral of the kings of France,
and its Treasury includes an array of sacred
vessels and coronation regalia. ■

The village of Frise and its fields run down to the marshes beside the Somme River.

Area of map detail

★ **Paris**

C

B

E L G I U M

St-Armand-les-Eaux
Valenciennes
Denain
le Quesnoy   **Maubeuge**
IORD   Givet
                      Avesnes-sur-Helpe
                              Fumay
D
        Hirson
N43   *N43*
Guise   *Ardennes*
Vervins   **Charleville-**
              Mézières
                    Sedan   LUXEMBOURG
AISNE   GERMANY
aon   **ARDENNES**   Montmédy Longwy   E
                        Stenay   Longuyon
oissons   Rethel   **Thionville**
      N31   Vouziers   Briey   Hagondange
                                                              F
Reims   Ste.-Menehould   Verdun Jarny Forbach Sarreguemines Wissembourg
A4 **Hautvillers**   A4   **Metz** N3 St-Avold
Dormans   **MARNE**   N3   Ars
Épernay Vertus   **Châlons-en-**   Pont-à-   **MOSELLE**   Haguenau
hierry   **Champagne**   Mousson Château-Salins   **BAS-**
        C   *Lorraine*   Sarrebourg   **RHIN**
        h   N4   Commercy   **MEURTHE-**   N4 Saverne **STRASBOURG**
Sézanne   Vitry-le- **Bar-le-Duc**   Toul **Nancy**   Marlenheim
              François   **St.-Dizier** N4   Lunéville   Rosheim
                          Vaucouleurs   Baccarat Obernai
Romilly-   Joinville Domrémy-   A31   Château d'Haut-
sur-Seine A26   la-Pucelle   St.-Dié Koenigsbourg
        N19   Neufchâteau Charmes   **MOSELLE**   Riquewihr Ribeauvillé
Troyes   **AUBE**   Mirecourt **Épinal** Bruyères Turckheim **Colmar**
                Bar-sur-Aube   Vittel   Gérardmer 1362m **HAUT-**
        A5   **HAUTE-** **VOSGES**   le Hohneck Guebwiller
              Chaumont **MARNE**   Remiremont Éloyes 1424m
N77   Plombières- le Thillot le Grand Ballon
        Langres   Bourbonne- les-Bains Cernay **RHIN** **Mulhouse**
                        les-Bains   Thann A36
YONNE   HAUTE-SAÔNE   TERRITOIRE- St.-Louis
p. 191   p. 191   DE-BELFORT Altkirch
        CÔTE-D'OR   p. 191
        p. 191   SWITZERLAND

0 ————— 60 kilometers
0 ————— 30 miles

Food & drink

ALSACE AND LORRAINE ARE THE GASTRONOMIC GIANTS OF THE NORTH, home of quiche lorraine, foie gras, suckling pig, and free-range goose. Alsatian cooks bring French elegance to such German staples as sauerkraut, dumplings, and stews—try the traditional *baeckenoffe*, a stew with beef and lamb. Lorraine has wonderful preserves and fruit tarts, such as bilberry, mirabelle plum, and red currant, and *jambon d'Ardennes* is one of the world's great cured hams.

Along the northern coast of France and in Flanders, along the Belgian border, you find delicious winter stews: *hochepot* (meat and root vegetable stew), *waterzooi* (fish stew), and *carbonnade de boeuf à la flamande* (beef stewed in beer). In summer there are light fish dishes to search out: herrings around Boulogne (look for *craquelot*—a dish using grilled, smoked herring). Marvelous vegetables come from the market gardens of the marshy Somme and Flanders, including endive and the raw ingredients for *flamiches* (leek, onion, or pumpkin tarts made with a pizza crust). Champagne offers extraordinarily imaginative cabbage dishes, and the Ardennes and the forests of the Vosges Mountains yield an

equally astonishing array of mushrooms.

Amiens is famous for duck pie and pastry-encased pâtés; Arras and Troyes for *andouillettes*—spicy chitterling sausages. Pork is a specialty of Troyes; Ste.-Ménéhould is celebrated for pig's trotters slow-cooked for 48 hours. Expect to find rabbit, hare, partridge, venison, wild boar, and truffles on

Country beers

Northern France and Belgium share a long-established tradition of brewing. But only about 40 non-industrialized breweries are left in France. A French pressure group for traditional beer, Les Amis de la Bière, works hard to support them. Although Strasbourg is the great brewing city, the best beer is brewed around Lille in the heart of Flanders. You could make a satisfying *brasserie* (brewery) tour of Nord and Picardie, including the brasseries of St.-Sylvestre, near Steenvoorde; Jeanne d'Arc in Ronchin, near Lille; Lepers at Annoeullin and Castelain at Bénifontaine, both near Lens; the Brasserie Duyck at Jenlain, near Valenciennes; and Les Enfants de Guyant in Douai.

Alsace still has a few independent breweries, notably Fischer in Schiltigheim, which also produces Adelscott beer, flavored with malt whiskey, and Meteor, which makes an unpasteurized pilsner beer. ■

menus in the Ardennes, as well as in the Vosges Mountains.

Visitors touring the Champagne vineyards may be surprised to find still wines produced there too. Bouzy, for example, is a still red made from the Pinot Noir grapes grown on the Montagne de Reims; Rosé des Riceys is a still rosé from Les Riceys in the southern vineyard area.

France's reputation for great wines overshadows its tradition of beer (see sidebar p. 106) and cider. Cider, though typically a Norman and Breton drink, is also produced in Champagne and by the Cidrerie Georges Maeyaert in Milly-sur-Thérain by Beauvais. ■

Kugelhopf, a rich dough cake similar to brioche, is a specialty of Alsace.

Specialties

First course Jambon sec: raw smoked ham

Main courses Carbonnade de boeuf à la flamande: beef stewed in beer

Choucroute à l'Alsacienne: casserole of meats and charcuterie with sauerkraut

Flamiche à la picardie: leek tart

Marcassin à l'ardénnaise: roast boar with celeriac

Potée champenoise: champagne stew with pork, ham, sausages, and vegetables

Poularde en gelée champenoise: cold chicken in aspic of still champagne

Quiche lorraine: open tart of egg, cream, and bacon

Desserts Galette au sucre: sponge cake with a sugar crust

Tarte aux myrtilles: bilberry tart

An ancient mill in the Créquoise Valley near Montreuil

Nord & Picardie

The rolling, wooded Nord area includes the French part of what was historically Flanders (the rest is now in Belgium). Flanders resembles the Low Countries, with canals and windmills, and towns with cobbled squares and gabled houses. North from Lille, capital of the region, are the medieval Flemish walled towns of Bergues and Wormhout, surrounded by canals. Fortified towns are a feature. Cambrai, for example, still has its old gatehouse, citadel, and keep. Farther south, Picardie has splendid cathedrals and notable Gothic churches, including the 16th-century abbey church of St. Riquier, near Abbeville.

Picardie is the larger of the two northern regions, with three départements. Of these, the peaceful Aisne in the east is a region of open plain crossed by rivers and interspersed with pockets of pastureland, villages, churches, and châteaus. Aisne's capital is the cathedral town of Laon, once a royal city. The western département, the Oise, is heavily wooded and the fine forests were favorite hunting grounds of the French kings, whose summer palace was at Compiègne. The Oise has many architectural gems, especially the Château de Chantilly and the beautifully preserved cathedral town of Senlis with its ancient ramparts. The Somme to the north will always be associated with the battles of World War I. Its capital, Amiens, is graced by one of the greatest Gothic cathedrals. ■

Eurotunnel (channel tunnel)

Eurotunnel, built by British and French engineers, opened in 1994, 192 years after it was first mooted. This rail system consists of two tunnels, one each way, a smaller service tunnel, and numerous interconnecting ones. Le Shuttle's Calais–Folkestone service takes vehicles on special wagons; the Eurostar passenger service has trains up to a quarter of a mile long. Calais Terminal's Exhibition Centre relates how the tunnel was constructed and is maintained.

Le Shuttle travels at 87 mph (140 kph) and takes 35 minutes to go through the tunnel, up to four trains an hour at peak times. Eurostar's trains, propelled by 16,000-horsepower cars at each end, achieve 186 mph (300 kph), and carry more than 6 million passengers a year. Paris to London takes two and a half hours; Brussels to London is two hours and 40 minutes. All Eurostar trains stop at Lille. ■

Lille

Lille

🗺 104 B4

Visitor information

www.univ.lille1.fr

✉ 42 Palais Rihour,
place Rihour

☎ 03 20 21 94 21

Apply for a permit
to visit the Citadelle
at the tourist office.

**Hôtel de Ville
& belfry**

✉ place Roger
Salengro

☎ 03 20 49 50 49

⊕ Belfry: Closed
indefinitely for
major restorations

**Palais des
Beaux-Arts**

✉ place de la
République

☎ 03 20 06 78 00

⊕ Closed Tues.

💲 $$

**Musée d'Art
Moderne**

✉ 1 allée du Musée,
Villeneuve d'Ascq

☎ 03 20 19 68 68

⊕ Closed Tues.

LILLE IS A FRONTIER TOWN, THOUGH FRANCE'S BORDER with its European Union partner Belgium is scarcely noticeable. During its thousand-year history Lille has belonged variously to Flanders, Burgundy, the Spanish Netherlands, France, and Germany. One of its best-preserved buildings is its star-shaped Citadelle, a great fort designed by Louis XIV's military engineer Vauban in 1667, for protection against the Spanish Netherlands when Lille became part of France.

From the visitors' gallery high up in the 345-foot (105-m) belfry of the 1930s **Hôtel de Ville,** you get a notion of the scale of the largest industrial city in northern France. Its spreading suburbs embrace surrounding towns all the way to the Belgian border, 6 miles away. The charming Place Général de Gaulle in the heart of the city, surrounded by old, steep-gabled Flemish houses, comes as a pleasant surprise. One of its most attractive buildings is the **Vieille Bourse** (the old stock exchange), built in 1652–53 in Flemish Renaissance style. But many of Lille's historic buildings were destroyed by bombing in 1940–44, though its old northern quarter is being restored.

Northern France's most important railroad and expressway junction, Lille is a lively regional center with excellent shopping, theater, music, and cinema. The **Palais des Beaux-Arts** displays works by Flemish, French, Dutch, Italian, and Spanish masters from the 15th century to the 20th, as well as Italian and French drawings, sculptures, and ceramics, and a renowned collection of works by Goya.

Villeneuve-d'Ascq, a suburb northeast of Lille, has the outstanding **Musée d'Art Moderne,** with a respected cubist collection, including works by Braque, Kandinsky, Klee, Léger, Miró, Modigliani, and Picasso. ■

The belfry of Lille's Hôtel de Ville is a 1930s neo-Flemish extravaganza.

Battlefields

Arras

⬛ 104 B4

Visitor information

✉ Hôtel de Ville,
place des Héros

☎ 03 21 51 26 95
Les Boves tours
from tourist office

THE MAP OF NORTHERN FRANCE, FROM DUNKERQUE TO
Verdun and from Cambrai to beyond the Somme River, is a map of
battlefields now buried beneath towns and villages, woods and fields.
The most recent saw action just over half a century ago—it was only
in 1940 that hundreds of thousands of retreating British troops evac-
uated the beaches of Dunkerque. Six centuries earlier, Edward III's
English soldiers vanquished Philippe VI's army at Crécy-en-
Ponthieu, in 1346. Memorials, cemeteries, and museums all over the
region explain the actions in these wars, recent and long gone.

Map Key:

✕ Battlefield
(with date)

† Memorial/
cemetery

Ⓜ Museum

Many monuments, some of great
artistic distinction—Edwin
Lutyens' British monument at
Thiepval in the Somme; Walter
Seymour Allward's Canadian War
Memorial on Vimy Ridge near
Vimy—mark the battle sites where
more than a million young soldiers

were killed in 1914–18. World War I
laid waste to the entire region, from
Amiens to Alsace and Reims to
Belgium, and it is scattered with
trenches, cemeteries, and
memorials to French, British,
Australian, New Zealand,
American, Moroccan, Indian,
Nepalese, and Chinese troops.

Many visitors make the journey
to see the site of a particular battle,
or to visit a certain graveyard or a
memorial to a division. Alternatively, you might follow one of
the signposted memori-
al routes that trace
the line of a

**Monument detail of
trench warfare**

ENGLAND

BELGIUM

Ardennes

Dunkerque †✕1940
Calais
Forêt
d'Eperlecques
Boulogne-
sur-Mer   Ⓜ ✕1944
             St-Omer
LILLE
le Touquet   Fruges   Béthune
Azincourt   Ⓜ✕1415   Lens
Hesdin   Vimy   Douai
Crécy-en-   Arras   Valenciennes
Ponthieu   Beaurains   Cambrai   Maubeuge
✕1346   †   ✕1917
Abbeville   Bapaume †
             Thiepval†   Bony
             Pozières† ✕1916 †
                        Rancourt Bellicourt
             Albert †   †
Chipilly   Ⓜ Péronne †
Amiens   St.-Quentin   Charleville-
                                     Mézières
Rouen   Laon
             Biérancourt Ⓜ
Beauvais   Soissons
Dieppe
Évreux   Reims
             Meaux   Chalons-en-
PARIS   Champagne

front or the battles in a campaign, or visit one of several very moving museums of the wars.

Here are some of the battle sites most worth visiting:

ARRAS

Beneath the Grand'Place in Arras are **Les Boves,** a network of caves thought to have been dug out more than 1,000 years ago. They have provided a refuge for locals during the region's frequent conflicts. During World War I, British troops were sheltered and their wounds dressed in Les Boves. To visit some of the caves, inquire at the tourist office.

CAMBRAI

The first full-scale tank battle in 1917 occurred near Cambrai.

ÉPERLECQUES BUNKER

The Nazi Germans built their first factory and launch base for V2 mis-

siles aimed at London during World War II, in the Forêt d'Éperlecques northwest of St.-Omer. The bunker, now a museum called **La Coupole,** shows everything from the liquid oxygen factory to the launch pad, accompanied by audiovisual displays.

HUNDRED YEARS' WAR

The lookout tower at the site of the battle of **Crécy** in 1346 displays an orientation table showing the battle plan. A small museum focuses on the Battle of Agincourt in **Azincourt** village (*closed Wed.*). An orientation table and model archers and horsemen on the field of battle itself enable visitors to follow the battle of 1415, in which the English soldiers of Henry V overcame superior French forces.

THE SOMME

A Tour of Remembrance follows the front lines of the two World War I battles of the Somme (information from the Somme tourist office). Among the signposted sights are two blockhouses at Pozières taken by Australian divisions, the British memorial at Thiepval, the French cemetery at Rancourt, and the memorial at Bellicourt to American soldiers. The tour encompasses trenches, shelters, and the rail supply line. The **Historial de la Grande Guerre** is a museum beside Péronne's medieval fortress.

VERDUN

The 17th-century citadel now holds a museum commemorating the 1916 German attack that destroyed this barracks town. There are tours of the battlefield in summer (ask at the tourist office). ∎

Vimy
🅼 104 B4

Canadian War Memorial, Vimy Ridge
☎ 03 21 58 19 34 (underground museum)
🕐 Open 10 a.m.– 6 p.m. Guided tours: April–Nov.

St. Omer
🅼 104 B5
La Coupole
✉ Forêt d'Éperlecques
☎ 03 21 93 07 07

Somme Regional Tourism
✉ rue Vincent Auriol, Amiens
☎ 03 22 22 32 66

Peronne
🅼 104 B4
Visitor information
✉ 1 rue Louis I
☎ 03 22 84 42 38

Historial de la Grande Guerre
✉ place du Château
☎ 03 22 83 14 18
🕐 Closed Mon. in winter & mid-Dec.–mid-Jan.

Verdun
🅼 105 D3
Visitor information
✉ place de la Nation
☎ 03 29 86 14 18
🕐 Open daily. Minibus tours: May–Sept., daily at 2 p.m. (reservations must be made a.m.)
$ $$$

Statue on the Canadian War Memorial at Vimy Ridge

From Arras to the coast

WEST OF ARRAS, THE PICARDIE PLAIN SLOPES GENTLY TO the coast. The countryside is patched with woodland and threaded by rivers: the picturesque Authie, the majestic Somme, and the Canche, overlooked by the medieval hill town of Montreuil. Le Touquet on the Canche Estuary is the most sophisticated of the resorts clustering along the sandy north-coast beaches.

Arras
A 104 B4
Visitor information
✉ Hôtel de Ville,
place des Héros
☎ 03 21 51 26 95

Le Touquet
A 104 A4
Visitor information
✉ Palais de l'Europe
☎ 03 21 05 62 62

The town of Le Touquet has long beaches as well as boutiques and villas set among trees.

With its underground shelters (see p. 111) and moving memorial to the many French Resistance members who were shot here during World War II, Arras is an important site on any battlefield tour. The late Gothic **Tel de Ville** overlooks the **Place des Héros,** one of Arras's two great central squares. You can look down on it from the town hall's 250-foot (80-m) belfry, but you get a better sense of its scale from within. Medieval cloth and corn markets were held in these immense squares. During the 1914–18 fighting, bombardments destroyed the Tel de Ville and many of the 16th-century houses surrounding the squares. However, the houses had been built to strict stylistic directives laid down by the town council, and after the war they were faithfully reconstructed.

Halfway between Arras and Lille is the ancient university town of **Douai** (*Visitor information, place d'Armes, tel 03 27 88 26 79*). During the Reformation, English Roman Catholics opened a college here to train priests, who returned to England to work secretly under threat of death. Here, they made the first Roman Catholic English translation of the Old Testament, the Douay Bible. Douai is a charming old town with 18th-century houses overlooking narrow streets and a famous 62-bell carillon in the exuberant belfry above the town hall.

A trip to **Le Touquet**, an elegant resort town, makes a pleasant morning's drive from Arras. Take the N39 via the pretty town of **Hesdin** (near the site of the Battle of Agincourt, see p. 111) and the D340 along the Canche River to the hill town of **Montreuil** with its well-preserved ramparts.

Le Touquet (nicknamed Paris-Plage) was fashionable when the Prince of Wales (later King Edward VIII) brought his guests there. Today it is a period piece, with art nouveau and art deco buildings. But with its airport, casino, horse racing, golf, hotels, fine restaurants, and Paris boutiques, it is still the most sophisticated north-coast resort. It also has great beaches, with activities such as sand-sailing, discothèques and nightclubs, and, nearby, Bagatelle, a children's amusement park. ■

Amiens

AMIENS, ON THE SOMME RIVER, WAS HEAVILY BOMBED IN 1918, and shelling in 1940 destroyed much of its ancient heart. But the grand cathedral has survived centuries of war and revolution. A classic model of the French Gothic style, it is the main reason to visit Amiens.

The Cathédrale de Notre-Dame (*place Notre-Dame, tel 03 22 91 79 28*) is France's tallest cathedral. Its nave, built between 1220 and 1236, was then the highest in France, at 139 feet (42 m). Stand at the west end of the nave and look toward the altar. Instantly, the soaring piers and pointed arches sweep your gaze heavenward, fulfilling one of the ideals of Gothic architecture.

The dramatic interior of this vast church is illuminated by windows that seem to replace the upper walls of the nave, choir, and chapels of the apse. The rose window in the west front still has its 16th-century glass, but much of the ancient glass was shattered during World War II bombardments. Local woodcarvers at the beginning of the 16th century decorated the 110 oak choir stalls with more than 400 scenes from the Old Testament, the life of the Virgin Mary, and scenes from everyday life.

The west front, with its asymmetrical towers, is less harmonious than the interior, but its three great portals are masterpieces of stonecarving. Statues of the Virgin adorn the right doorway, ones on the left venerate St. Firmin, who brought Christianity to Picardie in the fourth century. The "weeping angel," a hugely popular putto crying on a tomb, is by local sculptor Nicolas Blasset. Pilgrims followed the maze on the nave floor on their knees.

The streets around the cathedral contain painstakingly restored buildings, such as the medieval belfry, the **Musée de Picardie** (*48 rue de la République, tel 03 22 97 14 00, closed Mon.*), and the 17th-century **Tel de Berny** (*36 rue Victor Hugo, tel 03 22 97 14 00, closed Mon.*), now a museum with local decorative arts displayed in period settings.

Though Amiens cannot be described as a beautiful city, it has good restaurants, museums, and entertainments. Waterways flow around its St.-Leu district, and you can stroll the towpaths and bridges, or punt among its vegetable gardens—the *hortillonnages*—in traditional high-prowed boats. ∎

Amiens

🅰 104 B4

Visitor information

✉ 6 bis rue Dusevel

☎ 03 22 71 60 50

🕐 Closed Sun.

The biblical "Marriage at Cana," a 16th-century carving on the choir stalls of Amiens cathedral

Gothic cathedrals

The towers and spires of the Gothic cathedrals of northern France rise high above its spreading plains and cities, like spiritual landmarks. This is the birthplace of Gothic architecture—the style dates from circa 1140–44, when the choir of the abbey church of St.-Denis, north of Paris (see p. 101), was built.

Building a church, from an illuminated manuscript

Amiens cathedral nave, looking toward the west end, showing the maze

Though Gothic arches and flying buttresses were already appearing in some churches around Paris, the combination of pointed vaults (ceilings) and arches and thin, buttressed walls pierced by rows of large windows identify St.-Denis as a full-fledged Gothic building.

Notre-Dame in Paris, begun in 1163, was the next monumental church to be built in the new style, with a nave 109 feet (33 m) high. In a burst of cathedral building within a 100-mile (160-km) radius of Paris, the style evolved from the simplicity of Laon (see below) to the dramatic vertical lines of the mature Gothic style at Amiens (see p. 113) and Chartres (see pp. 98–99) and to the late or high Gothic style of Reims (see pp. 118–19), with its complex system of flying buttresses. Strasbourg cathedral (see p. 124), begun in the 13th century and finished in the 15th, reflects this evolution from the Romanesque style (see pp. 324–25) all the way through to the Flamboyant, the ornate late form of high Gothic.

Cathedral tour

A round-trip of 240 miles (380 km) will take you to six of France's most magnificent Gothic cathedrals. Begin at the cathedral of **Amiens,** whose interior is the supreme example of the mature French Gothic style. Follow the D934 east to **Noyon,** whose lovely cathedral, begun around 1150, is transitional in style between Romanesque and Gothic. Take the N32 and N44 across the Aisne département to **Laon,** once the royal city of the Carolingian kings. Here the 12th-century cathedral of Notre-Dame, begun in the 1160s and completed in 1230, is a fine example of early Gothic style. It has beautiful rose windows and captivating sculptures of exotic animals—a hippopotamus gargoyle, for instance—on its facade. Clustered around it are the bishop's palace and the Dauphin's court, medieval abbeys and streets of charming old town houses.

From Laon, it is a short journey southeast along the N44 (or the A26) to **Reims,** with its high Gothic cathedral.

Then take the N31 west to **Soissons** to admire the cathedral, restored after shelling in 1918. Started in the 12th and not finished until the 14th century, it shows the evolution of the Gothic style.

Continue westward along the N31 via Compiègne to **Beauvais,** whose cathedral was a daring attempt to build the tallest such edifice ever. In 1284, 12 years after its completion, the choir collapsed and had to be rebuilt with reinforcing buttresses. However, this grand project overstretched the town's resources, and the cathedral was never finished; today you see the choir and transepts built onto the tiny, early 11th-century Romanesque nave, which the new cathedral was intended to replace. From Beauvais the A16 returns you to Amiens. ■

Structure of a Gothic cathedral

The classic, three-stage structural system of the Gothic cathedral, shown below, consists of a nave arcade at ground level; a triforium (arcaded passage) above it; and a clerestory (upper wall zone, pierced by windows) above that. The high walls are buttressed for stability. In order to raise the nave roof to unprecedented heights, the builders constructed flying buttresses to transmit the thrust of the brick or stone vaults down to the sturdy main vertical buttresses. The pointed arches characteristic of Gothic architecture take the thrust from the vaults downward, so buildings could have thin walls pierced by large windows. These windows were divided by a tracery of delicate stonework, which reached astonishing heights of complexity in the round rose windows. ■

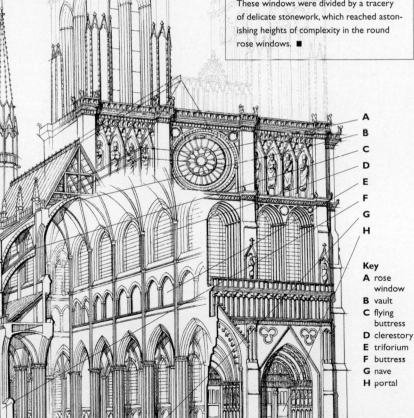

Key
A rose window
B vault
C flying buttress
D clerestory
E triforium
F buttress
G nave
H portal

Royal forests

**The beautiful
setting of the
Chantilly
châteaus**

THE FORESTS STILL SURVIVING IN THE SOUTH OF PICARDIE
are just remnants of those that originally covered much of northern
France. Kings and nobles came here from Paris and built hunting
lodges, palaces, and châteaus in and around the forests.

CHANTILLY

Once famous for its lace, Chantilly
is now best known for its châteaus
set on an island in a lake and
surrounded by gardens designed by
André Le Nôtre. The two châteaus,
the 16th-century **Petit Château**
and the adjoining 17th-century
Grand Château, showcase collections of fine and decorative arts,
and a priceless library, all assembled
by the Duc d'Aumale in the 19th
century. Treasures include the *Très
Riches Heures du Duc de Berry,* a
15th-century book of hours (not
always on display), and paintings by
Raphael and by French masters.
The beautiful 18th-century stables
are now the **Living Museum of
the Horse.**

SENLIS

One of the most ancient towns in
France, Senlis was founded before
the Romans conquered Gaul. Its
Gallo-Roman walls thread through
the town; 16 of its 28 towers still
stand, though hidden by houses.

Cathédrale Notre-Dame,
begun in 1155, is on a more modest
scale than many such Gothic
edifices. It has superb sculptures of
the Virgin and a 13th-century spire.
From the cathedral, explore the old
town, castle remains, and ancient
walls. The 18th-century **Château
de Raray** nearby so enraptured
Jean Cocteau that he set his film *La
Belle et la Bête* (1945) in it.

COMPIÈGNE

Set on the edge of the forest,
Compiègne is dominated by the
palace built in 1754 for Louis XV.
Inside are the apartments of
Napoleon I and his wife Marie-
Louise and the Hunting Gallery
decked with Gobelins tapestries.

A clearing in the Forêt de Laigue,
4 miles (6 km) east of Compiègne
off the N31, contains the **Musée
de l'Armistice** (*Tel 03 44 85 14
18, closed Tues. and a.m. Dec. & Jan.*)
in a reconstruction of the railroad
car in which the armistice that
ended World War I was signed. ∎

Vineyards at Verzenay spread across Champagne's undulating chalk hillsides.

Champagne

The vineyards of the Champagne region carpet the wide river valleys and climb gentle slopes to wooded escarpments that overlook some of the most beautiful countryside in northern France. Venerable villages with Romanesque churches and medieval market towns dot the countryside. Reims, the northern, and Troyes, the southern, capitals of Champagne have superb Gothic cathedrals and splendid museums. Both are little more than an hour's drive from Paris.

The size and splendor of the half-timbered medieval merchants' houses that survive in the old towns testify to Champagne's past prosperity. During the Middle Ages, it lay at the crossroads of northern Europe's trade routes. From the 14th to the 16th century, cloth from Italy, Flanders, and the German states, furs from Scandinavia, leather from Catalonia, and costly woods, spices, and gold from the Mediterranean were traded in great, six-week-long summer fairs held in Troyes, Lagny, Bar-sur-Aube, and Provins. The Champagne fairs are still held, but are now local summer festivals.

History has also left a legacy of castles and fortifications, built in strong defensive positions high on the edges of escarpments right across the region to repel invaders. From the fifth century, when Attila the Hun's army was routed near Châlons-en-Champagne, to the Nazi invasions of 1940, this part of France has been an entry point for armies marching on Paris.

Grapes have been cultivated in the chalky soils of Champagne for 2,000 years. In the late 17th century, Pierre Pérignon, cellarer at the Benedictine abbey of Hautvillers near Épernay, is said to have discovered how to make wine sparkle. Wine historians debunk this myth—wine produced in Champagne tends naturally to sparkle—but they recognize the part played by Dom Pérignon in the evolution of champagne. He produced still white wine from black grapes and he blended wines from different vineyards to make a richer, more subtle wine. ■

Reims

Reims

105 C3

Visitor information

✉ 2 rue Guillaume de Machault

☎ 03 26 77 45 25

Cathédrale Notre-Dame

✉ place du Cardinal-Luçon

☎ 03 26 47 55 34

🕐 Mass daily at 9 a.m. & 10:15 a.m.

IN 498, IN REIMS'S FIRST CATHEDRAL, ST. RÉMI BAPTIZED Clovis, king of the conquering Frankish tribe from the upper Rhine. Subsequently, almost every king of France from Philippe II in 1180 to Charles X in 1825 was crowned here.

The fittingly majestic **Cathédrale Notre-Dame,** begun in 1211 after a fire destroyed the previous cathedral, was designed for coronations. To create room for the ceremonies, the nave and choir were broadened to embrace the transepts, so that the interior appears luxuriously spacious, and the nave, with its avenues of piers, seems to soar. No expense was spared in its construction or its decoration—Reims was intended to surpass in concept and ornament even the great cathedrals at Chartres and Amiens. Its beautiful windows with their delicate bar tracery seem to eliminate the upper walls of the church and flood the great building with light. Much of its old glass was lost as a result of World War II bombing; the modern

Palais du Tau

✉ place du Cardinal
   Luçon

☎ 03 26 47 81 79

$ $$

Maison Mumm

✉ 34 rue du Champ
   de Mars

☎ 03 26 49 59 69

🕐 Closed Sat., Sun.
   a.m. in winter

**The two west
towers of Reims
cathedral soar
above the city and
the statue of
Jeanne d'Arc.**

windows of the Lady Chapel are by Marc Chagall.

Although built in stages between the 13th and 15th centuries, Reims has a unity of style representing the pinnacle of mature French Gothic. Its flying buttresses are daringly thin and light, a clear expression of the confidence medieval architects had achieved by the 13th century. One of its glories is the wealth of sculpture on its facade, though some are copies of originals damaged beyond repair. The central doorway is devoted to the Virgin with groups of the Annunciation and Purification. The statue of the Coronation of the Virgin that used to grace the central gable is now in

Visiting the champagne houses

Among the Reims champagne houses offering tours and tastings are Veuve Clicquot, whose *chef de caves*, Antoine Müller, perfected the technique of *remuage* (see p. 121) in 1818; Charles Heidsieck, who first exported champagne to the United States in 1851; Pommery, which produced the first *brut* or dry champagne, popular in England; Roederer, producer of Cristal, probably the world's most prestigious *cuvée*; and Ruinart, Champagne's oldest *maison*.

Maison Mumm, founded in 1827 by two German Protestant winemakers from the Rheingau, runs daily guided tours of its cellars, followed by tastings, and has a small museum focusing on champagne and an Oenothèque— an archive of vintages, with bottles dating back to 1893.

Ask at the Reims tourist office for details of tour times, durations, and charges. ∎

the Palais du Tau. Above the rose window on the west front look for the colossal statues of the kings of France, and by the left-hand portal the smiling "Angel of Reims."

The bishop's palace next to the cathedral, the **Palais du Tau,** displays coronation regalia, original carvings and statues rescued from the war-damaged cathedral, and several tapestries.

At the south end of the town, the **Basilique St.-Rémi** (*rue Simon*), founded in the 11th century, is the largest Romanesque church in northern France, though with later additions. This great abbey church was built over the chapel of St. Christophe where St. Rémi was buried.

These great ecclesiastical buildings are reason enough to visit Reims, but the city has much more to offer. Beneath its streets are the foundations of Durocorter, the metropolis of a Gaulish tribe called the Remes, who in 55 B.C. made an alliance with Julius Caesar during his invasion of Gaul. You can visit the **Cryptocorticus** (*place du Forum, closed a.m. & all Mon. mid-June–mid-Sept., & all mid-Sept.–mid-June,*)—vaulted galleries, perhaps a former temple, beneath Durocorter's forum—and the **Porte de Mars**—the largest triumphal arch in the Roman world. Limestone for these edifices and for aqueducts, roads, and dwellings was cut from beneath the city. Centuries later, these subterranean quarries make ideal, temperature-constant storage cellars for maturing wine.

In medieval times, Reims was a textile town, but during the 15th century wine production overtook cloth in importance. Today Reims, at the heart of the vineyards, is home to over 20 top champagne houses, many of which offer tours and tastings (see sidebar, left). ∎

Champagne country

MINOR ROADS CRISSCROSSING THE CHAMPAGNE REGION
connect the many pretty wine villages. A leisurely drive is the best way
to experience Champagne, with stops here and there to visit the
vignerons—small independent wine producers—to taste their
distinctive, often excellent champagnes.

Épernay

 105 C3

Visitor information

 7 avenue de
Champagne

 03 26 55 33 00

🕐 Closed Sun.
in winter

EXPLORING THE CHAMPAGNE COUNTRYSIDE

Meandering east from Reims
around the Parc Naturel de la
Montagne de Reims, the 40-mile
(70-km) "Route Touristique"
explores the heart of the
Champagne countryside, pausing at
vineyards and historical villages
filled with architectural marvels.
The vines you see along the way
bear the Pinot Noir grape, used to
enrich a champagne blend.

Begin by taking the D380 southwest out of Reims and follow the
signposts; soon you'll be driving east
along the D26. The route rises to
magnificent viewpoints at the St.-Lie
chapel beyond Jouy-lès-Reims.
Farther east, climb the woodsy path
above Verzy to an observation point
at **Mont Sinai** for a marvelous view
of the vineyards.

The road drops to the Vallée de
la Marne in the southwest corner of

How champagne is made

After the grapes have been harvested and pressed, the juice, or must, is fermented in vats until the following spring, when the wine is blended and bottled. Blending is what makes champagne the drink it is; there are many sparkling wines made by the champagne method (*méthode champenoise*), but the blenders of champagne marry wines from the current vintage with reserve wines from other vintages. Once blended, sugar and yeast mixed with reserve wine are added to each bottle, which is then corked and stored in V-shaped racks called *pupitres*. The yeasts convert the sugar into carbon dioxide which, trapped inside the bottle, dissolves into the wine, forming tiny bubbles. The bottles are turned every day and gradually tilted, a process known as *remuage*, or riddling. After fermentation, the cork is removed so that escaping gas expels the residue that settled on the cork. A small amount of wine also escapes, to be replaced by a mix of champagne and sugar. Champagne must be aged for at least a year, and a fine vintage may be aged for a decade or more. ■

Above: Extracting the juice from grapes for champagne in a wine press near Épernay

Top right: Rows of wooden racks containing bottles of maturing champagne line the cellars dug in the limestone.

the Champagne region. Here the grapes are Pinot Meunier, which impart a spiciness to the wine.

Soon you'll come to the quiet town of **Épernay,** the capital of Champagne country. The prestigious **Avenue de Champagne** is lined with sumptuous Champagne houses, including industry giant **Moët & Chandon** (see p. 383), founded in 1743. Opposite is the **Trianon Palace**—two pavilions and a lovely orangery surrounded by typically French formal gardens—built in the early 1800s by Jean-Rémy Moët to entertain his friend Napoleon Bonaparte.

The impressive **Château Perrier,** built in the 19th century by Charles Perrier, a former mayor of Épernay, now accommodates the town museum, where you can learn more about champagne production. Another museum is housed in the **Maison de Castellane,** identifiable by its ornate tower. The **Maison Pol Roger** is headquarters of the eponymous firm founded in 1849; its champagne was Winston Churchill's favorite.

OTHER TOURIST ROUTES

West from Épernay, you can follow another "route touristique" along the Marne River, flanked on both sides with Meunier grapevines. On the way to **Dormans,** a peaceful riverside town, it passes through **Hautvillers,** where you can visit the abbey where Dom Pérignon (see p. 117) was a monk. Another interesting town en route is **Boursault,** with a 19th-century castle built for the enterprising Madame Clicquot, who sold her champagne to the Russian court.

A different tourist route heads south of Épernay to Vertus, through a region called the **Côte des Blancs** for the white Chardonnay grapes that are almost exclusively planted here. ■

More places to visit in Champagne

CHÂLONS-EN-CHAMPAGNE

The third, with Reims and Épernay, in Champagne's triangle of wine towns, Châlons is threaded with picturesque canals overlooked by half-timbered houses. The town gate, the Porte Ste.-Croix, was erected in 1770 for Marie-Antoinette to pass through on her way to marry Louis XVI. In 1791, during the Revolution, the royal couple were recognized and arrested at Ste.-Ménéhould (*Visitor information, place Général Leclerc, tel 03 26 60 85 83,*

Detail from "The Creation of the World," one of the fine stained-glass windows dating from as early as the 13th century in Troyes cathedral

closed a.m. Sept.–July), 15 miles (25 km) to the east, on their flight from Paris. The queen's prayer book is displayed in Châlons's public library.

🅜 105 C3 **Visitor information** ✉ 3 quai des Arts ☎ 03 26 65 17 89 🕐 Closed Sept.–March

LANGRES

You enter this fortified town through 17th-century gateways. Built on a hill overlooking the Langres plateau, Langres was first fortified by the Romans and has a triumphal arch embedded in its curtain wall. The charming old town has several beautiful stone Renaissance mansions with charming courtyards that can be visited.

🅜 105 D2 **Visitor information** ✉ place O. Lahalle ☎ 03 25 87 67 67 🕐 Closed Sun. Oct.–April

SEDAN

The impressive **Château Fort** (*1 place du Chateau, tel 03 24 27 73 73*), begun in 1424 on the site of 11th-century fortifications, still dominates this border town. Vast and towering, it is one of the largest castles in Europe, still containing its sinister *oubliette* dungeons (the name comes from the French *oublier*, to forget) and lord's living quarters.

Southeast of Sedan is **Fort La-Ferté** (*Tel 03 24 27 50 50*), the northernmost fort on the Maginot Line, which was overrun in 1940.

🅜 105 D3

TROYES

Half-timbered, 16th-century houses overlook the cobbled streets in Troyes's atmospheric St.-Jean district. The European Center of Hebraic Study commemorates a medieval center of Jewish learning here. The **Cathédrale St.-Pierre-et-St.-Paul** has beautifully preserved stained glass, some dating from the 13th century. Troyes's other attractions include a medieval apothecary shop on a quayside.

🅜 105 C2 **Visitor information** ✉ 16 boulevard Carnot ☎ 03 25 82 62 70 🕐 Closed Sun. ∎

Vineyards on the rolling hills above the village of Hunawihr

Alsace & Lorraine

Half plateau and half forested mountain range, half French and half German, Alsace and Lorraine share a history, landscape, and cultural identity that are unique in France. Along their eastern edge, they follow the German border, marked by the Rhine, from Lauterbourg in the northwest to Basel in the southeast, where Alsace, Germany, and Switzerland meet. They have a common history, having been part of a German state since the ninth century, entering the kingdom of France only in the 17th and 18th centuries respectively. Several times since then, they have been conquered by Germany and later returned to France. French and German influences create an interesting mix in archaeology, architecture, and art, and are strongly evident in food, folklore, and festivities.

Lorraine's southern département is the mountainous, forested Vosges, an ancient, low massif that spreads eastward into Alsace. In winter there is skiing at St.-Maurice-sur-Moselle, la Bresse-le-Hohneck, Bussang, and Gérardmer.

The highest peak of the Vosges, the 4,672-foot (1,424-m) Grand Ballon, is in Alsace, with vineyards blanketing the foothills of the massif. Few visitors can resist following the Route du Vin through wine villages that are among the prettiest in France. And most visitors take time to explore Colmar and the other towns on the plain below. Medieval town centers preserve unspoiled streets of old houses

and ancient churches. Strasbourg, on the border with Germany, is one of the largest ports on the Rhine River. It rejoices in one of Europe's most magnificent cathedrals, set in the medieval old town. And, like Brussels, it contains many European institutions, such as the European Parliament, European Court, and Council of Europe.

Stretching between the region's two great capitals, Metz and Nancy, the Parc Naturel Régional de Lorraine, a quiet countryside crossed by rivers, is dotted by ancient fortifications and sites associated with past wars. Growing numbers of visitors now come to follow the traces of these conflicts. ∎

Strasbourg
105 F2
Visitor information
✉ 17 place de la
Cathédrale
☎ 03 88 52 28 28

**Cathédrale
Notre-Dame**
✉ place de la
Cathédrale
Stairs up the tower:
entrance at the
bottom of the tower
in place du Château
💲 $
Astronomical clock:
🕐 Clock strikes at
12:30
💲 $

Strasbourg

STRASBOURG IS FRANCE'S BIGGEST RIVER PORT AND ITS
sixth largest city, yet it has extraordinary charm and beauty. Founded
more than 2,000 years ago, the city grew on marshy ground around
branches of the Ill River, which thread through its picturesque old
quarter. The Rhine port and outlying districts are busily industrial,
but the city has all the vitality of a student town—its university,
founded in 1566, is one of the oldest in France. Strasbourg faces
Germany, just a bus ride away across the Rhine, and with some of
Europe's most powerful institutions in its northeast quarter, it feels
more like the capital of Europe than the old capital of Alsace.

"I have seen many magnificent
buildings in Switzerland, France,
Italy and Greece. But the most
beautiful thing of all is the interior
of the Strasbourg cathedral with its
great jewels, the miracle of its
stained-glass windows." Thus
wrote the sculptor Hans Jean Arp
(1887–1966), who was born in a
house near the **Cathédrale
Notre-Dame**. The glass, dating
from the 12th to the 13th centuries
and set in two rose windows with
beautiful tracery, was removed and
hidden for safekeeping during
World War II.

In the 1220s, when construction
of the cathedral began, Strasbourg
was an independent city. The
cathedral's transept was built first in
Romanesque style. Little more than
a decade later, the nave was rebuilt
in the French Gothic style. The plans
show that the architect modeled the
building on Notre-Dame in Paris,
but because it was built in stages
until the 15th century, it perfectly
reflects the progression from
Romanesque to high Gothic styles.
The plans show twin towers, both
with spires, only one of which was
completed, in 1439. It is worth

climbing the many steps to the platform on top of the tower to admire the statuary that decorates the spire.

The west front is remarkable for its medieval sculptures, especially the figures of the Wise and Foolish Virgins in the right portal. Many, however, are copies of those disfigured during the Revolution: The originals are displayed in the **Musée de l'Oeuvre de Notre-Dame** (*Tel 03 88 52 50 00*), opposite the cathedral.

In the cathedral transept is an astronomical clock. Made in the 16th century, it was given a new movement in the 19th. Its crowd of little figures can be seen in action at 12:30 p.m. every day when it strikes 12—it runs half an hour slow.

Notre-Dame and the medieval streets around it survived terrible bombardments in 1940–44. Across the Place du Château next to the cathedral, the 18th-century **Château des Rohan** (*Tel 03 88 52 50 00*), once the archbishop's palace, now houses the city's principal museums, the Musée des Beaux-Arts and the Musée des Arts Décoratifs et d'Archéologie. Close by is the 13th-century **Pharmacie du Cerf** in the Place de la Cathédrale, thought to be Europe's oldest surviving apothecary's shop. West of the city center in Place Hans Jean Arp stands the **Musée d'Art Moderne et Contemporain** (*Tel 03 88 52 50 00*), with works by Hans Jean Arp among others. The **Musée Alsacien** (*Tel 03 88 52 50 00*), on the Quai St.-Nicolas, displays regional costumes and furniture.

Take time to stroll around Strasbourg's old quarter built round canals once used by tanners and fishermen. The Ponts Couverts (the name means covered bridges, but they lost their tops in the 18th century) cross the canals under the restored 14th-century city wall. Tall houses line the quays, and the area is full of restaurants and bars. ■

EUROPEAN CAPITAL

Overlooking pretty Parc de l'Orangerie in northeast Strasbourg are the buildings of the European Union institutions, the Palais de l'Europe. Here, members of the Parliamentary Assembly of the Council of Europe debate. The Council's judicial body, the European Court and Commission for Human Rights, has its own building within the Palais. The oldest European institution in Strasbourg is the Central Commission for Navigation on the Rhine, which was founded in 1816. ■

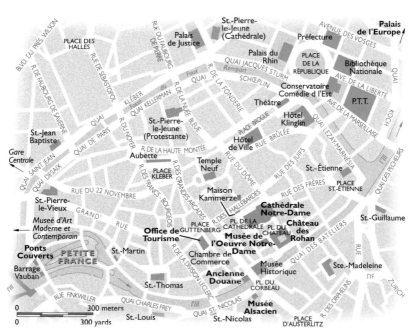

Drive along the Alsace wine route

The Route du Vin winds through the Vosges foothills, threading between the valley floor and the fringes of woods blanketing higher slopes.

The Alsace vineyards stretch for over 130 miles (200 km) across the foothills of the wooded Vosges Mountains from Marlenheim in the north to Thann in the south. Alsace wines were not widely known before World War II and were sold mainly as *vin ordinaire*; today, these dry, full-bodied wines have a reputation for quality, and Alsace now boasts 50 *grands crus* vineyards.

Mainly white wines are produced in Alsace, varying from bone-dry Rieslings to the *grands crus* made from very late harvested grapes that give sweet dessert wines labeled *Vendanges Tardives*. Most independent producers (who sell wines made from grapes grown in their own vineyards) offer wine tastings and vineyard tours; their cellars and wineries are signposted along the way. You can also try wines at the many wine fairs and festivals (*ask at the Maison du Vin in Colmar, 12 avenue de la Foire aux Vins, Tel 03 89 20 16 20*).

The Route du Vin passes such ancient castles as Eguisheim in the south, and abbeys such as Andlau farther north, whose ninth-century church was part of a convent. Towns and villages have cobbled streets, overhanging eaves, fountains, wells, and hanging baskets of flowers. The whole route takes days to enjoy, but the section between Colmar and Rosheim makes a fine day trip.

From Colmar (see pp. 130–31), take the D417 west to **Wintzenheim** ❶ and turn north onto the minor road that leads across the pretty Fecht River to **Turckheim,** with its three medieval gateways. From here, follow the Route du Vin signposts along mountain roads, climbing through vineyards to the flower-decked village of **Niedermorschwihr;** then go east and back west to Katzenthal, known for its Rieslings; and north to the village of **Ammerschwihr.** From here, follow the N415 north to **Kaysersberg** ❷—birthplace of the missionary doctor and Nobel Prize winner Albert Schweitzer—set among woods.

Turn eastward through vineyards along the D28 and then left onto the D1B. A detour along the D3 takes you to the popular walled village of **Riquewihr** ❸ (see p. 132). Then follow the D1B north through medieval **Ribeauvillé** ❹. Still on the D1B, continue to Bergheim, where a Wednesday market is held in the cobbled square, and **St.-Hippolyte** ❺, whose medieval ramparts are overlooked by the spectacular towers of **Château d'Haut-Koenigsbourg** (see p. 132).

From St.-Hippolyte, the D35 then meanders north through a string of wine villages— **Orschwiller,** with a small wine museum; Riesling-producing **Scherwiller** ❻; the old commune of **Dambach-la-Ville** ❼; **Ottrott** ❽, which makes red wine from its Pinot Noir grapes; and finally to **Rosheim** ❾, whose Maison des Païens may be the oldest domestic dwelling in Alsace (circa 1170). ■

Grape varieties

Alsace wines are varietal (pressed from one grape variety) and are identified by grape and the maker's name. Most are made from one of the five "noble" grapes. However, rosé and red wines are also produced from the Pinot Noir grape in a few vineyards around Ottrott in the north of Alsace and Herrenweg in the south. Crémant d'Alsace is a sparkling wine made by the champagne method (see p. 121) from a blend of wines.

The **noble grapes** and the characteristics of the wine they make are:

Gewürztraminer: powerful, aromatic wines with a fruity, spicy bouquet

Muscat d'Alsace: citrusy, slightly aromatic, and essentially dry wines

Pinot Blanc: fresh, harmonious wines

Riesling: fruity, floral, but delicate wines

Sylvaner: light, refreshing white wines

Tokay Pinot Gris: richly flavored wines with complex aromas ■

⚠ See area map p. 105
▶ Colmar
⏱ 52 miles (85 km)
🕐 one day
▶ Rosheim

HIGHLIGHTS
- Turckheim
- Riquewihr
- Ribeauvillé
- Château d'Haut-Koenigsbourg
- Rosheim

0   6 kilometers
0   3 miles

Rosheim ⑨

Bœrsch

Obernai

Ottrott ⑧

Ehn

Heiligenstein

823m

Barr

Château d'Andlau

Andlau   Eichhoffen

D35

Itterswiller

Scheer

Blienschwiller

Dambach-
la-Ville ⑦

662m

N422

Glasson

Dieffenthal

⑥

D35

Scherwiller

Liepvrette   N59

Châtenois

Sélestat

Château d'Haut-
Kœnigsbourg

530m

A35-E25

Orschwiller

St.-Hippolyte ⑤

Bergheim

D1B

Strengbach

④
Ribeauvillé

Zellenberg

Riquewihr
③ D3
Beblenheim

D1B

② D28 Bennwihr

Kaysersberg

Weiss

Sigolsheim

Ammerschwihr

N415

Katzenthal

Niedermorschwihr   Ingersheim

Turckheim

D10

COLMAR

D417

Wintzenheim ①

Fecht

Eguisheim

START

A352
D422
D35

The village of Riquewihr situated in the
middle of vine-covered hills

**PARC RÉGIONAL DES
BALLONS DES VOSGES**

The wine villages have
half-timbered houses
wreathed in flowers.

The oldest surviving
wine cask in the world,
made in 1715, in Hugel's
cellars at Riquewihr

Metz

THE IMMENSE SCALE OF THE DEFENSES OF METZ CONVEY something of the importance of this city, once one of the great frontier fortresses of France. A fortified bridge connects the Porte des Allemands, with its crenellations and lofty 13th-century towers, to the two huge bastions on the opposite bank of the Seille River.

Metz
🗺 105 E3
Visitor information
✉ place d'Armes
☎ 03 87 55 53 76

St.-Pierre-aux-Nonnains
✉ just off boulevard Poincaré

Cathédrale St.-Étienne
✉ place d'Armes

Musée d'Art et d'Histoire
✉ rue des Jardins
☎ 03 87 75 10 18
💲 $$. Free on Wed.

"Sacrifice d'Abraham," one of the stained-glass windows by Marc Chagall in Metz cathedral

Metz was already an old capital when the Romans invaded Gaul, and was the capital of the Frankish Merovingian dynasty before becoming a free city under the Holy Roman Empire.

The Romans first fortified the city, bringing water along an aqueduct whose remains can still be seen at Jouy-aux-Arches, some

4 miles (7 km) southwest of Metz on the N57.

Set at the strategic confluence of the Seille and Moselle Rivers, the city center with its many churches is still crisscrossed by old bridges. **St.-Pierre-aux-Nonnains,** built on the site of a fourth-century Roman basilica, is thought to be France's earliest Christian church.

The **Cathédrale St.-Étienne** was built between the 13th and 16th centuries in ocher-colored Jaumet sandstone. At 138 feet (42 m), its nave is the third highest of any French cathedral, lit by great windows with their original medieval glass. The glorious west rose window is the work of 14th-century artist Hermann of Munster.

The Petits-Carmes convent, between the cathedral and an arm of the Moselle River, became a museum in 1839. During expansion in the 1930s, the remains of the city's Roman baths were discovered beneath it. You can see them in the archaeology section of the **Musée d'Art et d'Histoire.** The beaux arts collection here includes works by Rembrandt, Dürer, van Dyke, and Titian.

Though Metz is an easy day trip from Nancy or Strasbourg, the medieval houses and views across the Moselle Valley make it a delightful place to stay. It is a good base for excursions to the battlefields of Verdun (see p. 111) and the Maginot Line forts at Fermont, Entrange, and Hackenberg. Metz also has the region's best nightlife and entertainment. ■

Nancy

THE CAPITAL OF LORRAINE MAY BE AN UP-TO-DATE manufacturing city, but its historic heart is still caught in the 18th century. Nancy grew up in the 12th century around the stronghold of the dukes of Lorraine, but its transformation came in the 18th, when it was elegantly replanned and rebuilt under Stanislas Leszczynski, the dethroned king of Poland. In 1738 Leszczynski was created Duke of Lorraine by Louis XV, his son-in-law, and he made Nancy the seat of his brilliant court.

Gilded wrought-iron gates in Place Stanislas by Lamour, the 18th-century master ironworker

Nancy
🅰 105 E2
Visitor information
✉ 14 place Stanislas
☎ 03 83 35 22 41

Musée des Beaux-Arts
✉ 3 place Stanislas
☎ 03 83 85 30 72
🕐 Closed Tues.
💲 $

Musée Historique Lorraine
✉ 64 Grande'Rue
☎ 03 83 32 18 74
🕐 Closed Tues.
💲 $$

Musée de l'École de Nancy
✉ 36–38 rue du Sergent-Blandan
☎ 03 83 40 14 86
🕐 Closed Mon. a.m. & Tues.
💲 $

This charming town beside the Meurthe River is green with parks and gardens. **Place Stanislas,** in the center of Nancy and focus of the 18th-century town planning, is a spacious square. In the middle, a statue of Stanislas is flanked by two ornate fountains and enclosed by magnificent gilded wrought-iron railings. Surrounding the square are several 18th-century palaces and the Hôtel de Ville by Emmanuel Héré, a student of Gabriel Boffrand, leading architect of French rococo style.

A hotel occupies the palace on one side of the square; another is the **Musée des Beaux-Arts.** The original 18th-century facade remains, but the building has been extended to accommodate its collection of important works by 19th- and 20th-century artists as well as decorative arts, including glassware from Nancy's Cristalleries Daum.

The 16th-century ducal palace, west of Parc de la Pepinière, now houses the **Musée Historique Lorraine,** with displays of jewelry, arms, armor, and illuminated manuscripts, and a section devoted to the furniture, textiles, and even tombstones of the city's Jewish community.

Walking is the best way to appreciate the vistas from Place Stanislas along the tree-lined Place de la Carrière, flanked by gracious 18th-century residences, to the Palais du Gouvernement.

ART NOUVEAU

As if Nancy's fine baroque town planning was not enough, a group of artists led by the glass craftsman Émile Gallé helped found the celebrated school of art nouveau here. Look for the artists' work on the west side of town, ranging from the 1903 Maison Huot by the architect Émile André to the 1910 interior of the Brasserie Excelsior. Southwest of the railroad station, the **Musée de l'École de Nancy** displays the art nouveau style, with emphasis on furniture, ceramics, and glassware. ∎

Colmar

AN IMPORTANT FORTIFIED TOWN IN THE MIDDLE AGES, Colmar has kept many of its ancient churches and much of its medieval center. Half-timbered houses sport colored roof tiles and, in the Petite Venise quarter of the town, winding streets cross the canals that link to the Ill River, which in turn joins Colmar to the Rhine.

Colmar
- 105 E2

Visitor information
- rue d'Unterlinden
- 03 89 20 68 92

Musée d'Unterlinden
- place Unterlinden
- 03 89 41 89 23
- Closed Tues. Nov.–March
- $$

ISENHEIM ALTARPIECE

One of France's most visited buildings is the former Dominican convent of Unterlinden (named after its linden trees), founded in the 13th century and still retaining its arcaded cloister. Converted into the **Musée d'Unterlinden** in 1849, it became the repository for works of art from surrounding religious institutions. The convent's most celebrated exhibit is the remarkable altarpiece originally painted for the convent at Isenheim, 14 miles (22 km) south of Colmar. This inspirational work is one of the few extant paintings by the great 16th-century artist Mathias Grünewald, court painter at Mainz.

Southwest of the Unterlinden Museum, the 13th- to 14th-century **Basilique St.-Martin** contains some beautiful 14th-century stained glass. The Dominican church nearby boasts the exquisite "Virgin in the Rose Bower," painted by the 16th-century Colmar artist, Martin Schongauer.

Cars are banned in old Colmar, so it is pleasant to stroll around, past some of ancient Colmar's superb buildings. The **Maison Adolphe,** built around 1350, and the former **Corps de Garde,** with a Renaissance balcony, are on Rue Mercerie, close to the St.-Martin basilica. The **Maison des Têtes** on Rue des Têtes, near the

Unterlinden Museum, has a carved oriel window. The **Ancienne Douane** (Old Customs House) is 15th century and stands on the Grand'Rue, appropriately by a canal. End your walk in La Petite Venise, the former leather-tanners' district, where the Lauch River and its canals are overlooked by picturesque old town houses, hung with flower baskets in summer.

The birthplace of master sculptor Frédéric-Auguste Bartholdi is now the **Musée Bartholdi** (*30 rue des Marchands, tel 03 89 41 90 60, closed Tues.*), a local history museum, where his studies for the Statue of Liberty are displayed. The **Fontaine du Vigneron,** a fountain dedicated to Alsatian vineyard owners, adorns the streets of Colmar. To the west, vineyards climb the slopes of the Vosges Mountains. As the capital of the Alsace wine district, Colmar hosts its August wine fair. ■

Above: Colmar's colored roof tiles Below: The Isenheim altarpiece

More places to visit in Alsace & Lorraine

CHÂTEAU D'HAUT-KOENIGSBOURG

The D159 loops its way up from St.-Hippolyte toward this castle, giving startling vistas across the Alsace plain, 2,500 feet (757 m) below. The present castle is a 19th-century restoration of 15th-century fortifications around a 12th-century keep. Guides in period dress describe the building and its defenses.
🄼 105 E2 ☎ 03 88 82 50 60 🕒 Closed Jan.–Feb. 🛒 $$

DOMRÉMY-LA-PUCELLE

In this Vosges village about 45 miles (74 km) southwest of Nancy, you can see the modest house where Jeanne d'Arc was born in 1412. In the surrounding fields she heard the voices of saints who urged her to deliver France from English domination and restore the Dauphin Charles to the French throne. In the chapel of **Notre-Dame de Bermont** (*1 mile /1.5 km north in Brixey, open first Sat. of month*) where she prayed, a fresco uncovered during restoration in 1997 has been dated to the 15th century. It shows a teenage girl with blond hair and blue eyes in peasant dress, and may be a portrait of the warrior saint.
🄼 105 D2

MULHOUSE

A medieval town that was once a free city attached to the Swiss Confederation, Mulhouse was an attractive old town until World War II. The 16th-century Hôtel de Ville survived and is now a museum of local history. The **Musée de l'Automobile** (*avenue de Colmar, tel 03 89 33 23 23, closed Tues.*) displays the Schlumpf collection, including 123 Bugattis, Juan Fangio's Maserati, and Charlie Chaplin's 1937 Rolls-Royce Phantom III.
🄼 105 E1 **Visitor information** ✉ 9 avenue Maréchal-Foch ☎ 03 89 35 48 48

RIQUEWIHR

Layers of fortifications still protect the 16th-century houses and courtyards of this picturesque little wine town. The main street is defended by a medieval fortified gate, now a museum of archaeology. The Cour des Bergers is the original town gate, complete with portcullis and a prison with torture chamber.
🄼 105 E2 **Visitor information** ✉ rue 1ère Armée ☎ 03 89 49 08 40 🕒 Closed Sun. and school holidays

ROUTE DES CRÊTES

The most spectacular drive in northern France scales the Route des Crêtes (literally the Road along the Crests), a strategic route cut across the peaks of the Vosges by French army engineers during World War I. From the orientation table on the summit of the 4,672-foot (1,424-m) **Grand Ballon,** the vista on a clear day embraces the entire Vosges range to the Black Forest in Germany, south to the Jura, and across the Alps to Mont Blanc. (Check the weather forecast before setting out; low clouds are prevalent and will blanket out the views.)

The Route des Crêtes begins at Cernay, about 5 miles (9 km) west of Mulhouse. Take the D5 north to Uffholtz and turn west on the D431. The road twists and turns its way up the steep sides of the **Grand Ballon,** the highest peak in the Vosges, its name said to be a corruption of *bois long* (long wood—the mountaintops were once clothed with trees). Past the Grand Ballon the road forks: Follow the D430 to **Le Hohneck** (4,467 feet/1,362 m), where the grassy summit gives lovely views across wooded mountainsides. Continue on the D430 to its junction with the D417, then take the D61 northward past **Lac Noir** and **Lac Blanc,** mountain lakes in extinct volcanic craters, surrounded by woods.

The route ends as the D61 joins the D148. Follow signs south to Lapoutroie and the pretty town of Kaysersberg, or follow the D148 around Le Brézouard (4,027 feet/1,228 m) to Ste.-Marie-aux-Mines, where the old silver mine is open to visitors in July and August. From here the D416 descends to Ribeauvillé.

WISSEMBOURG

On the Alsace–Germany border, Wissembourg (*see map on p. 105, F3*) has a beautiful old center, partly enclosed by ramparts and encircled by the Lauter River. The 13th-century **Église de St.-Paul-et-St.-Pierre** (*avenue de la Sous-Préfecture*) was built on the site of a seventh-century Benedictine abbey. ■

These two provinces are northern European, historically more influenced by Norsemen and Celts than by Romans. A mild climate makes farming successful, and softens the light so enticing to artists.

Normandy & Brittany

Normandy & Brittany

NORMANDY AND BRITTANY TOGETHER FORM THE NORTHWESTERN corner of France and combine a largely agricultural hinterland with a coast that has long been popular with both French and foreign vacationers. Both regions are major agricultural producers: Normandy is particularly famous for its dairy products and apples and Brittany for its vegetables, though both now also produce substantial quantities of meat and cereals.

The extensive coastline has made fishing an important industry, along with the cultivation of mussels and oysters. The shoreline of northern Normandy and northern Brittany is bordered by the English Channel (la Manche), while to the south, Brittany's coast juts out into the Atlantic Ocean.

All along the coast, fishing harbors and ferry ports see constant traffic between France and Britain. The entire shoreline offers a wonderful variety of landscape: rugged granite headlands, or chalky cliffs interspersed with sandy beaches.

The climate is relatively gentle, affected by the Gulf Stream and warmed by west winds that bring humidity and mild winters. However, harsher winds from the northwest and west can lower the temperatures and create sudden storms, especially along the coast. Brittany has some of the largest tides in the world around the bay of Mont-St.-Michel.

Southern Normandy and Brittany cover what is known as the Armorican Massif, ancient granite mountains that have eroded into gently rolling hills. In the west, the hard granite produces the dramatic coastline of Brittany. To the east the granite gives way to the limestone of the Paris basin, the source of the pale, easily carved Caen stone used to build many cathedrals and churches, and the chalk cliffs of the upper Normandy Channel coast.

The Seine is the main river of the region, looping its way through Normandy from Paris to Le Havre, a major communications route that has carried trade (and occasionally invading armies) for millennia. The main cities of the area are Rouen and Caen, regional capitals of Normandy; and Rennes, capital of Brittany. Brest is a great naval port, Nantes and Le Havre are important commercial ports.

Despite their proximity, the histories of

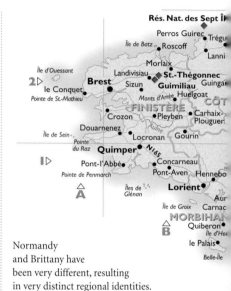

Normandy and Brittany have been very different, resulting in very distinct regional identities.

Normandy, on the Seine River and on the way to Paris, has always been an easy target for invaders. The Vikings began their raids up the Seine in the ninth century and eventually settled and colonized the land that took its name from these Norsemen. Traffic with Britain, and the success of William the Conqueror's 1066 invasion, meant significant cultural exchange, exemplified in the many churches in the Romanesque style (referred to as Norman style in England) on both sides of the English Channel.

British Celts colonized the Armorican Peninsula in the sixth century, and it became known as "la Petite Bretagne" (Little Britain), a designation eventually shortened to Bretagne (Brittany is the anglicized version of Bretagne). They established a culture and spoke a language utterly different from those of the rest of France and these endure to this day. ■

CHANNEL
ISLANDS
(U.K.)

Cap de la Hague
Nez de Jobourg
Pointe de Barfleur
Cherbourg St.-Vaast-la-Hougue
Valognes
Cap de Carteret **Utah Beach**
la Cambe **Omaha Beach**
Colleville-sur-Mer
Lessay Arromanches
Coutances **Bayeux** Cabourg
St.-Lô
MANCHE **Caen**

Cap d'Antifer Étretat
Côte d'Albâtre
Fécamp St.-Valery-en-Caux **Dieppe** Eu Blangy-sur-
Bresle
Neufchâtel-en-Bray
Bolbec **LE HAVRE** Trouville-
sur-Mer
Honfleur **Rouen** **SEINE-
MARITIME**
Lillebonne Forges-
les-Eaux
Jumièges Gournay-en-Bray
Fleury
Pont-Audemer Lyons-la-Forêt
Deauville Louviers les Andelys
Calvados **Lisieux** Bernay **EURE** Vernon
N13 **Évreux** Giverny
Coutances Livarot Conches
Granville Clécy Falaise Gacé **YVELINES**
Vire Flers **Argentan** Sées
le Mont- **St.-Michel** Avranches **Normandie** l'Aigle Verneuil-sur-Avre
ORNE
Domfront **Alençon** Mortagne-au-Perche
Fougères Bellême
MAYENNE St.-Céneri- EURE-ET-LOIR
le-Gérei
SARTHE

Golfe de St.-Malo
le Bréhat
bles d'Or- **St.-Malo**
les-Pins **St.-Michel**
St.-Brieuc Dinard Cancale
Rothéneuf **Dol-de-Bretagne**
Lamballe
ARMOR **Dinan**
Moncontour Combourg
udéac St.-Méen- les Iffs
le-Grand Montfort
ativy **RENNES**
Josselin Paimpont Vitré
né Guéhenno Ploërmel
Anne-d'Auray **ILLE-ET-VILAINE**
Vannes Redon Bain-de-Bretagne
la Roche- **LOIRE-
ATLANTIQUE**
Bernard
l'Hoëdic

0 | 60 kilometers
0 | 30 miles

Area of map detail
★Paris

Cafés, restaurants, and art galleries line the old harbor at
Honfleur, now mostly used by yachts.

Food & drink

BOTH NORMANDY AND BRITTANY REJOICE IN A LONG COASTLINE THAT yields an abundance of fish and shellfish. Combined with the produce of the lush dairy farms and orchards of Normandy and the vegetable farms of Brittany, this rich trawl of seafood has shaped the gastronomy of the region.

Along the coast you can dine sumptuously on all manner of seafood, especially mussels, oysters, and lobster. Fish, particularly sole, is often served with *sauce normande*, containing cream, mussels, shrimps, and mushrooms. Pork and pork products are popular, especially the wide range of *andouille* (chitterling) sausages made locally. The lamb here is excellent, acquiring a delicate salty flavor from grazing on the coastal salt marshes (*pré-salé*). A favorite dish is *tripes à la mode de Caen*, a hearty stew of tripe and vegetables with cider (traditionally eaten as a mid-morning snack).

Normandy is famous for its dairy products, the apples that go into cider, traditionally drunk with meals instead of wine, and Calvados (apple brandy). Apples and cream are often combined with Calvados to make delicious sauces for meat. The rich milk of Normandy cows produces France's finest butter and some of its best cheeses. Apples come sliced, caramelized, sunk in almond cream, fried in fritters, or doused in Calvados. Calvados (or affectionately, Calva) is widely used, enhancing the flavor and cutting the richness of the ubiquitous cream sauces. It is often drunk mid-meal as a *digestif* known as *le trou Normand* (literally "Norman hole," clearly intended to be filled with more food). Another specialty is Benedictine liqueur, made to an herbal recipe developed by monks.

The harsher landscapes of Brittany yield a gastronomy that is, not surprisingly, less rich. The sea dominates local menus: Among the bewildering variety of fish available, sole, turbot, and whiting come together in the spectacular *cotriade*, a fish soup, often with potatoes or, occasionally, cream.

Most famous of all Breton dishes is the *plateau de fruits de mer*, a giant spread of all kinds of seafood, including oysters, crabs, langoustines, prawns, shrimps, cockles, clams, and winkles. Watch a French family out for Sunday lunch dive into one of these; hours

later they will still be there, surrounded by piles of picked-clean shells and empty glasses.

Cancale is the center of the Breton oyster industry and worth a visit specifically to sample its wares, usually served raw with a dip of shallot vinegar or just a squeeze of lemon.

Breton food is not all fish, pork, and *pré-salé* lamb. Brittany produces vast quantities of vegetables. Artichokes have now become the symbol of the region (not least when they are used to block the roads to protest European Union agricultural policy).

Crepes, both sweet and savory (*galettes*), are mainstays of the Breton diet, served either as a main course with ham or cheese fillings, or with eggs on top, or lacily thin as exquisite desserts, known appropriately as *crêpes dentelles*. ∎

Specialties
Normandy
Main courses Canard au sang: Rouen duck in blood-thickened sauce
Pieds de cochon farcis: stuffed pig's trotters
Tripes à la mode de Caen: tripe cooked slowly with root vegetables and cider
Desserts Beignets de pomme à la normande: apple fritters with Calvados
Camembert, Livarot, Pont-l'Évêque: cheeses
Brittany
First courses Mouclade: mussel soup
Moules marinières: mussels cooked in white wine, shallots, onions, and parsley
Main courses Gigot d'agneau à la bretonne: roast lamb with white haricot beans
Palourdes farcies: grilled clams on the half-shell stuffed with shallots and herbs
Desserts Crêpes Suzette: sweet pancakes with orange juice and Grand Marnier
Kouign-Amann: pastry topped with caramelized sugar

Oysters are farmed and sold all along the coasts of Normandy and Brittany.

LA
DOUZAINE **29**F**50**

The Rouvre Valley in Normandy, where livestock graze on rich pastureland

Normandy

Sheer variety of landscape is Normandy's most immediately striking feature. The craggy grandeur of the coastline on the Cotentin Peninsula in the west gives way to the endless golden sands of the Calvados département, the belle epoque elegance of the Norman Riviera of Deauville and Trouville-sur-Mer, and the looming cliffs of the Côte d'Albâtre. Inland, take time to wander through the rural landscapes, from the cozy hills and streams of the Suisse Normande to the sweeping plateau of the Pays de Caux, and on to the lush patchwork *bocage* and orchards of the Pays d'Auge. This is the land of cheese producers, Calvados distilleries, and small restaurants for serious, leisurely lunches. And everywhere, pretty stone villages and half-timbered manors and farmhouses evince an architectural heritage that has managed to survive even the devastation of World War II.

The scenes of picturesque rural contentment that typify Normandy today belie the region's momentous and often somber history. Conflicts of many ages are made tangible in the great cathedral city of Rouen, and in the majestically ruined medieval abbeys studded along the meandering course of the Seine River. Most awe inspiring of all is the Abbaye de Mont-St.-Michel, a place of pilgrimage for ten centuries on its perilous rocky island above the sea. Bayeux still treasures its astonishing tapestry, a priceless record of William the Conqueror's invasion of Britain from these shores in 1066. Nearby, the Allied landing beaches mark a more recent story of invasion, serving as a permanent reminder of a period of heroism and extreme suffering.

Other, gentler, images of Normandy are owed to the Impressionist artists who sought inspiration in its seascapes and watery skies. Eugène Boudin's windblown dresses on the beach at Trouville and Raoul Dufy's gaily bobbing yachts at Le Havre often capture this aspect of Normandy. Above them all towers Monet who, in his exquisite gardens at Giverny (see p. 102), created compositions of light, reflections, and color that no visitor to Normandy should willingly miss. ■

Rouen

THE ANCIENT CAPITAL OF THE DUCHY OF NORMANDY, founded as a Roman settlement on the Seine, Rouen today is a huge, industrial city and port. The old city to the north of the river has been sensitively restored after the widespread destruction of World War II, and a stroll here will reveal a mass of museums, fine churches, and half-timbered Norman houses.

Monet painted the west front of Rouen cathedral many times, to catch the effect of changes in light.

Start as Monet did, at the **Cathédrale Notre-Dame,** the glorious Gothic west front of which he painted in so many different lights. Springing from 12th-century foundations are soaring Gothic arches, intricate Flamboyant carving, and two mismatched towers flanking the facade. Above the doorways, delicate openwork gables top rows of statues. The interior is a cool retreat of tall columns, luminous stained glass, and ancient tombs, including that of Rollo, first duke of Normandy.

To discover the heart of old Rouen, head along the pedestrians-only Rue du Gros-Horloge, lined with fine half-timbered buildings and elegant stores, passing under the medieval great clock set in a Renaissance arch. At the western end is **Place du Vieux-Marché,** where Jeanne d'Arc was burned at the stake in 1431. The site of her pyre has been unearthed and a modern church built in her honor. The **Musée Jeanne d'Arc** (*33 place du Vieux-Marché, tel 02 35 88 02 70*) contains one of the few known portraits of Joan, a sketch from 1429.

Back toward the cathedral stands the **Palais de Justice,** a remarkable example of 16th-century Gothic Flamboyant architecture, delicate and exuberant at the same time. West of Place du Vieux-Marché lies the **Hôtel-Dieu,** Rouen's old hospital, where the novelist Gustave Flaubert was born in 1821. It is now the **Musée**

Flaubert et Histoire de la Médecine (*Tel 02 35 15 59 95, closed Sun.–Mon.*), devoted to his life and to medical history.

To the north on Square Verdrel, the **Musée des Beaux-Arts** (*Tel 02 35 71 28 40, closed Tues.*) houses an excellent collection of European paintings, including one of Monet's Rouen cathedral series.

Beyond the cathedral are the beautifully restored **Église de St.-Ouen,** and another Flamboyant Gothic masterpiece, the **Église de St.-Maclou.** ■

Rouen
🅜 135 E3
Visitor information
✉ 25 place de la Cathédrale
☎ 02 32 08 32 40

Cathédrale Notre-Dame
✉ place de la Cathédrale

Seine Valley drive: Rouen to the coast

Beyond Rouen, the Seine River snakes its way slowly to the sea past wooded valleys, chalk cliffs, and apple orchards. This lovely drive along the north bank is also known as the Route des Abbayes, after the string of abbeys founded on the banks of the river in the seventh century, which were to become powerful centers of learning.

Follow the D982 west from Rouen to the village of **St.-Martin-de-Boscherville** ❶. The **Abbaye de St.-Georges** (*Tel 02 35 32 10 82*) here is a Romanesque church on the site of Roman temples. The interior is simple and atmospheric, the apse superbly carved, and the remains of a 12th-century chapter house include some beautifully carved capitals. Begun in 1050, the church escaped destruction during the Revolution because the village adopted it as their parish church. Today it is celebrated as one of the best preserved examples of Norman Romanesque architecture.

Continue on the D982 to **Duclair,** where you can take in fine views of the river. Then fork left to detour along the D65, following a great meander of the Seine past the apple and cherry orchards around Le Mesnil-sous-Jumièges. After the village, the great white towers of the **Abbaye de Jumièges** ❷ (*Tel 02 35 37 24 02*) soon loom into sight above the distant trees. These haunting ruins, the most majestic in Normandy, bear witness to their turbulent past. Founded in 654, the abbey was sacked in the ninth century by the Vikings, only to be refounded again in 1067 in the presence of William the Conqueror. At its height, in the 13th and 14th centuries, the monastery housed over 2,000 monks and lay brothers. After the violence of the Revolution, only the two great 11th-century towers, one

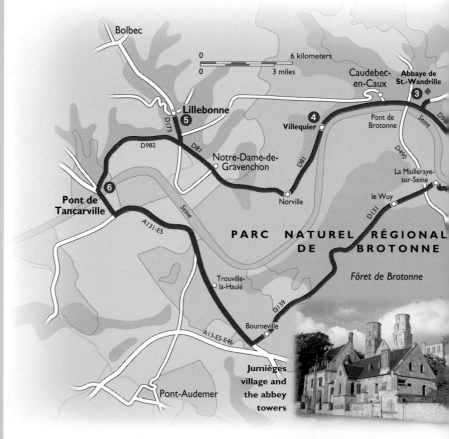

Jumièges village and the abbey towers

supporting arch of the lantern tower, and part of the now roofless nave survive.

Proceed along the D143 back to the D982, and go northwest to the Fontenelle Valley and the **Abbaye de St.-Wandrille** ❸ (*Tel 02 35 96 23 11*), which by contrast is a thriving Benedictine community, revived in 1931. Founded in the seventh century by St. Wandrille, then sacked by the Vikings, the abbey was refounded in the tenth century and flourished until the Revolution. The church, dating from the 13th and 14th centuries, remains in ruins, but the 14th-century cloister has been restored. The monks found a new church in the 1960s in an ancient wooden tithe barn, brought here from 30 miles (48 km) away and lovingly rebuilt piece by piece. Try and time your visit to attend a sung Mass of Gregorian chant (*weekdays 9:25 a.m., Sun. 10 a.m.*).

Drive on to Caudebec-en-Caux on the D982, then take the D81 to **Villequier** ❹, where the **Musée Victor-Hugo** (*via rue Ernest Binet, tel 02 35 56 91 86*) tells about the drowning of the writer's daughter, which inspired some of his most poignant poetry. **Lillebonne** ❺, farther west along the D81 and D173, has impressive Roman remains. Return to the D982 and cross the Seine on the **Pont de Tancarville** ❻, a stunning feat of engineering offering great views of the estuary.

From here, take the A131 to the D139 turn-off to Bourneville. Follow the D139 and D131 to La Maillersaye-sur-Seine and then take the D65 south through the Forêt de Brotonne to Jumièges via the ferry (*for times and fares tel 02 35 37 24 23*) and return to Rouen. ∎

🅼 See area map p. 135
▶ Rouen
↔ 90 miles (145 km)
🕓 4 hours
▶ Pont de Tancarville

HIGHLIGHTS
- Abbaye de St.-Georges
- Abbaye de Jumièges
- Abbaye de St.-Wandrille de Fontenelle
- Musée Victor Hugo, Villequier

The St.-Wandrille abbey church is in ruins, but its monastery buildings remain.

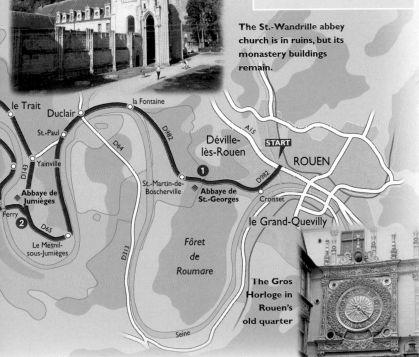

The Gros Horloge in Rouen's old quarter

Bayeux

Bayeux

135 D3

Visitor information

✉ Pont St.-Jean

☎ 02 31 51 28 28

Tapisserie de la reine Mathilde

✉ Centre Guillaume-le-Conquérant, rue de Nesmond

☎ 02 31 51 25 50

$ $$

Ticket also gives entry to Musée Baron Gérard, place de la Liberté (Italian primitives, Bayeux porcelain, needlepoint lace), and Musée d'Art Religieux, 6 rue Lambert-Leforestier.

Follow the details in the frieze at the top and bottom of the tapestry as well as the main events in the middle.

EVEN WITHOUT THE BAYEUX TAPESTRY, THE HISTORIC town of Bayeux would merit a leisurely visit for its beautifully preserved medieval center and impressive cathedral. But it is, of course, the world-famous tapestry (actually an embroidery on linen) that makes Bayeux so irresistible.

Recounting the 1066 Norman invasion of England under William the Conqueror, the staggering 230-foot-long (70-m) tapestry is an extraordinary historical document as well as a unique work of art. Age has dimmed some of the dyes (green in particular), but the wit and vigor of its execution are still superb. Panel by panel (58 in all), it tells a dramatic story rich in incident and amusing detail, from the original meeting of Harold and William, to the blessing of William's invasion fleet, the appearance of Halley's comet, and the fatal arrow that felled King Harold of England, ensuring victory for the Normans. The minutiae of medieval and military life are graphically detailed: Suits of chain mail are carried on portable hangers, soldiers picnic off their shields, while dukes dine at a table on roast chicken and kabobs.

Protected behind bulletproof glass in the **Centre Guillaume-le-Conquérant,** this medieval forerunner of the strip cartoon was probably commissioned by William's half brother, Bishop Odo of Bayeux, for the consecration of the cathedral in 1077—certainly Odo himself figures large in the story. Known by the French as the "Tapisserie de la reine Mathilde," it may have been the work of French or English embroiderers, but is usually attributed to Saxon weavers or English nuns. Allow plenty of time for a visit in order to take full advantage, not only of the tapestry itself, but also of the highly illuminating audiovisual displays that precede it and set it in context.

Emerging from the exhibition, stroll into the heart of medieval Bayeux. The town was particularly fortunate in being the first to be liberated by the Allies in 1944, thus escaping the devastation suffered by many others.

Overlooking the town are the Gothic spires of the **Cathédrale Notre-Dame** (*rue du Bienvenu*), with its beautiful 11th-century crypt and towers remaining from Bishop Odo's original Romanesque church. The chapels and crypt showcase delightful 15th-century frescoes, and the 12th-century chapter house has a maze depicted in its 15th-century tiled floor. The cobbled streets around the south of Rue St.-Martin contain many fine stone and timber-framed houses dating from the 15th to the 17th centuries. The Aure River runs through the town, spanned by a humpback bridge with water wheels still turning in the old mill.

Saturday is market day in **Place St.-Patrice,** a huge bustling affair recalling something of the flavor of medieval Bayeux. You can find all kinds of local fruits and vegetables,

along with flowers and meat and regional specialties. Bayeux lace is still made in the town and is worth seeking out.

On the southern edge of the town is the **Musée Mémorial de la Bataille de Normandie** (see p. 144), with a poignant British war cemetery almost opposite it. ∎

The mainly 13th-century Gothic Cathédrale Notre-Dame had a central tower added in the 15th century.

Normandy landing beaches

EARLY ON JUNE 6, 1944—D DAY—AN INVASION FORCE OF thousands of craft landed on the beaches of the Normandy coast, henceforth to be immortalized under the code names Utah, Omaha, Gold, Juno, and Sword. This was Operation Overlord, the meticulously planned and desperately fought Allied offensive to reclaim Normandy from its German occupiers—the last great set-piece battle of the Western world, according to war historians. Two months later, some 100,000 soldiers had died, along with thousands of French civilians, and many of the towns and villages of Normandy lay largely in ruins. But the Battle of Normandy had been won, and the tide of the war had turned irrevocably in the Allies' favor.

American assault troops land on Omaha Beach.

Musée Memorial de la Bataille de Normandie
- ✉ boulevard Fabian-Ware, Bayeux
- ☎ 02 31 92 93 41
- 🕐 Closed Jan. 1–15
- 💲 $$. Free for World War II veterans

Arromanches
- 🗺 135 D3
- **Visitor information**
- ✉ 2 rue du Maréchal Joffre
- ☎ 02 31 22 36 45

Today, more than 50 years later, the debris of war can still be seen in places, and some of those who visit the landing beaches have personal memories of those somber days.

To make sense of the deserted bunkers, tangles of barbed wire, and rusting hulks, begin by visiting one of the museums devoted to the subject. Almost every town in the area has its own small museum with a poignant display of mementoes, but a useful overview of the battle—complete with a wealth of photographs and contemporary uniforms, weapons, and docu-

ments—is presented in the **Musée Mémorial de la Bataille de Normandie** in Bayeux.

All along the beaches, the remains of German bunkers have been converted into memorials, providing a terrifying intimation of the challenge faced by the troops in the landing craft. The vast expanses of open sand stretched out at low tide, in particular, make it chillingly clear why it was so critical to time the landing to coincide with high tide.

Tales of heroism abound. At the west end of **Omaha Beach** rises the **Pointe du Hoc,** where an advance force of U.S. Rangers scaled the cliffs at dawn to knock out the German batteries. They were fiercely attacked and by the end only 65 U.S. Rangers, out of the initial 225, survived. **St.-Laurent-sur-Mer** has an Omaha museum (*rue de la Mer, tel 02 31 21 97 44, closed mid-Nov.–mid-Feb.*).

Overlooking Omaha Beach, where nearly 10,000 Americans perished in the face of the most effective German resistance of the battle, is the largest American military cemetery in Normandy at **Colleville-sur-Mer** (*Tel 02 31 51 62 00*). Most of the French soldiers who died now lie in their home towns and villages, but the cemeteries for the American, British,

Canadian, and Polish casualties dot the Normandy landscape. The heartrending rows of crosses and Stars of David stretching to the horizon are overwhelming. Grimmest of all are the German cemeteries: The largest, at La Cambe, contains 21,160 graves under the bleak inscription, "Here lie German soldiers." Some of them were as young as 16.

The town of **Arromanches** (near the beach code-named Gold) preserves part of the famous

thick entangling hedges of Normandy's *bocage* country, and villages caught in the crossfire were pulverized.

Two months of fighting left many historic towns in smoking ruins. St.-Lô and Falaise were the epicenters of the battle and suffered massive damage, but **Caen** was also ravaged. Three-quarters of the city was destroyed and thousands of its citizens killed or buried beneath the rubble. Its rebuilding, like that of many other ports and

Le Mémorial (Musée pour la Paix)

✉ esplanade Eisenhower, Caen

☎ 02 31 06 06 44

🕑 Closed Jan.

💲 $$. Free for World War II veterans

Mulberry Harbors, perhaps the most striking remains of the hardware of war. The **Musée du Débarquement** (*place du 6 Juin, tel 02 31 22 34 31, closed Jan.*) here tells the scarcely believable story of these artificial harbors, towed stealthily across the Channel to land 135,000 men, 20,000 vehicles, mountains of ammunition, and stores to support the troops.

In the days and weeks after D Day, land was gained inch by inch across Normandy by dint of bitter fighting. Tanks struggled in the narrow sunken lanes and the

towns in Normandy, took years. The town center has been completely reconstructed, the castle, churches, and the two great Romanesque abbeys restored.

Caen commemorates the war in **Le Mémorial,** a museum for peace opened in 1988. This high-tech building, on the German headquarters site of June 1944, tells the story of D Day through archive film and audiovisual displays. With its thoughtful tone and emphasis on the sacrifice rather than the glory of war, it is a fitting place to end a tour of the landing beaches. ■

Some of the 9,386 U.S. war graves in the cemetery at Colleville-sur-Mer

BATTLEFIELD ROUTE

A "Normandie Terre-Liberté" signposted route traces some key battle sites, starting from the famous Pegasus Bridge near Caen, the site of the first airborne assault. ■

Mont-St.-Michel

Mont-St.-Michel
🅰 135 D2
Visitor information
✉ boulevard de
l'Avancée
☎ 02 33 60 14 30
Guided tours
(I hour)
💲 $$

BUFFETED BY FEROCIOUS TIDES AND WINDS, RINGED BY treacherous quicksands and accessible only via a narrow causeway, the Abbaye de Mont-St.-Michel rises magnificently from its pinnacle of rock. Symbol of Normandy and now a World Heritage site, described by Guy de Maupassant as a "gigantic granite jewel, delicate as lace, thronged with towers and slender belfries," the abbey has been a place of pilgrimage for well over a thousand years.

In the eighth century this was a simple rock in the sea, a Celtic funeral mount covered in woods. Then in 708, according to legend, Aubert, Bishop of Avranches, had a vision of the Archangel Michael who instructed him to build an oratory on this rock, accessible only at low tide. In the church of St. Gervais in Avranches you can see Aubert's skull with a dent where the Archangel is said to have tapped him on the head.

In the tenth century, Richard I, duke of Normandy, founded a Benedictine abbey on the island, and gradually it was encased in monastic buildings. Through the centuries, these have been altered, have expanded, or have fallen down.

Over the original oratory the monks built the church of Notre-Dame-sous-Terre, which is now the crypt of the Romanesque abbey church, begun in the 11th century. As the monastery increased in importance, the French monarchy took a greater interest in its strategic potential, and more monastic buildings, known as La Merveille, were added in the new Gothic style. This soaring Gothic masterpiece encompasses three levels. At the top the monks remained enclosed in the abbey church with its exquisite marble cloisters and the superbly lit refectory. On this

The spire of the abbey church and the little island of Mont-St.-Michel at sunset

level, a terrace on the seaward side gives superb views of the bay. The second story accommodated the abbot, noble guests, and knights: The rib vaulting and decorated capitals of the knight's room are particularly magnificent. Humble pilgrims found succor at the almonry on the lower level.

Even though medieval pilgrims risked being sucked into

the quicksands surrounding the rock or overtaken by the incoming tide, Mont-St.-Michel steadily prospered to become one of the most prominent sites of pilgrimage in France. In the 12th century, the influence of the great abbey was ensured when it hosted peace negotiations between Louis VII of France and Henry II of England.

Today, the rock is joined to the mainland by a causeway, which has restricted the scouring action of the waves, thereby contributing to the gradual silting up of the bay.

Visiting the abbey is like a journey back in time. The **Porte de l'Avancée,** the only breach in the abbey's defenses, gives access to the **Grande Rue,** lined by 15th- and 16th-century houses, which in turn leads steeply up to the abbey's stairway, the **Grand Degré.** At the top are the abbey buildings.

During the Revolution, the abbey buildings were requisitioned and turned into a prison, and it was not until the mid-19th century, after a public outcry led by Victor Hugo, that restoration began. In addition to repair work, a spire was added to the church. The architect moved in, along with his maid, who married the baker's son and established a hotel. She was the legendary Mère Poulard. Her restaurant on the lower slopes of the mount remains to this day.

In 1966, monks returned and Mont-St.-Michel is once more a Benedictine foundation: Monastic life continues despite the tourists. Visit early or late, or attend the daily lunchtime Mass. ∎

BRIDGING THE TIDE

A footbridge is scheduled to replace the causeway which may help to prevent the silting up of the bay, and keep Mont-St.-Michel an island. ∎

Looking down from the abbey of Mont-Saint-Michel past Gothic spires to the sea below

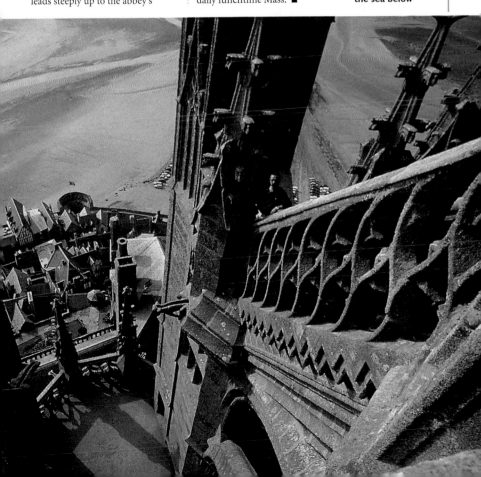

More places to visit in Normandy

CAEN

Heavily restored after the damage of World War II, Caen nevertheless retains some magnificent vestiges of its past. This was the site chosen by William the Conqueror for his castle in the 11th century. As penance for their consanguineous marriage, he and his wife, Matilda, endowed the city with two Romanesque jewels, the **Abbaye aux Hommes** and the **Abbaye aux Dames,** built of the lovely pale Caen stone. The great church of St.-Étienne, in the Abbaye aux Hommes, sheltered hundreds of citizens during the 1944 bombardment; Matilda's church of **La Trinité,** in the Abbaye aux Dames, contains her tomb. William's castle (much restored), surrounded by its impressive, largely original ramparts, contains the fine **Musée des Beaux-Arts.** Also worth visiting is the D-Day museum **Le Mémorial** (see p. 145). ⚑ 135 D3 **Visitor information** ✉ place St.-Pierre ☎ 02 31 27 14 14

CHERBOURG

The great port of Cherbourg, on the tip of the Cotentin Peninsula, is famed chiefly for its harbor—and justly so: The building of its great breakwater, 2 miles out to sea, was a heroic achievement spanning two centuries.

Fort du Roule, overlooking the town, offers panoramic views of the harbor. Cherbourg also saw ferocious German resistance in 1944, and now houses the **Musée de la Guerre et de la Libération.** The **Musée Thomas-Henry** contains works by painter Jean-François Millet, who was born in the nearby village of Gruchy. ⚑ 135 D3 **Visitor information** ✉ 3 quai Alexandre III ☎ 02 33 93 52 02

CÔTE FLEURIE

The string of sandy beaches and fashionable resorts west of Honfleur, known as the "flowery coast," was popularized in the 19th century by artists and writers. In the 1860s Napoleon III started bringing his court for summer visits to **Trouville-sur-Mer** (*Map 135 E3, Visitor information, boulevard F. Moureaux, tel 02 31 14 60 70*). Fashionable Paris flocked in his wake, the journey facilitated by the new railroad. Even grander is **Deauville** (*Map 135 E3, Visitor information, place de la Mairie, tel 02 31 14 40 00*), the 19th-century creation of one of Napoleon's dukes, who also built its racecourse. The casino followed, along with the famous esplanade, Les Planches. Both Trouville-sur-Mer and Deauville boast exuberant villas and some very grand hotels.

The Falaise d'Aval at Étretat, steep chalk cliffs typical of much of the Normandy coast, is being steadily eroded by the sea.

Farther west is **Cabourg** *(Map 135 E3, Visitor information, Jardins du Casino, tel 02 31 91 01 09)*, immortalized in all its belle epoque elegance by Marcel Proust in *À la recherche du temps perdu (Remembrance of Things Past)*, under the name Balbec. The glorious beach is still there, as is the astonishing seaside architecture, including the Grand Hôtel where Proust stayed (and where madeleines are served for breakfast, naturally).

DIEPPE

Dieppe, one of the deepest harbors in the English Channel, prospered through trade in the 16th and 17th centuries, but its heyday was as a 19th-century beach resort, the nearest to Paris and very fashionable. Today, you can enjoy the grand esplanade of the seafront, the casino, amusement parks, and seawater pools, as well as the busy port.
🄰 135 E3 **Visitor information** ✉ pont Jehan-Ango ☎ 02 32 14 40 60

LE HAVRE & THE CÔTE D'ALBÂTRE

Aside from the St.-François quarter around the old docks, Le Havre has little to show for its long history as a major port. But the new town built by architect Auguste Perret on the ruins left by World War II is an example of bold 20th-century urban planning. The glass and steel **Musée des Beaux-Arts** (*closed Tues.*) is an outstanding example of modern gallery design, housing works by Boudin, Dufy, Dubuffet, and others.

North of Le Havre across the estuary now spanned by the vast new Pont de Normandie stretch the white cliffs of the Côte d'Albâtre (alabaster coast). Here the chic little town of **Étretat**, nestling between two huge cliffs, is famous for the spectacular tunnels and arches of its rock formations.
🄰 135 E3 **Visitor information** ✉ 186 boulevard Clemenceau, Le Havre ☎ 02 32 74 04 04

HONFLEUR

This delightful harbor town at the mouth of the Seine has retained much of the charm that attracted artists in the 19th century, among them Boudin and Pissarro. It remains a magnet for artists: Painters with their easels perch on the quaysides, and exhibitions of contemporary works are held in the converted 17th-century warehouses around the Vieux Bassin, the old fishing port. The **Musée Eugène-Boudin** tells the story of Honfleur's artistic past, with works by Boudin, Dufy, and Monet. One of Monet's subjects was the 15th-century **Église Ste.-Catherine,** built of wood and a rare surviving example of the medieval shipwright's craft.
🄰 135 E3 **Visitor information** ✉ place Arthur-Boudin ☎ 02 31 89 23 30

PAYS D'AUGE

A rural region southeast of Caen and south of Lisieux (*Map 135 E2, Visitor information, 11 rue d'Alençon, tel 02 31 48 18 10*), the Pays d'Auge is the quintessence of Normandy, with lush pastures and orchards around ancient farmhouses. Be led by food, and follow the signposted Route du Cidre and Route du Fromage (Camembert, Pont-l'Évêque, and Livarot). The roads wind through pretty villages, past half-timbered manors, such as the 16th-century moated one at Coupesarte, northwest of Livarot. This is the Calvados area, where the best of the apple brandy is made. ■

The granite rocks around the coast of Brittany are as formidable as they are picturesque.

Brittany

Wave-lashed and windswept, Brittany's breathtaking coastline stretches for over 700 miles (1,100 km), a world of rocky peninsulas and headlands, mist-wreathed islands and tiny harbors, secret coves and hidden inlets. Its strength is in fortified towns such as St.-Malo and Vitré, and its wealth in the great ports that shelter its fishing fleet and the lovely old fishing villages that now double as summer resorts. Its drama lies in the towering waves and cliffs of Finistère to the west, and the fantastic—and treacherous—rock formations of the Côte de Granit Rose to the north.

Here the sea is an elemental force to be treated with respect. But the mild climate, sheltered bays, and magnificent beaches also make Brittany a perfect place for family vacations, and a paradise for bird-watchers. Its clear skies and wild beauty have inspired generations of artists, including Turner, Monet, Picasso, and perhaps most famously Gauguin, who exulted: "I love Brittany. There is something wild and primitive about it. When my wooden clogs strike this granite, I hear the dull, muffled, powerful tone I seek in my painting."

Inland from the "Armor," the Celtic name meaning land of the sea, lies the "Argoat," or land of forests, the mysterious interior that was the legendary haunt of King Arthur. This is the heart of rural Brittany, a landscape of wild woodland, remote moorland, and fertile fields, threaded by rivers and studded with historic towns and villages. In Brittany, the rich legacy of the past is everywhere apparent, in great Gothic cathedrals and medieval castles, Renaissance manors and solid granite farmhouses, frescoed churches and Finistère's unique parish closes.

Far older in geological terms than the "mainland" of France, Brittany has a timeless quality. Nowhere else in Europe has such a wealth of megalithic monuments, including the mysterious alignments at Carnac. The Celtic legacy of Cornish settlers in the fifth century B.C. still permeates Brittany's language and culture. Independent of France until the 16th century, the province retains a fierce pride in its local traditions: The Breton language is still alive among the old, who remember it, and the young, who are taught it. Visitors may enjoy a taste of Breton culture in the many summer festivals and *pardons* (religious processions). ■

Rennes

THE CAPITAL OF BRITTANY SINCE 1561, RENNES TODAY IS A lively university town and telecommunications research center. Although few of its inhabitants actually speak Breton, it is the focal point for the revival of academic interest in Breton culture. The town is at its most spectacular in early July, when it erupts into a street festival (*Les Tombées de la nuit*), celebrating music, poetry, and dance.

Rennes
⬛ 135 C1
Visitor information
✉ 11 rue St.-Yves
☎ 02 99 67 11 11

Although Rennes flourished in the Middle Ages, it lost most of its medieval buildings in a disastrous fire in 1720. In rebuilding, its citizens redesigned as well, and the result is a city of fine 18th-century buildings around a small medieval nucleus. Most of the old streets, of charmingly crooked half-timbered houses, are in a relatively small area around the **Place des Lices.** Once the medieval jousting lists, this square to the north of the Vilaine River now has an excellent market on Saturday mornings. Look particularly for the medieval houses around place Ste.-Anne, Rue de la Psalette, Rue St.-Georges, and Rue du Chapitre. The Auberge St.-Sauveur on Rue St.-Sauveur still has a Renaissance interior.

Sadly the magnificent 17th-century **Palais de Justice** (*place du Palais*), the parliament building and survivor of the 1720 fire, was almost completely burned during fishermen's riots in 1994. It has recently reopened after major renovation. The **Cathédrale St.-Pierre** (*Tel 02 99 30 12 03*) in the center of old Rennes dates from 1844, but has a 16th-century Flemish altarpiece.

The stately public buildings and grand town houses of Rennes are laid out in a geometric arrangement around the Place de l'Hôtel de Ville. Worth noting are the Hôtel de Ville itself, the superb arcading of the Théâtre, and the Palais du Commerce. To the east lies the **Jardin du Thabor,** a delightful botanical and rose garden. South of the river is the **Musée des Beaux-Arts** (*20 quai Émile Zola, tel 02 99 28 55 85, closed Tues.*), noted for its Georges de La Tour "Virgin and Child" and works from the Pont-Aven school. ■

Intricately patterned half-timbering fronts Rennes's medieval houses.

St.-Malo

St.-Malo

⚠ 135 C2

Visitor information

✉ esplanade
St.-Vincent

☎ 02 99 56 64 48

**Musée d'Histoire
de la Ville et du
Pays Malouin**

✉ Château's Great
Keep and main
tower

☎ 02 99 40 71 57

🕐 Closed Mon. in
winter

💲 $$

ON A ROCKY PROMONTORY IN THE RANCE ESTUARY, THIS virtually impregnable fortified port was known for centuries as the city of pirates. Its privateers plundered shipping in the English Channel, building themselves fine houses inside the city walls with the proceeds, while more law-abiding seafarers sailed the oceans far and wide. Corsairs from St.-Malo explored the distant Falkland Islands, and Jacques Cartier, who discovered the St. Lawrence River and began the colonization of Canada in the 16th century, also sailed from the harbor here. Novelist Gustave Flaubert described its gray granite walls as a "crown of stone above the waves," and the most impressive view of St.-Malo is undoubtedly from the sea.

The first community here was founded on the neighboring island of Aleth (now part of St.-Servan), by the Welsh monk Maclou or Malo in the sixth century. Two centuries later, attacks by Franks drove the population onto the island of St.-Malo, then linked to the mainland only by a causeway. Behind their fortifications, the townspeople gained a livelihood from the sea.

The narrow streets of the old walled city (the citadel), grouped around the partly 12th-century **Cathédrale St.-Vincent,** are lined with the tall 17th- and 18th-century houses of wealthy shipowners. It is all so authentic that it is hard to believe that they were largely rebuilt, stone by stone,

after the bombardments of World War II. Place Chateaubriand has some fine houses and good cafés, and the elegant dwellings on Rue Chateaubriand include the turreted **Maison de la Duchesse Anne.** The same duchess was responsible for the building of the late 15th-century **Château,** which now houses the town museum. A walk around the ramparts provides exhilarating views out to sea, and inland across the harbor and citadel. At low tide, you can walk out from the beach below the ramparts to the island of Grand-Bé, last resting place of the 19th-century writer Chateaubriand, and to the Fort National, built by Vauban on a small promontory to the north. ■

The first settlement of St.-Malo was on the peninsula that is now St.-Servan (foreground). St.-Malo's original island (behind) is now linked by the port and road bridges.

Côte d'Émeraude & Côte de Granit Rose

THE "EMERALD COAST" EXTENDS FROM THE POINTE DE Grouin, west of St.-Malo and north of the oyster port of Cancale, to le Val-André to the west, via a string of good beaches, pretty resorts, and headlands with spectacular views. Côte de Granit Rose is characterized by pink rocks weathered into fantastic shapes.

Rothéneuf
Rothéneuf, just east of St.-Malo, has a rock face of bizarre sculptures, carved by an eccentric 19th-century cleric. Facing St.-Malo across the Rance Estuary is **Dinard,** described at the beginning of the 20th century as "the most aristocratic and elegant seaside resort in northern Europe." In the mid-19th century, this fishing village was adopted by wealthy British and American visitors. They proceeded to make it their own by lining its cliffs and shore with an extravaganza of villas, with turrets, cupolas, verandas, and other belle epoque embellishments. Dinard and St.-Malo are now linked by a road across the **Rance Barrage** *(Tel 02 99 16 37 86)*, the dam of the world's first and largest tidal power station, which is open to visitors.

To the west some splendid beaches and attractive small resorts include **St.-Briac-sur-Mer** with its delightful little coves, the small fishing port of **St.-Jacut-de-la-Mer,** and the sands of **Sables-d'Or-les-Pins** and **Erquy.** The medieval **Fort la Latte** (with two drawbridges) overlooks the bay of La Frenaye, and **Cap Fréhel** offers wonderful views along the coast and over to the **Île de Bréhat.** The island is accessible by ferry from the Pointe de l'Arcouest. The cliffs here are a bird sanctuary: Keep an eye out for cormorants, razorbills, and guillemots.

Farther west, running from the Pointe de l'Arcouest to Trégastel, is the **Côte de Granit Rose,** where winds and tides erode the pink granite rocks into extraordinary shapes. The most dramatic section is around the resort of **Perros-Guirec.** From here the Sentier des Douaniers ("path of customs officers") leads over cliffs to Ploumanac'h, giving views to Les Sept-Îles, a wildlife sanctuary. ■

Rothéneuf
🅰 135 C2
Visitor information
✉ Les Rochers Sculptés
☎ 02 99 56 97 64

Dinard
🅰 135 C2
Visitor information
✉ 2 boulevard Féart
☎ 02 99 46 94 12

Perros-Guirec
🅰 134 B2
Visitor information
✉ 21 place
   Hôtel de Ville
☎ 02 96 23 21 15

The setting sun enhances the pink hues of the rocks at Ploumanac'h.

Breton customs

The key to the character and traditions of Brittany—so markedly distinct from anything else in France—lies not only in the rugged nature of the land but also, and more significantly, in the influence of the Celts. The Celtic colonizers from Britain of the sixth century B.C. were Druidic nature-worshipers, whose beliefs embraced a world of mystical beings and sorcery. Their monuments were adapted by the Roman invaders who subjugated them, and again by the second wave of British Celts who arrived in the fifth and sixth centuries, bringing Christianity with them.

From this mix of influences a distinctive culture developed with its own customs, a strong tradition of music and dance, and a separate language. The Breton language spoken today (by upwards of a quarter of a million people) bears no resemblance whatever to French, but has close links with Welsh, Gaelic, and Cornish.

Against heavy odds, Brittany retained its independence until the 16th century. Only with the death of the formidable Anne, Duchess of Brittany, in 1532 did the French King François I take possession of her daughter and her lands. The province became officially French, and the Breton language, culture, and customs were suppressed.

Celtic spirit

The indomitable Breton spirit survived down the centuries, nevertheless, and the 20th century has seen a great revival of all things Breton (though advocating independence from France remains a criminal offense). The language is taught in schools, and Celtic music has experienced a tremendous upsurge in interest.

Major festivals of Celtic culture, involving music, theater, dance, and poetry, are now held each year in Rennes (Les Tombées de la Nuit, the first ten days of July), Quimper (the Festival de Cornouaille, in the week up to the fourth Sunday in July), and Lorient (the Inter-Celtic Festival, biggest of all, from the first Friday to the second Sunday in August).

Left: Each village has a characteristic shape for the lace headdresses or *coiffes*; these are at Pont-l'Abbé. Right: Breton processions are accompanied by the music of bagpipes.

The *pardon* procession starts and ends at the church and involves everyone, young and old; here at Le Folgoët, northeast of Brest.

Pardons

Celtic Christians had a particular reverence for nature, and they were content to integrate their faith with other beliefs and religious customs, adopting local saints and holy wells and springs. The pagan figure of Ankou, a grim reaper figure representing death, made unique and vivid appearances in Breton religious imagery, as may be seen in the *danse macabre* in the 13th-century chapel of Kermaria, just off the D786 between St.-Brieuc and Paimpol. The early missionaries were elevated from being dragon-slaying miracle workers to the status of saints, revered within Brittany but largely unknown to the Vatican.

The Breton passion for music and dance, ritual and religion come together in the *pardons*: Annual processions to the shrines of local saints in order to make a vow or seek forgiveness. A Mass is followed by a procession; participants carry statues and relics, sing hymns, and some wear traditional costume.

These pardons offer an opportunity to admire the men's intricately embroidered vests and the women's headdresses: magnificent confections of lace and starched linen, sometimes with holes to let the wind pass through. Each village has a traditional shape and style of headdress. After the procession, the whole village then celebrates with traditional music and dancing.

Of the many pardons that take place some of the most impressive are those of St.-Yves, the patron saint of Brittany, an ecclesiastical lawyer who helped poor clients, at Tréguier (on May 19); of Ste.-Anne at Ste.-Anne-d'Auray (July 25 & 26); and of the Petite Troménie at Locronan (second Sun. in July), when the procession climbs a hill, a place of retreat (Tro Minihy—tour of the retreat—Troménie in French). The Grande Troménie, when the procession goes right round the hill, takes place every six years; next will be on the second and third Sundays of July 2001. ∎

Pays des Enclos et des Monts d'Arrée

✉ 12 avenue Foch, Landivisiau

☎ 02 98 68 48 84

Parish closes of Finistère

THE *ENCLOS PAROISSIAUX*, OR PARISH CLOSES, OF FINISTÈRE are a phenomenon unique to Brittany, enshrining in this remotest part of a far-flung region not only the devoutness of traditional Breton Catholicism but also its somber preoccupation with death.

The 16th-century restored calvary at Guehénno, depicting the Crucifixion

Dating mainly from the 15th century to the 17th, these walled churchyards typically contain, alongside the church and graveyard, a triumphal arch symbolizing entry into paradise, an ossuary, and, most importantly, a calvary. Stone carvings—intricate, sometimes primitive, and often very moving—frequently digress to include local legends, with figures clearly based on local characters. This was a pros-

perous period in Breton history, and villages made rich by the linen trade vied with each other in the extravagance of their parish closes. Two of the most flamboyant lie close together south of Morlaix, at St.-Thégonnec and Guimiliau.

St.-Thégonnec (*see map on p. 134, B2*) spared no expense in attempting to outdo Guimiliau, its rival, in splendor, employing the finest craftsmen from as far away as England. The result is a rather indigestible but undeniably impressive interior to its vast church, with an especially fine pulpit. The calvary contains a wealth of detail and intriguing figures, including St. Thégonnec himself, shown with the wolves he harnessed to his plow after they consumed his horses. The events surrounding the Crucifixion appear slightly muddled. This is because many of the elements of the calvary, hidden for safekeeping before the Revolution, were put back afterward in the wrong order.

The even more fabulous calvary at **Guimiliau** (*see map on p. 134, B2*), a few miles away, teems with more than 200 figures depicting scenes from the life of Christ. A riot of other figures include Kate Gollet (Katharine the Damned), who suffered a variety of deaths according to different calvaries. Here she is shown being torn apart at the gates of hell for stealing a holy wafer.

Other fine—and sometimes refreshingly simple—parish closes are to be seen nearby at Sizun, Commana, Ploudiry, La Martyre, and Guehénno near Josselin. ■

A faience shop in Quimper advertises its wares.

Quimper

Brittany's oldest city and capital of the ancient duchy of Cornouaille, Quimper has a history that starts in legend. King Gradlon founded Quimper after the flooding of his fabulous city of Ys, off Douarnenez. The spot he chose lay at the confluence (*kemper* in Breton) of the Odet and Steir Rivers, and the Odet threads through the cobbled streets of the medieval quarter, crossed by low, flower-decked bridges.

The delightful old town, with good shopping on Rue Kéréon, is dominated by the huge 13th-century Gothic **Cathédrale St.-Corentin,** its nave strangely set at an angle to the choir. The

Musée des Beaux-Arts, on Place St.-Corentin, has an outstanding collection of 19th- and 20th-century works, including some from the school of nearby Pont-Aven, where Paul Gauguin painted.

Quimper is also famous for its distinctive and very pretty faience, a local industry since the 17th century. The **Musée de la Faïence Jules-Verlingue** (*Tel 02 98 90 12 72*), overlooking the river on the Allées Locmaria, charts its history. The best place to shop for it lies behind the museum, at H.B. Henriot (*Tel 02 98 90 09 36, closed Sat.–Sun.*), Quimper's oldest factory. ■

Quimper

134 B1

Visitor information

✉ place de la Résistance

☎ 02 98 53 04 05

Musée des Beaux-Arts

☎ 02 98 95 45 20

🕑 Closed Tues. except July & Aug., & Sun. a.m. Oct.–March

💲 $

Concarneau

A major fishing port and now also a resort, Concarneau's chief attraction is its **Ville Close,** the walled old town on an island in the bay. This rocky perch had been inhabited for centuries before its fortifications were started in the 13th century. The Hundred Years' War increased its strategic importance, and the defenses were strengthened again in the 17th century by Louis XIV's military architect Vauban. There are wonderful views from the ramparts,

and the tiny streets are full of restaurants and souvenir shops. The old barracks now houses the **Musée de la Pêche** (*3 rue Vauban, tel 02 98 97 10 20, closed Mon. & last 3 weeks Jan.*), devoted to the local fishing industry. In the second half of August, the Ville Close comes alive with the Fête des Filets Bleus (blue nets), a festival of Breton music and dancing that has developed from the traditional ceremony of blessing the fishing nets. ■

Concarneau

134 B1

Visitor information

✉ quai d'Aiguillon

☎ 02 98 97 01 44

Carnac & its menhirs

BRITTANY IS STREWN WITH MEGALITHS—MENHIRS, cairns, passage graves, and dolmens—hewn from solid granite and put in place by a shadowy Neolithic civilization. How or why, no one knows for certain. Of them all, the stone circles and alignments at Carnac, which means the place where there are piles of stones, are the most staggering in their sheer size, number, and complexity. Possibly dating back as far as 5000 B.C., making them far older than Stonehenge, they are now recognized as the most important prehistoric site in Europe. Some of the lines may originally have been as much as 2.5 miles (4 km) long, containing thousands of menhirs. A construction on this scale was clearly of enormous significance to the civilization that built it. Archaeologists generally favor the theory that it formed some kind of vast astronomical observatory. Visit in the early morning or at dusk to avoid the crowds and savor the atmosphere.

In order to make the leap back in time necessary to set the stones in context, it is a good idea to start with the comprehensive **Musée de Préhistoire** in Carnac itself. The stones themselves are in three main locations: The largest, at **Le Ménec,** just north of Carnac

beyond the D196, consists of two oval-shaped enclosures, one of which has a medieval village built on top. Here 12 lines of menhirs (with over a thousand stones in the principal alignment) extend for nearly a mile (1.6 km). Access is restricted in order to protect the

site from erosion: The Archéoscope provides a viewing platform and audiovisual displays.

The best preserved alignments are at **Kermario.** Over a thousand menhirs are arranged in ten lines, with the giant of Le Manio, at 21 feet (6.5 m) the largest menhir still standing here, surrounded by a clutch of smaller stones beyond. **Kerlescan** has another 594 stones, arranged in 13 lines, with a covered passageway. Just to the east of Carnac rises the **Tumulus St.-Michel,** a tremendously ancient burial ground probably laid out around 4000 B.C. At the summit, the little chapel of St.-Michel has an orientation table overlooking the entire area.

Carnac-Ville itself is a pretty town of gardens and avenues with a 17th-century church, just inland from the resort of Carnac-Plage. ∎

Boat trips round Golfe du Morbihan

From Vannes, Locmariaquer, Port Navalo, La Trinité-sur-mer, or Auray

☎ 02 97 46 60 00

💲 $$$–$$$$$

Menhirs stand in alignment at Le Ménec near Carnac.

Menhirs

Marching silently over the land, row after row and mile after mile, Brittany's thousands of megaliths manage to impress us with a sense of deep significance while remaining unfathomably mysterious. As the archaeologist R.P. Giot remarked: "We may conclude, simply, that they are religious monuments, and in resorting to this vague, easy description we may attempt to conceal our ignorance."

According to legend, the megaliths are Roman soldiers turned to stone by St. Cornély as they pursued him to the sea. Earlier centuries thought they were part of Roman or Celtic burial rites or that they were intended to help sailors find their bearings. Not until the late 18th century was the astronomical significance of the alignments first noted, and no other theory since has dislodged this one.

Was Carnac an observatory for following the motions of the stars, with a view to predicting the days of the summer solstice and the equinoxes? This would have enabled the designers to establish a calendar for sowing and harvesting.

The gigantic menhir at nearby Locmariaquer was probably part of the same huge complex. Toppled by an earthquake in the 18th century and now lying in four pieces, this colossus originally stood some 65 feet (20 m) high. Near it stands the famous dolmen known as the Table des Marchands, decorated with spirals and curves. The same designs cover the burial chamber on the Île de Gavrinis in the Golfe du Morbihan. A boat trip around the islands in the gulf offers a glimpse of innumerable dolmens, menhirs, and stone circles, some now half engulfed by the waves. ∎

GLOSSARY
alignment:
row of upright stones
dolmen:
two uprights roofed with a third. Probably the supports of a burial chamber originally covered with earth
menhir:
upright stone

More places to visit in Brittany

BREST

Brest, one of France's most important naval ports, suffered heavy damage during World War II. But you can still see the remains of the 11th-century château and tour the naval town. **Océanopolis,** an important oceanographic research center, is a major attraction with models of different marine environments.

◪ 134 B2 **Visitor information** ✉ place de la Liberté ☎ 02 98 44 24 96

CROZON PENINSULA & POINTE DU RAZ

The most magnificent spots on the coastline of southern Finestère are the rocky fingers of the Crozon Peninsula and the Pointe du Raz. Cliff paths lead out to the westernmost points: to Pointe du Raz from Lescoff, and to Pointe de Pen-Hir on the Crozon Peninsula from Veryach beyond Camaret.

◪ 134 A2

DINAN

A lovely walled citadel, Dinan has been tactfully restored. Picturesque medieval cobbled streets, two splendid churches, and a 14th-century keep lie within its 13th-century defenses.

◪ 135 C2 **Visitor information** ✉ 6 rue de l'Horloge ☎ 02 96 39 75 40

FOUGÈRES & VITRÉ

These two fortified frontier towns guarded the old border between Brittany and France. In its spectacular position on a loop of the Nançon River, the stronghold at **Fougères** (Map 135 D2, Visitor information, place A. Briand, tel 02 99 94 12 20) is a feudal fortress par excellence. A rocky moat surrounds the 11th-century core and it was reinforced in the 14th and 15th centuries by 13 splendid towers.

Standing guard over the Vilaine Valley, the fairy-tale turrets and drawbridge of the castle at **Vitré** (Map 135 D1, Visitor information, prom. St.-Yves, tel 02 99 75 04 46) were also begun in the 11th century. The ramparts offer views over a maze of half-timbered houses to the 15th-century Flamboyant Gothic church.

JOSSELIN

The three slate-roofed turrets of Josselin's mighty castle, rising from a wall of granite that drops straight down into the Oust River, make one of the most famous Breton silhouettes. Built by the powerful Rohan family in the 14th century, it remains their home to this day but is open to the public for tours.

◪ 135 C1 **Visitor information** ✉ place de la Congrégation ☎ 02 97 22 36 43

TRÉGUIER

The hill town of Tréguier is dominated by the spire of its 14th-century cathedral dedicated to the dragon-slaying St. Tugdual. The *pardon* of St. Yves takes place here on May 19.

◪ 134 B2 **Visitor information** ✉ 1 place du Général Leclerc ☎ 02 96 92 30 19 ∎

The ramparts of the castle of Fougères have walls over ten feet thick.

With its mild climate, delicate light, and gentle landscapes, the Loire Valley is often considered the most quintessentially French of all the regions. Visit its medieval and Renaissance châteaus to feel the pulse of French history.

Loire Valley

Louis XII's porcupine emblem decorates the Château de Blois.

Loire Valley

THE CHIEF GLORY OF THE LOIRE VALLEY LIES IN THE MAGNIFICENT châteaus studding the banks of the river and its tributaries like jewels. The playground of medieval kings and nobles, the valley was to become the cradle of the artistic explosion of the French Renaissance. Today these sumptuous palaces and castles and their noble gardens are among France's chief attractions; some smaller ones even offer accommodations, so visitors may sample firsthand *la vie de château.*

The Loire is France's longest river, flowing some 600 miles (1,000 km) from its source in the Ardèche to its estuary at St.-Nazaire on the Atlantic coast. Most of the time the river is a wide, slow stream, but sometimes it floods and breaks its banks. Raised embankments, *levées*, have been built up to contain it, but controversy rages over proposals to control it further with barrages and dams. Although the Loire was a crucial trade and communications route for centuries, today much of it is so silted up and shallow that it is barely navigable.

The Loire region is now divided into two administrative areas, Centre and Pays de la Loire. Centre has the great city of Orléans as its capital, and includes Tours in the west and Bourges to the south. Its landscapes encompass vast wheatfields in the Beauce, the area north of the Loire, and the lakes and forests of the Sologne south of the river, historically a favored royal hunting ground. Farther south still, the rolling hills of the Berry region are one of the most deeply rural parts of France.

Touraine, the old name for the area around Tours, is the heart of the Loire Valley, its rich soils producing melons, asparagus, plums, strawberries, and some of the Loire's best wines. Many of the ravishing châteaus are in Touraine.

The Pays de la Loire starts just west of Tours and includes Angers, Le Mans, Nantes (the capital), and the Vendée to the south. Anjou, the old name for the region around Angers, was once a powerful duchy, with lands as far afield as Provence and Sicily. It was in the Loire Valley that the English were most memorably defeated by Joan of Arc at Orléans, and her memory is still cherished throughout the region.

Poets have for centuries hymned *la*

douce vie, the gentle life, of this great valley straddling the heart of France, neatly dividing north from south. The fertile alluvial soil and an exceptionally mild climate combine to yield fine wines and a cornucopia of fruit and vegetables.

Most of the great châteaus lie close to the banks of the Loire or its tributaries, and the great river itself runs like a silver thread through any journey here. Crisscrossing it in order to be on the right side at the right time is an art requiring careful planning, especially as the levées sometimes obscure the river from the road. Be prepared to forsake the Loire from time to time to explore its quiet backwaters and tributaries. ■

"One of the most wonderful rivers in the world, mirroring from sea to source a hundred cities and five hundred towers."
Oscar Wilde
(1880)

The entrance to the Château d'Azay-le-Rideau, a Renaissance gem, showing the loggia windows of the Italian-style staircase

0   60 kilometers
0   30 miles

★Paris

Area of map detail

NCHE
p. 135
p. 135
p. 93
p. 93
p. 93
p. 93
p. 191
p. 191
DEUX-SÈVRES
p. 232
VIENNE
p. 232
HAUTE-VIENNE
p. 232
CREUSE
p. 232
ALLIER
p. 191
232

ORNE

EURE-ET-LOIR

EURE-ET-LOIR

ESSONNE

SEINE-ET-MARNE

Mayenne
Alpes
Mancelles
Mamers
Nogent-le-Rotrou
A11
Brou
Bonneval
Malesherbes
Pithiviers

MAYENNE
Evron
la Ferté-Bernard
Châteaudun

Laval
Château-Gontier
Sablé-sur-Sarthe
le Mans
SARTHE
Poncé-sur-le-Loir
Trôo
Areines
Beaugency
Olivet
Châteauneuf-sur-Loire
Montargis

Orléans
LOIRET
Orléanais

A81

A23

Segré
la Flèche
le Lude
Lavardin
A10
Mer
Gien
Briare

le Plessis-Bourré
Baugé
Château-Renault
Vendôme
Blois
Chambord
N152

Angers
Château-la-Vallière
Chaumont-sur-Loire
Cheverny
A71

Serrant
A85
Tours
Amboise
LOIR-ET-CHER
Salbris
Aubigny-sur-Nère

MAINE-ET-LOIRE
Langeais
Villandry
Montrichard
Romorantin-Lanthenay
Sancerre
NIÈVRE

Rochemenier
Saumur Ussé
Azay-le-Rideau
Chenonceau
N76
Vierzon

Chemillé
Turquant
Montsoreau
INDRE-ET-LOIRE
Montrésor
Mehun

Doué-la-Fontaine
Chinon
Loches
Bourges
CHER

Cholet
Montreuil-Bellay
Fontevraud
Richelieu
Touraine
Châtillon-sur-Indre
Issoudun
St-Florent
N76

Châteauroux
INDRE

Marais-Poitevin
le Blanc
A20
Nohant
la Châtre
A71

HARENTE-MARITIME
Argenton-sur-Creuse
St-Amand-Montrond

Food & drink

VINEYARDS FLANK THE LOIRE ALONG MUCH OF ITS LENGTH, THOUGH THE Loire wines do not yet rank with those of Burgundy or Bordeaux. But for relaxation between visiting the châteaus and hearing the history of noble pleasures, try the excellent wines and regional dishes so graciously offered today.

Vines were first planted in the Loire Valley by the Romans, then grown assiduously by the monks who established important abbeys here, and their wines were drunk enthusiastically by the kings, queens, and courtiers who made the Loire Valley their playground. In recent years, the Loire vineyards have made great efforts to improve their wines and to promote those that have always been revered. Restaurants in the Loire area will have a good list of local wines, and there are signs everywhere for *dégustation*, or wine tasting (and buying, of course) at the vineyards themselves. Ask at a town's *syndicat d'initiative* or tourist office for a list of the nearby vineyards that welcome visitors.

The Loire Valley wines are light, fresh, and relatively low in alcohol. White wines predominate, based on the Chenin Blanc, Muscadet, and Sauvignon Blanc grapes, from the Muscadet of the Nantais area, perfect with shellfish, to fine Vouvrays and Sancerres farther east. Of the rosé wines, Rosé d'Anjou is the best known, and the Cabernet Franc grape, special to this region, makes a number of good reds. Seek out the fruity reds of Chinon and Bourgeuil. In Saumur, look for the *méthode champenoise* (champagne method) sparkling wines. Most voluptuous of all are the sweet dessert wines of the Coteaux du Layon.

These local wines go perfectly with the regional cuisine, which, like the climate of the Loire, is gentle, agreeable, and never extreme. The key is simplicity: Local game, fish, vegetables, and fruit are so good they need only a subtle sauce to bring out the flavor.

The Loire Valley is the garden of France: young white asparagus tips in season, salad crops, squashes, mushrooms (grown in caves along the riverside cliffs near Saumur), and tiny potatoes. Raspberries and strawberries flourish in the market gardens, while orchards yield apples, pears, and quinces as well as plums, especially greengages (*reines claudes*). Fish from the river feature on many menus, and include carp and pike, often served with a sauce of shallots, butter, and vinegar; salmon (with sorrel sauce); and eel, often made into a succulent red wine stew. Tiny fish are served simply fried, and great platters of seafood are available in profusion near the coast.

In Tours pork is cooked with prunes, game comes from the Sologne region south of the Loire, and chicken and fat capons are the basis for fricassees and casseroles. Keep an eye out for fresh cheeses, especially goat cheese. Desserts include open tarts of apples and plums, and fritters flavored with eau-de-vie. ■

"Artichokes and salad greens, asparagus, parsnips and the melons of Touraine, all are more tempting than great mounds of royal meats." Pierre de Ronsard (1524–1585)

Specialties

Main courses *Caneton de Nantes aux navets:* duck with turnips
Friture de la Loire: fried tiny freshwater fish
Matelote d'anguilles: eels in a red wine stew
Rillettes du Mans: shredded pork conserved in its own fat
Rillons de Tours: chunks of pork cooked till crisp and golden
Sandre au beurre blanc: pike perch (like walleye) with a sauce of butter, shallots, and vinegar
Saumon à l'oseille: salmon in a sorrel sauce
Desserts *Gâteau Pithiviers:* puff pastry almond cake
Tarte Tatin: caramelized upside-down apple tart
Cheeses Valençay, Crottin de Chavignol, Sainte-Maure de Touraine, Crémet de Nantes

Produce from the Loire: goat's cheese, fruit, tarte tatin, and light white wines

Orléans

Orléans

🅰 163 E3

Visitor information

✉ place Albert 1er

☎ 02 38 24 05 05

Maison Jeanne d'Arc

✉ 3 place du Général-de-Gaulle

☎ 02 38 52 99 89

🕐 Closed Mon. a.m. Nov.–April, April 28–29 & May 1, 8

💲 $

Parc Floral de la Source

✉ Orléans-la-Source

☎ 02 38 49 30 00

💲 Park $. Park & greenhouse $$

Jeanne d'Arc rallied the French troops against the English and lifted the siege of Orléans. Her statue stands in Place du Martroi.

BECAUSE OF ITS STRATEGIC BUT VULNERABLE POSITION ON a great bend of the Loire, Orléans has suffered greatly over the centuries, culminating in the devastation of World War II, when most of the city center was destroyed. Nevertheless, it has fine restaurants, excellent shopping (especially on Rue Royale), and beautiful parks.

Start your visit in Place du Martroi, dominated by a statue of Joan of Arc, and explore the rebuilt medieval streets of the old quarter. On Place du Général-de-Gaulle is the reconstruction of the **Maison Jeanne d'Arc,** where she spent ten days in 1429 after her defeat of the English and the lifting of the siege of Orléans. **Hôtel Groslot** on Place d'Étape is the best of the Renaissance buildings in the city.

Cathédrale Ste.-Croix (*place Ste.-Croix*), built in Gothic style in the 17th and 18th centuries, has always aroused controversy (Proust thought it the ugliest building in France), but it is interesting for its bizarre wedding cake towers, towering nave, and huge rose window. Museums include the **Musée des Beaux-Arts** (*place Ste.-Croix, tel 02 38 79 21 55, closed Mon.*), with works by Tintoretto and Velázquez; and the **Musée Historique et Archéologique** (*place de l'Abbé Desnoyers, tel 02 38 79 25 60, closed Mon., also Tues., Thurs., Fri. Sept.–June*), whose exhibits include some interesting second-century Celtic bronze statues.

Outside Orléans, head south for Olivet, where you can boat on the river and visit the glorious **Parc Floral de la Source,** a 245-acre (100-ha) nature reserve surrounding a 17th-century château. ∎

Jeanne d'Arc

The Maid of Orléans is honored annually in Orléans on May 7 and 8, the anniversary of the days in 1429 when she liberated the city from the besieging English forces, thus becoming one of French history's most potent heroines.

This young peasant girl from Lorraine (see p. 132) was first noticed when she came to Chinon and recognized the Dauphin, Charles VII, amongst a crowd of courtiers. She claimed that heavenly voices had instructed her to save him. She succeeded in rallying the French troops and relieving Orléans. The English were driven away, and she led Charles to Reims to be crowned. But a series of disasters led to her capture by the English, who tried her as a witch and burned her at the stake in Rouen on May 30, 1431. She was canonized a saint in 1920. ∎

Blois

Blois

🅰 163 D3

Visitor information

✉ Pavillon Anne de
Bretagne, 3 avenue
Jean-Laigret

☎ 02 54 90 41 41

Château de Blois

✉ place du Château

☎ 02 54 74 16 06

💲 $$

**Musée des
Beaux-Arts Déco-
ratifs & Musée
Archéologique**

✉ place du Château

☎ 02 54 74 16 06

💲 Ticket included in
entry to château

CLINGING PRETTILY TO THE HILLS OVERLOOKING THE
Loire, Blois makes an exceptional touring base, small enough to be
accessible and well situated for exploring both up- and downriver.
The surrounding farmland (strawberries and asparagus are special-
ties) and the game forests of the nearby Sologne area keep the restau-
rants here supplied with delicious local produce on which to feast at
the end of a day's sightseeing. Its steeply winding streets, lined with
half-timbered medieval buildings, little alleys, and hidden courtyards,
have preserved both the architecture and the atmosphere of the
town's illustrious past.

Blois is still dominated by its
magnificent **Château.** The great
13th-century Gothic hall and tower
remain from the original fortress.
Additions made during subsequent
centuries present an extraordinary
mixture of architectural styles.
Louis XII (R.1498–1515)
transformed it into an opulent
Renaissance palace (his emblem,
the porcupine, is everywhere). His
son, François I (R.1515–1547),
created its greatest single feature,
the magnificent octagonal open
spiral staircase that forms part of
the dazzling François I wing.

The cabinet of Catherine de
Médicis is intriguing for its secret
closets in which she reputedly hid
her poisons. The château is also
notorious for the murder of the
Catholic Duc de Guise at the
instigation of his Protestant
brother, Henri III (R.1574–1589),
fearful of the growing power of the
Catholics. Little good it did Henry,
who was himself murdered only six
months later.

The Louis XII wing of the
château now houses the **Musée
des Beaux-Arts Décoratifs**
and **Musée Archéologique,**
and the terrace gardens offer a good
view of the town, the Loire River,
the 18th-century bridge over the
river, and the 12th-century church
of St.-Nicolas. A fine restaurant is
set in the Orangerie (see p. 358). ∎

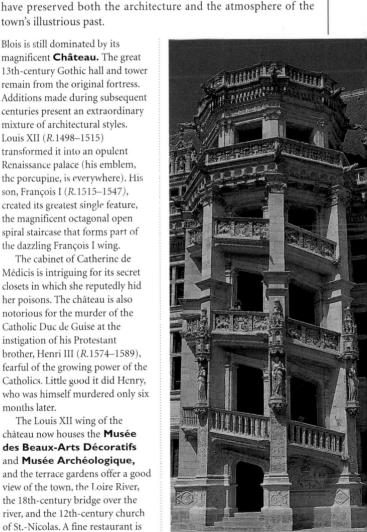

The octagonal
open spiral
staircase in
the **Château de
Blois** once
thronged with
the court of
François I.

Chambord

THE LARGEST OF THE LOIRE CHÂTEAUS, CHAMBORD IS A Renaissance masterpiece on an enormous scale, with 440 rooms, 85 staircases, and 365 chimneys—a fireplace for every day of the year. Until 1519 it was a simple hunting lodge, when François I decided to build himself the ultimate château. He was greatly inspired by Italian architecture, and had invited Leonardo da Vinci to live at Amboise. It seems more than likely that Leonardo may have drawn the first plans for the château including a scheme to divert the Loire to flow past it.

For 25 years almost 2,000 craftsmen and masons labored to build the Château de Chambord. Designed in the shape of a cross, the central keep is flanked by four towers and enclosed by a courtyard. The Grand Staircase rises through the keep to a lantern tower that was originally open, though glass was later added. This famous double spiral staircase was designed so that two people going up and down could always see each other but could only meet at the top and bottom.

Apartments flank the staircase on four sides, and everywhere you see the image of the salamander, emblem of François I. Grandest of all the rooms are the state apartments; in particular, the sumptuous bedchamber hung with richly embroidered velvet, added by Louis XIV who finished the château in 1685, while he waited for Versailles to be built.

Most extraordinary of all is the roof, a riot of gables, turrets, and spires, likened by Vivian Rowe to an Oriental town, "the skyline of Constantinople on a single building." The roof terraces were designed for the court to watch summer spectacles or herald the king on his return from the hunt. They make a splendid vantage point to survey the vast estate of 13,600 acres (5,550 ha) that still surrounds the Château. ■

⚠ 135 E3 ☎ 02 54 50 40 00
🕐 Closed Jan. 1 & May 1 💲 $$

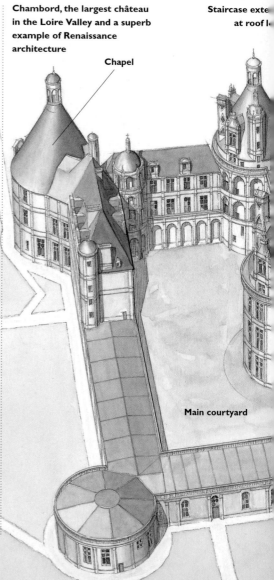

Chambord, the largest château in the Loire Valley and a superb example of Renaissance architecture

Staircase exte at roof l

Chapel

Main courtyard

Central staircase

A bedchamber, with gold-coffered ceiling, tapestry-hung walls, and a luxuriously huge fireplace

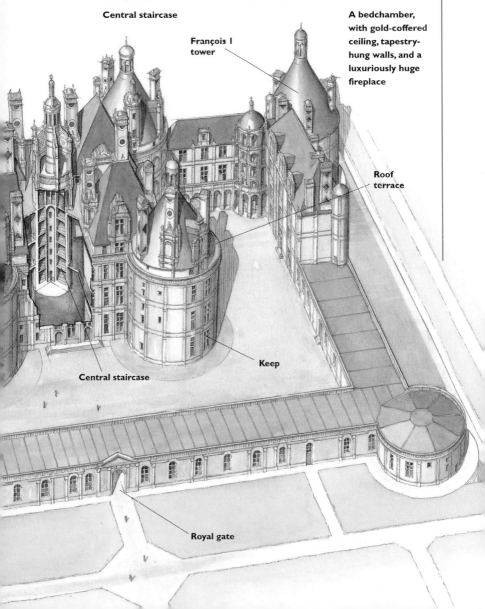

François I tower

Roof terrace

Keep

Central staircase

Royal gate

Amboise

ALTHOUGH ONLY A FRACTION NOW REMAINS OF THE original Château d'Amboise, its creamy walls and slate roof turrets still make a lovely sight, dominating the Loire and the charming narrow streets of the old town. For much of the 15th and 16th centuries, Amboise was a favorite residence of French kings, and it was here that the art of the Renaissance first came to France from Italy.

Amboise
163 D2
Visitor information
quai du Général de Gaulle
02 47 57 09 28

Château Royal d'Amboise
02 47 57 00 98
$$

Manoir du Clos-Lucé
2 rue du Clos-Lucé
02 47 57 62 88
$$

François I established a glittering court life at Amboise, enlivened by tournaments, masked balls, and fireworks designed by none other than Leonardo da Vinci. But in 1560, a Protestant conspiracy to murder the young François II (married to Mary, Queen of Scots) was put down with appalling ferocity, and hundreds of corpses hung from the battlements.

Nowadays, after a great deal of demolition and a period as a jail, this elegant château is again in royal hands, administered by the Comte de Paris, heir to the French throne. Enjoy the view of the Loire Valley from the terrace, visit the royal apartments in the 15th-century Gothic Logis du Roi, and climb the Tour des Minimes with its extraordinary spiral ramp

designed to give access to carriages. The jewel of Amboise is the late 15th-century Chapelle St.-Hubert, a dazzling example of Flamboyant Gothic that allegedly contains the tomb of Leonardo da Vinci.

It was in 1516 that Leonardo came to Amboise as painter, engineer, and architect to the king, bringing with him some of his favorite paintings, including the "Mona Lisa." François I installed him in the **Manoir du Clos-Lucé,** just outside Amboise, where you can visit his rooms. A museum dedicated to his technical drawings and experiments shows computer-generated models of some of his astonishing inventions. His architectural drawings suggest he may also have designed the staircases at Blois and Chambord. ■

Model of Leonardo da Vinci's invention of a paddleboat, which you can see at Clos-Lucé, the château where he lived outside Amboise

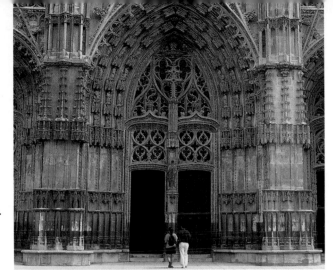

The intricate carving of Cathédrale St.-Gatien's Flamboyant Gothic west facade was completed in the 16th century.

Tours

LOUIS XI'S CAPITAL, TOURS TODAY IS A BIG, PROSPEROUS city, well worth exploring for its museums, stores, restaurants, and handsomely restored old buildings.

Tours
- 163 D2

Visitor information
- 78-82 rue Bernard-Palissy
- 02 47 70 37 37

Musée de l'Hotel de Gouin
- 25 rue du Commerce
- 02 47 66 22 32
- $

Musée des Vins de Touraine/Musée du Compagnonnage
- Cloître St Julien, 8 rue Nationale
- 02 47 61 07 93
- Closed Tues.
- $

An important city even in Gallo-Roman times, Tours enjoyed great wealth and celebrity in the Middle Ages thanks to the tomb of its famous bishop, St. Martin (now in the crypt of the New Basilica). The town flourished during the Renaissance, becoming famous for its silks, jewels, and arms. But several centuries of decline followed, culminating in the devastation of World War II. In 1959, the city began the process of regeneration that has made it a model of urban development.

The **Quartier St.-Julien,** bordered by the river, is today all trendy restaurants and antique shops. Start with lively Place Plumereau, lined with cafés and restored half-timbered buildings. Nearby is the Hôtel Gouin, a lavishly sculptured Renaissance building that houses the **Musée de l'Hotel de Gouin** with its art and archaeological collection. On the other side of Rue Nationale

(running across the Pont Wilson, a faithful 1978 reconstruction of the 18th-century stone bridge partly washed away by the river), in the former abbey of St.-Julien, is the **Musée des Vins de Touraine.** Equally fascinating is the **Musée du Compagnonnage** next door, devoted to the history of craft guilds and trades.

The **Cathédrale St.-Gatien** (*place de la Cathédrale*), currently being restored, was built from the 13th to the 16th centuries. It is a superb example of the development of the Gothic style. Especially fine are the Gothic facade, the richly colored medieval stained-glass windows, and 14th-century fresco of St. Martin and the beggar. Next door, in the 17th- and 18th-century former Bishop's Palace, is the **Musée des Beaux-Arts** (*18 place François-Secard, tel 02 47 05 68 73, closed Tues.*), which has two parts of a triptych by Andrea Mantegna (1431–1506). ■

Chenonceau

Château de Chenonceau

🗺 163 D2

☎ 02 47 23 90 07

💲 $$

BUILT BY WOMEN FOR WOMEN, CHENONCEAU IS PERHAPS the most romantic château in France, spanning the gentle waves of the broad Cher River on a series of graceful arches. Designed by Catherine Briçonnet in the early 16th century on the foundations of a manor house and watermill, this gem of Renaissance architecture was given by Henri II to his mistress Diane de Poitiers. It was she who in 1556 called in the great architect Philibert Delorme to build a bridge across to the other side of the river, so that she could go hunting more easily. When the king died, she was ousted by his jealous wife, Catherine de Médicis, who made Diane de Poitiers move out to the gloomy château of Chaumont. In 1570, Catherine commissioned Delorme to construct a two-story gallery on top of the bridge, for which he produced a design of classical elegance and symmetry.

The "Three Graces" by Van Loo hangs in the François I bedchamber.

These two remarkable women both laid out magnificent formal gardens at Chenonceau. They were succeeded by the widow of Henri III, Louise, who retired here for an 11-year vigil, hanging her bedchamber with black velvet decorated with symbols of death.

THE CHÂTEAU TODAY

An avenue of plane trees leads to the forecourt of the château. To the right is the 13th-century keep with a carved Renaissance doorway. Within the château, the rooms are lavishly furnished with painted ceilings, monumental stone fireplaces, gorgeous Flemish tapestries, and many fine paintings.

The Cabinet Vert, Catherine de Médicis's delightful study overlooking the river, was originally hung with green velvet and is still sumptuously decorated in fine brocade, while the tragic Queen Louise's bedchamber has been refurbished in funereal black. There is also a little private chapel with stained-glass windows designed by Max Ingrand (replaced after being bombed in 1944). Do not miss the extraordinary kitchens, deep in the hollow piers supporting the house.

In the 17th century the château fell into oblivion, resurfacing in the 18th century, when philosopher Jean-Jacques Rousseau stayed here. It escaped damage in the

Revolution, and became a military hospital during World War I.

Since 1913, Chenonceau has been owned by the Menier family, chocolate manufacturers, who maintain it impeccably. It is extremely popular, so try to visit early in the day, or out of high season. Spend a day here, viewing the château, boating on the river, and strolling in the gardens, perhaps attending one of the son-et-lumière performances. The old stables house a restaurant, and you can buy Chenonceau's own wines.

The neighboring village is Chenonceaux (*Visitor information,13 rue Bretonneau, tel 02 47 23 94 45),* oddly spelled differently from the château. ∎

The elegant classic structure of the gallery of Chenonceau, built atop a bridge, reaches 197 feet (60 m) across the Cher River.

Villandry

THE GLORY OF THE CHÂTEAU DE VILLANDRY IS ITS garden, faithfully re-created in 16th-century Renaissance style, with flowers, vegetables, and herbs laid out in formal geometric patterns.

Less than a hundred years ago the Château was closed in by woodland. It was rescued early in the 1900s by a Spanish doctor, Joachim Carvallo, and his wife, Ann, a steel heiress from Philadelphia. After restoring the Château, with its moat on three sides, they furnished it in Renaissance style. Then they replanted the gardens as they would have been in the 16th century.

The gardens are on three levels, linked by shady pergolas and fountains. On the upper terrace is the **Jardin d'Eau,** where a huge basin feeds water to the moat and fountains. A linden tree avenue forms the main axis of the gardens. Below is the **Jardin Potager,** or vegetable garden, laid out in geometric patterns, with fruit trees and herbs.

On the south terrace is the **Jardin d'Ornement,** a garden on the theme of love—a confection of geometric box parterres shaped in flames, butterflies, hearts, and daggers, symbolizing the different manifestations of love. ∎

Château de Villandry

🗺 163 D2
☎ 02 47 50 02 09
🕐 Closed mid-Nov.– mid-Feb.
💲 $$

French gardens

The French Renaissance garden—a stylized and beautiful combination of broad avenues and geometrical patterns, terraces and clipped hedges, statues and water gardens, fountains and pools—was heavily influenced by Italian ideas, then so prevalent in all the arts. André Le Nôtre (1613–1700) was the master of this style, creating château gardens all over France, most famously at Vaux-le-Vicomte and Versailles. In the 18th century Marie-Antoinette was largely responsible for the vogue for picturesque and informal gardens à l'anglaise, loosely inspired by the English landscape tradition. Fine examples of this style can be seen at the Grand Trianon at Versailles and the Jardin de Bagatelle at the Bois de Boulogne. Today, interest in French landscape gardening is reviving. An international garden festival takes place at Chaumont-sur-Loire every August and Blois has a school of landscape gardening. ∎

A drive along the Indre River

This drive takes you along the Indre River from Rigny-Ussé as far as Loches. Start at Ussé, picturesquely located to the south of the Indre near its junction with the Loire, between Tours and Saumur.

The **Château d'Ussé** ❶ (*Tel 02 47 95 54 05, closed mid-Nov.–mid-Feb.*) on the D7 is a treat: a truly fairy-tale castle of romantic turrets silhouetted against a dark forest. It is the setting of the original *Sleeping Beauty* (*La Belle au bois dormant*), a 17th-century tale by Charles Perrault. From Rigny-Ussé, the D7 runs parallel to the Indre River, and its great sister the Loire is visible across a fertile floodplain. Flanking the other side of the road is the forest of Chinon. Several turnings into the forest offer a chance for further exploration of its little hamlets.

Just past the village of Rivarennes, turn right on the D17, which follows the Indre River and soon passes the little town of **Azay-le-Rideau** ❷ across the water; don't miss the lovely **Château** here (see p. 178). Turn south off the D17, to the D57 and the village of **Villaines-les-Rochers** ❸, famous for its baskets made from rushes that grow beside the Indre. You can buy anything from a breadbasket to a baby's crib, and see the basket weavers at work. Return to the river on the D217 and stay south until you reach **Saché** ❹, a small village with a 16th-century manor house set among chestnut trees. In 1835 Balzac wrote *Le Père Goriot* here, having fled from his creditors. It is now a museum

(*Château de Saché, tel 02 47 26 86 50*), with his rooms perfectly preserved (particularly his bedroom: the bed made up, his coffee pot ready, and his inkwell and quill pen on the little wooden desk). Exhibits include first editions of his works and even his own carefully annotated proofs.

From here to **Montbazon** ❺, both banks of the river are equally rewarding. This is a gentle landscape of little wooded valleys and waterside villages with the river curving past orchards, châteaus, and mills. At Montbazon, the huge 11th-century stone keep now lies in ruins but is well worth climbing for the view. You might also stop at **Château d'Artigny** just outside the town, a luxury hotel and restaurant in an early 20th-century mansion.

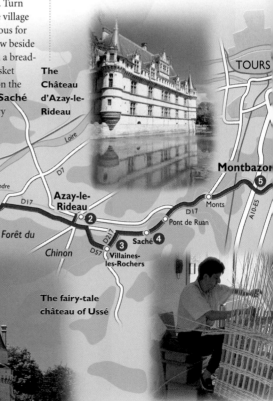

The Château d'Azay-le-Rideau

The fairy-tale château of Ussé

The D17 proceeds north of the river to the charming little town of **Cormery** 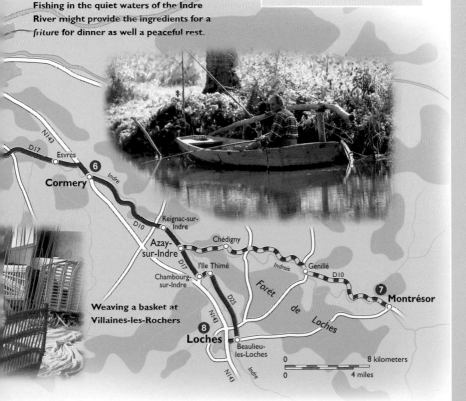, where the remains of a medieval Benedictine abbey stretch along Rue de l'Abbaye, and the 12th-century Église de Notre-Dame has a wealth of frescoes, statues, and carvings. Cormery is famed for its macaroon cookies. At Azay-sur-Indre, the Indrois River joins the Indre, and a delightful detour on the D10 takes you up beside the Indrois to **Montrésor**, a tranquil little town beside an ancient château (*Tel 02 47 92 71 04, closed Oct.–mid-April*). The walls and towers of the 11th-century fortress enclose a much-restored 16th-century residence overlooking the river.

From Azay-sur-Indre, the main route follows the D17; at Chambourg-sur-Indre cross the river and take the D25 along the valley past the forest of Loches, fronted by orchards and meadows. **Loches** (*Visitor information, place de la Marne, tel 02 47 91 82 82*) itself is a splendid town, its medieval core high on a rock overlooking the river. Stroll around the ramparts, admire the town's fine Renaissance doorways, and explore the 11th-century keep, the dungeons, the manor, and the royal apartments in the **Château**. Here Agnès Sorel (1422–1450), the mistress of Charles VII, lived in great luxury; look for her tomb and Jean Fouquet's painting of the Virgin whose face is said to be that of Agnès.

From Loches you can continue up the river, return down the D25 to explore the forest, or take the N143 straight back to Tours. ■

- 🅼 See area map p. 163
- ▶ Rigny-Ussé
- 🔁 50 miles (80 km)
- 🕒 Half a day
- ▶ Loches

NOT TO BE MISSED
- Château d'Azay-le-Rideau
- Villaines-les-Rochers basket weavers
- Cormery
- Loches

Fishing in the quiet waters of the Indre River might provide the ingredients for a *friture* for dinner as well a peaceful rest.

Weaving a basket at Villaines-les-Rochers

Château d'Azay-le-Rideau, built in the creamy-colored tufa stone of the Cher Valley

Azay-le-Rideau

AZAY-LE-RIDEAU IS ONE OF THE LOVELIEST OF THE LOIRE châteaus, famously described by Balzac as "a many-faceted diamond set in the Indre." With its delicate turrets and purely decorative fortifications reflected in the peaceful river moat against a background of trees, this is a château unquestionably built for pleasure rather than defense. While the building remains Gothic in its outlines, the delicate decorative work is of Italianate Renaissance inspiration.

Château d'Azay-le-Rideau
- 163 D2
- rue de Pineau
- 02 47 45 42 04
- $$

Building at Azay started in 1518 for a wealthy financier, Gilles Berthelot (a relation of Catherine Briçonnet, who built Chenonceau), whose wife, Philippa Lesbahy, oversaw the work. It entered royal hands when it was confiscated by François I still unfinished (it did not receive its final touches until the 19th century).

Perhaps the most striking feature of Azay is the harmony achieved between the Château and its setting, a virtuoso composition of pale stone, limpid water, and lush greenery. Set on an island between two arms of the Indre River, the Château is almost surrounded by water. Azay is also noted for its grand staircase, a major innovation at that time, consisting of three zigzag flights of stairs, with open loggia windows in Italianate style on each landing.

The interior, though luxuriously appointed, has an authentic, somewhat domestic feel. It has been furnished with period pieces, hung with sumptuous brocades, and some fine tapestries. The impressive kitchen is equipped with huge stone fireplaces, oak doors, and an intriguing selection of antique cooking equipment. A son-et-lumière show tells the Château's story every night from May to September.

The little town of Azay-le-Rideau is delightful, too. Look for the decorative Renaissance stone carving on a number of doors and windows in the old streets. The 11th-century **Église de St.-Symphorien,** close to the château, has a double-gabled front with fragments of a sixth-century facade and a row of little statues over the door. ■

Chinon

🅰 163 D2

Visitor information

✉ 12 & 16 rue
   Voltaire

☎ 02 47 93 17 85 or
   02 47 93 36 91

**Château de
Chinon**

✉ route de Tours

☎ 02 47 93 13 45

💲 $

Musée Rabelais

✉ La Devinière, D117,
   Seuilly

☎ 02 47 95 91 18

💲 $

Chinon

THE BEST VIEW OF CHINON—A SMALL TOWN STEEPED IN history and still dominated by the sprawling ruins of its great fortress—is from the opposite bank of the Vienne River. The formidable fortifications tell their own tale. Always a site of major strategic importance, the Château played a key role in Anglo-French skirmishes throughout the Middle Ages.

English king Henry II lived in the most ancient part of the stronghold—the Fort St. Georges, now demolished, east of the Château du Milieu and the Vieux Logis—and died here in 1189. The French Crown took possession of the castle, and a keep and other fortifications were added in the following century. The best preserved parts date from the 14th century.

Ruinous as it is, the castle's massive walls, lofty ramparts, and tall towers make it a dramatic place to explore. On the walls of the Château de Coudray you can still see the melancholy graffiti carved in 1308 by imprisoned Knights Templar awaiting death by burning.

But Chinon is most famous as the place where Jeanne d'Arc had her fateful interview with the Dauphin, Charles VII, when she recognized him hidden amongst a crowd of courtiers and recounted

her dream that he would be crowned king. Her memory is evoked at every turn.

The cobbled streets of the old town are charming; the main street, Rue Voltaire, is lined with half-timbered houses, their carved windows and doorways fine examples of Renaissance work. Off this street are the Caves Peintes (painted cellars), old quarries below the castle, where the local wine confraternity holds meetings. They are also the scene of Pantagruel's carousings in Rabelais's *Gargantua* and *Pantagruel*. Rabelais, whose name has entered the language as a synonym for bucolic excess, was born in the late 15th century 3 miles (5 km) southwest of Chinon. His birthplace at La Devinière, a modest manor house, is now the **Musée Rabelais** and has been restored and furnished in 15th-century vernacular style. ∎

**Across the Vienne
River loom the
forbidding ruins of
the Château de
Chinon.**

Fontevraud

ALLOW PLENTY OF TIME TO SEE FONTEVRAUD, ONE OF THE most complete surviving (though heavily restored) collections of medieval monastic buildings anywhere. The church, cloisters, kitchens, refectory, and gardens provide an unrivaled picture of monastic life over 600 years from the 12th century to the 18th.

Abbaye Royale de Fontevraud

163 C2

place des Plantagenêts

02 41 51 71 41

$

Founded in 1099 by a devout hermit, Robert d'Arbrissel, who embraced the ascetic and silent rule of St. Benedict, Fontevraud consisted of five separate religious establishments with different vocations. It was unusual in including both monks and nuns in the community, and unique in being governed by a woman. The abbesses were women of considerable influence, frequently of royal blood, and Fontevraud became a favorite royal sanctuary. This was the retreat chosen by Eleanor of Aquitaine, one-time queen first of

France and then of England, and the abbey church became the burial place of the Plantagenets. The painted 13th-century effigies of Eleanor, her husband Henry II, their son Richard the Lion-Hearted, and their daughter Isabelle of Angoulême are here.

After the Revolution, parts of the monastery were destroyed, and it was used as a prison from 1804 until 1963. It has been restored by the State, and excavation work still continues. Visitors may wander freely outside the abbey buildings, through the medieval gardens, the orangery, and the old stables.

The church is a superb Romanesque building, with an ambulatory and three apses. The simple lines of the nave are superb, and the great columns are topped by intricately and mysteriously carved capitals (binoculars are useful).

The magnificent Renaissance chapter house has fine vaulting, carved doorways, and 16th-century wall paintings. The lovely cloisters also date from the Renaissance, and the vast refectory has Romanesque walls and a Gothic vaulted ceiling. The most intriguing building is the perfectly (some say over-) restored Romanesque kitchen (the Tour d'Évraud). Octagonal in shape, it has a large central tower and a cluster of chimneys with pepperpot roofs. Inside are no fewer than six hearths, over which meals were once prepared for several hundred members of the community. The abbey buildings are now used as a conference center. ■

Left: The painted effigies of four Plantagenets, rulers of England and much of France, lie in the church at Fontevraud. Above: The abbey kitchens

The watchtower of the Château de Saumur commands views of the Loire and Saumur's old town.

Saumur

Saumur

⚐ 163 C2

Visitor information

✉ place de la Bilange

☎ 02 41 40 20 60

Château de Saumur

☎ 02 41 40 24 40

🕐 Closed Tues. Oct.–May

💲 $$

École Nationale d'Équitation

✉ St.-Hilaire-St.-Florent

☎ 02 41 53 50 50

🕐 Closed Sat. p.m.– Mon. a.m. & Tues. from Oct.–May

ONE OF THE MOST CHARMING TOWNS OF THE LOIRE Valley, Saumur is renowned for its sparkling wine, its Château, and its crack cavalry school. The graceful white turrets of the 14th-century château rise over the town and river today, just as they do in the luminous illustration to the *Très Riches Heures du Duc de Berry,* a book of hours now in one of the Châteaus at Chantilly (see p. 116), painted shortly after the château was built.

Once under the control of the kings of England, Saumur became the property of France in the 12th century. Today the **Château de Saumur** contains an excellent museum devoted to horseback riding as well as superb collections of furniture, paintings, and porcelain.

A survivor of heavy bombing in 1940, the château is surrounded by elegantly restored stone houses, while the little winding streets of the town below are lined with half-timbered dwellings, among which Balzac set his novel *Eugène Grandet.* On Place St.-Pierre stands the medieval **Église de St.-Pierre,** containing some fine 16th-century tapestries.

The **École Nationale d'Équitation** (National Riding School), in St.-Hilaire-St.-Florent just west of Saumur, stages spectacular riding displays given by the French army's skilled horseback riders. All along this village you can sample the local sparkling wine in tufa caves looking out over the river. Vast quantities of mushrooms are grown in caves, too; learn more in the **Musée du Champignon** (*Tel 02 41 50 31 55*). ■

Troglodyte dwellings

The Loire region has the highest concentration of troglodyte dwellings in Europe. For centuries, cave houses were cut out of cliff faces or dug out around a central pit, and are sometimes detectable only by the chimney poking up in the middle of a field. Between **Saumur** and **Montsoreau**, the banks of the Loire contain entire villages hewn from the soft, white tufa limestone. **Doué-la-Fontaine** has an underground zoo (*103 rue de Cholet, tel 02 41 59 18 58*), **Turquant** has several troglodyte dwellings, and the Loire River cliffs are riddled with houses dug out of the rock.

   Rochemenier, 3.5 miles (6 km) north of Doué-la-Fontaine on the D69, has a well-preserved troglodyte village museum, the **Musée**

Paysan de Rochemenier *(Tel 02 41 59 18 15, closed Dec.–Jan., Mon.– Fri., & Sat. & Sun. a.m. during Nov., Feb., & March except school vacations).* Its honeycomb of caves includes barns, wine cellars, and stables as well as dwelling places, in use until the 1930s. There is also a meeting room where the entire village was able to congregate for the *veillée,* long winter evenings spent spinning flax, shelling walnuts, even singing and dancing under the ground. ∎

Many troglodyte dwellings have been modernized with the addition of central heating, and sometimes verandas, as here.

Angers

Angers
🗺 163 C2
Visitor information
✉ place Kennedy
☎ 02 41 23 51 11

The Four Horsemen of the Apocalypse from the tapestry

ANGERS, ANCIENT CAPITAL OF ANJOU, IS THE GATEWAY TO the western Loire Valley. A civilized town with an old quarter rich with museums, cafés, and elegant shops, it is dominated by the impressive walls and 17 towers of its formidable 13th-century Château. Built by Louis IX (St. Louis, *R.*1226–1270) within the space of 20 years, this colossus of granite and black schist is approached by a drawbridge across a broad dry moat, now bright with flowers. From the battlements (leveled off at their present height in the 16th century in order to accommodate cannon), there are fine views of the town and river. Within the Château is Angers's pride, the famous Apocalypse Tapestry (see sidebar below).

Château d'Angers
✉ promenade du Bout-du-Monde
☎ 02 41 87 43 47
$ $$

Tapisserie de l'Apocalypse
✉ Château d'Angers
☎ 02 41 87 17 50
$ $$

Apocalypse Tapestry

No other treasure in Angers can rival the magnificent Apocalypse Tapestry, which is displayed in the château. Woven in the 14th century to a commission by Duke Louis I of Anjou, this extraordinary tour de force was torn up for blankets and doormats in the chaos of the Revolution.

Miraculously, 338 feet of the tapestry (originally 440 feet long, divided into 70 huge panels) survived and have been exquisitely restored. Their glowing red, blue, and gold threads illustrate surreally dramatic scenes from the Apocalypse of St. John in the Book of Revelation. ■

The fine Gothic **Cathédrale St.-Maurice** (*4 rue St.-Christophe, tel 02 41 87 58 45*) has an elaborate facade, tall vaulted nave, and 12th-century stained-glass windows. Nearby the **Maison d'Adam** is a fine half-timbered, 15th-century building. Two Renaissance palaces in the old quarter house museums: The **Hôtel Pincé** (*32 bis rue Lenepreu, tel 02 41 88 94 27, closed Mon. except June–Sept.*) contains a classical and Oriental collection, and the Logis Barrault is home to the **Musée des Beaux-Arts** (*10 rue du Musée, tel 02 41 88 64 65, closed Mon. except June– Sept.*). The intriguing 13th-century **Abbaye de Toussaint** (*33 bis rue Toussaint, tel 02 41 87 21 03, closed Mon. except mid-Sept.–mid-June*) displays the work of the 18th-century sculptor David d'Angers. Across the river from the Château is the medieval **Hôpital St.-Jean** (*4 boulevard Arago, tel 02 41 24 18

45, closed Mon.*), one of the oldest surviving hospital buildings in France. It displays "Le Chant du monde," a modern tapestry (1957–1966) by Jean Lurçat, inspired by the Apocalypse Tapestry. ∎

The black Château of Angers with its defensive battlements and flower-planted moat

Le Loir & Vendôme

To the north of the great Loire is the river of Le Loir, which runs from Illiers-Combray to just above Angers. **Vendôme,** on a network of islands formed by the Loir, is one of France's most attractive towns. In the Middle Ages it was famed for its tanneries, mills, and kid gloves. Now the old houses and mills provide second homes for Parisians.

Jean-Baptiste de Rochambeau (1725–1807), who led the French troops during the American Revolution, was born in Vendôme. His statue dominates the Place St.-Martin. The finest sight in town is the **Abbaye de la Trinité**, with a Gothic facade and some of the oldest stained glass in Europe.

Downriver from Vendôme is **Lavardin,** with medieval houses, a

Romanesque church, and a looming fortress. **Trôo** (*Visitor information, tel 02 54 72 51 27*) contains troglodyte houses built around an ancient burial mound. Across the river, the church in **St. Jacques-des-Guérets** has Romanesque wall paintings. From Trôo, follow signs to **La Possonnière,** where the poet Ronsard was born in 1524.

Farther downstream, the 15th-century **Château du Lude** (*Tel 02 43 94 60 09*) overlooks the river. From here continue on to the charming town of **La Flèche,** or southwest to **Baugé,** where you can see the Vraie Croix d'Anjou, a small double-armed cross brought back from the Crusades. During World War II it was the symbol of the Free French forces. ∎

Vendôme

🔺 163 D2

Visitor information

✉ 47 rue Poterie

☎ 02 54 77 05 07

Vraie Croix d'Anjou

✉ 8 rue de la Girouardière, Baugé

☎ 02 41 89 12 20

🕐 Closed p.m. except Tues.

Bourges

IN THE HEART OF RURAL BERRY, THE REGION SOUTH OF the Loire Valley, lies the historic town of Bourges, with its many architectural treasures. Its celebrated Gothic Cathédrale St.-Étienne (made a World Heritage site in 1993) is considered one of the most outstanding examples of Gothic architecture in France.

Built quickly, mostly between 1195 and 1260, the cathedral is unusual in having no transepts, so that the interior with its soaring pillars seems unusually spacious and airy. The facade has five beautifully carved doorways, three towers, and a gorgeous rose window dating from the 15th century. Within, the whole cathedral glows with stained glass; especially notable are the windows telling the story of the Annunciation in the chapel of Jacques Coeur.

Stone watcher at the window of Jacques Coeur's palace

Bourges
🅰 163 E2
Visitor information
✉ 21 rue Victor-Hugo
☎ 02 48 24 75 33

Cathédrale St.-Étienne
☎ 02 48 65 49 44

Musée des Arts Décoratifs
✉ Hôtel Lallemant, 6 rue Bourbonnoux
☎ 02 48 57 81 17
🕐 Closed Sun. a.m. & all day Mon.

Musée du Berry
✉ Hôtel Cujas, 4 rue des Arènes
☎ 02 48 57 81 15
🕐 Closed Sun. a.m. & all day Tues.

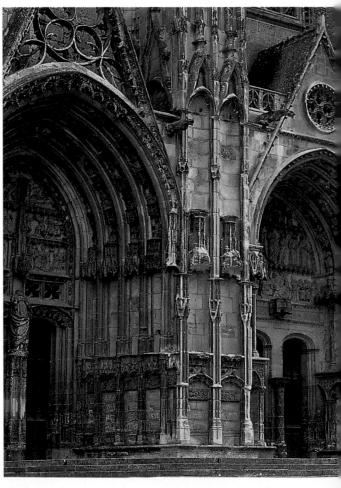

You can't go far in Bourges without encountering Jacques Coeur, one of the most powerful men in 15th-century France. Having sailed to the East, trading in silks, spices, and precious metals, he returned to Bourges to build a superb mansion. His **Palais Jacques Coeur** (*rue Jacques Coeur, tel 02 48 24 06 87*) incorporates some of the Roman wall of Bourges and was designed in part for defense. But once within the walls, its lovely patterned-tile floors, stone fireplaces, and painted ceilings reveal just how elegant Renaissance life could be.

The medieval and Renaissance quarter around the cathedral contains many other highlights, including a 17th-century garden designed by Le Nôtre, a medieval tithe barn adjoining the cathedral cloister, and many half-timbered, cantilevered houses. Among the grander town houses (*hôtels*), look for the Hôtel des Échevins and the Hôtel Lallemant, which now houses the **Musée des Arts Décoratifs.** The Hôtel Cujas, built in 1515 for a Florentine merchant, contains the **Musée du Berry**, devoted to the history of the Berry region. ■

The tympanum above the main portal of the cathedral's west front shows the Last Judgment, sculptured in exquisite detail with the dead rising from their graves.

More places to visit in the Loire Valley

LESSER CHÂTEAUS

The many smaller châteaus of the Loire beckon from every side. **Montreuil-Bellay** (*Map 163, C2, Visitor information, place de la Concorde, tel 02 41 52 32 39*), a riverside town south of Saumur, has an 11th-century fortress enclosing an elegant and beautifully furnished 15th-century mansion with a medieval kitchen, extensive wine cellars, and a row of intriguing little chapels.

The construction of the **Château de Serrant** (*Map 163 C2, tel 02 41 39 13 01*) near Angers, surrounded by a moat and attendant swans, took place over two centuries—though you would never guess from the harmonious coherence of the design. Inside, the Château is opulently decorated, and boasts an enormous library and a bedroom designed for Napoleon.

A drawbridge leads to the small, typically Angevin **Château du Plessis-Bourré** (*Map 163 C3, tel 02 41 32 06 01*), perfectly set in a pastoral landscape and encircled by a moat that reflects its white walls, blue slate roof, and spires. The Renaissance interior is designed for elegance rather than defense.

Medieval fortress on the outside—complete with moat, drawbridge, arrow-slit windows, towers, and crenellations—Renaissance palace on the inside, 15th-century **Langeais** (*Map 163 D2, tel 02 47 96 72 60*) contains fine tapestries and ingenious *tableaux vivants* evoking its long history.

The **Château de Cheverny** (*Map 163 E3, tel 02 54 79 96 29*), built between 1620 and 1634, has a classically regular facade and a lavishly painted interior.

The 19th-century novelist Georges Sand (1804–1876) lived in **Nohant** (*Map 163 E1, tel 02 54 31 06 04*), a little village north of La Châtre. Her house and garden, preserved much as she left them, are open to the public. Here she entertained her many lovers, Chopin among them, and wrote her novels.

LE MANS

Le Mans today is most famous for the 24-hour automobile race, celebrated in detail at the **Musée de l'Automobile de la Sarthe.** But there is much more to Le Mans,

including an old town of Renaissance and medieval houses, Roman walls, and the Gothic **Cathédrale St.-Julien,** noted for its flying buttresses and carved Romanesque doorway.

🏠 163 D3 **Visitor information** ✉ rue de l'Étoile ☎ 02 43 28 17 22

NANTES

The Loire meets the sea just beyond the great estuary city of Nantes, now capital of the Pays de la Loire (though it still considers itself a Breton city and the seat of the Dukes of Brittany). Its wealth was derived from its maritime activity.

The massive Château, currently undergoing major renovation, is mainly 15th century. The 19th-century neo-Gothic **Palais Dobrée** houses a rich private collection of art, furniture, tapestries, and manuscripts.

The 19th-century **Quartier Greslin** in the center of town is a feast of neoclassic facades and wrought-iron balconies, belle epoque shopping arcades, and art nouveau cafés. Don't miss the celebrated brasserie, La Cigale, opposite the theater.

🏠 162 B2 **Visitor information** ✉ place du Commerce ☎ 02 40 20 60 00

SANCERRE

Far up the Loire, Sancerre, a red-roofed town of old streets winding up a hill, is surrounded by vineyards and produces a fine dry white wine.

🏠 163 F2 **Visitor information** ✉ Nouvelle Place ☎ 02 48 54 08 21

THE VENDÉE

South of Nantes is the Vendée area of the western Loire, notorious in the late 18th century for its counter-revolutionary uprisings and guerilla warfare. It culminated in the massacre of 1794, in which more than 80,000 royalists died. War memorials and museums detailing the uprising may be found in **Cholet** and **Challans.** The Atlantic coast has long beaches and a string of small resorts. A bridge links Fromentine to the island of **Noirmoutier,** a haven of secluded beaches. Inland, canals thread the **Marais Poitevin,** a marshy landscape dotted with bird sanctuaries. ■

From the Auvergne down to the rich lands around the Rhône and Saône Rivers, and up to the Alps, this region offers a variety of grand landscapes: the old mountains of the Massif Central, the new mountains of the Alps, and many river valleys.

Central France & the Alps

Gate detail, Palais des Ducs, Dijon

Central France & the Alps

THIS REGION INCLUDES THE PROVINCE OF BURGUNDY and the quiet mountains of the Jura in the north, the Rhône Valley to the south, the Alps in the east, and in the west the mountains at the heart of France, the Massif Central. Burgundy is primarily an agricultural region, dominated by its prestigious wine industry, but with considerable expanses of unspoiled wilderness. The Rhône Valley has been an important trade route for millennia and now has many substantial cities and industrial centers. The rugged heights, deep gorges, clear lakes, and open spaces of the Alps attract walkers and skiers, and provide opportunities for a huge range of sports. The province of the Auvergne, largely encompassing the Massif Central, was until lately an undeveloped region but facilities here are improving rapidly.

The history of this area has left a rich legacy. The Romans maintained a major presence here, leaving many surviving remains. Burgundy is rich with religious and architectural sights, from the pilgrimage Basilica at Vézelay to the Abbey at Fontenay. The power of the medieval duchy of Burgundy rivaled that of the kingdom of France; its dukes held court in Dijon.

The most important river in the region is the Rhône, which has its source in Switzerland, flowing from Lake Geneva. The Isère, Drôme, and Durance Rivers all feed it with melted alpine snow. Lyon, at the confluence of the Rhône and the Saône Rivers, is the second largest city in France, a huge industrial metropolis. Lyon was for centuries a major producer of silk fabrics.

The French Alps to the east are dominated by the great peak of Mont Blanc at 15,770 feet (4,807 m). The mountains of the Jura along the Swiss border, meanwhile, are formed of limestone plateaus cut by deep valleys, heavily wooded and full of rivers, lakes, and waterfalls.

At the heart of the Massif Central are the granite and crystalline rocks produced by volcanoes—the *puys* that form the highest points of the massif. It is the source of many of France's major rivers: Loire, Dordogne, Tarn, Ardèche, and Hérault. ■

★Paris

Area of map detail

0   60 kilometers
0   30 miles

AUBE
p. 105

HAUTE-MARNE
p. 105

VOSGES
p. 105

HAUT-RHIN p. 105

Tonnerre

Châtillon-sur-Seine

Luxeuil-
les-Bains

N19

Lure   Ronchamp

Chablis

Cravant

Fontenay

Vesoul

Belfort

Montbard
Semur-en-
Auxois

Vénarey-les-
Launes

A31

HAUTE-
SAÔNE

Montbéliard

TERRITOIRE-
DE-BELFORT

Avallon

N6

Vézelay

CÔTE-D'OR

Gray

Pouilly-en-
Auxois

Dijon

Pesmes

A36

Besançon

Doubs

Maîche

Saulieu

A38

Clos de Vougeot

Auxonne

DOUBS

N57

Ornans   Morteau

Nuits-
St.-Georges

Cîteaux

Dole

Arc-et-Senans

Meursault   Beaune

Seurre

N5

Salins-les-Bains

hâteau-
hinon

Autun

Chagny

Arbois

Pontarlier

Monts de Morvan

le Creusot

Chalon-
sur-Saône

N73

Cirque de Baume

Lons-le-Saunier

Poligny

JURA

Champagnole

Montceau-
les-Mines

SAÔNE-
ET-LOIRE

N78

Doucier   Cascades du Hérisson

Bourbon-
Lancy

N79

Digoin

Tournus

Louhans

Morez

Charolles

Cluny

A6

A39

St.-Claude

Divonne-
les-Bains

Lac Léman

Evian-les-Bains

Paray-
le-Monial

Berzé-la-Ville

Mâcon

A40

1689m
Mont
Colomby
de Gex

Oyonnax

Thonon-
les-Bains

Juliénas

Chablais

Beaujeu

Fleurie

481m ▲ Mt. Brouilly

Bourg-
en-Bresse

Bellegarde

A40

St-Julien-en-
Genevois

Annemasse

Bonneville

Morzine

Roanne

Villefranche-
sur-Saône

Oingt

Pérouges

AIN

Rumilly

A41

Lac d'Annecy

HAUTE-SAVOIE

Annecy

Cluses

Chamonix

Tarare

A46

RHÔNE

A42

N75

Rhône

Lac du
Bourget

Megève

4807m ▲
Mont Blanc

▲ 3842m
Aiguille du Midi

Lyonnais

LYON

le Châtelard

Albertville

LOIRE

Feurs

N89

Aix-les-Bains

3747m
▲ Grande
Sassière

Monts du Forez

A72

1634m

Montbrison

Givors

A43

la-Tour-
du-Pin

Chambéry

A430

les Arcs

Ambert

A47

Rive-de-
Gier

Bourgoin-Jallieu

Vienne

A18

A43

Moutiers

la Plagne

Val d'Isère

St.-Chamond

ISÈRE

Méribel   Courchevel

SAVOIE

Tignes

ST.-ETIENNE

Pélussin

Voiron

St.-Pierre-
de-Chartreuse

Val Thorens

3676m
▲ Ciamarella

la Chaise-Dieu

Firminy

N82

Hauterives

A49

A41

Valloire

Arc

Modane

HAUTE-
LOIRE

Annonay

Tain-
l'Hermitage

Romans-
sur-Isère

PARC NAT.
Lans-en-Vercors
RÉGIONAL

Grenoble

Vizille

le-Bourg-
d'Oisans

3983m
le Meije

Tunnel
du Fréjus

ITALY

Yssingeaux

le-Puy-en-Velay

Lamastre

Isère

Valence

DU VERCORS

la Mure

3946m
Mt. Pelvoux

Massif des Écrins

Briançon

Monastier-
ur-Gazeille

1753m
Mt. Mezenc

Monts du Vivarais

Vercors

2086m
Mont Aiguille

Die

Valouise

St.-Véran

Langogne

ARDÈCHE

Privas

Drôme

Crest

DRÔME

Gap

Embrun

HAUTES-ALPES

Guillestre

Aubenas

Montélimar

Serres

N94

F

Largentière

ce,
nimie

1699m
▲ Mt. Lozère

Vallon-
Pont-d'Arc

A7

Nyons

N75

Durance

ALPES-DE-HAUTE-PROVENCE

lorac

Pont d'Arc
Gorges de
l'Ardèche

Aven de
Marzal

St.-Martin-
d'Ardèche

p. 281 E

leyrueis

Aven d'Orgnac

VAUCLUSE
p. 281

D

GARD
p. 281 C

SWITZERLAND

Monts du Charolais

Canal du Centre

N71

N70

Monts du Lyonnais

Saône

Ain

Rhône

Drac

Food & drink

BURGUNDIANS AND THE LYONNAIS BOTH LAY CLAIM TO BEING THE epicenter of French food. Their attitude to eating is summed up in the saying, "Better a good meal than fine clothes." It is a robust cuisine, varying from the acme of sophistication to peasant dishes made according to the produce and resources available.

This is a cuisine rich in protein, with quantities of meat and cheese, and sauces of wine and cream. Fine ingredients are plentiful: Bresse is famous for its *appellation contrôlée* chickens, Charollais for its beef. The Burgundian snail must be the plumpest in France, served with a rich emollient of butter and garlic; the Morvan produces one of France's best raw hams. Fish is plentiful too, and treated in imaginative ways: *Pochouse* is a kind of freshwater bouillabaisse, made with white wine; *quenelles de brochet* are delicate fishballs of pike.

Lyon is celebrated for its many starred restaurants and superstar chefs. Its traditional cuisine is famous for its *charcuterie*, the sausages and other pork products that go so well with Beaujolais Nouveau. Dijon is famous for mustard, and for spices that flavor *pain d'épices*, a delicious spice and honey cake.

Once you get into the mountains the food becomes more robust, with warming stews, soups, and gratins. *Gratin dauphinois* is a substantial dish of potatoes cooked with eggs, butter, milk, and cheese. Fondue is justly famous, and if you get the opportunity try raclette: a cozy ritual involving melting pieces of cheese, best on a snowy night. The mountains produce fine butter and cheese: The Jura is the home of Vacherin, the Savoie makes indispensible Gruyère, the Massif Central produces Cantal, another staple of every French larder, and the incomparable ewe's milk Roquefort.

The Auvergne volcanic center of the Massif Central also has a strong peasant cuisine, which has been absorbed by the rest of France, often via the small Paris cafés traditionally run by Auvergnats. The key ingredients are potatoes and cabbage; try *potée Auvergnate* (pork with stuffed cabbage). The Auvergne is also noted for its salted hams and dried sausages, and Le Puy is famous for its superior green lentils.

Cherries, raspberries, plums, and apricots feature on menus. Blackcurrants, with their intense flavor, come deliciously in tarts and preserves, and are distilled into the liqueur Cassis. Cassis combined with white wine makes the aperitif of the region, *kir*. Cassis combined with champagne is *kir royale*.

No visit to this region would be complete without sampling the aristocratic wine of Burgundy: The fragrant whites of Chablis and Meursault, and the velvety reds of Gevrey-

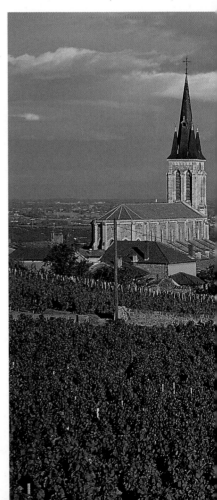

Chambertin or Nuits-St.-Georges. Expensive, maybe, but the top-of-the-tree always is. ∎

Specialties

First courses *Escargots à la bourguignonne:* snails in garlic and parsley butter

Jambon persillé: ham and parsley in aspic

Soupe à l'oignon: onion soup with grated Gruyère

Soupe aux cerises: cherry soup

Main courses *Boeuf bourguignon:* beef stewed slowly with baby onions, mushrooms, and red wine

Coq au vin à l'ancienne: cock cooked in red wine with baby onions and mushrooms

Oeufs en meurette: eggs poached in red wine sauce

Perdrix aux lentilles: braised partridge with lentils

Pintade aux choux: guinea hen with cabbage and sausages

Pochouse: freshwater fish (carp, pike, eel, trout) stewed in white wine

Vegetables *Aligot:* potato purée with cheese and cream

Pommes Lyonnaises: potatoes with onions

Desserts *Gâteau de noix et de marrons:* walnut and chestnut cake

Tarte à la lyonnaise: almond, kirsch, and breadcrumb tart

Drinks *Vin jaune:* strong yellow sherrylike wine, best drunk as an aperitif

Vin de paille: sweet white wine made from grapes sun dried on straw mats

Some of the best wine of the Beaujolais region comes from the town of Fleurie.

The little town of Irancy near Chablis, famed for cherries as well as its wine

Burgundy & the Jura

For much of its history, Burgundy was a powerful independent state, and it retains a strong sense of pride in its regional identity. There is also misty-eyed nostalgia for its glorious past—for tales of Vercingétorix and the last stand of the Gauls. The vanquishing Romans founded several of Burgundy's cities, and left remains in places such as Autun.

Burgundy is one of the richest regions of France and its historic towns and cities are the product of many centuries of civilization. The region is best known for producing some of the world's finest wines—a tour of the Côte-d'Or and a visit to the wine town of Beaune is an opportunity for any wine lover to savor.

Austere Cistercian abbeys and superb examples of Romanesque churches testify to the importance of Christianity here throughout the Middle Ages. The Benedictine Abbey of Vézelay was one of the starting points for pilgrimages to Santiago de Compostela (see pp. 266–67). Two of Christendom's monastic orders reached their apogee in Burgundy: Between the 10th and 12th centuries, the Benedictine rule reached its time of greatest influence at Cluny. Dissatisfaction with the increasing luxury and slackening discipline amongst the Benedictines led St. Bernard to found a new order in the 12th century, the Cistercians. The Abbey of Fontenay stands as a tribute to the industry and austerity of Cistercian monastic life. In Burgundy you can see the architectural development in church building from the Romanesque barrel vault to the Gothic naves of the cathedrals of Sens and Auxerre.

The 13th and 14th centuries saw the rise of the dukes of Burgundy, a golden age evoked in the magnificent palaces, noble mansions, and art collections of Dijon. The châteaus that dot the countryside tell of the wealth of the rulers of Burgundy and their nobles.

Outside its towns and cities, Burgundy is full of wonderful landscapes, from the regional park of the Morvan to the pastures of the Brionnais. To the east, the mountainous region of the Jura is a tranquil land of deep valleys and waterfalls.

Burgundy spans a watershed. The Saône River runs south to the Mediterranean; the Yonne flows north to join the Seine. In addition, canals link the main towns. A boat ride along Burgundy's waterways makes a truly delightful way to float through history. ■

Dijon

BOURGEOIS, COMFORTABLE DIJON HAS FOR ALMOST 2,000 years been a merchant city on an international trade route. Medieval trade in Eastern spices brought the ingredients for its two most noted gastronomic specialties: mustard and *pain d'épices*. What makes Dijon so pleasurable to visit is its balance of splendid architecture with a serious attitude toward food—and lots of good restaurants.

During the 14th century Dijon was the capital of the grand dukes of Burgundy, and it is their palace, the **Palais des Ducs,** that dominates the city. The oldest parts remaining are the 14th-century Tour de Bar and 15th-century vaulted ducal kitchens. The Tour Philippe-le-Bon, also 15th century, gives terrific views over the city. In the 17th century, the States General of Burgundy extended the palace as their parliament house. Part of this vast building, a mini-Versailles, now houses the collection of the **Musée des Beaux-Arts,** noted for its Dutch and Flemish masters.

Walk around old Dijon to see its dignified buildings enlivened with statuary and carvings. Rue Verrerie has 15th-century half-timbered houses with stained-glass windows. Rue des Forges, north of the Palais des Ducs, is equally historic: The **Hôtel de Chambellan** (now the tourist office) with its Gothic courtyard and stone spiral staircase dates from the 15th century, while the arcaded facade of the **Hôtel Aubriot** is 13th century. But it was in the 17th and 18th centuries, when Dijon flourished as a strong regional power, that most of its grand mansions were built. The **Hôtel de Vogüé** has distinctive Burgundian polychrome roof tiles and a pink marble courtyard; the **Maison des Cariatides** has stone caryatids around its windows.

Fine churches include the cathedral; and former **Abbaye St.-Bénigne,** with a beautiful, 11th-century Romanesque crypt beneath it. The superb Gothic **Église de Notre-Dame** has a medieval Jacquemart clock on the facade.

There is a food market every Tuesday, Friday, and Saturday in Les Halles. Do try Dijon's famous aperitif, *kir,* in a café on Place François-Rude. ∎

Dijon

[M] 191 D5

Visitor information

[✉] place Darcy & 34 rue des Forges

[☎] 03 80 44 11 44

Palais des Ducs et des États de Bourgogne

[✉] place de la Libération

[☎] 03 80 74 52 70

[🕐] Closed Tues.

[$] $$

Église de Notre-Dame

[✉] place Notre-Dame

The sculptured effigy of Duke Philip the Bold (1363–1404), carved by Claus Sluter, in the Salle des Gardes of the Palais des Ducs

Beaune

Beaune
🗺 191 D5
Visitor information
✉ rue de l'Hôtel-Dieu
☎ 03 80 26 21 30

Musée des Beaux-Arts
✉ rue de l'Hôtel de Ville
☎ 03 80 24 56 92
🕐 Closed a.m. & Nov.–March (except during wine auction—third weekend in Nov.)
💲 $

Musée du Vin de Bourgogne
✉ rue d'Enfer
☎ 03 80 22 08 19
💲 $

TASTING NOTES

Find out whether you are expected to pay for a tasting, and where you should spit—the floor may not always be acceptable! To assess the wine, look at its color, then swirl it in the glass to release its aroma and smell it. Sip it and savor it in your mouth, then spit it out. Remember that wines are often offered in ascending order of quality, so don't be too enthusiastic about the first one, or you may not be offered anything better! ∎

A SMALL TOWN WITH A BIG REPUTATION, BEAUNE IS THE true nerve center of the wine business in Burgundy. Set among some of the most distinguished vineyards in the world, it is *the* best place to go if you want to sample a variety of different wines from the region. It is also home to one of Burgundy's most celebrated sights, the Hôtel-Dieu.

To gain an overall view of this handsomely preserved old town, enter it through the 18th-century triumphal arch of Porte St.-Nicolas to the north. Walk around the remains of the 11th- to 15th-century ramparts and explore narrow lanes and cobbled courtyards, peering up at the fine Gothic and Renaissance details of the houses. Head for Place Monge, with its 15th-century bell tower and splendid houses such as the 16th-century Hôtel de la Rochepot. North from Place Monge runs Rue de Lorraine, lined with mansions and courtyards richly embellished with Renaissance carving, elaborate ironwork, and stone staircases. The Hôtel de Ville, a former 17th-century convent, houses the **Musée des Beaux-Arts,** featuring Dutch and Flemish paintings and a collection of works by Félix Ziem, born in Beaune in 1821.

The much-altered **Église de Notre-Dame** was built in the 12th century in Cluny Romanesque style, with Gothic and Renaissance decorations added later. In its chancel is a beautiful series of five 15th-century tapestries depicting the life of the Virgin Mary.

At the heart of Beaune is Place de la Halle, site of the medieval corn market. On Saturdays the market hall and stalls around it are laden with the gastronomic bounty Burgundy produces to complement

its wine. The streets all around are lined with wine cellars, many of which offer tastings. If you want to know about the mysteries of wine, make for the **Musée du Vin de Bourgogne.** It is housed in the splendid stone and timber 14th- to 16th-century mansion that was once a private residence of the dukes of Burgundy. The entire history of winemaking is recounted, with a fascinating exhibition of old equipment and presses.

THE HÔTEL-DIEU

The exterior of Beaune's most celebrated building, the Hôtel-Dieu (*rue de l'Hôtel Dieu, tel 03 80 24 45 00*), is forbidding and unadorned. Not until you step into the galleried courtyard do you realize its full glory, with its domes and turrets and polychrome roof tiles.

the Hospices de Beaune. The Hôtel-Dieu's last patient left only in 1971.

Patients were nursed by nuns in the Grande Salle des Malades. Rows of curtained four-poster wooden beds line the sides, each intended to accommodate two people, and all within sight of the great altar at the end. Above, the magnificent barrel-

Inset opposite: Wine *pichet* in the wine museum Below: The courtyard of the Hôtel-Dieu

This extraordinary building was founded as a hospital by Nicolas Rolin, chancellor to the dukes of Burgundy, and his wife, Guigone de Salins, in 1443. The Hundred Years' War had just ended and Burgundy was in chaos, with marauding gangs of disbanded soldiers, starving poor, and wolves on the streets. Succor for the poor was clearly necessary. Rolin endowed the hospice with vineyards to finance it, resulting eventually in the foundation of

vaulted timbered roof is carved and painted. Other rooms open to the public include the linen room and pharmacy, but best of all is the kitchen, with its great fireplace, age-old spit, and copper utensils.

Among the Hôtel-Dieu's many fine tapestries and paintings, the most famous is the 15th-century altarpiece, the "Last Judgment" by Rogier van der Weyden, its richly painted figures resplendent against a gold background. ∎

Drive down the Côte-d'Or

The Côte-d'Or is a 30-mile (48-km) strip of land that produces Burgundy's most venerated wines. The Route des Grands Crus, from Dijon via Beaune to Santenay, is a must for any serious wine connoisseur. The D122 and the N74 will take you through or past all the main towns with detours to smaller places; Beaune and Meursault make good places to stay or stop for lunch.

Vines fill the landscape, growing right up to the houses so as not to waste a handful of the precious soil, with the best vineyards on slopes facing east and south. The land is divided into a myriad of tiny plots with different owners, all of whom make their own wine. Often the wine is blended, but a few are so distinguished they are bottled and sold individually; here the winemaker is as important as the *domaine* (similar to the Bordeaux château).

Go in late summer when the weather is still warm but the grapes are ripening, or best of all at harvest time, in early fall. Then the air is heavy with the scent of yeast and grape juice, and every village has its cellar doors open and is full of pickers with their traditional wicker panniers. In these exclusive vineyards the harvest is still mostly done by hand.

CÔTE DE NUITS

Vines have been grown here for centuries, tended by the monks of the great abbeys. Start your tour at **Chenôve** ❶, on the D122, which runs parallel to, and west of, the N74. Here you can see a gargantuan 13th-century wine press in the former press house of the dukes of Burgundy. This is the beginning of the Côte de Nuits region, starring the finest red wines, produced from the Pinot Noir grape. Continue to **Gevrey-Chambertin** ❷, with more *grands crus* than any other village in Burgundy. The **Clos de Bèze** is purportedly the oldest vineyard in Burgundy, planted by the Abbey of Bèze in the sixth century. Continue on the D122 to Chambolle-Musigny. Just south is celebrated **Clos de Vougeot** ❸, founded in the 12th century by the monks of Cîteaux. Today, its 120 acres (50 ha) are divided between 80 owners. The 16th-century **Château du Clos de Vougeot** is the headquarters of the Confrérie des Chevaliers du Tastevin, the wine brotherhood founded to promote Burgundy. Visitors are welcome for tastings and to visit its wine

museum (*Tel 03 80 62 86 09*). Join the N74 and continue south to **Vosne-Romanée,** which can claim six *grands crus* including the majestic Romanée-Conti. A little stone cross marks its treasured patch of soil. **Nuits-St.-Georges** ❹ (*Visitor information, tel 03 80 61 22 47*) has numerous cellars to visit and a 13th-century church; the town gives its name to this section of the Côte d'Or: the Côte de Nuits.

CÔTE DE BEAUNE

South of Nuits-St.-Georges on the N74 comes the Côte de Beaune. The soil here is lighter and chalkier, perfect for the Chardonnay grape. Head first for **Aloxe-Corton** ❺ on the D2, home of distinguished red and white wines. Look for signs to the bewitching **Château Corton-André,** roofed in shining colored tiles, and open to visitors for tastings. Then continue north up the D18 to **Pernand-Vergelesses,** one of the prettiest of the wine villages. Go back down the D18, and continue on the D2 to **Savigny-lès-Beaune,** with the vineyards spread out below.

After the great wine town of **Beaune** ❻ (see pp. 196–97), take the D973 southward. The Côte de Beaune continues with some of the best white wines of Burgundy. A good place to taste them is in **Meursault** ❼, at the **Château de Meursault** (*Tel 03 80 26 22 75*) with its 14th-century cellars and an art gallery. **Puligny-Montrachet** ❽, down the D113, is a quiet little village with a very distinguished wine. A simple stone gateway leads to the vineyard of Montrachet, regarded by many as the best dry white wine in the world. The D113 continues south to **Santenay.** You could return to Beaune via the Hautes-Côtes, a route that combines vineyards with more spectacular scenery than the Côte-d'Or has to offer. Take the D33 up via St.-Aubin to the **Château de la Rochepot** ❾ (*Tel 03 80 21 71 37*), then take the D17 to **Orches,** where there are views over the Saône to the Jura. ■

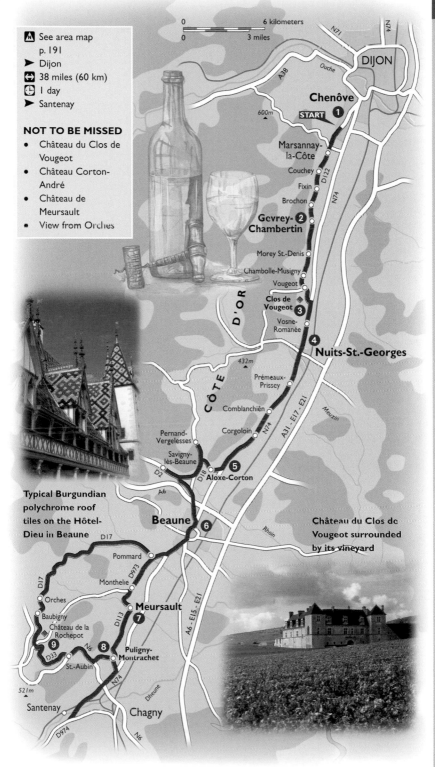

See area map
p. 191

► Dijon

↔ 38 miles (60 km)

🕐 1 day

► Santenay

NOT TO BE MISSED

- Château du Clos de Vougeot
- Château Corton-André
- Château de Meursault
- View from Orches

0   6 kilometers
0   3 miles

N71   N74

DIJON

Ouche

A38

Chenôve

600m   START ①

Marsannay-la-Côte

Couchey   D122

Fixin

Brochon

Gevrey-Chambertin ②

Morey St.-Denis

Chambolle-Musigny

Vougeot

Clos de Vougeot ③

Vosne-Romanée

④

Nuits-St.-Georges

432m

Prémeaux-Prissey

Comblanchiên

Corgoloin   N74

Pernand-Vergelesses

Savigny-lès-Beaune

D2   D18   ⑤ Aloxe-Corton

A6

Beaune ⑥

Rhoin

Château du Clos de Vougeot surrounded by its vineyard

Typical Burgundian polychrome roof tiles on the Hôtel-Dieu in Beaune

D17

Pommard

D973

Monthelie

D17

Orches

Baubigny

Château de la Rochepot

⑨   N6   ⑧

D33

St.-Aubin

Meursault ⑦

Puligny-Montrachet

A6 - E15 - E21

521m

Santenay

D974

N6

Chagny

Dheune

N74

D'OR

CÔTE

D'OR

Meuzin

A31 - E17 - E21

D113

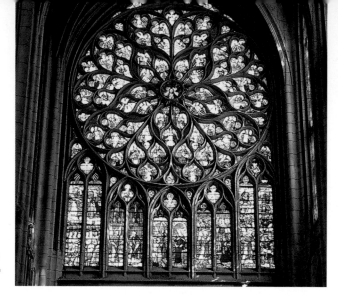

Glowing 16th-century stained glass in one of the rose windows of the Cathédrale St.-Étienne

Sens

IF YOU ARRIVE IN BURGUNDY FROM THE NORTH, SENS IS the first major town you come to. Always an important crossroads, its period of greatest influence was the 12th century when it was an archbishopric with control over most of northern France, including Paris and Chartres.

Sens
🅼 190 B6
Visitor information
✉ place Jean-Jaurès
☎ 03 86 65 19 49

Cathédrale St.-Étienne
✉ place de la République
☎ 03 86 64 15 27
💲 Crypt & Treasury: $

Musée de Sens
✉ place de la Cathédrale
☎ 03 86 64 46 22
🕐 Closed Tues. except June–Aug.
💲 $

The magnificent **Cathédrale St.-Étienne,** one of the first of France's great Gothic cathedrals, shows Sens's medieval importance. Building began in 1130; later additions spanned subsequent developments in the Gothic style. Archbishop Henri le Sanglier, who commissioned the building from William of Sens, was a close friend of St. Bernard of Clairvaux, and the influence of Cistercian austerity is clearly apparent in the simplicity of the structure, intended as a thing of beauty in its own right.

The proportions are mathematically calculated (the width of the nave being twice that of the side aisles), but the overall effect is one of harmonious space. Stained glass fills the tall windows, some of which survive from the 12th century. It was intended to "call to mind the walls of sapphires, of

rubies, of topaz and emerald of the Heavenly Jersualem."

The west portal is particularly beautiful, despite having lost one of its towers and much of its statuary. In the central doorway look for the statue of St. Étienne, a 12th-century Gothic work that survived destruction during the Revolution.

The adjoining archbishop's palace has been restored and is now the **Musée de Sens,** with one of the richest Treasuries in France: a glittering collection of religious art, Byzantine silks, shrouds, altar cloths, reliquaries, and vestments. Other displays in the museum recount the development of Sens from prehistoric times.

A stroll around the cathedral quarter of the town reveals streets of picturesque stone and half-timbered houses dating from the 16th to the 18th centuries. ■

Auxerre

AUXERRE IS A SLEEPY LITTLE TOWN ON THE BANKS OF THE
Yonne River, a perfect starting point for trips on the waterways of
Burgundy. From across the river you can see the steep roofs of the old
town and of the churches for which it is famous.

Dominating all the buildings is the
Cathédrale St.-Étienne. In
1215, Bishop Guillaume de
Seignelay decided to rebuild the
existing Romanesque cathedral in
the new Gothic style. Two centuries
later, the main body of the building
was complete, but it was 1560
before the cathedral was finished.
The columns and rib vaulting are
so subtly arranged they seem to be
carrying no weight at all. The airy
lightness is increased by the jewel-
like colors of the stained glass. The
Romanesque crypt stands in
complete contrast, its barrel vault
and sturdy pillars intact. The apse
still has remarkable 12th-century
frescoes of Christ on horseback
surrounded by angels, vestiges of a
scheme that once covered the
entire church.

A short walk up Rue Cauchois
will bring you to the **Abbatiale
de St.-Germain.** Hidden
beneath the neo-Gothic church is a
dim, vaulted Carolingian crypt with
ancient stone sarcophagi of long-
forgotten bishops and the tomb of
St.-Germain. The ninth-century
frescoes of the stoning of St.Étienne
are among the oldest religious wall
paintings in France.

The 17th-century town gate, the
Tour de l'Horloge, has a moon
dial as well as a sun dial in its 15th-
century clock face. ■

Auxerre
🗺 190 B5
Visitor information
✉ 1–2 quai de la
     République
☎ 03 86 52 06 19

Chablis

Chablis is the northernmost of
the great Burgundian vineyards, a little stone town with one
overwhelming interest—the
fragrant white wine, pale and dry,
to which it has given its name. In
spring there is a scent of laburnum
and a cool freshness in the air,
reminiscent of the wine itself.
There are good restaurants and
hotels here, and several *domaines*
open their cellars for tastings. To
drive around the vineyards (planted
with the Chardonnay grape), follow
the course of the Serein River on
the D91 north toward Maligny; to
your right are the *grands crus* vineyards, facing south and southeast.
Return on the D131 heading for
Milly, from where there is an
excellent view of the surprisingly
few Chablis vineyards. ■
🗺 191 C6 Visitor information ✉ 1 quai
du Biez ☎ 03 86 42 80 80

Cathédrale St.-
Étienne (left) and
the Abbatiale de
St.-Germain
(right) across the
Yonne River

Vézelay

Vézelay

🅼 191 C5

Visitor information

✉ rue St.-Pierre

☎ 03 86 33 23 69

THE GREAT BASILIQUE DE STE.-MADELEINE IN VÉZELAY rises on a rock from a deep valley. The best way to approach it is to climb the steep main street, following in the steps of the medieval pilgrims who flocked here to worship the (supposed) relics of St. Mary Magdalene.

The tympanum of the basilica with the nave and choir beyond

Vézelay's spiritual reputation still draws crowds, and the medieval streets of the town are crammed with bookstores, antique shops, and art galleries. Its ramparts give lovely views of the lush, rolling hills of the surrounding countryside.

Founded in 864, the **Basilique de Ste.-Madeleine** (*place de la Basilique, tel 03 86 33 24 36*) thrived until 1280, when it emerged that the bones of Mary Magdalene were still at St.-Maximin in Provence and that the relics at Vézelay were fakes. Virtually abandoned, damaged by Protestants in the 16th century, and neglected during the Revolution, the basilica was in a ruinous state when architectural historian Viollet-le-Duc began the 19th-century restoration.

Walk around the outside to view the apse with its radiating chapels, the chapter house which is all that remains from the 12th-century monastery, and the west facade with its restored 13th-century window and tower. Then enter the vast narthex, added to accommodate the crowds of pilgrims in the 12th century. The famous tympanum over the inner door is the pièce de résistance of Burgundian Romanesque. With tremendous movement and feeling it depicts the events of Pentecost: Rays of light streak from the fingers of Christ to the Apostles.

Looking through the door and straight down the aisle, the round Romanesque arches of the nave with alternating light and dark stones lead your eye to the soaring Gothic points of the choir beyond. The carvings of the capitals dwell heavily on the torment awaiting unbelievers. For an insight into the medieval mind-set, go down to the crypt to see the discredited relics. ■

Abbaye de Fontenay

FONTENAY IS THE OLDEST CISTERCIAN MONASTERY STILL surviving, and has been superbly restored to give an intriguing picture of monastic life. It was founded by St. Bernard of Clairvaux in 1118 in a quiet wooded valley and named after the spring there.

From the wooded hill above Fontenay you can see its entire layout, beautifully set in the valley and most dramatically defined in winter when the trees are bare. Aside from the 17th-century abbot's lodging at the western end of the church, all the buildings are the original 12th-century structures built by the monks, albeit restored. Remarkably, many of the brown Burgundian roof tiles are original, too. The architecture embodies beauty in its purest, most austere form, in accordance with St. Bernard's belief that any super-fluous decoration was a distraction from a building's spiritual purpose.

At the heart of the former monastery is the cloister, a square of open galleries arcaded with double columns of golden stone. Abutting the north gallery is the church, its facade unadorned. Inside, aisles flank the long nave; only the merest trace of decoration is detectable on the capitals, and there are no frescoes or any other

decoration. Its spartan beauty is enhanced by a subtle glow from the windows in the aisles and choir and the seven windows of the facade. In the north transept, a 13th-century statue of the Virgin stands serene and maternal, the Child on her hip.

The chapter house has exquisite rib vaulting and columns. In the dormitory above, the monks slept on straw pallets on the floor, and in the scriptorium they copied manuscripts; the warming room next to it kept the inks (and incidentally the monks' hands) from freezing in winter. The forge, where the monks worked the iron they dug from the hills, stands near the little river.

Fontenay received many endowments and thrived until the turmoil of the 16th-century religious wars. During the Revolution the abbey was sold and became a paper mill (the church was used for storage). In 1906 new owners, a branch of the Montgolfier ballooning family, undertook to restore it to its original Cistercian form. ■

Monasteries

The spread of Christianity, and in particular the development of the monasteries, was central to the growth and stability of the kingdom of France in the Middle Ages. Burgundy played a key role in the development of the monasteries in the ninth and tenth centuries. Two of the greatest medieval foundations were at Cluny and Cîteaux, in the heart of this powerful duchy, which was both a crossroads and a relatively safe region.

Benedictines

The Benedictine order, founded in Italy by St. Benedict in 529, spread rapidly throughout Europe, with monasteries regulated according to the Benedictine rule of chastity, obedience, renunciation of the material world, and physical labor: "To work is to pray" was the motto. The monks were meant to do six to eight hours of work plus four hours of prayer and four of reading. They were permitted no private property other than the habit they wore, a rope and scapular (cloak), a belt, and a knife.

In contrast to the hermetic principles of earlier monasteries, the Benedictines emphasized community—sleeping, praying, reading, and eating together according to a precise daily routine of work and worship. All power resided in the abbot, and each

monastery was self-supporting. The first monks built their church and dwellings on virgin territory, then supported themselves by farming, planting vineyards, and raising livestock.

Oases of order at a time of chaotic temporal government, the monasteries established a hierarchy of power that quickly made them influential throughout Europe. Large (an important monastery might have a thousand or more people attached to it—more populous than most towns at the time), prosperous, secure, and disciplined, they were often centers of learning and culture.

Cluny

By the tenth century, the Benedictines had become victims of their own success. The abbots were increasingly corrupt, and monks neglected their vows. In response to this decadence, Cluny (see p. 207) was founded in 910, reforming the Benedictine order and spreading its influence over much of Europe. Eventually Cluny established some

Prison

Forge

Infirmary

Scriptorium

Dormitory

The dormitory (right) and cloisters (far right) at Fontenay Abbey embody the principles of austerity and simplicity followed by the Cistercians.

1,450 daughter houses and the original monastery grew so huge that it required 40 farms, each with its own chapel, to support it.

Cistercians

But Cluny, too, fell into decadent ways. In reaction, the Cistercian order was founded at Cîteaux, near Dijon, in 1098. Its austerity attracted a young nobleman named Bernard, who was destined to become one of the most influential religious leaders of his age. Swiftly finding a following, Bernard established his own monastery at Clairvaux in northern Burgundy. Thousands came to hear him preach, and it was his passionate oratory that launched the Second Crusade from Vézelay. The Cistercian movement grew rapidly, founding hundreds of new monasteries, including Pontigny and Fontenay (see p. 203) in Burgundy.

Bernard revived the Rule of St. Benedict, stressing the importance of manual work, poverty, and simplicity, and railing against the excesses of Cluny. "Silence and perpetual remoteness from all secular turmoil" was his ideal, in order to "compel the mind to meditate upon celestial things." His veto on superfluous decoration had a profound effect upon Cistercian architecture: For the Cistercians, form followed function, and the austerity of their buildings reflected the asceticism of their lives.

By the time of the Revolution, however, even these great abbeys had become corrupt, exploiting the people and abusing their influence. Deep popular resentment against the power of the church and the monasteries was expressed in brutal dismemberment of the buildings during and after the Revolution. Cluny was totally destroyed; Cîteaux is still a monastery though most of the buildings are not old; Pontigny and Fontenay have been restored to offer a vision of monastic life as it was intended to be. ■

A Cistercian monastery, built according to the principles laid out by Bernard of Clairvaux. Bernard believed that monasteries should be self-supporting and provide everything necessary to sustain life.

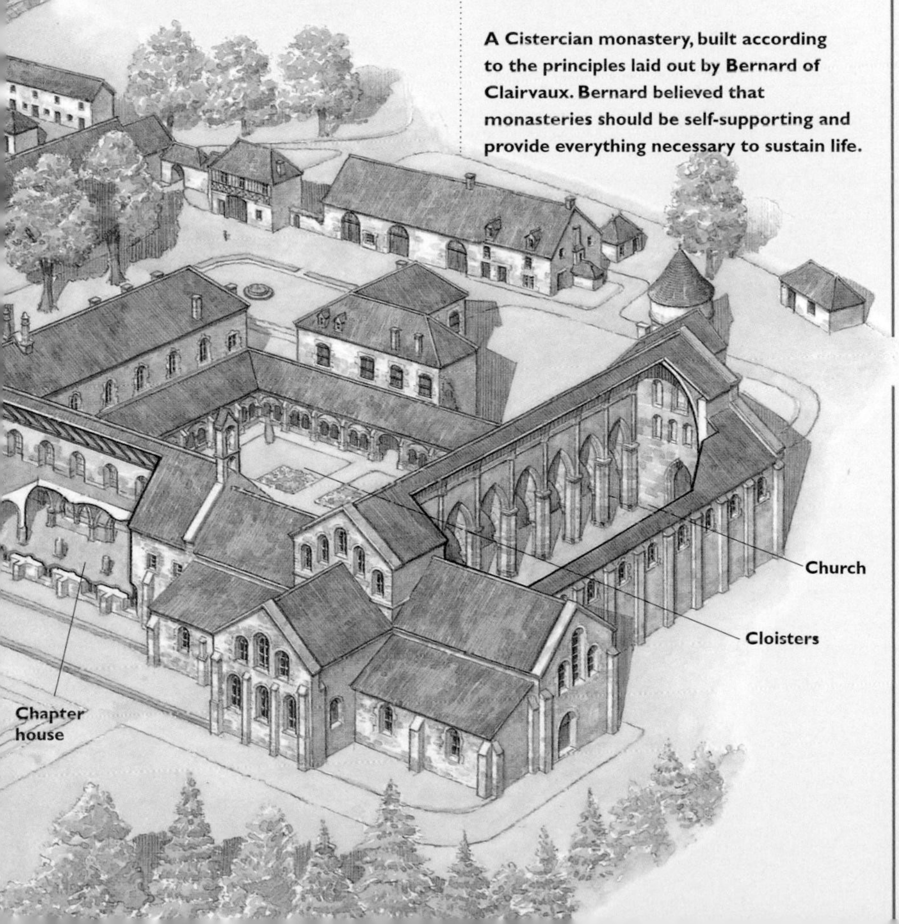

Church

Cloisters

Chapter house

Autun

FROM A HILL JUST SOUTH OF AUTUN THERE IS A GLORIOUS view of the city, revealing its Roman origins and its medieval heart. Founded by the Emperor Augustus in the first century B.C., Autun was one of the most important cities of Roman Gaul.

The ancient town of Autun around the Romanesque Cathédrale St.-Lazare. The Flamboyant spire was added in the 15th century.

Autun

◪ 191 C4

Visitor information

✉ 3 avenue Charles-de-Gaulle

☎ 03 85 86 80 38

The substantial legacies of that period include the sanctuary of the Temple of Janus, the Porte d'Arroux with its sculptured arcades and columns (still the main entrance to the town from the north), and the Porte St.-André, designed with separate arches for chariots and for pedestrian traffic. The remains of the Roman theater come to life every August with an evocative spectacle of Gallo-Roman life, complete with chariot races.

But this is also a medieval city, still partly cinched by ramparts. Its greatest treasure, the 12th-century Romanesque **Cathédrale St.-Lazare,** is famed for its incomparable sculpture. Gislebertus d'Autun was one of the greatest sculptors of an age that yields the names of few individual artists, and

the tympanum over the west portal was his masterpiece. It was saved from destruction during the Revolution because it had been plastered over earlier in the 18th century. His vivid rendering of the Last Judgment, carved between 1130 and 1135, prompted André Malraux to describe him as "a Romanesque Cézanne." The chapter house contains more of his work, including capitals depicting the "Suicide of Judas" and the "Dream of the Three Kings" (in bed with their crowns on).

The **Musée Rolin** (*5 rue des Bancs, tel 03 85 52 09 76, closed Tues.–Mon. Oct.–March &Tues. April–Sept.*) is housed in the adjacent 15th-century mansion, built by Nicolas Rolin, who founded the Hôtel-Dieu in Beaune (see p. 197). It contains Gallo-Roman antiquities, as well as Romanesque and Gothic works. The jewel of the collection is again by Gislebertus, a carved fragment taken from the cathedral and discovered built into a wall in 1856. This "Temptation of Eve" depicts Eve with sensuality and subtlety, as she takes the apple.

On the summit of Mont Beuvray, southwest of Autun, is **Bibracte,** a Gallic *oppidum* (camp). Here Vercingétorix called a council of war of the Gallic tribes in 52 B.C. in a doomed attempt to defeat the Romans. The **Musée Bibracte** (*St.-Léger-sous-Beuvray, closed mid-Nov.–mid-March*) documents this important site.

Autun is a gateway to the Morvan, rolling country ideal for walking or horseback riding. ∎

Cluny

THE NAME OF CLUNY, FOUNDED IN 910, ECHOES THROUGH the centuries. For hundreds of years the abbey was the most influential power in Christendom, described by Pope Urban II as the "light of the world." But the great abbey buildings, the pinnacle of Romanesque architecture, were torn down after the Revolution, leaving only gutted remains.

Cluny

191 C4

Visitor information

✉ 6 rue Mercière

☎ 03 85 59 05 34

🕐 Closed Nov.–March

Paray-le-Monial

191 C4

Visitor information

✉ avenue Jean-Paul II

☎ 03 85 81 10 92

Berzé-la-Ville

191 C4

Chapelle aux Moines

☎ 03 85 36 66 52

🕐 Closed Nov.–March

Belfry of the Blessed Water, part of the remaining south transept of Cluny, once the greatest abbey in Christendom

Of the original building only the south transept and tower still stand. The town of Cluny covers much of the rest, though excavations show the west end of the nave. The church was 600 feet (180 m) long with two towers and double aisles, the interior painted in glowing Byzantine colors. For centuries it resounded to the strains of Gregorian chant, and as if to emphasize the importance of music here, some surviving capitals are carved with scenes of musicians and their instruments. The work of the unknown "master of Cluny," these carvings, now displayed in the **Musée Ochier** in the 15th-century abbey palace, had a major influence on other sculptors, notably at Vézelay and Autun.

To set Cluny in context, visit the Burgundian churches, large and small, that were influenced by it. The architecture of the slightly older abbey church of **Tournus** (*Visitor information, place Carnot, tel 03 85 27 00 20*), 20 miles (33 km) to the northeast, is powerful and confident, with perfect round arches and attenuated columns. The 11th-century basilica of **Paray-le-Monial** to the west gives an idea of what Cluny actually looked like, on a reduced scale. Soaring to a daring 71 feet (22 m), the nave is crowned by austere, graceful vaulting. Clerestory windows provide the only clue as to how Cluny was lit.

The **Chapelle aux Moines,** part of a Cluniac foundation at

Berzé-la-Ville, southeast of Cluny, hints at how magnificently the abbey was decorated. The apse and walls are covered in frescoes of Christ in Glory surrounded by saints, in rich tones of ocher, blue, gold, and violet—"the golden gloom of Byzantium."

The **Circuit des Églises Romanes** (*details from Mâcon tourist office, p. 210*) is a self-guided driving tour that takes in ancient churches including the priory of Anzy-le-Duc; Iguerande; and St.-Hilaire at Semur-en-Brionnais, with its octagonal belfry. ∎

The Jura

THE MOUNTAINOUS REGION OF THE JURA, ON THE SWISS
border, covers much of the old region of Franche-Comté, once ruled
by the great duchy of Burgundy and only part of the nation of France
since the 17th century. The Jura's ancient mountains, which give their
name to the Jurassic period, have yielded several important dinosaur
remains. Deep valleys with rushing torrents divide the rolling
plateaus: The lakes and rivers teem with trout, carp, and pike, and
forests of black spruce, pine, and broad-leaved trees cover the slopes.

**Comité
Départemental du
Jura, Visitor
information**

✉ 8 rue Louis-
Rousseau, Lons-le-
Saunier

☎ 03 84 87 08 88

Arbois

🗺 191 D4

Visitor information

✉ rue de l'Hôtel de
Ville

☎ 03 84 66 55 50

Arc-et-Senans

🗺 191 D5

Visitor information

☎ 03 81 57 43 21

Ornans

🗺 191 E5

Visitor information

✉ 7 rue Pierre-Vernier

☎ 03 81 62 21 50

**Musée de la
Maison Natale
de Gustave
Courbet**

✉ Maison Natale de
l'Artiste, place
Robert-Fernie,
Ornans

☎ 03 81 62 23 30

🕐 Closed Tues.
Nov.–April

💲 $$

Visitors come to enjoy nature,
walking on the lower slopes, canoe-
ing on the rivers, and, in the winter
months, skiing. This is also France's
wettest region, though there is a dry
period in midsummer. Although it
is no longer as inaccessible as it
used to be, the Jura still is home to
plenty of wildlife, including the
lynx, otter, and mountain hare. The
high rainfall waters peat bogs,
which provide a habitat for rare
birds, butterflies, and mosses.
Cirque-de-Baumes, near Lons-
le-Saunier, curiously, shelters a
pocket of Mediterranean flora and
fauna amid its limestone cliffs.
Throughout the region, wildflowers
carpet the roadsides and meadows
in spring and summer.

Dotting the valleys are the Jura's
distinctive wooden houses, with
enormous chimneys serving as
rooms, smokehouses, or even
escape hatches when snow buries
the house.

The Jura yields some of France's
favorite cheeses, such as Morbier
and dense, creamy Vacherin. The
region also produces its own wine,
mostly from a small region around
the pretty town of **Arbois,** best
known for its Tavel rosé. You
should try *vin jaune*, a sherrylike
wine from Château-Chalon. You
may also find the increasingly rare
dessert wine known as *vin de paille*,
made from grapes left out in the
sun on straw mats before they are
pressed. Arbois is also famed as the
birthplace of Louis Pasteur, the
inventor of pasteurization, whose
house and laboratory are preserved
in the **Maison de Pasteur.**

LOUE VALLEY

For a brief visit to the Jura, you
could not do better than to follow
the course of the Loue Valley for
stunning scenery, cascading water-
falls, and eye-stretching mountain
views. Start from **Arc-et-Senans,**
with its ambitious 18th-century
new town, the Saline Royale. Built
to exploit the local salt mines, it was
never completely finished. Take the
D17 north to Quingey. Now follow
the D101 east, changing to the
D102 and D103 successively to fol-
low the river upstream to **Ornans,**
the most charming town in the
valley, with flower-decked balconies
overhanging the river. Famous as
the birthplace of the great realist
painter, Gustave Courbet, who
loved the region and frequently
portrayed it, the town boasts
several of his paintings, displayed
in his childhood home, now the
Musée Courbet.

Continue up the valley on the
D67, which provides stopping
places for admiring the view. Two
miles (3 km) past Mouthier, you
reach the dramatic source of the
Loue, springing in a great torrent
from a cavern in the rock, only a
short walk from the road. East of
Salins-les-Bains, the source of the
Lison River makes another beautiful

sight, a waterfall plunging into a deep green pool.

The **Région des Lacs,** strung out along the Ain Valley south of Champagnole, is a landscape of villages and waterfalls, mountains and forests. One of the most glorious sights is the spectacular cataracts of the **Cascades du Hérisson.** Reach them on foot from the village of Doucier, below the Pic de l'Aigle. The path climbs, steeply at times, through forest to the stunning Cascade de l'Éventail and then on to the Cascade du Grand Saut, where the path passes behind the falling waters.

To the west is **Lons-le-Saunier** (*Visitor information, place du 11 Novembre, tel 03 84 24 65 01*), a pleasant little town to stay in, handy for many of the region's sights. It was built over a thermal spring first used by the Romans and now supplying both its thermal baths and its swimming pool. ■

The pretty town of Arbols, center of the Jura's wine region and the childhood home of Louis Pasteur

More places to visit in Burgundy & the Jura

The 17th-century Vauban citadel in Besançon offers a good view of the old town.

BESANÇON

Set in a loop of the Doubs River, the ancient fortress town of Besançon is the capital of Franche-Comté. It now specializes in watch-making. Appropriately, a 19th-century astronomical clock adorns the 12th-century Gothic **Cathédrale St.-Jean.** Birthplace of novelist Victor Hugo and the Lumière brothers, pioneers of cinema, it is a historic town with some noble 17th-century architecture. The **Musée des Beaux-Arts** has works by Courbet, Ingres, and Boucher.

🏰 191 E5 **Visitor information** ✉ 2 place de la 1ère Armée Française ☎ 03 81 80 92 55

CHÂTILLON-SUR-SEINE

Châtillon, near the source of the Seine River, is the proud possessor of the Treasure of Vix, shown in the **Musée Archéologique** (*7 rue du Bourg, tel 03 80 91 24 67*). This Gaulish cache was unearthed in 1953 in Vix, 4 miles (6 km) northwest of Châtillon. A sixth century B.C. Celtic princess was buried here in a chariot, decked in jewels and gold, and surrounded by artifacts, notably the great Krater of Vix, the largest surviving bronze vessel from antiquity.

🏰 191 C6 **Visitor information** ✉ place Marmont ☎ 03 80 91 13 19

MÂCON

The southernmost of the Burgundy wine towns, Mâcon gives its name to the Mâconnais wine region, which produces red, rosé, and white wines, most notably Pouilly-Fuissé and the similar Saint-Véran. Visit the **Maison des Vins** (*484 avenue-le-Lattre-de-Tassigny, tel 03 85 22 91 11*) for information and tastings (and a good restaurant). An early center of Protestantism, Mâcon destroyed all 14 of its Romanesque churches. The pleasant **Place des Herbes** has a market and an extraordinary 15th-century timber-framed building (conveniently, a café), elaborately carved with monsters and risqué figures. The nearby **Rocher du Solutré,** a huge lime-stone outcrop where the bones of hundreds of thousands of prehistoric reindeer and horses have been found, has an excellent underground museum.

🏰 191 D4 **Visitor information** ✉ place St.-Pierre ☎ 03 85 21 07 07

NEVERS

Famous for its faience, which originated with Italian artists in the 16th century, Nevers has a good collection displayed in the **Musée Municipal** (*rue St.-Genest*). You can buy faience from the 17th-century Faïencerie Montagnon (*rue de la Porte du Croux, tel 03 86 71 96 90*). Architectural highlights in Nevers include well-preserved 12th-century ramparts, the 15th-century Palais Ducal, the Romanesque Église St.-Étienne, and the **Cathédrale St.-Cyr,** with the remains of a sixth-century bap-tistry and a 13th-century Gothic nave.

🏰 190 B4 **Visitor information** ✉ Palais Ducal, rue Sabatier ☎ 03 86 68 46 00

RONCHAMP

The chapel of **Notre-Dame-du-Haut** at Ronchamp is a technical and aesthetic tour de force, built in 1950–54 by the architect Le Corbusier. The most revolutionary work of his sculptural, antirationalist period, it is molded expressively in concrete, and creates the perfect atmosphere for prayer and meditation.

🏰 191 E5 **Visitor information** ✉ place du 14 Juillet ☎ 03 84 63 50 82 ∎

Mont Blanc and Lac Blanc combine to produce stunning alpine scenery.

Rhône Valley & the Alps

From the snowfields of the Alps to the olive groves of the Drôme Valley, from the starry restaurants of Lyon to remote mountain refuges, the Rhône–Alpes region embraces a huge variety of landscapes and activities. Wine lovers, skiers, walkers, and culture vultures will all feel at home here.

The mighty Rhône River flows right through the region, a critically important trade route connecting north and south. Towns and cities that have thrived as a result stud its banks. The Alps provide a dramatic backdrop, a skyline of peaks dominated by Mont Blanc, the highest mountain in Europe.

The main hub of the region is Lyon, France's second city, an important industrial metropolis with a lively cultural life. Its museums are world class, with a fine arts museum second only to the Louvre in Paris. It is also justly famed for its cuisine, with a wealth of exceptional restaurants.

The Romans colonized the area in the second century B.C., and substantial Roman remains can be found in Lyon as well as at Vienne and St.-Romain-en-Gal.

The Alps boast some of the world's top-flight ski resorts, such as Chamonix and Courchevel. But the mountains also make a beguiling summer retreat, with limpid blue lakes for swimming and boating, and gracious spa towns. Several major nature reserves protect the rare wild flora and fauna that abound in the higher reaches.

The peasant life of the mountain farmers and shepherds is not as hard as it once was, but they retain the distinctive vernacular architecture. The large timber or stone farmhouses still have the wide balconies essential for winter stores. Imaginative regional museums pay tribute to centuries of traditional life.

To the north lies the rich farmland of the Bresse province, known for its *appellation contrôlée* chickens. To the south is Nyons, famous for its huge variety of olives. The Beaujolais and Côtes du Rhône vineyards yield good everyday drinking wines as well as individual appellations of Beaujolais and Hermitage. Farther south the region meets Provence in the gorges of the Ardèche, and the lavender fields, olive groves, and sunflower fields of the Drôme Valley. ∎

Lyon

A FEW DAYS IN THE GREAT CITY OF LYON IS A TREAT, NOT least because it has every right to call itself the gastronomic capital of France. Lyon is the second largest city in France: Its key position at the confluence of the Rhône and Saône Rivers has historically made it a major hub on a vital trade route.

Lyon

[A] 191 D3

Visitor information

[✉] place Bellecour

[☎] 04 72 77 69 69

Musée de la Civilisation Gallo-Romaine

[✉] 17 rue Cléberg

[☎] 04 72 38 81 90

[⏱] Closed Mon.–Tues.

[$] $

Musée Historique de Lyon & Musée de la Marionnette

[✉] Hôtel Gadagne, 1 place du Petit-Collège

[☎] 04 78 42 03 61

[⏱] Closed Tues.

[$] $

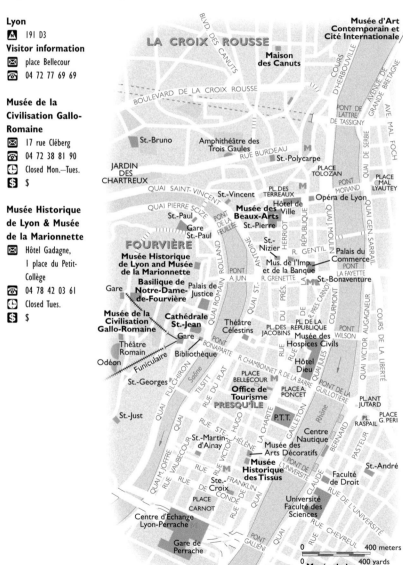

The history of Lyon can be read in its monuments and streets. It was founded by the Romans as Lugdunum in 43 B.C., and their great amphitheater on the hill of **Fourvière** is a good place to start a visit. To get there, walk up the winding Chemin du Rosaire, or take the funicular railroad from opposite the cathedral. The view from the top reveals the city on its peninsula (the Presqu'île) between the Rhône and the Saône. On a clear day you can see the Alps.

The ruins constitute the earliest Roman site outside Rome. The **Musée de la Civilisation Gallo-Romaine**—a modern building cleverly tucked into the hillside, with vast windows overlooking the amphitheater—does a splendid job of evoking everyday Roman life. Its superb collection includes mosaics (notably of a chariot race), inscriptions, statues, and coins. Since Roman times, Fourvière has been a site of sanctuaries, the most recent one being the 19th-century **Basilique Notre-Dame-de-Fourvière**

(*place Fourvière*), all turrets, marble, and stained glass.

OLD LYON

At the bottom of the Fourvière hill, on the west bank of the Saône, lies old Lyon. One of the largest ensembles of Renaissance buildings in Europe, it is now a protected area, its facades all freshly painted. In the 15th century Louis XI granted Lyon the right to hold fairs that attracted merchants from all over Europe. Magnificent *hôtels particuliers*, or town houses, were built and, since many of the merchants were Italian, there is a distinct Florentine quality to the architecture. Each mansion had its own alley (*traboule*) off the street, an internal courtyard with a well, and often a turret with a spiral staircase. The 16th-century Hôtel Gadagne houses the **Musée Historique de Lyon** and the **Musée de la Marionnette,** devoted to the famous puppets of Lyon. At the heart of the old quarter is the **Cathédrale St.-Jean,** a perfect synthesis of Romanesque

The view across Lyon from the Basilique Notre-Dame-de-Fourvière

Musée de la Résistance et de la Déportation
- 14 avenue Berthelot
- 04 72 73 33 54
- Closed Mon. & Tues.
- $

Musée Historique des Tissus
- 34 rue de la Charité
- 04 78 38 42 00
- Closed Mon.
- $

Musée des Beaux-Arts

- ✉ 20 place des Terreaux
- ☎ 04 72 10 17 40
- 🕐 Closed Mon. & Tues.
- 💲 $

Musée d'Art Contemporain

- ✉ Cité Internationale, 81 quai Charles-de-Gaulle
- ☎ 04 72 69 17 17
- 💲 $

Traboules, covered passageways, linked houses, since space was too restricted for roads.

and Gothic styles, built between 1180 and 1480.

The Presqu'île is the center of modern Lyon, where life revolves around Place Bellecour and its fountains, flowers, and statues. The best stores are here, especially around Rue de la République, Rue Émile-Zola, Rue Gasparin, and Rue du Président Herriot. Silk scarves make good souvenirs, recalling Lyon's famous silk industry.

To the north of the city, the hill of La Croix-Rousse is stacked with the houses of the silk workers (*canuts*) who made Lyon's fortune in the early 19th century. Their houses had to be tall to accommodate the huge Jacquard looms that transformed the industry from 1804 on. Visit the **Maison des Canuts** (*10 rue d'Ivry, tel 04 78*

28 62 04, closed Sun.) to see a traditional loom in operation. Many of the houses have been converted into fashionable lofts, but the area is still riddled with traboules. These passages played a key part in sheltering members of the Resistance during World War II, and it was here that their leader Jean Moulin was captured by the Nazis. The **Musée de la Résistance et de la Déportation,** housed partly in the cells in which the Gestapo tortured their prisoners, makes a thought-provoking memorial.

The history of Lyon's silk industry and fabrics in general is shown in the **Musée Historique des Tissus.** Set in an 18th-century town house, it displays a superb collection of silks, ancient and modern, Western and Oriental.

The artistic life of the city revolves around Place des Terreaux. Here the **Musée des Beaux-Arts,** in a former Benedictine convent, displays one of the largest collections in France. There are works by Veronese, Tintoretto, Rubens, and El Greco as well as flower paintings by the Lyon school which inspired many silk designs. Jean Nouvel's glass-and-steel dome for the neoclassic opera house towers over the Place des Terreaux, embellished by the modern sculpture of Daniel Buren. The **Musée d'Art Contemporain** is in the Cité Internationale, a modern development on the east bank of the Rhône.

And then, of course, there is the food. As an introduction, you might visit the market on Quai St.-Antoine or the indoor market at Les Halles. Restaurants range from grand establishments run by star chefs to small family-run *restaurants du quartier.* Finally, there are the *bouchons*: bistros serving local specialties such as tripe or sausages, washed down with Beaujolais. ■

Beaujolais country

BEAUJOLAIS IS ONE WINE REGION WHERE THE LANDSCAPE
doesn't play second fiddle to the vines: Rolling, wooded hills are
punctuated by golden-stone châteaus and *vignerons'* houses with
wine cellars on the ground floor, external staircases, and verandas.

The best wine comes from the
north, where a day's drive could take
in most of the ten Beaujolais *crus*,
allowing time for leisurely *dégustations*. **Villefranche-sur-Saône,**
20 miles (32 km) north of Lyon, is
the main town of Beaujolais, a
miniature version of Lyon with its
Italianate mansions, elegant courtyards, and small cafés serving fresh
Beaujolais with *saucisson*. **Beaujeu,**
northeast of Villefranche, is another
ancient wine town, where the
Hospices de Beaujeu have held wine
auctions since the 12th century.
Taste local wine in the **Place de
l'Hôtel de Ville,** where there is
also a museum of local traditions.

Quiet winding roads (D26 and
D18 northeast from Beaujeu) lead
to the **Terrasse de Chiroubles,**
where you have wide views of the
vineyards. Continuing north on the
D26 you come to **Juliénas,** where
every building appears to be a wine
cellar, even the church. Next stop
might be the eponymous windmill
of **Moulin-à-Vent** (to the south of
Juliénas on the D266), for wide-
ranging views of the Saône Valley,
and a chance to taste the oldest *cru*
in Beaujolais. **Romanèche-
Thorins,** nearby, is home to
enthusiast Georges Duboeuf,
whose Hameau du Vin offers a
wide variety of wines. In **Fleurie,**
west on the D32, look for the
Chapelle de la Madone in the vineyards, and try the local specialty,
andouillettes au Fleurie—chitterling sausages cooked in Fleurie
wine. **Villié-Morgan,** south on
the D68, offers wine tastings in the
cellar of an 18th-century mansion.
Nearby are **Château de Pizay,**
with its splendid topiary gardens,
and the Renaissance **Château de
Corcelles,** painted by Maurice
Utrillo (1883–1955). Farther south
are the village of **Brouilly** and
the **Côte de Brouilly,** vineyards
on the slopes of Mont Brouilly,
followed by **La Chaise,** a fine
17th-century château with gardens
designed by Le Nôtre.

For delightful château accommodations combined with good
Beaujolais wine try the **Château
de Bagnols** (*Tel 04 74 71 40 00*),
southwest of Villefranche. ■

**Villefranche-
sur-Saône**
🄰 191 C3
Visitor information
✉ 96 rue de la Sous-
Préfecture
☎ 04 74 07 27 40

Beaujeu
🄰 191 C3
Visitor information
✉ sq. de Grandhan
☎ 04 74 69 22 88

**Chapelle de
la Madone
overlooks
the vineyards
of Fleurie.**

The Mer de Glace glacier above Chamonix

Mont Blanc & the mountains

Chamonix-Mont Blanc
🅰 191 E3
Visitor information
✉ 85 place Triangle-de-l'Amitié
☎ 04 50 53 00 24

Parc National de la Vanoise Information
✉ 135 rue du Docteur-Julliand, Chambéry
☎ 04 79 68 65 76

Visitor information
Thonon-les-Bains
✉ place du Marché
☎ 04 50 71 55 55
Évian-les-Bains
✉ pl. Pont d'Allinges
☎ 04 50 75 04 26

FROM LAKE GENEVA ALMOST TO THE MEDITERRANEAN, the majestic snowy peaks of the French Alps offer awe-inspiring mountain landscapes. Most dramatic of all is Mont Blanc, Europe's highest peak at 15,770 feet (4,807 m).

At the foot of Mont Blanc sits **Chamonix,** the world capital of mountaineering. Its **Musée Alpin** presents a history of Mont Blanc and its early explorers. Non-climbers can make the spectacular ascent of neighboring summits by cable car: 12,609 feet (3,842 m) up the **Aiguille du Midi,** or 8,408 feet (2,526 m) up **Le Brevent,** both of which give fabulous views of Mont Blanc. Go early to avoid the crowds and midday mists, and take warm clothes. If you have no head for heights, take the rack railroad up to the glacier of the **Mer de Glace.** Chamonix today is a year-round resort, with swimming, golf, and tennis, as well as its winter skiing.

You do not have to be an aficionado of snow to enjoy the Alps. In summer, the air is fresh and clear and the light sharp, the high mountain passes are open, and drifts of alpine flowers cover the pastures. The best way to experience the beauty of the region is by hiking (*see p. 385 for sources of information, or ask at the Chamonix tourist office*). Never forget, though, that these are major mountains and always take the usual precautions, since even in summer the weather can change quickly. Make sure you have warm clothing, good boots, a whistle, food, and a map, and tell someone where you are heading and when you should arrive.

The mountain region east of the Rhône formed the independent principality of Savoie until it was ceded to France in 1860. It remained poor and remote until first alpinism and then skiing transformed its economy. Now the mountains and crystalline lakes attract visitors year-round.

NATURE RESERVES

The Alps remain a haven for a rich variety of flora and fauna. Savoie contains five major nature reserves, most notably the Vanoise, France's first national park. In this superb high mountain habitat lying between Courchevel and Val-d'Isère, you might see chamois, ibex, and even golden eagles. Remote pastures support countless wildflower species, including crocuses, blue and yellow gentians, numerous lilies and orchids, alpine anemones, and tulips.

LAKES

Ringed by snowy mountains, the lakes are an unforgettable sight. **Thonon-les-Bains** and **Évian-les-Bains** are both charming spa towns on the banks of Lac Léman (Lake Geneva); from both towns

passenger boats cross the lake to Switzerland. **Aix-les-Bains,** on the banks of Lac du Bourget, is a popular spa town; a boat trip on the lake can include a visit to the Benedictine **Abbaye de Haute-combe.** Rebuilt in 19th-century neo-Gothic, the abbey church contains the tombs of the Savoie kings.

Annecy, on the banks of Lac d'Annecy, makes an ideal base for touring the region. It rejoices in a charming old quarter with pastel facades, a château dating from the 12th century, canals and bridges, lakeside cafés, and beaches. ∎

Visitor information

Megève

☒ Masion des Frères

☎ 04 50 21 27 28

Morzine

☒ place de la Crusaz

☎ 04 50 74 72 72

Albertville

☒ 11 rue Pargoud

☎ 04 79 32 04 22

Val-d'Isère

www.val-disere.com

☒ Maison de Val-d'Isère

☎ 04 79 06 06 60

Annecy at night, with the street-lights reflected in the Thiou canal

Ski resorts

With high altitudes, reliable snow, the very latest in lifts and snowmaking systems, and a wide variety of *pistes* (trails),. France offers some of the best skiing in the world for all levels of expertise. Connections between the valleys and pistes are good, enabling you to ski long distances from one valley to the next and really explore the mountains.

Accommodations range from four-star hotels to self-catering chalets, and there are plenty of restaurants. Most of the resorts are within a three-hour drive of the airports at Chambéry, Geneva, or Lyon; Chamonix, Mégève, and Morzine are one hour from Geneva.

Chamonix-Mont Blanc is the capital of alpine skiing and site of the first Winter Olympics in 1924. ∎

Annecy

🅰 191 E3

Visitor information

☒ Bonlieu, 1 rue Jean-Jaurès

☎ 04 50 45 00 33

Grenoble

Grenoble
191 D2
Visitor information
14 rue de la
République
04 76 42 41 41

Musée Dauphinois
30 rue Maurice-Gignoux
04 76 85 19 01
Closed Mon.
$

The cable car
across the Isère
River in Grenoble

Capital of the old province of Dauphiné, Grenoble is the only large city in the Alps, handsomely set at the confluence of the Isère and Drac Rivers.

Grenoble prospered from the 19th-century discovery of hydro-electricity, and rapidly developed into a center of chemical and nuclear research. The pace of change has accelerated even further since it hosted the Winter Olympics in 1968. A fine base for visiting the region, the city also has a lively cultural life, animated by its large student population.

The best way to see the city is to take the vertiginous cable car up over the city to the **Fort de la Bastille,** where orientation tables help to interpret the mountain views; there is also a good café on the terrace. Walk down from the fort through the Jardin des Dauphins to

the **Musée Dauphinois,** an excellent regional museum in a 17th-century convent building.

To see the old quarter, with its 13th-century buildings and church, head for Place St.-André. The cathedral and the bishops' palace are on Place Notre-Dame. Place Grenette and Place Victor Hugo are both lively squares, good for cafés and shopping. The former Hôtel de Ville houses the **Musée Stendhal** (*1 rue Hector Berlioz, tel 04 76 54 44 14, closed Mon.*), devoted to the Grenoble-born writer; there is a Stendhal route in town. The arts are well supported by the **Musée de la Peinture et de la Sculpture** (*5 place de Lavalette, tel 04 76 63 44 44, closed a.m. & Tues.*) and **Le Cargo Maison de la Culture** (*4 rue Paul Claudel, tel 04 38 49 95 95, closed Sun.– Mon.*), for dance, music, and theater. ∎

Chambéry

The historic capital of once-Italian Savoie, Chambéry is another good base for a visit to the Alps. Its dignified old quarter is full of Italianate mansions and little covered passages. The extraordinary Fontaine des Éléphants on the Boulevard de la Colonne is a monument to the Comte de Boigne, who amassed a fortune in India in the 18th century and left much of it to the municipality. The fountain has become the symbol of the town.

For a hundred years or so in the 15th and 16th centuries, the Holy Shroud was kept here in the Chapelle des Ducs de Savoie, and Chambéry became a pilgrimage town. But in 1578, the shroud was taken to Turin, when that city became the administrative capital of the House of Savoie.

Just southeast of Chambéry is **Les Charmettes,** the country retreat of philosopher Jean-Jacques Rousseau, now restored just as he described it in his *Confessions.* ■

Chambéry
- 191 E3
Visitor information
- ✉ 24 boulevard de la Colonne
- ☎ 04 79 33 42 47

Musée Jean-Jacques Rousseau
- ✉ 22 chemin des Charmettes
- ☎ 04 79 33 39 44
- 🕐 Closed Tues.
- 💲 $

The Fontaine des Éléphants in Chambéry, nicknamed *quatre sans culs* (four without behinds)

Gorges de l'Ardèche

THE GORGES DE L'ARDÈCHE, IN THE FAR SOUTH OF THE
Rhône Valley and the Alps region, make a truly stunning tour. For
some 20 miles (32 km) between Vallon-Pont-d'Arc and St.-Martin-
d'Ardèche, the D290 twists along the rim of the gorge above the river.

**Gorges de
l'Ardèche**
🅰 191 C1
Visitor information
✉ 1 place de
l'Ancienne Gare,
Vallon-Pont-d'Arc
☎ 04 75 88 04 01

Before heading out, take a good
look at **Pont d'Arc** itself, a natural
limestone bridge hollowed out by
the fast-flowing waters of the
Ardèche River. Along the route
there are heart-stopping views at
every turn, especially on the Haute

Corniche, perched dizzyingly high
above the river.
    Adventurous alternatives to dri-
ving include kayaking and white-
water rafting on the Ardèche: You
can rent kayaks in Vallon-Pont-
d'Arc and find transportation back

The limestone
cliffs of the
Gorges de
l'Ardèche,
overlooking the
fast-flowing
river below

at St.-Martin-d'Ardèche (*Visitor information at Vallon-Pont-d'Arc*). The Ardèche is one of France's fastest, and potentially most treacherous, rivers; early summer is the safest time for tackling its waters.

The limestone plateau around the gorge is riddled with caves. The huge **Grotte de la Madeleine,** just off the D290, bristles with stalagmites and stalactites; **Aven d'Orgnac** (*aven* means pothole), just to the west, has spectacular rock formations, colored red by iron oxides and sparkling with crystals. The museum here includes a reconstruction of a Stone Age settlement. The interior of **Aven de Marzal,** a little to the north, glitters with colored crystals like some Byzantium of the natural world. A museum of speleology includes centuries-old equipment used to explore the cave when it was first discovered. Pretty villages upstream of the gorge include 12th-century **Balazuc,** on a cliff above the Ardèche River, and **Vogüé,** tucked between cliff and river, with a 12th-century château. ■

More places to visit in the Rhône Valley & the Alps

BOURG-EN-BRESSE

The market town of Bourg-en-Bresse is famous gastronomically for its chickens, and culturally for the **Abbatiale de Brou,** just outside town. This example of Flamboyant Gothic architecture, built between 1505 and 1536 by Margaret of Austria, has a superbly carved facade, choir stalls, and rood screen. Most gorgeous of all are the tombs of Margaret; her husband, Philibert le Beau; and his mother, Margaret of Bourbon; sculpted in exquisite detail from Carrara marble.

 191 D3 **Visitor information** ✉ 6 ave. Alsace-Lorraine ☎ 04 74 22 49 40

BRIANÇON

The highest town in Europe, at 4,300 feet (1,310 m), Briançon is strategically placed on one of the main passes into Italy. A major stronghold, it was heavily fortified by Vauban, Louis XIV's indefatigable military architect. He also designed the solid Église de Notre-Dame set high on the defensive hill chosen for the citadel. Streams run down the narrow streets of this old part of town, and the views over the surrounding mountains are superb.

🔼 191 E2 **Visitor information** ✉ place du Temple ☎ 04 92 21 08 50

HAUTERIVES

Located about 15 miles (24 km) north of Romans-sur-Isère on the D538, the **Palais Idéal** at Hauterives (*Tel 04 75 68 81 19*) is an astonishing sight. This bizarre palace was built by a local postman, Ferdinand Cheval, using stones he collected on his route. His odd creation jumbles together a variety of Oriental architectural styles. Inside, Cheval inscribed how long it took him to build: "1879–1912: 10,000 days, 93,000 hours, 33 years of toil."

NYONS

Famous for its olives, Nyons is a charming town, with a climate resembling that of the Riviera thanks to sheltering mountains. The **Musée de l'Olivier** tells the story of olive cultivation. The best time to visit is market day (Thursday), when you can buy a huge variety of olives, as well as olive oil products such as soap and olive-based delicacies.

🔼 191 D1 **Visitor information** ✉ place de la Libération ☎ 04 75 26 10 35

PARC NATUREL RÉGIONAL DU VERCORS

The Vercors regional park protects the dense pine forests, magnificent waterfalls, and steep mountain gorges of the Vercors massif. A marked trail leads through the forest on the high plateau, which is a nature reserve. This quiet area was a center of the Resistance during World War II. Poignant cemeteries and memorials (in villages such as Nizier and Vassieux) commemorate the tragic events that took place here, in particular the German air attack in 1944 that destroyed several villages.

 191 D2 **Visitor information**
 Maison du Parc, Lans en Vercors
 04 76 94 38 26

PÉROUGES

Some 19 miles (30 km) northeast of Lyon, the ancient town of Pérouges perches atop a hill. Its prosperity, based on hand weaving, declined when 19th-century mechanization made its fabrics uneconomic. Careful restoration and an influx of artisans have brought it back to life. You can still see its original fortifications, old town gates, cobbled streets, timbered balconies, and the market place shaded by an ancient linden tree.

 191 D3 **Visitor information**
 Syndicat d'Initiative, Entrée de la Cité
 04 74 61 01 14

VIENNE

Vienne is one of France's most ancient cities. It boasts a tremendous architectural heritage: the **Temple d'Auguste et Livie,** built in 25 B.C. in the heart of the earlier Roman town, with a noble facade of Corinthian columns; the remains of the **Théâtre de Cybèle;** and the **Théâtre Antique,** once one of the largest amphitheaters in France. The **Musée des Beaux-Arts et d'Archéologie** has informative displays about the Roman city. The **Cathédrale St.-Maurice** is the most imposing of Vienne's ancient churches.

 191 D3 **Visitor information**  3 cours Brillier  04 74 53 80 30 ∎

On the road to Italy via the Col de Montgenèvre

The road southeast from La Malène snakes up the mountainside.

Massif Central

At the very center of France lies the mountainous region of the Massif Central. Its ancient core is the Auvergne, settled by humans probably longer than anywhere else in France. With a reputation for being tough and thrifty, the Auvergnats, who like to describe France as "the Auvergne with a bit of land around it," have traveled far in search of work. Their influence throughout France is considerable, from the many Auvergnat-run Paris cafés to the positions of power occupied by such Auvergnat politicians as Valery Giscard-d'Estaing, Georges Pompidou, and Jacques Chirac.

The Massif Central is a land with many faces. Most spectacular are the great volcanoes, their summits offering views of a lunar landscape pitted with huge craters. The rugged river gorges of the Tarn and the Jonte thrill countless visitors, whether they drive the canyons or navigate the rivers by kayak. South of the Auvergne, the wild uplands of the Cévennes plateau make a haven for wildflowers and rare birds. Such natural beauty and open countryside makes this an ideal region for walking, hiking, and sports of all kinds from river rafting to hang gliding. Those who prefer gentler occupations can choose from a host of scenic drives, or take a short break at one of the elegant spas, enjoyed for their therapeutic properties since the time of the Roman occupation.

The history of the Massif Central, so ancient that it can be appreciated only on a geological time scale, is explained in a number of museums, including a major new museum of volcanology under construction near Clermont-Ferrand. Regional museums evoke a firmly rooted traditional life, dependent on industries such as silkworm cultivation, knife production, agriculture, and cheesemaking. The magnificent blue sheep's cheese of Roquefort is an unrivaled classic even in this land of cheeses. Local architecture features granite farms, heavy schist-tiled roofs with dormer windows, and open wooden verandas for drying winter stores. The region is rich in medieval castles, Renaissance châteaus, and Romanesque churches. ■

Le Puy-en-Velay

DON'T RUSH INTO THE TOWN OF LE PUY: TAKE TIME TO gaze upon its extraordinary setting. The town sits in the middle of a high-rimmed plateau from which erupts a forest of volcanic cones. Perhaps its bizarre surroundings contributed to Le Puy's importance as an early place of worship. For centuries, pilgrims sought it out and it was the starting point for the first recorded pilgrimage to Santiago de Compostela, led by its bishop in A.D. 951.

Once in the town, start by climbing the **Rocher Corneille** for its panoramic view over the old town. Topping this volcanic cone is the massive statue of **Notre-Dame-de-France,** which you can climb up inside as far as the neck. It was made from melted-down cannon seized after the fall of Sebastopol in the Crimean War.

The old town clusters around the Rocher in a maze of narrow streets. Dominating them is the **Cathédrale Notre-Dame-du-Puy,** built on another volcanic pinnacle with a dramatic approach up the stone steps of Rue des Tables. Currently being restored, this 12th-century edifice demonstrates the Muslim influence that filtered along the pilgrim route: Its domes and the west facade, with pointed arches,

mosaics, and striped stonework, are unmistakably Eastern in flavor. Inside, the cathedral has lovely 13th-century frescoes and a copy of the Black Madonna, brought back from the Crusades and burned during the Revolution.

Just to the north of the Rocher Corneille there is an even more distinctive sight, the 11th-century Romanesque chapel of **St.-Michel-d'Aiguilhe** perched on the steepest of the volcanic cones. A 268-step climb leads to the chapel, which also displays an Eastern influence in the graceful curves and diamond patterns of the facade.

Lacemaking is a traditional industry in Le Puy, and the **Musée Crozatier** (*Jardin Henri Vinay, tel 04 71 09 38 90*) has a collection of handmade lace. ■

Le Puy-en-Velay
🅰 191 C2
Visitor information
✉ place du Breuil
☎ 04 71 09 38 41

Cathédrale Notre-Dame-du-Puy
☎ 04 71 05 45 52
Ⓢ Treasury, cloisters, & museum: $

St.-Michel-d'Aiguilhe
✉ Aiguilhe
☎ 04 71 09 50 03
🕐 Closed mid-Nov.–mid-Feb.
Ⓢ $

Volcanic cones dominate Le Puy-en-Velay, one topped with a chapel, another with a statue.

Volcanoes
of the Auvergne

**Parc Régional des
Volcans
d'Auvergne**

**Centre
d'Information et
de Découverte
Montlosier**
✉ 1.6 miles (2 km)
from Pic de La
Vache et de Lassolas
☎ 04 73 65 64 00

**Parc Régional
Livradois-Forez
Centre
d'Information**
✉ St.-Gervais-sous-
Meymont
☎ 04 73 95 57 57

AN EXTRAORDINARY LUNAR LANDSCAPE OF PURPLE CONES
and craters lies in the middle of France. Most of these *puys* (or peaks)
are included in the nature reserve of the Parc Régional des Volcans
d'Auvergne, based in the Puy-de-Dôme département to the west of
Clermont-Ferrand. Today they are all (we are assured) extinct, but
three million years ago regular eruptions spewed out the lava that has
created this strange and desolate terrain. A major new center,
Vulcania, due to open in 2001, is part of the Parc Régional des Volcans.

The volcanoes fall into three
groups: The Monts Dôme only
became extinct some 4,000 years
ago and are still dramatically
volcanic in shape. The Monts Dore
stopped erupting much longer ago
and their cones have been eroded
away to a smoother silhouette. The
Cantal volcano, originally huge, has
mostly eroded, leaving lava plugs in
a system of radiating valleys.

The whole area makes magnificent walking country, but the most
spectacular excursion is undoubtedly to the the summit of **Puy de
Dôme.** The most famous volcano

of all, it is the oldest and highest, at
4,805 feet (1,464 m), of the Monts
Dôme chain.

To the Celts, the Puy de Dôme
was a royal mountain, on which
they worshiped their god of war.
The Romans subsequently built a
huge temple of lava stones and
marble, dedicated to the god
Mercury. Not until the mid-18th
century was it confirmed that these
strange formations were actually
volcanoes. Until that time people
believed that the Romans had constructed them. The Auvergne is still
reputed to be a place of sorcery and

Long-distance footpaths

**Sign on the route
of a Grande
Randonnée**

The most celebrated account of
a walk in the Massif Central is
Robert Louis Stevenson's *Travels
with a Donkey in the Cévennes.* He
walked with his donkey Modestine
from le Monastier-sur-Gazeille,
south of Le Puy, to
Langogne. His journey
took him over the granite
massif of Mont Lozère to
Florac, and then on to St.-
Jean-du-Gard, and along the
Cévennes Corniche, a remarkable route with superb views of the
causses. Walkers can follow a similar path today, and Stevenson's actu-
al route is marked on the *Institut
Géographique National* (IGN) maps

of the area. This is magnificent
walking country and there are all
kinds of marked trails to follow.
The Grande Randonnée (GR)
routes are long-distance footpaths
for walks of several days or weeks;
for these, you will need information
on accommodations along the way
(see p. 383). The Petite Randonnée
(PR) routes are shorter walks,
varying from a few hours to one or
two days. They generally pass
through the best scenery in the
region. Never forget that in the
Massif Central, as in all mountain
regions, the weather changes quickly, so be sure that you are always
suitably equipped. ■

enchantment; some people believe that witches and sorcerers meet at the summit of the Puy de Dôme to perform magic rituals.

You can drive to the summit up a spiraling road (*toll*), or walk up the original zigzagging Roman track (*park at Ceyssat Pass*). Before choosing to walk up, bear in mind that this is considered one of the toughest legs on the grueling Tour de France bicycle race. At the top are an information center, observation tables, a restaurant, and a geology museum. The ruins of the Roman temple to Mercury lie just below the summit (*no access for visitors*).

From the top of the Puy de Dôme, the view encompasses, on a very clear day, almost an eighth of France. Certainly it surveys a chain of over a hundred volcanic puys—although often their peaks wore down or were blown off long ago. Many of the resulting craters filled with lakes. The view changes by the minute according to the weather and time of day; it's at its most awe inspiring at sunset, starring a stunning palette of colors and dramatic shadows. Sometimes the summit is above cloud level, and you look down from bright sunshine onto a white, fleecy sea.

To the south rises the Monts Dore chain. Topping this range is the **Puy de Sancy,** the highest point in central France at 6,185 feet (1,885 m) and source of the Dordogne River. You can reach the peak by cable car from the town of Le Mont-Dore, followed by a walk. ■

The rugged Puy de Sancy is the highest point in the entire Massif Central.

Drive along the Gorges du Tarn

South of the Massif Central, the Tarn and the Jonte Rivers have cut deep into the limestone plateaus, known as *causses*, creating spectacular canyons and gorges.

Not surprisingly, the Tarn Gorges are a highly popular tourist destination. As well as traveling by car or bicycle, you can rent kayaks or river rafts and go through the gorge on the river itself. Visit early or out of season to avoid the crowds. That said, nothing can detract from the grandeur of the plunging gorges, the colors of the cliffs changing subtly with the light.

The old tanning town of **Millau 1** makes a good touring base (*Visitor information, tel 05 65 60 02 42*) for the Tarn Gorges. Leave Millau going north on the N9-E11 and take the D907 northeast along the Tarn River. Near **Les Vignes 2**, about halfway along the canyon, zigzag up the D995 and then take the D46 to **Point Sublime 3**. From this vantage point you get a terrific view of the gorge and the river below. The most spectacular part of the gorge, Les Détroits, comes between Les Vignes and **La Malène 4**, a little village that has always been a key crossing place of the canyon. It is a good place from which to take a boat trip downriver (*Visitor information, tel 04 66 48 50 77 mid-June–mid-Sept., 04 66 48 53 44 out of season*). Farther on, the 15th-century **Château de la Caze** (*Tel 04 66 48 51 01*) has an excellent restaurant.

Once you arrive at **Ste.-Énimie 5**, you have a choice of routes. The longer one takes the D907 east to just beyond Ispagnac, then right on the N106 to **Florac 6**, then the D907 south into the Parc National des Cévennes. At the junction of the D996 and D983 you can take the D996 to Meyrueis (see below) or follow the D983, D9, and D260 along the **Corniche des Cévennes** for 31 miles (50 km) to **St.-Jean-du-Gard 7** (*Visitor information, tel 04 66 85 32 11*). The corniche has superb views. It was originally cut by Louis XIV in pursuit of the Camisards, the local Protestant rebels who fought hard for their religious independence in the early 18th century. St.-Jean-du-Gard has a good museum of local life, the **Musée des Vallées Cévenoles** (*95 Grande-Rue, tel 04 66 85 10 48*).

Alternatively, you can head south from Ste.-Énimie on the D986 to Meyrueis across the **Causse Méjean.** This glorious plateau, spread with flowers in spring, nurtures rare birds including the griffon vulture, recently reintroduced here. From **Meyrueis 8** (*Tourist information, tel 04 66 45 60 33*), the D996 follows the **Gorges de la Jonte** back toward Millau, passing some famous caves on the way: **Aven Armand**, a vast grotto full of colored stalactites, and **Grotte de Dargilan**,

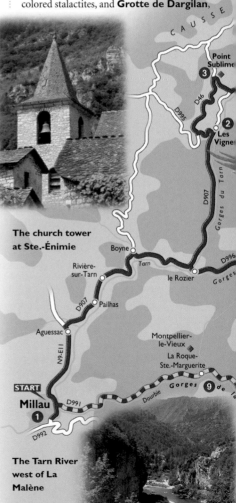

The church tower at Ste.-Énimie

The Tarn River west of La Malène

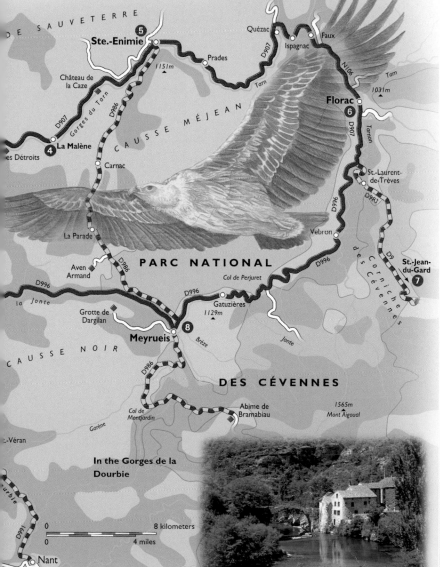

> ⛰ See area map p. 191
> ▶ Millau
> ↔ 60 miles (90 km)
> 🕐 Half a day
> ▶ Millau
>
> **NOT TO BE MISSED**
> - Point Sublime
> - La Malène
> - Corniche des Cévennes
> - Meyrueis
> - Aven Armand
> - Grotte de Dargilan

where staircases take you down into a series of caves and lakes. Southeast of Meyrueis off the D986 is the **Abîme de Bramabiau,** an abyss with an underground river.

Another drive from Millau takes you along the **Gorges de la Dourbie** ❾ on the D991. To the north is the weird rock formation of **Montpellier-le-Vieux,** which looks like a ruined town. South of Millau, via the D992 and D23, is **Roquefort-sur-Soulzon,** where you can visit caves in which Roquefort cheese, made from ewe's milk, is matured. ∎

In the Gorges de la Dourbie

More places to visit in the Massif Central

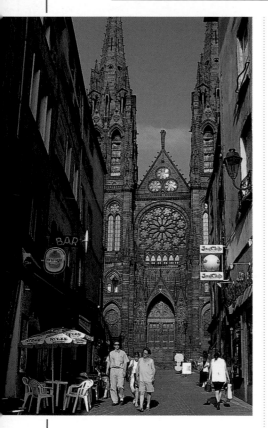

Rue des Graces leading to the cathedral in Clermont-Ferrand

CLERMONT-FERRAND

A bustling commercial town that owes its fortunes to the Michelin tire company, founded here in 1830, Clermont-Ferrand was two towns until 1731. Clermont, the older half, had a cathedral as early as the sixth century. The counts of Auvergne founded Montferrand, the other town, to counter the power of the bishops; but by the 17th century it had declined and in 1731 Clermont annexed its neighbor. The difference is still evident. Clermont has a daily market in Place St.-Pierre and the **Cathédrale Notre-Dame-de-l'Assomption,** with exquisite 12th- to 15th-century stained glass set off by somber basalt walls. Farther east is the **Basilique**

Notre-Dame-du-Port, a superb example of the Auvergnat Romanesque style. Montferrand is a quieter enclave of restored Renaissance houses. The much-altered old palace was imaginatively modernized around a courtyard, in the style of the Solomon R. Guggenheim Museum in New York, to display the collection of the **Musée des Beaux-Arts.**

🅼 190 B3 **Visitor information** ✉ place de la Victoire ☎ 04 73 98 65 00

THIERS

A visit to Thiers is worth it for the views alone. From its perch on the side of the ravine made by the Dorelle River you can see the volcanic peaks of the Monts Dôme and Monts Dore. The river waters made Thiers's fortune, powering the grinding wheels of the knifemakers, and making the town the most important center of cutlerymaking in France. On the old streets of half-timbered houses with finely carved corbels you can investigate the history of cutlery at the **Musée de la Coutellerie,** as well as shop for a huge variety of utensils and knives.

🅼 190 B3 **Visitor information**
✉ Chateau du Pirou ☎ 04 73 80 65 65

VICHY

Vichy has long been famous as a spa, reaching its fashionable heyday in the 19th century. You can still stroll around the **Parc des Sources** and take the waters, drink in the Grand Café, see the art nouveau Casino and cast-iron arcades, and seek out the **Source des Célestins** and other springs of Vichy water. Luxury hotels, fine restaurants, and glamorous stores abound, contributing to a seductive fin de siècle charm. Between 1940 and 1944, Vichy found notoriety as the headquarters of the collaborationist French government, close to the border between occupied and unoccupied France. In 1963, Vichy's fortunes changed again when the Allier River was dammed, creating a vast recreational lake.

🅼 190 B3 **Visitor information** ✉ 19 rue du Parc ☎ 04 70 98 71 94 ■

Southwest France combines the vacation attractions of sun, sea, and sand with a rich historical and cultural legacy and beautiful scenery. The great rivers Garonne, Dordogne, Lot, and Tarn thread through it, and vineyards abound.

Southwest France

Fattened geese In Périgord

★Paris

Area of map detail

0   60 kilometers
0   30 miles

6▷ MAINE-ET-LOIRE p.163

INDRE-ET-LOIRE p.163

Thouars
Loudun
Bressuire
Châtellerault
Parthenay
Futuroscope
Poitiers
VENDÉE p.163
DEUX-SÈVRES
Chauvigny
St.-Savin
INDRE p.163
5▷
St.-Maixent-l'Ecole
A10
Montmorillon
VIENNE
Poitou
Crozant
Niort
Île de Ré
Melle
Marche
Gué
St.-Martin-de-Ré
la Rochelle
N11
Bellac
la Souterraine
Surgères
A20
Fouras
A10
Ruffec
Confolens
HAUTE-VIENNE
Rochefort
St.-Jean-d'Angély
Angoumois
Plateaux
Île d'Oléron
Marennes
CHARENTE-MARITIME
Chorente
Limoges
St.-Léonard-de-Noblat
du Limousin
Saintes
Cognac
Jarnac
CHARENTE
la Rochefoucauld
4▷
Royan
Saujon
Angoulême
Nontron
Limousin
CORRÈZE
Pointe de Grave
Soulac-sur-Mer
N10
Barbezieux-St.-Hilaire
Puyguilhem
Uzerche
St.-Fort-sur-Gironde
Jonzac
St.-Jean-de-Côle
Thiviers
Tu
Lesparre-Médoc
Mirambeau
Aubeterre-sur-Dronne
Brantôme
Hautefort
Massi
Pauillac
Dronne
Périgueux
Isle
Brive-la-Gaillarde
Étang d'Hourtin-Carcans
Blaye
DORDOGNE
N89
Collonge
Lacanau-Océan
Grotte de Rouffignac
Vézère
Grotte de
la Rouge
Étang de Lacanau
GIRONDE
Libourne
N89
les Eyzies-de-Tayac
Lascaux
Arger
St.-Emilion
Beynac-et-Cazenac
Sarlat-la-Canéda
Gouffre
Padirac
Andernos-les-Bains
BORDEAUX
Lormont
Bergerac
Cadouin
Castelnaud
Rocamadour
Domme
Gra
3▷
Arcachon
A63
Monbazillac
Dordogne
Monpazier
LOT
Dune du Pilat
Bassin d'Arcachon
Biron
Grotte du Ste.-Eula
Étang de Cazaux et de Sanguinet
la Réole
Monflanquin
Bonaguil
Pech-Merle
Langon
Cénevières
Cajarc
Étang de Biscarrosse et de Parentis
Parentis-en-Born
Bazas
Marmande
A62
Cahors
St.-Cirq Lapo
Casteljaloux
Villeneuve-sur-Lot
A20
Mimizan
Marquèze
LOT-ET-GARONNE
Agen
Golfe
Sabres
Caussade
de
Roquefort
Nérac
TARN-ET-GARONNE
Cor
Castets
LANDES
A62
Moissac
Gascogne
les Landes
N10
Mont-de-Marsan
Castelsarrasin
Montauban
Tartas
Condom
Gers
Gaill
Hossegor
N124
Eauze
Rabasten
2▷
Dax
Aire-sur-l'Adour
Graul
Adour
GERS
Gimont
Lavau
A68
Biarritz
A64
Orthez
Auch
HAUTE-
TOULOUS
St.-Jean-de-Luz
Bayonne
Sauveterre-de-Béarn
Mirande
GARONNE
A63
Hendaye
Espelette
Pau
Muret
Ainhoa
PYRÉNÉES-ATLANTIQUES
Gave de Pau
A64
HAUTE-
N117
1▷
St.-Jean-Pied-de-Port
Pays Basque
Béarn
Oloron-Ste.-Marie
Tarbes
Grotte du
Mas-d'Azil
Pamiers
Mirep
Grottes de
Bétharram
Lourdes
Lannemezan
St.-Gaudens
N20
Lescun
Laruns
Argelès-Gazost
St.-Savin
St.-Lizier
Roquefixade
Gabas
Cauterets
Luz St.-Sauveur
St.-Bertrand-de-Comminges
Foix
Montségur
2884m
Pic du Midi d'Ossau
PYRÉNÉES
Massif de l'Arize
Bédeilhac
Tarascon-sur-Ariè
3298m
Vignemale
Parc Nat.
des Pyrénées
Bagnères-de-Luchon
ARIÈGE
Cirque de
Gavarnie
Grotte
de Niaux
Lombrives
Ax-les-Thermes
SPAIN
3115m
Pic d'Estats
Montaill
ANDORRA

A   B   C   D

Southwest France

TRAVEL THROUGH SOUTHWEST FRANCE AND YOU CROSS SOME OF THE country's richest agricultural land before climbing to the high Pyrenees. In the middle is the Aquitaine Basin, created by the great Garonne River flowing from the Pyrenees to the Atlantic via Toulouse and Bordeaux. On the way it is fed by the Tarn and Lot flowing down from the Massif Central. The Dordogne, which shares the Gironde Estuary with the Garonne, also flows from the Massif Central. For centuries these rivers were the region's main arteries of communication and trade. Wine, wood, and paper were shipped downstream to the port of Bordeaux, the boats returning with salt, sea fish, sugar, and other staples. But the coming of the railroad in the 19th century dealt a deathblow to river transport and now these great waterways are used more for pleasure than trade.

Flat and sandy, sometimes swept by the wind into high dunes, the Atlantic coast is laced with inland lakes. Until a century ago the coast was wild and inhospitable, and the sands were steadily encroaching inland. To stabilize the land, grasses were sown, followed by the pine trees that now form the great forest of the Landes, the largest pine forest in Europe. The once-threatening sands of the coast provide the wide beaches beloved by vacationers, pounded by rolling Atlantic breakers that are the delight of surfers.

To the south, the great mountain range of the Pyrenees stretches from the Mediterranean to the Atlantic, forming a natural frontier between France and Spain. The southwest's biggest cities are Bordeaux and Toulouse. Bordeaux was capital of the ancient duchy of Aquitaine, which in the Middle Ages included Gascony, Périgord, Poitou, and Limousin as well as Aquitaine. Toulouse was the seat of the powerful counts of Toulouse and the heart of the glittering troubadour culture. It was the capital of Languedoc, broadly embracing the whole of southern France from Aquitaine to Provence.

By the 12th century, southwest France, ruled autonomously but owing allegiance to the French Crown, was thriving both economically and culturally. But with the dynastic marriages of Eleanor of Aquitaine, and the spread of the Cathar heresy in Languedoc, the stage was set for trouble. Eleanor first married the French king, Louis VII, in 1137, but the marriage was annulled and in 1152 Eleanor married Henry Plantagenet, Count of Anjou and Duke of Normandy, who inherited the English Crown. Between them they ruled most of Britain and western France from Normandy to Aquitaine. Centuries of claims and counterclaims ensued, with the territorial ambitions of the rival French and English kingdoms finally erupting into the Hundred Years' War.

In Languedoc, the Albigensian Crusade against the Cathar heresy enabled the power-hungry French Crown to put an end to the autonomy of the counts of Toulouse.

The solid evidence of these conflicts can still be seen in the fortified *bastide* towns, the castles that pepper the banks of the Dordogne and the Lot, the gaunt Cathar fortresses of the Pyrenean foothills, and the fortified churches of Toulouse and Albi. Paradoxically, these relics of a strife-torn past are now some of the loveliest features of this diverse region. ∎

Food & drink

FROM PÉRIGORD, THE REGION NORTH OF THE DORDOGNE RIVER, TO THE Basque country along the Spanish border, southwest France glories in some of the finest produce and culinary skills that even France has to offer.

The Aquitaine coast yields fish and seafood in abundance—mussels, scallops, prawns, and most of all oysters—and the Gironde even produces caviar.

Périgord is synonymous with foie gras and truffles (see sidebar p. 249), such luxuries being the ultimate embellishment of what is effectively a peasant cuisine lifted to gastronomic heights. The traditional cooking medium is goose or duck fat as opposed to the butter used in Normandy or the olive oil ubiquitous in the Mediterranean. So do try the rich confits (duck or goose preserved in its own fat) and the many other delicious duck and goose dishes. Succulent local pork, beef, and lamb are variously enhanced with garlic, herbs, and truffles, and nothing is wasted. *Tripons* (tripe) and *ris de veau* (calf's sweetbreads) are particularly prized.

The local harvest of wild mushrooms such as chanterelles, morels, and ceps is served simply cooked in butter, as a filling for omelettes, or in sauces. Truffles, so expensive they are dubbed black gold, may be savored in slivers used to perfume an omelette. This region produces more walnuts than anywhere else in France. They are added to salads and sauces, crushed to make walnut oil, and distilled into eau-de-vie.

Bordeaux enjoys an enviable gastronomic reputation, with sophisticated food to complement its sublime wines. Toulouse and farther south is cassoulet country, with numerous contenders for the authentic recipe for this slow-cooked casserole of white beans with sausages and meat, often duck, pork, or mutton, usually topped with a crust of bread crumbs. Farther south still, in the Basque country, the pimiento is king, combined most deliciously with egg in *piperade*. Bayonne ham is justly famous for its aromatic flavor.

Fruit here is superlative, in both quantity and variety. The delicious plums of Agen make the best prunes in France. These are often combined with meat dishes, notably rabbit.

Wines

Bordeaux, with Burgundy, produces some of the most exquisite wines in the world. Visit a few of its châteaus to try the aromatic reds, dry fruity whites, and sublime sweet white wines. Local wines usually represent the best value in restaurants. Aside from the châteaus of Bordeaux, other names to look for include Bergerac, Buzet, Cahors, Gaillac, and the

Basque wine, Irouléguy. The unsurpassed brandies include Cognac and Armagnac. ∎

Specialties

First courses *Chipirons:* squid, often cooked in its own ink

Garbure béarnaise: thick soup made with cabbage, bacon, and confit of goose or pork

Sobronade: bean and bacon soup

Tourain bordelais: soup of onions, tomatoes, bread, and egg yolks

Main courses *Boeuf à la sarladaise:* fillet of beef stuffed with *pâté de foie gras*

Canard aux cèpes: duck with mushrooms

Cou farci: stuffed goose neck

Coquilles St.-Jacques à la bordelaise: scallops sautéed with shallots and parsley

Daube bordelaise: beef stewed in red wine

Enchaud Périgourdin: roast pork with garlic

Miques: little dumplings of bread, boiled in stock

Poulet basquaise: chicken with tomatoes, pimientoes, and Bayonne ham

Zakiro (a Basque dish): mutton grilled on an open fire

Desserts *Kanougas:* chocolate taffy

Touron: loaf of marzipan (almond paste) with nuts

Geese waiting to be sold at market

The sands of the Aquitaine coast pile high on the Dune du Pilat, Europe's highest sand dune.

Aquitaine & the Atlantic Coast

France's southern Atlantic coast is a revelation: one great sweep of beach unfolding from the tip of the Gironde Peninsula to the Spanish border, its dazzling light and pounding white waves earning it the poetic name of the Côte d'Argent, or Silver Coast.

For vacationers looking for sand and sea (and more particularly surf), this is paradise—a fact not lost on the French, who descend here in droves at vacation time, while oblivious foreigners rush through on their way to Spain or the Mediterranean. Beaches, dunes, and huge lakes interspersed with small resorts and fishing ports make this coast perfect for family vacations. For more sophisticated tastes, glamour is delivered in faded imperial fashion by Biarritz, with its classic belle epoque hotels, luxury shops, casinos, and golf clubs. Inland stretches the tremendous wooded expanse of the Landes, Europe's largest pine forest, planted in the 19th century to contain the shifting sands of the coast, and now a peaceful green retreat dotted with tiny rustic settlements and nature reserves.

In the north of the region lies the quiet city of Poitiers, with a magnificent heritage of Romanesque churches, and now perhaps best known—in startling contrast—for its 21st-century cinematic theme park, Futuroscope.

World famous for its exquisite porcelain and enamels, Limoges to the south has some of the finest museums devoted to the decorative arts to be seen anywhere.

North of the great Gironde Estuary lies the irresistibly unspoiled resort of La Rochelle, an ancient port that now contains more yachts than anywhere else on the coast.

Always an important port, the metropolis of Bordeaux offers a gracious 18th-century center, excellent museums and restaurants, and, of course, world-famous wines. No wine lover should miss the chance to visit the surrounding wine country, with its litany of magical names such as Château Mouton-Rothschild, Haut-Brion, St.-Émilion, and Château Margaux.

Finally, rising into the high Pyrenees in the far south is the French Basque country, a land apart, with its own language, racial identity, cuisine, and customs, which offers an intriguing glimpse into an ancient but still thriving culture with a piquant flavor all its own. ■

Poitiers

Poitiers

232 C5

Visitor information

www.pcl.fr/poitiers

✉ 8 rue des Grandes-Écoles

☎ 05 49 41 21 24

Information on guided tours available from the "Ville d'Art et d'Histoire" section of the tourist office

Notre-Dame-la-Grande

✉ Grande Rue

Baptistère de St.-Jean

✉ rue Jean-Jaurés

🕐 Closed Tues. (except July–Aug.) & a.m. all Nov.–March

💲 $

Parc de Futuroscope

www.futuroscope.fr

232 C5

✉ Jaunay-Clan—4 miles (6 km) north of Poitiers via N10

☎ 05 49 49 30 80. Recorded information: 08 36 68 50 20

💲 $$$–$$$$$. Entry variable for one, two, or three days—low, middle, or high season. Special prices for two-day visit including one night at Hôtel Futuroscope

POISED BETWEEN NORTHERN AND SOUTHERN FRANCE, Poitiers is an ancient city now reclaiming its heritage after years of decline. Its riches include a great concentration of Romanesque architecture. The city's position on a rocky promontory in a bend of the Clain River is best appreciated from the opposite bank, a view that also shows a cluster of church towers. Battles around this strategic stronghold have changed the course of French history, most famously in 732 when Charles Martel, founder of the Carolingian dynasty, turned the tide on the invading Saracens. In 1356, the Black Prince retained Poitiers and Aquitaine for England with a victory here.

Echoes of this history can still be seen in the city's architectural heritage. The 12th-century **Eglise de Notre-Dame-la-Grande** exemplifies the Poitevin Romanesque style. The west front is a mesmerizing gallery of idiosyncratic medieval sculpture—once brilliantly painted—flanked by a pair of pinecone pinnacles that are the hallmark of this style. The **Palais de Justice** *(rue Gambetta)* nearby contains magnificent vestiges of the 12th-century palace of the dukes of Aquitaine.

The 11th-century church of **St.-Hilaire-le-Grand** *(rue Doyenné)* is unique in Europe in having seven aisles, supported by an extraordinary forest of columns, many of them with fascinating carved capitals. The fourth-century **Baptistère de St.-Jean,** said to be the oldest Christian building in France, contains Roman marble columns, frescoes, and the pool in which converts were originally baptized by full immersion. ■

Parc de Futuroscope

The 21st-century architecture of Futuroscope (the European Park of the Moving Image) could not be in greater contrast to the stately Romanesque buildings of nearby Poitiers: Half-buried white cubes, white spheres, and mirrored crystalline shapes erupt out of the flat landscape. Every imaginable kind of visual technology is exploited here: screens seven stories high; a "magic carpet" with a screen below as well as in front of you; auditoriums with chairs simulating the movement on screen; 3-D projections that suck you into the

action; and a circular cinema. Since it opened in 1987, this brainchild of a local politician has become a huge success, attracting some three million visitors annually. ■

The port of La Rochelle, one of the best natural harbors along the Atlantic coast

La Rochelle

WITH ITS LOVELY OLD HARBOR, SPLENDID TOWERS, AND pedestrians-only medieval streets, La Rochelle is one of the prettiest and best preserved ports anywhere on the French Atlantic coast. Now also the biggest yachting center in western France, it is a fashionable and lively place for vacations, buzzing with restaurants and cafés. The narrow arcaded streets in the old town are lined with stately mansions, picturesque shops, and half-timbered houses.

La Rochelle
⚉ 232 B5
Visitor information
✉ place de la Petite Sirène, Le Gabut
☎ 05 46 41 14 68

Musée du Nouveau Monde
✉ 10 rue Fleuriau
☎ 05 46 41 46 50
🕐 Closed Tues. & Sun. a.m.
💲 $

This important port was granted privileges by Eleanor of Aquitaine in the 13th century that made it free of feudal obligations. Later it became a hotbed of Protestantism thanks to its trading links with northern Europe. Its most tragic—and heroic—moment came in 1627, when it was besieged by the Catholic forces of Cardinal Richelieu for 15 months. When a triumphant Richelieu entered the town, he found it full of emaciated corpses: Only 5,000 of the original population of 25,000 survived.

The town walls were razed, but the harbor entrance is still guarded by two 14th-century towers, the **Tour de la Chaîne** and the **Tour St.-Nicolas.** A huge chain used to be slung between them to protect the harbor at night and in times of war. A third tower, the **Tour de la Lanterne** west of the Tour de la Chaîne, was originally a lighthouse, with a giant wax candle for its light. You can climb to the top for a good view of the port.

From the old harbor, the Porte de la Grosse Horloge leads into the town, a feast of Renaissance and 18th-century architecture in distinctive Rochelais style, with arcaded shop fronts and roofs hung with fishtail slates.

A grand 18th-century mansion built by wealthy shipowners now houses the **Musée du Nouveau Monde** (Museum of the New World). Exhibitions concentrate on the links between La Rochelle and the Americas, and its influence on Louisiana, Canada, and the West Indies, though there is no permanent collection at the museum.

Just off the coast of La Rochelle, and reached by a 2-mile-long road bridge, is the **Île de Ré.** A peaceful retreat of salt marshes, vineyards, and shallow lagoons, the island attracts all manner of bird life, including curlew, teal, and geese. The capital, **St.-Martin-de-Ré,** is a fishing port of cobbled streets and whitewashed cottages protected by 17th-century ramparts. ■

Limoges & Aubusson

FOR ANYONE WITH A PASSION FOR THE DECORATIVE ARTS —and particularly for porcelain, enamels, and tapestry—Limoges and Aubusson offer rare delights. The discovery of a major deposit of kaolin nearby in 1768 made the name of Limoges synonymous with fine, pure white porcelain, because kaolin uniquely remains white after firing. It was to be the foundation of a major industry that produced some of the finest china ever made.

The **Musée National Adrien-Dubouché** contains a superb collection of more than 11,000 items of porcelain, chinaware, and metalwork from earliest times to the present.

Centuries before the porcelain industry started, Limoges was already famed throughout Europe for its virtuoso enamels. An unrivaled collection, from the 11th century on, is displayed in the **Musée Municipal de l'Évêché** (*place de la Cathédrale, tel 05 55 45 61 75, closed Tues. Oct.–June*). The museum also has a collection of paintings including Renoir's "Portrait of Madame le Coeur," given by the artist to his native city.

Limoges's soaring Gothic **Cathédrale St.-Étienne** has some magnificent stone carving, especially its famous rood screen.

AUBUSSON

The little town of Aubusson has been the tapestry capital of the world since the 15th century. In the mid-17th century, the town's workshops received the royal warrant, but the revocation of the Edict of Nantes in 1685 forced the Huguenot work force to flee. A revival in the 18th century ended with the Revolution.

In 1937 designer Jean Lurçat came to Aubusson and revived its fortunes. The **Musée Départemental de la Tapisserie** shows work from the 17th, 18th, and 20th centuries. A traditional workshop has been set up in the **Maison du Tapissier** (*rue Vieille*), a 16th-century weaver's house. At the **Manufacture St.-Jean** (*3 rue St.-Jean, tel 05 55 66 10 08, closed Sat.–Sun. Oct.–June*) you can watch tapestries and carpets being made. ■

Limoges
🅜 232 D4
Visitor information
✉ boulevard Fleurus
☎ 05 55 34 46 87

Musée National Adrien-Dubouché
✉ place Winston Churchill
☎ 05 55 33 08 50
🕐 Closed Tues. & a.m. July–Aug.
💲 $

Aubusson
🅜 232 E4
Visitor information
✉ rue Vieille
☎ 05 55 66 32 12

Musée Départemental de la Tapisserie
✉ avenue des Lissiers
☎ 05 55 66 33 06
🕐 Closed Tues. except p.m. July & Aug.
💲 $

Inset: Limoges enamel plate showing the crowning of the Virgin, circa 1340

Bordeaux

ONE OF FRANCE'S GRAND 18TH-CENTURY CITIES, FORMAL, solid, and sophisticated, Bordeaux enjoys an illustrious reputation as the hub of the largest region of vineyards producing some of the finest wines in the world. The trade in wine began in Roman times, when Bordeaux shipped wine from the Midi; then in the first century A.D. the vineyards around Bordeaux itself began to be cultivated. For much of the 13th, 14th, and 15th centuries the city lay in English hands, as the French and English fought out their claims to Aquitaine (indeed, Bordeaux was ranked the fourth city in England, after London, York, and Winchester). Even after the city became French again in 1453, the wine trade with England continued to grow, and the English taste for claret (red Bordeaux) has never waned since.

Bordeaux
🅐 232 B3
Visitor information
www.bordeaux-tourisme.com
✉ 12 cours du 30 Juillet
☎ 05 56 00 66 00

Grand Théâtre
✉ place de la Comédie
🕐 Closed Sun., & Mon.—Fri. mid-Sept.—June. Guided visits by reservation. Information and reservations at the tourist office. Tour: 1 hr.
💲 $$

Musée d'Art Contemporain
✉ 7 rue Ferrère
☎ 05 56 00 81 50
🕐 Closed Mon.
💲 $$. Free 1st Sun. of month

It is the 18th-century city that you see today, the result of a massive civic rebuilding scheme imposed by Paris, filled in with fine mansions built by wealthy wine merchants. After decades of restoration and cleaning, the golden stone of the city's arcades and statues, the elegant ironwork and classical facades, all exude elegance and prosperity.

ALONG THE RIVER
Start your visit on the waterfront, a great curve of wine warehouses on the cobbled quays from which the precious commodity was shipped. From the **Pont de Pierre,** a magnificent view takes in the classical facades lining the wharves fronting the grandeur of the St.-Pierre quarter. A stroll along the quays brings you to the stately **Hôtel de la Bourse,** the old maritime exchange, standing on one of the city's most impressive 18th-century squares. Farther along the waterfront you reach the vast Esplanade des Quinconces, with fountains and statues. Towering above it is the **Monument aux Girondins,** erected in memory of local deputies sent to the guillotine by Robespierre. The Resistance dismantled it and spirited it away by night to save it from being melted down by the German occupying forces during World War II.

Inland from the river, the broad tree-lined avenues of Cours de l'Intendance, Cours Georges Clemenceau, and Allées de Tourny, known as the Triangle, enclose the heart of Bordeaux life, full of fashionable shops and traditional cafés. A visit to the **Maison du Vin** (*3 cours du 30 Juillet*) is an indispensable prelude to any wine tour or tasting. The same street opens out into Place de la Comédie, dominated by the neoclassic masterpiece of the **Grand Théâtre,** impeccably restored to its formidable former glory. Built by Victor Lewis between 1773 and 1780, it boasts a staircase taken by Charles Garnier as his inspiration for the Opéra Garnier in Paris, and an auditorium now fabulously refurbished with its original gold, blue, and white decor.

To the north of Esplanade de Quinconces lies the old merchants' quarter, now a fashionable bustle of antique shops. Cours Xavier-Arnozan is resplendent with the great family houses built by the wine merchants in order to be near the port, their classical facades adorned with splendid wrought-iron balconies. Here, too, is the new **Musée d'Art Contemporain,**

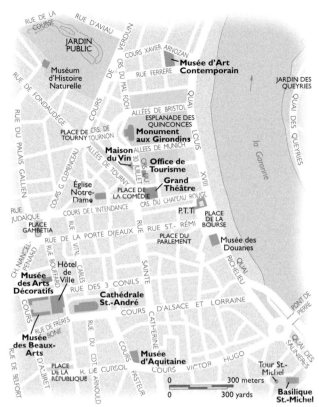

Musée d'Aquitaine

✉ 20 cours Pasteur

☎ 05 56 01 51 00

⊕ Closed Mon.

$ $. Free 1st Sun. of month

Musée des Beaux-Arts

✉ 20 cours d'Albret

☎ 05 56 10 20 56

⊕ Closed Mon.

$ $. Free 1st Sun. of month

Musée des Arts Décoratifs

✉ 39 rue Bouffard

☎ 05 56 00 72 50

⊕ Closed a.m. & all Tues.

$ $. Free 1st Sun. of month

housed in a converted 19th-century spice warehouse. The stone arches of the massive building provide a powerful setting for a variety of modern works.

The most interesting of the city's other museums cluster around the Cathédrale St.-André: The **Musée d'Aquitaine** provides an imaginative overview of local history, both rural and urban. The collection of the **Musée des Beaux-Arts** has a notable number of Renaissance paintings, together with two famous Eugène Delacroix canvases, "Greece on the ruins of Missolonghi" and "The Lion Hunt," and a number of Impressionist works. The **Musée des Arts Décoratifs,** meanwhile, gives a sense of life inside the city's 18th-century mansions with rooms displaying period furniture, porcelain, glassware, and the wrought iron for which Bordeaux is famous.

The **Cathédrale St.-André** is a vast 11th-century foundation, with later additions including a soaring Flamboyant Gothic choir and transepts. The 13th-century Porte Royale, on the south facade, has a notable tympanum of the Last Judgment. The almost equally immense **Basilique St.-Michel,** off the waterfront to the south of the city, has a free-standing Gothic belfry that at 374 feet (114 m) is the highest tower in southwest France. The terrace halfway up the tower affords a commanding view of the city. ■

Drive through the Haut-Médoc

In a region that produces the noblest wines in the world, with some 4,000 named, single-vineyard (or château) wines, the Médoc boasts the lion's share of the most aristocratic growths.

An unpromising marshy area to the northwest of Bordeaux, the Médoc was drained and planted only in the 18th century but soon it established a preeminence that it has never lost. When the wines of the Gironde region were classified in 1855, all 62 crus classés were from the Médoc. This short tour (allow a day) of the Haut-Médoc (the upper part of the Médoc) stars some of the most celebrated vineyards in the world. The best time to visit is just before the grapes are harvested in mid-September, when the vine leaves have turned golden, and the grapes hang tantalizingly heavy and luscious.

If you prefer to visit another of the Bordeaux wine regions—perhaps St.-Émilion, Entre-Deux-Mers, Sauternes, Graves, Côtes de Bourg, or Côtes de Blaye—the **Conseil des Vins du Médoc** (cours du 30 Juillet, tel 05 56 48 18 62) in Bordeaux will be able to provide all the information you need; they also organize bus tours. If you wish to travel independently, plan carefully: Try to contact each vineyard you want to visit to make an appointment (for some at least two weeks in advance) and remember that you may not be welcome during the grape harvest.

.
THE TOUR
For this tour of the crème de la crème, take the D2 (Route du Vin) north out of Bordeaux, through row upon row of vines planted in the gravelly ground flanking the Gironde Estuary between the river and the forest of the Landes. Stop first at **Château Siran** ❶ (Tel 05 57 88 34 04), once home to the Toulouse-Lautrec family, and splendidly furnished, with paintings that include a copy of Caravaggio's "The Young Bacchus." **Château Margaux** ❷ (Tel 05 57 88 83 83, closed Sat.–Sun. & Aug.), east of the D2 about 2 miles (3.5 km) farther on, dubbed the Versailles of the Médoc, is perhaps the most outstanding of the châteaus, with a grand avenue of trees leading to the Doric colonnades of the facade. But you won't see much more than the cool dark cellars

(chais) where the superlative wine is stored. Skip the town of Margaux and take a detour on the D5 to **Château Maucaillou** ❸ and the **Musée des Arts et des Métiers de la Vigne et du Vin** (Tel 05 56 58 01 23). From Vauban's star-shaped 17th-century **Fort Médoc** ❹ (Tel 05 56 58 98 40) there is an all-encompassing view of the Gironde Estuary and, beyond, the vineyards of Blaye.

Back on the wine route, the D2, you come next to **Château Beychevelle** ❺ (Tel 05 59 73 20 70), set in a beautiful 18th-century building where tasting is offered. Farther on, **Château Latour** ❻ is named after the tower that stands next to the château. Then take a deep breath as you approach the river port of **Pauillac**, where signs point to some of the most hallowed names in wines, including Mouton-Rothschild and Lafite-Rothschild. At **Château Mouton-Rothschild** ❼ (Tel 05 56 73 21 29, visits by appointment only) you may visit the reception rooms and banqueting hall of the château, and the display of wine labels commissioned from artists such as Pablo Picasso, Salvador Dali, Jean Cocteau, and Henry Moore (remunerated, naturally, in bottles of wine). Part of the cellars is now a museum, with paintings, sculpture, tapestries, ceramics, and glass all devoted to wine.

At **Château Lafite-Rothschild** ❽, another fine château building in a grand park, there are guided tours (by appointment only, tel 05 56 73 18 18). Just a little farther on the D2, **Château Cos d'Estournel** ❾, a bizarre 18th-century "Oriental" palace, produces one the five crus classés from St.-Estèphe. This little river port has one of the oldest vineyards of the Haut-Médoc, predating even the drainage work carried out in the 18th century.

From here on down the estuary, the land becomes the Médoc rather than the Haut-Médoc and the wines are classified accordingly as Médoc (but still very distinguished).

Retrace your steps, or take the fast route back to Bordeaux on the N215 and D1.

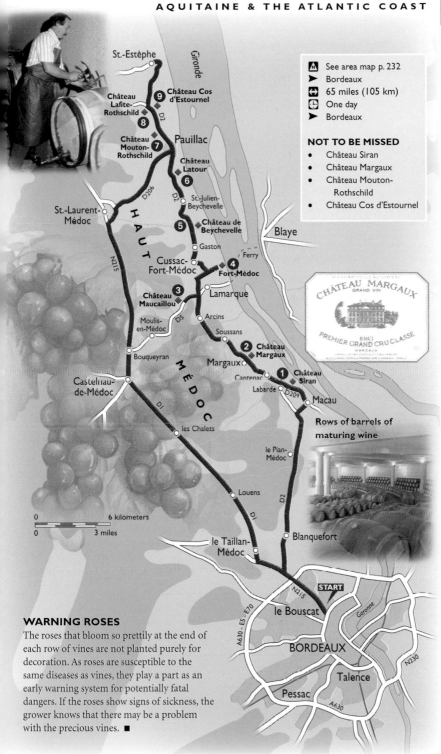

St.-Estèphe

Gironde

⑨ Château Cos d'Estournel

Château Lafite-Rothschild

⑧

⑦ Château Mouton-Rothschild

Pauillac

Château Latour

⑥

D2

D206

D2

St.-Julien-Beychevelle

St.-Laurent-Médoc

HAUT

⑤ Château de Beychevelle

Blaye

N215

Gaston

Ferry

Cussac-Fort-Médoc

④ Fort-Médoc

Château Maucaillou ③

Lamarque

Moulis-en-Médoc

D5

Arcins

Soussans

Bouqueyran

MÉDOC

② Château Margaux

Castelnau-de-Médoc

Margaux

Cantenac

① Château Siran

Labarde

D209

Macau

D1

les Chalets

le Pian-Médoc

D2

Louens

0 — 6 kilometers
0 — 3 miles

le Taillan-Médoc

Blanquefort

🗺 See area map p. 232
► Bordeaux
⟷ 65 miles (105 km)
🕐 One day
► Bordeaux

NOT TO BE MISSED
- Château Siran
- Château Margaux
- Château Mouton-Rothschild
- Château Cos d'Estournel

CHÂTEAU MARGAUX
GRAND VIN

PREMIER GRAND CRU CLASSE
MARGAUX

Rows of barrels of maturing wine

START

A630 · E5 · E70

N215

Geronne

le Bouscat

BORDEAUX

N230

Talence

Pessac

A630

WARNING ROSES

The roses that bloom so prettily at the end of each row of vines are not planted purely for decoration. As roses are susceptible to the same diseases as vines, they play a part as an early warning system for potentially fatal dangers. If the roses show signs of sickness, the grower knows that there may be a problem with the precious vines. ■

Biarritz

THE SWANKIEST AND LARGEST RESORT ON THE FRENCH
Atlantic seaboard, Biarritz enjoys a mild climate, invigorated by its
perfect position between the Pyrenees and the rugged coast.

The Hôtel du Palais lords over the beach at Biarritz.

Biarritz
- 🅰 232 B2
- **Visitor information**
- ✉ 1 square d'Ixelles
- ☎ 05 59 22 37 10

Musée de la Mer
- ✉ esplanade de la Rocher de la Vièrge
- ☎ 05 59 22 75 40
- 🕐 Closed 1st week of Jan.
- 💲 $$

When sea bathing became fashionable in the 19th century, the little whaling village of Biarritz soon attracted attention. Its fortunes were sealed when the Empress Eugénie persuaded her husband, Napoleon III, to build the Villa Eugénie, now the **Hôtel du Palais.** Queen Victoria followed, along with such an assortment of European crowned heads that the resort became known as the beach of kings. Coco Chanel added a note of chic, and the town still has a wealth of designer stores. After World War II, Biarritz became a haunt for American movie stars, while its aristocratic pedigree continued with the Duke and Duchess of Windsor. The casino, now

restored to all its art deco magnificence, attracted the world's gamblers, and Biarritz gained its reputation as the Monte Carlo of the Atlantic coast.

While these splendors are now slightly faded, the coastline is still gorgeous, with wide sandy beaches, huge rocks, and crashing Atlantic breakers. The **Grande Plage** is the most fashionable stretch of beach. The **Vieux Port** shelters a gentler one, while great waves break on the **Plage de la Côte des Basques,** a place of annual pilgrimage for Basques. It all makes a perfect setting for nonchalant strolling, with cliff walks and promenades lush with tamarisk and purple and blue hydrangeas, and lined with an eclectic combination of English villas, Andalusian haciendas, and Swiss chalets. A footbridge from the promontory at the south end of the Grande Plage takes you to the **Rocher de la Vièrge** with its statue of the Virgin, and an exhilarating view down the coast to Spain. The top of the lighthouse north of the Grande Plage (up 248 steps) offers an even more thrilling panorama.

On the promontory above the Virgin stands the **Musée de la Mer,** which has displays on local fishing and pools of sharks and seals. More esoteric interests are catered to in the **Musée du Chocolat** (*4 avenue de la Marne, tel 05 59 41 54 64*), offering tours and a tasting; as well as at the thalassotherapy center at **Les Thermes Marins** (*80 rue Madrid, tel 05 59 23 01 22*), where you can take mud baths and seawater steam baths. ∎

Bayonne

NOW THE ATTRACTIVE, ELEGANT CAPITAL OF THE FRENCH
Basque country, Bayonne was for centuries hotly disputed for its
strategic position on the frontier between France and Spain.

Constantly besieged, and controlled
by the English for almost 300 years,
Bayonne found prosperity in priva-
teering, shipbuilding, and arms
manufacture (and gave its name to
the bayonet). The tall, narrow streets
around the **Cathédrale Ste.-
Marie** are a pleasure to explore. The
cathedral, begun in the 13th century,
is a monument to changing times
and masters. Its soaring Gothic nave,
built by the English in the 14th century, is in the northern Gothic style,
rare in the region, and French fleur-
de-lis are on the keystones. Nearby,
the **Musée Bonnat** has an excellent art collection including works
by Rubens, Poussin, and Goya. The
Musée Basque is currently closed
but has temporary exhibitions in
Château Neuf (*place St.-André, tel 05
59 59 08 98*).

Bayonne is a good place to buy
Basque specialties such as the
famous beret, espadrilles, linen,
woolen blankets, and aromatic
Bayonne chocolate. Try the arcades
of Rue Pont-Neuf, between the
cathedral and the Hôtel de Ville. ■

The Basques

Basque country spans the
border between France and
Spain. The Basques have managed
to retain their separate identity
more than any other ethnic group
in Europe, and their language,
Euskara, is unlike any other
European tongue. The origin of
these remarkable people, and of
their language, is unknown. Basque
village houses are whitewashed,
with shutters painted green or red.

The game of *pelota* is a Basque
tradition. Played in a high-walled
court, known as a *fronton*, it is fast
and furious and involves hitting a
hard ball against a wall with a sort
of wicker glove or the bare palm.

Typical Basque towns (see map
p. 232, B2) include **St.-Jean-de-
Luz**, a fishing port, the walled town
of **Aïnhoa**, and **Espelette**, famous
for pimientoes, an essential part of
Basque cuisine. ■

Traditional giant
figures parade at
a Basque festival.

Bayonne
🗺 232 B2
Visitor information
✉ place des Basques
☎ 05 59 46 01 46

Musée Bonnat
✉ 5 rue J.-Lafitte
☎ 05 59 59 08 52
🕐 Closed Tues.

More places to visit in Aquitaine & the Atlantic Coast

COGNAC

The port of Cognac on the Charente River is now known for one thing: the fine brandy distilled from the wine of the local vineyards. The town is full of producers offering free tastings, but the best one is **Distillerie Otard** in its 15th-century château. Look for the black fungus that grows on the warehouses, fed by brandy evaporates, called the angels' share.

 232 C4 **Visitor information** ✉ rue du 14 Juillet ☎ 05 45 82 10 71

CÔTE D'ARGENT

The Aquitaine coast has Europe's highest sand dune, **Dune du Pilat,** and ideal beaches for swimming and surfing in a string of resorts. The main one is **Arcachon** (*Map 232, B3, Visitor information, esplanade Georges-Pompidou, tel 05 57 52 97 97*), on the Bassin d'Arcachon, where oysters are cultivated. It is a beguiling 19th-century place with a marina and whimsical vacation villas. Farther south are **Hossegor,** on a saltwater lake, and **Cap-Breton,** with its ancient lighthouse.

LES LANDES

A century ago, Les Landes were marsh and scrub threatened by drifting sands from the coast. In the 18th century the coastal dunes were stabilized and the marshes drained by the planting of marram grass and pines. The **Écomusée** (*Tel 05 58 08 31 31*) at Marquèze (*Map 232 B3*) shows the hard nature of traditional life in Les Landes.

ST.-ÉMILION

A medieval walled citadel, St.-Émilion is the very essence of a wine town. The handsome houses of golden limestone make it a picturesque base for visits to the nearby wine country. St.-Émilion wines include the appellation of Pomerol and the great Château Pétrus.

 232 C3 **Visitor information** ✉ place des Creneaux ☎ 05 57 55 28 28

SAINTES

Saintes, in the Charente Valley, contains a rich heritage of Roman and medieval architecture. The **Arc de Germanicus** (now in Place Bassompierre) once stood on a Roman bridge, and there are also the remains of baths and an amphitheater. The 12th-century **Abbaye aux Dames,** a lovely Romanesque building, has beautifully carved portals.

232 B4 **Visitor information** ✉ 62 cours National ☎ 05 46 74 23 82 ■

Tapping the pine trees for resin in the forests of Les Landes

Evening falls over the Dordogne River.

The Dordogne & Midi-pyrénées

The Dordogne touches the hearts and stirs the senses of visitors more than any other region of France—except, perhaps, Provence. In the dark days following the outbreak of World War II, its meandering streams, rolling hills, and quiet villages prompted Henry Miller to write in a kind of optimism: "France may one day exist no more, but the Dordogne will live on just as dreams live on and nourish the souls of men."

Although the Dordogne is first and foremost a river, and technically a small administrative département, for many foreigners the name conjures up a large area of elegiac river country. The climate is gentle, the summer sun never as unrelenting as farther south. The Dordogne, the Lot, and the Tarn Rivers water the land, ensuring a rich variety of crops.

North of the Dordogne River is Périgord, some of France's richest agricultural land. South of the river the limestone *causse* is not so lush but there are treasures of a different kind: underground chasms and grottoes, and some of the finest medieval religious architecture in France. The many castles and *bastides* (fortified towns) are relics of the bitter fighting throughout the Middle Ages.

Throughout the Dordogne region market towns such as Sarlat-la-Canéda, Cahors, and Périgueux have historic centers full of shady arcades and ornately carved buildings.

To the south lies the Midi-pyrénées. Its capital, Toulouse, is Mediterranean in atmosphere and humming with life. To the east, pink-brick Albi, with its great cathedral and lovely old streets, has an unrivaled collection of works by its famous son, Toulouse-Lautrec. West of Toulouse is the rolling farmland of Gascony, home of Armagnac brandy.

In addition to its impressive religious architecture, the region has some of the most enchanting rural architecture in France. Weathered farms of golden limestone beneath steep slate roofs bristle with dormer windows, little turrets, and elaborate dovecotes. Terracotta tiles and vine-shaded verandas herald the deep south. Restored, many of these fine old buildings are now vacation homes. ∎

Around Périgord

Périgueux
⚠ 232 C4
Visitor information
✉ 26 place
Francheville
☎ 05 53 53 10 63

Brantôme
⚠ 232 C4
Visitor information
✉ Pavillon Renaissance,
boulevard Charle-
magne
☎ 05 53 05 80 52

**Château de
Puyguilhem**
⚠ 232 D4
✉ 05 53 54 82 18
🕐 Closed Mon.,
Oct.–May, & first 3
weeks in Jan.
💲 $$

**Château de
Hautefort**
⚠ 232 D4
☎ 05 53 50 51 23
🕐 Closed Oct.–April
& Sun. p.m.
💲 $$

"Here [at Vienne] we supped and lay, having amongst other dainties, a dish of truffles, which is a certain earth nut, and found out by a hog trained to it…It is in truth an incomparable meat."
John Evelyn (1644)

THE ANCIENT TERRITORY OF PÉRIGORD (LARGELY covered by the present département of Dordogne) matches the ideal image of provincial France: lush, gently rural, and dotted with farms and manor houses. The region is united by its rivers, the Dronne, Isle, Vézère, and Dordogne, all of which have provided routes for transporting goods and people since the Gallo-Roman era. Today they make ideal routes for exploring the countryside.

Périgord—so green and tranquil—was the epicenter of the Hundred Years' War and the front line between the kingdom of France and English-held Aquitaine. The fortified towns and châteaus that are such a delight to visit today testify to this belligerence.

Traditionally, this historic region has been divided into Périgord Blanc (so-called for the white of its limestone), centered on Périgueux and the Isle River; and Périgord Noir (because of its dense woodland) around Sarlat-la-Canéda in the southeast. More recently, the color scheme has been broadened to include Périgord Vert (the green pastureland of the north) and Périgord Poupre (the vineyards around Bergerac).

PÉRIGUEUX
The regional capital, Périgueux, lying in a loop of the Isle River, makes a good base for touring the region. Dominating its skyline are the exotic domes and turrets of the **Cathédrale St.-Front,** the largest cathedral in southwest France. Originally built in the 12th century, it was restored in the 19th century by architect Paul Abadie, who later used it as an inspiration for the Basilique de Sacré-Coeur in Paris. Its remarkable roof offers a good view of the old town clustered at its feet, a tangle of cobbled streets, mullioned windows, and hidden courtyards.

From the **Tour Mataguerre,**

part of the medieval ramparts, you can enjoy another splendid view over the rooftops, including the ruins of a Gaulish amphitheater and temple. The little streets and squares come alive on market days, especially at the winter sales of foie gras and truffles (head for the Pierre Champion shop on Rue Taillefer for *foie gras truffé*).

BRANTÔME
North of Périgueux, in the tranquil valley of the Dronne River, lies Brantôme, one of the most charming towns in the whole of Périgord. Stroll along the riverbanks to admire its bridges and riverside garden, its ancient abbey church, and its exceptionally fine 11th-century bell tower. The first monks here simply carved their monastery out of the cliffs behind the abbey, in caves that are now open to the public: The **Cave of the Last Judgment** has stunning carvings of the Crucifixion and the Triumph of Death. Pierre de Bourdeille, abbot here in the 16th century, was to earn notoriety with his scurrilous tales of ladies at court, written under the pen name Brantôme.

A few miles northeast of Brantôme, the **Château de Puyguilhem** is a gracious example of French Renaissance architecture. East of Périgueux, the magnificent 17th-century **Château de Hautefort** stands in wooded parkland embellished with topiary and mosaic parterres. ∎

Truffles & foie gras

Truffles and foie gras are the heavenly twins of epicurean indulgence in Périgord, unsurpassed anywhere. Capricious and mysterious, resistant to all attempts at cultivation or scientific analysis, truffles must be snuffed out from their underground hiding places among the roots of certain oak trees by specially trained pigs or dogs. Their incomparable flavor is not only exquisite but also highly pungent. Sold in specialist markets such as those at Périgueux and Sarlat, truffles fetch as much as 1,400 francs a pound (about $15 an ounce). They may also be bought in cans, carefully graded.

The 19th-century essayist and wit, the Reverend Sydney Smith's definition of heaven was "eating *pâté de foie gras* to the sound of trumpets." Foie gras is made by force-feeding geese or ducks with corn to enlarge their livers, resulting in a rich and deliciously smooth meat. Although many people regard the practice (known as *gavage*) as cruel, it has to be said that the geese flock to be fed. Foie gras comes in many forms, in jars or cans; *foie gras d'oie entier* indicates the best goose liver, presented whole; *bloc de foie gras* describes pieces pressed together to form a block; *mi-cuit* denotes that the liver is cooked enough to keep for about a month. Finest of all is *foie gras truffé*, perfumed with black flowers of truffle. ■

Dogs can smell where a truffle lies below ground and are trained to point their master to the knob of precious fungus.

Dordogne Valley drive

One of the most beautiful drives in the Dordogne is upstream along the river valley from Bergerac to Sarlat-la-Canéda, a comfortable two-day excursion of 80 miles (170 km) or so. Here the great river cuts a swath between wooded valleys, fertile farmland, and craggy limestone cliffs topped by picturesque villages and castles at every turn. With its outstanding reputation for fine food and wine, this lovely region provides a perfect combination of the pleasures of the table, the landscape, and history. Take this drive at a leisurely pace, allowing for frequent stops for exploratory detours, contemplating views, and happily enjoying the moods of the river—brilliant in the sun, silvery in the diffuse light of dusk.

The Dordogne flows wide at **Bergerac** ❶ (*Visitor information, rue Neuve d'Argenson, tel 05 53 57 03 11*), forming a broad alluvial plain that is the main area of tobacco production in France. The old port, once a flourishing center of the wine trade, spans both sides of the river, and the town has winding streets of medieval half-timbered houses. The **Musée du Tabac** in the elegant 17th-century Maison Peyrarède (*place du Feu, tel 05 53 63 04 13, closed Sun. a.m. & all Mon.*) presents a fascinating survey of the evolution of tobacco smoking, with a huge variety of snuff boxes and pipes including Native American peace pipes. The **Musée du Vin** (*5 rue des Conférences*) celebrates the local wines, and

they may be tasted at the wine center in the medieval **Cloître des Récollets** (*place du Docteur-Cayla*).

The most celebrated of the local vintages is the sweet white wine of Monbazillac. The moated 16th-century **Château de Monbazillac** (*Tel 05 53 63 65 00, closed Nov.–March*), on the crest of hills just south of

---

🅰 See area map p. 232
▶ Bergerac
⬌ 80 miles (128 km)
🕐 2 days
▶ Domme

NOT TO BE MISSED

- Château de Monbazillac
- Cingle de Trémolat
- Abbaye de Cadouin
- Beynac-et-Cazenac
- La Roque-Gageac

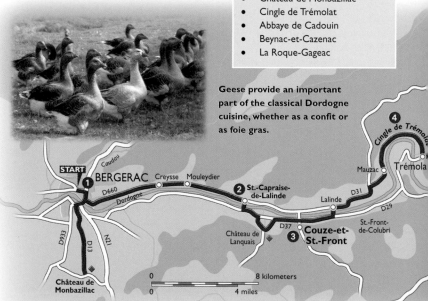

Geese provide an important part of the classical Dordogne cuisine, whether as a confit or as foie gras.

Bergerac on the D13, has an interesting local craft museum as well as wine tasting and a good restaurant.

Return and take the D660 along the north bank of the river from Bergerac. Cross the river at **St.-Capraise-de-Lalinde** ❷ on the D37 to **Château de Lanquais** (*Tel 05 53 61 24 24, closed Tues. & Oct.– March*). Part medieval fortress, part Renaissance palace, the castle occupies a magnificent site above the pretty old village of Lanquais. A reminder of the region's turbulent past can be seen in the damage inflicted by cannonballs during the Wars of Religion. The little town of **Couze-et-St.-Front** ❸, just to the east, is famous for papermaking, once a major industry here. The traditional methods are still used at the **Moulin du Larroque** (*Tel 05 63 61 01 75, closed Tues. & a.m. mid-Oct.–April*). Farther along the south bank, the picturesque village of **St.-Front-de-Colubri** perches on a cliff, offering a superb view of the Dordogne and the Gratusse rapids upriver, the most dangerous stretch to navigate when the riverboats traded upstream.

The river now executes one of its extraordinary horseshoe bends, known as *cingles*, at the **Cingle de Trémolat** ❹. Cross to the north bank of the river at St. Front to go round the cingle and enjoy a panoramic view of the rich pastureland contained in the loop. Trémolat itself is a charming little village, made famous by director Claude Chabrol as the setting for the film *Le Boucher* (1969). Between Trémolat and Limeuil, the D31 follows the cliff, overlooking the river.

Limeuil lies at the confluence of the Vézère and the Dordogne; here, rocky terraces frame the river, and the little village, with its Renaissance houses and 12th-century church, winds up the hill, providing glorious views. Follow the D51 beside the wide river, flanked by cliffs, then cross it to make a short detour on the D25, through a valley of chestnut woods, to **Cadouin** ❺ (*Tel 05 53 35 50 10, closed Tues. in winter & mid-Dec.–early Feb.*). This austerely beautiful Cistercian abbey of golden stone has a fine Gothic cloister. From Cadouin, a tiny road loops east to **Urval,** with its vast 12th-century fortified church. From Urval go north to the D25 and then east to **Siorac-en-Périgord** ❻, which has a 17th-century château and a little river beach.

Cross the river back to the north bank and follow the D703E upstream to the market town of **St.-Cyprien** ❼ (*Visitor information, tel 05 53 30 36 09*), clustered around its 14th-century church and massive bell tower

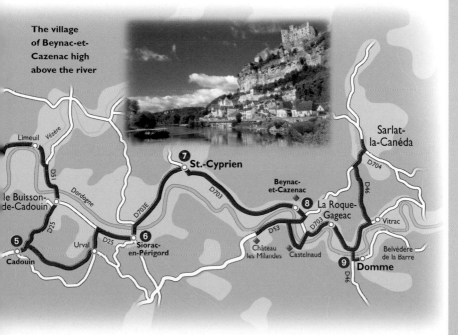

The village of Beynac-et-Cazenac high above the river

Houses in La Roque-Gageac are piled up the cliffside above the Dordogne.

on a wooded hillside. Continue upstream on the D703; now the valley starts to narrow. Towering above it is the formidable Château at **Beynac-et-Cazenac** ⑧ (*Visitor information, tel 05 53 29 43 08*), sitting like a stone crown on its rock, accessible by a steep footpath or via a detour inland through the pretty little village. Restoration work is gradually bringing this tremendous fortress back to its 13th-century appearance, with drawbridge, portcullis, and medieval kitchen. The vaulted great hall has lovely naive frescoes, and the views from the castle keep are not for the faint-hearted.

Beynac was a French bastion during the Hundred Years' War, and glowering opposite it on the south bank is the fortress of **Castelnaud** (*Tel 05 53 31 30 00*), intermittently an English stronghold. It now houses a museum of siege warfare, including primitive cannons and a reconstructed catapult. Cross the river from the D703 to the D53 under the Château de Castelnaud and make a short detour downstream on this road to visit the 15th-century **Château les Milandes** (*Tel 05 53 59 31 21, closed Nov.–April*), once the much-loved home of the remarkable Josephine Baker. Here the American twenties jazz singer and cabaret artist planned to realize her dream of a "world village" with a "rainbow tribe" of 12 children adopted from all over the

world. Financial difficulties and frail health forced her to abandon the idea, heartbroken, in 1969.

Retrace your steps to Castelnaud, then cross the river and continue east along the D703 to **La Roque-Gageac.** This irresistible place to pause shelters beneath the great craggy cliffside. Relax at a riverside café, stroll around the village, with its ocher houses and craft shops, or climb the steep narrow streets to the 12th-century church to admire the view.

Continue along the D703 then cross to the south of the river again on the D46. Just south of the river, take the D50 winding steeply up to **Domme** ⑨ (*Visitor information, tel 05 53 31 71 00*), the best preserved and possibly the loveliest of the *bastide* towns (see p. 262). High up on a crag above the river, the narrow, flower-decked streets still shelter within its 12th-century walls. Beneath the 17th-century covered marketplace is a cavern (now reached by an elevator), where it is supposed that the citizens of Domme took refuge during the Hundred Years' War and the Wars of Religion. The **Belvédère de la Barre,** at the end of the Grand-Rue, offers breathtaking panoramas of the river and the surrounding countryside. From Domme, the D50 and D46 take you to **Sarlat-la-Canéda** (see p. 253). ■

Sarlat-la-Canéda

NESTLING IN A LITTLE WOODED VALLEY A FEW MILES north of the Dordogne River, Sarlat is like a living architectural museum, with one of the best ensembles of medieval, Renaissance, and 17th-century buildings in France. Its narrow cobbled streets, surrounded by ramparts, are full of houses from all these prosperous eras, rich in carving, their steep roofs sometimes tiled with the traditional limestone slabs. Substantially rebuilt between 1450 and 1500, after the devastation of the Hundred Years' War (thus accounting for its architectural coherence), it was happily neglected during the 19th and 20th centuries (with the regrettable exception of the boulevard driven right through the middle of town). In 1962 Sarlat became one of the first towns in France to be restored and protected as a whole under a national policy of restoration.

Sarlat-la-Canéda
232 D3
Visitor information
Hôtel de Maleville
05 53 31 45 45

A street of age-old houses beside the abbey graveyard in Sarlat

Rue de la République (the unfortunate 19th-century boulevard that bisects the town) is lined on both sides with a warren of medieval streets and many handsome buildings. One of the most beautiful, on Place du Peyrou, is the pinnacled 16th-century **Maison de la Boétie,** house of poet Étienne de la Boétie, with graceful arches on the ground floor and delicately carved mullion windows. A relic of the town's powerful 12th-century abbey can still be seen in the **Chapelle des Pénitents Bleus** *(place du Peyrou).* The bizarre conical tower of the **Lanterne des Morts,** in the abbey graveyard, was built to commemorate the sermons and miracles of St. Bernard in Sarlat in 1147.

Place de la Liberté, the lovely main square, has lots of cafés and is the focus of Sarlat's famous market on Wednesdays and Saturdays. Then stalls offer truffles, walnuts, and foie gras, as well as everyday items for locals, and souvenirs for visitors. Not surprisingly, Sarlat is a tremendously popular tourist destination, and, if you can, it is best to visit out of season. Take time to wander its fascinating streets, poking into nooks and crannies; best of all, see it by night, when its history and atmosphere are enhanced by a modern system of gas lighting. For a good overall view, drive to the village of **Temniac,** which overlooks Sarlat from the north. ■

Lascaux & prehistoric cave paintings

THE PAINTED CAVES AT LASCAUX HAVE BEEN CALLED THE Sistine Chapel of prehistory for the powerful quality of the work. But they can now be seen only in replica at Lascaux II. Though a visit there is still an amazing experience, the beautiful Vézère Valley is rich in original marvels, so there are other choices as well.

Many buildings at Les Eyzies-de-Tayac back onto the overhanging cliff shelters.

The area is honeycombed with limestone caves, creating an underground network of tunnels and caverns protected from the light, with constant temperature and humidity that would be the envy of many modern museums.

Until about 17,000 years ago, people lived in dwellings of skin

A NOTE ON TERMINOLOGY
The French word for a cave is *grotte*; *gouffre* is a chasm with a wide surface opening; *cave,* on the other hand, means cellar or storeroom, often for wine. Signs pointing to a *cave* usually indicate wine for sale and probably tasting.

and turf, under rock overhangs, and sometimes in cave entrances. Yet the paintings are usually buried deep within the caves' dark interiors, painted or engraved by the light of stone oil lamps or torches. These areas were probably religious sanctuaries devoted to the worship of the animals that sustained Cro-Magnon life. The range of animals depicted includes horses, bison, deer, boars, wolves, foxes, birds, and reptiles, with the occasional mammoth and rhinoceros. Very often the animals are shown

pregnant, as if invoking fertility. Human figures appear only rarely. These early artists used charcoal, ocher, and red and yellow pigments made from oxidized iron, applied with fingers or brushes or blown through tubes. They also scratched and carved with horn, stone, or bone, often incorporating the natural contours of the rock as part of their design.

Some of the cave paintings were seen by earlier generations—there are signs of 16th-century graffiti at Rouffignac, for example—but nobody at that time would have believed them to be so old. The first scientific excavations began in the mid-19th century, revealing evidence of lives tens of thousands of years ago, along with entire periods of prehistory: The Mousterian, Magdalenian, and other early cultures were named after the finds here. The first skeletons of Cro-Magnon man were discovered in 1868, during excavations for a new railroad line at Cro-Magnon. Prehistory is a subject of passionate interest to local people. Farmers look out for worked flints in their fields, and small village museums display local finds.

LES EYZIES-DE-TAYAC
The best place to set these wonders in context is Les Eyzies-de-Tayac, known as the prehistoric capital of the world. Here the **Musée National de Préhistoire** displays local discoveries, diagrams,

timelines, and items from every prehistoric period to give an excellent introduction to the subject (though all the information plaques are in French). The terrace in front of the museum gives a good view of the beautiful Vézère River.

A number of caves lie nearby. **Font-de-Gaume,** discovered in 1901, has some of the best art still open to the public, with drawings of deer, horses, and mammoths and a frieze of bison. The **Grotte de Combarelles,** in the Beune Valley east of Les-Eyzies-de-Tayac, discovered in 1910, shelters over 200 engravings and drawings of animals and magic symbols. Tickets for both of these sites are subject to daily limits, so arrive early. The rock shelter of **Cap Blanc,** farther up the Beune Valley, contains a frieze of horses sculptured in relief. The caves at **Rouffignac** to the north have been known since the 15th century: Almost 5 miles (8 km) of caves and galleries can now be toured by electric train to see drawings of ibex, rhinoceros, mammoths, and fighting stags.

LASCAUX

Lascaux itself, close to Montignac farther up the Vézère Valley, lay buried beneath a landslide for thousands of years before being accidentally discovered in 1940, by children looking for their lost dog (so the story goes). What they found was a prehistoric art gallery of over 150 paintings and 1,500 engravings, perfectly preserved by a fortuitous glaze of crystals.

Drawings of animals in movement, executed in ocher and red pigments with strong lines of black charcoal, show an astonishingly sophisticated level of artistic skill. Opened to the public in 1948, the caves attracted such huge numbers of visitors that in 1963 the decision was made to close them, after green algae and white calcite were found to be spoiling the paintings. A splendid replica was built nearby at **Lascaux II,** where the paintings were painstakingly copied over 11 years, using identical tools and pigments to those of the original artists—an extraordinary phenomenon in itself. ■

Prehistoric artists at Lascaux cave used the cave contours to bring animals to life.

Les Eyzies-de-Tayac
- 🄰 232 D3
- **Visitor information**
- ✉ place de la Mairie
- ☎ 05 53 06 97 05

Musée National de Préhistoire
- ☎ 05 53 06 45 45
- 🕐 Closed Tues. mid-Nov.–mid-March
- 💲 $

Lascaux II
- 🄰 232 D3
- ✉ On the D704E, Montignac
- ☎ 05 53 51 95 03
- 💲 $$

Cahors

THE HILLS TO THE NORTH AND SOUTH OF CAHORS AFFORD panoramic views of the handsome ensemble of towers, ramparts, and bridges that make up the town, almost encircled in a snug loop of the Lot River. Cahors was of significance in the Middle Ages as the capital of Quercy, the limestone area around the Lot River.

Cahors

⚠ 232 D3

Visitor information

✉ place François-Mitterrand

☎ 05 65 53 20 65

The medieval Pont Valentré, originally built to defend Cahors against invaders

Prosperous, well defended, and proud of its ancient university, medieval Cahors was an important center of trade, banking, and learning. But in 1360, during the Hundred Years' War, it was handed over to the English. The population fled, and the nearly deserted city never fully recovered. One outstanding relic of its medieval grandeur survives: the famous 14th-century Pont Valentré spanning the river on seven Gothic arches guarded by three fortified towers. According to local legend, the master builder made a pact with the Devil in order to finish the bridge, but by cunning managed to retain his eternal soul.

Lined with plane trees, the main street of Cahors is Boulevard Gambetta, named for the famous 19th-century radical politician Léon Gambetta, a native of the city. The shops here and the nearby covered market supply all manner of local delicacies, including the rich, plummy wine of Cahors known as *vin noir*. To the east of Boulevard Gambetta clusters the old quarter, where houses show plenty of evidence of former glories. Alleys crossed by bridges stripe the streets with shadows, while the light reveals the Renaissance windows, stone carvings, and finely worked wooden corbels of these impressive mansions. One of the most entrancing is the **Hôtel Roaldès** (*quai Champollion*), with its south facade of timber and weathered redbrick, Italian-style loggia and tower, and north facade carved with suns, trees, and the rose emblem of Quercy.

At the heart of the old town is the Romanesque **Cathédrale St.-Étienne** (*place Aristide-Briand*). The two great domes decorated with 14th-century frescoes give a spacious feel to the interior and the Flamboyant Gothic cloister has beautiful carvings. But the cathedral's most splendid feature is the 16th-century tympanum over the north door, depicting the Ascension of Christ, supported by angels. ∎

Rocamadour

IN A CLEFT OF THE GREAT GORGE OF THE ALZOU RIVER, Rocamadour is one of the most impressive—and the most visited—sites in France. In the 12th century, the village exploded into fame with the discovery of the body of a man, believed to be Zacchaeus, husband of St. Veronica, who was rechristened St. Amadour. Buried beneath an existing chapel dedicated to the Virgin, the remains were soon credited with miracles, and pilgrims came from far and wide.

The grand stairway leads from the village up to the shrine of the Black Virgin and the saint's tomb. The devout climbed the steps on their knees (some still do). Within the **Chapelle de Notre-Dame,** carved into the rock, stands the famous statue of the Black Virgin. Probably 12th century, the statue is crudely carved but moving in its simplicity, the wood smoothed and darkened by time. Above it is a ninth-century bell, which is said to ring unaided to foretell a miracle. Down steps to the left of the chapel is the 12th-century crypt with the tomb of St. Amadour. The **Musée d'Art Sacré** displays a tremendous collection of sacred art.

Above the chapel the climb continues, either past the Stations of the Cross or up to the ramparts of the original fort, built to protect the shrine from the west. ■

Rocamadour
- ⊠ 232 D3

Visitor information
- ✉ rue de la Couronnerie
- ☎ 05 65 33 62 59
- ✉ Maison de Tourisme l'Hospitalet
- ☎ 05 65 33 22 00

Musée d'Art Sacré
- ✉ parvis des Églises
- ☎ 05 65 33 23 30

Gouffre de Padirac
- ⊠ 232 D3
- ☎ 05 65 33 64 56
- 🕐 Closed mid-Oct.–March
- 💲 $$ round-trip

The roofs of Rocamadour

Gouffre de Padirac

The Gouffre de Padirac, east of Rocamadour on the D673, is a vast chasm in the limestone, some 330 feet (100 m) wide and 800 feet (246 m) deep. It leads to a series of grottoes that reach at least 9 miles (15 km) underground. In the Middle Ages it served as a refuge in turbulent times, but only in the late 19th century did speleologists begin to explore it, discovering a prehistoric site as well as the huge caves. Elevators and stairs descend to the bottom of the chasm, and flat-bottomed boats ferry you along the subterranean river and into the illuminated caves. After about 350 yards (315 m) you arrive at the Salle du Grand Dôme, a cavern 295 feet (90 m) high, one of the world's loftiest. ■

Around the Lot Valley

AS IT FLOWS TOWARD CAHORS, THE LOT RIVER CUTS through *causses*—limestone plateaus. At one moment it is overhung by creamy yellow or pink cliffs, with picture-postcard villages and turreted fortresses clinging to their flanks the next moment it meanders gently through bucolic landscapes of meadows and vineyards. To the north its tributary, the Célé, fringed with graceful poplars, flows to meet it through a romantic valley studded with prehistoric caves and Renaissance castles. Cahors (see p. 256) makes a good base for excursions here. This round-trip follows the Lot up to the market town of Figeac, returning down the Célé Valley.

St.-Cirq-Lapopie
🅜 232 D3
Visitor information
☎ 05 65 31 29 06

Cajarc
🅜 232 D3
Visitor information
☎ 05 65 40 72 89

Figeac
🅜 233 E3
Visitor information
✉ place Vival
☎ 05 65 34 06 25

Musée Champollion
✉ place Champollion
🕐 Closed Mon. (except July & Aug.) & a.m. Nov.–Feb.
🆂 $$

Musée du Plein Air de Quercy
✉ Sauliac-sur-Célé
☎ 05 65 30 24 00
🕐 Closed Sat., a.m. Sept.–Oct., & Nov.–April
🆂 $$

Tourism has come in a gentle way here, with horseback riding, boating, several intriguing small museums, and caves in abundance: Everywhere you will see signs pointing to the *Grottes*.

Leave Cahors on the D653, heading east on the D662 to reach **St.-Cirq-Lapopie,** officially—and justly—designated one of the most beautiful villages in France. The winding cobbled streets, fortified church, and timber-framed houses with their Renaissance details and corbelling have all been lovingly restored. Artists have colonized the place since the 1950s, most famously the surrealist writer André Breton (1896–1966). Not surprisingly, it is a honeypot for tourists.

The Lot Valley bristles with castles; at **Cénevières** you can visit the 13th-century Château (*Tel 05 65 31 27 33, closed Nov.–Easter*) overlooking the river and admire its Renaissance additions including the stone staircase, gallery, and coffered ceilings. You can also enjoy the views from the terraces, which take in the trogolodyte village carved out of the opposite cliff.

The next major settlement is the pretty riverside resort of **Cajarc,** where the **Musée Georges-Pompidou** (Georges Pompidou, President of France from 1969 to 1974, used to have a house here)

stages exhibitions of contemporary European art (*Tel 05 65 40 78 19*). Continue up the valley to **Montbrun-les-Bains,** which has another spectacularly positioned ruined fortress. At **Larroque-Toirac** the fairy-tale medieval castle was rebuilt after the English burned it down in the 14th century.

ROSETTA STONE

A few miles farther on, the D662 cuts across the causse to reach **Figeac,** a beautiful old market town. Tanning was an important industry here, and many of the handsome medieval houses in the old town have octagonal chimneys and open *soleilhos*, drying rooms, on the top floor. The tourist office and local museum are housed in the 13th-century **Hôtel de la Monnaie,** the old mint. Jean-François Champollion, the 19th-century Egyptologist who first deciphered Egyptian hieroglyphics using the trilingual inscription of the Rosetta Stone, was born in Figeac. His birthplace is now the **Musée Champollion,** devoted to his life and work. The Place des Écritures is floored with an enlarged copy of the stone.

Leave Figeac on the D13, then turn left on the D41 to follow the lovely valley of the Célé River. Stop to visit the beautiful village of **Espagnac-Ste.-Eulalie** and the

atmospheric ruins of the aptly named 13th-century **Prieuré du Val-Paradis.** Continue past peach-colored cliffs and fortified caves to the Benedictine **Abbaye de Marcilhac.** About 3 miles (5 km) farther on stop at **Sauliac-sur-Célé** for its living museum of 19th-century farm work, the **Musée du Plein Air de Quercy.** Two reconstructed farms illustrate traditional agriculture and crafts, complete with authentic crops and animals, old wagons, tractors, milling, and breadmaking.

Beyond Cabrerets and its two commanding castles lie the incomparable treasures of the painted **Grotte de Pech-Merle,** discovered in 1922 by two local boys. This remarkable gallery of prehistoric paintings, a staggering 20,000 years old at the most conservative estimate, are still open to public view. You can explore almost a mile of

spectacular caves and galleries decorated with glorious paintings of bison and mammoths, silhouettes of horses, female figures, and mysterious handprints.

BÉRENGER'S FOLLY

West of Cahors towers the **Château de Bonaguil,** the ultimate military fantasy. In the late 15th century, Bérenger de Roquefeuil set about fortifying and enlarging the existing 13th-century keep, determined to build a totally impregnable castle. Forty years later, he was the proud lord of a masterpiece of military engineering. Sadly, nobody ever attacked him, so Bérenger was never able to prove his point. ∎

"St.-Cirq has cast a spell on me, the one which lasts for ever. I have no desire to go anywhere else."
André Breton (1951)

The village of St.-Cirq-Lapopie and the Lot River

Grotte de Pech-Merle
✉ Cabrerets
☎ 05 65 31 27 05
🕐 Closed Oct.–May
💲 $$

Château de Bonaguil
☎ 05 53 71 90 33
🕐 Closed Dec.–Jan.
💲 $$

Conques

THE LITTLE VILLAGE OF CONQUES IS TUCKED AWAY IN the steep valley of the Dourdou River. This unlikely setting hides one of the great pilgrimage churches of France, the Abbaye de Ste.-Foy.

Conques

🅰 233 E3

Abbaye de Ste.-Foy

☎ 05 65 69 85 12

The three great towers of the abbey rise above the village, tiled with the same local slates as the houses. Pilgrims began to come here in the 11th century when the monks at Conques stole the relics of St. Foy, an early Christian martyr, from Agen. Soon the abbey became a stopping place on the way to Santiago de Compostela (see pp. 266–67) as well as a place of pilgrimage itself.

The 11th-century interior of the church is pure Romanesque with a

soaring nave, beautifully decorated capitals, and three chapels at the rounded east end, built to provide more altars for the pilgrims. The most celebrated feature of the church is the tympanum over the west door, a masterpiece of 12th-century sculpture depicting the Last Judgment. Unusually, it still has traces of the original color.

The abbey's Treasure survived the Revolution intact, hidden by the villagers. Its precious pieces include enamel work, vestments, and reliquaries, but the star of the collection is the ninth-century reliquary for St. Foy herself, made to hold the bones of the young saint. It is in the form of a statue, made of gold and studded with jewels, cameos, and intaglios, some of which may date from Roman times.

The little village itself is sometimes overwhelmed by visitors to its church, but it has some charming old houses along its steep streets. ■

The Abbaye de Ste.-Foy and the village of Conques cling to the steep slopes of the valley of the Dourdou River, a tributary of the Lot.

Bastide towns

ALONGSIDE ITS NOBLE HERITAGE OF CASTLES AND ABBEYS, southwest France provides, through its *bastide* towns, insights into life in the war-torn Middle Ages.

Cordes
232 D2
Visitor information
Maison Fonpayrouse
05 63 56 00 52

Monpazier
232 D3
Visitor information
place des Cornières
05 53 22 68 59

Monflanquin
232 D2
Visitor information
place des Arcades
05 53 36 40 19

Arcades surround the central square of Monpazier, a well-preserved bastide town.

Built in the 13th and 14th centuries, bastides were new towns designed to protect the beleaguered country population during the Hundred Years' War. Those settling the new towns were granted land to support a family, or "to light a fire," and benefited from privileges stated in a town charter, which included freedom from feudal service and the right to hold a market and to elect a council.

The basic design—always with an eye to defense—was a grid of streets around a central arcaded square. Built by both the English and French on strategic sites, they were fortified with massive walls. Since a bastide's inhabitants did not owe allegiance to an overlord, there was no castle for refuge, so churches were fortified as sanctuaries.

SOME BASTIDE TOWNS

Cordes, 50 miles (90 km) southeast of Cahors, is one of the earliest of the bastides, founded by the

Count of Toulouse in 1222. It is also one of the loveliest, with perfectly preserved ramparts and town gates, and impeccably restored narrow cobbled streets lined with Gothic houses. Beside the vast covered marketplace is the well, bored 375 feet (114 m) deep to provide the town with water during sieges.

Monpazier, southeast of Bergerac, is one of the most complete bastide towns. It retains its exquisitely arcaded central square, covered market hall, fortified church, a rectangular pattern of streets, and ancient walls.

At **Monflanquin,** on a hill southeast of Bergerac, the market square is still complete. Passages between the houses afford glimpses of the country around.

Some other fine examples of bastides include Montauban (see p. 265), Mirepoix (see map p. 232, D1), Domme (see p. 252), and Lauzerte southwest of Cahors. ∎

Toulouse

A COSMOPOLITAN METROPOLIS, REGIONAL CAPITAL, AND thriving center of technology and aeronautical research, Toulouse still holds at its heart the lovely old *ville rose*, the pink-brick streets making up the old town. History may be powerfully tangible in Toulouse but this is still a lively city, with the biggest student population in France outside Paris. Visit the ancient city on foot, then for a startling change of pace take a trip on the state-of-the-art Métro, with each station credited to a different team of architect and artist.

Start in the **Place du Capitole,** the vast central square lined with cafés. It is dominated by the Capitole itself, the 18th-century **Hôtel de Ville** named after the city's medieval consuls, or *capitouls.* Beginning in the tenth century, Toulouse was the seat of the powerful counts of Toulouse and the focus of the most exciting civilization in Western Europe. All this came to a brutal end with the Albigensian Crusade of the 13th century, when Toulouse lost its autonomy. In the 15th century the city enjoyed another heyday, thanks to the *pastel* or woad plant cultivated here; it yielded a blue dye, to be supplanted by the arrival of indigo from the East in the 16th century.

Merchants and capitouls grew rich, building themselves ever more splendid mansions in Italian Renaissance style. Look for the lovely **Hôtel d'Assézat** on Rue de Metz, and **Hôtel Bernuy** on Rue Gambetta. The **Basilique,** built in honor of St. Sernin, is the largest Romanesque church in Europe (consecrated in 1096, though the nave and tower are from the 13th century) and was the most beautiful of all the pilgrim churches. Follow in the pilgrims' footsteps through the south portal with its tremendous carvings, down the nave, past glowing frescoes and tapestries, painted capitals, and

carved choir stalls, to the 11th-century altar. Then walk around the ambulatory and its radiating chapels before descending to the crypt, with its Treasury including some priceless reliquaries.

Don't miss the Gothic church of **Les Jacobins** (*rue Lakanal*), with its single row of columns that crescendo into sensational palm tree vaulting over the apse. Outstanding Romanesque sculptures from the city's churches and cloisters have been gathered together in the **Musée des Augustins** (*21 rue de Metz, tel 05 61 22 21 82*). Newly opened is **Espace d'Art Moderne et Contemporain** (*76 allés Charles-de-Fitte, tel 05 62 48 58 00, closed a.m. & all Mon.*) in the old abbatoirs of St. Cyprien district. ■

Toulouse

A 232 D2

Visitor information

✉ Donjon du Capitole

☎ 05 61 11 02 22

Basilique St.-Sernin

✉ place St.-Sernin

🕓 Closed to visitors Sun. a.m.

Espace d'Art Moderne

✉ Les Abbatoires, 76 Allées Charles-de-Fitte

☎ 05 62 48 58 00

🕓 Closed Mon.

💲 $

Cité de l'Espace

✉ avenue Jean-Gonord

☎ 05 62 71 64 80

🕓 Closed Mon except school vacations

💲 $$

Carved capital depicting the death of John the Baptist in the Musée des Augustins

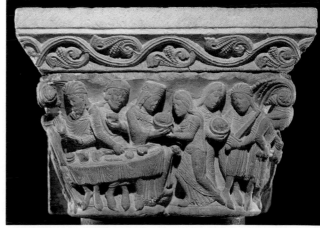

Albi

Its position on the steep banks of the Tarn River, and its fortress-church, made Albi a formidable city.

VIEWED FROM THE 11TH-CENTURY PONT VIEUX OVER THE Tarn River, Albi presents an unforgettable sight, its pink and ocher houses rising in tiers to the soaring bulk of its cathedral fortress.

Like Toulouse, Albi is a *ville rose,* built of the same pink brick. Its single most breathtaking feature is the great **Cathédrale Ste.-Cécile.** The mighty brick walls, buttressed by tremendous piers, are as daunting as they are astonishing. In the spacious nave, built without pillars or transept, is a colorful world of 16th-century Italian wall paintings and ethereally delicate carving. Most remarkable are the filigree rood screen and the fresco of the Last Judgment that covers the west wall. In the formal gardens of the 13th-century bishop's palace, the **Palais de la Berbie,** the ramparts offer ravishing views of the Tarn. Inside the palace lies Albi's other treasure: an extensive collection of works by Henri de Toulouse-Lautrec, who was born in Albi (see sidebar below).

In the old town you will find the **Maison Enjalbert** and **Hôtel de Reynes,** both built in the 16th century, and the Romanesque **Église de St.-Salvy** (*rue Mariès*), with a lovely 13th-century cloister. ∎

Albi
🅜 233 E2
Visitor information
✉ Palais de la Berbie, place Ste.-Cécile
☎ 05 63 49 48 80

Palais de la Berbie:
Musée de Toulouse-Lautrec
✉ place Ste.-Cécile
☎ 05 63 49 48 70
🕐 Closed Tues. except July & Aug.
💲 $

Toulouse-Lautrec

Born in Albi in 1864, Henri de Toulouse-Lautrec was descended from the counts of Toulouse. Crippled and stunted in his youth by what may have been brittle bone disease, he sought solace in painting, and freedom in the bohemian world of the Montmartre quarter of Paris. A superb draftsman with a wide technical range, he used just a few expressive strokes to convey the scenes that caught his eye. The **Musée de Toulouse-Lautrec,** in the Palais de la Berbie, has a collection of over 600 of his works, ranging from early landscapes and portraits to sketches and book illustrations, drawings and paintings, lithographs and posters. ∎

**The arcaded
central square**

Montauban

Montauban

△ 232 D2

Visitor information

✉ Ancien Collège

☎ 05 63 63 60 60

Musée Ingres

✉ Palais Épiscopal

🕐 Closed Mon. except
July & Aug. & Sun.
a.m. mid-Oct.–mid-
April

💲 $

Another pink-brick town on
the Tarn River, Montauban was
founded in the 12th century by the
Count of Toulouse. In the 16th century it became a major center of
Protestantism and even resisted a
siege by Louis XIII—despite the
fact that the king had arranged a
special lunch to view the assault.

The focus of the town is the
Place Nationale, which owes its
satisfying unity to the fact that it
was rebuilt in the 17th century

following a fire. The fortified
Église de St.-Jacques, largely
dating back to the 13th century,
stands near the Pont Vieux, which
is similar in style to the bridge at
Albi. At the end of the bridge stands
the former bishop's palace, now the
Musée Ingres. On his death,
Jean-Auguste-Dominique Ingres
left his studio contents to his native
town, including Greek vases and
Roman sculpture, as well as many
of his drawings. ■

Moissac

Moissac

△ 232 D2

Visitor information

✉ 6 place Durand-de-
Bredon

☎ 05 63 04 01 85

**Abbaye de
St.-Pierre**

✉ place St.-Pierre

💲 $. Tickets from
tourist information
office

The small town of Moissac on the
north bank of the Tarn River is
famed for the carvings on the abbey
church. In the 11th century, the
Abbaye de St.-Pierre at Moissac
became a daughter foundation of
the abbey of Cluny (see p. 207).

The church, part Romanesque
and part Gothic, is impressive, but
the 12th-century carvings on its
south portal will stop you in your
tracks. A scalloped decoration
frames the doorway and a central
column entwined with lions supports the tympanum. In minute

and still perfect detail (even the
revolutionaries stayed their
hammers), it depicts St. John's
vision of the Apocalypse from the
Book of Revelation. In the middle
sits Christ in Majesty surrounded
by the Evangelists, angels, and
symbolic beasts. The flowing figure
of Jeremiah on the western door
jamb has a melancholy beauty. On
the east side Avarice and Unchastity
writhe in torment. In the arcaded
cloisters, the 76 slender columns
support graceful arcades, their capitals carved with infinite delicacy. ■

The road to Compostela

The symbol of the scallop shell crops up all over southwest France, marking stages on the great pilgrim route to Santiago de Compostela in northwest Spain. Along with Jerusalem and Rome, this was one of the greatest shrines of medieval Christendom. Four main pilgrim routes threaded across France: from Paris; from Vézelay in Burgundy; from Le Puy-en-Velay in the Auvergne; and from St.-Gilles, near Arles in Provence. All converged in the southwest to cross the Pyrenees at the passes of Roncesvalles or Somport, continuing through Navarre on a single path.

Thousands of pilgrims and travelers still follow the routes today, passing through the same towns and villages as the original pilgrims. They, too, worship in the great churches of Conques or Toulouse, wonder at the finely carved cloisters and tympanum of Moissac, pause to pray at wayside shrines and crosses, or seek shelter in tiny frescoed chapels. They may have different reasons for making this pilgrimage: Some may still walk the route for religious reasons, some to better understand their forebears, some just to enjoy the scenery along the way. But, like the medieval pilgrims, they find satisfaction in the journey.

The object of the pilgrims' travels is the shrine of St. James (Santiago), the disciple who is believed to have brought Christianity to Spain, then part of the Roman Empire. On his return to Judea he was executed by Herod, and his followers returned with his martyred body to Galicia in Spain. As they approached the shore, they saw a vision of a man covered in scallop shells rise out of the waves on horseback; the scallop shell became the pilgrimage emblem. The body of St. James was buried, and subsequently most of Spain fell to the Moors. Then, in 814, a vision of stars (*compostela* means field of stars) showed the way to the saint's tomb, and on July 25 (now the feast of Santiago) the body was discovered. Soon a church was built on the spot: The present building at Compostela is a vast Romanesque church with an elaborate baroque facade added later.

Pilgrims were lured with the promise of indulgences—forgiveness of their sins and remission of time in purgatory—and pilgrimages became enormously popular. The first recorded pilgrimage to Compostela was carried out by the bishop of Le Puy in 951.

Vital encouragement for the pilgrimage route was provided by the formidably powerful Benedictine abbey of Cluny in Burgundy (see p. 207), which established daughter houses, churches, and shrines along the way, and donated relics to enhance their prestige and power. No shrine or place of pilgrimage was complete without a relic preserved in reliquaries of gold and silver embellished with jewels. Bones of saints were treasured, and pieces of the True Cross were especially valuable. Santiago de Compostela boasted the body of St. James, and many pilgrims would, en route, have prayed at shrines containing parts of no fewer than five Apostles and, at the Basilique de St.-Sernin in Toulouse (see p. 263), a sliver of the True Cross. It was many centuries before the authenticity of these relics was called into question. Intense and sometimes unseemly competition raged for the most potent relics. A monk from the abbey at Conques stole the relics of Ste. Foy from Agen. Vézelay was equally unscrupulous in refusing to return the remains of Mary Magdalene, sent to them (somewhat ironically) for protection.

Often pilgrims doggedly tramped the sacred path for years, suffering hardship and danger. Moved by their plight, at the end of the 12th century a monk from Poitou by the name of Amery Picaud penned the *Liber Sancti Jacobi*. This early guidebook gave details of the best places for sustenance, the most reliable sources of water, and the most rewarding chapels or monasteries to visit on the way.

Pilgrims wore the sign of the scallop shell to denote their calling. Even today it still works its magic. In 1987 the European Community officially recognized a system of signposting that had been devised using the scallop shell. It described the pilgrim route to Compostela as "one of the oldest signs of European cooperation and enterprise...a key part of our European heritage." ■

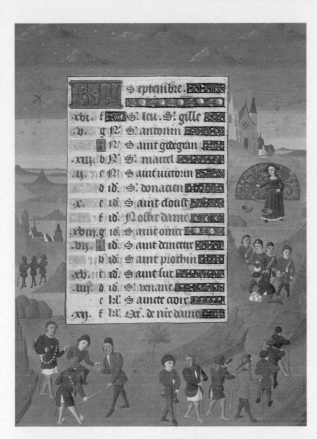

Left: Groups of pilgrims on their way to Santiago de Compostela shown on an illuminated manuscript of 1450

Two places where pilgrims worshiped on the way to Compostela were the Basilique de St.-Sernin, Toulouse (above right), and the abbey at Moissac, with its lovely cloisters (below).

Red sandstone turrets are characteristic of houses in Collonges-la-Rouge.

More places to visit in the Dordogne & Midi-Pyrénées

BIRON

Just south of the *bastide* town of Monpazier (see p. 262), the gargantuan Château de Biron dominates a great swath of countryside as it has since its 12th-century beginnings. The original keep was added to by generation after generation of the Gontaut family, until it was taken over by the local département authorities in 1978. Restoration is now in progress, and the château serves as an arts center during the summer. The feudal core of the buildings was enlarged with graceful Renaissance additions in the 16th century, including the beautiful double chapel—to house the family tombs above, with space for villagers to worship below.

🅰 232 D3 ☎ 05 53 63 13 39 ⊕ Closed Mon. Oct.–June

COLLONGES-LA-ROUGE

The lords of Turenne built this red village, its delightful mansions, towers, turrets, market hall, and château forming an almost bizarre homogeneity. The white limestone tympanum of the otherwise red church (11th–12th centuries) comes almost as a relief. Stroll along Rue Noire in the oldest quarter to gain a good sense of the whole.

🅰 232 D3

ST.-CÉRÉ

St.-Céré is a charming little market town, well situated for excursions to the Lot Valley. The Bave River ripples past its handsome streets, market square, and 15th-century balconied mansions. Above it to the north loom the two keeps (12th and 15th centuries) of the castle of **St.-Laurent-les-Tours,** home of the artist Jean Lurçat from 1945 to his death in 1966. Now it houses a museum of his work, and galleries in the town sell both original works and prints.

🅰 232 D3 **Visitor information** ✉ place de la République ☎ 05 65 38 11 85 ■

The path to the **Cirque de Gavarnie in the high Pyrenees**

The Pyrenees

Visible from the flat Plain of Aquitaine and—on a clear day—from the fringes of the Massif Central, the glittering peaks of the Pyrenees fill the horizon with unsurpassed grandeur. Here you will find all the majesty and solitude of high mountains, combined with the gentler delights of lush, green valleys, rushing waterfalls, and rare flora and fauna. In spring and summer, the alpine meadows are embroidered with flowers—turk's-cap lilies and columbines, fritillaries and gentians, violets and geraniums, asphodels and orchids—while in winter the mountains offer a variety of ski slopes. But perhaps the best time of all is the *arrière-saison*, the drowsy golden days of autumn when wisps of woodsmoke scent the air.

Spanning the frontier between Spain and France, the Pyrenees really belong to neither. For centuries, the main part of the Pyrenees consisted of a patchwork of tiny republics. The region still retains a sense of independent little states, each proud of its history and traditions.

The Pyrenees are a paradise for walkers, with the GR10, one of France's most famous long-distance footpaths, crossing the entire range from the Mediterranean to the Atlantic. There can be few better ways of experiencing the mountains at close hand. But do always check the weather forecast and go properly equipped; these are serious mountains, with attendant dangers. Public transportation in the Pyrenees is erratic, with the delightful exception of some mountain trains and cable cars. But the roads are usually good and well signposted, though gas stations are few and far between and snow closes many higher roads between October and May. Remember your passport if you plan to cross to Spain. ■

Parc National des Pyrénées Occidentales

GOLDEN EAGLES, GRIFFON VULTURES, LYNX, IBEX, EVEN (a few) Pyrenean brown bears: These are only a few of the rare and endangered species for which the Western Pyrenees National Park now provides sanctuary. Established in 1967 and covering 113,000 acres (45,700 ha), the park encompasses some of the most spectacular scenery in the Pyrenees including the breathtaking Cirque de Gavarnie. Firmly controlled and carefully husbanded, the park has no permanent human inhabitants. Hunting and flower picking are strictly prohibited, and camping in the wild is permitted only at distances equivalent to over an hour's trek from the road (and you must be off by sunrise).

A number of magnificent valley roads climb up into the park, following the courses of the many rivers flowing from the mountains. The surrounding towns and villages are well equipped with hotels, restaurants, campsites, and mountain guides. Maisons du Parc are official information centers advising about walks, weather, wildlife, and the rich flora of the region.

COL DU SOMPORT

To the west of the park, the N134 follows a Roman road along the valley of the Aspe from Oloron-Ste.-Marie, climbing to 5,354 feet (1,632 m) to enter Spain at the Col du Somport. This was the crossing place of the Saracen army on its way to defeat by Charles Martel in 732 and was trodden for centuries by pilgrims on their journey to Compostela (see pp. 266–67). Work has already begun here on a controversial highway and tunnel project that threatens the last habitat of the Pyrenean brown bear. This highway has become a *cause célèbre* among environmentalists. The ancient village of **Lescun,** huddled about halfway up the valley, offers exhilarating views of the sheer rock amphitheater and pinnacles of the Cirque de Lescun.

Just to the east, the D934 heads up the valley of the Ossau, leaving Pau behind to climb through spa towns perched between river and mountainside, and past magnificent waterfalls. Look for the large raptors—golden eagles, goshawks, peregrines, and vultures—for which this valley is famous.

Continue through Laruns and Gabas, then turn southwest on the D231 to reach the artificial **Lac de Bious-Artigues,** part of the great Pyrenean hydroelectric network. From here, a marked footpath takes you on a spectacular four-hour walk round the **Lacs d'Ayous.** The path passes through forests and mountain pastures covered with sheets of wildflowers in spring. Above you towers the extinct volcano of the **Pic du Midi d'Ossau** at 9,460 feet (2,884 m). Herds of the famous *isard,* a wild goat, graze its slopes. A cable car runs from Gabas to Pic de la Sagette, at 7,550 feet (2,134 m), giving marvelous views.

Retrace your steps to Laruns to head east on the D198, a superb drive that swoops over two dramatic *cols* (passes) to reach Argelès-Gazost. Heading south on the D921 to Gavarnie you pass the tiny village of **St.-Savin,** the site of an 11th-century abbey that once

A waterfall descends from the sunlit mountaintop into the darkness of the Cirque de Gavarnie.

La Vallée d'Aspe
Visitor information
✉ Moulin Bladé, Accous
☎ 05 59 34 71 48

Maison de la
Vallée d'Ossau
✉ Laruns
✉ 05 59 05 31 41

Cauterets
⚠ 232 C1
Visitor information
✉ place du Maréchal
   Foch
☎ 05 62 92 50 27

Cirque de
Gavarnie
⚠ 232 C1

Gavarnie
Visitor information
☎ 05 62 92 49 10

controlled the entire valley; the lovely 12th-century Romanesque church survives, together with the chapter house. Opposite rise the ruins of the Château of Beaucens, now a sanctuary for birds of prey.

From Pierrefitte-Nestalas, you have the choice of two remarkable valleys. The D920 runs along the narrow gorge to **Cauterets,** a grand old spa town of sulfurous vapors, colonnaded mansions, and wrought-iron balconies that makes an excellent base for skiing or walking. From here, a fine walk leads you past waterfalls to the **Pont d'Espagne,** where three cataracts converge in a tumult of spray. Farther up lies the **Lac de Gaube** at 5,660 feet (1,725 m), a deep lake in a barren landscape dominated by the snowy peak of Vignemale (at 10,814 feet, 3,298 m, the highest of the frontier summits) and its glacier.

The D921, the other route from Pierrefitte-Nestalas, runs up the Gorge de Luz to **St.-Sauveur,** once an important frontier post and a fashionable 19th-century spa with impressive ramparts. The

gorge opens out to allow a glimpse of the Pyrenees' most famous sight: the **Cirque de Gavarnie.**

From Gavarnie village you must walk or ride by donkey or horse to the cirque itself, a breathtaking rocky amphitheater carved out by rivers and glaciers, rimmed by peaks up to 10,000 feet (3,048 m) high. Waterfalls cascade down the cirque, the most spectacular of all being the **Grande Cascade de Gavarnie.** Plunging 1,385 feet (422 m), it is the highest waterfall in Europe. To the right is the Brèche de Roland, where, in the medieval epic poem *La Chanson de Roland*, the hero tried to break his enchanted sword rather than relinquish it to the infidel, and instead hacked a crevasse 400 feet (120 m) deep.

From Luz-St.-Sauveur follow the D918 via Barèges to the **Col de Tourmalet.** This pass, at 6,941 feet (2,115 m), is the highest in the mountains accessible by car. A cable car swings up from **La Mongie** to the spectacular new astronomical museum and observatories at the **Pic du Midi de Bigorre.** ◼

Pyrenean wildlife

The Pyrenees are home to more than 400 species of flowers, 160 of which are found nowhere else—including Pyrenean ramonda and saxifrage, separate species of columbines and lilies, tiny purple crocuses and pink androsace. This diverse and rich flora supports a number of unique butterflies, such as the Gavarnie blue and the Gavarnie ringlet.

On the upper mountain slopes, large raptors are able to breed relatively undisturbed. The magnificent birds circling high in the sky are vultures: the griffon vulture, lammergeyer (or bearded vulture), and Egyptian vulture.

Mammals include the *isard*, or Pyrenean antelope. The symbol of the park, its horns curve distinctively back at the tip. Its numbers are now increasing, and they may be spotted (with binoculars) on rocky outcrops high in the mountains. Other rare species include the snow partridge, the marmot, and the Pyrenean desman, a curious shrewlike part-aquatic mammal with long whiskers. Only a handful of brown bears remain. Even these are threatened with extinction as they are driven farther away from their natural habitat in the lower stretches of the park and into the high reaches of the mountains. ◼

Pau

PAU IS A FINE PLACE TO START A VISIT TO THE PYRENEES. The Boulevard des Pyrénées, below the château, offers a glorious panorama of the mountains encompassing no fewer than 83 peaks on a clear day. The historic capital of the ancient province of Béarn, and now the préfecture of the Pyrénées-Atlantiques département, Pau owes much of its elegance, curiously, to the British. The original British residents were retired officers of Wellington's army who decided to stay on after the Peninsula Campaign (1807–1814). They were joined later in the 19th century by compatriots attracted by the fashionably healthy air.

Pau
🅰 232 C2
Visitor information
✉ place Royale
☎ 05 59 27 27 08

Musée National du Château de Pau
✉ rue du Château
☎ 05 59 82 38 19
💲 $

Musée des Beaux-Arts
✉ rue Mathieu-Lalanne
☎ 05 59 27 33 02
🕐 Closed Tues.
💲 $

THE BRITISH CONNECTION
The British brought with them cricket and rugby (now an obsession in southwest France), polo, croquet, golf (the first golf course in France was laid out here), and foxhunting. ∎

A whimsical fountain in Pau, an elegant and historic town

Elegant and relaxed, Pau invites you to saunter down its leafy boulevards, past elegant mansions and art nouveau villas, and along the narrow cobbled streets lined with half-timbered houses. At the western end of the Boulevard des Pyrénées, overlooking the Gave de Pau River fringed by banana trees, rises the château of Pau. Originally a hunting lodge built by the counts of Foix, its great red-brick keep was added in the 14th century by the redoubtable Gaston Fébus, defender of the duchy of Foix from all comers.

In the 16th century, Margaret of Angoulême transformed the château into a Renaissance palace, with finely carved doorways, windows, and archways. This was the birthplace of her grandson, Henri of Navarre, who ascended to the throne of France in 1589 as Henri IV. A tour of the château is most memorable for the fine Gobelins tapestries in the state rooms, the magnificent second Empire apartments of Empress Eugenie, the 16th-century kitchens, and a giant tortoise shell that reputedly served as the infant Henri's cradle.

The **Musée des Beaux-Arts,** northeast of the château, has an impressive collection including works by El Greco, Rubens, and Degas, plus a section devoted to painters of the Pyrenees.

The vineyards of **Jurançon,** just across the Gave de Pau River, make an interesting and worthwhile visit from Pau. The wine is uniquely Béarnais, as the Gros and Petit Manseng and Courbu grapes from which it is made are grown nowhere else. A wine route is signposted to guide you through the vineyards. Ask at the Pau tourist office for information on the route and about vineyards that welcome visitors. ∎

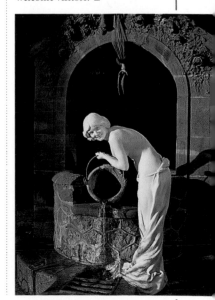

Lourdes

Lourdes

◮ 232 C1

Visitor information

✉ place Peyramale

☎ 05 62 42 77 40

Musée Pyrénéen d'Art et de Traditions Populaires

✉ Le Château Fort

☎ 05 62 42 37 37

💲 $

The shrine of St. Bernadette in Lourdes

THE MOST POPULAR CHRISTIAN SHRINE IN THE WORLD, Lourdes is also the gateway to the valleys of the Arrens, Cauterets, Ossau, and Gavarnie Rivers. Five million pilgrims flock to Lourdes annually, and the town has more hotels than anywhere else in France outside Paris. The faithful come in search of miracle cures for sickness and disability, many making the trip of a lifetime. Despite its formidable commercial trappings, Lourdes does not disappoint them.

It all began in January 1858, when a 14-year-old girl called Bernadette Soubirous claimed to have seen visions of the Virgin Mary. Divine directions led her to the spring in the Grotte de Massabielle, and ever since her last vision in 1862, pilgrims have come to the tiny cave to fill their bottles with miraculous waters and abandon their crutches. Some visit the humble little house on Rue des Petits-Fossés where she lived with her family.

A church was built over the miraculous grotto where a statue of the Virgin stands in the apparition niche. In addition to the **Basilique du Rosaire,** built in honor of Bernadette in 1889, a vast underground church, the **Basilique St.-Pie X,** was consecrated in 1958, the centenary of the visions. It can hold nearly 30,000 people.

The range of entertainment offered in the town includes a waxworks museum depicting the life of Christ and the life of Bernadette, a miniature stone model of Lourdes as it was in the time of Bernadette, and even a McDonalds Lourdes.

The older part of Lourdes, by the castle on the other side of the Gave de Pau River, contains the **Musée Pyrénéen d'Art et de Traditions Populaires.** Devoted in part to the *pyrénéistes,* pioneer climbers in these mountains, the museum displays early equipment, maps, and drawings alongside exhibits devoted to local crafts and costumes, and Pyrenean wildlife.

Some 9 miles (15 km) southwest of Lourdes are the spectacular **Bétharram caves** (*Tel 05 62 41 80 04, closed Dec.–March*), where a miniature railroad and barges ferry visitors on an underground river through a landscape of fantastic limestone formations. ∎

St.-Bertrand-de-Comminges

ONCE AN IMPORTANT ROMAN TOWN, ST.-BERTRAND-DE-Comminges still contains vestiges of this former glory. These include traces of thermal baths, a theater, and a temple, together with the ruins of a broad arcaded market place and a Christian basilica added in the fifth century. Barbarian invasions from the north and the plague combined to destroy the town, which lay in ruins until the 11th century. It was at this point that a local count, later to be canonized as St. Bertrand, embarked on the building of the cathedral.

St.-Bertrand-de-Comminges

🄰 232 C1

Visitor information

✉ Les Olivetains,
parvis de la
Cathédrale

☎ 05 61 95 44 44

Dubbed the Mont-St.-Michel of the Pyrenees, the **Cathédrale Ste.-Marie** completely overwhelms the tiny 15th- and 16th-century village that clusters beneath it. The beauty of its setting, the grandeur of its architecture, and the artistic treasures it contains make this one of the most outstanding buildings in the Pyrenees.

The church is Romanesque with later Gothic additions, notably in the exquisite cloister. The superb carvings of its capitals frame sublime views of the mountains beyond. Within, the cathedral contains a virtuoso feast of 16th-century woodcarving in its organ loft, and most particularly in its choir stalls and misericords. Here the medieval craftsmen depicted in riotously entertaining detail a gallery of devout, humorous, and even satirical figures and scenes, no doubt based on local characters known to them all.

In the shadow of this magnificent monument are the streets of the little village, its stone and timber-framed houses painstakingly restored. A couple of miles down the valley, the lovely 12th-century Romanesque **Église de St.-Just-de-Valcabrère** incorporates a patchwork of Roman masonry, from capitals to marble sarcophagi, recycled from the ruins of the Roman city. ■

The mountain-
top stronghold of
Montségur, the
greatest of the
Cathar castles

Around the Ariège Valley

RICH WITH INTEREST—FROM CATHAR CASTLES TO PAINTED
prehistoric caves—and easily accessible (about an hour's drive) from
Toulouse, the valley of the Ariège is one of the best areas of the
Pyrenees for a short visit.

St.-Lizier
🅰 232 D1
Visitor information
www.ariege.com/st-lizier
✉ place de l'Église
☎ 05 61 96 77 77

Foix
🅰 232 D1
Visitor information
✉ 45 cours
    Gabriel-Fauré
☎ 05 61 65 12 12

From Toulouse, approach the
Ariège along the beautiful valley of
the Lèze River. Though the wild
mountain scenery is dramatic, the
driving is not too hair-raising. At
Pailhès, make a pretty detour west
along the D119 to **Grotte du
Mas d'Azil,** a spectacular cave
featuring a tunnel so vast that the
road goes right into it. Leading off
the main cave are smaller ones that
prehistoric peoples inhabited for
some 20,000 years; a guided tour
takes in some of the prehistoric
artifacts, bones, tools, and painted
stones discovered here. More
recently, the caves have served as a
place of sanctuary for Protestants,
Cathars, and even earlier religious
refugees: A little chapel found here
dates back to the third century.

Proceed along the D119 and
turn right onto the D117 to reach
St.-Lizier, a fortified medieval
hilltop village distinguished by two
cathedrals. The **Cathédrale
St.-Lizier,** in the lower town, has
Romanesque frescoes and a delightful two-story cloister. Its exquisite
pink-brick Gothic bell tower,

modeled on St.-Sernin in Toulouse (see p. 263), makes a stunning sight against the distant mountain peaks beyond. The **Cathédrale de la Sède** dates from the 12th century.

Farther east, **Foix,** capital of the Ariège, was the power base of the turbulent counts of Foix in the Middle Ages. Four times Simon de Montfort besieged the castle before finally capturing this bastion of the Cathar faith in 1211. Nowadays it is a pleasant town of winding old streets, dominated by the three keeps of its castle, the earliest dating from the 11th century and well worth climbing for its commanding views over the town and the foothills of the Pyrenees.

A little way to the south on the N20, **Tarascon-sur-Ariège** is in the middle of a number of prehistoric caves (see sidebar this page). **Bédeilhac** (*Map 232 D1, tel 05 61 05 95 06*), northwest of Tarascon-sur-Ariège, is a gigantic cave bristling with stalagmites, its walls covered with paleolithic images of animals painted some 15,000 years ago. **Lombrives** (*Map 232 D1, tel 05 61 05 98 40*), to the southeast, has a vast 380-foot-high (117 m) cavern known as La Cathédrale, where a little train takes you right through the caves. Most impressive of all the caves, however, are those at **Niaux** (*Map 232 D1, tel 05 61 05 88 37*), just south of Tarascon-sur-Ariège. Here are some of the finest cave paintings in Europe: vigorous drawings of bison, horses, and deer, with delicately rendered details. Unlike the caves at Lascaux in the Dordogne (see pp. 254–55), the caves at Niaux are still open to the public; entrance is strictly controlled, so book ahead, either by phone or in person at the caves. The village of Niaux has the **Musée Pyrénéen** (*Tel 05 61 05 88 36*), devoted to crafts, costumes, and traditional life in the Ariège.

Heading back northward on the N20, turn right just before Foix onto the twisting D9. The road passes under the walls of two Cathar fortresses, Montgaillard and Roquefixade, before reaching **Montségur,** the tragic last bastion of Catharism.

After the Treaty of Meaux gave legal backing to the Albigensian Crusade (see pp. 322–23), this region became the center of Cathar resistance. As fortress after fortress fell, the lord of Montségur turned this bleak, comfortless castle into a refuge for all Cathar heretics. In 1244, however, after a ten-month siege and despairing of relief, the Cathars surrendered. Under the terms of the truce, those who recanted their faith would go free. Two weeks later, more than 200 Cathars—men, women, and children—who refused to recant were burned alive on a vast pyre. The little **Musée de Montségur** is devoted to the Cathars. ■

PREHISTORIC CAVES

The caves described in the text open at varying times throughout the year, and some may be seen only by appointment, as numbers are limited. Before visiting, check times with the tourist office in Foix, or phone the site directly for information.

Musée de Montségur
☎ 05 61 01 06 94
🕐 Closed Jan.,
　 a.m. Oct.–Feb.,
　 Mon.–Tues. in Dec.
💲 $

Mas d'Azil, in the Ariège, is one of many caves that have provided shelter and sanctuary for thousands of years.

The ancient bridge in St.-Jean-Pied-de-Port and the whitewashed houses of the old town

More places to visit in the Pyrenees

MIREPOIX

The 13th-century *bastide* town of Mirepoix, northeast of Foix, is celebrated for the beautiful half-timbered arcading of its main square, and for the enormous Gothic nave and graceful spire of its cathedral. The liveliest time to visit is market day (Thurs. or Sat.) or during the twice-monthly cattle market, one of the biggest in the region.

232 D1 **Visitor information** ✉ place du Maréchal Leclerc ☎ 05 61 68 83 76

OLORON-STE.-MARIE

This little market town, on the N134 at the junction of the Ossau and Aspe Valleys, is distinguished by its two churches: the Cathédrale Ste.-Marie with its Romanesque doorway of carved marble, and the Église Ste.-Croix with its 13th-century Spanish stonework. This is also the place to buy the famous Basque beret, manufactured here.

232 B1 **Visitor information** ✉ place de la Résistance ☎ 05 59 39 98 00

ST.-JEAN-PIED-DE-PORT

On the D933 at the foot of the Roncesvalles Pass, St.-Jean-Pied-de-Port was on one of the pilgrim roads to Santiago de Compostela. It is also famous as the site where Roland was defeated by the Basques, immortalized in the medieval poem *La Chanson de Roland* (which substituted Saracens for Basques, the greater to glorify its hero). The cobbled old town, and the new town on the opposite bank of the Nive River, are both enclosed by 15th- to 17th-century fortifications.

232 B1 **Visitor information** ✉ place Charles de Gaulle ☎ 05 59 37 03 57

SAUVETERRE-DE-BÉARN

A lovely town on the N124 with fine river views, a 13th-century church, castle ruins, and the remains of a fortified bridge, Sauveterre is best known today as the venue for the annual world salmon-fishing championships in July.

232 B2 **Visitor information** ✉ place Royale ☎ 05 59 38 58 65

TARBES

An important agricultural town, Tarbes stands on the west bank of the Adour River east of Pau and just off the east–west motorway, La Pyrénéenne. Within a fine park, the Jardin Massey, in the center of town lies the **Musée Massey,** devoted mainly to the Hussars. The World War I commander Maréchal Foch was born in Tarbes, and his birthplace now houses an exhibition of photographs, medals, and memorabilia. The stud farm, **Le Haras,** stages displays of horsemanship in summer.

232 C1 **Visitor information** ✉ 3 cours Gambetta ☎ 05 62 51 30 31 ■

Embracing the Côte d'Azur, Provence, and Languedoc–Roussillon, between Italy and Spain, the South of France excels in vacation delights. Roman monuments, medieval villages, sandy beaches, and sleek modern edifices are all bathed in a perfect climate.

South of France

Lavender fields in Provence

South of France

THE SOUTH OF FRANCE IS A HUGELY POPULAR VACATION region, and a highly desirable place to live. It remains warm for much of the year, with pockets of the Côte d'Azur, sheltered by mountains, being particularly mild. Summers are very hot and dry. The only blight is the cold wind of the Mistral, which howls down from the north in winter. Millions come to the South of France: to the Côte d'Azur, the villages of Provence, and the vacation lands of Languedoc-Roussillon.

The Massif Central and the Alps divide the Mediterranean coast geographically from the rest of France. This coast's main connection with the north is the great Rhône River. To the east, the mountains drop almost to the sea, and much of the Côte d'Azur is a rocky coast. Beyond the Rhône Delta to the west, the coast sweeps round in a great arc, fringed with newly developed beach resorts and washed by clear waters. The plain of Languedoc-Roussillon is intensively cultivated, producing a wide range of fruit and particularly wine, which increases in importance as it improves in quality. Shellfish are cultivated in the saltwater lagoons that edge the coast. To the north are the *Garrigue*-covered foothills of the Cévennes, and farther south, the Pyrenees form a natural frontier with Spain.

Marseille is the biggest city in the south, and France's largest port. Sète, to the east, is another important port. Nîmes and Montpellier are both significant and highly attractive cities, centers of high-tech industry and key links in the developing Mediterranean sunbelt.

Corsica, however, continues to embrace a separatism that has helped to restrain development and keep it one of the most unspoiled islands in the Mediterranean.

Historically, the Romans played a key role throughout the region. The whole of the south coast was their Provincia with Narbonne as its capital. Many of their buildings survive to this day, notably the Pont du Gard, the amphitheaters of Arles and Nîmes, and the theater at Orange.

Throughout the Middle Ages, Provence and Languedoc were famous for the "courts of love" and the poetry of the troubadours, and in the 19th century local enthusiasts made efforts to revive the Provençal language and identity. Like much of the rest of France, the region suffered during the 16th-century Wars of Religion, when many towns and cities were seriously damaged.

Area of map detail

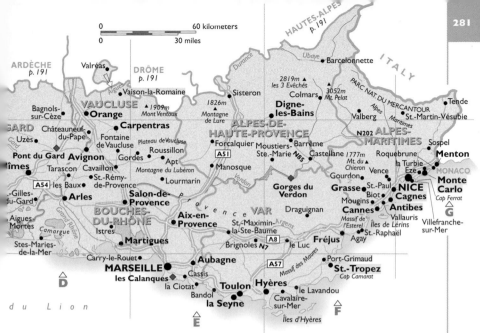

In the 18th and 19th centuries, the English came to the south of France for health cures and winter holidays. By the 1920s, sunbathing became fashionable and the Côte d'Azur became the land of summer vacations that it remains today. In the 1960s, the Languedoc-Roussillon coast was developed as a vacation playground with beach resorts, but keeping some areas as nature reserves.

The light and color of the south have always attracted artists, giving rise to such important artistic movements as cubism and fauvism—a legacy clearly evident in the many fine art museums of the region. ■

The harbor at Nice with the wooded slopes of the castle hill beyond

Food & drink

CUISINE DU SOLEIL, CUISINE OF THE SUN, IS THE NAME GIVEN TO THE FOOD of this blessed region. It is a Mediterranean cuisine, luscious, aromatic, and, as it happens, healthy. Market stalls are laden with seasonal local produce like peppers, tomatoes, figs, melons, cherries, peaches, and olives. It is the olive that is most central to southern cooking, its oil used almost exclusively instead of animal fat. Garlic is the other keynote, along with herbs like rosemary, thyme, and marjoram, which grow wild all over the countryside. These elements combine most satisfyingly in *aïoli*, a rich golden mayonnaise made from olive oil, garlic, and egg yolk, served with raw vegetables, fish, or soup.

To the east the cuisine has an Italian accent, and local specialties include *socca* (chickpea flour) pancakes; *pissaladière*, a pizza with onions, anchovies, and black olives; *pistou*, vegetable soup with basil; stuffed zucchini flowers; and the ubiquitous *pan bagnat*, a large roll stuffed with *salade Niçoise*. Farther west the influence is Spanish. In Roussillon, look for *cargolade*, a grill of snails and sausages (and aïoli, of course). Anchovies are another specialty, good with grilled red peppers.

All along the Mediterranean coast there is excellent fish and seafood. In Languedoc–Roussillon the saltwater lagoons produce mussels, oysters, and more obscure marine delicacies such as sea urchins and crayfish. Bouillabaisse fish stew is a key specialty. Fierce argument prevails over the exact recipe, but general agreement says that it should include monkfish, mullet, eel, tomatoes, and saffron. Traditionally, a fish broth is served first, and the fish follows. A simple *soupe de poisson* is also delicious, served with croutons and *rouille,* a hot red pepper mayonnaise. *Bourride* is another fish stew, with aïoli added at the last moment. Simple fish dishes like grilled sardines or red mullet are always good, as is *brandade*, a puree of salt cod and olive oil.

The south is certainly the best place in France to be a vegetarian, but there are plenty of good meat dishes, too. Lamb from the Sisteron area, grazed on fragrant herb-rich vegetation, is a great delicacy. Rich, slow-cooked *daubes* are serious affairs. Usually beef stewed in red wine (often with olives and tomatoes), they are also made with other ingredients including calamari. In the Camargue you should try *gardiane de taureau*, bull's meat stew, usually served with the delicious nutty rice grown locally.

What to drink with your meal is never a problem. Languedoc-Roussillon produces most of France's table wine, and its wines are becoming increasingly respected. Drink the local *vin de pays* or sample slightly more expensive local wines from the Corbières, Nîmes, Minervois, Fitou, and the Côtes de Roussillon. In Provence look for Châteauneuf-du-Pape or Gigondas. Along the coast, the local selection is more limited; try the Côtes de Provence rosé or Bandol. Aniseed-flavored pastis is a popular aperitif, and sweet dessert wines include Banyuls and Muscat, especially from Beaumes-de-Venise and Rivesaltes. ■

Specialties

First courses Anchoade: anchovy dip
Salade Niçoise: tomatoes, anchovies,
    hard-boiled eggs, and olives, sometimes tuna
    and beans
Tapenade: puree of olives and anchovies
Main courses Aubergines farcies à la
    provençale: eggplant stuffed with meat,
    onions, and herbs, served with tomato sauce
Perdrix à la Catalane: partridge with orange
    and pepper sauce
Stockfish à la Niçoise: dried cod stewed with
    onions, tomatoes, garlic, and herbs
Vegetables Artichauts à la barigoule: small arti-
    chokes stewed in oil and white wine
Fleurs de courges farcies: stuffed zucchini
    flowers
Ratatouille: a stew of eggplant, zucchini,
    peppers, and tomatoes
Desserts Calissons d'Aix: almond cookies
Crème Catalane: caramelized egg-custard
    dessert

A huge variety of different olives are on sale in Provençal markets.

Villefranche harbor, lined with restaurants

Côte d'Azur

Breathtaking beauty, clear blue waters, and a superb climate have earned the French Riviera, or "azure coast," an unrivaled position among the world's stylish vacation playgrounds. The Romans built spas and villas designed to catch the sea breezes, but only in the 19th century, with the arrival of the English aristocracy in search of health cures and botanical specimens, was the Côte d'Azur invented. Wealthy visitors from America and Europe followed, building villas and playing the tables at Monte Carlo's casino. In the 1920s, Coco Chanel invented sunbathing and F. Scott Fitzgerald wrote the jazz age into existence. After World War II, Brigitte Bardot and other starlets launched St. Tropez as a symbol of the new Côte d'Azur.

Despite the crowds, the coast retains its glamour and its place in the social calendars of the elite. The harbors are full of mega-yachts; superb restaurants, nightclubs, and casinos cater to serious eating and partying; and the exclusive beaches gleam with oiled bodies. But the coast offers more. Its museums are filled with modern art (much of it created here), and world-class jazz musicians play in Roman amphitheaters on starry nights. The simplest delights are perhaps the most potent and enduring: the brilliant blue sea, pine-shaded beaches, and cliff-top views; the scent of herbs and lavender, mimosa and pine; and terra-cotta villages perched among spectacular rocky landscapes a few miles inland. ■

Gardens of the Côte d'Azur

SHELTERED TO THE NORTH BY MOUNTAINS, UNTOUCHED by frost throughout the winter, and blessed with an early, balmy spring, the Côte d'Azur is a paradise for gardeners and garden lovers.

The opulent villas that sprang up along the coast in the 19th and early 20th centuries were surrounded by equally sumptuous gardens. Wealthy amateur enthusiasts and professional garden designers rushed to introduce exotic plants, from palms and cacti to avocados. Glamorous and eclectic, the gardens they created reveled in the lavish planting possibilities, while at the same time tending to retain an innately French restraint.

Cosseted **Menton** boasts a particularly impressive clutch of these subtropical paradises, in which fountains and shady terraces, statuesque planting and distant vistas combine irresistibly. For sheer variety of palms and subtropical species, the **Jardin Botanique du Val Rameh** is hard to equal.

The English landscape designer Lawrence Johnston made his only French garden at **Jardin de la Serre de la Madone** (*Val de Gorbio*), outside Menton. Here he grew the plants too delicate for England that he had collected from China, South Africa, and elsewhere.

At Cap Ferrat, visit the **Jardin & Musée Ephrussi-de-Rothschild.** Gardens of every inspiration —from Italian to Japanese, by way of grottoes, a temple of Diana, and a cactus collection—cluster in the shade of umbrella pines against a backdrop of aquamarine sea. In Hyères, **Parc St.-Bernard** (*follow signs from Cours de Strasbourg*) is a cornucopia of Mediterranean flora. And **Parc Ste.-Claire** (*boulevard Victor Basch*) contains ravishing terraced gardens made by American writer Edith Wharton. ∎

Jardin Botanique du Val Rameh, the Mediterranean arm of the Paris Natural History Museum

Menton
🅰 281 G3
Visitor information
✉ 8 avenue Boyer
☎ 04 92 41 76 76

Jardin Botanique du Val Rameh
✉ avenue St.-Jacques, Menton
☎ 04 93 35 86 72
💲 $

Jardin & Musée Ephrussi-de-Rothschild
✉ Cap Ferrat
☎ 04 93 01 33 09
🕒 Closed Mon.— Fri. a.m. Nov.—mid-Feb.

Nice

COMBINING A PROVENÇAL HEART WITH A WELCOMING joie de vivre, and a wealth of museums with a profusion of gardens, fountains, and palm trees, the wonderful city of Nice raises life alfresco to an art form.

Nice has three distinct parts: Vieux Nice, the old town and port, Italianate and heavy with character; the stately 19th-century city center behind the Promenade des Anglais; and chic Cimiez overlooking the city to the north, favored by the Romans and Queen Victoria.

The maze of tall, narrow streets of old Nice, once deliciously dangerous and seedy, is now a fashionable enclave of bistros, nightclubs, and galleries, all distressed ocher walls and turquoise shutters. But the authentic aroma of dried fish and garlic still hangs in the air, and its little shops remain the best place to buy your virgin olive oil. The daily outdoor market on Cours Saleya is famous for its flowers and local produce. Lunch on delicious Niçois specialties in one of the cafés—an inexpensive treat.

The tiny squares and lovely chapels of the old town are dominated by the huge dim cathedral with its glinting dome of glazed tiles. Of the palaces and *hôtels particuliers* (mansions) built by former illustrious residents and émigrés, the grandest is the 17th-century **Palais Lascaris** (*15 rue Droite, tel 04 93 62 05 54, closed Mon.*), with frescoed ceilings and rococo silver inlaid doors. Take the elevator up to the park where the château once stood to enjoy the waterfall, shady café, and amazing views.

Old Nice ends at the Paillon River, now site of spacious gardens, squares, and fountains, as well as the striking glass-and-marble **Musée d'Art Moderne**

et Contemporain (MAMAC).
The collections here focus on
French and American avant garde
art from the 1960s onward.

Stretching along the shoreline
to the west of the old town is the
Promenade des Anglais. Built
by the English community and
lined with grand hotels, it is the
last word in 19th-century elegance.
The doyen of these hotels is the
magnificent Negresco, with its
huge Baccarat chandelier.

Beyond the river lies 19th-
century Nice: dignified arcaded
squares, Italianate apartment buildings, and fashionable shops. There
is an exhilarating array of art galleries. The **Musée International
d'Art Naïf** (*Château Sainte-
Hélène, avenue Val Marie, tel 04 93
71 78 33, closed Tues.*) is in a pink
château; and the **Musée des
Beaux-Arts** has works by

Monet, Degas, and Sisley. Frescoes
and icons are displayed in the
ornate Russian Orthodox cathedral,
Cathédrale-St.-Nicolas, on
Boulevard Tzaréwitch.

Unmissable art treasures lie in
the wealthy suburb of **Cimiez,**
a cradle of hills to the north
sheltering whimsical villas. The
fabulous **Musée Marc Chagall**
(*Musée National Message Biblique,
avenue du Dr. Ménard, tel 04 93 53
87 2*) contains Chagall's "Biblical
Message" canvases.

Farther up the hill the **Musée
Matisse** is housed in a 17th-
century Genoese villa with a modern gallery wing. It contains
Matisse's personal collection
including still lifes, as well as the
"Tempête à Nice" and an array of
personal *objets*. There are also
many sketches for Matisse's
Chapelle de la Rosaire in Vence. ■

Nice
🗺 281 G3
Visitor information
www.nice-coteazur.org
✉ Acropolis,
  1 esplanade
  J.F. Kennedy
☎ 04 93 92 83 80
✉ 5 promenade des
  Anglais
☎ 04 92 14 48 03

**Musée d'Art
Moderne et
Contemporain**
✉ promenade des Arts
☎ 04 93 62 61 62
🕐 Closed Tues.
💲 $. Free 1st Sun.
  of month

**Musée des
Beaux-Arts**
✉ 33 avenue des
  Baumettes
☎ 04 92 15 28 28
🕐 Closed Mon.
💲 $

Musée Matisse
✉ 164 avenue des
  Arènes de Cimiez
☎ 04 93 81 08 08
🕐 Closed Tues.
💲 $

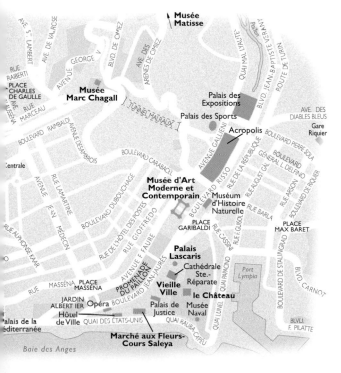

The Corniches

Villefranche-sur-Mer

🅰 281 G3

Visitor information

✉ square François-Binon

☎ 04 93 01 73 68

Beaulieu-sur-Mer

Visitor information

✉ place Georges-Clemenceau

☎ 04 93 01 02 21

IN A REGION WITH SUCH A WEALTH OF SPECTACULAR beauty, the stretch of coast between Menton and Nice is particularly outstanding. The best way to drink in the glorious views of cliffs, blue sea, and extravagant villas set among palm trees is to take the corniche roads. Of the three, the Grande and Moyenne Corniches offer the most sweeping panoramas, while the Corniche Inférieure, closest to the sea, has the worst traffic and the best views of luxurious resorts. This round-trip takes the lower road from Nice to Menton, returning on the upper roads.

From Nice, the N98 circles the Cap de Nice and passes through the port to reach **Villefranche-sur-Mer.** Here, narrow, enclosed streets rush steeply down to the exceptionally deep natural harbor, which has turned this small fishing village into an important naval port, lending it a more raffish flavor than most of this opulent coast. Pretty, pastel-colored houses and

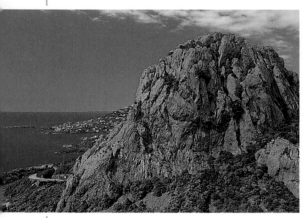

Along the Corniche the rocks drop steeply to the sea.

lively cafés line the tiny harbor, overlooked by the **Chapelle St.-Pierre,** a beguiling little church decorated by Jean Cocteau in 1957.

Jutting out into the sea just beyond Villefranche, the peninsula of Cap Ferrat, together with those of Cap-d'Ail and Cap Martin farther along the coast, is famously the preserve of the seriously rich, its natural beauties embedded with

fabulous villas and luxuriant gardens. Do not miss the **Musée Ephrussi-de-Rothschild,** a pink and white villa with marble floors and Tiepolo ceilings, housing a superb decorative arts collection and surrounded by magnificent gardens (see p. 285). At the end of the *cap,* the rocky end of the peninsula, is the **Grand Hôtel du Cap-Ferrat,** featuring among other luxuries a funicular railroad to the beach. The little fishing and yachting village of **St.-Jean-Cap-Ferrat** makes a picturesque place for lunch; relatively quiet **Plage des Fossés** leads to a path around the peninsula with fantastic views.

A couple of miles farther east of Villefranche on the N98, sheltered **Beaulieu-sur-Mer** enjoys a sybaritic climate and, not surprisingly, has some extremely grand hotels. Its most bizarre and delightful offering is the remarkable **Villa Kérylos** *(rue Gustave-Eiffel),* an authentic reproduction of an ancient Greek villa, in which the eccentric archaeologist Théodore Reinach lived in the manner of an Athenian citizen. One of his few concessions to the 20th century was glass in the windows.

Continuing around the coast, the road threads past rocky bays and caps. As it nears **Monaco** (see pp. 290–91), avoid the worst of the traffic by diverting onto the Moyenne Corniche (N7) as far as Menton.

Menton (see p. 285), only a mile (1.5 km) from the Italian border, remains the grande dame of the littoral: genteel, cradled by mountains, with tropical gardens. The steep streets of old Menton drop down to the **Promenade du Soleil,** lined with cafés, restaurants, and palm trees.

This is Cocteau's town: See the **Musée Jean-Cocteau** *(quai Napoléon, tel 04 93 57 72 30),* housed in a 17th-century fort, to enjoy a collection of his drawings, mosaics, and ceramics that combine simple lines with brilliant pyrotechnic effects. Best of all, visit the **Hôtel de Ville** *(rue de la République),* where he decorated the Salle des Mariages in his own inimitable fashion. The 17th-century **Église de St.-Michel** *(place St.-Michel)* is the setting for a chamber music festival in August.

From Menton, head back on the N7 to Roquebrune-Cap-Martin.

Turn inland onto the Grande Corniche (the D2564) to **Roquebrune,** a still-fortified medieval village of steep streets and vaulted alleys, opening to magnificent sea views.

Follow this spectacular road westward for about 4 miles (6 km) to **La Turbie,** dominated by the towering Trophée des Alpes, a sixth-century monument to Roman power. A quiet little garden on the cliff edge offers fabulous views out to sea and a superb aerial panorama of Monaco, far below.

At Col d'Èze, 4 miles (6 km) farther, the D45 leads to the tiny village of **Èze,** perched dizzyingly over the Mediterranean, its exquisitely restored streets, covered alleyways, and steep, twisting stairways now thronged with visitors.

Follow the winding Moyenne Corniche (N7) from Èze to Nice, stopping at the pull-offs provided to savor the ravishing views. ∎

Lemons grow year-round in Menton, thanks to the warm climate. Residents create extraordinary figures for the festival held every February to celebrate the lemon crop.

Monaco

SMALLER THAN NEW YORK'S CENTRAL PARK, THE TINY independent state and tax haven of Monaco is a magnet for those in search of glamour. Monégasque residency is highly sought after, but visitors flock to Monaco for its glittering nightlife, luxurious hotels, and expensive restaurants. Since his accession in 1949, Prince Rainier III, the autocratic head of state, has transformed his principality into a successful mega-business, extending it vertically and horizontally with skyscrapers and landfill, and earning it the epithets Hong Kong on the Mediterranean and Las Vegas *plage*.

Monaco
- 281 G3

Visitor information
- 2A boulevard des Moulins, Monte-Carlo
- 377 92 16 61 16

Palais du Prince
- place du Palais
- 377 93 25 18 31
- Closed Nov.–May
- $

Musée Océanographique
- avenue St.-Martin
- 377 93 15 36 00
- $$

Jardin Exotique
- boulevard du Jardin Exotique Moneghetti
- Garden: 377 93 30 33 65. Museum: 377 93 15 80 06
- Closed mid-Nov.–Dec. 25
- $$

The old town of Monaco, out on the jagged promontory of the Rocher, is an immaculate affair of elegant mansions, charming little squares and fountains, and, of course, lots of souvenir stores. The **Palais du Prince,** seat of the Grimaldi family, has sections dating from every century since 1000. Packed with gorgeous furniture, paintings, and frescoes, it is open to visitors only when the prince is away. But the changing of the palace guard outside is a daily spectacle. The great white 19th-century neo-Romanesque cathedral nearby contains the tomb of Princess Grace, perpetually strewn with roses. On the cliff is the world-class **Musée Océanographique,** with a superb aquarium.

South of the Rocher lie the new marina of **Fontvieille,** the **Princess Grace Rose Garden,** and the port of **La Condamine,** now a vast yachting marina with promenades for yacht-ogling. On the cliffs behind rise the magnificently situated **Jardin Exotique,** sheltering a huge range of exotic plants, as well as prehistoric caves and an anthropological museum.

The Grimaldis

The Grimaldi family has owned the independent principality of Monaco since the 14th century, making it the longest reigning dynasty in Europe. In its heyday, Monaco stretched from Menton to Antibes, living off taxes levied on the lemons and olives of Menton. When Menton was ceded to France in 1860, financial disaster loomed, but the reigning prince, Charles III, had the inspired idea of opening a casino (gaming rooms were banned in France at this time) on the hill, named Monte-Carlo in his honor. New railroad connections along the coast helped to attract a dazzling clientele, and the venture proved so lucrative that Charles was able to waive taxation for his subjects.

Thus has Monaco prospered, and along with it the Grimaldis. The right touch of glamour was added in 1956 when the present prince, Rainier III, married American actress Grace Kelly. For years they were a fairy-tale couple, but since her death in a car accident in 1982 the family has been dogged by problems: The heir, Albert, remains firmly unmarried; Princess Caroline's first husband was killed in a boat race; and her sister, Princess Stephanie, has been a source of scandal, leaving behind a trail of broken romances and abandoned careers. ■

Monaco hosts a constant round of festivals, fireworks, and rallies, culminating in the Grand Prix every May, when the roads are closed to traffic and the entire port becomes a racetrack. In 1997 the principality celebrated 700 years of independence with concerts, boat races, and a historic Grand Prix with classic cars (a passion of Prince Rainier III).

"Business tourism" flourishes, with plans for further developments.

MONTE-CARLO

Beyond the port is Monte-Carlo, with its fabled casino and opera, which should not be missed. To make sure visitors look the part, there's a dress code. Designed by Charles Garnier, who was also responsible for the Opéra Garnier in Paris, the interiors retain their extravagant belle epoque glamour, and the Salons Privés still provide a vicarious thrill.

The palm tree gardens around the Casino and the wonderful terrace surrounding them afford beautiful views over the Mediterranean. More ostentatious opulence is provided by a string of Monte-Carlo's sumptuous hotels, most notably the **Hôtel de Paris** and the **Hôtel Hermitage,** with its famous winter-garden foyer luxuriating under a glass roof designed by Gustave Eiffel. ■

Monte-Carlo, beyond the port (top), and its Casino (above)

Around St.-Paul-de-Vence

SET IN THE HILLS BEHIND THE BAIE DES ANGES, ST.-PAUL-
de-Vence is a perfectly preserved hill village, encircled by 16th-
century ramparts, overlooking terra-cotta roofs, cypresses, and azure
swimming pools. Though tiny, it has gained an international reputation from the illustrious catalog of artists and writers who have lived
and worked here. Today its galleries and restaurants attract thousands
of visitors. At the famous Colombe d'Or hotel-restaurant, you can
dine on the terrace surrounded by a priceless collection of art: a Léger
mosaic on the garden wall and a Braque dove by the swimming pool,
amid works by Picasso, Dufy, Modigliani, and a great many others, all
donated by impecunious artists in exchange for their keep.

St.-Paul-de-Vence

🅰 281 F3

Visitor information

✉ Maison de la Tour,
2 rue Grande

☎ 04 93 32 86 95

Fondation Maeght

✉ Montée des Trious

☎ 04 93 32 81 63

💲 $$

Entering the chic little village
through the 13th-century gate, you
follow Rue Grande past the foun-
tain to the 12th-century Gothic
church and the local history muse-
um. The museum features an
intriguing photo call of the celebri-
ties who have visited St.-Paul—
Simone de Beauvoir, Catherine
Deneuve, F. Scott Fitzgerald, and

many more. But the village is famed
for the **Fondation Maeght,** one
of the world's most distinguished
modern art museums, surrounded
by a labyrinth of witty, colorful
modern sculpture and tinkling
fountains by Miró, Calder, and oth-
ers. Attenuated Giacometti figures
stroll across the courtyard, and the
chapel is decorated by Braque. The

A haven for the creative

In a satisfying circular movement, the works of artists and writers that this region inspired now inform our image of it. Picasso's nymphs and sea urchins, Matisse's views of the sea, and Renoir's golden light and olive trees are constant presences. It was the intensity of the light that attracted the Impressionists. Now we see the luminous skies and seas through their eyes in galleries and museums amid the settings that inspired them.

Writers, too, have flocked here. Colette penned evocative portraits of Provençal life. Ford Madox Ford and Aldous Huxley worked here; and Katherine Mansfield and D. H. Lawrence died here. F. Scott Fitzgerald portrayed the beautiful people who partied here. ■

founders, Aimé and Marguerite Maeght, commissioned the Spanish architect José-Luis Sert to design a building conceived in harmony with the works within, and the result is extremely impressive.

CAGNES

The best part of nearby Cagnes is the original village of **Haut-de-Cagnes,** with its narrow medieval village streets and steep stairways, crowned by the 14th-century **Château Grimaldi** (*Tel 04 93 20 85 57, closed Tues.*). Within its fortress walls is a spectacular Renaissance interior that now houses a museum devoted to the olive; a collection of modern Mediterranean art with works by Matisse, Chagall, and more; and the wonderful Suzy Solidor collection: 40 portraits of the 1930s nightclub singer by artists including Cocteau, Dufy, and Tamara de Lempicka.

Renoir spent the last 20 years of his life in Cagnes, at the Maison Les Collettes, where the heat helped to ease the pain of arthritis. The fine old house, set among the ancient olive trees that fascinated him, is now the **Musée Renoir,** with one studio preserved just as he left it, complete with palette and easel (at which he painted with the brush strapped to his hand when his fingers were too painful). There are ten great paintings in the house and sculptures in the shady garden.

VENCE

Another haven for artists and writers, the town of Vence perches high surrounded by rose farms. Just outside is the remarkable **Chapelle du Rosaire** (*avenue Henri-Matisse, tel 04 93 58 03 26*), decorated by Matisse at the end of his life when he, too, was afflicted by arthritis. In an otherwise white interior, the pared-down monochrome drawings of the Stations of the Cross, and the aqueous blues, greens, and yellows of the stained glass are arresting, a tribute to the artist's dedication. ■

Cagnes
🅼 281 F3
Visitor information
✉ boulevard Maréchal Juin
☎ 04 93 20 61 64

Musée Renoir (Maison les Collettes)
✉ 19 chemin des Colettes
☎ 04 93 20 61 07
🕑 Closed Tues. & mid-Oct.–early Nov.
💲 $

Vence
🅼 281 F3
Visitor information
✉ place du Grand-Jardin
☎ 04 93 58 06 38

F. Scott Fitzgerald led the 1920s American invasion of the Côte d'Azur.

The Gallimard perfume house, one of the great perfumeries of Grasse

In & around Grasse

NESTLING IN A CRADLE OF HILLS BEHIND CANNES LIES THE perfume capital of the world, charming, sleepy Grasse. The surrounding landscape is a fragrant sea of flowers: Golden mimosa clothes the hillsides in January and February, followed by summer roses and lavender and autumn jasmine, all heady with scent. The town itself is an intriguing warren of steep, arcaded streets, with Renaissance details betraying the influence of Italian merchants. Tanning was the main industry here in the Middle Ages, and it was the 16th-century vogue for scented gloves, encouraged by Catherine de Médicis, which acted as the catalyst for the perfume industry.

By the 18th century Grasse was the world center of scent, and it remains so today. Using imported flowers such as patchouli as well as ton upon ton of home-grown blooms, it produces essences that are then sold, mostly to prestigious couture houses. The Molinard and Fragonard perfume companies have museums and provide tours. The **Musée International de la Parfumerie** provides a splendid introduction to the art of perfumery, with a beautiful collection of bottles from all over the world,

and its own rooftop garden of fragrant plants. Every shop in Grasse seems to sell perfume and flower waters, and the daily market in Place aux Aires sells irresistible dried flowers and herbs.

The artist and engraver Jean-Honoré Fragonard (1732–1806) was born in Grasse. The **Villa-Musée Fragonard,** where he lived with his family, contains some of his drawings and copies of wall panels. A rare religious work by him hangs in the **Cathédrale Notre-Dame-du-Puy** (*place du*

Petit-Puy), started in the 12th century, as well as three works by Rubens and a 16th-century triptych by Bréa.

GOURDON

To the north of Grasse, a wonderful drive past the rocky ravines and rushing waterfalls of the **Gorges du Loup** takes you up to Gourdon, one of the most spectacular *villages perchés* (hill villages) in the region. From the approach road you can see the precipitous drop of several hundred feet below Gourdon's castle walls, and the view from the top is just as dramatic. The castle, with 17th-century formal gardens on the cliff edge designed by André Le Nôtre, houses the **Musée Historique et Musée d'Art Naïf** (*Château de Gourdon, tel 04 93 09 68 02, closed a.m. Oct.–June*), an eclectic historical museum and a collection of naive paintings, including a good Henri Rousseau self-portrait.

PICASSO COUNTRY

The coast south of Grasse is first and foremost Picasso country. The artist spent much of his life in Juan-les-Pins, Antibes, and Cannes. He died in **Mougins**, now a chic little hilltop village with splendid views and numerous art galleries. The **Musée de la Photographie** (*67 rue de l'Église, tel 04 93 75 85 67*) has a collection of photos of Picasso by Lartigue (who lived in neighboring Opio), Doisneau, and Villiers. Mougins is also a place for serious eating. Most serious of all is the **Moulin de Mougins** (see p. 372). Run by the great Provençal chef Roger Vergé, the restaurant is famous for his light, imaginative *cuisine du soleil*, using local produce with masterful simplicity.

Vallauris, in the hinterland of Cannes, owes its fame to Picasso, who revived its fortunes as a pottery

center by working in a ceramic studio there. The main street, avenue Georges-Clemenceau, packed with shops selling pottery, was described by Picasso's companion Françoise Gilot as a "citadel to bad taste." The Galerie Madoura here, where Picasso worked, is still the place for high-quality pots at a price. In 1952 the artist painted the Romanesque chapel of the 16th-century Renaissance château with his tremendous "War and Peace" composition, and in the same year he gave the town his life-size bronze, "Man with Sheep," which stands in Place Paul-Isnard.

Just up the coast, the ancient and animated village of **Biot** has a charming medieval quarter and a famous glass factory. The **Musée National Fernand-Léger** (*chemin du Val-de-Pome, tel 04 92 91 50 30*), just outside the village, houses the artist's own collection of his powerful and positive work in a custom-built museum, its exterior adorned with brilliant ceramic panels and mosaics. ■

Antibes

CAP D'ANTIBES REMAINS ONE OF THE TRULY EXCLUSIVE hideaways of the Côte d'Azur, its exotic belle-epoque and modernist villas and fabulous hotels discreetly veiled by dense vegetation, through which paths lead to private beaches. But the public beaches here, though mostly rocky, are unspoiled; try Plage de la Sales, on the eastern shore, or tiny Plage de la Garoupe. Antibes itself is an ancient town facing Nice across the Baie des Anges.

Antibes

📍 281 F3

Visitor information

✉ 11 place du Général de Gaulle

☎ 04 92 90 53 00

Musée Picasso/ Château Grimaldi

✉ place Mariejol

☎ 04 92 90 54 20

🕐 Closed Mon.

💲 $$

Musée d'Histoire et d'Archéologie

✉ Bastion St-André, avenue Adm. de Grasse

☎ 04 92 90 54 35

🕐 Closed Mon.

💲 $

A Greek settlement (Antipolis) that later became a frontier town (neighboring Nice was in Savoie), Antibes had its fortress and port reconstructed by Vauban in the 17th century. Above the harbor is the old town, a maze of narrow streets with one of the region's best markets every morning (and a great flea market twice a week). On the ramparts, overlooking the sea, looms the 16th-century **Château Grimaldi.** Here, Picasso was given a studio after World War II, and in gratitude he gave the town paintings, drawings, and ceramics of the period, including "La Joie de Vivre," "Night Fishing at Antibes," and the "Antipolis Suite." The Château is now the **Musée Picasso,** and the works are beautifully displayed in the lustrous sea light pouring in through the windows. Paintings by Nicolas de Staël are also on show, along with works by artists of the school of Nice. The terrace garden provides the perfect setting for sculptures silhouetted against the sea. The **Musée d'Histoire et d'Archéologie,** farther along the ramparts, presents Greek, Roman, and other finds in two huge barrel-vaulted chambers.

By day, **Juan-les-Pins** (*Visitor information, tel 04 92 90 53 05*), west of Antibes, seems much like other resorts along the coast, but by night it comes alive, and the July jazz festival under the eponymous pines is hard to beat. ∎

Cannes

A PERFECT RIVIERA BASE AND ONE OF SOUTHERN FRANCE'S most glamorous cities, Cannes is big enough to have all the grand hotels, restaurants, beaches, and shopping you could ever want and small enough to walk around. It also offers easy access to inland beauty spots such as Grasse and Mougins.

Cannes
🗺 281 F3
Visitor information
✉ Palais des Festivals
☎ 04 93 39 24 53

**Boat to Îles de
Lérins from Cannes**
☎ 04 93 39 11 82
💲 $$$$$

In 1834, when Cannes was just a fishing village, the former British Lord Chancellor, Lord Brougham, was on his way to Nice when he was held up here by a cholera scare. Falling in love with the place, he built a summer villa; other foreigners soon followed, and Cannes blossomed. Now Cannes is best known for the International Film Festival held every May. The action centers on **La Croisette,** lined with palm trees, grand boutiques, and world-famous hotels such as the Carlton.

The Carlton terrace is the place favored by movie moguls for cocktails during the film festival. The beach is wide, sandy, and mostly private: Cannes is chic and expensive and determined to stay that way. To the west of the new **Palais des Festivals,** the main venue for the film festival, lies the yacht-filled harbor of the old port, also the scene of the morning flower market. The covered **Marché de Forville,** two blocks inland, offers a mouthwatering array of all the local delicacies.

From the market, little lanes lead up to the old town of **Le Suquet,** a charming alternative to the ostentatious pleasures of the seafront, with lots of restaurants to choose from. If you climb as far as the 11th-century **Tour du Mont Chevalier,** you will be rewarded by a splendid view along the coast. Above Cannes the immodestly named and exclusive **Corniche du Paradis Terrestre** also offers spectacular views, particularly of the Bastille Day (July 14) fireworks.

From Cannes you can take a boat to the peaceful **Îles de Lérins,** visible across the bay. The monastery on St.-Honorat once controlled much of the coast; now the monks cultivate lavender and grapes, and the simplicity of their lives is in startling contrast with that on the worldly shores opposite. Ste.-Marguerite is still forested. In the 17th century, the prison here held the Man in the Iron Mask. ■

The Carlton Hotel, the grandest of the hotels that line La Croisette

St.-Tropez

UNTIL FAIRLY RECENT TIMES JUST A TINY FISHING VILLAGE more easily reached by sea than land, St.-Tropez has become one of the hot spots for which the Côte d'Azur is famous.

Part of the harbor at St.-Tropez may still look like the archetypal unspoiled fishing village, but the town has different aspirations now.

Guy de Maupassant moved here in the 1880s, followed soon after by painter Paul Signac, whose villa became a haven for artists. Another bohemian influx came in the 1930s, led by Jean Cocteau and Colette. And in the 1950s Brigitte Bardot arrived as the ultimate crowd puller. Now celebrities moor their yachts or have villas here, attracting hordes of visitors. Rich bohemians rent restored village houses on the surrounding hills and spend their days on Plage de Pampelonne

(the hippest by far) and other inviting beaches.

And yet the little town remains charming: Visit the market on Place des Lices in the morning, and in the evening head for the cafés around the harbor. The 16th-century citadel offers evocative views. The same panoramas translated into paint are on view in the **Musée de l'Annonciade.** The old chapel of the Annunciation now houses the art collection given to St.-Tropez by patron of the arts Georges Grammont. Excellent examples of Postimpressionist works include some by Derain, Signac, Seurat, Dufy, and Braque, many of whom were pilgrims to the beauty and quiet of old St.-Tropez.

At the eastern end of the town, above the harbor, the hilltop citadel (*rue de la Citadelle*) guarded the town. The hexagonal keep, built in the 16th century, has three towers and ramparts giving views out to sea. Inside is a maritime museum, a branch of that in the Palais de Chaillot in Paris (see p. 92). ∎

St.-Tropez
🗺 281 F2
Visitor information
✉ quai Jean-Jaurès, avenue Général de Gaulle
☎ 04 94 97 45 21

Musée de l'Annonciade
✉ quai St.-Raphael
☎ 04 94 97 04 01
🕐 Closed Tues.
💲 $

Brigitte Bardot

In 1956, movie director Roger Vadim and a film crew burst into St.-Tropez to make a film starring his little-known actress wife. The film was *Et Dieu créa la femme (And God Created Woman)*, the actress was Brigitte Bardot, and St.-Tropez never looked back. The daughter of bourgeois Parisian parents, Bardot had been working as a model when she met Vadim at the age of 15. The nudity and love scenes in *And God*

Created Woman caused a scandal, and the film was a huge success. B.B. shot to stardom, and her sun-kissed, barefoot, *femme-enfant* brand of sexuality made her an icon for a whole generation. Bardot still lives in her villa outside St.-Tropez. But after three marriages and many love affairs, she has turned her attention to animals, and has since devoted herself to animal rights causes. ∎

Hyères & Îles d'Hyères

FERRIES

Ferries to the Îles d'Hyères run from Hyères harbor (90 minutes, tel 04 94 58 21 81); from Le Lavandou (35 minutes, Gare Maritime, tel 04 94 71 01 02); and from Cavalaire-sur-Mer (45 minutes). Round-trip fare: $$$$

The most venerable and southerly of the Côte d'Azur's resorts is dignified and old-fashioned Hyères. In the 19th century, it was a favorite wintering place for the Empress Eugénie, Queen Victoria, Robert Louis Stevenson, Edith Wharton, and members of the British aristocracy in search of health cures. But it never attracted the crowds that flocked to Nice and Cannes.

Despite wholesale development of its coastal suburbs, with mile upon mile of sandy beach, Hyères has kept its slightly faded charm, and is much in demand as a film set for belle epoque dramas.

A profusion of palm trees and Moorish architecture imparts an exotic quality on the broad 19th-century boulevards. Through a medieval gatehouse is the old town, with streets climbing the slopes of Casteau hill, lovely gardens, and sea views. The 12th-century **Tour St.-Blaise** and **Église de St.-Paul** hint at Hyères's former status.

The three exotically beautiful Îles d'Hyères, former haunt of pirates and now partly given over to the French armed forces, are remarkable, unspoiled, protected environments. Cars are restricted, so the islands are ideal for gentle walks among the scented *maquis* and for bathing in clear waters.

On **Porquerolles,** the largest island, you can rent bicycles to explore the rocky creeks of the north coast (not safe for swimming) and the sandy coves of the south. Watered with natural springs and rich in flora and fauna, **Port-Cros,** a national park since 1963, is strictly protected. Offshore is a marine nature reserve: From the beach at La Palud you can dive along an underwater trail to see a fantastic range of sea creatures, including sponges, sea urchins, octopuses, and moray eels. And for real nature lovers, the **Île du Levant** contains the world's oldest naturist colony, Héliopolis. ∎

Marseille

FRANCE'S OLDEST AND LARGEST PORT IS TOUGH, RAFFISH, colorful, and cosmopolitan. Founded by the Greeks in the seventh century B.C., it remained independent of France until the 15th century, after which it made a specialty of its own Mediterranean brand of turbulence: The Revolutionary hymn "La Marseillaise" owes its name to the fervor of the Marseillais rebels.

Marseille

⬛ 281 E2

Visitor information

✉ 4 La Canebière

☎ 04 91 13 89 00

Musée des Docks Romains

✉ place du Vivaux

☎ 04 91 91 24 62

🕐 Closed Mon.

$ $

France's gateway to the Middle East and to North Africa, Marseille has always been a cultural melting pot. The great boulevard of **La Canebière,** still a bustling though slightly run-down thoroughfare, was once where Western magnates and Eastern potentates met, while their ships moored in the harbor.

The **Vieux Port** remains the focus of the city, its old forts now overlooking a fish market and some superb seafood restaurants.

To the north of the port, the old quarter of Le Panier was largely dynamited by the Germans during World War II. A few historic buildings remain, including the restored 17th-century Hospice of **La Vieille Charité.** Nearby, the 19th-century **Cathédrale de la Major** (*esplanade de la Tourette*) dwarfs the 12th-century **Ancienne Major,** the original

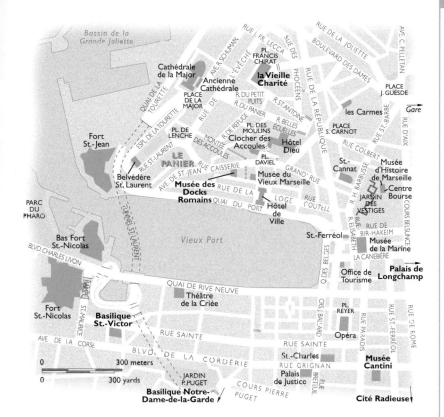

cathedral that was partially destroyed to make space for the new one. The **Musée des Docks Romains** displays finds from the excavation of the Roman port.

East of the port, the Palais de Longchamp is a 19th-century folly now housing the **Musée des Beaux-Arts** (*boulevard Longchamp*). And to the south stands Marseille's most ancient church, the fifth-century foundation of the **Basilique St.-Victor** (*quai de Rive Neuve*) with atmospheric crypts and catacombs. Nearby, dominating the whole city, is **Basilique Notre-Dame-de-la-Garde** (*parvis de la Basilique de Notre-Dame-de-la-Garde*), a 19th-century Byzantine basilica topped by a golden statue of the Virgin.

The city's commitment to modern architecture is evident in Le Corbusier's **Cité Radieuse** near the **Musée Cantini** (*19 rue Grignan, tel 04 91 54 77 75, closed Mon.*), a contemporary art gallery, and in architect Will Alsop's Hôtel du Département.

Marseille's corniche, Boulevard J. F. Kennedy, offers views to the island prison of the **Château d'If,** and paths to the Malmousque promontory. At the end is the city's main beach, the Plage du Prado.

Eastward to **Cassis,** the coast is notched with *calanques,* fjordlike inlets in white cliffs. Best viewed by boat, the beaches are only accessible by scrambling down the cliffs. Cassis is a delight, with good fish restaurants around its harbor. West of Marseille lie the calanques and villages of the **Côte Bleue.** ■

Detail from the Opéra in Place Reyer

Cassis
🅰 281 E2
Visitor information
✉ place Baragnon
☎ 04 42 01 71 17

More places to visit in the Côte d'Azur

ESTEREL MASSIF

The Esterel Massif boasts a rare stretch of unspoiled coastline in the Côte d'Azur, a landscape of jagged cliffs and forested ravines. A spectacular corniche road winds through pine forests, past porphyry cliffs and aquamarine *calanques*. Stop at **Pointe de l'Esquillon** for a grand view of the Mediterranean, the Esterel Massif, and the cliffs of Cap Roux. From **Agay** (*Visitor information, boulevard de la Plage, tel 04 94 82 01 85*), in its beautiful bay, you can walk across the Cap du Dramont to Le Dramont, where American troops established a beachhead in 1944.

281 F3

FRÉJUS

A Roman port (Forum Julii) founded by Julius Caesar, Fréjus is particularly rich in Roman and medieval remains. Though the port is silted up, a sizable amphitheater remains, along with parts of an aqueduct, a gateway, and a theater. Highlights of the medieval **Cité Épiscopale** include the Gothic and Renaissance cathedral with its elegant cloister, the 14th-century bishops' palace, and one of the oldest baptistries in France, probably fifth century—an octagon of Corinthian columns pilfered from the forum.

281 F3 **Visitor information** ✉ 325 rue de Jean-Jaurès ☎ 04 94 51 83 83

PORT-GRIMAUD

Port-Grimaud, across the bay from St.-Tropez, is an intriguing 1960s precursor of the return of vernacular architecture—a clever pastiche of a Provençal fishing village, built by architect François Spoerry in 1968. Designed around the yachting needs of the residents, the Venetian-style lagoon village has matured well to resemble a genuine ancient village.

281 F2

TOULON

The great naval port of Toulon lies on a deep natural harbor dramatically set against steep hills crowned with fortifications. The harborside **Quai de Stalingrad,** rebuilt after the war, is now lined with lively shops and cafés. To the north is the old town, a picturesque jumble of ancient buildings, including the 11th-century **Cathédrale Ste.-Marie-Majeure,** remodeled in the 17th century. The **Musée de la Marine** (*place Monsenergue, tel 04 94 02 02 01*) presents the city's long and eventful maritime history.

281 E2 **Visitor information** ✉ place Raimu ☎ 04 94 18 53 00 ■

The clear waters and red porphyry rocks of the Esterel corniche near St.-Raphaël

Lavender fields near Forcalquier

Provence

Land of lavender fields and olive groves, scented hillsides and fertile valleys, dazzling colors and limpid light, Provence is lauded for all its ravishing natural gifts. According to Provençal tradition, this blessed land came into being when God decided to use all the best parts left over from the Creation to make his own paradise. Only the maddening winter Mistral wind blights this garden of Eden: To withstand it, the traditional blue-shuttered farmhouses (*mas*) are built without windows in their north-facing walls.

Always coveted by foreigners, Provence was colonized by the Greeks before the Romans called it Provincia and left behind great amphitheaters and monuments at Arles and Orange, among the finest in France. Medieval popes based themselves in Avignon, where the Palais des Papes remains, a testament to their power. Great Cistercian abbeys bear witness to the less worldly side of medieval Christianity. The strong regional identity is evident in the cosmopolitan city of Aix-en-Provence, with its long literary and cultural history, and in Arles, home to proud Provençal folklore.

The region's natural wonders are simply breathtaking, ranging from the Gorges du Verdon—the Grand Canyon of Europe—to the mysterious Fontaine de Vaucluse. Mont Ventoux is the highest point of the region; its most individual and unusual part is the wide expanse of the Camargue.

Perhaps most delightful of all are the simple, enduring pleasures: a quiet pastis on a shady café terrace; a game of boules under the linden trees in a village square; produce-laden market stalls, local lavender and honey, and traditional Provençal fabrics. And no aspect of Provence is more evocative than the lovely, unspoiled *villages perchés* (hill villages) of areas such as the Lubéron. For a perfect day you can explore one of these ancient terra-cotta-roofed villages, visit an art gallery, and stroll past fields of wildflowers or aromatic herbs.

In this land of sensual delights, fine restaurants—splendid and simple—abound. But a picnic is a perfect way to savor the fragrant melons, peaches, and cherries, the goat's cheeses, tomatoes, and olives that ripen here. Or simply take a siesta in the shade of an olive tree and enjoy *la vie en plein air*. You will want to stay forever. ■

Avignon

Avignon
📍 281 D3
Visitor information
✉ 41 cours Jean-Jaurès
☎ 04 32 74 32 74

SECURE WITHIN ITS GREAT WALLS, AVIGNON RETAINS THE grand self-assurance of its 14th-century heyday, when a series of popes lived here. Then the narrow streets teemed with the comings and goings of the papal court. These days the city is a thriving cultural center, animated every summer by its music and drama festival, when palace courtyards and grand mansions serve as backdrops for the events. The focus at festival time is the Place de l'Horloge, with its Gothic clock tower and lively cafés.

The Palais des Papes, described by Prosper Merimée as "more like the citadel of a tyrant than the residence of the Vicar of God"

The coldly magnificent **Palais des Papes** (*place du Palais, tel 04 90 27 50 74*) dominates the historic city. Actually two palaces, begun in 1334, most of the interior of this great white edifice is strangely empty after the depredations of the Revolution, but six magnificent Gobelins tapestries and remarkable frescoes by Matteo Giovanetti reflect its former glory. The Chambre du Cerf, study of Clement VI, has beautiful ceramic tiles and

frescoes, skillfully restored. The lovely 14th-century **Petit Palais** (*Tel 04 90 86 44 58, closed Tues.*) opposite contains distinguished medieval painting and sculpture—an impressive introduction to the International Gothic style pioneered in Avignon by 14th-century Italian artists. Treats here include works by Simone Martine and a Botticelli "Madonna and Child."

Next to the palace stands the cathedral of Notre-Dame-des-Doms, and behind it the lovely park of the **Rocher des Doms.** Below are the Rhône River and the celebrated remains of the **Pont St.-Bénézet,** usually known as the Pont d'Avignon. Sadly truncated, the 12th-century bridge was partly swept away by the Rhône in the 17th century. Only four spans of the original 22 remain.

To the south are the narrow streets of the old town, one of the prettiest of which is Rue des Teinturiers, beside the Sorgue River. Here, until the 19th century, dyers produced the Provençal patterned cottons known as Indiennes, inspired by Indian calicos brought back from the Crusades. Museums here include the **Musée Calvet** (*65 rue Joseph-Vernet, tel 04 90 86 33 84, closed Tues.*), with its eclectic art collection, and the **Fondation Angladon-Dubrujeaud,** which cherishes the only van Gogh painting still in Provence, "Les Wagons de Chemin de Fer." ∎

In & around Orange

VISIT ORANGE FOR ITS MAGNIFICENT ROMAN HERITAGE: Its triumphal arch and theater are among the best Roman remains in the world. Lying in the Rhône Valley on the Roman Via Agrippa, Orange was (and still is) the gateway between north and south. Under the Emperor Augustine it was a thriving city, some three times its present size, with temples, baths, and a stadium, as well as other grand buildings. In the 16th century, Orange was inherited by William, Prince of Nassau, ancestor of the Dutch royal family.

Orange
📍 281 D4
Visitor information
✉ 5 cours Aristide-
Briand
☎ 04 90 34 70 88

Théâtre Antique
✉ place des Frères-
Mounet
💲 $

**Châteauneuf-du-
Pape**
📍 281 D3
Visitor information
✉ place du Portail
☎ 04 90 83 71 08

Vaison-la-Romaine
📍 281 D4
Visitor information
✉ place du Chanoine-
Sautel
☎ 04 90 36 02 11
🕐 Closed Tues. in
winter

The triumphal arch through which visitors still enter the city from the north is a monumental master piece. Built about 20 B.C. to commemorate Julius Caesar's victory over the Greeks at Massina (Marseille), it is encrusted with intricately carved battle scenes. But even this is dwarfed by the theater. The most complete surviving example anywhere, the theater still has most of its original seating (for 8,000), some of its columns and arches, and its tremendous stage wall, dwarfing a huge statue of Augustus. The acoustics are perfect, and the theater provides a superb setting for a music festival each July, with concerts, and opera.

To the south is **Châteauneuf-du-Pape,** planted by the popes and the most distinguished of the Côtes du Rhône vineyards.

VAISON-LA-ROMAINE

Northeast of Orange is Vaison-la-Romaine, an attractive town with a venerable history. Excavations revealed sections of the Roman city here (*Fouilles de Puymin, place du Chanoine-Sautel, tel 04 90 36 02 11, closed Sun.–Tues.*), complete with a basilica, baths, and a theater with seats carved out of rock, now the venue for a music festival each July. The excellent **Musée Municipal** contains a number of finds, notably an exquisite peacock mosaic. Over the river, across the Roman bridge that managed to survive terrible

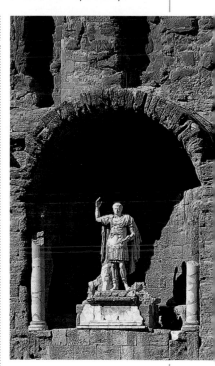

floods in 1992, is the **Haute Ville,** little cobbled streets twisting through restored 14th-century houses, rising up to the ruins of its château. The Romanesque cathedral has a sixth-century apse and marble altar, and a 12th-century cloister with wonderful carvings. ∎

"As if in answer to the insistent call of far-off Roman trumpets, I set out one early Autumn for Provence."
—Augustus John (1878–1961)

The statue of Augustus in the Roman theater at Orange is 10 feet (3 m) tall.

Around the Lubéron

THE RIDGE OF HILLS FROM MANOSQUE TO CAVAILLON, and the valleys on either side, form the Lubéron. A tour of this haven of lavender fields, vineyards, and orchards might offer any number of *villages perchés*, majestic mountain views, and fine walking.

Apt

🅼 281 E3

Visitor information

✉ 2 avenue Philippe-de-Girard

☎ 04 90 74 03 18

Maison du Parc Naturel Régional de Lubéron

☎ 04 90 04 42 00

Roussillon

🅼 281 E3

Visitor information

✉ place de la Poste

☎ 04 90 05 60 25

Gordes

🅼 281 E3

Visitor information

✉ place du Château

☎ 04 90 72 02 75

Abbaye de Sénanque

☎ 04 90 72 05 72

🕐 Closed Sun. a.m. March–Oct. & all a.m. Nov.–Feb.

💲 $

In the north of the region, steep ravines split the hills of the Lubéron massif, most of which lies in the Vaucluse département, and oaks grow down into the valleys. To the south, more fertile land slopes to the Durance River. The Grand Lubéron in the east has been designated a parc naturel régional, its headquarters in the little town of **Apt.**

The **Maison du Parc** in Apt has videos and information about local walks, wildlife, and vegetation. The town's main square offers *boules* and fountains in the shade of linden trees. The 11th-century **Cathédrale Ste.-Anne** shelters the saint's shroud, and a small archaeological museum documents the town's Roman past. Apt's Saturday market is a lively affair with specialties of local crystallized fruits, lavender oil, and handsome pottery.

Southeast of Apt, a strenuous walk from Auribeau leads up to the **Mourre Nègre,** the highest peak of the Montagne du Lubéron, with fine views in all directions.

Before the days of synthetic dyes, ocher quarrying was a major industry in the Lubéron. North of the Mourre Nègre are the abandoned quarries of the Colorado de Rustrel, a towering landscape in every shade of red and orange.

The walls and archways of the pretty village of **Roussillon,** just to the west of Apt, display the full palette of ocher, from brick red through rose to crimson. The **Falaises du Sang** (Cliffs of Blood) outside the village are

spectacular in the setting sun.

Beyond the Vaucluse plateau to the north looms the great summit of **Mont Ventoux,** over 6,000 feet high (1,900 m). The walk to the top (from Brantes, Malaucène, or Bédoin) is a breezy but fabulous climb; it is also possible to drive, or even cycle (the Tour de France has included the peak on its route).

The western Lubéron—the Petit Lubéron—is studded with delightful villages. Tiny **Bonnieux** *(Visitor information, place Carnot,*

Village des Bories

tel 04 90 75 91 90) clings to a hill-top, offering a glorious view of the valley, and the **Musée de la Boulangerie,** a bread museum (*Tel 04 90 75 88 34, closed Tues. & Nov.–March).* **Oppède-le-Vieux** has a ruined castle; and **Ménerbes** starred in British writer Peter Mayle's *A Year in Provence.* The picturesque village of **Gordes** clusters below the splendid 16th-century château, which displays contemporary art.

The nearby **Village des Bories** is a collection of ancient dwellings built on neolithic princi-ples, some of which were inhabited into the 20th century. Just north of Gordes is the Cistercian **Abbaye de Sénanque,** the pale stones of its chapel and cloister contrasting with the surrounding lavender fields.

Fontaine-de-Vaucluse sits along a gorge, at the foot of which lies the Sorgue River's source. In winter and spring a torrent from deep underground erupts into a deep (up to 1,008 feet!), dark green pool. It was here that Petrarch com-posed many of his sonnets to Laura.

The **Musée Pétrarque** dis-plays editions of his poems illus-trated by Braque, Picasso, Miró, and others. The **Moulin à Papier Vallis Clausa** has made paper here since the 16th century. ■

Fontaine-de-Vaucluse

🄼 281 D3

Visitor information

✉ chemin de la Fontaine

☎ 04 90 20 32 22

Musée Pétrarque

✉ rive Gauche de la Sorgue

☎ 04 90 20 37 20

🕐 Closed Tues. April–Sept., Mon.–Fri. Oct. & all Nov.–March

Moulin à Papier Vallis Clausa

✉ Chemin du Gouffre

Multicolored ocher rocks near Roussillon

Roussillon village

Arles

CLIMB TO THE TOP TIER OF THE ROMAN ARENA FOR THE best view of Arles, looking across the terra-cotta roofs and ocher walls to the Rhône River.

Arles
🅰 281 D3
Visitor information
✉ esplanade Charles-de-Gaulle
☎ 04 90 18 41 20

Arènes Romaines
✉ Rond-point des Arènes
☎ 04 90 49 36 86
💲 $

Musée de l'Arles Antique
✉ avenue de la 1ère Division des Français Libre
☎ 04 90 18 88 88
🕐 Closed Tues. & Oct.–March
💲 $

Museon Arlaten
✉ 29 rue de la République
☎ 04 90 93 58 11
🕐 Closed Mon. except July–Aug.
💲 $

Musée Réattu
✉ 10 rue du Grand Prieuré
☎ 04 90 49 36 74
💲 $

Fondation Vincent van Gogh
✉ 24 Rond-point des Arènes
☎ 04 90 49 55 49

Enough remains of this great Roman city to convey a powerful sense of history. Now used for bullfights and festival pageants, the vast first-century **Arènes Romaines** was once the scene of gladiatorial combats. Measuring 446 feet by 351 feet (136 by 107 m) with two stories each made up of 60 arches, it could seat 25,000 spectators. As you walk around the lower arcade of the arena, look for the tunnels through which wild beasts charged into the arena.

Nearby is the slightly earlier Roman theater, described by Henry James as "one of the most charming and touching ruins I had ever beheld." The two great columns of the stage wall (formerly used to hang prisoners) today provide a backdrop for performances during the Arles Festival in late June and early July.

The town's Roman remains are rivaled by its medieval buildings, notably the **Église St.-Trophime** (*place de la République*). A masterpiece of Provençal Romanesque, this cathedral is famed for its glorious cloister and an elaborately carved 12th-century portal.

Not content with being, in Chateaubriand's words, a great "open-air museum," Arles has a number of exceptional indoor museums. The new and impressive **Musée de l'Arles Antique** covers the city's Roman history; the **Museon Arlaten** is devoted to Provençal folklore, crafts, and costumes. The fine **Musée Réattu** includes 57 Picasso drawings donated by the artist, who reveled in the bullfights here.

But the artist most closely associated with Arles is without doubt Vincent van Gogh (1853–1890). It was here that he fell in love with the south and its brilliant colors, here in 1888 that he painted some of his

best known works including "Sunflowers" and "Chair," and here that shortly afterward he sliced off his ear in a fit of dementia. The **Fondation Vincent van Gogh** makes up for its lack of original van Gogh works with paintings inspired by him.

Arles today comes alive with a variety of festivals, including the Fête St.-Jean on June 24 and the Easter bullfights, when Arlésiens emerge wearing full costume, the men in cowboy outfits, the women in intricate lace headdresses and gorgeous embroidered shawls.

Just outside Arles, the Roman and early Christian burial ground of **Les Alyscamps,** painted by van Gogh, is a serene avenue of tombs and sarcophagi. ■

"The Midi fires the senses, your hand is more agile, your eye sharper, your brain clearer…"
—Vincent van Gogh (1853–1890) ■

The spectacle and color of bullfighting still attract huge crowds at the Roman-built arena in Arles.

The Camargue

EERILY BEAUTIFUL, THIS VAST WETLAND AREA FORMED BY the Rhône Delta is a world of infinite horizons, swaying grasses, and blue lagoons, all suffused with an extraordinary light.

Stes.-Maries-de-la-Mer

🅜 281 D3

Visitor information

✉ 5 avenue Van Gogh

☎ 04 90 97 82 55

St.-Gilles-du-Gard

🅜 281 D3

Visitor information

✉ place Mistral

☎ 04 66 87 33 75

Aigues-Mortes

🅜 281 D3

Visitor information

✉ Porte de la Gardette

☎ 04 66 53 73 00

The Camargue's unique ecology includes abundant wildlife, particularly numerous amphibians and waterfowl—most notably flamboyant flocks of pink flamingos. The glittering salt flats yield vast amounts of salt, and a delicious variety of rice grows here. The pastures are grazed by the famous native white horses, ridden by the Camarguais herdsmen known as *gardians*. These hardy people cling passionately to their traditional way of life, herding their small black bulls destined for the arenas of

Nîmes or Arles. The gardians still live in the low white cabins that are integral to the Camargue landscape.

The history and traditions of this extraordinary wilderness, now protected as a parc régional, are traced at the **Centre de Ginès** (*Tel 04 90 97 86 32*) at Pont-de-Gau, near Stes.-Maries-de-la-Mer, and at the **Musée Camarguais** southwest of Arles on the D570 (*Mas du Pont de Rousty, tel 04 90 97 10 82, closed Tues.*), a museum of Camargue life in a converted ranch, and the main center of the regional

park. It also provides information on walking and riding, and on ranches converted into atmospheric hotels and restaurants.

Endless empty beaches and unpretentious little resorts fringe the Camargue. **Stes.-Maries-de-la-Mer** nestles cozily round its vast fortified church (climb up to the rooftop for excellent views) and is now surrounded by stores bursting with all things Provençal (this is a good place to buy that Provençal cowboy shirt). Housed in the old town hall, the **Musée Baroncelli** (*rue Victor-Hugo, tel 04 90 97 87 60, closed Tues.*) has fascinating displays on Camargue traditions, and is named after a local *manadier* (rancher) who promoted the centuries-old gypsy associations with the town.

In a tradition dating back to the 16th century, every year on May 24 and 25, gypsy pilgrims flock to the town to take part in a procession carrying the statue of St. Sarah, patron saint of gypsies, to the sea to be blessed. During the festival, the streets throb with flamenco, horse races, and a kaleidoscope of costumes. Carmaguais dishes available in the restaurants here include *boeuf gardian*, a rich stew of bull's meat, best enjoyed with nutty Camargue rice.

To the north lies **St.-Gilles-du-Gard,** dubbed the Gateway to the Camargue, a tiny village dominated by an important church. Statues of the saints crowd around the three beautifully carved 12th-century portals, and a spiral staircase winds up its bell tower.

The far western edge of the Camargue is guarded by the haunting and remarkably intact medieval walled town of **Aigues-Mortes** (Place of the Dead Waters). Once an important port from which Louis IX set off on Crusades in the 15th century, it is now silted up and marooned 3 miles (5 km) from the sea. The best view of this strange town and the surrounding landscape is from the town walls, via the **Musée Archéologique** (*Tel 04 66 51 37 57, open July & Aug. only*). ■

Horses of the Camargue gallop freely across the open wetlands.

Nature reserve

One of Europe's major wetlands, the Camargue is an important haven for a wide variety of animals, grasses, and flowers, which thrive in its huge flat marshlands dotted with shallow saltwater lagoons (*étangs*). The great central **Étang de Vaccarès**, covering 16,000 acres (6,500 ha), has been designated a zoological and botanical reserve. Access is severely restricted (this is, for example, the only breeding site in France for the slender-billed gull and the red-crested pochard). A walk along the **Digue de la Mer** from Stes.-Maries-de-la-Mer provides good views of the reserve, and various points on the D37 and C134 may offer sightings of herring gulls and black-headed gulls, herons, avocets, egrets, and—most memorable of all—the famous flamingos (their distinctive pink color comes from the tiny crustaceans on which they feed). The visitor center at **La Capelière** (*Map 281 D3, closed Sun.*), on the east side of the Étang de Vaccarès, provides information on the reserve, along with an exhibition following the Camargue through the seasons. The **Parc Ornithologique** at Pont-de-Gau north of Stes.-Maries-de-la-Mer displays a variety of birds including predators such as Egyptian vultures, black kites, and eagle owls. ■

Les Baux-de-Provence

RISING ABOVE THE WHITE LIMESTONE CRAGS OF LES Alpilles, the ruins of the feudal citadel of Les Baux (as it's usually known) meld into the rocky outcrop on which they stand.

Les Baux
🔼 281 D3
Visitor information
✉ impasse du Château
☎ 04 90 54 34 39

Musée de l'Histoire de la Citadelle
✉ Château des Baux de Provence
☎ 04 90 54 55 56
💲 $

A limestone arch in the hills of Les Alpilles frames a view of Les Baux.

This was once the stronghold of the powerful, proud, and bloodthirsty lords of Baux. With their ancestry dating back to the Magi King Balthazar, the lords boldly placed the Star of Bethlehem on their coat of arms, and terrorized the region for much of the Middle Ages. Most infamous of all was the psychopathically violent Raymond de Turenne, known as the scourge of Provence. In the 14th century he amused himself by forcing his hapless prisoners to leap to their deaths from the castle walls.

In the 13th century, by contrast, Les Baux was the embodiment of romance, the most famous of the Provençal courts of love that lured troubadours from afar to serenade noble ladies. But the great citadel was to come to an ignominious end in 1632, when Cardinal Richelieu, finally tiring of the rebellious lords and inhabitants of Les Baux, ordered the entire edifice to be demolished. The result is the magnificent ruin visible today, strung out along a narrow and vertiginous spit.

Enter the **Ville Morte** (dead city) through the 14th-century **Tour du Brau,** which houses the castle's museum. From here, you can climb over the ruins of the castle and early village, discovering remnants of towers and walls. The edge of the escarpment offers tremendous views across the contorted rocks of **Val d'Enfer,** the legendary haunt of witches and reputedly the inspiration for the setting of Dante's *Inferno.*

The village below the citadel dates mainly from the 16th and 17th centuries, with a number of Renaissance chapels and mansions now containing museums. The **Fondation Louis Jou** in the Hôtel Jean de Brion displays the paraphernalia of a master typographer; the **Musée des Santons** in the Ancien Hôtel de Ville (*rue Porte Mage*) is devoted to the traditional clay figures that decorate Provençal Christmas cribs. Other notable museums include the **Musée d'Art Contemporain** (*Hôtel des Porcelets, place St.-Vincent*) and the intriguing **Musée de l'Olivier,** focusing on different artists' interpretations of olive trees. ■

Aix-en-Provence

"THE MOST BEAUTIFUL TOWN IN FRANCE AFTER PARIS," according to an 18th-century traveler, Aix is a chic and elegant city, with graceful boulevards, shady squares, and hundreds of beautifully carved stone fountains. Water is the raison d'être of the city, founded by the Roman consul Sextius, who was attracted by the hot springs that are still in use today.

At the heart of Aix lies the majestic **Cours Mirabeau,** the famous tree-shaded boulevard laid out on the site of the old ramparts, flanked by elegant 17th- and 18th-century houses and punctuated by beautiful fountains. Take time to watch the world go by from the terrace of one of the cafés here, such as Les Deux Garçons, a favorite haunt of artists and intellectuals since 1792.

To the north, the old town extends through a maze of squares. On Saturdays, when it is taken over by a market, this area is even more irresistible. Distinguished buildings include the 17th-century **Hôtel de Ville** and the old bishops' palace or Ancien Achevêché, which now houses the **Musée des Tapisseries,** with fine tapestries. Next door is the lovely Gothic **Cathédrale St.-Sauveur,**

unmistakable for its 16th-century carved doors, the cool columns of its fifth-century Merovingian baptistry, and its Romanesque cloisters. Among its treasures is Nicolas Froment's 15th-century triptych, the "Burning Bush."

South of Cours Mirabeau is the elegant Quartier Mazarin. Here the **Musée Granet** (*Tel 04 42 38 14 70, closed Tues.*) has several works by Paul Cézanne, Aix's most famous son. A Cézanne circuit leads you around the town, and you can visit the **Atelier Paul Cézanne** (*Tel 04 42 21 06 53*), where the artist worked from 1897 until he died in 1906. It has been re-created just as he might have left it. Here he painted "Les Grandes Baigneuses," and the window offers views of his beloved Mont Ste.-Victoire, inspiration for more than 50 of his paintings. ∎

Aix-en-Provence
- 281 E3

Visitor information
- 2 place Général-de-Gaulle
- 04 42 16 11 61

Musée des Tapisseries
- place de l'Ancien-Archevêché
- 04 42 23 09 91
- Closed Tues.
- $

Cathédrale St.-Sauveur
- place de l'Université

Gorges du Verdon

A GLIMPSE OF THE EMERALD GREEN WATERS OF THE Verdon River hundreds of feet deep in its limestone gorge is enough to explain the name "gift of green." The deepest, widest gorge in Europe, this great natural wonder and precious refuge is a parc naturel régional sheltering unusual flora and fauna. Geographically this is the meeting point of the Alps and the Mediterranean landscape, and the result is a huge variety of different habitats and a number of plants and birds, including species of fern and of birds of prey found nowhere else.

Left: The Gorges du Verdon cut dramatically through limestone mountains.

Right: Kayakers paddling down the gorge

Castellane
🏔 281 F3
Visitor information
✉ Route National 85
☎ 04 92 83 61 14

Moustiers-Ste.-Marie
🏔 281 F3
Visitor information
✉ Hôtel Dieu
☎ 04 92 74 67 84
🕐 Closed a.m. Oct.–May

FOR THE ACTIVE
The footpath at the bottom of the gorge provides an exhilarating 15-mile (24-km) hike. But most of the walk is limited to guided groups because of the terrain and the risk of hydro-electric dams being opened. The more intrepid can try white-water rafting or kayaking. ■

From its source in the High Alps, the Verdon River twists south for 40 miles (64 km) before plunging through the limestone canyon for 13 miles (24 km) at depths of 2,300 feet (700 m). For a circular tour starting from **Castellane,** an ancient town of ruined ramparts and now a busy tourist center, you need to allow a day and plenty of gas. Along the route are breathtaking views into the canyon—but beware of hair-raising bends and terrifying precipices.

Leave Castellane westward on the D952. The first superb viewpoint on the north bank is **Point Sublime;** from here, hikers can walk down 590 feet (180 m) to the bottom of the gorge. After Point Sublime, the D23 loops off to the south, providing spectacular views before rejoining the main D952 at **La Palad-sur-Verdon** to skirt the canyon.

Set in a deep ravine above the western end of the canyon is **Moustiers-Ste.-Marie,** a 15th-century settlement known for its pretty pottery. The noted chef Alain Ducasse has a restaurant here. From here head south on the D957 past the **Lac de Sainte-Croix,** an artificial lake of cobalt blue waters with ever present sailors and windsurfers, then turn left along the south side of the canyon on the Corniche Sublime, the D71. Views abound, particularly at **Pont de**

l'Artuby, spanning the gorge of the Artuby River, and at the **Balcons de la Mescla.** These "balconies" drop almost vertically to the churning waters far below.

To return to Castellane, follow the D71 east, turn north on the D90 (a steep, narrow road), and north again on the D955 to rejoin the D952. For an easier route, take the D71 east to the D21 at Comps-sur-Artuby. Turn east on this road, and almost immediately turn left on the D955 and proceed north to the D952. ■

More places to visit in Provence

HAUTE-PROVENCE
In the northeast corner of Provence is a mountainous region of remote villages, narrow river gorges, pine forests, and sheep pastures. In summer it offers fine walking; in winter the ski lifts prevail. An unbeatable way to discover this area is to take the narrow-gauge railroad, the **Chemin de Fer de Provence,** from Nice to **Digne-les-Bains** (*Visitor information, place du Tampinet, tel 04 92 36 62 62*). This spa town is the regional capital as well as the processing center for the lavender crop. Near the Italian border is the **Parc National du Mercantour** (*Visitor information, place F.-Mistral, Barcelonnette, tel 04 92 81 21 31*), an important natural reserve sheltering ibex, chamois, wild boar, golden eagles, and bearded vultures, and a huge range of plants and flowers.

ST.-RÉMY-DE-PROVENCE
On the fertile plain north of the Chaîne des Alpilles, St.-Rémy-de-Provence is a charming little market town. In 1889 Vincent van Gogh became a patient at the hospital of **St.-Paul-de-Mausile.** You can visit its gardens and 12th-century cloister, and also the **Centre d'Art Présence Van Gogh** in the 18th-century Hôtel Estrine. The **Musée des Arômes de Provence** is dedicated to the tradition of herb growing. St.-Rémy is most celebrated for the ruins of a Greco-Roman town, once a Roman spa, at nearby **Glanum.** 🄰 281 D3 **Visitor information** ✉ place Jean-Jaurès ☎ 04 90 92 05 22

TARASCON
Tarascon, on the Rhône bordering Languedoc, is dominated by its impressive white-walled, 15th-century Gothic château. This castle was a lively center of medieval culture, still evident in its graceful interior. The 12th-century **Église de St.-Marthe,** opposite, is dedicated to the saint who reputedly saved the town from an amphibious monster, the Tarasque, a victory still celebrated on the last weekend in June. The **Musée Souleïado** is devoted to antique and contemporary Provençal fabrics, with workshops and a shop selling the distinctive Souleïado designs. 🄰 281 D3 **Visitor information** ✉ rue des Halles ☎ 04 90 91 03 52 ■

Tarascon's terra-cotta tiled rooftops

Boats docked in the harbor at Sète

Languedoc-Roussillon

The "other" South of France, Languedoc-Roussillon, is every bit as dazzling as Provence and the Côte d'Azur, but flaunts itself less. These two provinces extend from the Rhône to the Pyrenees, and from the coast to the highlands of the Cévennes, the Corbières, and the Minervois. Languedoc owes its name to the medieval language of the troubadours *(la langue d'oc, see below)*. In Spanish-flavored Roussillon, the proud northern outpost of Catalonia that became part of France as late as the 17th century, the Catalan language is still common, and on village squares you may well see the national dance, the *sardaña*.

No other region of France encompasses such a variety of landscape. The wine villages of the coastal plain, surrounded by vineyards and thyme-scented *garrigue*, epitomize the sun-baked Midi; beneath the snowcapped Pyrenees, orchards of peach and plum, almond and cherry flourish among pastures rich with wildflowers in spring and threaded by paths. Walkers will relish the lonely Corbières hills and the uplands of the Haut-Languedoc. The fishing villages and saltwater lagoons are a paradise not only for wildlife, but also for artists.

There is a rich legacy of Roman *(romain)* and Romanesque *(roman)* architecture, from the Roman monuments of Nîmes and the Pont du Gard, to the Moorish-influenced Romanesque abbeys of Roussillon. ■

Langue d'oc

A romance language derived from Latin, the *langue d'oc* takes it name ultimately from the Roman formula for "yes," *hoc ille*. In the south of France this became *oc*, in the north *Il*. Thus the language of the south became known as *langue d'oc* and that of the north as *langue d'oïl*—modern French. The language of the troubadours and their lyric poetry, the *langue d'oc* survived determined efforts by the French to eradicate it. You can still hear it in the patois spoken by older people in markets and cafés, and in the Occitan (Provençal) language now taught in schools and universities. ■

Montpellier

FOUNDED IN THE TENTH CENTURY, MONTPELLIER IS NOW one of the liveliest cities in the south of France. Its ancient medical school and university still attract many students.

The Tour de la Babote defended the city in the 12th century.

Montpellier

🅰 280 C3

Visitor information

✉ allée Jean-de-Lattre de Tassigny

☎ 04 67 60 60 60

Life in Montpellier revolves around **Place de la Comédie,** bustling with cafés. At one end stands the 19th-century opera house that gives it its name and a fountain topped by Étienne d'Antoine's statue of the "Three Graces." North and west lie the car-free, winding medieval streets lined with 17th- and 18th-century mansions.

In the 16th and 17th centuries, Montpellier became a stronghold of Protestantism. In 1622 Louis XIII subjected it to a devastating eight-month siege, leaving little of its medieval fabric intact. But the city turned this to its advantage, building great mansions arranged around courtyards with stone staircases. Ones open to visitors are the **Hôtel de Manse** on Rue Embouque-d'Or and the **Hôtel des Trésoriers de la Bourse** on Rue Ancien-Courrier. The Hôtel Lunaret on Rue des Trésoriers de France, a masterpiece built by Jacques Coeur, Charles VII's treasurer, houses the **Musée Languedocien** *(Entrance at 7 rue Jacques Coeur, tel 04 67 52 93 03).*

The 17th-century former bishops' palace beside the cathedral, now the medical school, contains the French and Italian drawings of the **Musée Atger.** The **Musée Fabre** *(39 boulevard Bonne Nouvelle, tel 04 67 14 83 00)* specializes in French paintings, including Courbet's "Bonjour M. Courbet," Berthe Morisot's "L'Été," and Delaunay's "Nature Morte Portugaise."

To savor Montpellier's setting between the Cévennes and the sea, stroll along the **Promenade du Peyrou,** formal 18th-century gardens dominated by a graceful neoclassic *château d'eau,* an elaborate fountain, and the aqueduct that used to bring water to the city. North of the promenade is the **Jardin des Plantes,** one of the oldest botanical gardens in Europe.

Like its neighbor and rival, Nîmes, Montpellier prides itself on its modern architecture, including Ricardo Bofill's postmodern Antigone quarter (east of the Esplanade Charles-de-Gaulle) and squares based on a reinterpretation of classical architecture. ∎

Nîmes

NÎMES COMBINES ANCIENT HISTORY AND MODERN LIFE with tremendous brio and zest, at its most colorful during the Féria du Pentecôte, the annual bullfighting and folklore festival in May.

The city owes its chief glories to the Romans, who settled around the spring of Nemausus and built a range of fortifications and public buildings. The Emperor Augustus gave the city its walls and gates, as recorded by an inscription on the Porte d'Auguste. Most impressive is **Les Arènes** (*Tel 04 66 76 72 77*), a perfect oval arena two stories high, skillfully engineered and beautifully constructed in the first century A.D. Inside, the seating (for 24,000) was strictly segregated according to rank and sex.

The city's other Roman glory, the 2,000-year-old temple known as the **Maison Carrée** (now an exhibition space for current archaeological research), is all delicacy, grace, and exquisite proportions. Opposite stands the **Carrée d'Art,** a vast art gallery and library designed by British architect Norman Foster as a glass-and-aluminum tribute to the ancient temple.

The old town is a charming jumble of narrow streets, shady squares, and fountains. Many of the 16th- and 17th-century houses are a legacy of the textile industry (this is the birthplace of the fabric called "de Nîmes" or denim), founded by a number of enterprising Protestants, who, barred from public office, threw themselves into trade. If you need a quiet retreat, head for the **Jardin de la Fontaine** (*quai de la Fontaine*), which contains the springs and ruins of a Roman nymphaeum with limpid pools and cool stone terraces. The **Tour Magne** above, part of Augustus's city walls, offers good views over the city and the surrounding countryside. ∎

Nîmes
🅰 281 D3
Visitor information
✉ 6 rue Auguste
☎ 04 66 67 29 11

Maison Carrée
✉ place de la Maison Carrée
☎ 04 66 36 26 76

Carrée d'Art
✉ place de la Maison Carrée
☎ 04 66 76 35 35
🕐 Closed Mon. Library closed Sun. & Mon.
💲 $

Bullfights are still popular in the arena at Nîmes.

Bullfights

The Roman arenas of Nîmes and Arles, once the scene of gladiatorial fights, now echo to the drama of the *corrida*. A bull, selected for his nobility and courage, is released from a dark box into the blinding sunlight of the ring. There he is stabbed by the picadors, and speared by the *banderilleros*, before being engaged in a stylized dance of death—stately or grotesque, according to your point of view—by the matador. At the moment of truth, the animal is dispatched with a single sword thrust. ∎

Pont du Gard

Pont du Gard

 281 D3

Visitor information

✉ Maison de Tourisme, Remoulins

☎ 04 66 37 22 34

AS BEAUTIFUL AS IT IS FUNCTIONAL, THE PONT DU GARD IS an indication of the heroic scale on which the Romans built and thought. The problem was simple enough: The spring at Nîmes was not sufficient to supply the growing city with water. The solution was radical: Fresh water would be piped from springs at Uzès, some 30 miles (48 km) away, along a system of aqueducts, trenches, and tunnels carved out of the solid rock. The total drop was a mere 56 feet (17 m), and the engineering skills involved were immense.

Built by the Romans, the Pont du Gard is a testimony to their engineering skills.

Two millennia later, the aqueduct spans the river on its three great tiers of golden limestone arches virtually unchanged, despite the depredations of time. Even the marks of the original Roman builders can still be seen on some of the stones (the largest of which weighs a staggering six tons), along with graffiti left by young French *compagnons* or journeymen masons, for whom this used to be a place of pilgrimage.

Those who now picnic beneath the aqueduct, beside the Gardon River, may wonder why it was necessary to build on such a monumental scale. In winter, however, the river may swell to become a rushing torrent, capable of destroying modern bridges (as it did in 1958). The Roman engineers designed the aqueduct with a slight curve that enabled it to withstand a great pressure of water. Other technical refinements, on a par with this curve, are the almost imperceptible fall that carried the water along; and the waterproof rendering that sealed the inside of the channel along the top.

The best view of the aqueduct is from the truncated 18th-century road bridge that runs alongside it. Unfortunately, current renovation work means it is no longer possible to walk along the arcades at the top. ■

Carcassonne

Carcassonne

[M] 280 B2

Visitor information

[✉] 15 boulevard
Camille-Pelletan

[☎] 04 68 10 24 30

**Cité Medieval et
Château Comtal**

[☎] Visitor information:
04 68 10 24 35.
Chateau: 04 68 11
70 77.

[$] $

THE TURRETED AND MACHICOLATED DOUBLE WALLS OF
Carcassonne crystallize our notions of the perfect medieval citadel.
Sieges heroically resisted, knights in armor jousting in the lists, and
troubadour romance spring to mind in this evocative setting.

The largest and most impressive medieval citadel in Europe, Carcassonne was known to the Celts and fortified by the Romans. Commanding the communication route between Toulouse and the Mediterranean, it was coveted by Visigoths, Saracens, and Charlemagne. In the 13th century, Simon de Montfort's army arrived at Carcassonne, by then a Cathar stronghold, and—fresh from their massacre of the Cathars of Béziers—besieged and captured it.

De Montfort made the citadel the headquarters for his murderous raids. The inhabitants rebelled, but Louis IX moved them to the new bastide he built below the city. Thus the twin sites of Carcassonne evolved. In the late 13th century Philip the Bold massively strengthened the citadel's defenses, creating a bulwark against Spain.

But when the French annexed Roussillon in 1659, the Spanish border shifted southward, and the citadel became redundant. The

ville basse prospered and the cité declined so far that in the mid-19th century it was decided to demolish the remaining fortifications. Mercifully, the architect and medievalist Viollet-le-Duc stepped in to save this jewel. Thanks to him we can now see a complete medieval city. Wander between the two sets of ramparts, then penetrate the twin sandstone towers of the Narbonne Gate, with its portcullis and drawbridge. Inside is a warren of meticulously restored medieval houses (not to mention hotels, restaurants, and souvenir stores).

The core of the city is the 12th-century **Château Comtal.** You can walk around the ramparts past medieval defenses: watchtowers, posterns, and machicolations for hurling boiling oil and stones on attackers. The Romanesque and Gothic **Cathédrale St.-Nazaire** boasts superb stained glass and the 13th-century "siege stone," perhaps depicting the siege of Carcassonne in 1209. ■

**BURNING OF
THE CITY**

The annual Festival de
la Cité begins on July
8 and culminates in
the "Burning of the
city" (L'embrasement
de la cité) on July
14—Bastille Day,
the great French
national holiday. ■

**An aerial view
of the medieval
citadel of
Carcassonne**

Drive the Cathar trail

Follow this trail to the last strongholds of the Cathars, where they took refuge in perilously inaccessible castles and fortified hilltop villages, in the wild and inhospitable foothills of the Pyrenees.

The golden era of the Languedoc—mighty, independent, and home to a brilliant civilization—was cut short in the 13th century with the ferocious Crusade against the Cathar heretics. The Cathars (also known as Albigensians after the town of Albi) pursued a faith of high moral principles ("Cathar" is derived from the Greek *katharos*, meaning pure) and were fatally critical of the corruption of the established church. The key to their heresy lay in their Manichean belief in the dual powers of good and evil, and the resulting conviction that only the world of the spirit was good, while the material world was irredeemably evil. Their leaders, known as *perfecti*, traveled the countryside, preaching and teaching in the vernacular *langue d'oc*.

In 1209 the pope and the French king joined forces, launching a Crusade led by the ruthless Simon de Montfort. The heretics sought refuge in the isolated castles of the Corbières, whose names—Montségur, Quéribus, Peyrepertuse—are forever linked with the memory of the doomed Cathars they sheltered.

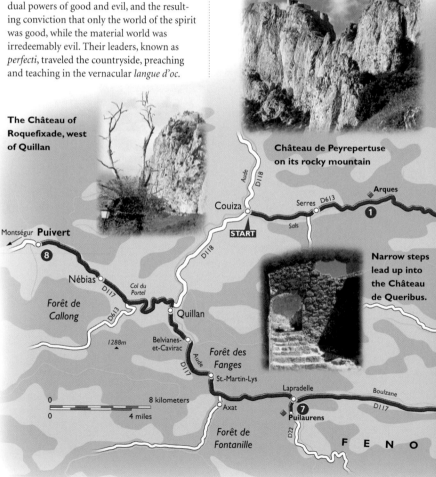

The Château of Roquefixade, west of Quillan

Château de Peyrepertuse on its rocky mountain

Narrow steps lead up into the Château de Queribus.

A day's drive through the mountains will take you to a number of the Cathar castles. Start from **Couiza** on the D118, 25 miles (40 km) south of Carcassonne, and take the D613 east to **Arques ❶** (*Tel 04 68 69 84 77*), with its perfectly preserved 13th-century keep. Turn north on the D40 for a difficult climb to the

---

🅜 See area map p. 281
➤ Cuiza
↔ 115 miles (180 km)
🕐 1 day
➤ Montségur

Driving: Though this is a
  mountainous route, the driving
  is not difficult.
Warning: Gas stations are few.
Meals: Take a picnic and plenty
  of water.

monumental ruins of **Termes ❷** (*Tel 04 68 70 09 20*) and the **Château de Durfort ❸**, perched over a ravine. De Montfort's capture of the apparently unassailable Termes in 1210 sent shudders of foreboding through all the other Cathar fortresses.

Return to the D613 and go east to the atmospheric village of **Villerouge-Termenès ❹**, which has grown up around the great stone circular towers of its castle (*Tel 04 68 70 09 11*). This was the refuge of the last Cathar "perfect," who was finally burned at the stake in 1321. A medieval banquet is held in the courtyard each year in his honor.

Double back on the D613 for 2 miles (3 km) to just beyond Félines-Termenès, then head south to Padern, through the rocky gorge of the Torgan River. Go west on the D14 to some of the most spectacular castles of all.

Château de Peyrepertuse ❺ (*Tel 04 68 45 03 26*) is reached by a single long and winding road, and an uphill drive of at least half an hour. So cramped is the site that the castle stretches out to fit its dizzy perch, in places only a few yards wide, with one narrow entrance. Inside is a simple Romanesque chapel, and beyond it another flight of exposed steps leads up to the final refuge. The wind takes your breath away, as does the view to the sea, to the void below, and to the peaks of the Pyrenees.

Visible from Peyrepertuse is the **Château de Quéribus ❻**, its keep and remarkable chapel dominating the Roussillon plain. Backtrack on the D14 for 5 miles (8 km) and take the D123 to reach this, the last stronghold of the Cathars. It proved impregnable to siege, finally surrendering peacefully in 1255. A single stairway is still the only access to the castle.

Proceed southwest on the D19 and D117 to the more accessible **Puilaurens ❼** (*Tel 04 68 20 52 07*), bristling with machicolations, arrow-slit windows, and ramparts. The single stone stairway, zigzagging precariously to the top, ensured that no assailant went unnoticed or unbombarded.

Take the D117 to Quillan, south of Couiza, and head west, still on the D117, to **Puivert ❽** (*Tel 04 68 20 80 98*), more palace than castle, despite its sturdy defenses. Farther west (on the D117 and D9) rises the great rock of **Montségur**, the Cathar headquarters (see p. 277), a fitting place to end your drive. ■

Romanesque abbeys

AMONG THE CHIEF GLORIES OF LANGUEDOC-ROUSSILLON are its Romanesque abbeys. These lovely buildings, dating from the 10th, 11th, and 12th centuries, combine simple, austere spaces—stone barrel-vaulted naves and serene cloisters—with exquisitely carved stone capitals and panels. Some are set in remote places, and preserve the peaceful monastic atmosphere. These abbeys have been beautifully restored, and you can see several in a tour of the Roussillon département around Perpignan. They also serve as wonderful venues for summer music festivals. Among these is the famous Pablo Casals Festival, held every August, which features concerts in the enormous ninth-century abbey church of St.-Michel-de-Cuxa.

St.-Michel-de-Cuxa
- 280 B1
- Codalet
- 04 68 96 15 35
- Closed a.m. Sun. & religious holidays
- $

Serrabone
- 280 B1
- Prieuré de Serrabone et Jardin Mediter- ranéen, Boule d'Amont
- 04 68 84 09 30
- $

Founded by the Benedictines in 878, the lovely monastery of **St.-Michel-de-Cuxa** in its wooded setting is actually pre-Romanesque. Its unusual keyhole-shaped arches are in the Mozarabic style, a legacy of the Moorish occupation of the region. The abbey's surviving great square tower, in bleached ocher-colored stone, is beautifully silhouetted against the dark massif of Mont Canigou. The finest of the capitals from the 12th-century pink marble cloister, looted after the Revolution, was found in Prades in 1909, and sold to the Metropolitan

Museum of Art in New York City.

On a crag set high up on the slopes of Mont Canigou, the silent, ascetic retreat of **St.-Martin-du-Canigou** (*Tel 04 68 05 50 03*) is accessible only by jeep or a 40-minute climb on foot. But its beauty and setting more than repay the effort. The best panorama is from a viewpoint above the abbey. Inside, you may visit the cloister and garden, the Romanesque chapel and church, and the tombs of Guifred, Count of Cerdagne—who founded the monastery in the 11th century in penance for killing his son and his wife.

The Augustinian priory of **Serrabone** also clings to the side of Mont Canigou, commanding a spectacular view of the surrounding peaks. It is set in a lovely garden of vines, shrubs, and fragrant herbs (where you may picnic). The beautifully simple 11th-century church houses a splendid tribune of pink marble columns and arches, carved with an astonishing array of mythical beasts, flowers, and human figures. The marble cloister arches frame the mountain views.

Among the orchards and vines south of Perpignan is the ancient town of **Elne,** which every year hosts a music festival in its 11th-century cathedral. Elne's incomparable treasure is its cloister, where the marble capitals have been vigorously carved; several feature monks peeking round doors. The oldest (12th century) and finest tell the Creation story: The panel of Adam and Eve is a masterpiece.

ST.-GUILHEM-LE-DÉSERT

Half hidden in the Hérault gorge, north of Montpellier, are the picturesque village and beautiful austere abbey of St.-Guilhem-le-Désert. Guilhem of Aquitaine, trusty lieutenant of Charlemagne, founded the abbey in the ninth cen-

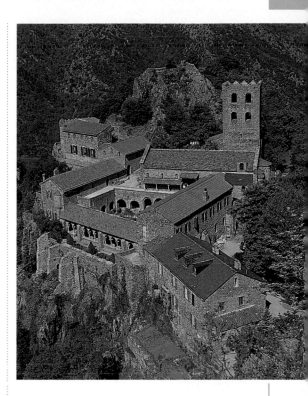

tury. His piety, coupled with a relic of the True Cross awarded him by Charlemagne, assured him a following even in this remote spot.

You climb up to the abbey through the charming village below, honeycombed by streams tumbling through gardens and under bridges, dotted with modest Romanesque houses lovingly restored, and dominated by the curves of the chapel apses. The abbey church is a perfect example of the simplicity and strength of Romanesque building, with a great barrel-vaulted nave, massive pillars, and sturdy arches.

Two galleries of the cloister are still here, but to see the rest you must go to New York—to the Cloisters, part of the Metropolitan Museum of Art. There, cloisters from St.-Guilhem-le-Désert join those from St.-Michel-de-Cuxa. ■

Looking down on the abbey of St.-Martin-de-Canigou

Elne
🅰 280 B1
Visitor information
✉ 2 rue Doctor Charles Bolte
☎ 04 68 22 05 07

St.-Guilhem-le-Désert
🅰 280 C3
Visitor information
✉ St.-Guilhem-le-Désert
☎ 04 67 57 44 33

Collioure &
the Côte Vermeille

Collioure

280 C1
Visitor information
place du 18 Juin
04 68 82 15 47

Banyuls-sur-Mer
280 C1
Visitor information
avenue République
04 68 88 31 58

THE CÔTE VERMEILLE (AN UNTRANSLATABLE MIXTURE OF "vermilion" and "silver gilt"), where the Pyrenees tumble into the cerulean blue Mediterranean, is by far the most beautiful section of the Languedoc coast. Red rocks carpeted with vines rise above the sandy bays, and the winding shoreline, threaded by corniche roads offering sensational views, shelters tiny coves and fishing villages all the way to Spain.

The jewel of the coast is the little port of **Collioure.** In the early 20th century, its brilliant light, gaily painted fishing boats, and colorful stuccoed houses inspired Matisse and other artists to experiment with the violent eruptions of pure color that earned them the soubriquet fauvist (literally "wild beast"). Art galleries, restaurants, and stores now cram the tiny cobbled streets, and you can follow a *chemin du Fauvisme* (ask at the tourist office

Collioure's harbor with the Château Royal and the former lighthouse

for details), with reproductions of views by Matisse and Derain in the places where they were painted.

The charm of Collioure remains essentially unchanged. Its perfect little harbor is flanked by the **Château Royal** (*Tel 04 68 82 06 43*), built by the Knights Templar in the 13th century and later reinforced by Vauban. It is now used for exhibitions of modern art. The fortified 14th-century **Église de Notre-Dame-des-Anges** has borrowed the former lighthouse as its bell tower. Three small sheltered beaches of pebble and sand extend beneath harborside restaurants with sunny terraces, where you can indulge in locally caught fish (anchovies are the main catch) and Collioure wine.

South of Collioure, the road roller coasts in and out of coastal towns and past the steeply terraced vineyards of **Banyuls-sur-Mer.** Stop at Cap Béar for a dazzling panorama of mountains and sea. Banyuls itself is as sweet as its wine (try it chilled as an aperitif), with palm-shaded cafés around the harbor, a little beach, and wine *caves* along the ancient narrow streets. On the southern side of the town is an oceanographic research institute with an aquarium of local sea life (*Tel 04 68 88 73 39*). At the most southerly point of the French coast, **Cerbère** flies the red and gold Catalan flag. ■

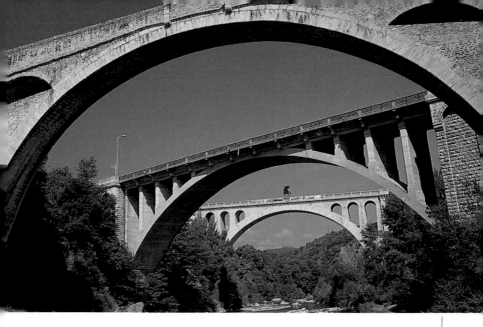

**Bridges spanning
the Tech Valley**

Céret & the Tech Valley

A 14TH-CENTURY SINGLE-SPAN BRIDGE ACROSS THE TECH River, the Pont du Diable, leads into the winding streets and shady squares of Spanish-style Céret, capital of the Vallespir (the Tech Valley). Catalan Céret is a lively center, with colorful Easter celebrations, an international festival in August, and bullfights in its arena.

Céret
🅰 280 B1
Visitor information
✉ I avenue Georges-
Clemenceau
☎ 04 68 87 00 53

Amélie-les-Bains
🅰 280 B1
Visitor information
✉ quai 8 Mai
☎ 04 68 39 30 83

Arles-sur-Tech
🅰 280 B1
Visitor information
☎ 04 68 39 11 99

Céret's charms once attracted a galaxy of avant garde artists, including Picasso and Braque. Here, they painted works such as "Landscape at Céret" (Picasso, 1911) and "Rooftops, Céret" (Braque, 1911). Their evenings at the **Grand Café** (*boulevard Maréchal-Joffre, tel 04 68 87 02 85*) left tangible evidence: several Picasso drawings on café notepaper.

Céret has an excellent **Musée d'Art Moderne** (*8 boulevard Maréchal-Joffre, tel 04 68 87 27 76, closed Tues. Oct.–April*). A modern building of ocher terraces, shady patios, and glass walls, the museum houses works by Catalan artists Capdeville and Tapiès, as well as canvases by Dufy and Chagall; a series of ceramic bowls from Vallauris by Picasso, depicting bull-

fighting and donated by the artist; and a fine early Picasso, "Portrait of Corina Père Romeu" (1902).

TECH VALLEY
The valley stretches westward from Céret through cherry orchards to the Roman spa town of **Amélie-les-Bains.** A few miles farther on the D115 is **Arles-sur-Tech,** where a Benedictine abbey was founded in 900. The massive Romanesque church was rebuilt in the 12th century and features an elegant 12th-century cloister.

Farther up this remote valley is the **Gorges de la Fou,** allegedly the narrowest gorge in the world. An iron walkway winds through the cliffs, accessible only on foot with the mandatory protective headgear. ∎

Catalonians
dancing the
sardaña

Perpignan &
French Catalonia

WITH ITS HISTORICAL ROOTS IN THE COUNTY OF
Barcelona and the kingdoms of Aragon and Majorca, it is not surprising that Roussillon often feels more Spanish than French. It is
proudly conscious of its distinct identity as French Catalonia: The
red-and-yellow Catalonian flag flutters everywhere, the national
dance, the *sardaña*, is danced solemnly in village squares, and many
people speak Catalan, sometimes still as a first language.

The sunny, southern city of
Perpignan is the capital of
French Catalonia, with a strong
Spanish influence underscored by
the large population of émigrés
from Franco's Spain.

The **Palais des Rois de
Majorque** takes up virtually a
quarter of the old town—in the
13th century the city was the capital
of the kings of Majorca. Within its
17th-century ramparts, built by
Vauban, the vast two-story palace
and its arcaded courtyard, its
beautifully frescoed and tiled royal
chapels, and its great Gothic hall,

building, the **Palais de la Députation.**

Le Castillet, a 14th-century gateway, houses the **Musée Casa Païral** a museum of Catalan traditions and crafts. **Musée Rigaud** shows work by Perpignan-born Hyacinthe Rigaud, along with paintings by Dufy and Picasso, and works by sculptor Aristide Maillol.

The 14th-century **Cathédrale de St.-Jean** dominates Place de Gambetta, a former parade ground lined with 16th-century houses. Built by the kings of Majorca, the cathedral is in the Roussillon style of red brick and pebbles, and has a typical southern Gothic wrought-iron bell tower. Inside, candlelight illuminates frescoed walls, stained glass, and a glowing gilt altar. In a chapel on the south side hangs the harrowing 14th-century wooden statue of the Devôt Christ, which is carried through the streets on Good Friday by a brotherhood of penitents. Bells toll, muffled drums roll, and the penitents pass through the town in scarlet or black robes topped by tall pointed hoods.

AROUND PERPIGNAN

The beaches of **St.-Cyprien-Plage** and **Canet-Plage,** both within convenient reach of Perpignan, are popular and sandy, but otherwise unremarkable. The remains of Europe's oldest human being, dating back to about 450,000 B.C., were discovered in 1971 at **Tautavel.** The **Musée de la Préhistoire** there tells the story and displays a reconstruction of the famous skull.

Dominating Perpignan is the snowy peak of **Mont Canigou** (9,138 feet, 2,785 m), sacred and mystical mountain of the Catalans, with a great iron cross perched on its summit. The climb to the top from Vernet-les-Bains-Cortalets is a magnificent experience. ∎

betray an unmistakable Spanish-Moorish influence.

The focus of the old town lies to the north, in **Place de la Loge.** Here, among pink marble paved streets and narrow alleys, stands the **Loge de Mer.** Built in exquisite 14th-century Gothic style as the city's stock exchange and maritime court, it boasts carved wooden ceilings and sculpted windows. The first floor now houses a fast food restaurant, where you can inspect the Loge's glories at close quarters. Its gargoyles and filigree balustrades, meanwhile, may be contemplated from one of the cafés on the square. Beside it stands the 14th-century **Hôtel de Ville,** with its superb 17th-century gates, and the 15th-century Roussillon parliament

Perpignan
🅰 280 B2
Visitor information
✉ place Armand Lanoux
☎ 04 68 66 30 30

Palais des Rois de Majorque
✉ 2 rue des Archers
☎ 04 68 34 48 29
$ $

Musée Casa Païral–Le Castillet
✉ place Verdun
☎ 04 68 35 42 05
$ $

Musée Rigaud
✉ 16 rue Ange
☎ 04 68 35 43 40
🕐 Closed Tues.
$ $

Tautavel
🅰 280 B2
Musée de La Préhistoire
✉ avenue Leon-Jean-Gregory
☎ 04 68 29 07 76
$ $$

More places to visit in Languedoc-Roussillon

BÉZIERS
Famous for wine, rugby, and bullfights, this large, lively, and ancient city climbs steeply up the left bank of the Orb River, to the vast 14th-century **Cathédrale St.-Nazaire,** with its fortified towers, stained glass, and frescoes. The original cathedral was burned during the sacking of Béziers in 1209, when terrified citizens vainly sought refuge within it. Southwest of Béziers stands **Oppidum d'Ensérune,** one of France's most important pre-Roman sites, documented by a fascinating museum.
 280 C2 **Visitor information** 29 avenue St.-Saens 04 67 76 47 00

CANAL DU MIDI
Stretching 150 miles (241 km) from Toulouse to the Mediterranean at Sète or Agde, the Canal du Midi is a monumental feat of engineering and an architectural masterpiece. It was the brainchild of Pierre-Paul Riquet, a

The narrow streets of the mountain village of Villefranche-de-Conflent

government official. Work began in 1667, with Riquet providing much of the finance.

NARBONNE
Capital of the largest Roman province in Gaul and a great port until the Middle Ages, when its harbor silted up, Narbonne is now prosperous again thanks to the surrounding wine region. The historic heart, north of the Canal de la Robine, bisects the town. Here looms the fortified **Palais des Archevêques,** the archbishops' palace, built in the 13th and 14th centuries. Beside it, the unfinished Gothic cathedral displays a fine cloister, 14th-century stained glass, and beautiful tapestries. Behind lies a vestige of Roman Narbo, underground warehouses known as the **Horreum.**
 280 B2 **Visitor information** place R. Salengro 04 68 65 15 60

SÈTE
An important port for three centuries, busy Sète has a network of canals and bridges lined with delightful buildings, all pink and blue facades and iron balconies. Stroll along the Grand Canal to discover a string of excellent seafood restaurants serving *fruits de mer* fresh from the sea. Sète is liveliest during the *joutes nautiques* in August: picturesque traditional water jousting tournaments, to the accompaniment of 300-year-old jousting songs.
 280 C3 **Visitor information** 60 Grand' Rue Mario-Roustan 04 67 74 71 71

VILLEFRANCHE-DE-CONFLENT
Founded by the counts of Cerdagne in the 12th century as a defense against Moorish invasion, Villefranche has a perfectly preserved medieval garrison. Its only alterations date from the 17th century, when Vauban added massive ramparts and gates, and **Fort Libéria.** High above the gorge, the fort is accessible by footpath or underground passage. Villefranche is the starting point for a round-trip up to the mountain plain of the Cerdagne, on the popular **Petit Train Jaune,** a charming narrow-gauge railroad that winds through gorges and over viaducts.
 280 B1 **Visitor information** place de l'Église (June–Sept.) 04 68 96 22 96 ■

Set in the Mediterranean 140 miles from Nice, but only 90 miles from Italy, Corsica is French now but was Italian for centuries, and briefly independent. Restrained tourism is bringing prosperity without spoiling Corsica's beauty.

Corsica

The Corsican hellebore is unique to Corsica.

Bonifacio, on the rocky cliffs of the southern point of Corsica

Corsica

PERHAPS THE BEST WAY TO SOAK UP THE FLAVOR OF CORSICA IS TO SIP AN aperitif on a café terrace in the early evening, and observe the *passagiata*, as locals take their nightly stroll, greeting their neighbors. Like the Corsican language, this custom is more Italian than French, but Corsica is far too independent to be described in terms of either. The island has been a province of France since 1769, after several centuries of control by either Pisa or Genoa. In the 18th century it even enjoyed a brief (and nostalgically evoked) period of autonomy under national hero Pasquale Paoli. Sometimes violent separatist struggle and a dislike of foreign (including French) intervention have insured that Corsica has only recently developed as a tourist destination.

The third largest island in the Mediterranean, Corsica is a wild and beautiful place, aptly described as a mountain in the sea. The coastline is glorious, with rugged cliffs, wonderful beaches, and unpolluted sea. Parts are now fully developed resorts with huge marinas, watersports of all kinds, and frenetic nightlife. Coastal ports such as Ajaccio, Bastia, and Bonifacio are as as colorful and lively as anywhere in the Mediterranean. But there are still plenty of remote coves and deserted beaches to discover, and the mountains are a paradise for walkers and nature lovers. Corsica also has a legacy of beautiful Romanesque churches and several important megalithic monuments, most notably the stone warriors of Filitosa.

The real Corsica lives on behind the coastal facade, shepherds still move their flocks from lowlands to higher pastures every year, and religious festivals are celebrated with medieval passion and ancient songs. And in the mountains and romantic fortified citadels, Corsica's stormy past of bandits and vendettas never seems very far away. ■

Around the island

THE MOST ROMANTIC WAY TO GET TO CORSICA FROM THE
sea is by ferry either into Bastia in the north or Bonifacio or Ajaccio
in the south. As you disembark, the fragrance of the herb-scented
maquis, for which the island is famous, greets you.

Bastia *(Map 333 C4)* makes
a good starting point and
offers a wonderful taste of the
island: a bustling, colorful
port, dominated by a great
16th-century Genoese
citadel above the old harbor.
Life revolves around **Place
St.-Nicolas** (the tourist
office is here, *tel 04 95 55 96
96),* with its shady esplanade, and
the warren of Italianate streets in
the old town. The port itself has a
lively waterfront with plenty of
cafés and restaurants
flanking the facade
of the 17th-century
**Église de St.-Jean-
Baptiste.**

North of Bastia
stretches the peninsula of
Cap Corse. You can drive
all the way around it in a day,
stopping at quiet beaches or
fishing ports.

Along the eastern
shore is **Erbalunga,** a
fishing harbor favored
by artists. A rewarding
detour might take in the
villages of **Macinaggio**
and, inland, **Rogliano** and
the castle of **San Colom-
bano.** Down the west coast the
corniche road is dramatic and
often precipitous, but the gorgeous views are ample compensation. **Canari** has a superb
12th-century Pisan Romanesque
church, with a fine view out to sea.
The Genoese watchtower at
Nonza also gives a magnificent
view over the **Golfe de St.
Florent** to the south of the cape.

Area of map detail
★Paris

Cap Corse
Port de Centuri
Rogliano ● ● Macinaggio
Pino ● Luri
Canari ● 1307m
Monte
Stella ▲
Nonza ▲
Golfe de ● Erbalunga
St. - Florent
Désert des
Agriates St.-Florent ● **Bastia**
l'Île-Rousse Patrimonio
Belgodère Oletta
Nebbio
Calvi Muro **San-Michele** ● Murato
Muro **de Murato**
Calenzana 1937m **HAUTE-**
Monte Grosso Ponte Leccia
Asco ▲ Morosaglia
2706m **CORSE** ● la Porta
Monte Cinto ▲ *Castagniccia* ● Piedicroce
Calacuccia
Golfe de
Porto **Gorges de la ● Corte** Cervione
Calanche Restonica
Réserve Naturelle
de Scandola
Capu Rosso Porto Evisa 2622m ● Venaco
Piana **Lac de Mélo** Monte
Vico Rotondo
Cargèse **CORSE-** ● Vizzavona
Golfe de **DU-** Bocognano ● Ghisoni ● Aléria
Sagone **SUD** 2352m ▲
Monte Renoso ● Ghisonaccia
Capo di Feno ● Bastélica
Ajaccio ●
Zicavo ●
Îles Sanguinaires Santa-Maria-Siché
Golfe d'Ajaccio 2136m ● Solenzara
Monte Incudine
Capu di Muru Petreto-Bicchisano Aullène ◗ Col de Bavella
Filitosa ◆ 1218m
● Zonza
Propriano ● Conca
Golfe de
Valinco Sartène ● Golfe de Porto-Vecchio
Porto-Vecchio
Golfe de Santa-Manza
● Bonifacio
Capo
Pertusato

0   40 Kilometers
0   20 miles

NEBBIO VALLEY & MONTE GROSSO

St.-Florent (*Map 333 C4, visitor information, tel 04 95 37 06 04*) in the Nebbio Valley basin is positively chic, with a marina full of yachts.

The **Île Rousse,** named for its red cliffs, is a major resort and ferry terminal, so popular it is best avoided in high summer. **Calvi** (*Map 333 B4*), enclosed on its promontory and dominated by a baroque church, is charming, but can also get very crowded.

A splendid drive leads inland from the Île Rousse to **Belgodère** and **Muro,** villages with superb views out to sea. **Calenzana** (*Map 333 B4*) is one of the starting points for Corsica's long-distance hiking trails, and for the route to the summit of Monte Grosso.

The **Golfe de Porto** is so beautiful that it is protected in its entirety; wonderful drives and boat trips go all around the coast. The red cliffs at **Calanche,** dipping straight into the sea, are best seen by boat (*ask at the information office in Porto*). **Porto** is a pretty little harbor but very popular; a better bet is **Piana,** up above the coast.

AJACCIO & PREHISTORIC CORSICA

The capital of southern Corsica is **Ajaccio** (*Map 333 A3, visitor information, boulevard du Roi Jerome, tel 04 95 51 53 03*). Cradled by mountains, this bustling town basks in Corsica's mildest climate. There is a distinctly Arab flavor to its white stucco houses, fountains, and palm trees. Napoleon Bonaparte was born here, and the evidence is everywhere. The **Maison Bonaparte** (*rue St.-Charles*), where he grew up, has family portraits and memorabilia. The **Palais Fesch,** built by Napoleon's uncle, houses a magnificent collection of Italian art plundered during Napoleon's Italian campaign. The **Chapelle Impériale** next door was built by Napoleon III as a Bonaparte family mausoleum. There is a splendid view of the town and the bay from the **Jetée de la Citadelle,** jutting out into the harbor. Ajaccio is as close as you can get to the Côte d'Azur in Corsica, with good restaurants and sidewalk cafés, a marina crowded with yachts, and a casino. At the northern tip of the bay rise the **Îles Sanguinaires,** rocky islets so named because they glow blood-red at sunset.

To the south is **Filitosa** (*Map 333 B2*) with 3,000-year-old menhirs carved to resemble armed warriors, making a haunting sight amid the chestnut trees. Some of the best are on display in the Musée de Préhistoire Corse in Sartène (see p. 335).

At the extreme south of Corsica is the port of **Bonifacio** (*Map 333 B1*), its fortified upper town set on craggy limestone cliffs hollowed into caves by the sea. From here there are glorious views, in clear weather as far as Sardinia. The 12th-century citadel was once the headquarters of the French Foreign Legion.

PORTO-VECCHIO & INLAND CORSICA

The **Golfe de Porto-Vecchio** (*Map 333 C2*) offers splendid

Calvi

⚠ 333 B4

Visitor information

✉ Port de Plaisance

☎ 04 95 65 16 67

Porto

⚠ 333 A3

Visitor information

✉ place de la Marine

☎ 04 95 26 10 55

Palais Fesch

✉ 50 rue Fesch

☎ 04 95 21 48 17

🕐 Closed Sept.–June, Mon. a.m. July–Aug.

💲 $$

Site Préhistorique de Filitosa

☎ 04 95 74 00 91

Napoleon was born in Corsica.

beaches and safe waters. This is the beginning of the Côte des Nacres (mother-of-pearl coast), with wide sandy beaches, huge marinas, bars, and discos. Inland is **Solenzara** (*Map 333 C2*); winding roads lead to the pass at Bavella, dominated by the enormous statue of Notre-Dame de Bavella.

SARTÈNE

A closed inland mountain town of somber granite walls and narrow cobbled streets above the Rizzanese Valle, Sartène (*Map 333 B2*) has shady plane trees and palms. The old Genoese palace here is now a wine center with *dégustations* of the local Sartènais wine. The **Église de Ste.-Marie** houses the wooden cross and iron chain used for the local religious procession, U Catenacciu (the chained one). On Good Friday an anonymous citizen,

disguised in red robes and hood, re-enacts Christ's struggle to carry the cross to Calvary, through the streets of Sartène. A candlelit procession follows in his wake. The **Musée de Préhistoire Corse** (*rue Croce, tel 04 95 77 01 09, closed until further notice, call for details*) in Sartène's old prison has archaeological finds from all over the island, notably from Filitosa.

CORTE

Corte (*Map 333 B3*), in the center of Corsica, is the main university town. From 1755 to 1769, it was the capital of a briefly independent Corsica. The steep streets of the old town and the citadel dominated by its Moorish bell tower sit on a rocky promontory above two rushing torrents. A good way to reach Corte is by the narrow-gauge railroad that runs between Bastia and Ajaccio. ■

Remote hilltop Montemaggiore I

Bonifacio
🅰 333 B1
Visitor information
✉ 2 rue Fred. Scamaioni
☎ 04 95 73 11 88

Sartène
🅰 333 B2
Visitor information
✉ 6 rue Borgio
☎ 04 95 77 15 40

Corte
🅰 333 B3
Visitor information
✉ Quartier des 4 Fontaines
☎ 04 95 46 26 70

Walking in Corsica

CORSICA IS GREAT WALKING COUNTRY. A LONG-DISTANCE trail (GR20) crosses the mountainous center of the island from north to south through the Parc Naturel Régional de la Corse, a vast conservation area of mountains and coastline.

For information on walking in Corsica, consult the **Agence du Tourisme de la Corse**

🕐 17 boulevard Roi-Jérôme, Ajaccio

☎ 04 95 51 77 77

Starting from Calenzana, just inland from Calvi, and ending at Conca on the Gulf of Porto Vecchio, the GR20 is about 130 miles (210 km) long and can take up to 15 days to walk. Basic mountain refuges are set along the way (bring your own food). The first section between Calenzana and Vizzavona is the most difficult: Experience of mountain walking is essential, but the rewards great.

An easier alternative is the **Mare e Monti Trail** between Calenzana and Cargese. You can take the train to Corte or Vizzavona from Ajaccio or Bastia. **Corte** makes a good base for walking; suggestions are the **Gorges de la Restonica, Lac de Melo,** and the **Forêt de Vizzavona,** where several hiking trails are marked. ■

Corsica's rugged mountains drop straight into the sea.

Wildflowers

Corsica is famous for its *maquis*, the aromatic undergrowth of shrubs and herbs that covers most of the island. Once, the island was forested, mainly by oak, like those at Porto-Vecchio. When the trees were felled, the vegetation became maquis, a spiny thicket of lentisk, Spanish broom and juniper, wild olive, rock rose, thyme, rosemary, and lavender. In World War II, partisans hid in the maquis of southern France, and the Resistance got its other name, the Maquis. Spring is the best time to see the maquis in flower, with unique species such as the Corsican crocus and Corsican hellebore. ■

Travelwise

Road signs in the Jura

TRAVELWISE INFORMATION

PLANNING YOUR TRIP

WHEN TO GO

Choosing when to go depends upon the sort of vacation you would like. The French Government Tourist Office (F.G.T.O.) has a number of offices outside France to advise you (see p. 344 for addresses). Air France offices abroad provide many vacation services besides booking flights (see p. 339 for telephone numbers).

Once you have decided which areas you want to visit, you can contact the region's Comité Departmental de Tourisme (C.D.T.) or the local visitor information office for brochures and information. Many tourist offices and visitor attractions now have web sites:
www.tourisme.fr
www.pariscope.fr
www.culture.fr/louvre
www.region-bretagne.fr/english/TOURISME
www.culture.fr
www.paris.org
www.info-france-usa.org
www.monaco.mc/usa
www.sncf.fr

CLIMATE

Spanning both northern and southern Europe, France has three different climates: Atlantic, Mediterranean, and Continental. Winter temperatures throughout most of France may drop below freezing, with winds and storms lashing the Atlantic coastal regions. Southern Atlantic and Mediterranean France, though much warmer, nevertheless have a chilly winter: Visitors planning a Christmas trip will need warm clothes. Snow is not unknown in the south, even close to the south coast. The Continental climate of eastern France is generally cooler in both winter and summer, but is subject to the greatest extremes, with cold winters followed by hot, humid, and sometimes stormy summers.

Overall, winter temperatures in France vary from around 15° to 50°F (-10° to 10°C), and summer temperatures from around 65° to 85°F (18° to 30°C) in the hottest areas along the southern Atlantic and Mediterranean coasts.

MAIN EVENTS

Throughout the year, France is alive with festivals, ranging from the major traditional fêtes such as the flower festival in Nice to tiny village celebrations of the local harvest of, say, garlic or chestnuts. Others, such as the famous *pardon* processions in Brittany, celebrate individual saints' days. More and more French towns and cities stage cultural events such as jazz, opera, and theater festivals, and these often take place in historic buildings from Romanesque abbeys to Roman amphitheaters.

Although most of the major festivals take place during the summer months, others are seasonal; wine festivals, for example, take place in October, after the *vendange* (grape harvest). Religious festivals are often celebrated with great ceremony, and Easter and Christmas both offer opportunities to see and participate in traditional local events.

January Paris fashion shows; Limoux Carnival.
February Menton Lemon Festival; Nice Carnival.
March Monte-Carlo festival of contemporary film music.
April Lourdes Sacred Music Festival; Easter celebrations; Paris marathon; Le Mans motorcycle race.
May Cannes Film Festival; Grasse international rose show; Mâcon wine fair; Stes.-Marie-de-la-Mer gypsy pilgrimage; Monaco Grand Prix; Nîmes feria.

June Strasbourg Music Festival; Les Imaginaires at Mont-St.-Michel; Chartres International Organ Festival; Noirlac Music Festival; Le Mans 24-hour car race; Chantilly Prix de Diane Hermès horse race.
July Tour de France; Aix-en-Provence Festival; Antibes Jazz Festival; Avignon Festival; Bastille Day: celebrated throughout France on the 14th; Nice Jazz Festival; Quimper Fêtes de Cornouailles.
August Antibes International fireworks festival; Lorient Celtic Festival; Marciac Jazz Festival; Menton International Chamber Music Festival; Dijon grape harvest and folk fair; Bagnères de Luchon flower festival.
October Dijon International Gastronomy Fair; Paris Motor Show; Paris Jazz Festival.
November Beaujolais Nouveau celebrations; Beaune Wine Auction; Dijon Gastronomic Fair.
December Paris Boat Show; Strasbourg Christmas market.

WHAT TO TAKE

You should be able to buy anything you need in France. Pharmacies offer a wide range of drugs, medical supplies, and toiletries, along with expert advice, but you should bring any prescription drugs you might need. If you wear them, a second pair of glasses or contact lenses is a good idea (and a legal requirement if you plan to drive). Sunscreen and anti-mosquito products are advisable in summer. Clothing will depend on your destination and when you travel; you will only need to really dress up for big city restaurants or casinos. Don't be too casual, however: Be prepared to dress for dinner after a day at the beach, and always dress appropriately for visiting churches (a scarf or shirt is useful as a cover-up). Most sports equipment can be rented, but bring personal equipment like walking boots with you. In France, electricity is 220 volts, 50 Hz, and most plugs have two round pins. If you bring electrical equipment, you will need an adapter, and, for U.S. appliances, a transformer. In cities and tourist towns you will be able to buy English-language newspapers and magazines.

Lastly, don't forget the essentials: passport, driver's license, travelers' checks (or ATM card), and insurance documentation.

INSURANCE

Make sure you have adequate coverage for medical treatment and expenses including repatriation, and baggage and money loss.

HOW TO GET TO FRANCE

PASSPORTS

U.S. and Canadian citizens need only a passport to enter France for up to 90 days' stay. No visa is required.

AIRLINES

All the major airlines have flights to France and many arrange package tours and budget-price flights. Air France has booking offices abroad and offers useful information. Direct schedule flights from North America all go to Paris (Delta also flies direct to Nice and Lyon). Package tours may fly into other airports.

Useful numbers
In France:
Air France, Tel 08 02 80 28 02
American Airlines, Tel 01 69 32 73 07
Continental, Tel 01 42 99 09 09
Delta, Tel 01 47 68 92 92
TWA, Tel 01 49 19 20 00
United, Tel 01 41 40 30 30
In the U.S. and Canada:
Maison de France, New York, Tel 212/838-7800
Maison de France, Los Angeles, Tel 310/271-6665
Maison de France, Montréal, Tel 514/288-4264

AIRPORTS

You will arrive in Paris from abroad either at Roissy-Charles de Gaulle or Orly Sud (south) airport.

Roissy-Charles de Gaulle
Tel 01 48 62 22 80
Roissy-Charles de Gaulle is 15 miles (26 km) north of Paris near the A1 autoroute. From here you can get on the Paris périphérique (beltway). If you plan to travel into the city by road, try to avoid the rush hours (7:30 a.m. to 10 a.m. and 4:30 p.m. to 7:30 p.m.). The airport bus from Roissy-C.D.G. (lines 1 and 2) will take you as far as Rue Scribe (near the Opéra Garnier); it runs every day between 5:45 a.m. and 11 p.m. An airport bus goes to the Gare de l'Est main line railroad station. There is also a rail service (RER B every 15 minutes) with stops at Gare du Nord, Châtelet, St.-Michel, Notre-Dame, Luxembourg, Port Royal, Denfert-Rochereau, and Cité Universitaire.

Orly Sud
Tel 01 49 75 15 15
Orly is 10 miles (15 km) south of Paris. A shuttle bus links Orly Sud (international flights) to Orly Ouest (national flights) every 12 minutes between 5:50 a.m. and 11 p.m. The jetbus from the Orly airports runs to Denfert-Rochereau Métro station from 6 a.m. to 10:30 p.m. The railroad service from Orly to central Paris (RER C every 15 minutes) takes approximately 40 minutes.

Tickets for rail services can be bought inside the airport terminals from a computerized ticket machine. If you need help, ask at the reception desk (*Accueil*). Buses to connect with rail services are within easy access. If you are not renting a car from the airport, the rail links are the easiest way to get into the city, and most railroad stations are close to a Métro station, or linked to one. Look for RER signs (Réseau Express

Régional: the high speed suburban branch of the Métro) for fast links between Métro lines and train stations (RER A & B), and between main stations (RER C & D).

Air-taxis (*avions-taxis*) are available from major airports, and a helicopter service (Comptoire Helifrance) has offices at both Roissy-C.D.G. and Orly airports. To reserve an air-taxi call 01 45 54 95 11.

An airport bus runs between Orly and Roissy-C.D.G. every 20 minutes. The Orlyval bus links up with the RER B rail line, which goes out to Roissy-C.D.G.

FROM THE UNITED KINGDOM

Eurotunnel (or the channel tunnel) now offers a fast, frequent rail service (Eurostar) between London (Waterloo), Lille (2 hours) and Paris (Gare du Nord, 3 hours). Tickets can be booked through French or British rail companies. The SNCF central reservation office is in Paris (Tel 08 36 35 35 35). Le Shuttle transports cars and passengers between Folkestone and Calais with a simple drive-on-drive-off system. The journey through the tunnel lasts about 35 minutes. Reservations are not essential. Le Shuttle runs 24 hours a day year-round.

Several ferry and hovercraft services operate from the U.K. to the northern French ports. For information contact Brittany Ferries (Portsmouth and Plymouth to St. Malo, Caen, and Roscoff), Wharf Road, Portsmouth PO2 8RU, Tel 08705-360 360, Fax 0879 011100. Hoverspeed (Dover to Calais and Folkestone to Boulogne), Marine Parade, Dover CT17 9TG, Tel 08705-240 241. P&O/Stena Ferries (Dover to Calais and Portsmouth to Le Havre, Cherbourg, and St. Malo) Channel View Road, Dover CT17 9TJ, Tel 0870-242 4999.

GETTING AROUND

TRAVELING IN FRANCE

BY AIRPLANE

There are internal flights to most major cities in France. Orly Ouest deals with internal flights from Paris. Flights within France are operated by Air France, Air Littoral, Air Liberté, and AOM.
Air France, Tel 08 02 80 28 02
Air Littoral, Tel 04 67 20 67 20
Air Liberté, Tel 08 03 80 58 05
AOM, Tel 08 03 00 12 34

BY TRAIN

The French national railroad, the SNCF (Société Nationale des Chemins de Fer) links Paris and all major cities. You can buy train tickets in advance from your travel agent or SNCF office, or at a station or travel agency (agence de voyage) in France.

Some services require a seat reservation as well as a ticket, and stations often have separate ticket and reservation desks. You can travel to all major cities from Paris by TGV (Train à Grande Vitesse), or by regular train services. The Motorail service transports passengers together with their cars or motorbikes. Both the TGV and the Motorail service require reservations.

For long-distance journeys you can travel overnight by couchette (sleeping car shared with up to six other people) or voiture-lit (private sleeping car for up to three people). Both of these services are available first and second class, and must be reserved in advance.

If you buy your train ticket in France you must punch it at the time-stamping machine (composteur) at the entrance to the platform, before you begin the journey. Once stamped, a ticket is valid for 24 hours. An unstamped ticket is not deemed to be valid.

Foreign visitors to France can buy a special vacation rail pass for up to one month. If you plan to travel mostly by train this saves having to buy tickets each time as well as costing less than individual tickets, and the pass often offers further advantages such as reduced rates on other forms of transportation. Ask for details of La Carte "France Vacances Pass." North Americans have a wide choice of passes, including Eurailpass, Flexipass, and Saver Pass, which can only be purchased in the United States (Tel 212/308-3103 for information, 800/223-636 for reservations). The France Rail 'n' Drive pass offers a flexible rail and car-rental package, while the Fly, Rail, and Drive pass combines internal flights with train travel and car rental. Discounts are available for students and senior citizens by showing a student card or passport.

SNCF central reservation office in Paris: Tel 08 36 35 35 35 for national information or 01 53 90 20 20 for Paris information.

BY CAR

France has a good network of roads, from small and often picturesque C and D roads to autoroutes, often called péages, because a toll (péage) must be paid. Occasionally you pay a fixed fee upon entering a section of autoroute; more often you are given a ticket as you enter, and you pay as you leave according to the distance traveled. Credit cards are accepted in the pay booths. The autoroutes may only be two lanes in each direction, but are the quickest routes.

There are gas stations with 24-hour service approximately every 15 miles (20 km), but there are also, more frequently, well-designed parking and picnic places (called Aires). The main routes nationales between towns and cities (N on maps) are generally in excellent condition. Many are two-lane for at least part of their length.

Renting a car

Renting a car in France is expensive. Arrange a car rental with your local travel agent before leaving home; it can be much cheaper. Otherwise there are desks in airports and major railroad stations in France. There are fly-drive options with most flights, and the SNCF offers a train/car rental package.

Central offices:
Autorent, Tel 01 45 54 22 45, Fax 01 45 54 39 69
Avis, Tel 01 55 38 68 60, Fax 01 46 21 65 60
Budget, Tel 08 00 10 00 01, Fax 01 46 86 22 17
Europcar, Tel 01 30 43 82 82, Fax 01 30 96 03 25
Hertz, Tel 01 39 38 38 38
Rent-a-Car, Tel 01 45 22 28 28

To rent a car in France you must have a current driver's license (held for at least three years) and be at least 21 years old. Some companies will not rent to people under 26 or over 60. Make sure you have information about what to do in case of an accident or breakdown; telephone numbers in case of emergencies; and the procedure to follow. You must carry the relevant car documents with you, and some identification.

Motoring information

Age limits and licenses The minimum age limit for driving in France is 18 years (21 if you are renting a car). Visitors from North America and the U.K. do not need an international driver's license but must carry their home driver's license.

Breakdown assistance Autoroutes and routes nationales have emergency telephones every mile (2 km). Police stations (gendarmeries) can give information about breakdown services or garages—call them at 17.
Accidents See p. 345.

Busy periods French roads will be busy from the beginning of July, when school vacations begin, and at their worst around August 15, a major national holiday. Special routes attempt to relieve summer traffic congestion; watch for the small green BIS (*Bison Futé*) signs that indicate these alternative routes. A brochure in English on the Bison Futé routes is available from French government tourist offices.

Children Children under ten must travel in the rear seat.

Distances All distances on signposts in France are shown in kilometers (1 km = 0.62 miles).

Drink-driving The French drink-driving limit is 50 mg alcohol per 100 ml of blood. This can mean that as little as one glass of beer can take you up to the limit.

Gas Fuel is sold by the liter (there are 3.75 liters to an American gallon). Most gas stations accept credit cards.

Headlights Motorcycles must have headlights on when moving, and cars must use headlights in poor visibility. All vehicles must carry a spare set of lightbulbs, and drivers who wear glasses or contact lenses must have a spare pair with them when driving.

On-the-spot fines On-the-spot fines may be levied by police for several offenses, including speeding, not wearing seat belts, and not having the car's documentation with you.

Parking Some French towns and cities have blue zones where parking is free for up to an hour. You need to display a parking disk (*disque de stationnement*), which you obtain from garages, *tabacs*, and tourist offices. Otherwise most towns have on-street parking machines (*horodateurs*) from which you buy a ticket to display in your car. Coins required vary from 2F to 10F. Multi-story car parking garages are common; check closing times: Some

close overnight and may shut by 8 p.m.

Priorité à droite Traditionally, priority on French roads was given to vehicles approaching from the right, except where otherwise indicated. Nowadays, on main roads, the major road will normally have priority, with traffic being halted on minor approach roads with one of the following signs:
• *Cedez le passage:* yield
• *Vous n'avez pas la priorité:* you do not have right of way
• *Passage protégé:* no right of way
A yellow diamond sign indicates that you have priority, the diamond sign with a diagonal black line indicates that you do not have priority.

Take care in small towns and rural areas without road markings where you may be expected to yield to traffic coming from the right—especially farm vehicles. If oncoming drivers flash their headlights, it is to indicate that they have priority, not the other way around. Priority is always given to emergency and public utility vehicles.

Road conditions For information about current road conditions, telephone the Inter Service Route line (Tel 48 94 33 33) or tune into the local radio frequency (often indicated on signs beside roads).

Road signs
• *Access interdit:* no entry
• *Allumez vos feux:* switch on lights
• *Interdiction de stationner:* no parking
• *Passage pour piétons:* pedestrian crossing
• *Rappel* (remember): reminder of a previous restriction
• *Sens unique:* one-way traffic
• *Virages sur....km:* curves for...km
• *Zone bleue:* parking disk required

Seat belts The wearing of seat belts is mandatory in both the front and rear seats.

Speed limits These are different speed limits for normal weather and times of poor visibility (heavy rain or fog). Autoroutes have limits of 75–85 mph (110–130 kph; slower limit applies in poor visibility). Two-lane roads 60–75 mph (90–110 kph) Other open roads 50–55 mph (80–90 kph) Towns (from entry name sign to exit name sign) 30 mph (50 kph).

Traffic circles Vehicles already on a traffic circle have priority, except very occasionally in small towns where *priorité à droite* still applies.

Traffic lights These are sometimes suspended high over the road and can easily be missed.

TRANSPORTATION IN PARIS

Taxis can be found outside every main line train station and airport, and at taxi ranks throughout the city. Taxi drivers in Paris operate on three tariffs:
• Tariff A, 7 a.m. to 7 p.m.
• Tariff B, 7 p.m. to 7 a.m.
• Tariff C, at night in the suburbs and during the day in the outlying districts of Hauts-de-Seine, Seine St.-Denis, and Val-de-Marne, when the taxi has no client for the return journey.
Extra charges are added for pickups at train stations, luggage weighing over 12 lbs/5kg, a fourth passenger (the driver can refuse to take more than three passengers), and an animal (except for a seeing-eye dog). A ten percent tip to taxi drivers is usual.

Any complaints about Paris taxis should be addressed in writing to Service des Taxis, Préfecture de Police, 36 rue des Morillons, Paris 75015.

Public transportation There are three kinds of public transportation in Paris: Métropolitan (Métro), Réseau Express Régional—high speed suburban rail lines (RER), and Autocar (the bus, sometimes called "car").

Using the Métro Maps are posted in every Métro station, or ask for a free *Plan du Métro* when you buy a ticket. Each line has a number and is identified by the station at either end: The east–west line 1, for example, is La Défense-Château de Vincennes.

A *carnet* (book) of ten tickets is a useful savings if you plan to use the Métro frequently. A Carte Orange is good for unlimited trips on Métro, RER, and buses for one week, or for a month. You will need a passport-size photograph for a Carte Orange. A Paris Visite card is available at Métro stations and is good for one, two, three, or five days and entitles you to unlimited use of public transportation and discounts at some sights. The Formule 1 card, also available at the Métro ticket booths, is good for all transportation for one day only. If you need advice on bus, Métro, or rail travel, ask at a tourist office.

PRACTICAL ADVICE

COMMUNICATIONS

POST OFFICES

Mail and telecommunication services are controlled by the same organization in France. This is called the PTT (pronounced pay-tay-tay), and offices open from 9 a.m. to 5 p.m. on weekdays and from 9 a.m. to noon on Saturdays (in smaller towns offices will close for lunch and, in villages may only be open for two or three hours on weekday mornings). Mail can be delivered to you at a post office if it is marked "Poste Restante" and with the postal code of the Bureau de Poste at which you collect it. The postal code is essential. You will have to pay a fee for each item of mail.

Mail boxes Yellow *boites postales* (mail boxes) are located outside every PTT and on walls in larger towns. They may have separate compartments for local mail, *départemental* (mail within the *département*), and *autres départements/destinations* (elsewhere in France and foreign).

TELEPHONES

Post offices contain telephones where you can make your call first and pay at the counter afterward. Telephone directories (*annuaires*) are no longer available in most post offices since the introduction of Minitel (see below). You can ask your hotel receptionist to find a number or call the operator at 12. Telephone numbers have ten digits usually written divided into pairs, for example 01 23 45 67 89.

Numbers in Paris begin with 01, numbers in the northwest of the country begin with 02, in the northeast with 03, southeast with 04, and southwest with 05.

To call a French number (for example, 01 23 45 67 89) from abroad dial the international code (011 from United States and Canada, 00 from U. K.) then the code for France (33), followed by the number, omitting the first 0: 011 33 1 23 45 67 89.

Phone booths *Cabines téléphoniques* stand outside larger post offices, in railroad stations and airports, or near roads or parking garages in towns and villages. They take either phone cards, money, or both. Phone cards (*télécartes*) in units of 50F and 120F can be bought at any tobacconist (*bureau de tabac*) distinguished by a red lozenge-shaped sign.

Making a call Follow the instructions that will appear on the telephone's screen: "*décrochez*" (pick up the receiver); "*inserrez votre carte*" (insert your card or coin); "*patientez*" (wait); "*numérotez*" (dial the number); "*raccrochez*"

(hang up). In villages with no telephone booths watch for a blue sign, *téléphone publique*, on a private house. The owner is required to let you use the telephone and charge you the regular rate for the call.

International calls To make an international call from France dial 00 followed by the country's international code. These can be found in the front of the *Pages Jaunes* section of the *annuaire* or posted in a telephone booth. Some useful ones are: Australia 61; Canada 1; Ireland 353; United Kingdom 44; United States 1.

For operator services dial 12. For international directory assistance, dial 00 33 12, followed by the country code.

To dial toll-free numbers (*numéros verts*), insert a card or money to make the connection (coins will be returned after the call, units will not be registered against cards). Reduced rate calls in France and Europe 7 p.m.–8 a.m. weekdays, noon Sat–8 a.m. Mon. for U.S. and Canada 7p.m.–1p.m., Mon–Fri, and all day Sat. & Sun. Reduced rates also apply on public holidays.

MINITEL

This is a screen reference system that provides information and telephone numbers for companies and establishments all over France. It also offers a multilingual information service designed to help you organize your vacation. It is still available in Post Offices but is rapidly being superceded by the Internet.

DÉPARTEMENTS

France is divided into 96 administrative départements, named after a principal river and identified by a number. When making any inquiries about a region it is helpful to know the département names and numbers; for example 09 (zero-neuf) Ariège.

CONVERSIONS

1 kilo = 2.2 lbs
1 litre = 0.2642 U.S. gallons
1 mile = 1.6 km

Women's clothing
American 8 10 12 14 16 18
French 38 40 42 44 46 48

Men's clothing
American 36 38 40 42 44 46
French 46 48 50 52 54 56

Women's shoes
American 6-6.5 7-7.5 8-8.5 9-9.5
French 38 39 40-41 42

Men's shoes
American 8 8.5 9.5 10.5 11.5 12
French 41 42 43 44 45 46

ETIQUETTE & LOCAL CUSTOMS

Etiquette is very important in France: Always be ready to shake hands when you are introduced, and when you meet friends and acquaintances. Kissing on both cheeks is also very common. When entering any establishment it is polite to offer a general *"Bonjour, messieurs/dames."* Remember to use the titles *"Monsieur"* and *"Madame."* Young women are addressed as *"Mademoiselle,"* a woman in her 20s or older is addressed as *"Madame."* Address a waiter as *"Monsieur,"* and call a waitress either *"Madame"* or *"Mademoiselle." "Garçon"* (boy) is not acceptable.

When visiting churches and cathedrals, dress appropriately and respect the sensitivities of those who are there for devotional purposes. Visitors are requested not to walk around religious buildings during services. Even though in most cases no fee is charged to visit a church or cathedral, it is polite to contribute to one of the boxes requesting donations.

HOLIDAYS

All banks, post offices and many museums, galleries, and stores close on these national holidays:
January 1 (Jour de l'An)
Easter Sunday and Monday (Pâcques)
May 1 (Fête du Travail)
May 8 (Victoire 1945)
Ascension (Assention)
Pentecost (Pentecôte)
July 14 (Fête Nationale)
August 15 (Assomption)
November 1 (Toussaint)
November 11 (Armistice 1918)
December 25 (Noël)

MEDIA

AMERICAN & BRITISH NEWSPAPERS

Newspapers and magazines are sold in Maisons de la Presse, many of which stock American or British newspapers (often the previous day's edition). International newspapers are available in airports, major railroad stations, and most large hotels.

Regional newspapers contain national and international as well as local news, and are often read more than the national press. The main national dailies are Le Monde, conservative Le Figaro, and left-wing Libération and L'Humanité. American and British dailies—The International Herald Tribune, The Times, and Daily Telegraph—are widely available in major towns and cities.

TV CHANNELS

French television offers five TV channels: TF1, France 2, France 3, 5 or La Cinquième (in the evening this one becomes Arte, a combined Franco-German transmission), and M6. TF1 occasionally shows undubbed American films with French subtitles, Arte more frequently shows subtitled international films and art programs. Most American films shown on French television are dubbed into French, as are all the American soaps and serials that make up the bulk of French TV. A

subscription channel, Canal + (Canal plus), has a monthly program of films, shown at least once in the original language (marked VO—*version original*), as well as sports. Cable TV is becoming more widespread. The main television news programs are at 1 p.m. and 8 p.m.

RADIO

The national radio station, France Inter (1892m long wave), broadcasts English-language news twice a day in summer (generally at 9 a.m. and 4 p.m.). During the peak holiday period, other local stations may have English broadcasts. On the Mediterranean, Riviera Radio (106.3 and 106.5 kHz) broadcasts 24 hours a day in English. In some areas, BBC Radio 4 can be received on long wave (198 kHz).

MONEY MATTERS

In December 2000, one U.S. dollar equaled approximately 7.5 French francs. The French franc is divided into 100 centimes. Francs are issued in 500, 200, 100, 50, and 20 franc bills, and 20, 10, 5, 2, and 1 franc coins. Centimes are issued in 50, 20, 10, and 5 centime coins.

On January 1, 1999, the euro became the official currency of France, and the French franc became a denomination of the euro. Franc notes and coins continue to be legal tender during a transitional period. Euro bank notes and coins are to be introduced by January 2002. (In December 2000 one U.S. dollar equaled 1.1 euros.)

Most major banks have ATMs outside for bank (ATM) cards and international credit cards with instructions in a choice of languages. You will need a four digit PIN number. Arrange this with your bank before you leave home. In France, credit cards now often have a chip containing the ID. Foreign cards usually have this information on a

PRACTICAL ADVICE

magnetic strip, which may occasionally cause problems. Currency can be exchanged in banks, and Bureaux de Change in railroad stations and airports. It is best to buy travelers' checks in francs before you leave home. To cash travelers' checks at the bank have some form of identification (passport) ready. To use a check you will not need a check card, but you may be asked for identification (with photo). Hotels often ask for your passport during your stay. French nationals must carry identification at all times, and visitors are advised to do the same.

Credit cards are widely accepted, Visa is by far the most common. Mastercard (Access/Eurocard) and Diners Club are also widely accepted, as is American Express In many places. Carte Bancaire (CB) is a French card encompassing both Visa and Mastercard.

OPENING TIMES

Nearly all stores and offices close for lunch from noon to 2 p.m., often to 3 p.m. or 4 p.m. in summer in the south. Many stores close for the morning or all day Mon. or Wed.
Banks 9 a.m.–5 p.m. Mon.–Sat., closing for lunch
Post offices 9 a.m.–6 p.m. weekdays, closing for lunch, 9 a.m. to noon Sat.
Stores 9 a.m.–7 p.m. Mon.– Sat., closing for lunch; some food stores also open on Sun a.m.
Grocery stores 9 a.m.–7 p.m. Mon.–Sat., some closing for lunch except Sat. and sometimes Fri.
Bureaux de Tabac and **Maisons de la Presse** 8 a.m.–7 p.m. Mon –Sat., 8 a.m.–noon Sun.
Gas stations usually close at 9 p.m. except on autoroutes.
Museums close for lunch from noon to 2 p.m., except perhaps during the months of July and/or August. Municipal museums usually close on Mon., national museums on Tues.

PETS

Animals under three months old are not allowed into France; older pets must have a certificate attesting that they have had an anti-rabies vaccination within the last 12 months, or an official declaration that they have been brought from a rabies-free area.

TIME DIFFERENCES

France runs to CET (Central European Time) one hour ahead of Greenwich Mean Time, six hours ahead of Eastern Standard Time. Noon in France is 6 a.m. in New York. Remember that France uses the 24-hour clock.

TIPPING

Most restaurant bills include a service charge. This is generally indicated at the bottom of the menu. If in doubt, ask: *Est-ce que le service est compris?* It is usual to leave a small additional tip for the waiter if the service has been good. It is customary to tip taxi drivers 10 percent, though this is not obligatory. It is usual to give porters, doormen, tour guides, and hairdressers a tip of 5–10F, usherettes and cloakroom attendants 2F. There is no need to leave a tip for hotel maids unless you have required out-of-the-ordinary service.

TOILETS

Self-cleaning toilet cabins on the street (not wheelchair accessible) cost 2F. Large department stores have public restrooms. You can always use the toilet in a bar or café, signposted *les toilettes* or *les WC* (pronounced lay vay-say). Public toilets vary considerably; some, particularly in the south, are still old-fashioned squat toilets. There may be an attendant; tip with small change.

TOURIST OFFICES

New York
Maison de la France
444 Madison Avenue, 16th Floor

New York, New York 10020
Tel 212/838-7800
Fax 212/838-7855
West Coast
9454 Wilshire Blvd., Suite 715
Beverly Hills, California 90212
Tel 310/271-6665
Fax 310/276-2835
Midwest
676 North Michigan Ave.,
Chicago, Illinois 60611-2819

CANADA
Montréal
1981 Ave. McGill College. Ste. 490
Montréal, Quebec H3A 2W9
Tel 514/288-4264
Fax 514/845-4868
Toronto
30 St. Patrick St., Suite 700
Toronto, Ontario M5T 3A3
Tel 416/593-4723
Fax 416/979-7587

IN FRANCE
Maison de la France
8–10 avenue de l'Opéra
Paris 75001
Tel 01 42 86 70 00

TRAVELERS WITH DISABILITIES

An information sheet for travelers with disabilities is published by the French Government Tourist Office. The guide "Où Ferons Nous Etape?" (in French) lists accommodations suitable for travelers with disabilities, including wheelchair users. It is available by mail from the Association des Paralysés, 22 rue du Père-Guérin, Paris 75013, Tel 01 44 16 83 83.

CNRH (Comité National de Liaison pour la Réadaptation des Handicapés), 236 bis rue de Tolbiac, Paris 75013, Tel 01 53 80 66 63, publishes "Paris-Île de France pour tous" tourist guide for disabled.
Information is also available on Minitel: 3614 Handitel.
E-mail: cnrh@worldnet. net

For additional information on vacations and accommodations, look up Le Quotedien du Handicap on the Internet at www.handitel.org

EMERGENCIES

EMBASSIES IN FRANCE

Canadian Embassy 35 avenue Montaigne, Paris 75008, Tel 01 44 43 29 00, **Consulate** 37 avenue Montaigne, Paris 75008, Tel 01 44 43 29 16.
British Embassy 35 rue du Faubourg St.-Honore, Paris 75008, Tel 01 44 51 31 00.
U. S. Embassy 2 avenue Gabriel, Paris 75008, Tel 01 43 12 22 22.
U. S. Consulate 12 boulevard Paul-Peytral, Marseille 13006, Tel 04 91 54 92 00.

EMERGENCY PHONE NUMBERS

15 SAMU (*Service d'Aide Medicale d'Urgence*) Ambulance
17 Police secours (police rescue)
18 Pompiers (fire rescue)
Both police and fire rescue have medical backup and work in close contact with SAMU. In the case of a serious car accident, phone either the police (17) or fire rescue (18), who, although a fire service, are used to attending accidents.

For legal assistance in an emergency, contact your embassy or consulate for a list of English-speaking lawyers.

WHAT TO DO IN A CAR ACCIDENT

There is no need to involve the police if you have an accident in which no one has been hurt. The official procedure is for each driver to fill out a *constat à l'amiable*, each signing the other's copy. Phone the rental company and explain what has happened.

If you are involved in a serious road accident, phone the police (17) or fire rescue (18). These numbers are free but in a phone booth you need to insert a coin to make a connection (it is returned to you after the call).

A number and address in the telephone booth will say where you are, and you may be asked the name of the nearest town so that the operator can identify which *département* you are in. Alternatively, you may find the local *police secours* number posted in the phone booth.

LOST PROPERTY

If you lose something on a bus or the Métro, first try the terminal to see if it has been handed in. In Paris, after 48 hours, you can go to the Bureau des Objets Trouvés, 36 Rue des Morillons, 75015 Paris, Tel 01 55 76 20 20, where you have to pay 4 percent of the value of any item reclaimed. To report a theft or loss, go to a *gendarmerie* or *commissariat de police*. Their telephone numbers are in the front of local directories; in an emergency, dial 17.

If you lose your passport, report first to the police, then to the nearest embassy or consulate (see above). If you are detained by the police for any reason, you are entitled to call the nearest consulate for a member of the staff to come to your assistance.

Lost credit cards
American Express: Tel 01 47 77 72 00
Diners Club: Tel 01 49 06 17 50
Visa: Tel 08 00 90 11 79
Mastercard: 01 45 67 84 84

HEALTH

Check that your health insurance covers visits to France. Pharmacies—recognizable by a green cross sign—are staffed by qualified pharmacists who can recommend treatment, and will tell you if you need to see a doctor and where to find one. The fee to see a doctor is 115F. To call the doctor out to see you will cost 140–300F.

For serious physical injury, go to a hospital emergencies department (*urgences*). A pharmacy will

will be able to direct you. To renew a prescription, take your medicine in its package to a pharmacy. If they do not have that product, they will try to find its equivalent. If they can only sell it to you with a prescription, they will direct you to the nearest doctor.

International Association for Medical Assistance to Travelers IAMAT is a non-profit organization that anyone can join free of charge. Members receive a directory of English-speaking IAMAT doctors on call 24 hours a day, and are entitled to services at set rates.
IAMAT offices
U.S.: 417 Center St., Lewiston, New York 14092, Tel 716/754-4883.
Canada: 1287 St. Claire Ave., W. Toronto, M6E 1B9, Tel 416/652-0137

MEDICAL EMERGENCIES
For an ambulance, dial 15, Service d'Aide Médicale d'Urgence.

French medical treatment is of a high standard, and facilities are generally excellent. In Paris the American Hospital is at 63 boulevard Victor-Hugo, Neuilly 92292, Tel 01 46 41 25 25.

FURTHER READING

The Cathedral Builders, Jean Gimpel. New York: Harper & Row, 1984.
The Food Lovers Guide to France, Patricia Wells. Workman Publishing, 1999.
Fragile Glory: A Portrait of France and the French, Richard Bernstein. New York: Plume, 1991.
The French, Theodore Zeldin. New York: Kodansha, 1996.
A Little Tour in France, Henry James. New York: Farrar, Straus and Giroux, 1983.
Montaillou, Emmanuel Le Roy Ladurie. Gallimard, 1978.
A Moveable Feast, Ernest Hemingway. New York: Scribner, 1964.
Two Towns in Provence, M.F.K. Fisher. New York: Vintage Books, 1983.

HOTELS & RESTAURANTS

Excellent and varied accommodation is available all over France, ranging from grand hotels to cozy farmhouses. You can splurge on some of the finest hotels in the world or stay at cheap motel-style chains such as Formule 1 or Balladins, which will accommodate a family of four for less than 200 francs per night. You can stay in grand châteaus, or seek out small farmhouses (chambres d'hôte) for bed and breakfast and meals of homegrown produce. Obviously, facilities will be reflected in the price, and in cheaper hotels you may not have private baths.

HOTELS

Many hotels offer pension or demi-pension accommodations. Demi-pension includes breakfast and dinner, while full pension includes lunch as well.

Grading system

French hotels are officially graded according to a star system, from four to one stars, indicating the minimum level of facilities. The requirements of the lesser grades are assumed in the higher ones. A few hotels in this selection, either restaurants with rooms or château hotels, are not star-rated.

✪✪✪✪ Four stars indicate a hotel with a restaurant and all rooms with private bath/shower rooms.

✪✪✪ Three-star hotels have at least 80 percent of the rooms with bath/shower, and offer breakfast in the room.

✪✪ Two-star establishments must have 40 percent of the rooms with bath/shower and a telephone in each room.

✪ One-star hotels offer plain but adequate accommodation.

The following is a selection of good quality hotels throughout the country (listed by price, then in alphabetical order). Wherever possible we have chosen hotels that are both individual and typical, perhaps with notable local or historic associations.

Please note that, **unless otherwise stated:**
1. Breakfast is not included in the price.
2. The hotel has a restaurant. If it is outstanding, the restaurant symbol is also given or reference is made to a separate entry for the restaurant.
3. All rooms have a telephone and television.

Room price categories are given only as guidance and do not take into account seasonal variations. Further taxes may be added to the price. Prices are per (double) room.

In high season, always try to book in advance, if possible confirming by fax. You may be asked for a deposit or credit card number.

Credit & debit cards

Many hotels accept all major cards. Smaller ones may only accept some, as shown in their entry. Abbreviations used are: AE (American Express), DC (Diners Club), MC (Mastercard), V (Visa).

Hotel chains & groups

U.S. contact numbers:
Concorde Hotels Tel 800/888-4747
Hilton Tel 800/HILTONS
Leading Hotels of the World Tel 800/223-6800
Relais & Châteaux Tel 212/856-0115
French contact numbers:
Maisons des Gîtes de France Tel 01 49 70 75 85
Many departments have a Loisirs Acceuil booking service to reserve hotels, gîtes, and camp sites; ask the French Tourist Office for a list or contact the nearest local tourist office.

RESTAURANTS

Wherever you go, you will find a wide variety of restaurants, from humble auberges to the great classics. Many hotels have their own restaurants, and some restaurants also rent rooms.

PRICES

HOTELS
An indication of the cost of a double room without breakfast is given by $ signs.
$$$$$	over $280
$$$$	$200–$280
$$$	$120–$200
$$	$80–$120
$	under $80

RESTAURANTS
An indication of the cost of a three-course dinner without drinks is given by $ signs.
$$$$$	over $80
$$$$	$50–$80
$$$	$35–$50
$$	$20–$35
$	under $20

Our selection (listed by price, then alphabetical order) suggests good regional restaurants offering typical local dishes, as well as including some of the great stars of French cuisine. In the regions it is always worth seeking out typical local restaurants and sampling the specialties of the area. See each regional food section for a guide to local cuisine and dishes, and the menu reader on pp. 387–88.
L = lunch   D = dinner

Dining hours in France

Lunch usually starts around midday and continues until 2 p.m. Dinner is eaten around 8 p.m. but may start about 7 p.m.; in smaller places or in the countryside you may be too late after 9 p.m. Dinner tends to be earlier in the north of the country, later as you go south.

At the height of the season, or if you have a particular place in mind, make a reservation.

Restaurants often have outdoor tables for good weather, and even in towns and cities you may find yourself sitting on the sidewalk or in a courtyard. Facilities for outside dining are mentioned here only where the view, or perhaps the garden, is of particular note.

Menus must by law be displayed outside any establishment serving food, and studying and comparing these before making your choice is part of the pleasure. Most restaurants offer one or more *prix-fixe* menus, set meals at a fixed price, sometimes including wine. Otherwise (and usually more expensively), you order individual items *à la carte*—from the menu.

The French usually eat a salad after the main course and sometimes with the cheese course, which always comes before dessert. Bread and water are supplied free. (French tap water is safe to drink.)

Wine lists in the regions are often dominated by local wines, and all restaurants offer a *vin de pays* by the carafe or demi-carafe. Although smoking is now forbidden by law in all public places in France, it is in fact still widely accepted, and you should specify if you prefer a non-smoking (*non-fumeurs*) section.

Cafés

Cafés remain a French institution, good for morning coffee, leisurely drinks, or modest meals. In small towns and villages they are very much the center of local life. Note that drinking at the bar is cheaper than sitting at a table.

Tipping

A service charge is usually included in the bill. Only add more if the service has been particularly good.

PARIS

ÎLE DE LA CITÉ

🏨 DU JEU DE PAUME
$$$ ✪✪✪✪
54 RUE ST.-LOUIS-EN-L'ÎLE, 75004
TEL 01 43 26 14 18
FAX 01 40 46 02 76
In the 17th century, Court (Royal) tennis was played in this building, now creatively converted into an attractive

hotel. Rooms may be somewhat small. Garden.
🛏 30 🚇 Pont-Marie ❐
❄ ✪ All major cards

🏨 DE LUTÈCE
$$$ ✪✪✪
65 RUE ST.-LOUIS-EN-L'ÎLE, 75004
TEL 01 43 26 23 52
FAX 01 43 29 60 25
Small and cozy. A fire burns in the lobby's fireplace, and the modest rooms each have an individual feature, like beams or a pretty mirror.
🛏 23 🚇 Pont-Marie ❐
❄ ✪ AE, MC, V

🍽 LA TOUR D'ARGENT
$$$$$
15 QUAI DE LA TOURNELLE, 75005
TEL 01 43 54 23 31
FAX 01 44 07 12 04
On a quay just across the Seine from the Île. Perhaps no longer the peak of excellence it once was, but it still has two Michelin stars and is a favorite with visitors for its duckling, and its view of the Seine River and Notre Dame.
🚇 Maubert-Mutualité
🕐 Closed Mon. ❐ ❄
✪ All major cards

LEFT BANK

🏨 MONTALEMBERT
$$$$$ ✪✪✪✪
3 RUE MONTALEMBERT, 75007
TEL 01 45 49 68 68
FAX 01 45 49 69 49
A 1920s beaux arts hotel, brought up to date with a rooms in contemporary or traditional style.
🛏 56 + suites 🚇 Rue du Bac ❐ ❄ ✪ All major cards

🏨 RELAIS CHRISTINE
$$$$$ ✪✪✪✪
3 RUE CHRISTINE, 75006
TEL 01 40 51 60 80
FAX 01 40 51 60 81
Discreet luxury in a former convent. No restaurant but breakfast served in the

vaulted, 13th-century kitchens. Garden.
🛏 35 rooms + 16 duplex
🚇 Odéon 🅿 ❐ ❄
✪ All major cards

🏨 DUC DE SAINT-SIMON
$$$$ ✪✪✪
14 RUE ST.-SIMON, 75007
TEL 01 44 39 20 20
FAX 01 45 48 68 25
A luxurious haven, with exquisite antique furnishings. There is a charming basement breakfast room and courtyard garden, but no restaurant.
🛏 29 + 5 suites 🚇 Rue du Bac ❐ ✪ AE, MC, V

🏨 LUTÉTIA
🍽 **$$$$ ✪✪✪✪**
45 BOULEVARD RASPAIL, 75006
TEL 01 49 54 46 46
FAX 01 49 54 46 00
Behind the striking facade of this enormous art deco pile, the interior has been elegantly restyled by designer Sonia Rykiel. Restaurant "Paris" has a Michelin star, and there's a brasserie too.
🛏 220 + 30 suites
🚇 Sèvres-Babylone ❐ ❄
✪ All major cards

🏨 D'ANGLETERRE
$$$ ✪✪✪
44 RUE JACOB, 75006
TEL 01 42 60 34 72
FAX 01 42 60 16 93
Individually decorated rooms and friendly staff add to the charm of this conveniently located hotel between the Boulevard St.-Germain and the Seine. No restaurant.
🛏 23 + 4 suites 🚇 St.-Germain-des-Prés ❐
✪ All major cards

🏨 STE.-BEUVE
$$$ ✪✪✪
9 RUE STE.-BEUVE, 75006
TEL 01 45 48 20 07
FAX 01 45 48 67 52
A pleasing and friendly hotel that combines antique furniture and contemporary artworks. No restaurant.
🛏 22 ❐ ❄ ✪ All major cards

HOTELS & RESTAURANTS

🏨 **DE L'UNIVERSITÉ**
$$$ ✪✪✪
22 RUE DE L'UNIVERSITÉ, 75007
TEL 01 42 61 09 39
FAX 01 42 60 40 84
Great attention to detail is evident in this hotel in the university area, with its atmosphere of a private residence.
🛏 27 🚇 Rue du Bac 🛗
💳 🅐 All major cards

🏨 **DE VIEUX PARIS**
$$$ ✪✪✪✪
9 RUE GIT LE COEUR, 75006
TEL 01 44 32 15 90
FAX 01 43 26 00 15
The famous Beat hotel that in the 1950s and 1960s accommodated writers William Burroughs and Allen Ginsberg. The 15th-century building has been refurbished but rooms are small.
🛏 13 + 7 suites 🚇 St.-Michel 🅐 All major cards

🍴 **LE JULES VERNE**
$$$$$
TOUR EIFFEL, 2ND FLOOR
75007
TEL 01 45 55 61 44
Dinner with a view, *bien sûr*, at this Michelin one-star restaurant in one of Paris's most famous monuments. Not surprisingly, it is essential to book—and weeks ahead.
🚇 Trocadéro 💳 🅐 All major cards

🍴 **CLOSERIE DES LILAS**
$$$$
171 BOULEVARD
MONTPARNASSE, 75006
TEL 01 40 51 34 50
This bar/brasserie/restaurant, once a hangout of Picasso, Hemingway, Apollinaire, Lenin, and more, is a good place to eat and drink amid the literary crowd.
🚇 Vavin 🅐 All major cards

🍴 **VIOLON D'INGRES**
$$$$
135 RUE ST.-DOMINIQUE, 75007
TEL 01 45 55 15 05
Christian Constant, the former chef at Les Ambassadeurs in

Hôtel de Crillon, provides the same high-quality cuisine at lower prices at this Michelin one-star restaurant.
🚇 Pont de l'Alma
🕐 Closed Sun., Mon., & Aug.
💳 🅐 AE, MC, V

🍴 **LES BOUCHONS DE FRANÇOIS CLERC**
$$$
12 RUE DE L'HÔTEL COLBERT, 75005
TEL 01 43 54 15 34
Fine food served in a friendly fashion. Wonderful wines and homemade breads.
🚇 St.-Michel 🕐 Closed Sat. L & Sun. L 💳 🅐 AE, MC, V

🍴 **LE DÔME**
$$$
108 BOULEVARD
MONTPARNASSE, 75014
TEL 01 43 35 25 81
A famous Montparnasse brasserie. Fish and seafood in a lively ambience.
🚇 Montparnasse 🕐 Closed Mon. 💳 🅐 AE, MC, V

🍴 **BISTRO CÔTÉ MER**
$$
16 BOULEVARD ST.-GERMAIN, 75005
TEL 01 43 54 59 10
Reliably good food, lively ambience, and attractive decor in one of famed chef Michel Rostang's bistros.
🚇 Maubert-Mutualité 💳 🅐 AE, MC, V

🍴 **BRASSERIE LIPP**
$$
151 BOULEVARD ST.-GERMAIN, 75006
TEL 01 45 48 53 91
Perhaps more noted for its historical and literary connections, and wonderful turn-of-the-century decor, than for the food.
🚇 St.-Germain-des-Prés 💳 🅐 AE, MC, V

🍴 **LA COUPOLE**
$$
102 BOULEVARD
MONTPARNASSE, 75014
TEL 01 43 20 14 20

A legendary art deco brasserie—everyone who was anyone (including, of course, Hemingway) came here in the 1920s. Good food, and great service, too.
🚇 Montparnasse 💳 🅐 All major cards

🍴 **LE PROCOPE**
$$
13 RUE DE L'ANCIENNE COMÉDIE, 75006
TEL 01 40 46 79 00
Restored to its 17th-century splendor, Le Procope (see p. 70) serves popular brasserie dishes. Sorbets and ice creams are a specialty.
🚇 Odéon 💳 🅐 All major cards

RIGHT BANK

🏨🍴 **BALZAC**
$$$$$ ✪✪✪✪
6 RUE BALZAC, 75008
TEL 01 44 35 18 00
FAX 01 44 35 18 05
The belle epoque building has huge rooms, sumptuous furnishings, and Pierre Gagnaire's restaurant (see p. 350).
🛏 56 + 14 suites 🚇 George-V 🛗 💳 🅐 All major cards

🏨 **BRISTOL**
$$$$$ ✪✪✪✪
112 RUE DU FAUBOURG ST.-HONORÉ, 75008
TEL 01 53 43 43 00
FAX 01 53 43 43 26
Luxury and discretion for the rich and/or famous, with fine works of art, tapestries, and Persian carpets. Garden.
🛏 195 + suites 🚇 St.-Philippe-du-Roule 💳 🅿 📺 🅐 All major cards

🏨🍴 **DE CRILLON**
$$$$$ ✪✪✪✪
10 PLACE DE LA CONCORDE, 75008
TEL 01 44 71 15 00
FAX 01 44 71 15 02
One of the great palace hotels, with views over the Place de la Concorde. Two restaurants: the Michelin two-star Les

Ambassadeurs and L'Obélisque. Winter garden.
[i] 163 + suites
[T] Concorde [-] [S]
[S] All major cards

FOUR SEASONS GEORGE V
$$$$$ ✪✪✪✪
31 AVENUE GEORGE V, 75008
TEL 01 47 23 54 00
FAX 01 47 20 06 49
Recent refurbishment has brought this venerable palace hotel luxuriously up-to-date. Courtyard garden.
[i] 260 [T] George V [-]
[S] [Z] [Y] [S] All major cards

MARIGNAN-ÉLYSÉES
$$$$$ ✪✪✪✪
12 RUE MARIGNAN, 75008
TEL 01 40 76 34 56
FAX 01 40 76 34 34
A Beauvais tapestry in the salon, antique furnishings, and comfortable rooms.
[i] 5 + 16 duplex suites
[T] Franklin-Roosevelt [-]
[S] [S] All major cards

PAVILLON DE LA REINE
$$$$$ ✪✪✪✪
28 PLACE DES VOSGES, 75003
TEL 01 40 29 19 19
FAX 01 40 29 19 20
Elegant, antique-furnished rooms, some with four-poster beds in this enviable location. Pretty courtyard.
[i] 31 + 14 suites + 10 duplex [T] St.-Paul [-] [S]
[S] All major cards

VERNET
[Y] $$$$$ ✪✪✪✪
25 RUE VERNET, 75008
TEL 01 44 31 98 00
FAX 01 44 31 85 69
A luxurious gem. Fireplace and piano in the lobby. Jacuzzis in rooms. The belle époque restaurant has two Michelin stars.
[i] 42 + 9 suites [T] George-V [-] [S] [S] All major cards

COSTES
$$$$ ✪✪✪✪
239 RUE ST.-HONORÉ, 75001
TEL 01 42 44 50 00
FAX 01 42 44 50 01
Stylish hotel noted for its up-to-the-minute design and elegant decor; some rooms look onto a delightful courtyard.
[i] 85 [T] Tuileries [S] [Z]
[Y] [S] All major cards

PERGOLÈSE
$$$$ ✪✪✪✪
3 RUE PERGOLÈSE, 75016
TEL 01 53 64 04 04
FAX 01 53 64 04 40
Modern designer decor and marble bathrooms. Near the Arc de Triomphe.
[i] 40 [T] Argentine [-]
[S] [S] All major cards

GALILÉE
$$$ ✪✪✪
54 RUE GALILÉE, 75008
TEL 01 47 20 66 06
FAX 01 47 20 67 17
A refined small hotel with elegant furnishings.
[i] 27 [T] George V [-]
[S] [S] AE, DC, MC, V

LE RELAIS DU LOUVRE
$$$ ✪✪✪
19 RUE DES PRÊTRES–ST.-GERMAIN-L'AUXERROIS, 75001
TEL 01 40 41 96 42
FAX 01 40 41 96 44
A cozy little hotel with a garden, between the Louvre and St.-Germain-l'Auxerrois.
[i] 20 [T] Louvre or Pont-Neuf [-] [S] All major cards

SAINT-MERRY
$$–$$$ ✪✪✪
78 RUE DE LA VERRERIE, 75004
TEL 01 42 78 14 15
FAX 01 40 29 06 82
Once the presbytery of the St.-Merri church, whose flying buttresses enter some rooms. Pricier rooms have wooden Gothic furnishings; others have showers not baths, but are charmingly decorated.
[i] 12 [T] Hôtel-de-Ville
[S] MC, V

¶ ALAIN DUCASSE
$$$$$
59 AVENUE RAYMOND POINCARÉ, 75116
TEL 01 47 27 12 27
Ducasse is the new star of haute cuisine in Joël Robuchon's former domain. Three Michelin stars.
[T] Victor-Hugo [+] Closed 22 Dec.–3 Jan., Sat., Sun., public hols., & mid-July–mid-Aug. [S] [S] All major cards

¶ L'AMBROISIE
$$$$$
9 PLACE DES VOSGES, 75004
TEL 01 42 78 51 45
Classic French food (too classic for some) and three Michelin stars in an exquisite setting on the lovely Place des Vosges. Reservations essential.
[T] St.-Paul [+] Closed Sun., Mon., first 3 weeks of Aug., & Feb. school vacation [S]
[S] AE, MC, V

¶ CARRÉ DES FEUILLANTS
$$$$$
14 RUE CASTIGLIONE, 75001
TEL 01 42 86 82 82
Chef Alain Dutournier offers traditional southwestern cuisine: variations on foie gras, truffles. Two Michelin stars.
[T] Concorde or Tuileries [+] Closed Sat. L, Sun., Aug.
[S] All major cards

¶ LUCAS-CARTON
$$$$$
9 PLACE DE LA MADELEINE, 75008
[☎] 01 42 65 22 90
An art nouveau setting and impeccable service enhance the experience at this temple of gastronomy with three Michelin stars.
[T] Madeleine [+] Closed Sat. L, Mon. L, all Sun., & 3 weeks Aug. [S] [S] All major cards

¶ PIERRE GAGNAIRE
$$$$$
6 RUE BALZAC, 75008
TEL 01 44 35 18 25
One of France's most innovative chefs; three Michelin

stars. Small, so book far ahead. 🚇 George-V 🕐 Closed Sat. & Sun. L, also Feb. school vacation, & July–mid-Aug. 🛗 🏧 All major cards

🍴 TAILLEVENT
$$$$$
15 RUE LAMENNAIS, 75008
TEL 01 44 95 15 01
A longstanding leader in haute cuisine with three Michelin stars, Taillevent has lovely dining rooms, perfect service, and a renowned wine cellar. Reservation essential.
🚇 George-V 🕐 Closed Sat., Sun., public hols., & Aug. 🏧 All major cards

🍴 LA MAISON BLANCHE
$$$$
15 AVENUE MONTAIGNE, 75008
TEL 01 47 23 55 99
A fashionable crowd and modern decor, but the uneven cooking may not live up to its views over the Seine.
🚇 Alma-Marceau 🕐 Closed Sat. L, Sun., Mon. L, 1–10 Jan. & Aug. 🛗 🏧 AE, MC, V

🍴 LE TRAIN BLEU
$$$
GARE DE LYON, 20 BOUL-EVARD DIDEROT, 75012
TEL 01 43 43 09 06
Breathtaking belle epoque decoration in this station rest-aurant. Typical brasserie food.
🚇 Gare de Lyon 🛗 🏧 All major cards

🍴 ANGÉLINA
$$
226 RUE DE RIVOLI, 75001
TEL 01 42 60 82 00
Join the fashion crowd for hot chocolate in this elegant tea-room. You may have to wait in line on the weekend to get in.
🚇 Tuileries 🕐 Closed D & Tues. in Aug. 🛗 🏧 AE, V

🍴 BOFINGER
$$
5 & 7 RUE DE LA BASTILLE, 75004
TEL 01 42 72 87 82
Huge mirrors at this classic

brasserie; try the *choucroute*.
🚇 Bastille 🛗 🏧 All major cards

🍴 LE MOULIN À VIN
$$
6 RUE BURQ, 75018
TEL 01 42 52 81 27
This little corner of old Montmartre serves traditional food and good wines, and there's group singing to the strains of an accordion.
🚇 Abbesses 🕐 Closed Sun., Mon., Wed., & Thurs. L, & Aug. 🏧 MC, V

🍴 AU PIED DE COCHON
$$
6 RUE COQUILLIÈRE, 75001
TEL 01 40 13 77 00
Lively, all-night restaurant serving brasserie dishes; specialties include pig's feet and shellfish platters.
🚇 Louvre or Les Halles 🏧 All major cards

🍴 CHEZ OMAR
$
47 RUE DE BRETAGNE, 75003
TEL 01 42 72 36 26
Excellent couscous, old-fashioned bistro decor.
🚇 Filles-du-Calvaire 🕐 Closed Sun. L 🏧 No credit cards

🍴 HARRY'S NEW YORK BAR
$
5 RUE DAUNOU, 75002
TEL 01 42 61 71 14
New York-style piano bar once popular with Heming-way and F. Scott Fitzgerald. Recommended Bloody Marys.
🚇 Opéra 🏧 AE, DC, V

OUTER PARIS

🍴 LE PRÉ CATELAN
$$$$
ROUTE DE SURESNES, 75016
TEL 01 44 14 41 14
Talented chef Eric Anton has livened up the cuisine of this lovely restaurant.
🚇 Porte-Maillot, then Bus 144 (till 8 p.m.) 🕐 Closed Sun., Mon. from 29 Oct.–8

May, & Feb. school vacation 🏧 All major cards

🍴 BRASSERIE FLO
$$
7 COUR DES PETITES-ÉCURIES, 75010
TEL 01 47 70 13 59
A sparkling, 19th-century brasserie where the menu has typical brasserie dishes. Friendly service.
🚇 Château-d'Eau 🛗 🏧 All major cards

NORTHERN FRANCE

NORD & PICARDIE

AIRE-SUR-LA-LYS 62100

🏨 HOSTELLERIE DES TROIS MOUSQUETAIRES
$/$$ ✪✪✪✪
CHÂTEAU DU FORT DE LA REDOUTE
TEL 03 21 39 01 11
FAX 03 21 39 50 10
A family-run hotel, in a large, wooded garden. The interior is in grand, traditional style; older, larger bedrooms are very elegant. Golf course.
🛏 33 🅿 🕐 Closed Mon & Tues except during July & Aug. and mid-Dec.–mid-Jan. 🏧 AE, MC, V

AMIENS 80000

🍴 MARISSONS
$/$$$
PONT DODANE
TEL 03 22 92 96 66
Converted 15th-century boathouse in Amiens's old quarter. Imaginative cooking and Amiens specialties such as *canard en croûte de foie gras*.
🕐 Closed Sat. L, all Sun., & 1st week Jan. 🛗 🏧 All major cards

BOULOGNE-SUR-MER 62200

🏨 MÉTROPOLE
$ ✪✪✪
51–53 RUE THIERS

TEL 03 21 31 54 30
FAX 03 21 30 45 72
Between the ramparts and
the sea, this quiet hotel has
a delightful garden. No
restaurant.
[1] 25 [P] [C] Closed late
Dec.–early Jan. [S] All major
cards

CALAIS 62100

[H] MEURICE
$/$$$ ✪✪✪
5 RUE EDMOND-ROCHE
TEL 03 21 34 57 03
FAX 03 21 34 14 71
Until World War II the
Meurice was one of France's
luxury hotels. It was restored
in 1953 and today offers
comfortable hospitality to
travelers. Restaurant La
Diligence serves good
standard French cuisine.
[1] 39 [C] Restaurant closed
Sat. L [S] All major cards

DOULLENS 80600

[H] CHÂTEAU DE
REMAISNIL
$$$/$$$$$ ✪✪✪✪
TEL 03 22 77 07 47
FAX 03 22 77 41 23
A beautiful 18th-century
mansion set on 35 acres of
parkland, once home to
Bernard and Laura Ashley and
now run by Americans.
Extremely grand with rococo
features, tapestries, and
luxurious bedrooms. Smaller,
more rustic rooms in the
coach house.
[1] 20 [S] All major cards

HESDIN-L'ABBÉ 62360

[H] CLÉRY
$/$$$ ✪✪✪
TEL 03 21 83 19 83
FAX 03 21 87 52 59
A dignified 18th-century
house surrounded by
parkland. Sitting room with
log fire; contemporary decor.
Dinner on weekday evenings
only. Tennis.
[1] 22 [C] Closed mid-Dec.–
Jan. [S] All major cards

LILLE 59000

[H] CARLTON
$$$$ ✪✪✪✪
3 RUE DE PARIS, 59800
TEL 03 20 13 33 13
FAX 03 20 51 48 17
A classic grand hotel, situated
in the heart of the city
opposite the Opéra. Decor
and furnishings in elegant
Louis XV style. Charming,
spacious bedrooms with
marble bathrooms.
[1] 57 + 3 suites [P] valet
[S] Rooms [S] [S] All major
cards

SOMETHING SPECIAL

[H] GRAND HÔTEL
BELLEVUE
Mozart once stayed in
this 18th-century
Bourbon hotel close to the
Opéra, the Palais de la
Musique, and the Palais de
Congrès. The building is a
fine example of Lille
architecture with classic
decor. No restaurant.
$$$ ✪✪✪
5 RUE JEAN-ROISIN, LILLE
59800
TEL 03 20 57 45 64
FAX 03 20 40 07 93
[1] 61 [S] All major cards

[H] L'HUÎTRIÈRE
$$$$/$$$$$
3 RUE DES CHATS-BOSSUS,
59800
TEL 03 20 55 43 41
A very fashionable establishment, with one Michelin star,
in the old town. An art deco,
blue-and-gold tiled entrance
leads to a richly furnished
dining room. Excellent
seafood and regional cuisine.
[C] Closed Sun. D, public hols.
D, & mid-July–mid-Aug.
[S] All major cards

MONTREUIL-SUR-MER
62170

[H] CHÂTEAU DE
[R] MONTREUIL
$$$ ✪✪✪✪
4 CHAUSSÉE DE CAPUCINS
TEL 03 21 81 53 04
FAX 03 21 81 36 43
Tastefully decorated bed-
rooms look out over the
gardens of this secluded
château on the edge of town.
The one-star Michelin restaurant specializes in seafood.
[1] 13 [P] [C] Closed mid-
Dec.–Feb. [S] All major cards

[R] AUBERGE DE LA
GRENOUILLÈRE
$$$/$$$$
LA MADELEINE-SOUS-
MONTREUIL
TEL 03 21 06 07 22
A charming Picardie farm-
house, particularly popular for
lunch on the terrace. Try
dishes like pré-salé agneau de
la baie de Somme, or the
house specialty, frogs legs with
garlic and fried parsley.
[1] 4 [C] Closed Tues. &
Wed. (except July & Aug.) &
Jan. [S] All major cards

CHAMPAGNE

REIMS 51100

[H] LES CRAYÈRES
[R] $$$$$
64 BOULEVARD
HENRY-VASNIER
TEL 03 26 82 80 80
A beautiful turn-of-the-20th-
century family château, home
to master chef Gérard Boyer
and the epitome of French
refinement and luxury.
A Michelin three-star restaurant offers dishes that include
lamb with truffles en croûte
and pig's trotters stuffed with
foie gras. Huge wine list and,
of course, lots of champagne.
Reservation essential.
[1] 16 + 3 suites [C] Closed
Tues. L, all Mon. & mid-
Dec.–mid-Jan. [S] All major
cards

🏨 DE LA PAIX
$/$$ ❂❂❂
9 RUE BUIRETTE
TEL 03 26 40 04 08
FAX 03 26 47 75 04
In the heart of the car-free center, this is a peaceful old hotel with a garden. Rich, warm interior decor and bedrooms that are modern and comfortably furnished.
ⓘ 106 🅿 🚫 🚫 🚆
🀫 All major cards

🍴 LE VIGNERON
$$/$$$$
PLACE PAUL-JAMOT
TEL 03 26 79 86 86
Reservations are essential for this popular restaurant serving authentic regional cuisine. It offers a good selection of champagne and also houses a champagne museum.
🕒 Closed Sat. Sun., Aug. 1–20, & Dec. 23–Jan. 2 🚫
🀫 MC, V

TROYES 10000

🏨 DE LA POSTE
$/$$ ❂❂❂❂
35 RUE ÉMILE-ZOLA
TEL 03 25 73 05 05
FAX 03 25 73 80 76
A charming hotel, close to the museums, furnished in comfortable modern style. Two restaurants, Le Carpaccio and Les Gourmets, renowned for seafood.
ⓘ 32 🅿 🚫 ♿ 🀫 All major cards

ALSACE & LORRAINE

COLMAR 68000

🏨 HOSTELLERIE LE 🍴 MARÉCHAL
$$$ ❂❂❂
4 PLACE SIX MONTAGNES NOIRES
TEL 03 89 41 60 32
FAX 03 89 24 59 40
A 16th-century. half-timbered hotel and restaurant, beautifully situated on the canalside in Colmar's "Little Venice." Specialties include *terrine de foie de canard à la*

gelée au muscat d'Alsace and lobster and monkfish salad with truffle vinaigrette.
ⓘ 30 🀫 AE, MC, V

🏨 GRAND HÔTEL 🍴 BRISTOL
$/$$ ❂❂❂
7 PLACE DE LA GARE
TEL 03 89 23 59 59
FAX 03 89 23 92 26
A beautifully decorated, central hotel with turn-of-the-20th-century elegance. Two good restaurants, the Michelin one-star Rendezvous de Chasse and the more informal l'Auberge.
ⓘ 70 🀫 All major cards

MARLENHEIM 67520

🏨 LE CERF 🍴
$$/$$$
30 RUE DU GÉNÉRAL-DE-GAULLE
TEL 03 88 87 73 73
FAX 03 88 87 68 08
This picturesque inn with a flowery courtyard, located in a village on the N4 21 miles (30 km) west of Strasbourg, contains a Michelin two-star restaurant specializing in Alsatian dishes such as *tête de veau* or sauerkraut with pork and foie gras.
ⓘ 15 🕒 Closed Tues. & Wed. 🀫 All major cards

NANCY 54000

🏨 GRAND HÔTEL DE 🍴 LA REINE
$$$$ ❂❂❂❂
2 PLACE STANISLAS
TEL 03 83 35 03 01
FAX 03 83 32 86 04
This exquisite 18th-century palace, one of the historic buildings on Place Stanislas in the heart of Nancy, was once the home of Marie-Antoinette, hence the hotel's name. Luxurious bedrooms are furnished in Louis XV style. The hotel's restaurant is also called Stanislas, after the dethroned Polish king.
ⓘ 48 ♿ 🀫 All major cards

PRICES

HOTELS
An indication of the cost of a double room without breakfast is given by $ signs.

$$$$$	over $280
$$$$	$200–$280
$$$	$120–$200
$$	$80–$120
$	under $80

RESTAURANTS
An indication of the cost of a three-course dinner without drinks is given by $ signs.

$$$$$	over $80
$$$$	$50–$80
$$$	$35–$50
$$	$20–$35
$	under $20

STRASBOURG 67000

🏨 MONOPOLE MÉTROPOLE
$/$$$ ❂❂❂
16 RUE KUHN
TEL 03 88 14 39 14
FAX 03 88 32 82 55
Close to the historic Petite France district, this peaceful, grand hotel offers rooms either in contemporary mode or in traditional Alsatian style. No restaurant.
ⓘ 90 🅿 🕒 Closed Christmas & New Year's Day 🚫 Rooms 🀫 All major cards

🍴 BUEREHIESEL
$$$$/$$$$$
4 PARC ORANGERIE
TEL 03 88 45 56 65
An Alsatian farmhouse, reconstructed in the Orangerie Park, is now a Michelin three-star restaurant. Chef Antoine Westermann offers seasonal delicacies such as Bresse chicken with potatoes and artichokes. Inventive desserts include brioche with pear and beer-flavored ice cream.
🕒 Closed Tues., Wed., mid–late Aug., late Dec.– early Jan., & Feb. school vacation 🚫 🀫 All major cards

---

🍴 AU CROCODILE

$$$$/$$$$$
10 RUE DE L'OUTRE
TEL 03 88 32 13 02
With luxurious surroundings,
impeccable service, and three
Michelin stars, the Crocodile
is the most stylish restaurant
in Strasbourg. Favorite dishes
served here include roast
monkfish with fennel confit
and saffron tomatoes.
🕒 Closed Sun., Mon., 3
weeks July–Aug., & late
Dec.–early Jan. 🔲 🏧 All
major cards

VERDUN 55100

🏨 LE COQ HARDI

$$/$$$ 😊😊
8 AVENUE DE LA VICTOIRE
TEL 03 29 86 36 36
A delightful hotel with a
typical Lorraine facade of
flowery window boxes and an
interior of polished oak.
Excellent restaurant.
🚪 34 + 3 suites 🕒 Closed
Fri. except on public hols.
🏧 🏧 All major cards

NORMANDY & BRITTANY

NORMANDY

AUDRIEU 14250

🏨 CHÂTEAU D'AUDRIEU
🍴 $$$/$$$$$

TEL 02 31 80 21 52
FAX 02 31 80 24 73
Between Bayeux and Caen,
this 18th-century château has
period decoration and a
Michelin one-star restaurant.
🚪 23 + 6 suites 🕒 Closed
late Dec.–end Jan. Restaurant
closed Tues. L & all Mon. 🏧
🏧 AE, MC, V

BAYEUX 14400

🏨 D'ARGOUGES
$ 😊😊
21 RUE ST.-PATRICE
TEL 02 31 92 88 86
FAX 02 31 92 69 16
Set in a peaceful garden, this
old family mansion is within

walking distance of the town's
center. No restaurant.
🚪 26 🕒 Closed Dec.
11–26 & Jan. 5–20 🏧 All
major cards

🏨 LION D'OR
🍴 $ 😊😊😊

71 RUE ST.-JEAN
TEL 02 31 92 06 90
FAX 02 31 22 15 64
An attractive 17th-century
post house round a central
courtyard boasts an excellent
restaurant serving dishes such
as duck foie gras with honey
and succulent sausages.
🚪 24 🅿 🕒 Closed late
Dec.–late Jan. 🏧 All major
cards

BEUVRON-EN-AUGE 14430

🍴 LE PAVÉ D'AUGE
$$$
TEL 02 31 79 26 71
Michelin one-star restaurant
in the covered market hall,
serving simply cooked, local
ingredients. Try lobster with
herb butter, and local cheeses
and Calvados.
🕒 Closed Mon. end Nov.–
end Dec., Feb. school hols. &
Tues. Sept.–April 🏧 MC, V

CABOURG 14390

🏨 GRAND HÔTEL

Cabourg's Grand Hotel
stylishly dominates the
sea front just as it did in
Marcel Proust's novel,
Remembrance of Things Past.
Proust often stayed here, and
the hotel still serves the
memorable madeleine cakes.
$$/$$$$$ 😊😊😊😊
PROMENADE MARCEL-
PROUST, CABOURG 14390
TEL 02 31 91 01 79
FAX 02 31 24 03 20
🚪 70 🕒 Restaurant
closed Jan. & Mon. &
Tues. from Dec.–May
🏧 All major cards

CAEN 14000

🍴 LA BOURRIDE
$$$/$$$$
15 RUE DU VAUGUEUX
TEL 02 31 93 50 76
This small but comfortable,
old restaurant with two
Michelin stars serves
specialties like local *andouille*
(chitterling sausages) and
pigeon. Reservation essential.
🕒 Closed Sun. and Mon.,
except public hols., 3 weeks
Jan., & mid-Aug.–early Sept.
🏧 All major cards

DEAUVILLE 14800

🍴 LE SPINNAKER
$$/$$$
52 RUE MIRABEAU
TEL 02 31 88 24 40
A highly regarded seafood
restaurant on the promenade,
serving traditional Norman
cuisine with lashings of cider
and Calvados. The baked
lobster in cider vinegar is a
special treat.
🕒 Closed Mon. Sept.–June,
Tues. Oct.–Easter, 1 week
Nov. 🏧 All major cards

DIEPPE 76200

🍴 LA MARMITE DIEPPOISE
$$$
8 RUE ST.-JEAN
TEL 02 35 84 24 26
A popular restaurant located
close to the harbor named
after its most famous local
dish: fish and shellfish in a
cream sauce.
🕒 Closed Thurs. D, Sun. D,
all Mon. Nov. 21–Dec. 10, &
Feb. school vacation
🏧 MC, V

DINARD 35800

🏨 LE GRAND HÔTEL
$$$/$$$$ 😊😊😊😊
46 AVENUE GEORGE V
TEL 02 99 88 26 26
FAX 02 99 88 26 27
Dinard's classic grand hotel
on the promenade.
🚪 90 🅿 🕒 Closed

March–Oct. & Dec. 28–Jan. 3
🏨 🏧 All major cards

🏨 ROCHE CORNEILLE
🍴 $$$ ✸✸✸
4 RUE GEORGES CLEMENCEAU
TEL 02 99 46 14 47
FAX 02 99 46 40 80
In central Dinard, this secluded
château hotel is elegantly
furnished and has a celebrated
fish restaurant. Price includes
breakfast.
🛏 28 🕒 Closed mid-Nov.–
mid-March. Restaurant closed
Mon. 🏧 AE, MC, V

ÉVREUX 27000

🏨 DE FRANCE
🍴 $$ ✸✸
29 RUE ST.-THOMAS
TEL 02 32 39 09 25
FAX 02 32 38 38 56
Traditional hotel in a central
but peaceful setting, with an
excellent restaurant serving
classic dishes. The restaurant
opens onto a pretty garden
beside the river.
🛏 16 🅿 🕒 Restaurant
closed Sun. D & all Mon.
🏧 AE, D, MC, V

HONFLEUR 14600

🏨 LA FERME SAINT-
🍴 SIMÉON
$$$/$$$$$ ✸✸✸✸
RUE ADOLPHE-MARAIS
TEL 02 31 89 23 61
FAX 02 31 89 48 48
This peaceful 17th-century
farmhouse was a favorite with
the Impressionists—who
would not recognize its
present luxury. The Michelin
one-star restaurant serves
specialties such as stuffed *pré-
salé* lamb. Sauna, solarium, and
hydrotherapy complex.
🛏 31 + 3 suites 🅿 🏊
🏧 AE, MC, V

🍴 L'ABSINTHE
$$/$$$$
10 QUAI DE LA QUARANTAINE
TEL 02 31 89 39 00
Charming restaurant in an
ancient 16th-century
presbytery by the harbor.

🕒 Closed mid-Nov.–mid-
Dec. 🛗 🏧 D, MC, V

🍴 L'ASSIETTE
GOURMANDE
$$/$$$$
QUAI PASSAGERS
TEL 02 31 89 24 88
This very popular one-star
Michelin restaurant offers
dishes like risotto St.-Jacques
and sweetbreads with snails.
🕒 Closed Sun. D & all Mon.
Jan. 15–Feb. 15 🛗 🏧 All
major cards

LA BOUILLE 76530

🏨 LE ST.-PIERRE
🍴 $$/$$$
GRAND COURONNE
TEL 02 35 18 01 01
A light, airy hotel-restaurant
with a pretty, covered terrace
overlooking the Seine. First-
class, inventive cuisine.
🛏 7 🕒 Closed Sun. D & all
Mon. Oct.–Feb. 🏧 AE, MC, V

LE BEC-HELLOUIN
27800

🏨 L'AUBERGE DE
L'ABBAYE
$ ✸✸✸
TEL 02 32 44 86 02
FAX 02 32 46 32 23
An 18th-century inn with a
terrace near Bec-Hellouin
monastery. The restaurant
serves regional specialties
based on cider and apples.
🛏 11 🕒 Restaurant
closed Mon. D & all Tues.
Nov.–Easter & Mon.
Easter–Oct. 🏧 AE, MC, V

LES ANDELYS 27700

🏨 LA CHAÎNE D'OR
$/$$$ ✸✸✸
27 RUE GRANDE
TEL 02 32 54 00 31
FAX 02 32 54 05 68
Overlooked by the ruins of
the Château Gaillard, this
18th-century auberge stands
beside the Seine. Picturesque
views from most rooms and
from the restaurant. Terrace.
🛏 10 🅿 🕒 Closed Sun.

D, all Mon. Tues. L in winter
& Dec. 24–Feb. 1 🏧 AE,
MC, V

MONT-ST.-MICHEL
50116

🏨 AUBERGE ST.-PIERRE
ET LOGIS DU
CHAPEAU BLANC
$/$$ ✸✸✸
GRANDE RUE
TEL 02 33 60 14 03
FAX 02 33 48 59 82
Situated at the foot of
the abbey, this 15th-century
timbered building is sheltered
by the ramparts. Quiet
rooms, many with beautiful
views.
🛏 21 🕒 Closed Jan. 🏧 AE,
MC, V

SOMETHING
SPECIAL

🍴 LA MÈRE POULARD
Visitors from Ernest
Hemingway to Margaret
Thatcher have sampled the
famous Omelette Mère
Poulard, made from a secret
recipe over an open fire, and
still as popular as ever at this
long-established restaurant.
Other specialties include
grilled pink lobster and rack
of lamb. Rooms available.
$$$ ✸✸✸
GRANDE RUE, MONT-ST.-
MICHEL 50116
TEL 02 33 60 14 01
🛏 27 🏧 All major cards

PONT-AUDEMER 27500

🏨 BELLE ISLE SUR RISLE
$$$/$$$$ ✸✸✸✸
112 ROUTE DE ROUEN
TEL 02 32 56 96 22
FAX 02 32 42 88 96
Beautiful grounds with
ancient trees surround this
handsome mansion on an
island in the Risle River.
Elegantly furnished bedrooms.
Sauna, tennis.
🛏 20 🕒 Closed Jan. & Feb.
🏊 🏧 All major cards

PORT-EN-BESSIN 14520

🏨 LA CHENEVIÈRE
🍴 $$$/$$$$ ✪✪✪✪
ESCURES-COMMES
(NW OF BAYEUX)
TEL 02 31 51 25 25
FAX 02 31 51 25 20
A noble Normandy mansion
dating from the 19th century,
with an excellent restaurant,
set in a tree-lined park a
short distance from the
sea and Omaha Beach golf
course. Each room has its
own little secret garden.
🛏 18 + 3 suites 🅿
🚫 Closed Jan. 2– Feb. 8 🚭
🆑 All major cards

ROUEN 76000

🏨 CATHÉDRALE
$ ✪✪
12 RUE ST.-ROMAIN
TEL 02 35 71 57 95
FAX 02 35 70 15 54
This old, half-timbered town
hotel has a flowery courtyard
and a salon du thé. No
restaurant.
🛏 24 🆑 MC, V

🍴 GILL
$$$$
9 QUAI DE LA BOURSE
TEL 02 35 71 16 14
Modern and elegant, one of
Rouen's top restaurants with
two Michelin stars. Fresh food
is cooked with great style
here. Sample such delicacies
as langoustine ravioli and the
Rouen specialty, pigeon stuffed
with liver and cooked in a
sauce of its own blood.
🚫 Closed Sun. D Oct.–April,
all Mon., 2 weeks April, 2
weeks Aug. & Jan. 2–9 🚭
🆑 All major cards

TROUVILLE-SUR-MER 14360

🍴 LES VAPEURS
$$
160 BOULEVARD FERNAND-
MOREAUX
TEL 02 31 88 15 24
A popular art deco brasserie
close to the fish market, with

fresh dishes to suit late
nighters and early risers. The
shrimps and the *moules frites*
(mussels with French fries) are
especially recommended.
🚫 Closed Dec. 24 🆑 AE,
MC, V

BRITTANY

BREST 29200

🏨 CORNICHE
$ ✪✪✪
1 RUE AMIRAL NICOL
TEL 02 98 45 12 42
FAX 02 98 49 01 53
A modern hotel built in the
old Breton style. On the coast
road west of the town. Tennis.
🛏 16 🆑 AE, MC, V

CANCALE 35260

🍴 MAISON DE BRICOURT
$$$/$$$$$
1 RUE DU GUESCLIN
TEL 02 99 89 64 76
Cozy little Michelin two-star
restaurant with a garden. It is
renowned for its dedicated
chef, Olivier Roellinger, who
specializes in imaginative
seafood dishes; try clams with
ceps, potatoes, and shallots.
Reservations essential.
🚫 Closed Wed. (except D
July & Aug.), all Tues., & mid-
Dec.–mid-March 🆑 All
major cards

CONCARNEAU 29900

🍴 COQUILLE
$$$
QUAI MOROS
TEL 02 98 97 08 52
Attractive Breton style restau-
rant in old port serving variety
of fresh fish and seafood.
🚫 Closed Sun. D. & Mon. &
first 2 weeks in May & Jan.
🆑 All major cards

🍴 CRÊPERIE DES REMPARTS
$
31 RUE THÉOPHILE-LOUARN
VILLE CLOSE
TEL 02 98 50 65 66
Situated in the Ville Close

(walled town), this is a good
place to sample excellent
crêpes and *galettes*.
🚫 Closed Mon. in winter
🆑 MC, V

DINAN 22100

🍴 MÈRE POURCEL
$$/$$$$
3 PLACE DES MERCIERS
TEL 02 96 39 03 80
Restaurant in a historic
15th-century Breton building.
Menu changes seasonally, and
the wine list is recommended.
🚫 Closed Sun. D, all Mon.
Sept.–June, & Feb. school
vacation 🆑 All major cards

LORIENT 56100

🍴 L'AMPHITRYON
$$/$$$$
127 RUE DU COLONEL
MULLER
TEL 02 97 83 34 04
Friendly, local restaurant
serving fresh seafood.
🚫 Closed Sat. L, all Sun.
(except public hols.),
April 23–30 & Sept. 4–14
🚭 🆑 MC, V

PONT-AVEN 29123

🍴 MOULIN DE ROSMADEC
$$/$$$
TEL 02 98 06 00 22
A one-star Michelin restaurant
in an old millhouse near the
bridge in the town center.
Traditional Breton decor.
Specialties include grilled
Breton lobster, *sauté de
langoustines*, and beautifully
prepared artichokes.
Reservation essential.
🛏 4 🚫 Closed Sun. D in
winter, all Wed., Feb., & 2
weeks Nov. 🆑 MC, V

QUIMPER 29000

🏨 CHÂTEAU DE GUILGUIFFIN
$$$
LANDULEC 29710 (ON THE
D874 SOUTH OF QUIMPER)
TEL 02 98 91 52 11

FAX 02 98 91 52 52
Large château surrounded by wild and magnificent parkland. No restaurant but brunch or buffet supper served by arrangement. Price includes breakfast.
🛈 3 + 2 suites 🕒 Closed early Nov.–Feb. 🚫 All major cards

🏨 LA TOUR D'AUVERGNE $/$$ ✪✪✪
13 RUE DES RÉGUAIRES
TEL 02 98 95 08 70
FAX 02 98 95 17 31
A refurbished inn situated in the town center, with a pretty courtyard. Comfortable rooms.
🛈 38 🅿 🚫 AE, MC, V

🍴 L'AMBROISIE $$$
49 RUE ELIE-FRÉRON
TEL 02 98 95 00 02
Conveniently situated close to the cathedral and well known for its excellent fish and imaginative desserts. Michelin one star.
🕒 Closed Sun. D in winter & school hols. in Nov. & Feb. 🚫 MC, V

QUIMPERLÉ 29300

🏨 CHÂTEAU DE KERLAREC $$
ARZANO (ON THE D22 NE OF QUIMPERLÉ)
TEL 02 98 71 75 06
FAX 02 98 71 74 55
Château on wooded grounds, built around 1860 and still retaining its period character. Fish, seafood, and Breton specialties prepared if requested beforehand. Tennis. Price includes breakfast.
🛈 4 🚫 No credit cards

RENNES 35000

🏨 CHÂTEAU DU BOIS GLAUME $$
POLIGNÉ 35320 (ON THE N137 S OF RENNES)
TEL 02 99 43 83 05

FAX 02 99 43 79 40
An early 18th-century château in a park with ancient trees and lake. Dinner by request only but restaurants nearby. Fishing, tennis.
🛈 2 + 2 suites 🚫 No credit cards

🍴 AUBERGE ST.-SAVEUR $$
6 RUE ST.-SAVEUR
TEL 02 99 79 32 56
A handsome half-timbered building that survived the great fire of 1750. Inside, it retains the traditional atmosphere. Specialties include Breton lobster and other shellfish, and fish dishes.
🕒 Closed Sat. L & all Sun. & Mon. L 🚫 AE, MC, V

RIEC-SUR-BELON 29340

🍴 CHEZ JACKY $$$
PORT DE BELON
TEL 02 98 06 90 32
The place to eat Belon oysters, a basic, authentic restaurant on the Belon River with oysterbeds right next to the restaurant. The *plateau de fruits de mer* is a treat. Reservation essential.
🕒 Closed Mon. & March.–early Oct. 🚫 MC, V

ROSCOFF 29680

🏨 BRITTANY 🍴 $$/$$$ ✪✪✪
BOULEVARD STE.-BARBE
TEL 02 98 69 70 78
FAX 02 02 98 61 13 29
Stone manor house facing the old port of Roscoff and L'Île de Batz, with a renowned restaurant, The Yachtsman. Sauna.
🛈 25 🕒 Closed Nov.–March Restaurant closed Sat. L & Sun. L 🚫 All major cards

ST.-MALO 35400

🏨 GRAND HOTEL DES THERMES $$$/$$$$$ ✪✪✪✪

100 BOULEVARD HÉBERT, COURTOISVILLE
TEL 02 99 40 75 75
FAX 02 99 40 76 00
Elegant hotel on the seafront with a garden, a sea-therapy center, and two restaurants.
🛈 181 + 7 suites 🅿 🕒 Closed 2 weeks Jan. 🛗 🚫 All major cards

🏨 LA KORRIGANE $$/$$$ ✪✪✪
39 RUE LE POMELLEC, ST.-SERVAN
TEL 02 99 81 65 85
FAX 02 99 82 23 89
Elegantly furnished turn-of-the-20th-century mansion near the harbor. Beautiful bedrooms, two sitting rooms, and a pretty garden. No restaurant
🛈 12 🅿 🚫 All major cards

🍴 LA DUCHESSE ANNE $$$
5 PLACE GUY-LA-CHAMBRE
TEL 02 99 40 85 33
A veritable institution with elegant decor and impeccable cuisine. Specialties include *foie gras de canard* and local grilled lobster. Michelin one star.
🕒 Closed Sun. D in winter, Wed., & Dec.–Jan. 🚫 MC, V

🔲 CAFÉ DE L'UNIVERS
$$
PLACE CHATEAUBRIAND
TEL 02 99 40 89 52
This popular restaurant within the walls of the old town offers excellent seafood, and serves a late dinner.
🔲 All major cards

ST.-THÉGONNEC 29410

🔲 AUBERGE ST.-THÉGONNEC
$/$$$
TEL 02 98 79 61 18
Traditional auberge in an intriguing village known for its parish close. Good simple Breton cooking. Rooms also available.
🔲 19 🔲 Closed Sun. D, Mon. & Dec. 20–Feb. 5 except July & Aug. 🔲 AE, MC, V

STE.-ANNE-LA-PALUD 29550

🔲 DE LA PLAGE
$$$$ ✿✿✿✿
TEL 02 98 92 50 12
FAX 02 98 92 56 54
Classic seaside hotel right on a tiny remote beach; a peaceful relaxing retreat. Wonderful seaviews and sunsets from the excellent Michelin one-star restaurant. Great for local crab and langoustines and the Breton speciality, a *pot au feu* of lobster and vegetables.
🔲 26 + 4 suites 🔲 Closed mid-Nov.–March & Tues. L except July & Aug. 🔲
🔲 All major cards

TRÉBEURDEN 22560

🔲 TI AL-LANNEC
$/$$$ ✿✿✿
14 ALLÉE DE MEZO-GUEN
TEL 02 96 15 01 01
FAX 02 96 23 62 14
On wooded grounds overlooking the Bay of Lannion, and a path to the sea. Some rooms have terraces or verandas. Tennis, sauna.
🔲 29 🔲 Closed mid-

Oct.–mid-March 🔲 🔲 All major cards

VANNES 56000

🔲 LA MARÉBAUDIÈRE
$ ✿✿✿
4 RUE ARISTIDE-BRIAND
TEL 02 97 47 34 29
FAX 02 97 54 14 11
A quiet, stylishly decorated hotel with a garden, near the old town. No restaurant.
🔲 41 🔲 AE, MC, V

LOIRE VALLEY

AMBOISE 37400

🔲 LE CHOISEUL
$$/$$$$ ✿✿✿✿
36 QUAI CHARLES-GUINOT
TEL 02 47 30 45 45
FAX 02 47 30 46 10
An elegant, 18th-century mansion, close to the château facing the Loire River, with a flower garden and a Michelin two-star restaurant.
🔲 29 + 3 suites 🔲
🔲 Closed Dec.–late Jan. 🔲
🔲 All major cards

🔲 LE LION D'OR
$ ✿✿
17 QUAI CHARLES-GUINOT
TEL 02 47 57 00 23
FAX 02 47 23 22 49
Traditionally run hotel, close to the château beside the Loire River.
🔲 21 🔲 🔲 Closed Dec. 1–15 & Jan. 🔲 MC, V

🔲 LE MANOIR ST.-THOMAS
$$/$$$
1 MAIL ST.-THOMAS
TEL 02 47 57 22 52
Splendid baroque manor house in a lovely garden, serving classic cuisine with a nouvelle touch. Try the honey-glazed duck with cinnamon and ginger. Exceptionally good wine cellar.
🔲 Closed Sun. D in winter, all Mon., Tues. L in summer, & mid-Jan.–mid-March
🔲 All major cards

ANGERS 49100

🔲 ANJOU
$/$$$ ✿✿✿✿
1 BOULEVARD MARÉCHAL FOCH
TEL 02 41 88 24 82
FAX 02 41 87 22 21
Large 19th-century hotel, beautifully renovated, close to the old town. The restaurant, Salamandre, has Renaissance decor as a backdrop to very good value food; try the ravioli stuffed with lobster or the excellent fish soups.
🔲 53 🔲 All major cards

🔲 FRANCE
$ ✿✿✿
8 PLACE DE LA GARE
TEL 02 41 88 49 42
FAX 02 41 86 76 70
Classic hotel conveniently situated near the railroad station and major sights, with Plantagenêts restaurant.
🔲 56 🔲 Closed Sat. L, Sun. D & 2 weeks Aug. 🔲 🔲
🔲 All major cards

🔲 LES TROIS RIVIÈRES
$$$
62 PROMENADE DE REUILÉE
TEL 02 41 73 31 88
Popular restaurant beside the river with fine views. Specializes in fish. Open daily.
🔲 All major cards

AZAY-LE-RIDEAU 37190

🔲 GRAND MONARQUE
$$/$$$
PLACE DE LA RÉPUBLIQUE
TEL 02 47 45 40 08
Friendly hotel-restaurant with a shady terrace. Delicious local fare; river salmon, and goat's cheese, for example, complemented by Azay-le-Rideau's wine.
🔲 24 🔲 Closed Sun. D, all Mon. & Fri. D, Oct.–March, & mid-Dec.–Jan. 🔲 AE, MC, V

BLOIS 41000

🔲 LE MÉDICIS
$/$$ ✿✿✿
2 ALLÉE FRANÇOIS 1ER

TEL 02 54 43 94 04
FAX 02 54 42 04 05
An elegant 19th-century hotel within walking distance of the château and close to the railroad station. Restaurant with classic cuisine.
🛏 12 🕐 Closed Sun. D Oct.–Easter & Jan. 🅢
🅢 All major cards

🏨 ANNE DE BRETAGNE
$ ✪✪
31 AVENUE JEAN-LAIGRET
TEL 02 54 78 05 38
FAX 02 54 74 37 79
Situated on a small square close to the château, this modest hotel is quiet and friendly. No restaurant.
🛏 28 🕐 Closed Jan. 9–Feb. 6 🅢 All major cards

SOMETHING SPECIAL

🍴 L'ORANGERIE DU CHÂTEAU
A lovely terrace restaurant in the château orangery. Specialties include perch with asparagus (in season), *filet de pigeonneau à la Vendômoise*, and *panier de poudre d'ail*.
$$/$$$$
1 AVENUE JEAN LAIGRET, BLOIS
TEL 02 54 78 05 36
🕐 Closed Sun. D, Wed., 1 week Aug., Feb. school vacation, & Tues. D from Nov. 1–Easter 🅢 AE, MC, V

🍴 AU RENDEZVOUS DES PÊCHEURS
$$$
27 RUE FOIX
TEL 02 54 74 67 48
Simple little bistro serving excellent fish dishes; try the asparagus and langoustine.
🕐 Closed Sun. & Mon. L, first 3 weeks Aug. & last 2 weeks Feb. 🅢 🅢 MC, V

BOURGES 18000

🍴 LE D'ANTAN SANCERROIS
$$
50 RUE BOURBONNOUX
TEL 02 48 65 96 26
Popular restaurant in a venerable building, with excellent local cooking.
🕐 Closed all Sun. & Mon. L
🅢 AE, MC, V

CHAMBORD 41250

🏨 LE GRAND SAINT-MICHEL
$ ✪✪✪
TEL 02 54 20 31 31
FAX 02 54 20 36 40
Quiet hotel close to the château and on the edge of the forest. Reservations strongly advised. The restaurant serves good traditional and regional cuisine on the terrace. Tennis.
🛏 38 🅿 🕐 Closed mid-Nov.–mid-Dec. 🅢 MC, V

CHENONCEAUX 37150

🏨 BON LABOUREUR ET CHÂTEAU
$/$$ ✪✪✪
6 RUE DU DR. BRETONNEAU
TEL 02 47 23 90 02
FAX 02 47 23 82 01
This village-center hotel has been family run for generations. Chintzy living rooms and pleasant bedrooms overlook a courtyard. Restaurant serves nouvelle cuisine.
🛏 22 + 5 suites 🅿
🕐 Closed mid-Nov.–mid-Dec & Wed. D & all Thurs. Nov. 1–Easter & Jan. 3, Feb. 5
🅢 🅢 🅢 All major cards

🏨 LA ROSERAIE
$ ✪✪✪
7 RUE DU DR. BRETONNEAU
TEL 02 47 23 90 09
FAX 02 47 23 91 59
A charming hotel with a garden, tastefully decorated rooms, and beamed dining room. Terrace for dining.
🛏 17 🅿 🕐 Closed mid-

Nov.–mid-Feb. 🅢 🅢 All major cards

CHINON 37500

🏨 CHÂTEAU DE MARÇAY
🍴 **$$/$$$$ ✪✪✪✪**
MARÇAY (4 MILES/6 KM S OF CHINON VIA D749 & D116)
TEL 02 47 93 03 47
FAX 02 47 93 45 33
A medieval, turreted château in its own parkland with a Michelin one-star restaurant. Tennis.
🛏 30 + 4 suites
🕐 Closed mid-Jan.–mid-March. Restaurant closed Sun. D & all Mon. mid-Nov.–end March 🈺
🅢 All major cards

🏨 DIDEROT
$ ✪✪
4 RUE BUFFON, 37500
TEL 02 47 93 18 87
FAX 02 47 93 37 10
A pretty, creeper-covered town house in a quiet courtyard. Breakfast served on the terrace or in the rustic dining room. No restaurant. No TV in rooms.
🛏 28 🅿 🅢 Rooms
🅢 All major cards

🍴 AU PLAISIR GOURMAND
$$/$$$
QUAI CHARLES-VII
TEL 02 47 93 20 48
An elegant mansion with a sunny terrace at the foot of the château houses this Michelin one-star restaurant. Try the ravioli escargots, or the "tasting menu" including potatoes with caviar, scallops in champagne, and squab with foie gras. Reservation essential.
🕐 Closed Sun. D, all Mon., & Feb. 15–March 10 🅢
🅢 AE, MC, V

🍴 HOSTELLERIE GARGANTUA
$$
73 RUE VOLTAIRE
TEL 02 47 93 04 71
Popular restaurant in a Renaissance palace over-

---

looking the river. Open until
11 p.m. Eight rooms available.
🕒 Closed Wed. 🅂 AE,
MC, V

FONTEVRAUD 49590

🏨 LA CROIX BLANCHE
$ ✪✪
7 PLACE DES PLANTAGENÊTS
TEL 02 41 51 71 11
FAX 02 41 38 15 38
A simple but agreeable hotel
close to the abbey with rooms
overlooking the garden.
🛏 21 🅿 🕒 Closed mid-
Jan.–early Feb. & 2 weeks
Nov. & Sun. L & all Mon.
Oct.–March 🅂 AE, MC, V

🍴 LA LICORNE
$$$$
ALLÉE STE.-CATHERINE
TEL 02 41 51 72 49
A Michelin one-star restaurant
in an 18th-century building.
Try the langoustine ravioli and
roasted Loire salmon with
vanilla butter. Reservations
necessary.
🕒 Closed Sun. D, all Mon.
except Jul. & Aug., Wed. D
Oct.–April, Oct. 8–16, &
mid-Dec.–end Jan. 🅂 All
major cards

SOMETHING SPECIAL

🏨 HOSTELLERIE PRIEURÉ ST.-LAZARE
This well-modernized
hotel is in the old St.-
Lazare priory, within the
abbey. The 19th-century
wing contains the bedrooms
and in summer the restaurant
tables spread out into the
cloisters.
$ ✪✪✪
RUE ST. JEAN DE L'HABIT
FONTEVRAUD
TEL 02 41 51 73 16
FAX 02 41 51 75 50
🛏 52 🅿 🕒 Closed
mid-Nov.–mid-March 🅂
🅂 AE, MC, V

🍴 LA ROUTE D'OR
$$
PLACE DE L'ÉGLISE,
CANDES-ST.-MARTIN
TEL 02 47 95 81 10
A tiny restaurant in the
village of Candes-St.-Martin
east of Fontevraud. Tables in
a cellar dining room or on
the cobbled square. Try perch
in foie gras or baby eels
flavored with Roquefort.
🕒 Closed Tues. D & all Wed.
in winter 🅂 MC, V

JOUÉ-LÈS-TOURS 37300

🏨 CHÂTEAU DE BEAULIEU
$$/$$$ ✪✪✪
67 RUE DE BEAULIEU
TEL 02 47 53 20 26
FAX 02 47 53 84 20
A 17th-century manor house
hotel in quiet surroundings
with a garden and beautiful
rooms.
🛏 19 🅂 🅂 AE, MC, V

LA FLÈCHE 72200

🏨 LE RELAIS CICERO
$/$$ ✪✪✪
18 BOULEVARD D'ALGER
TEL 02 43 94 14 14
FAX 02 43 45 98 96
A stately, 17th-century
mansion, with the peaceful
ambience of the convent it
once was. No restaurant.
🛏 21 🕒 Closed Sun. D lat
Dec.–early Jan. 🅂 AE, MC, V

LAMOTTE-BEUVRON 41600

🍴 TATIN
$$/$$$
5 AVENUE DE VIERZON
TEL 02 54 88 00 03
Small hotel-restaurant serving
simple local cuisine with
excellent game and fish.
Claims to be the originator of
Tarte Tatin, the upside-down
caramelized apple tart; it is
always available here.
🕒 Closed Sun. D, all Mon., &
Jan. 5–15 & Feb. 15–March 6.
🅂 🅂 All major cards

LE MANS 72000

🏨 CHANTECLER
$ ✪✪✪
50 RUE DE LA PELOUSE
TEL 02 43 14 40 00
FAX 02 43 77 16 28
Modern hotel close to the old
town. No restaurant.
🛏 32 + 3 suites 🅂 AE,
MC, V

LES ROSIERS-SUR-LOIRE 49350

🍴 AUBERGE JEANNE DE LAVAL
$$$$/$$$$$
54 RUE NATIONALE
TEL 02 41 51 80 17
Old-fashioned family inn with
a flowery terrace, now a
Michelin one-star restaurant
serving classic Loire cuisine,
particularly river fish with
exquisite *beurre blanc.*
🛏 4 🕒 Closed Mon. in
winter & late Nov.–late Dec.
🅂 🅂 AE, MC, V

LOCHES 37600

🏨 LE GEORGES SAND
$/$$ ✪✪
39 RUE QUINTEFOL
TEL 02 47 59 39 74
FAX 02 47 91 55 75
Former 17th-century coaching
inn beneath the castle
ramparts with stone staircases
and a medieval watchtower.
Rooms overlook the castle or
the river and meals are served
on the terrace in fine weather.
🛏 20 🅂 MC, V

MONTBAZON 37250

🏨 CHÂTEAU D'ARTIGNY
🍴 $$$/$$$$$ ✪✪✪✪
TEL 02 47 34 30 30
FAX 02 47 34 30 39
Beautiful white-stone château
in its own wooded parkland
southwest of Montbazon,
overlooking the Indre Valley.
Built for the *parfumier* Coty,
its sumptuous interior is
sometimes a venue for
musical evenings. Rooms in
the château and the lodge by

HOTELS & RESTAURANTS

the river. Excellent cuisine, and an impressive wine cellar. Sauna, tennis, small golf course. 🛈 48 + 4 duplex 🕒 Closed Dec. 3–Jan. 13 🚇 🖾 All major cards

MONTLOUIS-SUR-LOIRE 37270

🏨 CHÂTEAU DE LA BOURDAISIÈRE
$$$/$$$$
25 RUE DE LA BOURDAISIÈRE
TEL 02 47 45 16 31
FAX 02 47 45 09 11
Charming château in parkland, built for Marie Gaudin, the mistress of François I. The beautifully furnished rooms have period pieces. Tennis, horseback riding. Reservations only; confirmation by fax required.
🛈 10 🅿 🏊 🖾 MC, V

NANTES 44000

🏨 LA PÉROUSE
$ ○○○
3 ALLÉE DUQUESNE,
TEL 02 40 89 75 00
FAX 02 40 89 76 00
Situated in the Cours des Cinquante Otages right in the city center, this decidedly modern building has won awards for its minimalist design. No restaurant.
🛈 47 🖾 All major cards

SOMETHING SPECIAL
🍴 LA CIGALE
Famous belle epoque café/brasserie in the center of Nantes serving superb fish and seafood.
$$
4 PLACE GRASLIN, NANTES
TEL 02 51 84 94 94
🖾 MC, V

ORLÉANS 45000

🏨 DES CÈDRES
$ ○○○
17 RUE MARÉCHAL FOCH

TEL 02 38 62 22 92
FAX 02 38 81 76 46
A modern, well-run hotel on a quiet street, just outside the town center. Large rooms and a garden. No restaurant.
🛈 34 🖾 Rooms 🕒 Closed Dec. 24–Jan. 2 🖾 All major cards

🏨 LE RIVAGE
$ ○○
635 RUE REINE BLANCHE, OLIVET, 45160
TEL 02 38 66 02 93
FAX 02 38 56 31 11
Situated 3 miles (5 km) south of Orléans beside the Loire, this modern hotel offers meals on the terrace over-looking the river. Tennis.
🛈 17 🅿 🕒 Closed late Dec.–late Jan. Restaurant closed Sat. D Nov.–March
🖾 All major cards

🍴 LES ANTIQUAIRES
$$$
2–4 RUE AU LIN
TEL 02 38 53 52 35
Imaginative Loire cooking in a Michelin one-star restaurant; specialties include game from the Sologne such as duck, wild boar, hare, and venison.
🕒 Closed Mon. & 3 weeks Aug. 🖾 AE, MC, V

ROMORANTIN-LANTHENAY 41200

🏨 GRAND HÔTEL
🍴 LION D'OR
$$/$$$$
69 RUE CLEMENCEAU
TEL 02 54 94 15 15
FAX 02 54 88 24 87
Luxurious château with a beautiful garden and Michelin two-star restaurant, thought by some to be the best cooking in the Loire Valley. Wonderful local produce such as white asparagus and wild mushrooms in season; the frog's legs and the caramelized brioche with angelica sorbet are especially recommended.
🛈 13 + 3 suites 🕒 Closed mid-Feb.–mid March 🖾
🖾 All major cards

SACHÉ 37910

🍴 AUBERGE DU XIIÈME SIÈCLE
$$/$$$
RUE PRINCIPALE
TEL 02 47 26 88 77
Half-timbered inn with a medieval interior, opposite the manor house where Balzac used to write. Good value traditional cooking.
🕒 Closed Sun. D, all Mon. & Tues. L, June 13–20, Aug. 28–Sept. 4 & Jan. 10–31
🖾 AE, MC, V

SAUMUR 49400

🏨 ANNE D'ANJOU
$$ ○○○
32 QUAI MAYAUD
TEL 02 41 67 30 30
FAX 02 41 67 51 00
An 18th-century building overlooking the Loire. There is a good affiliated restaurant in the hotel gardens called Les Ménestrels (11 rue Raspail, Tel 02 41 67 71 10).
🛈 50 🅿 🖾 AE, MC, V

SOMETHING SPECIAL
🍴 LES CAVES DE MARSON
Delightful troglodyte restaurant near Saumur with candlelit dining rooms quarried out of the tufa caves. The specialty is fouaces, stuffed wheat pancakes cooked in a traditional wood-fired oven. Set menus include wine.
$
ROU-MARSON, SAUMUR 49400
TEL 02 41 50 50 05
🕒 Closed Mon.
🖾 MC, V

🍴 LES CLOS DES BÉNÉDICTINS
$$$
ST.-HILAIRE–ST.-FLORENT (W OF SAUMUR VIA N147 & D751)
TEL 02 41 67 28 48
In a new hotel overlooking

🏨 Hotel 🍴 Restaurant 🛈 No. of hotel bedrooms 🚇 Métro station 🅿 Parking 🕒 Closed 🛗 Elevator

the town and château of
Saumur; imaginative modern
French cooking and fine local
wine list.
🕐 23 🕒 Closed Dec.
12–Jan. 24 🔐 AE, MC, V

TOURS 37000

🏨 JEAN BARDET
🍴 $$$/$$$$$ ✪✪✪✪
57 RUE GROISON, 37100
TEL 02 47 41 41 11
FAX 02 47 51 68 72
An elegant 19th-century
mansion set in a large park
with beautiful vegetable
gardens. It contains the
celebrated two-star Michelin
restaurant where the famous
chef Jean Bardet uses the
herbs and produce from
the gardens to wonderful
effect.
🛏 16 + 5 suites 🕒 Closed
Sun. D, all Mon. Nov.–March,
& Mon. L April.–Oct. 🔐
🏊 🔐 All major cards

🏨 L'UNIVERS
🍴 $$$ ✪✪✪
5 BOULEVARD HEURTELOUP
TEL 02 47 05 37 12
FAX 02 47 61 51 80
Situated in the town center,
this grand hotel in the classic
style once hosted Henry
James. (He remarked upon
the overwhelming politeness
of the staff.) Frescoes of
famous visitors from 1846 to
the present day decorate the
walls. Most of the rooms face
the internal courtyard and
there is a highly rated affiliated
restaurant, La Touraine.
🕐 77 + 8 suites 🅿
🔐 rooms 🔐 🔐 All major
cards

🏨 DU MANOIR
$ ✪✪
2 RUE TRAVERSIÈRE
TEL 02 47 05 37 37
FAX 02 47 05 16 00
A small and charming hotel in
a 19th-century building close
to the railroad station and the
old town. Prettily decorated
rooms and renovated
bathrooms. No restaurant.

🕐 20 🅿 🔐 All major
cards

🏨 LES HAUTES ROCHES
Four miles upstream from
Tours, this elegant
troglodyte hotel on the north
bank of the Loire River has
rooms carved out of the rock.
The restaurant offers classic
Michelin one-star cooking,
served on a delightful terrace
overlooking the Loire River.
Try the rabbit and foie gras
terrine, and Grand Marnier
soufflé.
$$$/$$$$ ✪✪✪✪
86 QUAI DE LA LOIRE,
ROCHECORBON, 37210
TEL 02 47 52 88 88
FAX 02 47 52 81 30
🕐 15 🕒 Closed mid-
Jan.–mid-March.
Restaurant closed Sun. &
Mon. D in winter & Mon.
L (except public hols.)
🔐 AE, MC, V

AUXERRE 89000

🏨 PARC DES MARÉCHAUX
$/$$ ✪✪✪
6 AVENUE FOCH
TEL 03 86 51 43 77
FAX 03 86 51 31 72
A large 19th-century house
close to the town center, with
traditionally decorated rooms,
some looking out onto the
park. No restaurant.
🕐 25 🔐 All major cards

🍴 BARNABET
$$$
14 QUAI DE LA RÉPUBLIQUE
TEL 03 86 51 68 88
This 17th-century building
with a garden in the old town

houses a Michelin one-star
restaurant with an excellent
wine list; try the lamb with
truffled potatoes and gelée de
fruits au chablis.
🕒 Closed Sun. D, all Mon., &
late Dec.–early Jan. 🔐 AE,
MC, V

AVALLON 89200

🏨 CHÂTEAU DE VAULT-DE-LUGNY
$$$/$$$$$ ✪✪✪✪
TEL 03 86 34 07 86
FAX 03 86 34 16 36
A beautifully restored, 16th-
century country mansion
standing on its own grounds.
Some bedrooms have four-
poster or canopy beds. The
restaurant serves traditional
cuisine and is open only to
hotel guests. Tennis, fishing.
🕐 12 🅿 🕒 Closed mid-
Nov.–late March 🔐 AE, MC, V

BEAUNE 21200

🏨 LE CEP
$$$ ✪✪✪✪
27 RUE MAUFOUX
TEL 03 80 22 35 48
FAX 03 80 22 76 80
A 16th century hotel
decorated in Renaissance
style close to the Hôtel-Dieu.
No restaurant.
🕐 56 🅿 🔐 🔐 All
major cards

🍴 JARDIN DES REMPARTS
$$$$
10 RUE HÔTEL-DIEU
TEL 03 80 24 79 41
Dine on the garden terrace
of this popular Michelin one-
star restaurant known for its
wines as well as for its
excellent cuisine; try the
warm chocolate gâteau.
🕒 Closed Sun., Mon.
(except public hols.), Feb., 1
week Aug. 🔐 MC, V

🍴 LA BOUZEROTTE
$/$$$
BOUZE-LÈS-BEAUNE
TEL 03 80 26 01 37
A village restaurant with
simple country-style food

including rich omelettes with bacon and potatoes, delicious salads picked from the garden, and fruit tarts. Sunny terrace for outside dining or open fire indoors.
🕒 Closed Mon. D, all Tues., early Dec.–early Jan., & mid-Feb.–early March 🚇 MC, V

CHABLIS 89800

🏨 **HOSTELLERIE**
🍴 **DES CLOS**
$$ ✪✪✪
RUE JULES-RATHIER
TEL 03 86 42 10 63
FAX 03 86 42 17 11
This stylishly comfortable hotel in a medieval hospice has individually furnished bedrooms. The Michelin one-star restaurant serves dishes such as a *fricassée* of Burgundy snails and veal kidneys. A wide variety of local Chablis wines includes many by the glass.
🛏 26 🅿 🕒 Closed late Dec.–mid-Jan. 🔵 🚇 AE, MC, V

CHAGNY 71150

🍴 **LAMELOISE**
$$$$/$$$$$
PLACE D'ARMES
TEL 03 85 87 65 65
FAX 03 85 87 03 57
A 15th-century building with traditional wood-beamed Burgundian decor contains one of Burgundy's great restaurants—a Michelin three-star establishment, friendly and family run. Excellent local cheeses. Reservation essential.
🛏 16 🕒 Closed Thurs. L, all Wed. (except D July–Sept.), & late Dec.–late Jan. 🚇 AE, MC, V

CLUNY 71250

🏨 **DE BOURGOGNE**
$/$$ ✪✪✪
PLACE DE L'ABBAYE
TEL 03 85 59 00 58
FAX 03 85 59 03 73
A 19th-century mansion built over part of the remains of

Cluny abbey. Stone walls, period furniture, and objets d'art. The well regarded restaurant serves Burgundian cuisine.
🛏 12 + 3 suites 🅿
🕒 Closed mid-Nov.–mid-March. Restaurant closed Wed. L & all Tues. 🔵 🚇 All major cards

DIJON 21000

🏨 **HOSTELLERIE**
CHAPEAU ROUGE
$$/$$$ ✪✪✪✪
5 RUE MICHELET
TEL 03 80 30 28 10
FAX 03 80 30 33 89
This elegant historic hotel in the center of Dijon is a local landmark, with a restaurant offering Burgundian classics.
🛏 30 🔵 🚇 All major cards

🍴 **THIBERT**
$$/$$$$
10 PLACE WILSON
TEL 03 80 67 74 64
One of Dijon's star chefs, Jean-Paul Thibert, is celebrated for his modern way with traditional cuisine. Try his escargots de Bourgogne or the local specialty of freshwater fish in white wine. One Michelin star.
🕒 Closed Mon. L, all Sun., 3 weeks Aug., & Feb. school vacation 🔵 🚇 AE, MC, V

🍴 **LA TOISON D'OR**
$$$
HÔTEL PHILIPPE LE BON
18 RUE STE.-ANNE
TEL 03 80 30 73 52
The restaurant in this grand 15th-century mansion serves magnificent traditional dishes like coq au vin, snails in Meursault sauce, and the Dijon specialty, saddle of hare marinaded in *marc de Bourgogne*. It is also home to the *"Compagnie Bourgui-nonne des Oenophiles"* (Burgundian winelovers) so you can expect a superb selection of the region's wines.
🕒 Closed Sun. except public

PRICES

HOTELS
An indication of the cost of a double room without breakfast is given by $ signs.
$$$$$ over $280
$$$$ $200–$280
$$$ $120–$200
$$ $80–$120
$ under $80

RESTAURANTS
An indication of the cost of a three-course dinner without drinks is given by $ signs.
$$$$$ over $80
$$$$ $50–$80
$$$ $35–$50
$$ $20–$35
$ under $20

hols. & Sun. L from Aug. 1–15
🚇 All major cards

GEVREY-CHAMBERTIN 21220

🏨 **LES GRANDS CRUS**
$ ✪✪✪
ROUTE DES GRANDS CRUS
TEL 03 80 34 34 15
FAX 03 80 51 89 07
A modern hotel in the village center but in traditional Burgundian style gives superb views over the vineyards. Breakfast in the little flowery garden. No restaurant.
🛏 24 🅿 🕒 Closed early Dec.–late Feb. 🚇 MC, V

GEX 01770

🏨 **AUBERGE DES**
CHASSEURS
$/$$ ✪✪✪
NAZ-DESSUS, ECHENEVEX
TEL 04 50 41 54 07
FAX 04 50 41 90 61
Just south of Gex in the Jura Mountains, this delightful converted farmhouse has a well-tended garden and wonderful views. Tennis.
🛏 15 🕒 Closed Sun. D (except July–Aug.), all Mon. & Nov.–March 🛗 🚇 AE, MC, V

MARCIGNY 71110

LES RÉCOLLETS
$ ✪✪✪
PLACE DU CHAMP DE FOIRE
TEL 03 85 25 05 16
FAX 03 85 25 06 91
Once a convent, this charming
house on the edge of a little
market town is now a cozy
small hotel with open fires,
home-baked brioches,
handmade chocolates, and a
friendly atmosphere. No
restaurant.
🛏 9 AE, MC, V

MEURSAULT 21190

LES MAGNOLIAS
$$
8 RUE PIERRE-JOIGNEAU
TEL 03 80 21 23 23
FAX 03 80 21 29 10
An 18th-century mansion
with a beautifully decorated
interior set in a quiet court in
this famous wine village.
Large, comfortable rooms.
No restaurant.
🛏 12 Closed Dec.–
mid-March AE, MC, V

SAULIEU 21210

CÔTE-D'OR
$$$$$
2 RUE ARGENTINE
TEL 03 80 90 53 53
One of France's legendary
Michelin three-star
restaurants, where chef
Bernard Loiseau specializes in
cuisine légère, producing
imaginative dishes such as pike
in shallot fondue and snail and
nettle soup, served with
excellent wines. Dine inside or
in the garden.
🛏 23 + 7 suites + 3 duplex
 All major cards

VÉZELAY 89450

LE PONTOT
$$/$$$ ✪✪✪
PLACE DU PONTOT
TEL 03 86 33 24 40
FAX 03 86 33 30 05
An ancient fortified house,
American owned, within the

walls of the old town.
Breakfast in a lovely walled
garden in summer and a Louis
XVI-style breakfast room in
winter. No restaurant.
🛏 10 Closed Oct.–mid-
April DC, MC, V

L'ESPÉRANCE
$$$$$ ✪✪✪✪
ST.-PÈRE
TEL 03 86 33 39 10
In a village just south of
Vézelay. The charming country
hotel has an intimate restau-
rant in the hotel conservatory,
the setting for the Michelin
three-star cooking of chef
Marc Meneau, who treats
local ingredients with great
imagination. Try potato
pancakes with caviar, or turbot
in a crust of salt with lobster
butter, served with the wines
of Vézelay and Chablis. Some
rooms in a restored watermill.
🛏 30 + 5 suites
 Restaurant closed Tues.
(except D mid-June–mid-
Oct.) & Wed. L (except
public hols.) Restaurant
 All major cards

BAGNOLS 69620

CHÂTEAU DE
BAGNOLS
$$$$$ ✪✪✪✪
TEL 04 74 71 40 00
FAX 04 74 71 40 49
Beautifully restored moated
castle of golden stone with
exquisitely landscaped
gardens. Antiques and silk
draperies enhance the elegant
interior. The Michelin one-star
restaurant excels in regional
dishes such as fillet of beef
with *girolles* and a ravioli of
fresh peas.
🛏 16 + 4 suites
 Closed early Jan.–April
& Nov.–late Dec.
 Rooms All major
cards

CHAMONIX-MONT-
BLANC 74400

CHALET-HÔTEL
BEAUSOLEIL
$/$$ ✪✪
LE LAVANCHER
TEL 04 50 54 00 78
FAX 04 50 54 17 34
This quiet, family hotel
surrounded by fields and
mountains offers
homey cooking and a
charming garden. Tennis.
🛏 15 Closed mid-
Sept.–mid-Dec. AE, MC, V

COURCHEVEL 73120

LA SIVOLIÈRE
$$$/$$$$$ ✪✪✪
QUARTIER DES CHENUS
TEL 04 79 08 08 33
FAX 04 79 08 15 73
Charming, tasteful chalet hotel
at the foot of the Courchevel
ski runs. Very comfortable and
exquisitely decorated.
🛏 32 Closed
May–Dec. AE, MC, V

LE BATEAU IVRE
$$$$/$$$$$
HÔTEL POMME DE PIN
TEL 04 79 08 36 88
Two-star Michelin restaurant
with glorious panoramic
mountain views serving hearty
fare such as roast scallops or
stuffed pig's trotters.
 Closed mid-April–mid-
Dec. All major cards

GRENOBLE 38000

CHÂTEAU DE LA
COMMANDERIE
$/$$ ✪✪✪
AVENUE ÉCHIROLLES, EYBENS,
38320
TEL 04 76 25 34 58
FAX 04 76 24 07 31
Just outside Grenoble and
close to the ski slopes, this
historic château has a walled
garden, tapestry-hung rooms,
and beautiful bedrooms.
🛏 25 Closed Sat. L,
Sun. D, & all Mon., late
Dec.–early Jan. All
major cards

 Non-smoking Air-conditioning Indoor/ Outdoor swimming pool Health club Credit cards   **KEY**

HOTELS & RESTAURANTS

JULIÉNAS 69840

🍴 LE COQ AU VIN
$$
PLACE DU MARCHÉ
TEL 04 74 04 41 98
Beaujolais bistro in the wine
village famous for its special
recipe coq au vin and other
traditional favorites.
🕐 Closed Wed. & late
Dec.–early Feb. 🚫 All major
cards

LA MALÈNE 48210

🏨 CHÂTEAU DE LA CAZE
$$/$$$$ ✪✪✪✪
TEL 04 66 48 51 01
Wonderfully romantic,
turreted 15th-century château
on the banks of the Tarn,
perfect for a meal or a stay
while touring the Tarn
Gorges.
🛏 13 🕐 Closed Thurs. L
mid-Oct.–late April, all Wed.
Oct.–May, & late Nov.–mid-
March 🚫 AE, MC, V

LA ROCHETTE 73110

🏨 HOSTELLERIE LES CHÂTAIGNIERS
$/$$
RUE MAURICE-FRANCK
TEL 04 79 25 50 21
FAX 04 79 25 79 97
A Savoie mountain valley
retreat: The tall and elegant
house in its own park has a
cultured, cozy ambience with
books in different languages.
Reservation essential.
🛏 2 + 2 suites 🅿
🕐 Closed 2 weeks Jan.
🚫 MC, V

LYON 69000

🏨 LA TOUR ROSE
$$$$/$$$$$ ✪✪✪✪
22 RUE DU BOEUF, 69005
TEL 04 78 37 25 90
FAX 04 78 42 26 02
A 17th-century house with
rooms in elegant Renaissance
style and a garden of terraces
and waterfalls. The Michelin
one-star restaurant has an
excellent wine list.

🛏 6 + 6 suites + 4 duplex
🅿 🕐 Restaurant closed
Sun. 🚫 All major cards

🏨 VILLA FLORENTINE
$$$$/$$$$$ ✪✪✪✪
25 MONTÉE ST.-BARTHÉLEMY,
69005
TEL 04 72 56 56 56
FAX 04 72 40 90 56
Romantic hotel with a
wonderful view over the red
roofs of old Lyon, a favorite
with visiting heads of state.
Michelin one-star restaurant,
Les Terrasses de Lyon: Try the
lamb cooked in milk with
anchovies.
🛏 16 + 3 suites 🅿 🛗
🖼 🚫 All major cards

🍴 LÉON DE LYON
$$$$$
1 RUE PLENEY, 69001
TEL 04 72 10 11 12
One of Lyon's great rest-
aurants (two Michelin stars),
long established on a narrow
street off Quai St.-Antoine.
The menu includes the
traditional Lyon favorites,
such as sausages, lentils, and
rich potato gratin along with
more modern lightweight
fare. Superb cheese board
and wine list.
🕐 Closed Mon. L, all Sun.,
& 2 weeks Aug. 🛗 🚫 AE,
MC, V

🍴 PAUL BOCUSE
$$$$$
40 RUE DE LA PLAGE
COLLONGES-AU-MONT-D'OR
69660
TEL 04 72 42 90 90
Paul Bocuse's restaurant is 9
miles (16 km) north of Lyon,
but is worth the pilgrimage,
and plenty of people make it
to this Michelin three-star
restaurant. They find simple,
perfect food—exquisite roast
chicken, creamy potato gratin,
and luxuries like truffle soup,
grandly served. There's even a
jeunes gourmands menu for
children.
🛗 🚫 All major cards

MÉGÈVE 74120

🏨🍴 CHALET DU MONT D'ARBOIS
$$$/$$$$$ ✪✪✪✪
ROUTE MONT D'ARBOIS
TEL 04 50 21 25 03
This magnificent hotel in a
peaceful setting was once
home to the Rothschild family.
The restaurant serves choice
meals accompanied by an
excellent wine list.
🛏 23 + 6 suites 🚫 All
major cards

MÉRIBEL 73550

🏨 LE GRAND COEUR
$$$$/$$$$$ ✪✪✪✪
TEL 04 79 08 60 03
FAX 04 79 08 58 38
One of Meribel's grand hotels,
a luxury establishment with
every comfort, located in the
town center.
🛏 41 🅿 🕐 Closed mid-
April–mid-Dec. 🖼 🍴
🚫 All major cards

PÉROUGES 01800

🏨 HOSTELLERIE DU VIEUX PÉROUGES
$$$/$$$$ ✪✪✪/✪✪✪✪
PLACE DU TILLEUL
TEL 04 74 61 00 88
FAX 04 74 34 77 90
An old Bresse inn in this
restored medieval town.
Guest rooms in the 14th-
century parts of the building
are decorated in the style
of the original sleeping
quarters.
🛏 15 🅿 🚫 MC, V

MASSIF CENTRAL

SALERS 15140

🏨 LES REMPARTS
$ ✪✪
ESPLANADE BARROUZE
TEL 04 71 40 70 33
FAX 04 71 40 75 32
Perched on the edge of the
ancient fortifications of
medieval Salers, this hotel has
spectacular views and
delicious local cooking.

① 18 ⊕ Closed mid-Oct.–mid-Dec. ⊠ MC, V

VICHY 03200

▦ PAVILLON D'ENGHIEN
▯ $ ✿✿✿
32 RUE CALLOU
TEL 04 70 98 33 30
FAX 04 70 31 67 82
Small, old-fashioned hotel near the Enghien Gardens and Callou baths; with a restaurant, Jardins d'Enghien.
① 22 ⊕ Closed late Dec.–early Feb. Restaurant closed Sun. D and Mon. (except public hols.) ⊠ ⊠ All major cards

▯ L'ALAMBIC
$$/$$$
8 RUE NICOLAS-LARBAUD
TEL 04 70 59 12 71
Popular little restaurant with a welcoming atmosphere and beautifully presented cuisine. Try the mesclun salad with langoustine tails or chicken tournedos stuffed with snails. Superb wine list. Reservations advised.
⊕ Closed Mon. & Tues. L, also Mon. D late Feb.–early March, & late Aug.–early Sep.
⊠ ⊠ MC, V

SOUTHWEST FRANCE

AQUITAINE & THE ATLANTIC COAST

AINHOA 64250

▦ OHANTZEA
$ ✿✿
TEL 05 59 29 90 50
A simple, 17th-century farmhouse that has been in the same family for 300 years; some of the rustic bedrooms have balconies.
① 13 ▯ ⊕ Closed Dec.–Jan. ⊠ All major cards

▯ ITHURRIA
$$/$$$
PLACE DU FRONTON
TEL 05 59 29 92 11
A Michelin one-star restaurant

with peaceful gardens. Typical dishes include foie gras des Landes, roast pigeon with garlic, or Basque cassoulet with red beans.
① 27 ⊕ Closed Wed. (except July & Aug.) ⊠ AE, MC, V

ARCACHON 31320

▦ SÉMIRAMIS
$$$ ✿✿✿
4 ALLÉE DE REBSOMEN
TEL 05 56 83 25 87
FAX 05 57 52 22 41
Renovated 19th-century neo-Gothic mansion.
① 20 ⊕ Closed Nov. 15–30, Jan. 5–31, & Sun. mid-Oct.–mid-March ⊠ ⊠ MC, V

▯ CHEZ YVETTE
$/$$
59 BOULEVARD DU GÉNÉRAL LECLERC
TEL 05 56 83 05 11
A real sea-table with produce fresh from the market or the garden. Try the fricassée of octopus with Espelette peppers or soupe de poisson d'Arcachon.
⊠ ⊠ All major cards

BIARRITZ 64200

▦ CHÂTEAU DU CLAIR DE LUNE
$$ ✿✿✿
48 AVENUE ALAN-SEEGER
TEL 05 59 41 53 20
FAX 05 05 59 41 53 29
Elegant fin de siècle family house set in a quiet park south of Biarritz town. Breakfast around one large table. No restaurant.
① 15 ⊠ All major cards

▯ CAFÉ DE PARIS & BISTROT BELLEVUE
$$$$
5 PLACE BELLEVUE
TEL 05 59 24 19 53
The art deco dining room of this one-star Michelin restaurant serves stylishly presented classic cuisine. Or try the Bistrot Bellevue with its crab and lobster dishes.

⊕ Closed mid-Nov.–mid-March ⊠ All major cards

▯ CAMPAGNE ET GOURMANDISE
$$
52 AVENUE ALAN-SEEGER
TEL 05 59 41 10 11
Restaurant south of Biarritz with panoramic views of the Pyrenees. Typical dishes include fricassée de champignons en cappuccino d'herbes and oxtail with foie gras.
⊕ Closed Sun. D in winter, all Wed., & Feb., & Nov. school vacations ⊠ MC, V

BORDEAUX 33000

▦ BURDIGALA
$$$$ ✿✿✿✿
115 RUE GEORGES BONNAC
TEL 05 56 90 16 16
FAX 05 56 93 15 06
Beautifully decorated hotel with every comfort, just outside the city center.
① 68 + 15 suites ▯ ⊠ rooms ⊠ All major cards

▦ NORMANDIE
$$ ✿✿✿
7 COURS 30-JUILLET
TEL 05 56 52 16 80
FAX 05 56 51 68 91
Opposite the Maison du Vin, this central hotel is comfortable and welcoming. Some rooms have balconies.
① 100 ⊠ All major cards

▯ LA TUPINA
$$$
6 RUE PORTE DE LA MONNAIE
TEL 05 56 91 56 37
Savor chef Jean-Pierre Xiradakis's excellent regional cuisine, follow his good advice on wines, and enjoy the ambience of this popular restaurant close to the river.
⊕ Closed Sun. ⊠ All major cards

▯ LE VIEUX BORDEAUX
$$/$$$
27 RUE BUHAN
TEL 05 56 52 94 36
Relax in this Michelin one-star

restaurant's leafy courtyard in the heart of the city and enjoy its good value and quality.
🕒 Closed Sat. L, Sun., public hols., 3 weeks Aug., & Feb. school vacation 🅰 All major cards

CAP-FERRET 33950

🏨 **DES PINS**
$ 😊😊
RUE DE FAUVETTES
TEL 05 5 60 60 11
FAX 05 56 60 67 41
A small hotel in a quiet part of town, set in gardens.
ℹ 14 🅂 🕒 Closed early Nov.–Easter 🅰 AE, MC, V

CASTELNAU-DU-MÉDOC 33480

🏨 **CHÂTEAU DU FOULON**
$$
TEL 05 56 58 20 18
FAX 05 56 58 23 43
An elegant white château set in a large park just outside the village. Breakfast *en famille* at the magnificent grand table. No restaurant.
ℹ 4 + 4 suites 🅿 🅰 No credit cards

ESPELETTE 64250

🍴 **EUZKADI**
$$
TEL 05 59 93 91 88
This restaurant in a typical Basque house prepares excellent Basque specialties.
🕒 Closed Mon., & Tues. in winter 🅰 MC, V

EUGÉNIE-LES-BAINS 40320

🏨 **LES PRÉS D'EUGÉNIE**
🍴 **$$$$ 😊😊😊😊**
TEL 05 58 05 06 07
FAX 05 58 51 10 10
The empire of the legendary chef, Michel Guérard, inventor of *cuisine minceur* and holder of three Michelin stars. It encompasses two hotels, first Les Prés d'Eugénie and second Le Couvent des

Herbes, an 18th-century former convent. Two health spas, La Maison Rose and La Ferme aux Grives, complete the four establishments. All are individually decorated in exquisite taste. Restaurants serve both traditional and *minceur* cuisine and there are luxurious spa facilities. Go for your health, your tastebuds, or both. Tennis.
ℹ 60 rooms & 15 suites (in all four establishments)
🕒 Closed 2 weeks Dec., & early Jan.–end Feb. Ferme aux Grives closed Mon. & Tues. D mid-July–end Aug.
📶 🅰 All major cards

LA ROCHELLE 17000

🏨 **LES BRISES**
$$ 😊😊😊
CHEMIN DIGUE RICHELIEU
TEL 05 46 43 89 37
FAX 05 46 43 27 97
Close to the port with a fine terrace overlooking the sea. No restaurant.
ℹ 50 🅿 🅰 AE, MC, V

🍴 **LE YACHTSMAN**
$/$$
23 QUAI VALIN
TEL 05 46 41 20 68
A popular hotel-restaurant along the quayside where you can dine on the terrace with a view of the old port.
🕒 Closed Sun. D & Mon. in winter, & 1 week late Dec.
🅰 AE, DC, MC, V

LIMOGES 87000

🍴 **LES PETITS VENTRES**
$/$$
20 RUE DE LA BOUCHERIE
TEL 05 55 34 22 90
A 15th-century house with Old World charm and a terrace where you dine on the region's traditional cuisine. Try *tête de veau* (calf's head) or the *pot au feu*.
🕒 Closed Sun. D & all Mon. May 1–15 & Sept. 10–25
🅰 AE, MC, V

MARGAUX 33460

🏨 **LE PAVILLON DE MARGAUX**
$$
TEL 05 57 88 77 54
FAX 05 57 88 77 73
Built in typical 19th-century local style, this hotel has panache and a terrace where you can dine surrounded by the celebrated vineyards.
ℹ 14 🅿 🕒 Closed Dec. 15–Jan. 15 🅰 AE, MC, V

🍴 **AUBERGE DE SAVOIE**
$
TEL 05 57 88 31 76
A good value restaurant in this wine town, specializing in regional dishes such as a quiche of *foie de canard et jus de truffe*.
🕒 Closed Mon. D in winter, Sun., public hols., & Feb. school vacation, Nov. 6–13
🅰 V

PAUILLAC 33250

🏨 **CHÂTEAU COR-**
🍴 **DEILLAN BAGES**
$$$$ 😊😊😊😊
ROUTE DES CHÂTEAUX
TEL 05 56 59 24 24
FAX 05 56 59 01 89
An English country house-style

hotel situated in the heart of the Médoc with a Michelin one-star restaurant. Home of the "École de Bordeaux," which arranges wine courses and visits to the châteaux.
🛈 25 🅿 🕒 Closed early Dec.–early Feb. 🕼 All major cards

POITIERS 86360

🏨 NOVOTEL FUTUROSCOPE
$$ 😊😊😊
PORTES DU PARC
TEL 05 49 49 91 91
FAX 05 49 49 91 90
Modern hotel convenient to the popular Futuroscope visual technology park.
🛈 110 + 18 studios 🅿 🚫 🎕 🕼 All major cards

ST.-ÉTIENNE-DE-BAÏGORRY 66430

🏨 ARCÉ
$$ 😊😊😊
TEL 05 59 37 40 14
FAX 05 59 37 40 27
This mountain-village hotel has been in the same family for over a hundred years. A veranda sits out over the river, and some rooms have their own balconies. Beamed sitting room, library, and dining room with picture windows. Tennis.
🛈 23 🕒 Closed mid-Nov.–mid-March 🕼 MC, V

ST.-JEAN-DE-LUZ 64500

🏨 PARC VICTORIA
$$$$ 😊😊😊😊
5 RUE CÉPÉ
TEL 05 59 26 78 78
FAX 05 59 26 78 08
A 19th-century villa with a formal park and gardens. Luxuriously appointed rooms have marble bathrooms, and some balconies.
🛈 8 + 4 suites 🅿
🕒 Closed mid-Nov.–mid-March 🕼 All major cards

🍴 CHEZ MATTIN
$$
63 RUE BAIGNOL
TEL 05 59 47 19 52
Rustic decor, Basque specialties, and a warm family welcome. Sample the stuffed peppers or Basque gâteau.
🕒 Closed Mon. & Nov.–Feb. 🕼 AE, MC, V.

ST.-JEAN-PIED-DE-PORT 64220

🏨 LES PYRÉNÉES
$$$$ 😊😊😊😊
19 PLACE DU GÉNÉRAL DE GAULLE
TEL 05 59 37 01 01
An excellent hotel with a terrace. The restaurant (Michelin two stars) is well known for the quality of its Basque/Gascon cuisine. Excellent fish dishes include langoustine and they do a fine gazpacho.
🛈 20 🅿 🕒 Restaurant closed Mon. D Nov.–April, Tues. Oct.–June, 3 weeks Jan., & late Nov.–late Dec. 🍽
🏊 🕼 AE, MC, V

THE DORDOGNE & MIDI-PYRÉNÉES

ALBI 81000

🏨 HOSTELLERIE ST.-ANTOINE
$$/$$$ 😊😊😊😊
17 RUE ST.-ANTOINE
TEL 05 63 54 04 04
FAX 05 63 47 10 47
Charming 18th-century inn owned by the same family for five generations. Most rooms look out onto the garden.
🛈 44 🅿 🚫 🎕 🕼 All major cards

🍴 LE JARDIN DES QUATRE SAISONS
$$
19 BOULEVARD DE STRASBOURG
TEL 05 63 60 77 76
A restaurant of exceptional quality and good value. Try the terrine of escargots with

pig's feet and truffles, or the roast pigeon with charlotte of mushroom and rosemary.
🕒 Closed Mon. & Sun. D
🕼 AE, MC, V

AUCH 32000

🍴 FRANCE
$$$/$$$$
2 PLACE DE LA LIBÉRATION
TEL 05 62 61 71 71
Try the best of Gascon cooking in this hotel-restaurant, prepared by chef André Daguin, known for his promotion of the region's cuisine and its key elements of duck, goose, garlic, and wine.
🛈 31 🕒 Closed Jan. 2–14
🕼 All major cards

BERGERAC 24100

🍴 LE CYRANO
$$
2 BOULEVARD MONTAIGNE
TEL 05 53 57 02 76
Good value restaurant for the classic cuisine of Périgord accompanied by delicious Bergerac wines.
🕒 Closed Sun. D, & Wed. Sept. 15–June 15 🕼 All major cards

BRANTÔME 24310

🏨 DOMAINE DE LA ROSERAIE
$$ 😊😊😊
ROUTE D'ANGOULÊME
TEL 05 53 05 84 74
FAX 05 53 05 77 94
Renovated 17th-century hotel just outside Brantôme, located on nine acres of quiet parkland. Breakfast in the rose garden in summer; sit by the open fire in winter.
🛈 7 & 1 suite 🕒 Closed mid-Jan.–mid-March 🏊 🕼 All major cards

🍴 LE MOULIN DE L'ABBAYE
$$$
1 ROUTE DE BOURDEILLES
TEL 05 53 05 80 22
Dine on the terrace of this lovely old mill, once the house

of the Abbé Pierre de Bourdeilles and now a one-star Michelin restaurant. Watch the Dronne River roll by, and enjoy the excellent cuisine; pigeon with ceps, *foie gras de canard*, crème brûlée with strawberries.
🕒 Closed Nov.–April, & L except weekends & public hols., Mon. L July & Aug.
🖎 All major cards

LE BUISSON-DE-CADOUIN 24480

🏨 **MANOIR DE BELLERIVE**
$$/$$$ ✪✪✪
ROUTE DE SIORAC
TEL 05 53 22 16 16
FAX 05 53 22 09 05
Sample the *grande vie d'autrefois* (high life of past times) at this fine manor house dating from the time of Napoleon III and set on mature parkland. Breakfast on the terrace overlooking the river. Tennis and sauna.
ⓘ 24 🅿 🕒 Closed Jan. 3–end Feb. 🖎 🖎 All major cards

CAHORS 46000

🍴 **CLAUDE MARCO**
$$/$$$
LAMAGDELAINE (4 MILES/6 KM E OF CAHORS VIA D653) 46090
TEL 05 65 35 30 64
An old *bergerie* where you can eat inside beneath the vaulted ceiling or out on the terrace. Specialties at this one-star Michelin restaurant include *pot au feu* with duck or *filet de boeuf* with morel mushrooms.
🕒 Closed Sun. D, Mon. in winter, early Jan.–early March, & 10 days Oct. 🖎 AE, MC, V

CORDES 81170

🍴 **HOSTELLERIE DU VIEUX CORDES**
$$
RUE ST.-MICHEL
TEL 05 63 53 79 20
Sit on the terrace in the

shade of an ancient wisteria at this hotel-restaurant. Try authentic cassoulet or delicious fish dishes.
🕒 Closed Sun. D, Mon. in winter, & Jan. & Feb. 🖎 All major cards

CUQ-TOULZA 81470

🏨 **CUQ-LE-CHÂTEAU**
$$/$$$
TEL 05 63 82 54 00
FAX 05 63 82 54 11
In a hilltop hamlet just outside Cuq-Toulza, this former presbytery is charmingly decorated and has several terraces. Meals by reservation only.
ⓘ 8 🅿 🕒 Closed early Jan.–Feb. 🖎 🖎 D, MC, V

DOMME 24250

🏨 **DE L'ESPLANADE**
$$ ✪✪✪
TEL 05 53 28 31 41
FAX 05 53 28 49 92
Quiet hotel within the fortifications of this historic *bastide* town, with a terrace and lovely views over the Dordogne Valley. The Michelin one-star restaurant makes good use of local produce, particularly truffles.
ⓘ 25 🕒 Closed early Nov.–mid-Feb. Restaurant closed Mon. except D in season 🖎 All major cards

FIGEAC 46100

🍴 **LE DÎNÉE DU VIGUIER**
$$$
4 RUE BOUTARIC
TEL 05 65 50 08 08
Le Dinée is the restaurant of the hotel Viguier du Roy, a château spanning the 12th to 18th centuries. Try gigot of monkfish spiked with truffles, the Quercy tart with morels, or the warm shrimp omelette.
🕒 Closed Mon., also Sun. D in winter 🖎 All major cards

GRAMAT 46500

🏨 **CHÂTEAU DE ROUMÉGOUSE**
$$/$$$
ROUTE DE BRIVE
TEL 05 65 33 63 81
FAX 05 65 33 71 18
This romantic 19th-century château with its wooded parkland was a favorite with Général de Gaulle. The rooms are charming and there is even one in the tower. On fine evenings dine on the terrace with river views.
ⓘ 16 🕒 Closed Nov.–April & Dec. 20–31 🖎 🖎 All major cards

LES EYZIES-DE-TAYAC 24620

🏨 **CRO-MAGNON**
$/$$ ✪✪✪
TEL 05 53 06 97 06
FAX 05 53 06 95 45
This old family *relais* occupies a charming building in the village center. Dine on the terrace or in the garden.
ⓘ 22 🕒 Closed Wed. L, early Oct.–early May 🖎 All major cards

🍴 **LES GLYCINES**
$$
ROUTE DE PÉRIGUEUX
TEL 05 53 06 97 07
A little auberge among greenery with a rustic interior and a terrace beside the river. Rooms available.
🕒 Closed Sat. D (except hols. & July–Sept.) & mid-Oct.–mid-March 🖎 AE, MC, V

MONBAZILLAC 24240

🍴 **CHÂTEAU DE MONBAZILLAC**
$$$
TEL 05 53 58 38 93
Sample the exquisite sweet wine of Monbazillac in this beautiful château in the middle of the vineyard, best of all as part of a meal in its excellent restaurant.
🕒 Closed Sun. D, Mon., Feb., & Nov. 🖎 AE, MC, V

PÉRIGUEUX 24000

🍴 HERCULE POIROT
$$
2 RUE DE LA NATION
TEL 05 53 08 90 76
Dine on the best of Périgord cuisine beneath the low vaulted ceiling of this fine Renaissance building.
🗝 All major cards

PUYMIROL 47270

🏨 LES LOGES DE
🍴 L'AUBERGADE
$$$$ ✪✪✪✪
52 RUE ROYALE
TEL 05 53 95 31 46
FAX 05 53 95 33 80
In the center of a fortified town, this 13th-century residence once belonged to the counts of Toulouse. The owner-chef, M. Trama, serves excellent cuisine that has won him two Michelin stars, and also offers a huge selection of cigars. Terraced garden and rooms have Jacuzzis or massage showers.
🛏 11 🅿 🌡 🕐 Closed Mon. in winter & Feb. school vacations. Restaurant closed Sun. out of season 🗝 All major cards

ROCAMADOUR 46500

🏨 LES VIEILLES TOURS
🍴 $ ✪✪
ROUTE DE PAYRAC (2 MILES/4 KM WEST OF ROCAMADOUR)
TEL 05 65 33 68 01
FAX 05 65 33 68 59
This partly 13th-century manor house makes a comfortable hotel. Good restaurant, too.
🛏 17 🕐 Closed mid-Nov.– April 🌡 🗝 AE, MC, V

🍴 SAINTE-MARIE
$$
PLACE DE SENHALS
TEL 05 65 33 63 07
Rustic restaurant with a terrace where you can dine on excellent local cuisine.
🕐 Closed mid-Oct.–Easter 🗝 MC, V

ST.-CÉRÉ 46400

🍴 RIC
$$$
ROUTE DE LEYME
TEL 05 65 38 04 08
FAX 05 65 38 00 14
A small restaurant with a summer terrace, serving regional cuisine. Some rooms.
🛏 5 🕐 Closed Dec.–March 🌡 🗝 MC, V

ST.-CIRQ-LAPOPIE 46330

🏨 LA PELISSARIA
$$ ✪✪✪
LE BOURG
TEL 05 65 31 25 14
This popular hotel in a 13th-century building is perched on the edge of a hill village. Wonderful views.
🛏 8 & 2 suites 🕐 Closed mid-Nov.–early April 🌡 🗝 MC, V

🍴 AUBERGE DU SOMBRAIL
$$
TEL 05 65 31 26 08
A peaceful old house in the heart of this picturesque, medieval village where you can eat indoors or on the terrace. The regional cuisine includes local Quercy lamb.
🕐 Closed Tues. D, Wed. mid-Oct.–June, & mid-Nov.–end March 🗝 MC, V

ST.-CYPRIEN-EN-PÉRIGORD 24220

🏨 L'ABBAYE
$$ ✪✪✪
RUE DE L'ABBAYE
TEL 05 53 29 20 48
FAX 05 53 29 15 85
An extended 18th-century family mansion with views of hills and the medieval town. Dine in the original kitchen with its stone walls and fireplace or in the garden.
🛏 23 🕐 Closed mid-Oct.–mid-April 🗝 AE, MC, V

🏨 LA GRANDE MARQUE
$ ✪✪
MARNAC ST. CYPRIEN
TEL 05 53 31 61 63
FAX 05 53 28 39 55
This 18th-century house on a hill with remarkable country views has rooms in the renovated former tobacco drying sheds. Dine on the shady terrace.
🛏 5 🍴 Table d'hote meals available 🅿 🕐 Closed Nov.–Easter 🗝 No credit cards

SARLAT-LA-CANÉDA 24200

🍴 LA MADELEINE
$$
1 PLACE DE LA PETITE RIGAUDIE
TEL 05 53 59 10 41
A hotel-restaurant in Sarlat, the center of Périgord cuisine, which offers all the regional delicacies: goose, duck, ceps, truffles, and foie gras.
🕐 Restaurant closed mid-Nov.–mid March 🗝 AE, MC, V

SOUILLAC 46200

🏨 CHÂTEAU DE LA TREYNE
$$$/$$$$ ✪✪✪✪
LA TREYNE
TEL 05 65 27 60 60
FAX 05 65 27 60 70
A charming white château surrounded by parkland above the Dordogne River, southeast of Souillac. Tennis and canoeing.
🛏 14 + 2 suites 🅿
🕐 Closed mid-Nov.–Easter
🌡 🗝 MC, V

🍴 LA VIEILLE AUBERGE
$$/$$$
1 RUE DE LA RECÈGE
TEL 05 65 32 79 43
Old auberge beside a tributary of the Dordogne River, decorated in Louis XV style. Generous cooking includes local delicacies, such as artichokes stuffed with foie gras, and truffles. Some rooms.

HOTELS & RESTAURANTS

🕒 Closed Sun. D & Mon. Jan.–March & Nov. 15–Dec. 20 🐾 All major cards

TOULOUSE 31000

🏨 BEAUX-ARTS
$$$ ✪✪✪
1 PLACE DU PONT NEUF
TEL 05 34 45 42 42
FAX 05 34 45 42 43
This 18th-century building beside the river has been a hotel for 100 years. No restaurant, but beneath the hotel is the lively Brasserie des Beaux-Arts.
🛏 19 🔲 🔲 🐾 All major cards

🏨 GRAND HÔTEL
🍽 DE L'OPÉRA
$$/$$$ ✪✪✪✪
1 PLACE DU CAPITOLE
TEL 05 61 21 82 66
FAX 05 61 23 41 04
Centrally located, the hotel is in a courtyard hidden behind its two well-known restaurants. The Michelin two-star Les Jardins de l'Opéra has seasonal specialties on its inventive menus. The Grand Café de l'Opéra serves light meals.
🛏 45 + 5 suites 🔲 rooms 🔲 🐾 All major cards

🍽 JONQUE DU YANG TSÉ
$$$
BOULEVARD GRIFFOUL-DORVAL, 31400
TEL 05 61 20 74 74
Excellent and original Szechuan Chinese cooking in a converted barge on the Canal du Midi.
🕒 Closed Mon. L 🐾 All major cards

🍽 LE CANTOU
$$
98 RUE VELASQUEZ, 31300
TEL 05 61 49 20 21
A pretty restaurant where you can sample the best of regional cuisine, for example *fricassée* of langoustines and scallops, or *civet de canard* with calf's foot.
🕒 Closed Sat. & Sun, &

Aug. 10–17, Jan. 1–7 🐾 All major cards

🍽 FRÉGARE
$$$
1 RUE D'AUSTERLITZ
TEL 05 61 21 62 45
Toulouse institution overlooking Place Wilson, serving well thought out classics like cassoulet and duck.
🐾 All major cards

TRÉMOLAT 24510

🏨 LE VIEUX LOGIS
🍽 $$$/$$$$ ✪✪✪
TEL 05 53 22 80 06
FAX 05 53 22 84 89
This village hotel with its charming mix of buildings has been in the same family for 400 years. The Michelin one-star restaurant is run by the highly regarded chef Pierre-Jean Duribreux. Some of the rooms have four-poster beds and the galleried dining room looks out onto the pretty garden.
🛏 18 🅿 🔲 🐾 All major cards

THE PYRENEES

AX-LES-THERMES 09110

🍽 LE GRILLON
$$
RUE ST.-UDAUT
TEL 05 61 64 31 64
A hotel-restaurant up in the mountains offering a terrace with wonderful views. The duck *magret* with honey is recommended.
🕒 Closed Tues. D, Wed. (except vacations) 🐾 MC, V

FOIX 09000

🏨 LONS
$ ✪✪✪
6 PLACE GEORGES-DUTHIL
TEL 05 61 65 52 44
FAX 05 61 02 68 18
Situated next to the Ariège River, this friendly hotel has a terrace, a brasserie, and a

---

PRICES

HOTELS
An indication of the cost of a double room without breakfast is given by $ signs.
$$$$$ over $280
$$$$ $200–$280
$$$ $120–$200
$$ $80–$120
$ under $80

RESTAURANTS
An indication of the cost of a three-course dinner without drinks is given by $ signs.
$$$$$ over $80
$$$$ $50–$80
$$$ $35–$50
$$ $20–$35
$ under $20

restaurant.
🛏 40 🕒 Closed late Dec.–mid-Jan. 🐾 All major cards

GAVARNIE 65120

🏨 LA BRÈCHE
DE ROLAND
$ ✪✪
GÈDRE
TEL 05 62 92 48 54
FAX 05 62 92 46 05
An old mountain mansion, in a village 5 miles (8 km) N of Gavarnie on the D921. The hotel has a garden and a terrace where you can dine. The owner can arrange sporting trips into the mountains and helicopter rides.
🛏 28 🕒 Closed Oct.–Dec. & April 15–30 🐾 MC, V

LIMOUX 11300

🍽 MAISON DE LA
BLANQUETTE
$
46 BIS PROMENADE DU TIVOLI
TEL 04 68 31 01 63
A town restaurant with rustic decor and a very good wine selection, including, of course, sparkling Limoux *champenoise*.
🕒 Closed Wed. D mid-Sept.–mid-June 🐾 MC, V

MIREPOIX 09500

🏨 LA MAISON DES CONSULS
$$ 🌑🌑🌑
6 PLACE DU MARÉCHAL
LECLERC
TEL 05 61 68 81 81
FAX 05 61 68 81 15
In the central square of a
bastide town, this renovated
14th-century house has
spacious, historically themed
rooms overlooking the
medieval streets and passages.
No restaurant.
🛏 8 🔳 MC, V

PAU 64000

🏨 GRAND HÔTEL DU COMMERCE
$ 🌑🌑
9 RUE MARÉCHAL JOFFRE
TEL 05 59 27 24 40
FAX 05 59 83 81 74
A traditional hotel in the
town center close to the
château, with a good value
restaurant.
🛏 51 🔳 All major cards

🍴 CHEZ PIERRE
$$$
16 RUE LOUIS-BARTHOU
TEL 05 59 27 76 86
An elegantly decorated town
house restaurant. Try the
langoustine ravioli with
madras curry or veal with
morel mushrooms.
🕐 Closed Sat. L, Sun. (except
public hols.), 1 week early
Jan. 🔳 All major cards

🍴 LE TRESPOEY
$$/$$$
HÔTEL CORONA, 71 AVENUE
DU GÉNÉRAL LECLERC
TEL 05 59 30 64 77
A warm and welcoming
restaurant with modern decor
and several dining rooms;
specialties include baked
pigeon breast and gratin of
lobster. The proprietor pays
particular attention to the
wine list.
🕐 Closed Fri. D, Sat., & Aug.
🔳 AE, MC, V

ST.-BERTRAND-DE-COMMINGES 31510

🏨 L'OPPIDUM
$ 🌑🌑
RUE DE LA POSTE
TEL 05 61 88 33 50
FAX 05 61 95 94 05
Small hotel in the heart of the
medieval village, and walking
distance to the cathedral.
🛏 15 🕐 Closed Wed.
(except school vacations),
& mid-Nov.–mid-Dec.
🔳 AE, MC, V

🍴 LUGDUNUM
$$
VALCABRÈRE
TEL 05 61 94 52 05
Reservations are essential for
this unique and historic
culinary experience. Sample
recipes compiled by Apicius, a
first-century Roman gastro-
nome. Nothing too outlandish
but dishes such as young boar
or partridge served with
authentically spiced wines.
🕐 Closed Fri. & Sat. D &
Sun. L in winter, Sun. D in
season 🔳 MC, V

ST.-GIRONS 09200

🏨 EYCHENNE
🍴 **$$$ 🌑🌑**
8 AVENUE PAUL-LAFFONT
TEL 05 61 04 04 50
A beautiful old family-run
hostelry with a friendly
atmosphere. Well-equipped
bedrooms and a lovely
garden. The restaurant serves
traditional southwestern local
cuisine: Try monkfish with
saffron or the *confit de canard*
with ceps.
🛏 41 🕐 Closed Sun. D,
Mon. (Nov.–March except
public hols.), & late Dec.–end
Jan. 🔳 All major cards

SAUVETERRE-DE-BÉARN 64390

🏨 DU VIEUX PONT
$ 🌑🌑
RUE DU PONT DE LA
LÉGENDE
TEL 05 59 38 95 11

FAX 05 59 38 99 10
This picturesque hotel is built
on medieval arches above
the river beside a ruined
bridge. A terrace overlooks
the river and some rooms
have balconies. Access is by a
very steep and narrow road.
Fishing.
🛏 6 & 2 suites 🕐 Closed
mid-Dec.–mid-Jan. 🔳 MC, V

ANTIBES 06600

🍴 LE MARQUIS
$$$
4 RUE SADE
TEL 04 93 34 23 00
Quiet little restaurant in the
old town with solicitous
service and elegant cooking;
dishes include foie gras ravioli
with morel mushroom sauce
and lobster with olive butter.
🕐 Closed Mon. & Tues. L &
Nov. 1–11 & Jan. 5–15 🔳 All
major cards

At Cap d'Antibes
🏨 DU CAP-EDEN ROC
$$$$$ 🌑🌑🌑🌑
BOULEVARD KENNEDY, 06160
TEL 04 93 61 39 01
FAX 04 93 67 76 04
Favored by Cannes film stars,
this is the last word in luxury,
especially the 1930s terrace
and the pool hewn out of the
rocks where Zelda Fitzgerald
used to swim. Tennis.
🛏 121 + 9 suites 🅿
🕐 Closed Nov.–April
🚭 Rooms 🏊 🏋 🔳 AE,
MC, V

BEAULIEU-SUR-MER 06310

🏨 LA RÉSERVE
🍴 DE BEAULIEU
$$$$$ 🌑🌑🌑🌑
5 BOULEVARD DU MARÉCHAL
LECLERC
TEL 04 93 01 00 01
FAX 04 93 01 28 99
Fabulous Riviera hotel on the

seafront, founded by the famous James Gordon Bennett, proprietor of the *New York Herald Tribune*. It's called La Réserve for the seawater tank (*réserve*) the chef used to keep fish alive in. The restaurant, which has one Michelin star, still specializes in fish.

[i] 33 [P] [Closed] Closed Nov.–Dec. 22 & Jan. 21– March 3 [S] rooms [≈] [S] All major cards

BIOT 06410

[ff] LES TERRAILLERS
$$$/$$$$
11 ROUTE DU CHEMIN-NEUF
TEL 04 93 65 01 59
Large farmhouse restaurant south of Biot, with imaginative cuisine that has gained it one Michelin star. Try baby rabbit with *fines herbes*, foie gras ravioli with *fumet de morilles*, or monkfish with thyme butter.
[Closed] Closed Thurs. L July & Aug., & all Wed. [S] [S] AE, MC, V

CAGNES: HAUTE-DE-CAGNES 06800

[ff] JOSY-JO
$$$
4 PLACE PLANASTEL
TEL 04 93 20 68 76
Bistro in the old town with rustic decor and a huge fireplace. Superb ingredients simply cooked such as peppers marinated in olive oil, and *petits farcis* (stuffed vegetables).
[Closed] Closed Sat. L, all Sun. & 2 weeks early Aug. [S] [S] AE, MC, V

CANNES 06400

[h] CARLTON INTER-CONTINENTAL
$$$$$ ✪✪✪✪
58 LA CROISETTE
TEL 04 93 06 40 06
FAX 04 93 06 40 25
Luxury hotel with private beach, and a terrace where

film moguls do deals during the Cannes festival.
[i] 295 + 18 suites [P] [S] [≈] [S] [S] All major cards

[ff] LA SCALA
$$$
HÔTEL NOGA HILTON, 50 BOULEVARD DE LA CROISETTE
TEL 04 92 99 70 93
A fashionable restaurant with a terrace overlooking the Mediterranean, serving a gourmet Italian menu. Specialties include risotto with artichokes and foie gras, and pigeon with cep ravioli.
[S] All major cards

[ff] LA MÈRE BESSON
$$/$$$
13 RUE DES FRÈRES PRADIGNAC
TEL 04 93 39 59 24
A Cannes institution, this popular, modest little bistro serves a different fish dish every day.
[Closed] Closed Sat. Sun., & Mon. L [S] [S] All major cards

ÎLE DE PORQUEROLLES 83400

[h] [ff] LE MAS DU LANGOUSTIER
$$$$ ✪✪✪
CHEMIN DU LANGOUSTIER
TEL 04 94 58 30 09
FAX 04 94 58 36 02
Luxury island hotel on a rocky position overlooking the sea, with a one Michelin-star restaurant. Meals served in the garden. *Demi-pension* only. Tennis.
[i] 44 + 5 suites [Closed] Closed Oct.–May [S] All major cards

JUAN-LES-PINS 06160

[h] DES MIMOSAS
$$ ✪✪✪
RUE PAULINE
TEL 04 93 61 04 16
FAX 04 92 93 06 46
Quiet, 19th-century house with large modern rooms, many with balconies, and a shady garden. No restaurant.

[i] 34 [Closed] Closed Oct.–late April [≈] [S] AE, MC, V

MENTON 06500

[ff] LA VÉRANDA
$$$
LES AMBASSADEURS
3 RUE PARTOUNEAUX
TEL 04 93 28 75 75
The garden theme of the decor here is a reference to the nearby Jardin Val Rameh and is followed through in the cooking, with sauces based on flowers.
[Closed] Closed Sun. & Jan. 15–Feb. 15 [S] All major cards

MONACO: MONTE-CARLO 98000

[h] HERMITAGE
$$$$$ ✪✪✪✪
SQUARE BEAUMARCHAIS
TEL 377 92 16 40 00
FAX 377 92 16 38 52
A luxurious belle epoque palace with a huge, glass-domed winter garden, opulent restaurant and terrace of cool marble. Private swimming.
[i] 209 + 18 suites [P] [S] [S] All major cards

[ff] LOUIS XV
$$$$$
HÔTEL PARIS, PLACE DU CASINO
TEL 377 92 16 30 01
Monaco's most famous and expensive restaurant, a three-star Michelin establishment presided over by the celebrated Alain Ducasse. If you need to look at the prices, don't go. Typical dishes might be Provençal vegetables with black truffles, or pigeon with *foie gras de canard*.
[Closed] Closed Tues., Wed. (except D mid-July–late Aug.), 2 weeks Feb., & Dec. [S] All major cards

MOUGINS 06250

[ff] LE MOULIN DE MOUGINS
$$$$
AVENUE NOTRE-DAME-DE-VIE

TEL 04 93 75 78 24

This Michelin one-star restaurant in a 16th-century olive oil mill is run by Roger Vergé, the chef celebrated for his *cuisine du soleil* (cuisine of the sun)—a sophisticated twist on traditional Provençal food. Think of courgette flowers stuffed with truffles, or lavender blossom beignets.
🕐 Closed Mon. & late Jan.–early March 🚫 All major cards

NICE 06000

🏨 NÉGRESCO

The most famous and expensive hotel in Nice. This magnificent belle epoque building on the Promenade des Anglais has sumptuous furnishings and impeccable service. As grand as it gets—look for the vast Baccarat chandelier.
$$$$/$$$$$ ◊◊◊◊
37 PROMENADE DES ANGLAIS, 06300
TEL 04 93 16 64 00
FAX 04 93 88 35 68
🛏 134 & 18 suites 🚫
🚫 All major cards

🏨 BEAU RIVAGE
$$$/$$$$ ◊◊◊◊
24 RUE ST.-FRANÇOIS-DE-PAULE, 06300
TEL 04 93 80 80 70
FAX 04 93 80 55 77
Ideally located on the edge of the old town and with views over the sea, this large hotel has its own private beach club. It was here that Matisse stayed on his first few visits to Nice. (Ask for a room overlooking the sea.)
🛏 118 🚫 🚫 🚫 All major cards

🏨 LA PÉROUSE
$$/$$$$ ◊◊◊◊
11 QUAI RAUBA-CAPÉU
TEL 04 93 62 34 63

FAX 04 93 62 59 41
For a sea view that won't break the bank: flowery terrace and garden restaurant.
🛏 64 🚫 rooms 🏊 🚫 All major cards

🍴 LE GRAND PAVOIS
$$$
11 RUE MEYERBEER
TEL 04 93 88 77 42
One of the best fish restaurants in Nice. The art deco interior is an elegant backdrop for local dishes such as lobster *grillé et flambé* and an excellent bouillabaisse.
🚫 🚫 MC, V

🍴 LA MÉRENDA
$$$
4 RUE TERRACE 06300
Tiny bistro, famous for its traditional Niçois dishes: stockfish, beignets, stuffed sardines, beef daube. No phone and no booking. Get there early to reserve a table.
🕐 Closed Sat. & Sun., 1 week April, late July–mid-Aug., Christmas, & Feb. school vacation 🚫 🚫 No credit cards

🍴 LE COMPTOIR
$$
20 RUE ST.-FRANÇOIS-DE-PAULE, 06300
TEL 04 93 92 08 80
A 1930s-style bar/restaurant, particularly good for late night dining or for a light meal after the opera.
🕐 Closed Sun. 🚫 AE, MC, V

🍴 LE SAFARI
$$
1 COURS SALEYA
TEL 04 93 80 18 44
Big café with Mediterranean blue shutters, close to the market on Cours Saleya. Great for alfresco dining. Try the deep rich *calamari* (squid) daube, or *bagna cauda*, a hot anchovy dip with raw vegetables.
🚫 All major cards

ST.-JEAN-CAP-FERRAT 06230

🏨 GRAND HÔTEL DU
🍴 CAP FERRAT
$$$$$ ◊◊◊◊
BOULEVARD DU GÉNÉRAL DE GAULLE
TEL 04 93 76 50 50
FAX 04 93 76 04 52
One of the Riviera's legendary grand hotels, secluded in its own tropical gardens overlooking the sea, with a private funicular down to a terrace and the seawater pool. Magnificent interior furnishings and a Michelin one-star restaurant. Tennis.
🛏 44 + 9 suites 🅿
🕐 Closed Jan. 3–March 1
🚫 🚫 All major cards

ST.-PAUL-DE-VENCE 06570

🏨 COLOMBE
🍴 D'OR

Dine on the terrace at this celebrity-haunted hotel-restaurant amid a priceless collection of art donated as payment for meals and rooms by Picasso, Calder, Braque, and more. Try the serving of 15 hors d'oeuvres and the soufflés. Reserve rooms in advance.
$$$/$$$$ ◊◊◊
PLACE DES ORMEAUX-PLACE DE GAULLE
TEL 04 93 32 80 02
🛏 16 + 10 suites
🕐 Closed Nov.–late Dec.
🚫 All major cards

🏨 LE ST.-PAUL
$$$/$$$$ ◊◊◊◊
86 RUE GRANDE
TEL 04 93 32 65 25
FAX 04 93 32 52 94
Secluded, exquisitely furnished 16th-century town house, within the village walls.
🛏 15 + 3 suites 🚫 🚫 All major cards

HOTELS & RESTAURANTS

ST.-TROPEZ 83990

🏨 LE BYBLOS
🍴 $$$$$ ✪✪✪✪
AVENUE PAUL-SIGNAC
TEL 04 94 56 68 00
FAX 04 94 56 68 01
The famous hotel where
Mick Jagger married Bianca;
designed like a village with
sumptuous Moroccan decor,
a chic nightclub, and an
excellent restaurant, Les
Arcades.
🛏 86 + 11 suites 🅿
🕐 Closed mid-Oct.–April
🅂 ⛱ 🅂 All major cards

🏨 LE YACA
$$$$/$$$$$ ✪✪✪✪
1 BOULEVARD D'AUMALE
TEL 04 94 55 81 00
FAX 04 94 97 58 50
Old Provençal house in the
town center, built around a
swimming pool and garden.
🛏 27 🕐 Closed Jan. & Feb.
🅂 ⛱ 🅂 All major cards

🏨 LA PONCHE
$$$$ ✪✪✪✪
PLACE RÉVELIN
TEL 04 94 97 02 53
FAX 04 94 97 78 61
Charming ensemble of
former fishermen's cottages
behind the port, with stylish,
surprisingly large bedrooms.
🛏 13 & 5 suites 🕐 Closed
Nov.–late March 🅂 🅂 AE,
MC, V

🍴 L'ÉCHALOTTE
$$
35 RUE ALLARD
TEL 04 94 54 83 26
One of St.-Tropez's most
fashionable restaurants; try
Provençal specialties like
stuffed courgettes, or the
steak with shallots.
🕐 Closed Thurs. Oct.
15–Easter & Thurs. L end of
season 🅂 AE, MC, V

🍴 CAFÉ SÉNÉQUIER
$$
QUAI JEAN-JAURÈS
TEL 04 94 97 00 30
Favorite café on the port;
pricey but good for evening
aperitifs and watching celeb-
rities on yachts drink theirs.
🅂 No credit cards

PROVENCE

AIX-EN-PROVENCE
13100

🏨 PIGONNET
$$$/$$$$ ✪✪✪✪
5 AVENUE DU PIGONNET
TEL 04 42 59 02 90
FAX 04 42 59 47 77
Provençal country house in
its own park, charmingly
embellished in the 1920s.
🛏 52 🅿 🅂 ⛱ 🅂 All
major cards

🍴 LES DEUX GARÇONS
$
COURS MIRABEAU
TEL 04 42 26 00 51
Classic terrace café on the
Cours Mirabeau, a favorite
with artists and intellectuals
since the 18th century.
🅂 MC, V

APT 84400

🍴 AUBERGE DU
LUBÉRON
$$/$$$$
17 QUAI LÉON SAGY
TEL 04 90 74 12 50
Typical Provençal food in a
peaceful atmosphere, with a
terrace and garden. Duck foie
gras with fruit *confits*; Lubéron
lamb with *aubergine confits*.
Reservation essential.
🕐 Closed Sun. D in winter,
Mon. (except D in season),
& Dec. 23–Jan. 15 🅂 All
major cards

ARLES 13200

🏨 GRAND HÔTEL
NORD PINUS
$$$/$$$$$ ✪✪✪✪
14 PLACE DU FORUM
TEL 04 90 93 44 44
FAX 04 90 93 34 00
Although brought up-to-date,
this luxury hotel has kept its
individuality, with traditional
Provençal furniture and bulls'
heads mounted on the walls.
Very popular with bullfighters
at festival time.
🛏 25 🅿 🅂 rooms
🅂 All major cards

🏨 LE MAS DE PEINT
$$$$ ✪✪✪✪
LE SAMBUC
TEL 04 90 97 20 62
FAX 04 90 97 22 20
Converted stables attached to
an old Camargue farmhouse.
Exquisitely designed rooms
have wooden ceilings, white
linen furnishings, and antiques.
Cooking with homegrown
vegetables adds to the charm.
🛏 8 + 2 suites 🅿
🕐 Closed early Jan.–March
🅂 🅂 All major cards

🍴 CAFÉ LA NUIT
$
PLACE DU FORUM
TEL 04 90 96 44 56
Favorite local café, decorated
to look as it was in van Gogh's
painting "Café du Soir."
🅂 AE, MC, V

AVIGNON 84000

🏨 L'EUROPE
🍴 $$/$$$$$ ✪✪✪✪
12 PLACE CRILLON
TEL 04 90 14 76 76
FAX 04 90 14 76 71
Avignon's top hotel—even
Napoleon stayed here. The
grand entrance to this 16th-
century mansion leads on to
the peaceful terrace with a
fountain, and the elegant salon
is hung with tapestries. The
Michelin one-star restaurant,
La Vieille Fontaine, lives up to
the splendor of the establishment. Try courgette flowers
stuffed with artichoke or roast
sea bream with tomato tart.
🛏 44 + 3 suites 🅿
🕐 Restaurant closed Mon. L
& all Sun. & 2 weeks in Aug.
🅂 🅂 All major cards

🏨 DE LA MIRANDE
🍴 $$$$$ ✪✪✪✪
4 PLACE AMIRANDE
TEL 04 90 85 93 93
FAX 04 90 86 26 85
An 18th-century hotel close

to the Palais des Papes, with luxurious rooms and tasteful furnishings. The Michelin one-star restaurant offers Proven-çal specialties such as flavorsome Lubéron lamb.

🛈 19 🅿 🚭 🗷 All major cards

🍴 LE GRANGOUSIER
$$/$$$$
17 RUE GALANTE
TEL 04 90 82 96 60
A glassed-in courtyard is the setting for imaginatively prepared local produce: celery ravioli with shrimp and langoustines; lobster tart with beans and pistou.
🕒 Closed Mon. L (except July), all Sun., & 2 weeks Aug.
🗷 AE, MC, V

BONNIEUX 84800

🏨 HOSTELLERIE DU PRIEURÉ
$$ ✪✪✪
RUE JEAN-BAPTISTE AURARD
TEL 04 90 75 80 78
FAX 04 90 75 96 00
Tastefully renovated 18th century priory in traditional Provençal style.
🛈 10 🅿 🕒 Closed
Nov.–March 🗷 MC, V

CHÂTEAUNEUF-DU-PAPE 84230

🏨 LA SOMMELLERIE
$ ✪✪✪
ROUTE DE ROQUEMAURE
TEL 04 90 83 50 00
FAX 04 90 83 51 85
Charming 17th-century bergerie situated among the famous vineyards and now a delightful small hotel.
🛈 14 🕒 Closed March 1–13 🗷 AE, MC, V

GIGONDAS 84190

🍴 LES FLORETS
$/$$$
TEL 04 90 65 85 01
An attractive, quiet restaurant with Provençal decor and a terrace. Choices include monkfish braised with orange

butter, and lamb on a bed of eggplant. Some rooms available as well.
🕒 Closed Tues. D, all Wed. in winter, & Jan.–Feb. 🗷 All major cards

GORDES 84220

🏨 LA FERME DE LA HUPPE
$/$$
ROUTE D'APT
LES POURQUIERS
TEL 04 90 72 12 25
FAX 04 90 72 01 83
In peaceful Lubéron country-side, a beautiful 18th-century farm with an inner courtyard, renovated in Provençal style.
🛈 8 🕒 Closed Dec.–April
🚭 Some rooms 🏊
🗷 MC, V

🍴 LE MAS TOURTERON
$$$
LES IMBERTS, CHEMIN ST.-BLAISE
TEL 04 90 72 00 16
Old Provençal mas (farm-house) with a walled garden serving light, fresh, and imaginative cuisine using seasonal products.
🕒 Closed Tues. L Sept.–June, all Mon., & mid-Nov.– March
🗷 All major cards

LES BAUX-DE-PROVENCE 13520

🏨 LA BENVENGUDO
$$ ✪✪✪
(1 MILE/2 KM S OF LES BAUX)
TEL 04 90 54 32 54
FAX 04 90 54 42 58
Tucked beneath the Alpilles hills, a manor-hotel with an elegant garden. The lounge and dining room are in Provençal style; some rooms have private terraces. Tennis.
🛈 20 + 3 suites 🅿
🕒 Closed Nov.–mid-March
🚭 some rooms 🏊 🗷 AE, MC, V

🍴 OUSTAU DE BAUMANIÈRE
$$$$/$$$$$
TEL 04 90 54 33 07

A Michelin two-star restaurant in an elegantly furnished 16th-century building, famous for its gigot d'agneau en croûte and truffle ravioli.
🕒 Closed Thurs. L & all Wed. Nov.–March & late Jan.–March 10 🗷 All major cards

LOURMARIN 84160

🏨 HOSTELLERIE LE PARADOU
$$
COMBE DE LOURMARIN
TEL 04 90 68 04 05
FAX 04 90 08 54 94
Peaceful family hotel tucked into the Gorges de Lour-marin; rooms have views over fields and village.
🛈 9 🅿 🕒 Closed mid-Nov.–mid-Dec & Jan. 5–Feb. 5 🗷 MC, V

MOUSTIERS-STE.-MARIE 04360

🍴 LES SANTONS
$$$/$$$$
PLACE DE L'ÉGLISE
TEL 04 92 74 66 48
Tiny Michelin one-star restaurant near the Gorges du Verdon, run by the celebrated Alain Ducasse, chef of Hôtel de Paris in Monaco. Reservations necessary.
🕒 Closed Mon. D (except mid-July–mid-Aug.), Tues., & mid-Nov.–mid-Dec. 🗷 All major cards

ORANGE 84100

🍴 AUBERGE DE L'ORANGERIE
$$
4 PLACE DE L'ORMEAU, PIOLENC 84420
TEL 04 90 29 59 88
This 18th-century auberge with a charming shady stone-walled courtyard provides a traditional atmosphere for inventive cuisine, such as langoustine with truffle sauce and osso buco of langoustines with fresh pasta.
🗷 DC, MC, V

STES.-MARIES-DE-LA-MER 13460

🏨 LE MAS DE LA FOUQUE
$$$$ ✪✪✪✪
ROUTE DU PETIT RHÔNE
TEL 04 90 97 81 02
FAX 04 90 97 96 84
Traditional Camargue hotel;
large rooms with tiled floors
and wooden beams have
private terraces overlooking
the lagoon and park.
🛏 14 🅿 🕐 Closed
Nov.–April ⛵ 🔲 All
major cards

LANGUEDOC-ROUSSILLON

BOUZIGUES 34140

🍴 CÔTE BLEUE
$$/$$$
(2 MILES/4 KM E OF MÈZE)
TEL 04 67 78 31 42
Large family restaurant
overlooking the Bassin de
Thau, which is the best place
to sample the vast variety of
shellfish found here: mussels
and langoustines are excellent,
and do try the tiny sweet
Bouzigues oysters.
🕐 Closed Tues. D, all Wed.
Sept.–June & late Jan.–late
Feb. 🔲 AE, MC, V

CARCASSONNE 11000

🏨 CITÉ
$$$$/$$$$$ ✪✪✪✪
PLACE DE L'ÉGLISE
TEL 04 68 71 98 71
FAX 04 68 71 50 15
Grand neo-Gothic hotel built
into the ramparts of the old
city, with its own garden and
two restaurants.
🛏 55 + 6 suites 🅿
🕐 Closed Jan. ⛵ 🔲 All
major cards

🍴 BRASSERIE LE DONJON
$
2 RUE DU COMTE ROGER
TEL 04 68 25 95 72
Elegant restaurant in the
middle of the old walled city

serving such traditional dishes
as cassoulet and foie gras.
🕐 Closed Sun. D Nov.–March
🔲 All major cards

CASTELNOU 66300

🍴 LE VICOMTE
$$
CHÂTEAU DE CASTELNOU
TEL 04 68 53 32 08
Medieval château in restored
village, serving traditional
Catalan cuisine such as *boules
de Picoulat* (Catalan meatballs
in spicy sauce).
🕐 Closed D in winter, all
Tues., & Jan.–Feb. 🔲 MC, V

CÉRET 66400

🍴 LES FEUILLANTS
$$$/$$$$$
1 BOULEVARD LAFAYETTE
TEL 04 68 87 37 88
Charming terrace restaurant
with two Michelin stars
serving imaginative versions of
traditional Catalan cuisine.
🕐 Closed Sun. D & all Mon.
Sept.–June 🔲 AE, MC, V

COLLIOURE 66190

🏨 CASA PAIRAL
$/$$$ ✪✪✪
IMPASSE DES PALMIERS
TEL 04 68 82 05 81
FAX 04 68 82 52 10
A 19th-century Catalan villa
set in a shady garden with
palm trees and fountains—a
peaceful haven in the town
center. No restaurant.
🛏 28 🕐 Closed Nov.–
April ⛵ 🔲 AE, MC, V

🏨🍴 LES TEMPLIERS
$ ✪✪
12 QUAI DE L'AMIRAUTÉ
TEL 04 68 98 31 10
FAX 04 68 98 01 24
Hotel and restaurant in the
old town near the harbor.
Great platters of seafood
accompanied by Collioure
wine. The hotel is famous for
the artists who stayed here,
including Matisse and Braque,
and retains its authentic
atmosphere.

PRICES

HOTELS
An indication of the cost
of a double room without
breakfast is given by $ signs.
$$$$$	over $280
$$$$	$200–$280
$$$	$120–$200
$$	$80–$120
$	under $80

RESTAURANTS
An indication of the cost of a
three-course dinner without
drinks is given by $ signs.
$$$$$	over $80
$$$$	$50–$80
$$$	$35–$50
$$	$20–$35
$	under $20

🛏 21 + 50 annex 🕐 Closed
early Jan.–early Feb. Restaurant closed Sun. D & all
Mon. in winter 🔲 AE, MC, V

GANGES 34190

🏨 CHÂTEAU DES MADIÈRES
$$/$$$$ ✪✪✪✪
TEL 04 67 73 84 03
FAX 04 67 73 55 71
This 14th-century fortress has
spectacular views over the Vis
River gorge. Vaulted dining
rooms, a Renaissance fireplace,
and medieval arches combined
with modern comfort.
🛏 8 + 4 suites 🕐 Closed
Nov.–early April 🚩 🔲 All
major cards

MOLITG-LES-BAINS 66500

🏨🍴 CHÂTEAU DE RIELL
$$$/$$$$ ✪✪✪✪
TEL 04 68 05 04 40
FAX 04 68 05 04 37
Mock-Gothic château in the
foothills of the Pyrenees with
a view of Mont Canigou.
Nearby spa. The one-star
Michelin restaurant serves
traditional cuisine.
🛏 19 🕐 Closed Nov.–end
March ⛵ 🔲 All major cards

🏨 Hotel   🍴 Restaurant   🛏 No. of hotel bedrooms   🚇 Métro station   🅿 Parking   🕐 Closed   🚪 Elevator

MONTPELLIER 34000

🏨 DEMEURE DES BROUSSES
$/$$ ✪✪✪
538 RUE DU MAS DES
BROUSSES, ROUTE DE
VAUGUIÈRES
TEL 04 67 65 77 66
FAX 04 67 22 22 17
An 18th-century *mas*
(farmhouse) in a park, with an
excellent restaurant.
🛈 17 🅿 🅢 All major
cards

🍴 LE JARDIN DES SENS
$$$$/$$$$$
11 AVENUE ST.-LAZARE
TEL 04 99 58 38 38
Small, sophisticated, Michelin
three-star restaurant with
a garden in the middle of
Montpellier, celebrated for
its southern regional cooking.
🕒 Closed Mon. L & all Sun.
🅰 🅢 All major cards

NÎMES 30000

🏨 L'HACIENDA
$$ ✪✪✪
CHEMIN DU MAS DE
BRIGNON
MARGUERITTES 30320
(5 MILES/8 KM NE OF NÎMES)
TEL 04 66 75 02 25
FAX 04 66 75 45 58
Hotel in a large farmhouse
outside a village north of
Nîmes, with attractive
terraced garden.
🛈 12 🅿 🕒 Closed
Nov.–Feb. 🅰 🅢 MC, V

🍴 L'ENCLOS DE LA FONTAINE
$$$
HÔTEL IMPERATOR,
QUAI DE LA FONTAINE
TEL 04 66 21 90 30
Restaurant of the Hôtel
Imperator favored by bull-
fighters at *féria* time. Try local
specialties such as *brandade
de morue* (creamy salt cod),
escabèche (marinated fish), or
sea bass with fennel compôte.
🅢 All major cards

PERPIGNAN 66000

🍴 CASA SANSA
$$$
2 RUE FABRIQUE NADAL & 3
RUE FABRIQUE COUVERTE
TEL 04 68 34 21 84
This Perpignan favorite is
tucked away in a tiny alley
with paintings cramming the
walls. An excellent place to
sample Catalan specialties
such as roasted vegetables,
rabbit with figs, and beef
daube with orange.
🕒 Closed Mon. L & all Sun.
🅢 All major cards

SÈTE 34200

🏨 GRAND HÔTEL
$/$$ ✪✪✪
17 QUAI MARÉCHAL DE
LATTRE-DE-TASSIGNY
TEL 04 67 74 71 77
FAX 04 67 74 29 27
A charming belle epoque
hotel overlooking the Grand
Canal.
🛈 45 🅿 🅢 Rooms
🅢 All major cards

AJACCIO 20000

🍴 A LA FUNTANA
$$
9 RUE NOTRE DAME
TEL 04 95 21 78 04
In the old town of Ajaccio,
near the cathedral, serving
local products in classic style.
🕒 Closed Sun. & Mon. mid-
June–mid-July 🅢 All major
cards

BASTIA 20200

🍴 LA CITADELLE
$$/$$$
RUE STE.-CROIX
TEL 04 95 31 44 70
An old olive mill with a
terrace for alfresco dining on
excellent regional cuisine.
🕒 Closed Sat. L, all Sun.,
& mid-Feb.–mid-March 🅢
🅰 AE, MC, V

BONIFACIO 20169

🏨 GENOVESE
$$$$/$$$$$ ✪✪✪✪
HAUTE VILLE
TEL 04 95 73 12 34
FAX 04 95 73 09 03
The former Foreign Legion
barracks in the old town
transformed into a modern,
luxury hotel. No restaurant.
🛈 14 🅿 🕒 Closed
Nov.–April 🅢 🅢 All
major cards

🍴 STELLA DORO
$$
7 RUE DORIA
A family-run restaurant with
rustic decor and a friendly
ambience. Try the stuffed
mussels or the bouillabaisse
(order in advance).
🕒 Closed Oct.–Easter
🅢 All major cards

CALVI 20260

🏨 AUBERGE
🍴 DE LA SIGNORIA
$$$/$$$$ ✪✪✪
ROUTE DE FORÊT DE
BONIFATO
TEL 04 95 65 93 00
FAX 04 95 65 38 77
A 17th-century house set
peacefully in a park with pines,
palms, and orange trees to the
south of Calvi. Good restau-
rant with terrace where you
can dine by candlelight. Tennis.
🛈 20 🕒 Closed mid-
Oct.–April 🅢 Rooms 🅰
🅢 AE, MC, V

PORTO-VECCHIO 20137

🏨 GRAND HOTEL
🍴 CALA ROSSA
$$$/$$$$$ ✪✪✪
CALA ROSSA
TEL 04 95 71 61 51
FAX 04 95 71 60 11
Northeast of Porto-Vecchio, a
very pleasant hotel with shady
trees, a flowery garden, terrace
on the beach, and a Michelin
one-star restaurant specializing in fish dishes. Tennis.
🛈 49 🕒 Closed Jan.–mid-
April 🅢 🅢 All major cards

SHOPPING IN FRANCE

Shopping is one of the great pleasures of a visit to France. From the smallest streets to the grandest city boulevards, French stores offer delectable displays of patisserie, chocolates, and all manner of sweetmeats. Ordinary practical products are often beautifully designed and can make excellent presents: Stationery stores (*papeteries*) offer wonderful little notebooks and files, and *drogueries* (not drugstores but hardware stores) are Aladdin's caves of intriguing kitchen utensils and charming pottery. Town centers are now often car-free, with supermarkets and hypermarkets on the outskirts. These are ideal for bulk food shopping, often have a good selection of wine, and are also useful for buying stamps, newspapers, camera film, and gas.

MARKETS

Markets are still the best way to shop in France. Most towns and villages have at least a weekly market, and in bigger cities they may even be daily. They usually start early in the morning and close at noon—if you want to see them at their bustling best and have the pick of the produce, the best mushrooms or raspberries, then go early. Much of the fruit and vegetables are likely to be locally grown; look for signs saying *du pays*. The livestock section is not for the tender-hearted, as cages full of live ducks, geese, and chickens wait to be carried home for dinner. Look for local delicacies such as cheese, honey, olives, *charcuterie*, spices, herbs, and special breads and cakes.

France also has numerous flea markets (*marchés aux puces* or *brocantes*) selling secondhand goods, antiques, and local curios. Again, you need to arrive early to find the bargains.

DÉGUSTATIONS

Dégustation means tasting. All over France you will see signs inviting you to sample the local produce, particularly the wine. You are not obliged to buy, but it would be thoroughly uncivil not to purchase at least one bottle.

OPENING HOURS

Food stores, especially bakers (*boulangeries*), open early, around 7 a.m. Small stores and department stores (*grands magasins*) usually open from 9 a.m. Most stores close for lunch between noon and 2 or 3 p.m., staying open until 7 or 7:30 in the evening. Hypermarkets will usually stay open all day until quite late.

Many stores close on Mondays; food shops, and especially bakers, open on Sunday mornings, when it is fun to watch everyone buying their tarts and cakes for Sunday lunch.

PAYMENT

Supermarkets accept credit cards, but smaller stores often do not. Check the signs on the door before you go in. Some traders are reluctant to accept payment by American Express cards or travelers' checks.

EXPORTS

Most purchases include TVA (VAT or value-added tax) at a base rate running currently at 20.6 percent, rising to as high as 33 percent on luxury items. Visitors from outside the European Union may claim back TVA if they spend more than 2,000 francs in one place: Ask the store for a completed *bordereau* (export sales invoice), which must be shown, together with the goods, to customs officers when you leave the country. You then mail the form back to the retailer, who will refund the TVA—though this may take some time.

RETURNS

If you have a complaint about any purchase, return it as soon as possible to the store together with the receipt as proof of purchase. In the case of a serious dispute, contact the local Direction Départementale de la Concurrence et de la Consommation et de la Répression des Fraudes (find the number in the telephone directory).

WHAT TO BUY

The French are particularly good at little luxuries such as lingerie, soap, cosmetics, perfume, chocolate, and delicious jam. Every region of France has its own special products that make irresistible souvenirs. Often these are gastronomic delights such as honey, herbs, cookies, or foie gras; wine, brandies, or local liqueurs. Look for local pottery, baskets, and fabrics.

The following is a list of regional products, with a selection of especially good places to buy in each region.

NORTHERN FRANCE

CHAMPAGNE

The big champagne houses are in Reims or Épernay, and can be toured (see pp. 118–19, 121, and 383). To buy champagne, the following stores have a good selection:

La Vinocave 45 place Drouet, Reims 51100, Tel 03 26 40 60 07.
Le Vintage 1 cours Anatole France, Reims 51100, Tel 03 26 40 40 82.

CHEESE

Philippe Olivier 43–45 rue Thiers, Boulogne-sur-Mer 62200, Tel 03 21 31 94 74. Famous cheese store with hundreds of different cheeses.

CHOCOLATE

Chocolaterie de Beussent 66 Route de Desvres, Beussent 62170, Tel 03 21 86 17 62. Handmade chocolates.
Chocolaterie Jean Trogneux 1 rue Delambred, Amiens 80000, Tel 03 22 71 17 17. Handmade chocolates and macaroons from Amiens.
La Chocolaterie Thibaut Zone Artisanale, rue Max-Menu, Pierry 51530, Tel 03 26 51 58 04. Handmade chocolates including chocolate champagne corks filled with *marc de Champagne*.

ENAMELWARE
Société des Faïenceries et Émaux de Longwy 3 rue des Émaux, Longwy 54400, Tel 03 82 24 30 94.
Emaux Saint Jean l'Aigle rue de la Chiers, Herserange-Longwy 54400, Tel 03 82 24 58 20.

FOIE GRAS
Charcuterie Glasser 18 rue des Boulangers, Colmar 68000, Tel 03 89 41 23 69.
Jean Lutz, 5 rue du Chaudron, Strasbourg 67000, Tel 03 88 32 00 64.

GLASS
Cristal Daum Vannes-le-Chatel, near Toul, Tel 03 83 25 41 01.
Crystal engraving workshop 74 rue de Viller, Lunéville 54300, Tel 03 83 73 26 61.
Espace Verre rue de la Liberté, Vannes-le-Chatel, near Toul, Tel 03 83 25 47 44.

MARKETS
Amiens	Wed. & Sat.
Beauvais	Wed. & Sat.
Boulogne-sur-Mer	Wed. & Sat.
Calais	Wed., Thurs., & Sat.
Colmar	Thurs. & Sat.
Langres	Fri.
Le Touquet	Mon.–Thurs., Sat.
Lille	daily
Metz	Wed., Thurs., & Sat.
Nancy	Tues.–Sat.
Reims	daily
Strasbourg	Mon.–Sat.
Troyes	Sat.

NORMANDY & BRITTANY

BÉNÉDICTINE
Palais Bénédictine 110 Rue Alexandre-Le-Gran, Fecamp 76400, Tel 02 35 10 26 00. Taste and buy Bénédictine liqueur where it is made.

CALVADOS
Distilleries des Fiefs Ste.-Anne, Coudray-Rabut 14140, Tel 02 31 64 30 05.

Pierre Huet Manoir la Brière des Fontaines, Cambremer 14170, Tel 02 31 63 01 09.

CHEESE
Denis Thébault Boissey 14140 (southwest of Lisieux), Tel 02 31 21 64 00.
Durand-la-Heronnière. Camembert 61120 (south of Lisieux), Tel 02 31 39 08 08. Traditional Camembert and cider making.
Fromagerie Graindorge Livarot 14140, Tel 02 31 48 20 00. Livarot cheese.
Henry Pennec Pont l'Evêque 14130, Tel 02 31 64 25 38. Maker of Pont l'Evêque cheese.

CIDER
Route du Cidre, Pays d'Auge For information about this signposted route through cider country call 02 31 63 08 87.
Auberge "La Route de Cidre" Montreuil-en-Auge 14340, Tel 02 31 63 12 27. Rent bikes for the Route du Cidre.
La Ferme de Beuvron Beuvron-en-Auge 14130, Tel 02 31 79 29 19. Makers of cheese, Calvados, and cider.

CLOTHES
Coopérative des Marin Guilvinec 29730. Breton fishermen's sweaters and other gear.

COOKIES
Les Sources de l'Aven Pont-Aven 29930, Tel 02 98 06 07 65. Homemade butter cookies and Breton cake.

FAIENCE
Faïencerie Keraluc 14 rue de Troménie, Quimper 29000, Tel 02 98 90 09 36.
Faïence Carpentier 26 rue St. Romain, Rouen 76000, Tel 02 35 88 77 47.

LACE
You can buy Alençon lace at the following museums:
Musée des Beaux-Arts et de la Dntelle rue Julien, Alençon 61000, Tel 02 33 32 40 07.

Musée de dentelle au point d'Alençon rue du Mar, Lattre-de-Tassigny, Alençon 61000, Tel 02 33 26 27 26.

MUSTARD & OTHER FOOD SPECIALTIES
Épicerie Claude Olivier 16 rue St.-Jacques, Dieppe 76200, Tel 02 35 84 22 55.

SEA SALT
La Salorge de Guérande Buy from roadside stands amid the salt marshes south of Guérande.
La Maison du Sel Pradel 44350, Tel 02 40 62 01 25.

MARKETS
Bayeux	Wed. & Sat.
Brest	daily
Caen	Fri. & Sun.
Concarneau	Mon. & Fri.
Dieppe	Tues., Thurs., & Sat.
Dinan	Thurs.
Honfleur	Sat.
Lorient	Sat.
Quimper	daily
Rennes	Tues.–Sun.
Rouen	Thurs.–Sun.
Saint-Malo	Mon.–Sat.
Trouville-sur-Mer	Wed. & Sun.
Vannes	Wed. & Sat.

Apple fair Ste.-Opportune-la-Mare (north of Pont Audemer). First Sunday of the month between October and April.
Camembert fair Camembert (south of Lisieux). Last Sunday in July.
Cider fair Caudebec-en-Caux. September.

LOIRE VALLEY

BASKETS
Coopérative de Vannerie de Villaines 1 rue de la Chen-eillère, Villaines-les-Rochers 37190.

CHARCUTERIE
Charcuterie Hardouin Virage Gastronomique, Vouvray 37210, Tel 02 47 40 40 40.

SHOPPING IN FRANCE

CHOCOLATES, COOKIES, & PÂTISSERIE
La Chocolaterie Royale 53 rue Royale, Orléans 45000, Tel 02 38 53 93 43.
Épicerie Le Berry Îlot Victor-Hugo, 41 rue Moyenne, Bourges 18000, Tel 02 48 70 02 38.
La Petite Marquise 22 rue des Lices, Angers 49000, Tel 02 41 87 43 01.
Chocolat Benoit 1 rue des Lices, Angers 49000, Tel 02 41 88 94 52.

FAIENCE
Faïencerie de Gien place de la Victoire, Gien 45500, Tel 02 38 67 00 05.
Faïenceries du Bourg-Joly 16 rue Carnot, Malicorne-sur-Sarthe 72270, Tel 02 43 94 80 10.

WINE
Local *Maisons du vin* will give information on tastings and on producers for direct sales.

Grands Vins du Vouvray Manoir du Haut–Lieu, Vouvray 37210, Tel 02 47 52 78 87.
Maison des Vins du Pays Nantais Bellevue, La Haie-Fouassière 44690, Tel 02 40 36 90 10.
Maison du Vin de l'Anjou 5 bis place Kennedy, Angers 49100, Tel 02 41 88 81 13.
Maison des Vin de Bourgeuil Bourgeuil 37140, Tel 02 47 97 92 20.
Vins de Touraine 19 square Prosper-Mérimée, Tours 37000, Tel 02 47 05 40 01.

Cointreau
Distillerie Cointreau St.-Barthélemy-d'Anjou 49124, Tel 02 41 31 50 50. Distillery tour.

MARKETS
Amboise	Fri. & Sun.
Angers	daily
Blois	Tues., Thurs., & Sat.
Bourges	Thurs.–Sun.
Chinon	Thurs.
Nantes	daily
Orléans	Tues.–Sun.
Saumur	Sat.
Tours	daily

CENTRAL FRANCE & THE ALPS

CHARCUTERIE
Charcuterie Batteault 4 rue Monge, Beaune 21200, Tel 03 80 22 23 04.
Charcuterie Reynon 13 rue des Archers, Lyon 69000, Tel 04 78 37 39 08.

CHEESE
Abbaye Notre-Dame de Cîteaux Cîteaux 21700, Tel 03 80 61 11 53. Monks still produce the eponymous cheese.
Coopérative Fromagerie d'Arbois rue des Fosses, Arbois 39600, Tel 03 84 66 09 71.
Deloche Les Languières, Le Grand-Bornand 74450, Tel 04 50 27 00 20. Buy cheese and watch it being made.
Fromagerie Berthaut place Champ-de-Foire, Époisses 21460, Tel 03 80 96 44 44.
Fromagerie René Richard Les Halles, 102 cours Lafayette, Lyon 69000, Tel 04 78 62 30 78.
Les Caves Société Roquefort-sur-Soulzon 12250, Tel 05 65 59 93 30 or 05 65 58 58 58. Tours through the caves where the cheese is matured as well as for sale.

CHOCOLATE
Chocolaterie-Confiserie Bernard Laurent 6 rue du Lac, Annecy 74000, Tel 04 50 45 04 70.
Pâtisserie-Chocolaterie Bernachon 42 cours Franklin-Roosevelt, Lyon 69006, Tel 04 78 24 37 98.

MONTÉLIMAR NOUGAT
Suprême Nougat 3 avenue St.-Martin, Montélimar 26200, Tel 04 75 01 74 42.

MUSTARD
Grey-Poupon Maille, 32 rue de la Liberté, Dijon 21000, Tel 03 80 30 41 02.

NOUGAT
Chabert et Guillot 1 rue André-Ducatez, Montélimar 26200, Tel 04 75 00 82 00.

OLIVES
Coopérative Agricole du Nyonsais place Olivier-de-Serres, Nyons 26110, Tel 04 75 26 03 44.

PAIN D'ÉPICES
Mulot & Petitjean 13 place Bossuet, Dijon 21000, Tel 03 80 30 07 10.

SILK
L'Atelier de Soierie 33 rue Romarin, Lyon 69001, Tel 04 72 07 97 83.
La Maison des Canuts 12 rue d'Ivry, Lyon 69004, Tel 04 78 28 62 04. Silk weavers center.

WINE
Beaujolais
Maison des Beaujolais RN6 69220 St.-Jean d'Arbières, Tel 04 74 66 16 46.
Les Routes des Vins Le Pays Beaujolais, Villefranche-sur-Saône 69400, Tel 04 74 02 22 00.
Le Hameau du Vin Romanèche-Thorins 71570, Tel 03 85 35 22 22. Wine museum.

Burgundy
Marché aux Vins rue Nicolas-Rolin, Beaune 21200, Tel 03 80 25 08 20. Tasting (charge).
Le Vigneron 6 rue d'Alsace, Beaune 21200, Tel 03 80 22 68 21. Wine accessories.
Vins de Bourgogne 12 boulevard Bretonnière, Beaune 21200, Tel 03 80 25 04 80.

Chablis
La Chablisienne 8 boulevard Pasteur, Chablis 89800, Tel 03 86 42 89 89.

Jura
Societé de Viticulture du Jura avenue du 44ème RI, Lons-le-Saunier 39016.

Mâcon
Maison du Vin 520 avenue Maréchal de Lattre-de-Tassigny, Mâcon 71000, Tel 03 85 22 91 30.
Syndicat Viticole de Pouilly Les Loges, Pouilly-sur-Loire 58150, Tel 03 86 39 06 83.

Cassis
Cassis Boudier 14 rue de Cluj,
Dijon 21007, Tel 03 80 74 33 33.

Chartreuse
Les Caves de la Chartreuse
10 boulevard Edgar-Kofler,
Voiron 38500, Tel 04 76 05 81 77.

MARKETS

Aubusson	Sat.
Autun	Wed., Fri., & Sun.
Auxerre	Tues. & Fri.
Beaune	Wed. & Sat.
Besançon	Tues., Fri., & Sun.
Bourg-en-Bresse	Wed. & Sat.
Chablis	Sun.
Chambéry	Sat.
Clermont-Ferrand	Mon.–Sat.
Dijon	Tues., Fri., & Sat.
Grenoble	Tues.–Sun.
Louhans	Mon. Bresse poultry
Lyon	Tues.–Sun.
Nyons	Thurs.
Le Puy-en-Velay	Sat.
Vichy	Wed.

SOUTHWEST FRANCE

BASQUE LINEN
Boutiques Berrogain carrefour des Cinq-Cantons, Bayonne 64100, Tel 05 59 59 16 18.
Boutiques Berrogain boulevard de BAB, 64600 Anglet, Tel 05 59 57 31 31.

BAYONNE HAM
Maison Montauzer 17 rue de la Salie, Bayonne 64100, Tel 05 59 56 84 04.
Pierre d'Ibaïalde 41 rue des Cordeliers, Bayonne 64100, Tel 05 59 25 65 30.

CHOCOLATE & BASQUE CARAMELS
Chocolaterie Cazenave 19 Arceaux, Port-Neuf, Bayonne 64100, Tel 05 59 59 03 16.
Chocolaterie Henriet place Clemenceau, Biarritz 64200, Tel 05 59 24 24 15.

MAKHILA
(Traditional Basque walking sticks

in wood, often silver-tipped)
Ainciart Bergara (est. 1789), Larressore 64480, Tel 05 59 93 03 05.
M Leoncini 37 rue Vieille Boucherie, Bayonne 64100, Tel 05 59 59 18 20.

OYSTERS
B Pedemay impasse du Grand Coin, Petit Piquey, Lege-Cap-Ferret 33950, Tel 05 56 60 58 18.

PORCELAIN
Ancienne Manufacture Royale de Limoges 7 place des Horteils, Aixe sur Vienne 87700, Tel 05 55 70 44 82.
Musée Haviland Le Pavillon de la Porcelaine, Z1 Magré, Route de Toulouse, Limoges 87000, Tel 05 55 30 21 86.

TRUFFLES, FOIE GRAS, & CONFITS
Aux Armes du Périgord 1 rue de la Liberté, Sarlat-la-Canéda 24200, Tel 05 53 59 14 27.
Conserverie Godard Gourdon 46300, Tel 05 65 41 03 97.
La Ferme de Turnac Domme 24150, Tel 05 53 28 10 84.
Le Gers Gourmet Gayarin, St.-Germe 32400, Tel 05 62 69 61 07 or 05 62 69 60 37. (St.-Germe is on D935 east of Aire-sur-l'Adour.)
Pierre Champion 21 rue Taillefer, Périgueux 24004, Tel 05 53 03 90 29.
Pebeyre 66 rue Frédéric-Suisse, Cahors 46000, Tel 05 65 22 24 80 (Sat. & Sun.).

WINE & SPIRITS
For a good selection of Bordeaux wines try:
L'Intendant 2 allée de Tourny, Bordeaux 33000, Tel 05 56 48 01 29.
La Vinothéque 8 cours du 30 Juillet, Bordeaux 33000, Tel 05 56 52 32 05.

Maisons du Vin
Maison des Sauternes place de la Mairie, Sauternes 33210, Tel 05 56 76 69 83.
Maison des Vins de Graves 61 cours Maréchal Foch, Poden-

sac 33720, Tel 05 56 27 09 25.
Maison de Vins de Bergerac 2 place du Dr. Cayla, Bergerac 24100.
Maison du Tourisme et du Vin La Verrerie, Pauillac 33250, Tel 05 56 59 03 08.
Maison du Vin des Côtes de Blaye 11 cours Vauban, Blaye 33390, Tel 05 57 42 91 19.
Maison du Vin des Côtes de Bourg place de l'Éperon, Bourg 33710.
Maison du Vin de St.-Émilion place Pierre, Meyrat, St.-Émilion 33330, Tel 05 57 55 50 55.
Maison du Vin de St.-Estèphe place de L'Église, St.-Estèphe 33180, Tel 05 56 59 30 59.
Syndicat Interprofessionel du Vin de Cahors avenue Jean-Jaurès, Cahors 46000, Tel 05 65 23 22 21.

Armagnac
Jean-Gabriel Cénac Domaine de Laubuchon, Manciet 32370, Tel 05 62 08 50 29.
Janneau Fils SA 50 avenue d'Aquitaine, Condom 32100, Tel 05 62 28 24 77.

Cognac
Cognac Otard Château de Cognac, 127 boulevard Denfert-Rochereau, Cognac 16101, Tel 05 45 36 88 88.
Remy Martin 20 rue de la Société Vinicole, Cognac 16100, Tel 05 45 35 76 66.

MARKETS

Auch	Thurs. & Sat.
Bayonne	Mon.–Sat.
Bergerac	Wed. & Sat.
Biarritz	Mon.–Sat.
Bordeaux	Mon.–Sat.
Brantôme	Fri.
Cahors	Wed.
Lalbenque (truffle market)	Mon. Dec.–March
Pauillac	Sat.
Périgueux	Wed. & Sat.
St.-Émilion	Sun.
St.-Jean-de-Luz	Tues. & Fri.
Sarlat-la-Canéda	Wed. & Sat.

SHOPPING IN FRANCE

ANCHOVIES
Société Roque 17 route
d'Argelès, Collioure 66190,
Tel 04 68 82 22 30.

CHARCUTERIE
**La Maison du Saucisson
d'Arles** 3 avenue de la
République, St.-Martin-de-Crau
13310, Tel 04 90 47 30 40.

ESPADRILLES &
CATALAN FABRICS
Les Toiles du Soleil Le Village,
St.-Laurent-de-Cerdans 66260,
Tel 04 68 39 50 02.

GLASSWARE
Verrerie de Biot chemin des
Combes, Biot 06410, Tel 04 93
65 03 00.

HERBS
L'Herbier de St.-Rémy 34
boulevard Victor-Hugo, St.-
Rémy-de-Provence 13210, Tel 04
90 92 11 96.

OLIVES & OLIVE OIL
Alziari 14 rue St.-François-de-
Paule, Nice 06000, Tel 04 93 44
45 12.
Moulin de la Braque 2 route
de Châteauneuf, Opio 06650, Tel
04 93 77 23 03.

PERFUME
Parfumerie Fragonard
20 boulevard Fragonard, Grasse
06130, Tel 04 93 36 44 65.
Parfumerie Galimard
73 route de Cannes, Grasse
06130, Tel 04 93 09 20 00.
Parfumerie Molinard
60 boulevard Victor-Hugo,
Grasse 06130, Tel 04 93 36 01 62.

POTTERY
Céramique Girelli 11 avenue
du Tapis Vert, Vallauris 06220,
Tel 04 93 64 13 71.
Moustiers-Ste.-Marie Many
potteries along route de Riez,
Moustiers-Ste.-Marie 06430.
Syndicat des Potiers Éspace
Grandjean, avenue du Stade,
Vallauris 06220, Tel 04 93 64 17 93.

PROVENÇAL FABRICS
Souleîado 5 rue Joseph-Vernet,
Avignon 84000, Tel 04 90 86 47
67 (also in other locations).

SANTONS
**(Christmas crib figurines)
Atelier Carbonel**
47 rue Neuve Ste.-Catherine,
Marseille 13000, Tel 04 92 74
66 69.

WINE
Corbières
Chateau de Boulenuac, Tel 04 68
27 73 00.
Côtes du Roussillon
19 avenue de la Grande
Bretagne, Perpignan 66000, Tel
04 68 51 31 81.
Côtes du Provence
route national 7, Les Arcs-sur-
Argens 83460, Tel 04 94 99
50 10.
Fitou
La Palme, Tel 04 68 40 42 70.
**Maison du Tourisme et du
Vin** 41 cours Jean-Jaurès,
Avignon 84000, Tel 04 90 27
24 00.
Minervois
Tel 04 68 27 80 02.
**Vignerons de Beaumes-de-
Venise** quartier Ravel, Beaumes-
de-Venise 84190, Tel 04 90 12
41 00.

Corsican wine
Maison Verte, boulevard du
Fangu, Bastia 20000, Tel 04 95 31
37 36.

MARKETS

Aix-en-Provence	Tues., Thurs., & Sat.
Apt	Sat.
Arles	Wed. & Sat.
Avignon	Tues.–Sun.
Cannes	daily
Carpentras	Fri.
Ceret	Sat.
Hyères	Sat.
L'Isle-sur-la-Sorgue	Thurs. & Sun.
Marseille	Fish market daily a.m., general & flea markets Tues.–Sun.
Montpellier	daily
Nice	Tues.–Sun., flea market Mon.
Orange	Thurs.
Perpignan	daily
St.-Rémy-de-Provence	Wed.
St.-Tropez	Tues. & Sat.
Tarascon	Tues.
Toulouse	daily

ACTIVITIES IN FRANCE

Almost every possible kind of leisure activity can be pursued in France, and your preference may influence the regions you choose to visit. Virtually everywhere in the regions you can walk, ride, and play golf, and the coasts offer a huge variety of marine and bathing activities. Most towns have excellent public swimming pools and sports facilities. The cities offer more worldly entertainments, from casinos to opera, and nightclubs to local feast days—often the best way to sample the authentic flavor of a place. Within each region, we have indicated the best places or contacts for activities of particular interest, and listed the main festivals and events during the year. Below is a list of national numbers to contact for specific activities, some of which also have regional contacts. Local tourist offices will provide further information.

National addresses for sports and activities:

CANOEING & KAYAKING
Fédération Française du Canoë-Kayak 87 quai de la Marne, Joinville-le-Pont 94340, Tel 01 45 11 08 50.

CYCLING
Fédération Française du Cyclo-Tourisme 8 rue Jean-Marie-Jégo, Paris 75013, Tel 01 44 16 88 88.

FISHING
Conseil Supérieur de la Pêche 10 rue des Dardanelles, Paris 75017, Tel 01 56 68 90 50. The season opens around the second Saturday in March. For freshwater fishing you will need to buy a permit from a *tabac*.

GOLF
Fédération Française du Golf Levallois, Tel 01 41 49 77 00.

HORSEBACK RIDING
Delegation Nationale pour le Tourisme Équestre 9 boulevard. MacDonald, Paris 75019, Tel 01 53 26 15 50.

HYDROTHERAPY & HOT SPAS
Centre d'Informations Thermales 32 avenue de l'Opéra, Paris 75002, Tel 01 44 71 37 37.
Fédération Thermale et Climatique Française 18 rue de l'Estrapade, Paris 75005, Tel 01 43 25 11 85.

MOUNTAIN CLIMBING
Fédération Française de la Montagne et de l'Escalade 8 quai de la Marne, Paris 75019, Tel 01 40 18 75 50.

SAILING
Fédération Française de la Voile 55 avenue Kléber, Paris 75784, Tel 01 44 05 81 00, Fax 01 47 04 90 12.

SKIING
Fédération Française de Ski 50 rue des Marquis, Annecy 74000, Tel 04 50 51 40 34.
Écoles de Ski Français 6 allée des Mitaillères, Meylan 38246, Tel 04 76 90 67 36.

UNDERWATER SPORTS
Fédération Française d'Etudes et de Sports Sous-Marins 24 quai de la Rive-Neuve, Marseille 13284, Tel 04 91 33 99 31, Fax 04 91 54 77 43.

WALKING
FFRP (Fédération Française de la Randonnée Pédestre), 14 rue Riquet, Paris 75019, Tel 01 44 89 93 90, Fax 01 40 35 85 67.
Information Center, FFRP, 64 rue de Gergovie, Paris 75014, Tel 01 44 89 93 93.

WATER SKIING
Fédération Française du Ski Nautique, 16 rue Clément-Marot, Paris 75008, Tel 01 47 20 05 00, Fax 01 47 20 43 74.

TOURS & ORGANIZED SIGHTSEEING
Tourist circuits and routes are indicated all over France, and local tourist offices can help with suggestions.

The **Caisse Nationale des Monuments Historiques et des Sites** publishes a map of historic routes. Write to Hôtel de Sully, 62 rue St.-Antoine, Paris 75186, or call 01 44 61 21 00. Routes include great cathedrals, parks and gardens, and historic castles, as well as specific historic routes such as the William the Conqueror Trail in Normandy. For further information contact Demeure Historique, 57 Quai de la Tournelle, Paris 75005, Tel 01 55 42 60 00, Fax 01 43 29 36 44.

For tours by bus contact local information offices. Many sights offer guided tours, but bear in mind that they are often only in French and can be quite lengthy. At some sights, a tour may be obligatory.

NORTHERN FRANCE

ALSACE WINE ROUTE
Maison des Vins d'Alsace, 12 avenue de la Foire aux Vins, Colmar 68012, Tel 03 89 20 16 20.

CHAMPAGNE TOURS
Most of the big Champagne houses have their cellars in Reims or Épernay and can be toured. Some of the château vineyards also have tours. In some cases you will need to make an appointment, so it is always advisable to call first.

Lanson 66 rue de Courlancy, Reims 51100, Tel 03 26 78 50 50. By appointment.
Moët and Chandon 20 avenue de Champagne, Épernay 51200, Tel 03 26 51 20 20. Admission charge.
Mumm 34 rue de Champ de Mars, Reims 51100, Tel 03 26 49 59 70. Tours in several languages, tasting. Admission charge.
Piper-Heidsieck 51 boulevard Henry-Vasnier, Reims 51100, Tel 03 26 84 43 44.
Taittinger 9 place St.-Nicaise, Reims 51100, Tel 03 26 85 84 33. Tours in French, English, and

German. Admission charge.
Veuve Clicquot I place des Droits de l'Homme, Reims 51100, Tel 03 26 89 54 41. By appointment.

MAIN EVENTS
Sunday before Easter
Coulommiers Wine and cheese fair
May
Amiens Carnival
June
Chantilly Horse races
July
Boulogne-sur-Mer Fish festival
Douai Festival of Giants
August
Cambrai Festival of giants
Locon Garlic fair
Maroilles Fête de la Flamiche (leek tart)
Wimereux Mussel festival
September
Lille Grand flea market and mussel festival (*braderie*)
October
Neuilly-St.-Front Apple fair
St.-Augustin Apple & cider festival

NORMANDY & BRITTANY

BOAT TRIPS
Quimper Tel 02 98 95 32 33. Trips on traditional sailing boats.
Seine estuary Aboard *Stephanie*, 38 rue Bucaille, Honfleur, Tel 02 31 89 21 10.
Seine cruise Aboard *Salamandre*, Le Havre, Tel 02 35 42 01 31.
Les Sept Îles Perros-Guirec, Tel 02 96 91 10 00.

CYCLING
Ligue de Basse-Normande Tel 02 31 80 85 91. Cycling in Lower Normandy.
La Maison de la Randonnée Rennes, Tel 02 99 67 42 21.

GOLF
Ligue de Golf de Bretagne Rennes, Tel 02 99 31 68 80.

HORSEBACK RIDING
Tourisme Équestre du Calvados Tel 02 31 85 52 72.
Haras du Pin (National

Stud) Tel 02 33 36 68 68. Guided tours.

NORMANDY LANDINGS
Tourist information on D-Day landings organized tours, Tel 02 33 28 88 71.
Sea boat trips including Normandy beaches: Mme. Vicquelin, Tel 02 31 51 81 33.
Plane trips Aéro Nord, Carpiquet, Tel 02 31 26 62 06.
Helicopter Héli-time, Toques-Deauville, Tel 02 31 81 82 83.

OYSTER ROUTE
Association Ostréane à Surzur Tel 02 97 42 05 16.

SEA FISHING
Trouville Tel 02 31 65 21 49.

THALASSOTHERAPY
(Sea-water treatment)
Institut de Thalassotherapie Arzon, 56640, Tel 02 97 53 90 90.
Pornic Phytomer Pornic 44210, Tel 02 40 82 21 21.
Thalassa Dinard Dinard 35800, Tel 02 99 82 78 10.
Thermes Marin de St.-Malo St.-Malo 35400, Tel 02 99 40 75 75.

WALKING
Calvados Tel 02 31 27 14 14. Information on area walks.
Brittany Randonnée Pédestre, Tel 02 97 42 57 94.

MAIN EVENTS
NORMANDY
May
Coutances Jazz festival
Mont St.-Michel Spring festival
Rouen Joan of Arc festival Sunday nearest May 30
June
D-Day beaches June 6
Balleroy Hot-air balloon meeting mid-June
July
Le Havre International regatta
Mont St.-Michel Pilgrimage across the sands
August
Cabourg William the Conqueror procession
Carteret Festival of the Sea
Deauville Horse racing, Grand Prix
September

Lessay Holy Cross fair
Lisieux St. Thérèse festival: procession with relics
September–October
Haras du Pin Horse trials

BRITTANY
May
Tréguier Pardon of St. Yves
July
Locronan Petite Troménie (Grande Troménie every 6 years, 2001, 2007, and so on)
Rennes Les Tombées de la Nuit
Vannes Jazz festival
August
Carnac Menhir festival
Concarneau Festival of the Blue Nets
Erquy Festival of the Sea
Lorient Interceltic Festival
Ste.-Anne-la-Palud Grand Pardon
September
Carnac Pardon of St.-Cornély

LOIRE VALLEY

BALLOONING
France Montgolfières La Riboulière, Monthou-sur-Cher 41400, Tel 02 54 71 75 40.

CANOEING & KAYAKING
Ligue Pays de la Loire de Canoë-Kayak 75 avenue du Lac de Maine, Angers 49000, Tel 02 41 73 86 10.

CRUISES
Bateaux Nantais Tel 02 40 14 51 14. Cruises up the Loire River.

TOURIST ROUTES
La Route des Dames de Touraine Château de Montpoupon near Montrichard 41400, Tel 02 47 94 23 62.
Les Circuits sur les Pas de St. Martin, Tours 37000, Tel 02 47 70 37 36.

MAIN EVENTS
Most of the large châteaux have son-et-lumière (sound and light) performances throughout the summer season.
February

Angers Honey fair
Saumur Wine festival
May
Saumur International Horse Show
Orléans Joan of Arc festival
May–June
Chambord Festival de Chambord
July
Amboise Festival
Chinon Medieval market
Doué La Fontaine Rose festival
July
Tours Garlic and basil festival
August
Rochefort-sur-Loire Anjou folk festival
Vouvray Wine fair
October
Azay-le-Rideau Apple fair
Bourgeuil Chestnut fair

CENTRAL FRANCE & THE ALPS

CANALS/BOATING
Bateaux de Bourgogne 1–2 quai de la République, Auxerre 89000, Tel 03 86 72 92 10.

BALLOONING
Air Escargo Remigny 71150, Tel 03 85 87 12 30.

ROCK CLIMBING
Club Alpin Français (section Auvergne), 3 rue Maréchal Joffre, Clermont-Ferrand 63000, Tel 04 73 90 81 62.

SILK FARM
Ma Magnanerie Lieu-dit Les Mazes, Vallon-Pont-d'Arc 07150, Tel 04 75 88 01 27. Restored silk farm (*magnanerie*) now a living museum of silkworm farming.

SKIING
Bureau Info Montagne, Maison de Tourisme, 14 rue de la République, Grenoble 38019, Tel 04 76 42 45 90, Fax 04 76 15 23 91.
Ski France covers more than 100 resorts. Reservations for accommodations, and a 24-hour telephone ski bulletin from mid-Dec. to mid-April, Tel 01 47 42 23 32, Fax 01 42 61 23 16. For

information contact them at 61 boulevard Haussmann, Paris 75008.

STEAM TRAINS
Chemin de Fer du Haut-Rhône Maison d'Accueil, Montalieu Vercieu 38390, Tel 04 74 88 49 23.
Chemin de Fer du Vivarais 2 quai Jean-Moulin, Lyon 69001, Tel 04 78 28 83 34.

WALKING
Randonnée Pédestre Côte-d'Or M. Moussard, Hôtel du Departement, Dijon 21035, Tel 03 80 63 66 00.
Saône-et-Loire M Colin, M.J.C. de Bioux, 20 avenue Pierre-Benave, Mâcon 71000, Tel 03 85 34 40 17.
Yonne M. Raymond Bosco, 8 chemin de Chevannes, Vallan 89580, Tel 03 86 41 22 26.

MAIN EVENTS
Sunday before Palm Sunday
Nuits St-George Hospice wine auction.
Maundy Thursday
Le-Puy-en-Velay Penitents procession by torchlight
End May–1st week June
Beaune Foire de Beaune
June
Villefranche-sur-Saône Midsummer's night festivities
July
Arbois Wine festival
Gannat World folklore festival
Le-Puy-en-Velay Marian procession July 14–15
Vienne Jazz festival
September 8
Mont Brouilly Wine producers pilgrimage
September–December
Beaujolais Grape harvest. Festivities all over region
October–November
Dijon Annual gastronomic fair
Bourg-en-Bresse Gastronomic fair, 3rd Sunday in November
Beaune Hospice wine auction 4th Sunday in November
Chablis Wine festival, December 8
Lyon Festival of Light

SOUTHWEST FRANCE

The **Centre Loisirs Accueil du Périgord** offers information and advice on horseback riding, rambling, kayaking, golf, fishing, and tours by horse-drawn caravan. Tel 05 53 35 50 24 or Fax 05 53 35 50 00.

BOAT TRIPS ON THE LOT RIVER
Comité Départemental de Tourisme 107 quai Cavaignac, Cahors 46001, Tel 05 65 35 07 09, Fax 05 65 23 92 76.

GAMBLING
Casino de Biarritz 1 avenue Édouard VII, Biarritz 64201, Tel 05 59 22 77 77.
Casino La Rochelle allée du Mail, La Rochelle 17000, Tel 05 46 34 12 75.

GOLF
Biarritz Golf School 4 impasse Canegre, Biarritz 64200, Tel 05 07 04 39 90.
Centre International d'Entrainement au Golf de Biarritz avenue du Château, Bidart 64210, Tel 05 59 43 77 87.

HORSEBACK RIDING
Centre Hippique du Lycée Agricole et Forestier Bazas 33430, Tel 05 56 25 03 21.

SKIING & MOUNTAIN-CLIMBING IN THE PYRENEES
Centre d'Information Montagnes et Sentiers, St.-Girons 09200, Tel 05 61 66 40 10.

SURFING
Fédération Française de Surf Plage Nord, boulevard Front de Mer, Hossegor 40150, Tel 05 58 43 55 88.
Lacanau Surf Club Tel 05 56 26 38 84.
Surf Sans Frontières Lacanau 33680, Tel 05 56 26 36 14. Both these clubs are able to give instructions in English.

ACTIVITIES IN FRANCE

TENNIS
Biarritz Olympique Parc des Sports d'Aguilera, Biarritz 64000, Tel 05 59 43 71 38. Covered and outdoor courts.

THALASSOTHERAPY
Institut Louison-Bobet 11 rue Louison-Bobet, Biarritz 64200, Tel 05 59 41 30 01.
Les Thermes Marins 80 rue de Madrid, Biarritz 64200, Tel 05 59 23 01 22.

WINE COURSES
École du Vin Château Loudenne, Médoc, 33340 St. Yzans, Tel 05 56 73 17 80.

WALKING
L'Association Randonées Pyrénéennes Tarbes 65007, Tel 05 62 90 09 90.
Randonnée Dordogne, Le Port de Domme-Cénac, Domme 24250, Tel 05 53 28 22 01.
Parc National Régional des Landes de Gascogne Sabres 40360, Tel 05 58 07 52 70.

MAIN EVENTS
Pentecost
La Rochelle International sailing week
Vic-Fezensac. Bullfights
June 24
St.-Jean-de-Luz Fête de St. Jean; torchlight procession, Basque festivities
August
Arcachon Festival of the Sea
Biarritz Surfing contest
Gujan-Mestras Oyster fair
Rocamadour Torchlit Festival of the Assumption, 3rd Sunday in September
St.-Émilion Grape harvest festival
October
Nontron Chestnut fair
November
Bordeaux SIGMA festival of Theater and Dance

SOUTH OF FRANCE & CORSICA

CANOE & KAYAKING
Verdon Plus 4 allée Louis Gardiol, Riez 04500, Tel 04 92 77 76 36.
Comité Régional Corse de Kayak Suaralta Vecchia, Bastelicaccia 20129, Tel 04 95 23 80 00.

CASINOS
Casino Croisette Palais des Festivals, Cannes 06400, Tel 04 93 38 12 11.
Le Casino place du Casino, Monte-Carlo, Monaco, Tel 00 377 92 16 23 00.
Casino Ruhl, Promenade des Anglais, Nice, Tel 04 93 87 95 87.

HORSEBACK RIDING
Centre Équestre de la Ville de Marseille 33 Traverse Carthage, Marseille 13000, Tel 04 91 73 72 94.
Languedoc–Roussillon ATECREL 14 rue des Logis, Loupian, Mèze 34140, Tel 04 67 43 82 50.
Association Régionale du Tourisme Équestre Corse Piedigriggiu 20218, Tel 04 95 47 60 05, Fax 04 95 47 65 78.

NUDISM
Héliopolis Île du Levant, Hyères 83411.

RIVER FISHING
Fédération Interdépartementale de Peche et Pisciculture 19 avenue Noël Franchini, Ajaccio 20000, Tel 04 95 23 13 32.

SAILING & WINDSURFING
Cannes Station de Voile Port du Mourre Rouge, Cannes 06400, Tel 04 92 18 88 87.
Nautique 2000 Port Gallice, Juan-les-Pins 06160, Tel 04 93 61 20 01.
Station Voile place de la République, Port Bacarès 66420, Tel 04 68 86 16 56.

SCUBA DIVING
Centre de Plongée 2 ruelle des Moulins, Nice 06000, Tel 04 93 55 59 50.

SKIING
Isola 2000 Office de Tourisme, Tel 04 93 23 15 15.
Font Romeu Office de Tourisme, Tel 04 68 30 68 30.

MAIN EVENTS
CÔTE D'AZUR
February
Menton Lemon festival (Procession of the Golden Fruit)
Shrove Tuesday
Nice Carnival 2 weeks
May
Cannes International Film Festival
Monaco Formula One Grand Prix
July
Juan-les-Pins–Antibes World Jazz Festival
Nice Jazz festival

PROVENCE
May
Stes.-Maries-de-la-Mer Le Pelerinage (Gypsy Pilgrimage)
Whitsun
Nîmes Feria (Whitsun Festival)
July
Aix-en-Provence International Festival of Opera & Music
Arles Feria bullfights (Provençal) also Ferias (Spanish & Provençal). July to September
Avignon Festival of Theater, Dance & Music

LANGUEDOC–ROUSSILLON
Good Friday
Perpignan Procession des Pénitents de la Sanch
June
Tarascon Fête de la Tarasque
July
Carcassonne Embrasement de la Cité July 14
Prades Pablo Casals music festival July–August

CORSICA
Good Friday
Sartène Procession du Catenacciu

LANGUAGE GUIDE

USEFUL WORDS & PHRASES
General
Yes *Oui*
No *Non*
Excuse me *Excusez-moi*
Hello *Bonjour*
Hi *Salut*
Please *S'il vous plaît*
Thank you (very much) *Merci (beaucoup)*
You're welcome *De rien*
Have a good day! *Bonne journée!*
OK *D'accord*
Goodbye *Au revoir*
Good night *Bonsoir*
here *ici*
there *là*
today *aujourd'hui*
yesterday *hier*
tomorrow *demain*
now *maintenant*
later *plus tard*
right away *tout de suite*
this morning *ce matin*
this afternoon *cet après-midi*
this evening *ce soir*
Do you speak English? *Parlez-vous anglais?*
I am American *Je suis Américain* (man); *je suis Américaine* (woman)
I don't understand *Je ne comprends pas*
Please speak more slowly *Parlez plus lentement, s'il vous plaît*
Where is...? *Où est...?*
I don't know *Je ne sais pas*
No problem *Ce n'est pas grave*
That's it *C'est ça*
Here it is *Voici*
There it is *Voilà*
What is your name? *Comment vous-appelez-vous?*
My name is... *Je m'appelle...*
Let's go *On y va*
At what time? *À quelle heure?*
When? *Quand?*
What time is it? *Quelle heure est-il?*

In the hotel
Do you have...? *Avez-vous...?*
a single room *une chambre simple*
a double room *une chambre double*
with/without bathroom/shower *avec/sans salle de bain/douche*

Help
I need a doctor/dentist *J'ai besoin d'un médicin/dentiste*
Can you help me? *Pouvez-vous m'aider?*
Where is the hospital? *Où est l'hôpital?*
Where is the police station? *Où est le commissariat?*

Shopping
I'd like... *Je voudrais...*
How much is it? *C'est combien?*
Do you take credit cards? *Est-ce que vous acceptez les cartes de crédit?*
size (clothes) *la taille*
size (shoes) *la pointure*
cheap *bon marché*
expensive *cher*
Have you got...? *Avez vous...?*
I'll take it *Je le prends*
Anything else? *Avec ça?*
enough *assez*
too much *trop*
bill *la note*

Shops
bakery *la boulangerie*
bookshop *la librairie*
chemist *la pharmacie*
delicatessen *la charcuterie/le traiteur*
department store *le grand magasin*
fishmonger *la poissonnerie*
grocery *l'alimentation/l'épicerie*
junk shop *la brocante*
library *la bibliothèque*
supermarket *le supermarché*
tobacconist *le tabac*

Sightseeing
visitor information office *office de tourisme/le syndicat d'initiative*
open *ouvert*
closed *fermé*
every day *tous les jours*
all year round *toute l'année*
all day long *toute la journée*
free *gratuit/libre*
abbey *l'abbaye* (f)
castle, country house *le château*
church *l'église* (f)
museum *le musée*
staircase *l'escalier* (m)
tower *la tour* (La Tour Eiffel)
tour (walk or drive) *le tour*
town *la ville*
old town *la vieille ville*
Town Hall *Hôtel de ville/la mairie*

MENU READER

See regional food sections for recommended regional dishes.

breakfast *le petit déjeuner*
lunch *le déjeuner*
dinner *le dîner*
I am on a diet *Je suis au régime*
I'd like to order *Je voudrais commander*
Is service included? *Est-ce que le service est compris?*

Le menu
menu à prix fixe meal at set price
à la carte dishes from the menu, charged separately
entrée/hors d'oeuvre first course
le plat principal main course
boisson compris drink included
carte des vins wine list
l'addition the bill
Les boissons drinks
café coffee
  au lait ou crème with milk or cream
  decal/decaffeine decaffeinated coffee
  express/noir espresso/black
  filtre American filtered coffee
thé tea
tisane infusion of herbs or flowers, e.g., chamomile, verveine, limeflower
le lait milk
eau minérale mineral water
  gazeux fizzy
  non-gazeux still
limonade ginger ale
citron pressé fresh lemon juice served with sugar
orange pressée fresh squeezed orange juice
frais, fraîche fresh or cold
bière beer
  en bouteille bottled
  à la pression on tap
  panaché mixed
le panaché shandy
la carafe/le pichet pitcher of tap water or wine
la demi-carafe half liter
un quart quarter of a liter
vin de maison house wine
vin de pays local wine
digestif after-dinner drinks
Santé! Cheers!

Le repas the meal
le pain bread
le poivre pepper
le sel salt
le sucre sugar
le potage soup
Meat dishes
l'agneau lamb
l'andouille tripe sausage
le bifteck steak
  grillé grilled
  saignant rare
  bleu very rare
  à point just cooked
  bien cuit well done
  contre-filet cut of sirloin steak
  entrecôte rib steak
  faux-filet sirloin steak
  hachis chopped
blanquette stew of veal, lamb, or
  chicken with creamy egg
  sauce
boeuf à la mode beef in red
  wine with carrots,
  mushrooms, and onions
bordelaise with red wine and
  shallots
bourguignonne cooked in red
  wine, onions, and mushrooms
le canard duck
la carbonnade stew of beef in beer
la cargolade grill of snails
le carré d'agneau rack of lamb
le cassoulet stew of beans,
  sausages, pork, or duck
la choucroute sauerkraut
le confit duck or goose preserved
  in its own fat
le coq au vin chicken in red wine
le côte d'agneau lamb chop
les cuisses de grenouille frog's legs
la daube beef stew with red
  wine, tomatoes, and onions
le dinde turkey
l'escargot snail
le faisan pheasant
farci stuffed
le foie de veau calf's liver
le foie gras liver of force-fed
  duck or goose
le jambon ham
le lapin rabbit
le magret de canard breast of duck
le médaillon round piece of meat
l'oie goose
la perdrix partridge
le petit-gris small snail
la pintade guinea fowl
le porc pork
le pot-au-feu casserole of beef
  and vegetables

le poulet chicken
le poussin young chicken
les rognons kidneys
rôti roast
le sanglier wild boar
la saucisse fresh sausage
le saucisson salami
le veau veal
Fish dishes
l'anchois anchovy
l'anguille eel
le bar (or loup) similar to sea bass
la barbue brill
le belon Brittany oyster
le colin hake
le bigorneau sea snail
la bouillabaisse fish soup
le cabillaud cod
le coquillage shellfish
la coquille St.-Jacques scallop
la crevette shrimp
la daurade sea bream
l'encornet squid
le flétan halibut
les fruits de mer seafood
l'homard lobster
l'huître oyster
la langoustine large prawn
la limande lemon sole
la lotte monkfish
la moule mussel
moules marinières mussels in
  white wine and onions
la poulpe octopus
la raie skate
le saumon salmon
le thon tuna
la truite trout
Some sauces
américaine white wine,
  tomatoes, butter, and Cognac
béarnaise egg, butter, wine, and
  herbs
aïoli garlic mayonnaise
forestière mushrooms and bacon
hollandaise egg, butter, and lemon
meunière butter, lemon, and
  parsley
meurette red wine sauce
Mornay cream, egg, and cheese
paysan rustic style with local
  ingredients
pistou Provençal sauce with
  basil, garlic, and olive oil
Provençal usually tomatoes,
  garlic, and olive oil
Légumes vegetables
l'ail garlic
l'artichaut artichoke
les asperges asparagus
l'aubergine eggplant

l'avocat avocado
le champignon mushroom
le cèpe cep, boletus mushroom
le cornichon gherkin
la courgette zucchini
le chou cabbage
le choufleur cauliflower
le concombre cucumber
cru raw
les crudités raw vegetables
les épinards spinach
le haricot dried bean
les haricots verts green beans
les lentilles lentils
le maïs corn
le mange-tout snow pea
le mesclun mixed leaf salad
le navet turnip
la noix nut, walnut
la noisette hazelnut
l'oignon onion
le poireau leek
le pois pea
le poivron bell pepper
les pommes de terre potatoes
les chips potato chips
les pommes frites french fries
le radis radish
la roquette (arugula) rocket
  (arugula)
le riz rice
la salade verte green salad
la truffe truffle
Fruits
l'ananas pineapple
la cerise cherry
le citron lemon
le citron vert lime
la figue fig
la fraise strawberry
la framboise raspberry
la groseille redcurrant
la mangue mango
la mirabelle yellow plum
le pamplemousse grapefruit
la pêche peach
la poire pear
la pomme apple
le raisin grape
la prune plum
le pruneau prune
Snacks
le croque-monsieur ham and
  cheese toasted sandwich
l'oeuf à la coque boiled egg
oeufs au jambon ham and eggs
oeufs brouillés scrambled eggs
oeufs sur le plat fried eggs
le yaourt yogurt

ILLUSTRATIONS CREDITS

Abbreviations for terms appearing below: (t) top; (b) bottom; (l) left; (r) right.

Cover, (tl) Tony Stone Images. (tr) Pix. (bl) Powerstock. (br) Powerstock

1, Telegraph Colour Library. 2/3, Tony Stone Images. 4, Pix. 9, AKG. 11, Tony Stone Images. 12, Bruno Barbey. 13, James L. Stanfield. 14/15, Yann Arthus-Bertrand. 17, Adam Woolfit. 18/19, Stephanie Maze. 21, Colorific! 22, AKG. 23, Mary Evans. 24/5, E.T Archive. 26, Giraudon. 27, Giraudon. 28, Giraudon. 29, Hulton Getty. 31, AKG. 32/3, David Alan Harvey. 35, Robert Harding. 36, Images. 37, AKG. 38/39, James L. Stanfield. 40, Giraudon. 42/3, AKG. 43, AKG. 44, Giraudon. 45, Giraudon. 46, Pix. 47, Hulton Getty. 48/9, William Albert Allard. 50, Ronald Grant. 51, PowerStock. 52(t), Pix. 52(b), AA Photo Library/Ken Patterson. 54, James L. Stanfield & Victor R. Boswell, Jr. 56(t), Pix. 56(b), Maltings Partnership. 59, AA Photo Library/Ken Patterson. 60, Pix. 61, Giraudon. 63, AA Photo Library/Ken Patterson. 64, Colorific! 65, AA Photo Library/ J.A.Tims. 66, Pix. 67, AA Photo Library/J.A.Tims. 68, Giraudon. 69, Pix. 70(t), Pix. 70(b), Magnum Photos. 71, Gamma. 72, AA Photo Library/ P. Enticknap. 73, Pix. 77, Telegraph Colour Library. 78, Telegraph Colour Library. 79, Giraudon. 80, Maltings Partnership. 80(t), Giraudon. 80 (b), Giraudon. 81, Giraudon. 82, Giraudon. 83, Giraudon. 86, AA Photo Library/ T.Souter. 87, AA Photo Library/ J.A.Tims. 88, Pictor. 89, AKG. 90, Telegraph Colour Library. 91, AA Photo Library/ J.A.Tims. 92, AA Photo Library/ B Rieger. 93, Pix. 94, Pix. 94/5, Maltings Partnership. 95, Pix. 96, James L. Stanfield. 98, Pix. 99, AA Photo Library/D. Noble. 100, Pix. 102, AA Photo Library/C. Sawyer. 103, Pix. 105, Pix. 106/107, Anthony Blake. 108, Michael Busselle. 109, Pix. 110, AA Photo Library/D. Robertson. 111, AA Photo Library/D. Robertson. 112, Pix. 113, James L. Stanfield. & Victor R. Boswell, Jr. 114, Giraudon. 114b, Pix.114/5, Malting Partnership. 116, Pix. 117, Pix. 118, Pix. 120, Michael Busselle. 121, Michael Busselle. 122, Pix. 123, Pix. 124, J.Allan Cash. 127(t) AA Photo

Library/D. Robertson. 126(bl) AA Photo Library/T. Oliver. 126(br) AA Photo Library. 128, Giraudon. 129, Pix. 130, Pix.131, AKG. 133, Pix. 135, Pix. 137, AA Photo Library/ P.Kenward. 138, Michael Busselle. 139, Giraudon. 140, AA Photo Library/C. Sawyer. 141(t), AA Photo Library/C. Sawyer. 141(b) AA Photo Library/C. Sawyer. 142/3, Fotomas. 143, AA Photo Library/C. Sawyer. 144, Hulton Getty. 145, J.Allan Cash. 146, Mont St Michel, AA Photo Library/C. Sawyer. 146/7, Michael St. Maur Sheil. 148/9, AA Photo Library/C.Sawyer. 150, Pix. 151, AA Photo Library S.Day. 152, Pix. 153, Pix. 154(t), AA Photo Library/ R.Strange. 154(b), AA Photo Library/R.Strange. 155, R.Victor. 156, AA Photo Library/ R.Strange. 157, R.Victor. 158/9, Spectrum. 160, S.Day. 161, Pix. 163, AA Photo Library/R.Moss. 165, Michael Busselle. 166, AA Photo Library/R.Moss. 167, AA Photo Library/J.Edmanson. 168, AA Photo Library/R.Moss. 168/9, Maltings Partnership. 169(t), AA Photo Library/R.Moss. 169(b), Pix. 170, Pix. 171, AA Photo Library/ R.Moss. 172, Pix. 173, Pix. 174, AA Photo Library/ J.Edmanson. 174/5, Michael Busselle. 176(t) AA Photo Library/ A.Baber. 176(b) AA Photo Library/ J.Edmanson. 176c, AA Photo Library/J.Edmanson. 177, AA Photo Library/P.Kenward. 178/9, Pix. 179, Pix. 180, Pix. 181, AA Photo Library/ J.Edmanson. 182/3, Pix. 183, AA Photo Library/ R.Moss. 184, AA Photo Library/ R.Moss. 185, B.Smith. 186, Pix.187, AA Photo Library/R.Moss. 189, AA Photo Library/M.Short.192/3, AA Photo Library/R.Strange. 194, Michael Busselle. 195, AKG. 196, AA Photo Library/M.Short. 197, AA Photo Library/M.Short. 199(t), AA Photo Library/M.Short. 199(b), AA Photo Library/M.Short. 200, AA Photo Library/M.Short. 201, AA Photo Library/M.Short. 202, Pix. 203, Pix. 204(t), Pix. 20(b), AA Photo Library/M.Short. 204-5, Maltings Partnership. 206, Pix. 207, Pix. 209, AA Photo Library/ M.Short. 210, AA Photo Library/ M.Short. 211, J.Allan Cash. 213, Adam Woolfit. 214, Adam Woolfit. 215, AA Photo Library/R.Strange. 216, Pix. 217, Pix. 218, Telegraph Colour Library. 219, J.Allan Cash. 220/1, J.Allan Cash. 223, AA Photo Library/ R.Moss. 224, AA Photo Library/ T.Oliver. 225, AA Photo Library/ T.Oliver. 226, Pix. 227, Pix. 228a, AA Photo Library/R.Moore.

228b, AA Photo Library/T.Oliver. 229, AA Photo Library/T.Oliver. 243(t), AA Photo Library/ P.Kenward. 243(b), Spectrum Colour Library. 230, Pix. 231, Michael Busselle. 234/5, Anthony Blake. 236, Pix. 237, AA Photo Library. 238/9, Pix. 239, AKG. 240, AA Photo Library/ P.Kenward. 241, J.Allan Cash. 244, AA Photo Library/P.Bennett. 245, AA Photo Library/P.Bennett. 246, Aquitaine, Pix. 247, Michael Busselle. 249(t), Anthony Blake. 249(b), Anthony Blake. 250, Michael Busselle. 251, AA Photo Library/P. Kenward. 252, Michael Busselle. 253, Pix. 254, Pix. 255, AA Photo Library. 256, J.Allan Cash. 257, Pix. 259, Telegraph Colour Library. 260/1, Michael Busselle. 262, Michael Busselle. 263, Giraudon. 264, J.Allan Cash. 265, Pix. 267(tl), AKG. 267(tr), Pix. 267(b), Pix. 268, AA Photo Library/P.Kenward, 269, Pix. 270, Pix. 273, Pix. 274, AA Photo Library/B.Smith. 275, Pix. 276, Pix. 277, Pix. 278, Pix. 279, Michael Busselle. 281, Pix. 283, Tony Stone Images 284, Tony Stone Images. 285, Pix. 286, Tony Stone Images. 288, Pix. 289, Pix. 291(t), AA Photo Library/A.Baker. 291(b), AA Photo Library/A.Baker. 292, Chris Fairclough Colour Library. 293, AKG. 294, J.Allan Cash. 295, Pix. 296, Tony Stone Images. 297, Tony Stone Images. 298, Pix. 299, Pix. 300, Pix. 301, Pix. 302, Michael Busselle. 303, Michael Busselle.304, AA Photo Library/R.Strange. 305, AA Photo Library/R.Strange. 306, AA Photo Library/R. Strange. 307(t), AA Photo Library/A. Baker. 307(b), AA Photo Library/A. Baker. 308/9, William Albert Allard. 310, Pix. 312, Tony Stone Images. 313, AA Photo Library/ R.Strange. 314, Michael Busselle. 315, Pix. 316, AA Photo Library/R.Strange. 317, AA Publishing/R.Strange. 318, Montpellier, Pix. 319, Agence Vandystadt. 320, Images. 321, Tony Stone Images. 322(tr), AA Photo Library/P. Bennett. 322(tl), AA Photo Library/P. Bennett. 322(b), AA Photo LibraryK. Reynolds. 324, AA Photo Library/T.Oliver. 325, Pix. 326, Tony Stone. Images. 327, Pix. 328/9 Diaf. 330, Pix. 331, Oxford Scientific Films. 332, Pix. 334, Pix. 334/5, Tony Stone Images. 336, Pix. 337, AA Photo Library.

The world's largest nonprofit scientific and educational organization, the National Geographic Society was founded in 1888 "for the increase and diffusion of geographic knowledge." Since then it has supported scientific exploration and spread information to its more than nine million members worldwide.

The National Geographic Society educates and inspires millions every day through magazines, books, television programs, videos, maps and atlases, research grants, the National Geography Bee, teacher workshops, and innovative classroom materials.

The Society is supported through membership dues, charitable gifts, and income from the sale of its educational products. Members receive NATIONAL GEOGRAPHIC magazine—the Society's official journal—discounts on Society products, and other benefits.

For more information about the National Geographic Society, its educational programs, publications, or how to support its work, call 1-800-NGS-LINE (647-5463), or write to: National Geographic Society, 1145 17th Street, N.W., Washington, D.C. 20036 U.S.A.

Printed in the U.S.A.

Published by the National Geographic Society

John M. Fahey, Jr., *President and Chief Executive Officer*
Gilbert M. Grosvenor, *Chairman of the Board*
Nina D. Hoffman, *Executive Vice President,*
  President, Books and School Publishing
William R. Gray, *Vice President and Director, Book Division*
David Griffin, *Design Director*
Elizabeth L. Newhouse, *Director of Travel Publishing*
Barbara A. Noe, *Senior Editor*
Caroline Hickey, *Senior Researcher*
Carl Mehler, *Director of Maps*
Gary Colbert, *Production Director*
Richard S. Wain, *Production Project Manager*
DeShelle Downey, *Staff Assistant*

Edited and designed by AA Publishing (a trading name of Automobile Association Developments Limited, whose registered office is Norfolk House, Priestley Road, Basingstoke, Hampshire, England RG24 9NY. Registered number: 1878835).

Betty Sheldrick, *Project Manager*
David Austin, *Senior Art Editor*
Josephine Perry, *Editor*
Phil Barfoot, *Designer*
Simon Mumford, *Senior Cartographic Editor*
Nicky Barker-Dix, Helen Beever, *Cartographers*
Richard Firth, *Production Director*
Picture Research by Poppy Owen at I. S. I.
Drive maps drawn by Chris Orr Associates, Southampton, England
Cutaway illustrations drawn by Maltings Partnership, Derby, England

Updated 2001.

Library of Congress Cataloging-in- Publication Data
  The National Geographic traveler. France.
      p.   cm.
    Includes index.
    ISBN 0-7922-7426-1 (alk. paper)
    1. France—Guidebooks.   1. National Geographic Society
  (U.S.)
    11. Title: France.
  DC16.N37 1999
  914.404'839—dc21   98-54974
                                                          CIP

Printed and bound by R.R. Donnelley & Sons, Willard, Ohio.
Cover printed by Miken Inc., Cheektowaga, New York.

Visit the society's Web site at www.nationalgeographic.com

The information in this book has been carefully checked and to the best of our knowledge is accurate. However, details are subject to change, and the National Geographic Society cannot be responsible for such changes, or for errors or omissions. Assessments of sites, hotels, and restaurants are based on the authors' subjective opinions, which do not necessarily reflect the publisher's opinion. The publisher cannot be responsible for any consequences arising from the use of this book.

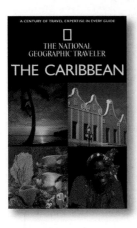
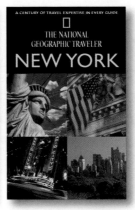